A New Star-Rating System & Other Exciting News from Frommer's!

In our continuing effort to publish the savviest, most up-to-date, and most appealing travel guides available, we've added some great new features.

Frommer's guides now include a new **star-rating system**. Every hotel, restaurant, and attraction is rated from 0 to 3 stars to help you set priorities and organize your time.

We've also added **seven brand-new features** that point you to the great deals, in-the-know advice, and unique experiences that separate travelers from tourists. Throughout the guide, look for:

Finds	Special finds—those places only insiders know about
Fun Fact	Fun facts—details that make travelers more informed and their trips more fun
Kids	Best bets for kids—advice for the whole family
Moments	Special moments—those experiences that memories are made of
Overrated	Places or experiences not worth your time or money
Tips	Insider tips—some great ways to save time and money
Value	Great values—where to get the best deals

Here's what the critics say about Frommer's:

"Amazingly easy to use. Very portable, very complete."
—*Booklist*

"Detailed, accurate, and easy-to-read information for all price ranges."
—*Glamour Magazine*

"Hotel information is close to encyclopedic."
—*Des Moines Sunday Register*

"Frommer's Guides have a way of giving you a real feel for a place."
—*Knight Ridder Newspapers*

Frommer's

Sicily
1st Edition

by Darwin Porter & Danforth Prince

WILEY

Wiley Publishing, Inc.

About the Authors

Darwin Porter and **Danforth Prince** are coauthors of a number of best-selling Frommer's guides, notably Italy, England, France, and Spain. Porter, a bureau chief for the *Miami Herald* at 21, was the author of the first-ever Frommer's guide to Italy and has traveled extensively throughout the country ever since. He is joined by Prince, who was formerly of the Paris bureau of the *New York Times*.

Published by:

Wiley Publishing, Inc.

111 River St.
Hoboken, NJ 07030

ISBN 0-7645-6718-7
ISSN 1541-6410

Editor: Alexis Lipsitz Flippin
Production Editor: Ian Skinnari
Cartographer: Nicholas Trotter
Photo Editor: Richard Fox
Production by Wiley Indianapolis Composition Services

Front cover photo: Family gathered at the table on Lipari, in the Aeolian Islands
Back cover photo: The Temple of Hercules, in Agrigento's Valley of the Temples

For information on our other products and services or to obtain technical support, please contact our Customer Care Department within the U.S. at 800-762-2974, outside the U.S. at 317-572-3993 or fax 317-572-4002.

Wiley also publishes its books in a variety of electronic formats. Some content that appears in print may not be available in electronic formats.

Manufactured in the United States of America

5 4 3 2

Contents

List of Maps

An Invitation to the Reader

In researching this book, we discovered many wonderful places—hotels, restaurants, shops, and more. We're sure you'll find others. Please tell us about them, so we can share the information with your fellow travelers in upcoming editions. If you were disappointed with a recommendation, we'd love to know that, too. Please write to:

Frommer's Sicily, 1st Edition
Wiley Publishing, Inc. • 909 Third Ave. • New York, NY 10022

An Additional Note

Please be advised that travel information is subject to change at any time—and this is especially true of prices. We therefore suggest that you write or call ahead for confirmation when making your travel plans. The authors, editors, and publisher cannot be held responsible for the experiences of readers while traveling. Your safety is important to us, however, so we encourage you to stay alert and be aware of your surroundings. Keep a close eye on cameras, purses, and wallets, all favorite targets of thieves and pickpockets.

New! Frommer's Star Ratings & Icons

Every hotel, restaurant, and attraction listing in this guide has been ranked for quality, value, service, amenities, and special features using a star-rating scale. In country, state, and regional guides, we also rate towns and regions to help you narrow down your choices and budget your time accordingly. Hotels and restaurants in the Very Expensive and Expensive categories are rated on a scale of one (highly recommended) to three stars (exceptional). Those in the Moderate and Inexpensive categories rate from zero (recommended) to two stars (very highly recommended). Attractions, towns, and regions are rated according to the following scale: zero stars (recommended), one star (highly recommended), two stars (very highly recommended), and three stars (must-see).

In addition to the rating system, we also use seven icons to highlight insider information, useful tips, special bargains, hidden gems, memorable experiences, kid-friendly venues, places to avoid, and other useful information:

| Finds | Fun Fact | Kids | Moments | Overrated | Tips | Value |

The following abbreviations are used for credit cards:

| AE | American Express | DISC | Discover | V | Visa |
| DC | Diners Club | MC | MasterCard | | |

FROMMERS.COM

Now that you have the guidebook to a great trip, visit our website at **www.frommers.com** for travel information on nearly 2,500 destinations. With features updated regularly, we give you instant access to the most current trip-planning information available. At Frommers.com, you'll also find the best prices on airfares, accommodations, and car rentals—and you can even book travel online through our travel booking partners. At Frommers.com, you'll also find the following:

- Online updates to our most popular guidebooks
- Vacation sweepstakes and contest giveaways
- Newsletter highlighting the hottest travel trends
- Online travel message boards with featured travel discussions

The Best of Sicily

The largest island in the Mediterranean Sea, **Sicily** is a land of beauty, mystery, and world-class monuments. It's an exotic mix of bloodlines and architecture from medieval Normandy, Aragonese Spain, Moorish North Africa, ancient Greece, Phoenicia, and Rome. Much of the island's raw, primitive nature has faded in modern times, as thousands of newfangled cars clog the narrow lanes of its biggest city, **Palermo.** Poverty remains widespread, yet the age-old stranglehold of the Mafia seems less certain because of the increasingly vocal protests of an outraged public. On the eastern edge of the island is **Mount Etna,** the tallest active volcano in Europe. Many of Sicily's larger urban areas (**Trapani, Catania,** and **Messina**) are relatively unattractive, but areas of ravishing beauty and eerie historical interest are found in the cities of **Syracuse, Taormina, Agrigento,** and **Selinunte.** Sicily's ancient ruins are rivaled only by those of Rome itself. Agrigento's **Valley of the Temples,** for example, is alone worth the trip.

1 The Best Travel Experiences

- **Wandering Around Palermo's La Kalsa:** The ancient quarter of La Kalsa, created during the city's Arab domination, is as close as Sicily comes to having a casbah typical of the North African cities to the south. Although there are safer places to be, this densely populated district of narrow streets and markets provides a view of local Sicilian life unlike anywhere else on the island. To make your experience more authentic, you'll naturally purchase some *babbaluci* from one of the many vendors. These are marinated baby snails sold in paper cornets for devouring on the spot. Head for Piazza della Kalsa, the heart of the quarter, and the day is yours. See "The Major Attractions" in chapter 4.

- **Walking Among the Dead:** Outside Palermo, the Catacombe dei Cappuccini amazingly preserve the lifelike corpses of some 8,000 Palermitans entombed here from the late 16th century until 1920, when the last victim, a 2-year-old *bambina,* was laid to rest. In dimly lit, damp, murky, subterranean corridors, you can wander among these mummies. It's a gory sight, but it's absolutely fascinating. Not only is the clothing preserved but so are the skin, hair, and eyes of some of these corpses, attired in their Sunday best, giving you gruesome smiles. See "The Major Attractions" in chapter 4.

- **Close Encounters with the Sicilian Apennines:** The island isn't all coastline, even though most visitors rarely dip into the hinterlands. For a close-up view of life as lived in the "Sicilian Alps," head inland to explore Sicily's greatest national park, Parco Naturale Regionale delle Madonie, sprawling across 39,679 hectares (98,007 acres). The town of Cefalù makes the best base for exploring the park. Castles dotting the park's lofty villages evoke the Middle Ages and the fiefdom of the ruling Ventimiglia families who presided over post-Angevin Sicily. This is the "bread-basket of Sicily," and you'll pass through pretty farms and vine-yards. There's no better place on the island to picnic in the summer, with fields giving way to downhill skiers in winter. See "Cefalù" in chapter 6.

- **Climbing the Volcano:** Follow in the footsteps of the "disgraced" Ingrid Bergman, who came here in 1949 with her "scandalous" lover and director, Roberto Rossellini, to make the ill-fated film *Stromboli.* On the Aeolian island of Stromboli, the most spectacular of its archipelago, you can witness showers of flaring rock and sparks from its volcano. For the most dramatic viewings, visit at night, when you can witness up close the channels from which the lava flows toward the sea along *sciara del fuoco,* or "trails of fire." At the top you're treated to fiery explosions, a great show that's gone on for centuries. Just wear something over your coiffure so that you, too, don't light up the night. See "Stromboli: Climbing the Volcano" in chapter 7.

- **Cooling Off in Gole dell'Alcantara:** Often visited from Taormina en route to Mount Etna, the Alcantara lava gorges are the best place to experience almost freezing waters when the temperatures in eastern Sicily soar to cauldron con-ditions. These gorges were carved by a river of the same name into rock-hard basalt, the creation of one of Mount Etna's ancient erup-tions. You can rent thigh-length boots, but many prefer to take along "a swimming costume," as Victorian guidebooks advised. This wonderland is the place to be a kid again, splashing around in the cooling waters off eastern Sicily from May to September. There's nothing quite like it in all of Sicily. See "Taormina: Farther Afield to the Alcantara Gorges" in chapter 8.

- **Visiting Medieval Erice:** This once heavily fortified and walled mountain town, left over from the Middle Ages, is suspended 755m (2,478 ft.) above sea level. Ancients called the city Eryx, and a glorious golden temple dedi-cated to Aphrodite at the pinnacle of the town was like a gleaming lighthouse for ancient mariners. You can wander its cobblestone streets and peer into hidden, flower-filled courtyards along twisting lanes. Nothing seems as foreboding as a walk down a *vanelle,* an alley so narrow that only one person can pass at a time. Many Sicilian men journey here looking for a wife, as the women of Erice have been considered the most beautiful in Sicily for cen-turies. See "Erice" in chapter 13.

2 The Most Romantic Getaways

- **Atelier Sul Mare** (Castel di Tusa; ℭ **0921-334295**): Sicily's most unusual hotel lies far off the beaten path. The most iconoclastic hotel on the island was created by an artist who has anointed himself the "Ambassador to Beauty." Some of the bedrooms are the creative statements of renowned artists who lived on the premises for months and made their rooms works of art. See page 145.

- **Hotel Villa Sonia** (Castelmola; ℭ **0942-28082**): High above the resort of Taormina, this 1974 old-style villa is one of Sicily's most appealing hotels and a retreat for escapists. Its rooms opening onto spectacular views, it is a cozy, tranquil nest, with beautiful public areas. Its restaurant is so excellent you won't want to leave the premises at night. See page 187.

- **Palazzo San Domenico** (Taormina; ℂ **0942-613111**): No other hotel in Sicily offers the sweeping majesty of this time-tested icon whose rooms were installed in a 15th-century monastery. Grand comfort on a deluxe level goes hand-in-hand with such charming ecclesiastical touches as Madonnas in wall niches and centuries-old depictions of saints praying in ecstasy. See page 181.
- **Villa del Bosco** (Catania; ℂ **095-7335100**): Few island hotels evoke the grand and stately aristocratic life of the 19th century as does this estate lying 5km (3 miles) south of the center of Catania. Once a private home, it has been

successfully converted into a first-class hotel that often attracts celebrities. Its on-site restaurant is another good reason to stay here. See page 209.

- **Eremo della Giubiliana** (Ragusa; ℂ **0932-669119**): A stone-built estate in sunny isolation, this is a baronial compound of refinement and grace. A stay here is like a visit to the grand country estate of some Sicilian don of the non-Mafia type. All the luxuries of the 21st century are found here, as well as fine dining, but the aura is definitely Old World. See page 273.
- **Foresteria Baglio della Luna** (Agrigento; ℂ **0922-511061**): This is one of the grandest country inns of Sicily, having been meticulously restored by an antiques dealer and turned into a glamorous oasis of style, comfort, and elegance. Agrigento never had such a stylish place to stay. See page 286.

3 The Best Museums

- **Galleria Regionale della Sicilia** (Palermo; ℂ **091-6164317**): This is the most magnificent collection of regional art in all of Sicily—in fact, the gallery is one of the finest in Italy itself. Housed in the Catalán-Gothic Palazzo Abatellis, its superb collections trace Sicilian painting and sculpture from the 13th to the 18th century. Some of its paintings, such as *Triumph of Death* from 1449 or *Eleanora of Aragon* from the same century, are among the most impressive masterpieces in the south of Italy. See "The Major Attractions" in chapter 4.
- **Museo Archeologico Regionale** (Palermo; ℂ **091-6116807**): One of the greatest archaeological museums in all of Italy is filled

with a virtual "British Museum" collection of rare finds that is particularly rich in artifacts from the Greek and Roman colonizations of the island. The metopes dug up from the city of Selinunte alone are worth the visit here, as it was one of the great cities of Magna Graecia. See "The Major Attractions" in chapter 4.

- **Museo Mandralisca** (Cefalù; ℂ **0921-421547**): Come here for no other reason than to gaze in wonder at Antonello da Messina's *Portrait of an Unknown Man,* painted in 1465. It is the masterpiece of this great Sicilian artist. While here, you can check out the other art treasures of this impressive regional museum, including everything from a Chinese puzzle in ivory to a 4th-century-B.C. vase. See "Cefalù: Seeing the Sights" in chapter 6.

- **Museo Regionale** (Messina; *©* **090-361292**): A former silk mill has been successfully converted into one of the island's most impressive regional museums, one that contains Sicily's greatest collection of art from the 15th to the 17th century. See "Messina: Exploring the City on Foot" in chapter 6.

- **Museo Civico** (Termini Imerese; *©* **091-8113557**): Housed in a 14th-century *palazzo* (palace) is one of the finest regional museums in Sicily, devoted to art and archaeology. The Hellenistic and Roman pottery is among its greatest treasures, and the museum is also rich in medieval and Renaissance art. See "Termini Imerese: Exploring the Town" in chapter 6.

- **Museo Archeologico Eoliano** (Lipari; *©* **090-9880174**): One of the great archaeological museums of Italy lies hidden away on the volcanic Aeolian island of Lipari. Among its many celebrated exhibitions are a stunning collection of ancient vases, many from the 4th century B.C., and a magnificent trove of theatrical masks unearthed from tombs of the same era. See "Lipari: Exploring the Island" in chapter 7.

- **Museo Civico Belliniano** (Catania; *©* **095-7150535**): This museum pays homage to the composer Vincenzo Bellini, who was born here on 1801. The rather drab five-room apartment evokes old Catania and is filled with Bellini memorabilia, including original folios of his operas, his death mask, and even the coffin in which his body was transferred from Paris. See "Seeing the Sights" in chapter 9.

- **Museo Archeologico Regionale Paolo Orsi** (Syracuse; *©* **0931-464022**): This is a showcase for some of the most important archaeological finds of southern Italy. Especially intriguing are the showrooms devoted to the Greek colonization of Sicily, including the celebrated *Landolina Venus.* See "Syracuse: Seeing the Ancient Sights" in chapter 10.

- **Museo Regionale di Arte Medievale e Moderna** (Syracuse; *©* **0931-69511**): One of Sicily's greatest art collections is housed in the 13th-century Palazzo Bellomo. The collections are the finest in the painting and decorative arts of southeastern Sicily and include such masterpieces as *The Burial of St. Lucia* by Caravaggio. See "Syracuse: Exploring Ortygia Island" in chapter 10.

4 The Best Cathedrals & Churches

- **Oratorio del Rosario di San Domenico** (Palermo): This 16th-century oratory is the stunning achievement of sculptor and baroque decorator extraordinaire, Giacomo Serpotta. To many, it is the equal of the also glorious Santa Cita oratory (see below). Serpotta's stucco designs are among the greatest in southern

Italy. See "The Major Attractions" in chapter 4.

- **Oratorio di San Lorenzo** (Palermo): This is yet another great oratory that shows the magnificent decoration of master sculptor Giacomo Serpotta, who created this masterpiece here between 1698 and 1710. See "The Major Attractions" in chapter 4.

- **Chiesa di Santa Cita/Oratorio del Rosario di Santa Cita** (Palermo): The church of Santa Cita, bombed in World War II, is visited mainly for its stunning oratory, representing the crowning architectural achievement of sculptor Giacomo Serpotta, who labored on it between 1686 and 1718. His oratory of cherubs and angels is a real romp. See "The Major Attractions" in chapter 4.

- **Monreale Duomo** (Monreale): This grand cathedral represents the pinnacle of the glory of Arab-Norman art and architecture. Launched in 1174 by William II, the Duomo is the most stunning of the Norman churches of Sicily, the mosaics in its interior rivaling those of the celebrated Cappella Palatina in Palermo. See "Monreale" in chapter 5.

- **Duomo** (Cefalù): One of Sicily's most magnificent Norman cathedrals, built by Roger II, stands in this charming little north coast town. The cathedral is known for its grand array of Byzantine-Norman mosaics completed in 1148. They are a virtual tour de force of this type of painstaking art. See "Cefalù: Seeing the Sights" in chapter 6.

- **Duomo** (Catania): Dedicated to the martyred St. Agatha, this cathedral was built on the orders of the Norman king, Roger I, and was largely destroyed in the earthquake that devastated Catania in 1693. What was left was redesigned with parts that survived the catastrophe. The great composer of operas, Bellini, is buried here, as are several Aragonese kings. See "Seeing the Sights" in chapter 9.

5 The Best & Most Evocative Ruins

- **Tyndaris** (Capo Tindari): Tyndaris was a bustling place at its founding by Dionysius the Elder in 396 B.C. Later destroyed by pillaging conquerors, Tyndaris has now been unearthed, and the ruins of everything from a basilica to a Roman theater can be seen. The view of the coast and sea is reason enough to visit. See "Cefalù: Easy Excursions" in chapter 6.

- **Teatro Greco** (Taormina): Opening onto a view of Mount Etna in the background, this Greek amphitheater was hewn out of a rocky slope on Mount Tauro. What you see today is what's left after destruction by the Arabs in the 10th century. See "Taormina: Exploring the Area" in chapter 8.

- **Ortygia Island** (Syracuse): Famous in Greek mythology, this island is filled with ancient ruins such as the Tempio di Apollo, the

Greek temple dedicated to Apollo that dates from the 6th century B.C. and the oldest peripteral (having a single row of columns) Doric temple still left in the world. See "Syracuse: Exploring Ortygia Island" in chapter 10.

- **Parco Archeologico della Neapolis** (Syracuse): Two of the greatest attractions of Sicily—both from the world of the ancients—lie in this city in southeastern Sicily. The Greek Theater is one of the great theaters of the classical period still remaining. The other attraction is the Latomia del Paradiso, or the "Ear of Dionysius," the most famous of the ancient quarries of Syracuse. See "Syracuse: Seeing the Ancient Sights" in chapter 10.

- **Villa Romana del Casale** (Piazza Armerina): This is one of the grandest of all Roman villas to have survived from the classical era. It contains a total of 40 rooms "carpeted" with 11,340 sq. m (37,800 sq. ft.) of some of the greatest and most magnificent mosaics in western Europe. Its most reproduced mosaics are those of 10 young women dressed in strapless two-piece bikinis that would not be out of style today. See "Piazza Armerina: Seeing the Sights" in chapter 11.

- **Valle dei Templi** (Agrigento): Containing the largest and greatest collection of ancient Greek ruins in all the world, the "Valley of the Temples" outside the city of Agrigento opens onto the southern coast of Sicily. The temples are especially stunning and evocative at night when they are floodlit. The most impressive temples are those dedicated to Juno (from the mid–5th c. B.C.) and to Concord. Concord is the most magnificent of all, with 13 wind-eroded columns still standing. See "Agrigento & the Valley of the Temples" in chapter 12.

- **Selinunte's Archaeological Garden** (Selinunte, west of Agrigento): Guy de Maupassant called these ruins an "immense heap of fallen columns," and so they are, but they are also the remains of one of the greatest colonies of ancient Greece. The temples date from the 6th century to the 5th century B.C. See "Selinunte" in chapter 12.

- **Tempio di Segesta** (Segesta): One of the world's most perfectly preserved monuments from antiquity, Tempio di Segesta was constructed in the 5th century B.C. Amazingly, 36 of its Doric columns, supporting entablatures and pediments, still stand. A visit to this remote site in western Sicily also gives you a chance to see a large Greek *teatro* (theater) in ruins. See "Segesta" in chapter 13.

6 The Best Beaches

- **Mondello Lido** (Mondello): This is where the citizens of Palermo flock on a hot summer day to escape the stifling heat of the capital city. In Sicily, Mondello Lido is only outclassed in fashion by the beaches at the foot of Taormina. Its wide, sandy beaches extend for 2km (1¼ miles) from Monte Pellegrino to Monte Gallo. See "Mondello: Fun at the Beach" in chapter 5.

- **Mortelle:** The best sands in northeast Sicily are found at the resort of Mortelle, which is where the Messinese themselves go to escape the scalding heat in their capital. The resort lies 12km (7½ miles) north of Messina at the northeast tip of the island. The area is filled with good sandy beaches so you can take your pick. The best-accessorized strip is called Lido dei Tirreno. See "Messina: Easy Excursions to the Beach" in chapter 6.

- **Spiaggia Sabbie Nere** (Vulcano): Completely off the beaten trail, "Black Sands Beach" is the finest in the Aeolian archipelago—that is, once you get over the fact that its sands are actually black and not powdery white. Beaching it here is something to tell the folks back home. See "Vulcano: Exploring the Island" in chapter 7.

- **Giardini-Naxos:** On the waterfront near Taormina, Giardini-Naxos is one of the best and most sophisticated seaside resorts of Sicily. The sandy beach, one of the island's best, lies between Capo Taormina in the northwest, sweeping south to Capo Schisò in the south. It may lack Taormina's medieval charm, but Giardini is filled with good hotels, fine swimming, and excellent restaurants. See "Giardini-Naxos" in chapter 8.

- **Lido Mazzarò** (Taormina): The best-equipped beach in Sicily, Lido Mazzarò is also one of the finest, a favorite sea-bordering strip of sand and gravel once frequented by the stars of Hollywood's Golden Age and still as interesting as ever. A 15-minute cable-car ride down from the medieval town of Taormina, the beach is a hot spot from April to October. Bars and restaurants border the sands. See "Taormina: Exploring the Area" in chapter 8.

- **Marina di Ragusa:** Southeastern Sicily has a number of beaches, some of them quite tacky, but Marina di Ragusa is the best of the lot. This is quite an appealing area, and if Ragusa is too hot in summer you might anchor here in a hotel and visit the ancient city on a day trip. The resort also has the best ice-cream bars, popular pubs, and watersports in the area. See "Ragusa" in chapter 11.

7 The Best Luxury Hotels

- **Villa Igiea Grand Hotel** (Palermo; ☎ **091-6312111**): This old villa built at the turn of the 20th century in the Art Nouveau style is the grandest address in Palermo. Surrounded by a park overlooking the sea, it provides an old-world atmosphere but has all the modern comforts. It was once a private villa but has been handsomely converted for guests. See page 51.

- **Grand Hotel Liberty** (Messina; ☎ **090-6409436**): This is one of the grandest hotels on the eastern coast of Sicily. It was transformed in the mid-1990s into a bastion of comfort and tranquility, with some of the island's best and most plush bedrooms. In all, a stay here is a beautiful way to visit "messy" Messina. See page 131.

- **Villa Meligunis** (Lipari; ☎ **090-9812426**): This hotel is as good as it gets in the volcanic Aeolian islands. A restored cluster of 17th-century fishermen's cottages forms the nucleus of the compound. All modern conveniences in this remote outpost have been added. See page 159.

- **Grand Hotel Timeo** (Taormina; ☎ **0942-23801**): Liz Taylor and Richard Burton have long vamoosed, but this deluxe hotel still attracts the rich and famous who want to enjoy the stately comfort of a 19th-century neoclassical villa near Taormina's Greek theater. It's lighthearted and baronial at the same time. See page 181.

- **Excelsior Grand Hotel** (Catania; ☎ **095-7476111**): This is the leading hotel of Sicily's second city, a monument to the modernism of the *La Dolce Vita* days of the 1950s when it was first constructed. The city may be in decay, but the hotel is completely up to date, housing its guests in luxury and comfort. See page 209.

- **Grand Hotel** (Syracuse; ☎ **0931-464600**): This turn-of-the-20th-century hotel is so old it's new again following a major upgrade and renovation in the 1990s. Its stately, old-fashioned charm has been preserved, but its comforts are definitely 21st century. It's the best place to stay if you plan to visit the archaeological gardens of Syracuse. See page 251.

8 The Best Moderately Priced Hotels

- **Palazzo Excelsior** (Palermo; ℂ **091-6256176**): With its faded 19th-century nostalgia, this is a very appealing choice lying on the most prestigious street of Palermo, but in an isolated spot. Much of the interior is appealingly dowdy. It's not for everyone, but it attracts those discerning guests who like staying in a living museum. See page 56.

- **Hotel Grotta Azzurra** (Ustica; ℂ **091-8449396**): On this remote island off the northern coast of Sicily is Ustica's finest accommodation, set on a wide plateau above the ocean. It's a lush resort-style Mediterranean vacation retreat, and the prices are most affordable. See page 122.

- **Villa Fabbiano** (Taormina; ℂ **0942-626058**): Romantically positioned in a hilltop village, this affordable hotel is a little gem. You're in a beautiful setting amid good furnishings, but you pay only a fraction of the price charged by nearby competitors such as the deluxe Grand Hotel Timeo. See page 184.

- **Villa Mora** (Giardini-Naxos; ℂ **0942-51839**): Its bedrooms opening onto views of the Ionian Sea, this is the ultimate beachfront retreat for those who prefer to be right on the water and not anchored in the hilltop medieval village of Taormina above. With private balconies opening onto the bay, this small hotel is an oasis of charm and tranquility, with good rooms and pleasantly aromatic Sicilian cuisine. See page 199.

- **Hotel Moderno** (Erice; ℂ **0923-869300**): In spite of its dull and misleading name, this is quite a good hotel in Sicily's most enchanting medieval town. Rooms are in an attractively decorated main building or in an annex. All units have hints of 19th-century styling and open onto private balconies or terraces with views in all directions. See page 301.

9 The Best Restaurants

- **La Scuderia** (Palermo; ℂ **091-520323**): At the foot of Monte Pellegrino, 5km (3 miles) north of the city, this is Palermo's grandest restaurant, with superb international and Italian cuisine. Talented chefs turn out a tempting array of dishes prepared with market-fresh ingredients and served on the town's prettiest flower terrace. See page 61.

- **Charleston Le Terrazze** (Mondello; ℂ **091-450171**): At Palermo's fashionable beach resort, this restaurant serves a better cuisine than that found in the capital city itself. It's housed in a building from 1913. The chefs use the finest ingredients in preparing the Sicilian/international cuisine. See page 117.

- **Osteria del Duomo** (Cefalù; ℂ **0921-421838**): Its location across from the town's most famous cathedral is touristy, but this first-rate restaurant is anything but. It's a bastion of some of the north coast's grandest cuisine, specializing in sophisticated Sicilian fare along with a discreet offering of international dishes that have attracted world celebrities. See page 142.

- **Casa Grugno** (Taormina; ℂ **0942-21208**): Taormina has never had such a temple of gastronomy. One of the most creative and exciting restaurants in Sicily is the culinary showcase for Andrea Zangerl, an Austria-born chef. His modern takes on Sicilian cuisine and sublime international dishes draw the world to his doorstep. See page 187.

- **Osteria I Tre Bicchieri** (Catania; ℂ **095-7153540**): Opening in 2002, this quickly became Catania's finest restaurant, immediately celebrated by the local press for its Continental cuisine. Naples-born wunderkind and chef Laquinangelo Carmine has won immediate acceptance with his succulent cuisine. He is known especially for his preparation of Mediterranean fish. See page 215.

- **Le Zagare** (Catania; ℂ **095-7476111**): There is no finer Grand Hotel–style dining on the eastern coast of Sicily than at this citadel of haute cuisine, serving the best of island dishes along with a well-chosen sampling of Continental recipes. The baroque city around it may be in decay, but the good life still holds forth here. See page 215.

- **Il Barocco** (Noto; ℂ **0931-835999**): Your finest dining in this ancient but decaying town west of Syracuse is at this restaurant in a building that was converted from an 18th-century stable block for a historic palace nearby. Today, it's the setting for excellent Sicilian dishes, especially seafood from the Ionian Sea. See page 266.

- **Locanda Don Serafino** (Ragusa; ℂ **0932-248778**): One of the finest restaurants in southern Sicily is set inside the cellars of a 17th-century palace. The Sicilian cuisine, based on market-fresh products, is elegantly presented here—dishes designed to appeal to the most discerning of tastes. See page 275.

- **Ristorante Il Dehor** (Agrigento; ℂ **0922-511061**): In a grand villa of a hotel, Foresteria Baglio della Luna, this is one of the six best restaurants in all of Sicily, serving top-notch and refined Sicilian and international cuisine. Winning rave reviews from the press in Europe, this place tempts you with an array of fixed-price menus from a very talented chef. See page 292.

10 The Best Down-Home Trattorie

- **Lo Scudiero** (Palermo; ℂ **091-581628**): The capital's finest moderately priced trattoria is set across from the landmark Politeamo Theater. Honest, straightforward Sicilian food is served here at very affordable prices. See page 62.

- **Bye Bye Blues** (Mondello; ℂ **091-6841415**): Even though the name doesn't sound very Sicilian, this is one of the best places to go for true island cooking. A casual, relaxed place outside Palermo, this trattoria is run by a husband-and-wife team full of "passion" about feeding you well from the island's bounty. See page 116.

- **E Pulera** (Lipari; ℂ **090-9811158**): For some of the best Aeolian cooking, head here for time-tested recipes and some of the best fish specialties in the island chain, including a delectable fishermen's soup. No one makes a better swordfish ragout than these folks. See page 160.

- **Granduca** (Taormina; ℂ **0942-24983**): The most atmospheric choice in this chic resort looks like an antiques store with potted plants. It also contains an alluring terrace with panoramic views. But most people come here for the excellent food and repertoire of both Sicilian and Italian specialties. See page 191.

- **La Grotta di Carmelo** (Acireale; ① **095-7648153**): The setting looks touristy and gimmicky, as you dine in a cave carved into a rock-face wall. Constructed of black lava rock from Mount Etna, the restaurant serves really good food, both seafood and typical Sicilian fare. Much of the fish is brought in daily after a harvesting in the Ionian Sea. See page 237.

- **Don Camillo** (Syracuse; ① **0931-67133**): One of the city's finest and most affordable dining rooms was constructed on the foundation of a 15th-century monastery.

The cuisine of seafood and Sicilian recipes is among the most creative in town. It's a charmer. See page 258.

- **Monte San Giuliano** (Erice; ① **0923-869595**): In the medieval hilltop village of Erice, the most spectacular in Sicily, you can dine at this undiscovered garden hideaway after making your way through narrow, labyrinthine streets. Most of the foodstuff is plucked from the sea, and is enjoyed in a rustic setting. Some of the dishes, such as a seafood couscous, are North African–inspired. See page 302.

2

Planning Your Trip to Sicily

To see most of Sicily's highlights, plan on spending at least 5 to 7 days and moving a few times. Everything is very spread out—Sicily is the largest island in the Mediterranean, 177km (110 miles) north to south and 281km (175 miles) wide. Taormina, the most popular resort, is a great place to relax and play in the sun for a couple of days; from here you can also visit Mount Etna. The town is rather isolated in the east, however, so it may not be the best base for seeing the island's other highlights. The quickest and most efficient way to see the majority of Sicily is to fly into Palermo, rent a car, and travel east to Taormina; then return your car and fly back to the mainland from Catania. (Conversely, you can fly into Catania, perhaps from Rome, and end your itinerary in Palermo, returning the car there before flying back to Rome.)

This chapter is devoted to the where, when, and how of your trip—the advance planning required to get it together and take it on the road. Because you might not know exactly where in Sicily you want to go or what surrounds the major city you want to see, we'll start off with a quick rundown of the various regions.

1 The Regions in Brief

A predominantly mountainous island, Sicily is separated from the mainland by the Straits of Messina. Culturally there is an even wider gap between Italy and its semi-autonomous island, Sicily, which feels a world apart.

This is a land of tempestuous elements, including active volcanoes and torrential rivers that can flood during the winter rainy season and dry up in the scorching summer months. While northern Sicily enjoys a milder clime, southern Sicily is often profoundly affected by the hot winds known as *sirocco* blowing in from the deserts of North Africa.

Sicily lies at the confluence of a trio of seas—in fact, the Greeks called it *Sikelia,* or "three points." The northern coast opens onto the Tyrrhenian Sea, the eastern coast (Catania and Taormina) onto the Ionian Sea, and the southern coast, the Sicilian Sea.

Sicily also controls a string of offshore islands, including Ustica, off the coast of Palermo; the Aeolians (mainly Stromboli, Vulcano, and Lipari); and the Egadis, lying off the cities of Marsala and Trapani on the west coast. Lonely Pantelleria lies off the western coast, and the southernmost Pelagians are almost in North Africa. Here's a rundown of the cities and regions covered in this guide.

THE AEOLIAN ISLANDS
From the mud baths of Vulcano to the fiery explosions at night from the crater on Stromboli, the Aeolian Islands (*Isole Eolie* in Italian) are mysterious and exciting places to be, different from anything else in Italy. Awash in the Tyrrhenian Sea, these islands lie off the northern coast and are within easy reach of the port of Milazzo by hydrofoil or ferryboat. The three main islands to visit are **Vulcano** (closest to the Sicilian mainland), **Lipari** (where most of the tourist facilities are found), and **Stromboli** (still

actively volcanic). Those travelers with unlimited time can also make day trips to such lesser islands as **Panarea, Filicudi, Salina,** and **Alicudi.**

AGRIGENTO

On the southern coastline of Sicily, Agrigento was one of the most important centers of Magna Graecia, and its **Valle dei Templi** (Valley of the Temples), a mammoth array of temple ruins, is reason enough to go to Sicily. The home of the 5th-century philosopher, Empedocles, and of the playwright, Luigi Pirandello, Agrigento was destroyed by Carthage in 406 B.C. But those invading armies left plenty of ruins for us to explore today. The town's Doric temples date from the 6th century to the 5th century B.C. and were erected to such deities as Hercules, Juno, and Jupiter.

CATANIA

The second city of Sicily opens onto the Gulf of Catania, lying at the foot of the southern slopes of Mount Etna, a volcano that has rained lava down on it for centuries. One of the oldest cities of Sicily, it dates from the 8th century B.C. Massively rebuilt after destruction by an earthquake in 1693, Catania today is called the "baroque city." You'll either love this massive sprawl or hate it. We love it, as did such hometown boys as the writer Giovanni Verga (1840–1922) and the composer Vincenzo Bellini (1801–35).

MESSINA

Overlooking the Straits of Messina on the northeast coast of Sicily, the city of Messina is for most visitors the gateway into Sicily. Although it's possible to fly into Palermo, most people arrive by hydrofoil or ferryboat from the Italian mainland, disembarking at the port of Messina where rail and bus connections can be made to other parts of Sicily. Shakespeare used the city as a setting for *Much Ado About Nothing,* although he never actually laid eyes on it. Messina today is a modern city, having been rebuilt after many disasters.

MOUNT ETNA

This is Sicily's greatest natural attraction and its highest mountain, and it's also the largest volcano in Europe and one of the most active in the world. The ancient Greeks viewed it as the home of Vulcan, god of fire, and home of the Cyclops, the one-eyed monster. Much of its surrounding landscape is covered with solidified lava, a surface for skiing in winter or hiking terrain in summer. The crater is dangerously active, so you always feel a sense of adventure or even danger while touring or hiking in the area.

PALERMO

The island's largest city and its capital is also filled with the most sightseeing treasures. Palermo opens onto the Gulf of Palermo on the northwest coast of Sicily, the largest settlement in Conca d'Oro, a fertile land planted with citrus. Founded by the Phoenicians, it contains innumerable fine monuments, particularly in the baroque vein, along with an array of art that spans the centuries. It's a messy city, difficult to navigate and crime-laden, but like its sister city Naples, it's worth the effort for those who don't mind a certain inconvenience.

PIAZZA ARMERINA

This is not a piazza (square) but an actual town, and a spectacularly sited one as well, lying inland in central Sicily. It is visited mainly by those who want to see the famous Roman hunting lodge from the 4th century B.C. The mosaics found here are among the most spectacular in the world, including some bathing beauties in bikinis.

RAGUSA

On the southern slope of the Iblei mountain range, Ragusa lies inland from the sea and is one of the most

Sicily

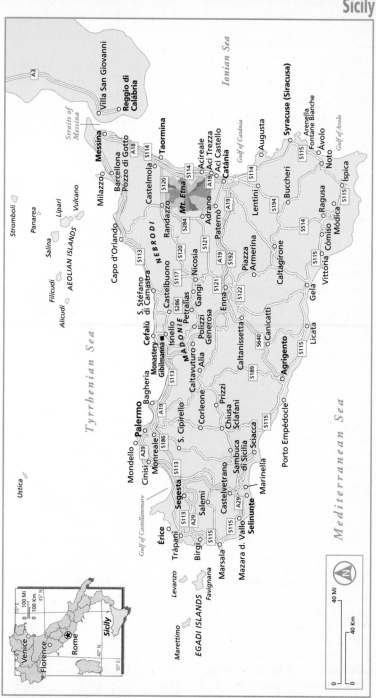

Ionian Sea

Tyrrhenian Sea

Mediterranean Sea

Straits of Messina

Gulf of Catania

Gulf of Avolo

Gulf of Castellammare

Villa San Giovanni
Reggio di Calábria

Messina
Barcellona
Pozzo di Gotto
Milazzo
Castelmola   S114   Taormina
Acireale
Aci Trezza
Aci Castello
Catánia
Mt. Etna
Randazzo   S120
S284   Adrano   A18
Paternò   A19
Syracuse (Siracusa)
Arenella
Fontane Bianche
Avolo
Noto   S115
Ispica
Augusta
Buccheri
Lentini   S194
Piazza
Armerina
Caltagirone
Ragusa   S115
Cómiso   S514
Módica
Vittória
Gela   S115
Comiso

Stromboli
Panarea
Lipari
Salina   Vulcano
Filicudi
Alicudi   AEOLIAN ISLANDS

Capo d'Orlando   S113
N E B R O D I
S. Stéfano
di Camastra   S120
Castelbuono   S117   Nicosia   S121
Cefalú   S286   Gángi
Isnello   Petralias
Polizzi   S121
Generosa   Enna   S192
M A D O N I E   S122
Caltavuturo
Alia
Caltanissetta
Canicatti
Licata
Agrigento   S115
S189
S640

Palermo
Bagheria
Monastery
Gibilmanna   S113
Mondello
Cinisi   A29
Monreale   S186
S. Cipirello
Corleone
Chiusa
Sclafani
Prizzi
Sciacca   S115
Sambuca
di Sicilia
Porto Empédocle

Segesta   S113
Salemi
Castelvetrano
Marinella   A29
Selinunte   S115
Érice
Trápani   S113   A29
Birgi   S115
Marsala   S115
Mazara d. Vallo

Ustica

Ionian Sea

40 Mi
40 Km

15° E.   100 Mi
0   100 Km
45° N.

Venice
Florence
Rome
Sicily
40° N.
10° E.

Marettimo   Levanzo
EGADI ISLANDS
Favignana

intriguing cities to visit in the southeastern sector of the island. It's actually two cities in one, both Ragusa Ibla and Ragusa Superiore. Of medieval origin, with narrow, twisting lanes, the old city, which suffered a major earthquake in 1693, retained much of its appearance when it was rebuilt.

SEGESTA & SELINUNTE
Your journey of discovery through Sicily should include these ancient ruins. Segesta lies in western Sicily in a setting of rolling hills. Its claim to fame is a Doric temple built around 430 B.C., with its 36 limestone columns still intact. On the southern coast, Selinunte was once a rival to Segesta until it was destroyed by Hannibal and the Carthaginians. Like Agrigento and Syracuse, Selinunte is visited for its impressive and scattered ruins of temple columns that speak of former glory.

SYRACUSE
Called *Siracusa* in Italian, this historic city, founded by the Greeks in the 8th century B.C., lies on the southeastern coast of the island. After Taormina and Palermo, it is the third most visited city in Sicily. Filled with medieval streets but with an essentially baroque aura in architecture, it is visited mainly for its classical ruins and works of art. These include a Greek theater and a Roman amphitheater, both from the 3rd century B.C.

TAORMINA
Sicily's grandest resort, first publicized by Goethe in 1787, has over time drawn a steady stream of celebrities, among other visitors, ranging from Oscar Wilde to Marlene Dietrich. Situated atop Monte Tauro, Taormina is not on the beach, but good sandy beaches are easily reached along its eastern flanks. In spite of the hordes who descend on it every year from April to October, Taormina retains some of its medieval aura.

TRAPANI & ERICE
The major city on the western coast, Trapani lies in the northwest, opening onto the Egadi archipelago of three islands. It offers superior transportation links to the rest of Sicily and easy road links to Palermo. Trapani was also founded by the Greeks, though eventually it fell to the Romans. The medieval hill town of Erice, to its immediate north, has far more antique charm, and if you have only 1 day to spend in the west, devote it to touring Erice. But if you have the time, Trapani and its monuments make for an intriguing day of sightseeing.

2 Visitor Information

For information before you go, contact the Italian Government Tourist Board.

In the United States: 630 Fifth Ave., Suite 1565, New York, NY 10111 (© 212/245-4822; fax 212/586-9249); 500 N. Michigan Ave., Suite 2240, Chicago, IL 60611 (© 312/644-0996; fax 312/644-3019); and 12400 Wilshire Blvd., Suite 550, Los Angeles, CA 90025 (© 310/820-1898; fax 310/820-6357; www.italiantourism.com).

In Canada: 175 Bloor St. E., South Tower, Suite 907, Toronto, ON, M4W 3R8 (© 416/925-4882; fax 416/925-4799).

In the United Kingdom: 1 Princes St., London W1R 8AY (© 020/7408-1254; fax 020/7493-6695).

You can also write directly (in English or Italian) to the provincial or local tourist boards of the areas you plan to visit. Provincial tourist boards **(Ente Provinciale per il Turismo)** operate in the principal towns of the provinces. Local tourist boards **(Azienda Autonoma di Soggiorno e Turismo)** operate in all places of tourist interest; you can get a list from the Italian Government Tourist Office. If you are in Sicily and need to get information, call the toll-free number (only within Italy, ☎ **800-117700**). If you are calling from another country, dial ☎ **06/874190 07**. The service is available daily from 8am to 11pm in five languages, dispensing information concerning transportation, health assistance, events, museums, safety, hotels, information points, and tourist assistance.

On the Web, the Italian Government Tourist Board sponsors the site **www.italiantourism.com**, and the Italian State Tourism Board sponsors **www.enit.it**.

3 Entry Requirements & Customs

ENTRY REQUIREMENTS

U.S., Canadian, U.K., Irish, Australian, and New Zealand citizens with a **valid passport** don't need a visa to enter Italy or Sicily if you don't expect to stay more than 90 days and don't expect to work there. If after entering Italy you want to stay more than 90 days, you can apply for a permit for an extra 90 days, which as a rule is granted immediately. Go to the nearest *questura* (police headquarters) or to your home country's consulate. If your passport is lost or stolen, head to your consulate as soon as possible for a replacement.

CUSTOMS

WHAT YOU CAN BRING INTO ITALY OR SICILY   Foreign visitors can bring along most items for personal use duty-free, including fishing tackle, a pair of skis, two tennis racquets, a baby carriage, two hand cameras with 10 rolls of film, and 400 cigarettes or a quantity of cigars or pipe tobacco not exceeding 500 grams (l.1 lb.). There are strict limits on importing alcoholic beverages. However, for alcohol bought tax-paid, limits are much more liberal than in other countries of the European Union.

WHAT YOU CAN TAKE HOME Rules governing what you can bring back duty-free vary from country to country and are subject to change, but they're generally posted on the Web.

Returning **U.S. citizens** who have been away for at least 48 hours are allowed to bring back, once every 30 days, $400 worth of merchandise duty-free. You'll be charged a flat rate of 10% duty on the next $1,000 worth of purchases. Be sure to have your receipts handy. On mailed gifts, the duty-free limit is $50. You cannot bring fresh foodstuffs into the United States, but tinned foods are allowed. For more information, contact the **U.S. Customs Service,** 1300 Pennsylvania Ave. NW, Washington, DC 20229 (☎ **202/354-1000**) and request the free pamphlet *Know Before You Go*. It's also available on the Web at www.customs.ustreas.gov (click on "Traveler Information," then on "Know Before You Go").

For a clear summary of **Canadian** rules, write for the booklet *I Declare,* issued by the **Canada Customs and Revenue Agency** (☎ **800/461-9999** in Canada, or 204/983-3500; www.ccra-adrc.gc.ca). Canada allows its citizens a C$750 exemption, and you're allowed to bring back duty-free one carton of cigarettes, 200 grams of tobacco, 40 imperial ounces of liquor, and 50 cigars. In addition, you're allowed to mail gifts to Canada valued at less than C$60 a day, provided they're unsolicited and don't contain alcohol or tobacco (write on the package, "Unsolicited gift, under C$60 value"). All valuables should be declared on the Y-38 form before departure from Canada, including serial numbers of valuables you already own, such as expensive foreign cameras. *Note:* The C$750 exemption can only be used once a year and only after an absence of 7 days.

Citizens of the U.K. who are **returning from a European Community (EC) country** will go through a separate Customs Exit (called the "Blue Exit") especially for EC travelers. In essence, there is no limit on what you can bring back from an EC country, as long as the items are for personal use (this includes gifts) and you have already paid the necessary duty and tax. However, Customs law sets guidance levels. If you bring in more than these levels, you may be asked to prove that the goods are for your own use. Guidance levels on goods bought in the EC for your own use are: 800 cigarettes, 200 cigars, 1 kilogram of smoking tobacco, 10 liters of spirits, 90 liters of wine (of this not more than 60 liters can be sparkling wine), and 110 liters of beer. For more information, contact **HM Customs & Excise National Advice Service,** Passenger Enquiry Point, 2nd Floor Wayfarer House, Great South West Road, Feltham, Middlesex, TW14 8NP (℗ **0845/010-9000**); or consult their website at www.hmce.gov.uk.

The duty-free allowance in **Australia** is A$400 or, for those under 18, A$200. Personal property mailed back from Italy or Sicily should be marked "Australian goods returned" to avoid payment of duty. Upon returning to Australia, citizens can bring in 250 cigarettes or 250 grams of loose tobacco, and 1,125 milliliters of alcohol. If you're returning with valuable goods you already own, such as foreign-made cameras, you should file form B263. A helpful brochure, available from Australian consulates or Customs offices, is *Know Before You Go.* For more information, contact **Australian Customs Services,** GPO Box 8, Sydney NSW 2001 (℗ **1300/ 363-262** within Australia, or 02/ 6275-6666 outside Australia). Or check www.customs.gov.au.

The duty-free allowance for New Zealand is NZ$700. Citizens over 17 can bring in 200 cigarettes, or 50 cigars, or 250 grams of tobacco (or a mixture of all three if their combined weight doesn't exceed 250g); plus 4.5 liters of wine or beer, or 1,125 milliliters of liquor. New Zealand currency does not carry import or export restrictions. Fill out a certificate of export, listing the valuables you are taking out of the country; that way, you can bring them back without paying duty. Most questions are answered in a free pamphlet available at New Zealand consulates and Customs offices: "New Zealand Customs Guide for Travellers, Notice no. 4." For more information, contact New Zealand Customs, The Customhouse, 17–21 Whitmore St., Box 2218, Wellington (℗ 04/473-6099 or 0800/428-786; www.customs.govt.nz).

4 Money

CURRENCY

The **euro,** the new single European currency, became the official currency of Italy and 11 other participating countries on January 1, 1999.

However, the euro didn't go into general circulation until early in 2002. The old currency, the Italian lira, disappeared into history on March 1, 2002, replaced by the euro, whose official abbreviation is "EUR."

The symbol of the euro is a stylized *E:* €. Exchange rates of participating countries are locked into a common currency fluctuating against the dollar.

For more details on the euro, check out **www.europa.eu.int/euro**.

The relative value of the euro fluctuates against the U.S. dollar, the pound sterling, and most of the world's other currencies, and its value might not be the same by the time you

The Euro, the U.S. Dollar, & the British Pound

Regarding the Euro At the time of this writing, the U.S. dollar and the euro traded almost on par (i.e., $1 approximately equals 1€). But that relationship can and probably will change during the lifetime of this edition. For more exact ratios between these and other currencies, check an up-to-date source at the time of your arrival in Europe.

For British Readers At this writing, £1 = approximately US$1.56, and approximately the same for the euro. These were the rates of exchange used to calculate the values in the table below.

Euro	US$	UK£	Euro	US$	UK£
1	1	0.64	75	75	48.23
2	2	1.29	100	100	64.30
3	3	1.93	125	125	80.38
4	4	2.57	150	150	96.45
5	5	3.22	175	175	112.53
6	6	3.86	200	200	128.60
7	7	4.50	225	225	144.68
8	8	5.14	250	250	160.75
9	9	5.79	275	275	176.83
10	10	6.43	300	300	192.90
15	15	9.65	350	350	225.05
20	20	12.86	400	400	257.20
25	25	16.08	500	500	321.50
50	50	32.15	1000	1000	643.00

actually travel to Sicily. A last-minute check is also advised before you begin your trip.

At this writing, the euro and the U.S. dollar were almost on par with one another, exchanging at a rate that was virtually 1 to 1. Because of that, no U.S. dollar equivalents are given for the euro-denominated prices designated within this travel guide.

Also as of this writing, Great Britain still uses the pound sterling, with 1 euro equaling approximately .64 pence.

Exchange rates are more favorable at the point of arrival. Nevertheless, it's often helpful to exchange at least some money before going abroad (standing in line at the exchange bureau of the Palermo airport isn't fun after a long overseas flight). Check with any of your local American Express or Thomas Cook offices or major banks. Or order in advance from the following: **American Express** (✆ 800/721-9768; cardholders only), **Thomas Cook** (✆ 800/223-7373; www.thomascook.com), or **Capital for Foreign Exchange** (✆ 888/842-0880; www.afex.com).

It's best to exchange currency or traveler's checks at a bank, and not at an exchange bureau, hotel, or shop. Currency and traveler's checks (for which you'll receive a better rate than cash) can be changed at all principal airports and at some travel agencies, such as American Express and Thomas Cook. Note the rates and ask about commission fees; it can sometimes pay to shop around.

ATMS

ATMs are prevalent in all Sicilian cities and even in smaller towns. ATMs are linked to a national network that most likely includes your bank at home. Both the **Cirrus** (② **800/424-7787;** www.mastercard. com) and the **PLUS** (② **800/843-7587;** www.visa.com) networks have automated ATM locators listing the banks in Italy that will accept your card. Or just search out any machine with your network's symbol emblazoned on it.

Important note: Make sure that the PINs (personal identification numbers) on your bank cards and credit cards will work in Sicily. You'll need a **four-digit code** (six digits won't work), so if you have a six-digit code you'll have to go into your bank and get a new PIN for the trip. If you're unsure about this, contact Cirrus or PLUS (above). Be sure to check the daily withdrawal limit at the same time.

TRAVELER'S CHECKS

These days, traveler's checks seem less necessary because most Sicilian cities and towns have 24-hour ATMs, allowing you to withdraw small amounts of cash as needed. But if you prefer the security of the tried and true, you might want to stick with traveler's checks—provided that you don't mind showing an ID every time you want to cash a check.

You can get traveler's checks at almost any bank. **American Express** offers denominations of $20, $50, $100, $500, and (for cardholders only) $1,000. You'll pay a service charge ranging from 1% to 4%. You can also get American Express traveler's checks over the phone by calling ② **800/721-9768;** Amex gold and platinum cardholders who use this number are exempt from the 1% fee. AAA members can obtain checks without a fee at most AAA offices.

Visa offers traveler's checks at Citibank locations nationwide, as well as at several other banks. The service charge ranges between 1.5% and 2%; checks come in denominations of $20, $50, $100, $500, and $1,000. Call ② **800/732-1322** for information. **MasterCard** also offers traveler's checks. Call ② **800/223-9920** for a location near you.

CREDIT CARDS

Credit cards are invaluable when traveling—they're a safe way to carry money and a convenient record of all your expenses. You can also withdraw cash advances from your cards at any bank (although this should be reserved for dire emergencies because you'll start paying hefty interest the moment you receive the cash). Some credit cards limit how much money you can withdraw daily in cash advances, so ask before you go.

Note: Many banks, including Chase and Citibank, have begun to charge a 2% to 3% service fee for transactions in a foreign currency.

5 When to Go

From April to June and **late September to October** are the best months for traveling in Sicily—temperatures are usually mild and the crowds aren't quite so intense. Starting in mid-June, the summer rush really picks up, and from **July to mid-September** the country teems with visitors. **August** is the worst month: Not only does it get uncomfortably hot, muggy, and crowded, but the entire island goes on vacation at least from August 15 to the end of the month—and many Sicilians take off the entire month. Many hotels, restaurants, and shops are closed (except at the spas, beaches, and islands, which are where 70% of the Sicilians head to). From **late October to Easter,** most attractions go on shorter winter hours or are closed for renovation. Many hotels and restaurants take a month or two off between **November and February,** when spa and beach destinations become padlocked ghost towns, and it can get much colder than you'd expect. The almond trees blossom in February, especially along the southern coast, and Taormina and Mount Etna are celebrated for their riot of spring flowers. Easter is a time of major celebration on the island, with many traditional, religion-oriented festivals.

High season on most airlines' routes to Rome/Palermo usually stretches from June to the beginning of September. This is the most expensive and most crowded time to travel. **Shoulder season** is from April to May, early September to October, and December 15 to 24. **Low season** is from November 1 to December 14 and December 25 to March 31.

WEATHER

It can be very hot in summery Sicily, especially inland. The high temperatures (measured in Sicily in degrees Celsius) begin in May, often lasting until sometime in October. Winters are mild.

For the most part, it's drier in Sicily than in North America, so high temperatures don't seem as bad because the humidity is lower. On islands, temperatures can stay in the 90s (30s Celsius) for days, but nights are most often comfortably cooler.

Months	Jan	Feb	Mar	Apr	May	Jun	Jul	Aug	Sept	Oct	Nov	Dec
PALERMO												
Temp.(°F)	54	55	56	60	66	72	78	79	75	69	62	56
Temp.(°C)	12	13	13	16	19	22	26	26	24	21	17	13
Rainfall/in.	2.80	2.60	2.30	1.70	1.00	.50	.20	.50	1.60	3.90	3.70	3.20
SYRACUSE (SIRACUSA)												
Temp.(°F)	54	54	55	59	60	72	78	79	75	69	58	56
Temp.(°C)	12	12	13	15	16	22	26	26	24	21	14	13
Rainfall/in.	2.40	1.70	1.30	.70	.50	1.00	.10	.20	1.00	3.10	2.00	2.80

HOLIDAYS

Offices and shops in Sicily are closed on the following **national holidays:** January 1 (New Year's Day), Easter Monday, April 25 (Liberation Day), May 1 (Labor Day), July 15 (Santa Rosalia), August 15 (Assumption of the Virgin), November 1 (All Saints' Day), December 8 (Feast of the Immaculate Conception), December 25 (Christmas Day), and December 26 (Santo Stefano).

SICILIAN CALENDAR OF EVENTS

For major events in which tickets should be procured well before you arrive, check with **Global Tickets** in the United States at ℂ **800/223-6108.**

January

Epiphania (Epiphany), Piana degli Albanesi. Located 29km (18 miles) from Palermo in one of the Albanian colonies founded in Sicily at the end of the 15th century, the celebration of Epiphany is an ostentatious affair. A joyous procession of residents in traditional Albanian costumes parades through the streets. January 6. Call ℂ **091-8571785** (http://www.pianalbanesi.it).

Carnevale, Acireale. Carnevale is celebrated all over Sicily, but this is the most beautiful. In a town north of Catania, the event is marked by a colorful parade of masked participants and giant floats. Lemons and oranges from nearby citrus fields are used in abundance, creating an aromatic atmosphere. It's a weeklong party of fun and revelry. Third week in January. Contact the Acireale tourist office at © **095-891999.**

February

Almond Blossom Festival, Agrigento. Literally thousands of almond trees are in bloom around the Valley of the Temples at this festival heralding the arrival of the first fruits of spring. In Phrygian myths, the almond tree was viewed as "the father of the world." The event is marked with exotic music, singing, beauty pageants, parades, and traditional puppet shows. All kinds of sweets made with almonds are sold. First half of February. Contact the Agrigento tourist office at © **0922-21899.**

Feast of Saint Agata, Catania. Of pagan origin, this is a beautiful all-night religious celebration of the martyred patron saint of the city. A procession of candle-bearers called *candelore* parades through the city, accompanied by the mayor and his entourage in gilded horse-drawn carriages. High church officials add clouds of incense and all the requisite pomp and circumstance. There's also street theater and fireworks. Sweets based on centuries-old recipes from nunneries are sold. All-around mayhem prevails. February 13 to 15. Contact the Catania tourist office (© **095-7306255**).

April

The Dance of the Devils, Prizzi. Unique in Italy, a grotesque dance of the devils *(Il Ballo dei Diavoli)* takes place on Easter in this medieval town a 2-hour drive south of Palermo deep in the Sicilian interior. The festival represents the age-old struggle between good and evil. Figures dressed as devils in red, their faces covered with grotesque masks, parade through the streets, searching for souls to devour. Death is seen dressed in yellow and carrying a crossbow. All ends well as "angels" appear later to subdue the devils. Call © **167-016681;** www.commune/prizzi.pa.it.

Holy Week Observances, island-wide. Processions and age-old ceremonies—some from pagan days, some from the Middle Ages—are staged in every city or town in Sicily. No matter where you are, you're likely to come across observances of this annual event. Particularly colorful and moving are the observances in Palermo and Catania along the coast. Trapani's procession of the *Misteri* is the island's most famous event staged during Holy Week. But the finest and most colorful observance, in our view, is in the inland city of Caltagirone, a 2-hour drive southwest of Catania. Events are staged on such days as Holy Tuesday, Good Friday, and, of course, Easter Sunday itself. The week leading up to Easter. Local tourist offices can supply details.

May

Infiorata, Noto. The residents of this little southeastern Sicilian town prepare a magnificent carpet of flowers along Via Nicolaci, in the historic core. Themes are taken from religion or mythology. The festival features crafts shows, performances of sacred music, and tours of religious sites, followed by dances and parades of flower-bedecked antique carriages. The beginning of the month. Check with the tourist office at © **0931-573779** for exact dates and information.

June

Festa del Muzzini, Messina. Muzzini are ancient vases draped in silk that are carried in parades. This observance is actually a pagan rite to honor Demeter, the goddess of earth and fertility. It is rumored that many young women trying to have a child find themselves impregnated on the night of this celebration. June 24. Contact the tourist office at Messina at © **090-64022.**

July

The Feast of Santa Rosalia, Palermo. Holding a special place in the hearts of many residents, this festival is the most famous and popular in Sicily. During the week of the festival the city becomes an open-air theater. The highlight is a 15m (50-ft.) high float known as the *carro,* which is paraded through the streets along with a statue of Santa Rosalia on a huge cart drawn by horses. Torchlight processions are conducted to the saint's shrine on Monte Pellegrino, where the saint is said to have appeared in a vision to a hunter. Bands, dancers, African drums, religious choruses, fantastic fireworks, theatrical performances, and feasts featuring everything from delectable tiny snails to fantastic gelato characterize the event. July 10 to 15. Contact the tourist office in Palermo at © **091-583847.**

August

Ferragosto (Assumption Day). This national holiday on August 15 virtually shuts down the island of Sicily, marking the event where Mary was said to have been "taken up and assumed into heaven." This mid-August event (date varies) always includes a feast of pagan origin and street parades and fairs with young girls dressed in virginal white, sitting on oxen carts, their virtue menacingly protected by spikes. They toss pomegranates and fruit at the spectators. This observance is at its most colorful in Palermo. Call the tourist office at © **091-583847.**

Palio dei Normanni, Piazza Armerina. Sicily's Norman past is observed in this historic celebration in which locals dress in ancient costumes for parades. Even jousting takes place as knights in period costumes looking like refugees from the pages of *Ivanhoe* appear. They fight against a puppet representing the dreaded Saracens. Mid-August. Contact the tourist office at Piazza Armerina (© **0935-680201**).

September

International Couscous Festival, San Vito Lo Capo. Outside Trapani, this annual event means 3 days of dancing to live music and a bounty of local foods. The couscous competition draws some of the best cooks in the world, including those from North Africa where the dish originated. You'll gain 10 pounds if you participate in all the feasting. Mid-September. Contact the tourist office in Trapani at © **0923-29000.**

October

Maritime Festival, Porticello Santa Flavia. This maritime festival takes place every year at a little fishing port to the east of Palermo. Sporting competitions include boat races among the fishermen, along with a village festival dedicated to fish, a mainstay of the port's economy, especially the harvesting of anchovies and sardines. At night a parade of boats illuminated with flaming torches is staged, and an image of Maria, "holiest of light," is hauled to the water to be blessed. Naturally, stalls sell all the fish dishes you can consume. The first Sunday in October. Contact the tourist office at Palermo (© **091-583847**).

November

Tutti Santi (All Saints' Day), island-wide. This ancient observance is celebrated all over Sicily as a national holiday including the "Day of the Dead." It's the Sicilian version of Halloween in which the spirits of the dead are said to roam about. Originally more pagan in origin, it was tamed by the Catholic Church with the introduction of saints who are celebrated. Children are costumed for parades around the main squares of various towns. Pastry shops prepare a delectable confection, the ominously named "bones of the dead." November 1 and 2. Check with local tourist offices.

December

Christmas Fair, Syracuse. The major holiday fair of the south is conducted in this ancient city, with the island's most colorful Christmas market. Many islanders drive for miles to purchase gifts for the holidays here, including sweets, clothing, special embroidery, decorations, ornaments, and other items. It's conducted in the Epipoli section of Syracuse. From the second Saturday of December to December 21. Contact the tourist office in Syracuse (① **0931-67710**).

6 Health & Insurance

TRAVEL INSURANCE AT A GLANCE

Since Sicily is far from home for most of us, and because a number of things could go wrong—lost luggage, trip cancellation, a medical emergency—consider the following types of insurance.

Check your existing insurance policies before you buy travel insurance to cover trip cancellation, lost luggage, or medical expenses. You're likely to have partial or complete coverage already. The cost of travel insurance varies widely, depending on the cost and length of your trip, your age, your health, and the type of trip you're taking.

For information on **car rental insurance,** go to the "By Car" section of "Getting Around Sicily," later in this chapter.

TRIP-CANCELLATION INSURANCE

There are three types of trip-cancellation insurance: one, in the event that you pre-pay for a cruise or tour that gets canceled and you can't get your money back; a second for when you or someone in your family gets sick or dies, and you can't travel (but beware that you may not be covered for a pre-existing condition); and a third for when bad weather makes travel impossible. For information, contact one of the following insurers: **Access America** (① 800/284-8300; www.accessamerica.com);

Travel Guard International (① 800/826-1300; www.travelguard.com); **Travel Insured International** (① 800/243-3174; www.travelinsured.com); and **Travelex Insurance Services** (① 800/228-9792; www.travelexinsurance.com).

MEDICAL INSURANCE Most health insurance policies cover you if you get sick away from home—but check, particularly if you're insured by an HMO. With the exception of certain HMOs and Medicare/Medicaid, your medical insurance should cover medical treatment—even hospital care—overseas. However, most out-of-country hospitals make you pay your bills up front, and send you a refund after you've returned home and filed the necessary paperwork. If you require additional medical insurance, try **MEDEX International** (① **888/MEDEX-00** or 410/453-6300; www.medexassist.com) or **Travel Assistance International** (① **800/821-2828;** www.travelassistance.com; for general information on services, call the company's Worldwide Assistance Services, Inc., at ① **800/777-8710**).

LOST-LUGGAGE INSURANCE On domestic flights, checked baggage is covered up to $2,500 per ticketed passenger. On international flights (including U.S. portions of international trips), baggage is limited to approximately $9.05 per pound, up to approximately $635 per checked bag. If you plan to check items more valuable than the standard liability, you may purchase "excess valuation" coverage from the airline, up to $5,000. Be sure to take any valuables or irreplaceable items with you in your carry-on luggage. Lost luggage may also be covered by your homeowner's or renter's policy or platinum and gold credit cards.

THE HEALTHY TRAVELER

In general, Sicily is viewed as a "safe" destination, although problems, of course, can and do occur anywhere. You don't need to get shots; most foodstuff is safe, and the water in cities and towns is potable. If you're concerned, order bottled water. It is easy to get a prescription filled in towns and cities, and nearly all places contain English-speaking doctors at hospitals with well-trained medical staffs.

In other words, Sicily is part of the civilized world.

The vegetarian can go into almost any restaurant in Sicily, even those specializing in meat and fish, and order a heaping plate of antipasti made with fresh vegetables.

WHAT TO DO IF YOU GET SICK AWAY FROM HOME

If you worry about getting sick away from home, consider purchasing **medical travel insurance** and carry your ID card in your purse or wallet. In most cases, your existing health plan will provide the coverage you need. See the section on insurance above for more information.

If you suffer from a chronic illness, consult your doctor before your departure. For conditions like epilepsy, diabetes, or heart problems, wear a **Medic Alert Identification Tag** (© **800/825-3785**; www.medicalert. org), which will immediately alert doctors to your condition and give them access to your records through Medic Alert's 24-hour hot line.

Pack **prescription medications** in your carry-on luggage, and carry prescription medications in their original containers. Also bring along copies of your prescriptions in case you lose your pills or run out. Carry the generic name of prescription medicines, in case a local pharmacist is unfamiliar with the brand name.

And don't forget sunglasses and an extra pair of contact lenses or prescription glasses.

Contact the **International Association for Medical Assistance to Travelers (IAMAT)** (© **716/754-4883** or 519/836-3412; fax 519/836-0102; www.iamat.org) for tips on travel and health concerns in Sicily and lists of local, English-speaking doctors; in Canada, call © **519/836-0102.** The United States **Centers for Disease Control and Prevention** (© **800/ 311-3435**; www.cdc.gov) provides up-to-date information on necessary vaccines and health hazards by region or country. (Their booklet, *Health Information for International Travel,* is $25 by mail; on the Internet, it's free.) Any foreign consulate can provide a list of area doctors who speak English. If you do get sick, ask the concierge at your hotel to recommend a local doctor—even his or her own doctor, if necessary. Or contact your embassy or consulate—they maintain lists of English-speaking doctors. For an emergency dial © **113** for the police or © **112** for the *Carabinieri* (army police corps): They can call an ambulance or help you in many ways. If your situation is life-threatening, go to the *pronto soccorso* (emergency department) at the local hospital.

Under the Italian national healthcare system, you're eligible only for free *emergency* care. If you're admitted to a hospital as an in-patient, even from an accident and an emergency, you're required to pay (unless you're a resident of the European Economic

Area). You're also required to pay for follow-up care.

If you do end up paying for health care, especially if you're admitted to a hospital for any reason, most health-insurance plans and HMOs will cover at least part of the out-of-country hospital visits and procedures. Be prepared to pay the bills up front at the time of care, however. You'll get a refund after you've returned to your country and filed all the paperwork.

THE SAFE TRAVELER

Don't think you'll be at the mercy of the Mafia the moment you step foot into Sicily, as popular belief around the world suggests. The Mafia is virtually invisible.

You'll face more danger from petty thieves such as pickpockets than you will from the Cosa Nostra. *Scippatori,* or purse snatchers and pickpockets, are the curse of such cities as Palermo, Messina, and Catania.

Country towns, of course, are far safer. Avoid walking on dark streets in the old towns of Sicily at night. Even relatively deserted inner-city streets during the day can put you at risk of robbery. Although many tourists are robbed, violence against visitors is rare.

Never leave valuables in a car, and never travel with your car unlocked. A U.S. State Department travel advisory warns that every car (whether parked, stopped at a traffic light, or even moving) can be a potential target for armed robbery. In these uncertain times, it is always prudent to check the U.S. State Department's travel advisories at **http://travel.state.gov**.

7 Tips for Travelers with Special Needs

TRAVELERS WITH DISABILITIES

Sicily is hardly in the vanguard of catering to travelers with disabilities. Only the most expensive first-class or deluxe hotels have facilities that accommodate persons with disabilities.

The narrow, cobblestone streets of Sicily's cities and villages, most of which date back to the Middle Ages, weren't built for people who get around in wheelchairs. Hysterical drivers and impossible parking don't help much either. Even if you're an Olympic athlete, getting across a street in the face of speeding traffic in Palermo is risky at any time.

It is our recommendation that a person with disabilities planning to tour Sicily do so only on an organized tour specifically geared to provide assistance, which is vitally needed.

ORGANIZATIONS

- **The Society for Accessible Travel and Hospitality** (© 212/447-7284; fax 212/725-8253; www. sath.org) offers a wealth of travel resources for all types of disabilities and informed recommendations on destinations, access guides, travel agents, tour operators, vehicle rentals, and companion services. Annual membership costs $45 for adults; $30 for seniors and students.

- **The American Foundation for the Blind** (© 800/232-5463; www.afb.org) provides information on traveling with Seeing Eye dogs.

FOR BRITISH TRAVELERS

The **Royal Association for Disability and Rehabilitation (RADAR),** Unit 12, City Forum, 250 City Rd., London EC1V 8AF (© 020/7250-3222; www.radar.org.uk), publishes three holiday "fact packs" for £2 each or £5 for all three. The first provides general information, including tips for planning and booking a holiday, obtaining insurance, and handling finances; the second outlines transportation available when going abroad and equipment for rent; the third deals with specialized accommodations. Another good resource is **Holiday Care,** Imperial Building, 2nd Floor, Victoria Road, Horley, Surrey RH6 7PZ (© **01293/774-535;** www.holiday care.org.uk), a national charity dispensing advice on accessible accommodations for the elderly and persons with disabilities. Annual membership is £35.

GAY & LESBIAN TRAVELERS

Even though Italy since 1861 has had rather liberal legislation regarding homosexuality, Sicily remains one of the major bastions of homophobia in Europe. Some of the islanders express anti-gay attitudes that might belong more appropriately to the Middle Ages. Open displays of affection between same-sex couples meets with obvious disapproval by intolerant islanders.

Don't be misled: Sicilian men are often very affectionate, linking arms with each other and kissing each other on the cheeks in saying hello or bidding goodbye. This is how straight men behave, and such affection is not to be construed as overtly sexual.

There are few gay businesses in Sicily. If you are gay and still want to go, your best bet is the more sophisticated resort of Taormina, following in the footsteps of former visitors like Tennessee Williams and his longtime companion, Frank Merlo.

If you really want a gay holiday in Italy, Sicily may not be for you. Head for *la dolce vita* as lived on the Isle of Capri (see *Frommer's Italy*).

If you're determined to go, however, the following may be helpful.

The International Gay & Lesbian Travel Association (IGLTA) (© **800/ 448-8550** or 954/776-2626; fax 954/ 776-3303; www.iglta.org) links travelers with gay-friendly hoteliers, tour operators, and airline and cruise-line representatives. It offers monthly newsletters, marketing mailings, and a membership directory that's updated once a year. Membership is $200 yearly, plus a $100 administration fee for new members.

SENIOR TRAVEL

Mention the fact that you're a senior when you first make your travel reservations. All major airlines and many Sicilian hotels offer discounts for seniors.

Members of **AARP** (formerly known as the American Association of Retired Persons), 601 E St. NW, Washington, DC 20049 (© **800/ 424-3410** or 202/434-2277; www. aarp.org), get discounts on hotels, airfares, and car rentals. Anyone over 50 can join.

AGENCIES/OPERATORS

- **Elderhostel** (© **877/426-8056;** www.elderhostel.org) arranges study programs for those ages 55 and over (and a spouse or companion of any age) in the U.S. and in more than 80 countries around the world, including Italy. Most courses last 2 to 4 weeks abroad, and many include airfare, accommodations in university dormitories or modest inns, meals, and tuition.

- **Elder Travelers,** 1615 Smelter Ave., Black Eagle, MT 59414 (www.eldertravelers.com), aids those who are over 50. Their stated purpose is to provide members with "zero cost lodging" anywhere in the world, including Sicily; seniors are hooked up with their counterpart hosts in the lands in which they travel. For $40 annually, subscriptions are given to their informative newsletter.

FAMILY TRAVEL

Sicilian love *bambini* but don't offer a lot of special amenities for them. For example, a kids' menu in a restaurant is a rarity. You can, however, order a half portion *(mezza porzione),* and most waiters will oblige. Most Sicilian hoteliers will let children 12 and under stay in a room with their parents for free. Sometimes this requires a little negotiation at the reception desk.

At attractions, inquire if a kids' discount is available. Italians call it *sconto*

bambino. For European Community young people under 18, a big break is offered. They are admitted free to all state-run museums.

Throughout the guide, look for our kid-friendly icons.

8 Getting There

BY PLANE

High season on most airlines' routes to Sicily is usually from June to the beginning of September. This is the most expensive and most crowded time to travel. **Shoulder season** is April through May, from early September to October, and from December 15 to 24. **Low season** is from November 1 to December 14 and December 25 to March 31.

There are no direct flights to Sicily. Most visitors fly first to Milan or Rome, then take a connecting flight to Sicily, most often using Palermo as their gateway to the island.

In the west, planes arrive at the **Aeroporto Falcone & Borsellini,** 31km (19 miles) west of Palermo at Punta Raisl. In the eastern part of the island planes land at Catania's **Aeroporto Fontanarossa,** 7km (4½ miles) south of the center. For airport information in Palermo, call ✆ **091-591698** daily from 5:30am to 9:30pm, and for the Catania airport, call ✆ **095-730266** daily from 8am to midnight.

Chances are you'll use Alitalia for the Sicilian flights. For Alitalia flight information in Palermo, call ✆ **091-7020313** daily from 5:30am to 7:30pm; in Catania, call Alitalia (✆ **095-252410**) daily from 5am to 9pm.

Flying time from Rome to Palermo is just 1 hour. **Alitalia** (✆ **800/223-5730** in the U.S., or toll free ✆ **8488-65641** for domestic flights within Italy) operates at least 17 flights a day from Rome to Palermo and about 13 from Milan. There is

one direct flight a day from Turin to Palermo (far more if you stop over in Milan or Rome and make a connecting flight). For most visitors who are already in the south of Italy, the daily flight from Naples to Palermo is the most heavily booked. There are also six daily flights from Bologna to Palermo.

Alitalia also operates 12 daily flights from Rome to Catania. There are also eight flights a day that stop first in Naples. From Milan to Catania, there are 16 direct flights daily, or nine with stops in Rome. From Turin, Alitalia offers two direct flights to Catania (or 16 with stops in Rome). From Bologna, the airline flies three times daily to Catania, or 16 times with stops in Rome or Naples.

Meridiana (✆ **06-478041** in Rome, or 091-323141 in Palermo) is the second major carrier serving Sicily. The airline shares some of its flights and reservations functions with Alitalia (see above). Most of Meridiana's flights to Sicily operate between Rome and Palermo (four direct flights daily) and can be booked separately or as part of a transatlantic itinerary through Alitalia.

In addition to its flights from Rome to Palermo, Meridiana offers two direct daily flights from Milan to Catania; one direct daily flight from Bologna to Palermo (three direct flights from Bologna to Catania); and one direct flight from Verona to Palermo (two direct flights from Verona to Catania). Surprisingly, Meridiana doesn't fly from Rome to Catania or from Naples to Catania.

> ### ⌒Tips   Cutting Air Costs
>
> Regardless of how you opt to fly, it's cheaper for transatlantic passengers to Italy to have a flight to Palermo written into the overall ticket when booking a flight to Italy from North America. If you book a flight to Palermo once you've arrived in Italy, it will cost much more.

Another, smaller carrier, less important than Meridiana or Alitalia, **AirEurope** (© 800-454000) has Sicilian links with three mainland Italian cities: one flight daily from Milan to Palermo; three flights daily from Milan to Catania; two flights daily from Venice to Palermo; and two flights daily from Venice to Catania, plus (the most heavily used flight) a Naples-to-Palermo air link once a day.

A final carrier serving Sicily is **Air One** (toll free © 848-848880, or 06-488800 in Rome). It flies from Rome to Palermo five times a day, and from Rome to Catania six times a day. There are three daily flights from Milan to Palermo, and six flights from Milan to Catania. There is also a daily flight from Turin to Catania.

But to fly to Sicily from North America, you must first reach Italy.

FROM NORTH AMERICA Flying time to Rome from New York, Newark, and Boston is 8 hours; from Chicago, 10 hours; and from Los Angeles, 12½ hours. Flying time to Milan from New York, Newark, and Boston is 8 hours; from Chicago, 9¼ hours; and from Los Angeles, 11½ hours.

American Airlines (© 800/433-7300; www.aa.com) offers daily nonstop flights to Rome from Chicago's O'Hare Airport, with flights from all parts of American's vast network making connections in Chicago. **Delta** (© 800/221-1212; www.delta.com) also flies from New York's JFK Airport to Milan, Venice, and Rome; separate flights depart every evening. **United** (© 800/241-6522; www.ual.com)

has service to Milan only from Washington Dulles Airport in Washington, D.C. **US Airways** (© 800/428-4322; www.usairways.com) offers one flight daily to Rome out of Philadelphia (you can connect through Philly from most major U.S. cities). And **Continental** (© 800/525-0280; www.continental.com) flies twice daily to Rome and Milan from its hub in Newark.

Air Canada (© 888/247-2262; www.aircanada.ca) flies daily from Toronto to Rome. Two of the flights are nonstop; the others touch down en route in Montréal, depending on the schedule.

British Airways (© 800/AIRWAYS; www.britishairways.com), **Virgin Atlantic Airways** (© 800/862-8621; www.virgin-atlantic.com), **Air France** (© 800/237-2747; www.airfrance.com), **Northwest/KLM** (© 800/374-7747; www.klm.com), and **Lufthansa** (© 800/645-3880; www.lufthansa-usa.com) offer some attractive deals for anyone interested in combining a trip to Sicily with a stopover in, say, Britain, Paris, Amsterdam, or Germany.

Alitalia (© 800/223-5730; www.alitaliausa.com) is the Italian national airline, with nonstop flights to Rome from different North American cities, including New York (JFK), Newark, Boston, Chicago, and Miami. Nonstop flights into Milan are from New York (JFK), Newark, Miami, and Boston. From Milan or Rome, Alitalia can easily book connecting domestic flights if your final destination is Sicily. Alitalia participates in the frequent-flier programs of other airlines, including Continental and US Airways.

FROM THE UNITED KINGDOM
Operated by the European Travel Network, **www.discount-tickets.com** is a great online source for regular and discounted airfares to destinations around the world. You can also use this site to compare rates and book accommodations, car rentals, and tours. Click on "Special Offers" for the latest package deals.

British newspapers are always full of classified ads touting slashed fares to Italy. One good source is *Time Out.* London's *Evening Standard* has a daily travel section, and the Sunday editions of almost any newspaper run many ads. Although competition is fierce, one well-recommended company that consolidates bulk ticket purchases and then passes the savings on to its consumers is **Trailfinders** (© 020/7937-5400; www.trailfinders. com). It offers access to tickets on such carriers as SAS, British Airways, and KLM.

Both **British Airways** (© 0845/ 773-3377 in the U.K.; www.ba.com) and **Alitalia** (© 020/8745-8200; www.alitaliausa.com) have frequent flights from London's Heathrow to Rome, Milan, Venice, Pisa (the gateway to Florence), and Naples. Flying time from London to these cities is from 2 to 3 hours. British Airways also has one direct flight a day from Manchester to Rome. Once on mainland Italy, you can make a connecting flight into Catania or Palermo, among other cities (see above).

The fastest way to get from the British Isles to Sicily is not via Alitalia or British Airways but through the smaller airline, **Meridiana** (© 0044-1293507-527), at London's Gatwick airport. Meridiana maintains offices at 15 Charles II St. SW1 in London (© 020/78392222). Meridiana flies

twice daily to Palermo from Gatwick with a stopover in Florence. There is also one daily flight from Gatwick to Catania, plus another daily flight to Catania with a stopover in Florence.

FLYING FOR LESS: TIPS FOR GETTING THE BEST AIRFARE

Passengers sharing the same airplane cabin rarely pay the same fare. Travelers who need to purchase tickets at the last minute, change their itinerary at a moment's notice, or get home for the weekend often get stuck paying the premium rate. Here are some ways to keep your airfare costs down.

- Passengers who can book their ticket **long in advance,** who can **stay over Saturday night,** or who **fly midweek or at less-trafficked hours** will pay a fraction of the full fare. If your schedule is flexible, say so, and ask if you can secure a cheaper fare by changing your flight plans. *Note:* The lowest-priced fares are often nonrefundable, require advance purchase of 1 to 3 weeks and a certain length of stay, and carry stiff penalties for changing dates of travel.

- You can also save on airfares by keeping an eye out for **promotional specials** or **fare wars,** when airlines lower prices on their most popular routes, with the competition often following suit. You rarely see fare wars offered during peak travel times, but if you can travel in the off season, you may snag a bargain.

- **Consolidators,** also known as bucket shops, are a good place to find low fares. Consolidators buy seats in bulk from the airlines and then sell them back to the public at prices usually below even the airlines' discounted rates. Their small ads usually run in Sunday newspaper travel sections. *Note:* Bucket shop tickets are usually nonrefundable or rigged with stiff cancellation penalties, often as high as 50% to 75% of the ticket price. Reliable consolidators include **STA Travel** (© **800/781-4040;** www.sta.travel.com),which offers good fares for travelers of all ages, and **Flights.com** (©**800/ TRAV-800;** www.flights.com), started in Europe and offering excellent fares worldwide. **Fly Cheap** (© **800/Y-CHEAP** (www. 1800flycheap.com) is owned by package-holiday megalith MyTravel and so has expecially good access to fares for sunny destinations.

• **Join frequent-flier clubs.** Accrue enough miles, and you'll be rewarded with free flights and elite status. It's free, and you'll get the best choice of seats, faster response to phone inquiries, and prompter service if your luggage is stolen, your flight is canceled or delayed, or you want to change your seat.

• **Search the Internet** for cheap fares. Among the more popular virtual travel agents are **Travelocity** (www.travelocity.com), **Expedia** (www.expedia.com), **Orbitz** (www.orbitz.com) and **Yahoo! Travel** (http://travel.yahoo.com).

BY CAR

If you're already on the Continent, particularly in a neighboring country such as France or Austria, you may want to drive to Italy. However, you should make arrangements in advance with your car-rental company.

It's also possible to drive from London to Rome, a distance of 1,810km (1,124 miles), via Calais/Boulogne/Dunkirk, or 1,747km (1,085 miles) via Oostende/Zeebrugge, not counting channel crossings by hovercraft, ferry, or the Chunnel. Milan is some 644km (400 miles) closer to Britain than is Rome. If you cross over from England and arrive at one of the continental ports, you still face a 24-hour drive. Most drivers play it safe and budget 3 days for the journey.

Most of the roads from western Europe leading into Italy are toll-free, with some notable exceptions. If you use the Swiss superhighway network, you'll have to buy a special tax sticker at the frontier. You'll also pay to go through the St. Gotthard Tunnel into Italy. Crossings from France can be through the Mont Blanc Tunnel, for which you'll pay, or you can leave the French Riviera at Menton and drive directly into Italy along the Italian Riviera toward San Remo.

If you don't want to drive such distances, ask a travel agent to book you on a Motorail arrangement where the train carries your car. This service, however, is good only to Milan, as no car and sleeper expresses run the 644km (400 miles) south to Rome.

Warning: You won't save a lot of money by driving to Sicily from another European country. Once you cross the frontier into Italy, you'll face a staggering number of tolls for riding the *autostrade* (express highways). Not only that, but gasoline costs are among the highest in Europe. Count on a lot of time, at least 17 hours of straight driving from the Swiss or French border to Villa San Giovanni, the point from which the car-carrying ferries sail to Messina in eastern Sicily.

BY TRAIN

For many visitors, this is the most convenient way to reach Sicily from the Italian mainland. Trains with connections from all over Europe, including Rome and Naples, arrive at the port of Villa San Giovanni, near Reggio di Calabria, in southern Italy.

Trains roll onto enormous barges for the 1-hour crossing into eastern Sicily. Passengers remain in their seats during the short voyage across the Straits of Messina, eventually rolling back onto the tracks once they reach

Sicily. The train from Rome to Palermo takes 11 to 13 hours, depending on the speed of the train. The rail route from Naples to Palermo takes 10 hours.

For fares and information within Italy, call © **892021.** See individual town or city listings for more detailed train information and fares.

If you plan to travel heavily on the European rails, you'll do well to secure the latest copy of the *Thomas Cook European Timetable of Railroads.* This 500-plus-page timetable accurately documents all of Europe's main-line passenger rail services. It's available from **Forsyth Travel Library,** 44 S. Broadway, White Plains, NY 10604 (© **800/FORSYTH;** www.forsyth. com), for $28 (plus $4.95 shipping in the U.S. and $6.95 in Canada), or at travel specialty stores such as **Rand McNally,** 150 E. 52nd St., New York, NY 10022 (© **212/758-7488;** www. randmcnally.com).

New electric trains have made travel between France and Italy faster and more comfortable than ever. France's **TGVs** travel at speeds of up to 185 miles per hour and have cut travel time between Paris and Turin from 7 to 5½ hours and between Paris and Milan from 7½ to 6¾ hours. Italy's **ETRs** travel at speeds of up to 145 miles per hour and currently run between Milan and Lyon (5 hr.), with a stop in Turin.

EUROPE-WIDE RAIL PASSES

EURAILPASS Many travelers to Europe who go on to Sicily take advantage of one of the greatest travel bargains, the **Eurailpass,** which permits unlimited first-class rail travel in any country in western Europe (except the British Isles) and Hungary in eastern Europe.

The advantages are tempting: There are no tickets; simply show the pass to the ticket collector and then settle back to enjoy the scenery. Seat reservations are required on some trains. Many of the trains have couchettes (sleeping cars), for which an extra fee is charged. Obviously, the 2- or 3-month traveler gets the greatest economic advantages. To obtain full advantage of a 15-day or 1-month pass, you'd have to spend a great deal of time on the train.

Eurailpass holders are entitled to considerable reductions on certain buses and ferries as well. You'll get a 20% reduction on second-class accommodations from certain companies operating ferries between Naples and Palermo.

A **Eurailpass** is $572 for 15 days, $740 for 21 days, $918 for 1 month, $1,298 for 2 months, and $1,606 for 3 months. Children 3 and under travel free, provided that they don't occupy a seat (otherwise, they're charged half fare); children 4 to 11 are charged half fare. If you're under 26, you can buy **a Eurail Youthpass,** entitling you to unlimited second-class travel for $401 for 15 days, $518 for 21 days, $644 for 1 month, $910 for 2 months, and $1,126 for 3 months.

Eurail Saverpass, valid all over Europe for first class only, offers discounted 15-day travel for groups of three or more people traveling together April through September, or two people traveling together October through March. The price is $486 for 15 days, $630 for 21 days, $780 for 1 month, $1,106 for 2 months, and $1,366 for 3 months.

The **Eurail Flexipass** allows you to visit both Italy and Sicily with more flexibility. It's valid in first class and offers the same privileges as the Eurailpass. However, it provides a number of individual travel days that you can use over a much longer period of consecutive days. That makes it possible to stay in one city and yet not lose a single day of travel. There are two passes: 10 days of travel in 2 months for $674, and 15 days of travel in 2 months for $888.

Many of the same qualifications and restrictions as those for the previously described Flexipass apply to the **Eurail Youth Flexipass.** Sold only to travelers under 26, it allows 10 days of travel within 2 months for $473, and 15 days of travel within 2 months for $622.

Eurail Selectpass is a Flexipass, meaning that travel days need not be consecutive. Passes are available for 5, 6, 8, or 10 days within a 2-month period. Prices vary, of course, depending on the days selected, beginning at $346 for a 5-day pass.

For more information, log onto the official Eurail website at **www. eurail.com.**

WHERE TO BUY A PASS

In **North America,** you can buy these passes from travel agents or rail agents in major cities such as New York, Montréal, and Los Angeles. Eurailpasses are also available through **Rail Europe** (℡ **800/848-7245;** www. raileurope.com). No matter what everyone tells you, you can buy Eurailpasses in Europe as well as in America (at the major train stations), but they're more expensive. Rail Europe can also give you information on the rail/drive versions of the passes.

For details on the rail passes available in the **United Kingdom,** stop in at or contact the **International Rail Centre,** Victoria Station, London SW1V 1JZ (℡ **08705/848-848**). The staff can help you find the best option for the trip you're planning. Some of the most popular are the **Inter-Rail** and **Under 26** passes, entitling you to unlimited second-class travel in 26 European countries. **Under 26** passes are a worthwhile option for travelers under 26. They allow you to move leisurely from London to Rome, with

as many stopovers en route as you want, using a different route southbound (through Belgium, Luxembourg, and Switzerland) from the return route northbound (exclusively through France). All travel must be completed within 1 month of the departure date.

BY BOAT & FERRY

As an island, Sicily is well connected via sea links to mainland Sicily. The major connection is from Villa San Giovanni in Calabria, the last mainland city approached before the ferry trip over to Messina in eastern Sicily. Ferries—called *traghetti*—depart frequently from Villa San Giovanni, making the trip of 12km (7½ miles) across the Straits. For complete details on the crossings, including fares, refer to "Getting There" in chapter 6. If you don't have a car, the fastest way to go is by hydrofoil from Reggio di Calabria.

If you're already in Naples, it's easy to go by sea from that city to Palermo. **SNAV** (℡ 081-2514781) operates hydrofoils that make 5-hour southern crossings to Sicily. There is also a car-carrying ferry service operated by **Tirrenia Lines** (℡ 081-199123199) taking 11 hours to reach Palermo from Naples. Boat schedules are dependent on weather conditions. For details, refer to "Getting There" in chapter 3.

If you're in the north of Italy, you can also sail to Palermo from Genoa. **Grandi Navi Vedloci,** Via Fieschi 1 (℡ 010-589331), runs daily service to Palermo from July 8 to September 21 (Mon–Sat otherwise). The journey takes 20 hours, costing 101€ for foot passengers or 170€ per person for those bringing a vehicle. Ferries in Genoa depart from Nuovo Terminale Traghetti.

Grand Navi Veloci, Varco Galvali (℡ 0586-409804), also operates ferries to Palermo from the port of Livorno. Three ferry departures a week make the 17-hour run. Foot passengers are charged 75€ one-way; a person in a vehicle pays 121€.

BY BUS

There is no direct bus service to Sicily from outside Italy. Europe's major bus carrier, **Eurolines** (✆ **0990/143219** in London), has its main office at Grosvenor Gardens, Victoria, London SW1. It runs buses to Rome in 33 hours. After that, you can take an Italian bus to Sicily unless you're completely exhausted. Buses leave England on Wednesday and Friday, heading for Milan and Rome. The cost ranges from £129 to £139.

If you're in Rome and want to travel overland by bus into Sicily, you can book tickets from **Segesta,** Piazza della Repubblica (✆ **06-4819676**), which has two departures daily from Rome's Piazza Tiburtina going to Messina in 9 hours for a one-way cost of 29€. The line also goes to Syracuse in 11 hours, with a one-way ticket costing 36€.

9 Package Deals, Escorted Tours & Special-Interest Vacations

Before you start your search for the lowest airfare, consider booking your flight as part of a package, whether in the form of an escorted tour or a special-interest tour, or simply purchasing the biggest elements of your vacation from package tour operators at the same time. A package that includes airfare, hotel, transportation, and sometimes extras often costs less than the hotel alone would have, had you booked it yourself. That's because packages are sold in bulk to tour operators, who resell them to the public at drastically reduced costs.

Many airlines offer package deals. Also check the Sunday travel section of your newspaper for package operators.

ESCORTED TOURS

Escorted tours are structured group tours, with a leader. The price usually includes everything from airfare to hotels, meals, tours, admission costs, and local transportation.

RECOMMENDED ESCORTED TOUR OPERATORS

Italiatour, a company of the Alitalia Group (✆ **800/845-3365;** fax 212/765-2183; www.italiatourusa.com), offers the best escorted tours of Sicily. The best deal is a 9-day, 7-night jaunt from $1,699 round-trip that takes in such highlights as Catania, Ragusa, Agrigento, Palermo, and Giardini-Naxos (the latter the "beachfront" for Taormina). Of all the tours we've studied, this one best encapsulates the highlights. In most cases, the company sells pre-reserved accommodations, which are usually less expensive than if you had reserved them yourself. Because of the company's close link with Alitalia, the prices quoted are sometimes among the most reasonable on the retail market.

The biggest operator of escorted tours is **Perillo Tours** (✆ **800/431-1515** or 201/307-1234; fax 201/307-1808 in the U.S.; www.perillotours.com), family-operated for three generations—perhaps you've seen the TV commercials featuring the "King of Italy," Mario Perillo, and his son. Since it was founded in 1945, it has sent more than a million travelers to Italy on guided tours. Perillo's tours cost much less than you'd spend if you arranged a comparable trip yourself.

Accommodations are in first-class hotels, and guides tend to be well qualified and well informed. Tours in Sicily also include time in southern Italy, including 3 nights in Rome and 3 nights in Sorrento. The swing through Sicily itself, part of a larger tour, usually takes in 2 nights in

Palermo, 1 night in Agrigento, and 3 nights in Taormina.

Amelia International, 176 Woodbury Rd., Hicksville, NY 11801 (© **900/742-4591** or 516/433-0696; fax 516/822-6220; www.ameliainternational.com), specializes in Sicily and its Mediterranean neighbors. Custom-designed tours of Sicily last for 11 days, costing from $3,300 per person double occupancy—land charges only. You spend 4 nights in Palermo, 2 nights in Agrigento, 1 night in Syracuse, and 3 nights in Taormina. Highlights of the trip include visits to the Aeolian Islands, a journey to the medieval village of Erice, and a jeep ride along the craters of Mount Etna.

Globus and Cosmos Tours, working jointly, comprise one of Perillo's top competitors. **Globus** (© **866/ 755-8581;** www.globusandcosmos. com) also offers a grand tour of Italy and Sicily, spread over 15 days. The tour allows 4 nights in Sicily, time to visit the Valley of Temples, among other attractions. **Cosmos** (© **800/ 276-1241**), the budget branch of Globus, sells the same itineraries. These tours must be booked through a travel agent and not directly.

Yet another offering is through **Insight Vacations** (© **800/582-8380;** www.insightvacations.com), which features art tours. Its 12-day tour of "The Country Roads of Southern Italy & Sicily" includes stopovers at the seaside resort of Giardini-Naxos (below Taormina) and visits to the temples at Agrigento and the art treasures of Palermo.

Abercrombie & Kent (© **800/ 323-7308** in the U.S., or 0845/ 0700610 in the U.K.; www. abercrombiekent.com) offers a variety of luxury tours. A special feature is its deluxe Rome-to-Palermo tour, with a cruise aboard the *Sea Cloud.* The ship sails into such ports as Trapani on the western coast of Sicily and goes on to Lipari (one of the Aeolian Islands),

calling at Catania, Syracuse, and Taormina.

SPECIAL-INTEREST VACATIONS

For many visitors, a theme tour is the best way to explore the island.

For those who'd like to cycle along volcanic craters and rugged coastlines, in sight of Greek ruins, an intriguing 8-day biking tour offered by **VBT** (© **800/BIKE-TOUR;** www.vbt. com) costs from $1,995 per person, including accommodations (airfare not included). Bike trips circle the craters of Mount Etna and go to Taormina and on to some of the Aeolian Islands, including Lipari and Salina.

Hikes through ancient Sicily are organized through **Mountain Travel-Sobek,** 6420 Fairmount Ave., El Cerrito, CA 94530 (© **888/687-6235** or 800/227-2384; www.mtsobek.com). Depending on the number in your group, 10-day tours (land costs only) range from $3,590 to $3,790 per person. Hikes go through Palermo, Piazza Armerina, and the temples of Agrigento, and even include winetasting in the Corleone of Mafia fame.

Academic Tours (© **800/875-9171** or 718/417-8782; www.academic tours.com) is a real Sicilian specialist. They offer the best archaeological tours of Sicily, visiting such ancient cities and sites as Segesta, Erice, Selinunte, Piazza Armerina, Noto, and Syracuse. Typical prices for land arrangements are $1,499 in a double room for a 15-day tour.

To Grandmothers House We Go (© 718/768-6197) features cooking and cultural tours of Sicily. No more than 12 participate at one time. Cooking classes concentrate on simple, delicious food. The tour comprises not only food, but historical sights as well as living history—that is, the shops of artisans, a high school, a winery, a tuna fishery, and more.

10 Getting Around Sicily

BY PLANE

Unlike in mainland Italy, flying around Sicily is rarely an option. Once you've made a choice to fly into Palermo as your western gateway or Catania as your eastern gateway, the train, the bus, or a private rental car are the chief means of getting about. There are domestic flights from Palermo to the Pélagie Islands close to North Africa and to the island of Pantelleria, also owned by Sicily.

BY TRAIN

Unless you're heading for remote towns and villages in Sicily, riding the rails is the best way to traverse the island without a private rented car. All the major cities such as Palermo, Catania, Messina, Syracuse, Agrigento, Taormina, and Trapani have rail links. Trains on weekends and holidays tend to be crowded, so book in advance.

Train fares are generally very affordable in Sicily. See "By Train" listings under the individual town and city recommendations for trip times and point-to-point fares. Trains are operated by **Ferrovie dello Stato (FS),** the Italian State Railways. For general information on connections through Sicily, call © **892021** from anywhere on the island or within Italy itself. For more information, search the website at **www.fs-online.com.**

An **Italian Railpass** (known in Italy as a **BTLC Pass**) allows non-Italian citizens to ride as much as they like on Italy's entire rail network, including Sicily. Buy the pass in the United States or at main train stations in Italy, have it validated the first time you use it at any rail station, and ride as frequently as you like within the time allowed. An 8-day pass is $330 first class and $222 second class, a 15-day pass costs $417 first class and $276 second class, a 21-day pass costs $484 first class and $320 second class, and a 30-day pass costs $579 first class and $348 second class. All passes have a $15 issuing fee per class.

With the Italian Railpass and each of the other special passes, a supplement must be paid to ride on certain rapid trains, designated **ETR-450** or **Pendolino trains.** The rail systems of Sardinia are administered by a separate entity and aren't included in the Italian Railpass or any of the other passes.

Another option is the **Italian Flexi-rail Card,** which entitles you to a predetermined number of days of travel on any rail line in a certain time period. It's ideal for passengers who plan in advance to spend several days sightseeing before boarding a train for another city. A pass giving 4 possible travel days out of a block of 1 month is $239 first class and $191 second class, a pass for 8 travel days stretched over a 1-month period costs $334 first class and $268 second class, and a pass for 12 travel days within 1 month costs $429 first class and $343 second class.

You can buy these passes from any travel agent or by calling © **800/848-7245.** You can also call © **800/4EURAIL** or **800/EUROSTAR.**

As a rule of thumb, second-class travel usually costs about two-thirds the price of an equivalent first-class trip. The relatively new **InterCity trains** (designated **IC** on train schedules) are modern, air-conditioned trains that make limited stops; compared with the costs of the far slower direct or regional trains, the supplement can be steep, but a second-class IC ticket will provide a first-class experience.

An IC couchette (private fold-down bed in a communal cabin) requires a supplement above the price of first-class travel. Children 4 to 11 receive a discount of 50% off the adult fare, and children 3 and under travel free with their parents. Seniors and travelers under age 26 can also purchase discount cards. Seat reservations are highly recommended during peak season and on weekends or holidays; they must be booked in advance.

Slower Sicilian trains—called **Diretto, Espresso,** and **Interegionale**—stop at only the major towns or cities. Try to avoid a Regionale train (sometimes known as the Locale), as they stop in every hamlet and take forever.

Available at ticket offices is an FS booklet, *Treno Sicilia,* updated twice annually and usually distributed free.

BY BUS

Where the train doesn't go, there is almost always a local bus to take you into the more remote villages and hinterlands, although you can generally go from city to city and town to town by bus as well. Bus fares are often more expensive than rail transportation. For individual city and town links, and for a general outline of fares, refer to the individual recommendations of cities and towns.

The major bus company is **SAIS** (© **091-616028** in Palermo, or 095-536168 in Catania), offering service from Palermo to Messina, Catania, and Syracuse. **Cuffaro** (© **091-6161510**) links Palermo in the north with Agrigento in the south. **Etna Trasporti** (© **095-530396**) travels between Catania and Piazza Armerina and between Catania and Taormina. **Interbus** (© **095-536201**) has service between the cities of Catania, Messina, Taormina, and Syracuse.

Sunday is a bad day to take the bus, as schedules are either curtailed or else shut down completely. Keep in mind that large cities can have a number of bus depots. In smaller towns, buses generally pull into one central square, often the rail station.

Tickets most often are purchased right on the bus. In bigger cities such as Palermo, you can buy a ticket in advance at the office of one of the local companies. That way, you'll be more confident that you'll have a seat.

Only the cities or larger towns offer a bus system to get you from point to point. Tickets for city buses are bought before boarding, and you must validate them once you hop on or else you'll be fined up to 25€ on the spot.

Tickets are generally purchased at ticket booths, tobacconists *(tabacchi),* or newspaper kiosks. Most city buses charge .77€ for a ticket whose validity is from 60 to 90 minutes. Sometimes a city will offer a 24-hour transit ticket that can save you money if you plan to use the bus network extensively going from attraction to attraction.

BY CAR

U.S. and Canadian drivers don't need an **International Driver's License** to drive a rented car in Italy or Sicily. However, if you're driving a private car, you need such a license.

You can apply for an International Driver's License at any **American Automobile Association (AAA)** branch. You must be at least 18 and have two 2-by-2-inch photos and a photocopy of your U.S. driver's license with your AAA application form. The actual fee for the license can vary, depending on where it's issued. To find the AAA office nearest you, check the local phone directory or contact **AAA's national headquarters** (© **800/ 222-4357** or 407/444-4300; www. aaa.com). Remember that an International Driver's License is valid only if physically accompanied by your original driver's license and only if signed on the back. In Canada, you can get the address of the **Canadian Automobile Association** closest to you by calling © **613/247-0117;** www.caa.ca.

RENTALS Many of the loveliest parts of Sicily lie miles from the main cities, far away from the train stations. For them, and for sheer convenience and freedom, renting a car is usually the best way to explore the island. But you have to be a pretty aggressive and alert driver who won't be fazed by super-high speeds on the autostrada or by narrow streets in the cities and towns. Sicilian drivers have truly earned their reputation as bad but daring.

However, the legalities and contractual obligations of renting a car in Sicily (where accident and theft rates are very high) are a little complicated. To rent a car here, a driver must have nerves of steel, a sense of humor, a valid driver's license, and a valid passport, and must be (in most cases) more than 25 years old. Insurance on all vehicles is compulsory, though any reputable rental firm will arrange it in advance before you're even given the keys.

In some cases, slight discounts are offered to members of the American Automobile Association (AAA) or AARP. Be sure to ask. Their toll-free numbers and agencies are used mainly by those who wish to rent a car on the mainland of Italy and then drive to Sicily, as not all of them have offices on the island itself.

It is generally cheaper to make arrangements for car rentals before you leave home. Of course, you can also rent cars once you arrive in Sicily. Although the price can vary greatly, depending on the vehicle, the average car rental on the island costs from 62€ to 70€ per day.

The main agencies for car rentals in Sicily include **Avis** (© **800/331-1212;** www.avis.com) and **Hertz** (© **800/654-3131;** www.hertz.com). Avis has locations at Aeroporto Fontanarossa in Catania (© **095-340500**), or in the city itself at Via Giuffrida 19-21 (© **095-445536**); and at the Aeroporto Falcone-Borsellino at Palermo (© **091-591684**) or in town at Via Francesco Crispi 115 (© **095-586940**).

Hertz has locations at Aeroporto Fontanarossa in Catania (© **095-341595**) and in town at Via Toselli

16C (© **095-322560**). It also has an office at the Aeroporto Falcone-Borsellini in Palermo (© **091-213112**), and in town at Via Messina 7E (© **091-331668**).

U.S.-based companies specializing in European car rentals are **Auto Europe** (© **800/223-5555;** www.autoeurope.com), **Europe by Car** (© **800/223-1516,** 800/252-9401 in California, or 212/581-3040 in New York; www.europebycar.com), and **Kemwel Holiday Auto** (© **800/678-0678;** www.kemwel.com).

The major Italian car-rental firm of **Maggiore** is found at Aeroporto Fontanarossa in Catania (© **095-340594**) and in town at Via Conte Ruggero 139 (© **095-591681**).

RENTAL INSURANCE Each company offers a **collision-damage waiver (CDW)** at $15 to $25 per day (depending on the car's value). Some companies include CDWs in the prices they quote; others don't. This extra protection will cover all or part of the repair-related costs if you have an accident. (In some cases, even if you buy the CDW, you'll pay $200 to $300 per accident. Ask questions before you sign.) If you don't have a CDW and have an accident, you'll usually pay for all damages, up to the car's replacement cost. Because most newcomers aren't familiar with local driving customs and conditions, we highly recommend you buy the CDW. (But first check your existing auto insurance and also see what's available through your credit cards. Note that credit cards might cover collision but will usually not cover liability.) In addition, because of Sicily's rising theft rate, all three of the major U.S.-based companies offer theft and break-in protection policies (Avis and Budget require it). For pickups at Sicilian airports, all companies must impose a 10% government tax. To avoid that charge, consider picking up your car at an inner-city location.

There's also an unavoidable 19% government tax, although more companies are including this in the rates they quote.

GASOLINE Gasoline (known as *benzina*) is expensive in Sicily. Be prepared for sticker shock every time you fill up even a medium-size car with *super benzina,* which has the octane rating appropriate for most of the cars you'll be able to rent. It's priced throughout the country at around 1€ per liter (about 3.75€ per gallon). Gas stations on the autostrade are open 24 hours, but on regular roads gas stations are rarely open on Sunday; also, many close from noon to 3pm for lunch, and most shut down after 7pm. Make sure the pump registers zero before an attendant starts refilling your tank. A popular scam in Sicily is to fill your tank before resetting the meter, so you pay not only your bill but also the charges run up by the previous motorist.

DRIVING RULES The Italian Highway Code follows the Geneva Convention, and Italy as well as Sicily uses international road signs. Driving is on the right; passing is on the left. Violators of the highway code are fined; serious violations might also be punished by imprisonment. In cities and towns, the speed limit is 50kmph, or 31 mph. For all cars and motor vehicles on main roads and local roads, the limit is 90kmph, or 56 mph. For the autostrade, the limit is 130kmph, or 81 mph. Use the left lane only for passing. If a driver zooms up behind you on the autostrada with his or her lights on, that's your sign to get out of the way. Use of seat belts is compulsory.

BREAKDOWNS & ASSISTANCE The **Automobile Club Italiano (ACI)** does not offer free roadside emergency help to stranded motorists in Sicily. If you call the ACI emergency number (℃ **116**) in the event of a breakdown,

you must pay a minimum of 93€, plus another 39€ to have your car towed to the nearest garage, plus tax and .85€ per kilometer. So getting stranded in Sicily is a serious cost. Not only that, but 20% is added to the bill between 10pm and 6am and on Saturday and Sunday. ACI offices are at Via delle Alpi 6 (℃ **091-300468**) in Palermo, and at Via Sabotino 1 (℃ **095-533324**) in Catania.

SICILIAN ROADS The autostrada does not exist as extensively on Sicily as it does on the Italian mainland. The most traveled route is the A19 between Palermo and Catania, a convenient link between the island's two major cities. The other much-traveled route is A20 going between Palermo and Messina. A18 links Messina and Catania on the eastern coast, whereas A29 goes from Palermo to the capital of the western coast, Trapani.

Sicily, of course, has nowhere near the burdensome tolls of mainland Italy but there are some: For example, Messina to Catania on the autostrada costs 2.50€.

Unless you're traveling from main city to main city, you'll use the state roads, or *Strade statali,* single-lane and toll-free routes. To reach remote villages, you'll sometimes find yourself going along a country lane and watching out for the goats.

BY BICYCLE

Most Sicilian cities have bike rental firms; otherwise, your hotel might help you make arrangements for one. Rentals in cities cost from 7.50€ a day or 51€ a week. Even though helmets and lights are not legally required, they are prudent to have. It is forbidden to bike along the autostrade. Bikes are transported free on Sicilian ferries, but you must pay to carry them on most trains. Fast trains generally do not allow bikes, although conductors on IC trains let you put a bike in the baggage train for an extra 5€.

BY TAXI

Taxi rates vary from town to town but in general are pricey. In most cities the meter begins at 3.50€, and then you are charged 2.25€ for the first kilometer, plus another .65€ per kilometer thereafter. There are supplements of 3€ from 10pm to 7am and on holidays. Depending on the size of the taxi, four or as many as five passengers are allowed. Taxis are found at all arrival terminals. In some cities they can be called. When you reserve by phone, the taxi meter goes on when the cabbie pulls out of his station. In Sicily, taxis rarely stop if hailed on the street.

SUGGESTED ITINERARIES

If You Have 1 Week

Day 1 Fly or sail into Palermo and allow 1 day to recover from travel fatigue. If you recover sufficiently, take our walking tour through old Palermo.

Day 2 Visit Palazzo dei Normanni and the Museo Archeológico Regionale in the morning. Head for Monreale and its mosaic-laden cathedral in the afternoon.

Day 3 Travel toward Messina for an overnight but spend most of the day exploring Cefalù, dominated by its Romanesque Duomo.

Days 4 & 5 After Messina, head down the coastline to spend 2 nights in the medieval hilltop town of Taormina. One day can be spent discovering the town and getting in some beach time. On the final day from your base in Taormina, you can visit the volcanic slopes of Mount Etna.

Day 6 From Taormina, continue south to the ancient city of Syracuse, where you can spend the rest of the day wandering through its archaeological gardens. Overnight in this ancient place.

Day 7 After bidding adieu to Syracuse, head west for another ancient city, Agrigento, exploring its Valle di Templi (Valley of the Temples), with some of the greatest Greek ruins in the world. With a little imagination, you'll know why Pindar called Agrigento "the most beautiful city built by mortal men." Overnight here before driving north the next day for your transportation links out of Palermo. If you have time in the morning, explore the ruins of the Greek temples at Selinunte before continuing on to Palermo and the end of your Sicilian sojourn.

If You Have 2 Weeks

Day 1 Instead of beginning the trip in Palermo, fly into Catania, where you can take our walking tour after you've recovered from jet lag.

Days 2 & 3 The following morning, head north to Taormina for some R&R on the beach, followed by a walk through the hilltop medieval quarter at night. Spend the third day exploring Mount Etna.

Day 4 Head north from Taormina for a day wandering around Messina followed by an overnight.

Day 5 Leave Messina in the morning, heading west to the nearby port of Milazzo. From here you can take a ferryboat or hydrofoil to either Lipari or Vulcano, both Aeolian Islands. Always reserve a room for the night before sailing to one of these islands. A visit to Lipari or Vulcano will give you a preview of what life is like on a volcanic island.

Day 6 Return to the port of Milazzo on the Sicilian mainland in the morning and drive west to Cefalù with its Romanesque Duomo. This is the most fascinating city on the north coast for overnighting.

Days 7, 8 & 9   Make it Palermo. The city contains the greatest treasure trove of artifacts and architecture in all of Sicily, and is a richly rewarding stopover in spite of some difficulty getting around. On day 8 explore the mosaics in the basilica of nearby Monreale, then head for Mondello, the beach resort of Palermo, for an afternoon in the sun. Spend day 9 taking in all of the architectural treasures and museums of Palermo you haven't seen thus far.

Day 10   Head west for Segesta in the morning, exploring its Greek ruins, which include Sicily's most magnificent ancient temple. Then continue on to Erice, a fascinating medieval hill town, for the night.

Day 11   After leaving Erice, drive along the coast to see the ruins of Selinunte in the morning, continuing east to Agrigento for the night. At night wander around the Valley of the Temples to see them illuminated by floodlights.

Day 12   From Agrigento, cut across country to Piazza Armerina, viewing the fabulous mosaics in a Roman villa here, before heading for Ragusa for the night.

Days 13 & 14   Visit the little city of Noto in the morning before continuing to Syracuse for the night. The following day, while you're still based in Syracuse, explore its vast architectural gardens. Overnight in Syracuse before continuing the next morning north to Catania, where you can make flight arrangements to the rest of the world.

 FAST FACTS: **Sicily**

American Express Travel agencies representing American Express interests in Sicily are found in large cities, including **La Duca Viaggi**, Viale Africa 14 (✆ **095-7222295**) in Catania; **La Duca Viaggi**, Via Don Bosco 39 (✆ **0942-625255**) in Taormina; and **Giovanni Ruggieri e Figli**, Emerico Armari 40 (✆ **091-587144**) in Palermo.

Business Hours Regular business hours are generally Monday through Saturday from 8 or 9am to 1pm and 4 to either 7 or 8pm. The *riposo* (mid-afternoon closing) is observed in Sicily. If you're on island in summer, when the heat is intense, you too may want to learn the custom of *riposo*, retreating back to your hotel for a long nap in the hottest part of the afternoon. Banking hours vary from town to town, city to city, but in general are Monday through Friday from 8:30am to 1:20pm and 3 to 4pm.

Climate See "When to Go," earlier in this chapter.

Consulates There's a **U.S. Consulate** at Via Vaccarini 1 (✆ **091-305857**) in Palermo. There's also a **United Kingdom Consulate** at Via Cavour 117 (✆ **091-326412**) in Palermo.

Currency See "Money," earlier in this chapter.

Drugstores At every drugstore *(farmacia)* there's a list of those that are open at night and on Sunday.

Electricity The electricity in Sicily varies considerably. It's usually alternating current (AC); the cycle is 50Hz 220V. It's recommended that any visitor carrying electrical appliances obtain a transformer. Check the exact local current at the hotel where you're staying. Plugs have prongs that are round, not flat; therefore, an adapter plug is also needed.

Emergencies For the police, dial ℂ **113**; for an ambulance, ℂ **118**; and to report a fire, ℂ **115**. For road assistance, dial ℂ **116**. For a general crisis, call the *Carabinieri* (military-trained police force) at ℂ **112**.

Language Except in the remote backwaters, Italian, of course, is the language of the land. English is often understood at attractions such as museums and at most hotels and restaurants catering to foreign visitors. Even if not all of the staff speaks English at a particular establishment, such as a restaurant, sometimes at least one member of the staff does and can aid you. Most islanders also speak a Sicilian dialect. This is a patois comprised of words left over from various conquerors, including Arabic, Greek, French, and Spanish. It's a sort of linguistic amalgam, reflecting centuries of occupation, including that by the Americans.

Legal Aid The consulate of your country is the place to turn for legal aid, although offices can't interfere in the Italian legal process. They can, however, inform you of your rights and provide a list of attorneys. You'll have to pay for the attorney out of your pocket—there's no free legal assistance. If you're arrested for a drug offense, about all the consulate will do is notify a lawyer about your case and perhaps inform your family. If the problem is serious enough, most nationals will be referred to their embassies or consulates in Rome.

Liquor Laws Wine with meals has been a normal part of family life for hundreds of years in Sicily. Children are exposed to wine at an early age, and consumption of alcohol isn't anything out of the ordinary. There's no legal drinking age for buying or ordering alcohol. Alcohol is sold day and night throughout the year because there's almost no restriction on the sale of wine or liquor in Sicily.

Mail Mail delivery in Italy is notoriously bad. Your family and friends back home might receive your postcards in 1 week, or it might take 2 weeks (sometimes longer). Postcards, aerogrammes, and letters weighing up to 20 grams sent to the United States and Canada cost .75€; to the United Kingdom and Ireland, .60€; and to Australia and New Zealand, .75€. You can buy stamps at all post offices and at *tabacchi* (tobacconists).

Newspapers/Magazines In major cities, it's possible to find the *International Herald Tribune* or *USA Today*, as well as other English-language newspapers and magazines, including *Time* and *Newsweek*, at hotels and news kiosks—but they're hard to find outside major cities. There is no English-language magazine or newspaper published in Sicily.

Police Dial ℂ **113**, the all-purpose number for police emergency assistance in Italy.

Restrooms All airport and rail stations, of course, have toilets, often with attendants who expect to be tipped. Bars, nightclubs, restaurants, cafes, gas stations, and all hotels have facilities as well. Public toilets are also found near many of the major sights. Usually they're designated WC (water closet) or *donne* (women) or *uomini* (men). The most confusing designation is *signori* (gentlemen) and *signore* (ladies), so watch that final *i* and *e!* Many public toilets charge a small fee or employ an attendant who expects a tip. Carry tissues in your pocket or purse—they come in handy.

Safety Refer to "The Safe Traveler," earlier in this chapter.

Taxes As a member of the European Union, Italy imposes a **value-added tax** (called **IVA** in Italy) on most goods and services. The tax that most affects visitors is the one imposed on hotel rates, which ranges from 9% in first- and second-class hotels to 19% in deluxe hotels.

Non-EU (European Union) citizens are entitled to a **refund of the IVA** if they spend more than 150€ at any one store, before tax. To claim your refund, request an invoice from the cashier at the store and take it to the Customs office *(dogana)* at the airport to have it stamped before you leave. **Note:** If you're going to another EU country before flying home, have it stamped at the airport Customs office of the last EU country you'll be in (for example, if you're flying home via Britain, have your Italian invoices stamped in London). Once back home, mail the stamped invoice (keep a photocopy for your records) back to the original vendor within 90 days of the purchase. The vendor will, sooner or later, send you a refund of the tax that you paid at the time of your purchase. Reputable stores view this as a matter of ordinary paperwork and are businesslike about it. Less-honorable stores might lose your dossier. It pays to deal with established vendors on large purchases. You can also request that the refund be credited to the credit card with which you made the purchase; this is usually faster.

Many shops are now part of the **"Tax Free for Tourists"** network (look for the sticker in the window). Stores participating in this network issue a check along with your invoice at the time of purchase. After you have the invoice stamped at Customs, you can redeem the check for cash directly at the Tax Free booth in the airport at Palermo or Catania or mail it back in the envelope provided within 60 days.

Telephone To call Italy from the United States, dial the **international prefix, 011;** then Italy's **country code, 39;** and then the city code (for example, **091** for Palermo or **095** for Catania), which is now built into every number. Then dial the actual **phone number.**

A **local phone call** in Italy costs around .10€. **Public phones** accept coins, precharged phone cards *(scheda* or *carta telefonica)*, or both. You can buy a *carta telefonica* at any *tabacchi* (tobacconists; most display a sign with a white T on a brown background) in increments of 2.50€, 5€, and 7.50€. To make a call, pick up the receiver and insert .10€ or your card (break off the corner first). Most phones have a digital display that'll tell you how much money you've inserted (or how much is left on the card). Dial the number, and don't forget to take the card with you after you hang up.

To **call from one city code to another,** dial the city code, complete with initial 0, and then dial the number. (Note that numbers in Sicily range from four to eight digits in length. Even when you're calling within the same city, you must dial that city's area code—including the zero. A Catanian calling another Catanian number must dial 095 before the local number.)

To **dial direct internationally,** dial **00** and then the country code, the area code, and the number. **Country codes** are as follows: the United States and Canada, 1; the United Kingdom, 44; Ireland, 353; Australia, 61; New Zealand, 64. Make international calls from a public phone, if possible, because hotels almost invariably charge ridiculously inflated rates for direct dial. Calls dialed directly are billed on the basis of the call's duration only. A reduced rate is applied from 11pm to 8am Monday through Saturday and all day Sunday. Direct-dial calls from the United States to Sicily are much cheaper, so arrange for whomever to call you at your hotel.

Italy has recently introduced a series of **international phone cards** (*scheda telefonica internazionale*) for calling overseas. They come in increments of 50, 100, 200, and 400 *unita* (units), and they're usually available at *tabacchi* and bars. Each *unita* is worth .15€ of phone time; it costs 5 *unita* (.65€) per minute to call within Europe or to the United States or Canada, and 12 *unita* (1.55€) per minute to call Australia or New Zealand. You don't insert this card into the phone; merely dial ✆ **1740** and then *2 (star 2) for instructions in English, when prompted.

To call the free **national telephone information** (in Italian) in Italy, dial ✆ **12**. **International information** is available at ✆ **176** but costs .60€ a shot.

To make **collect or calling card calls,** drop in .10€ or insert your card and dial one of the numbers here; an American operator will shortly come on to assist you (because Sicily has yet to discover the joys of the touch-tone phone, you'll have to wait for the operator to come on). The following calling-card numbers work all over Italy: **AT&T** ✆ 172-1011, **MCI** ✆ 172-401, and **Sprint** ✆ 172-1877. To make collect calls to a country besides the United States, dial ✆ **170** (free), and practice your Italian counting in order to relay the number to the Italian operator. Tell him or her that you want it *a carico del destinatario.*

Don't count on all Sicilian phones having touch-tone service. You might not be able to access your voice-mail or answering machine from Sicily.

Time In terms of standard time zones, Sicily is 6 hours ahead of Eastern Standard Time in the United States. Daylight saving time goes into effect in Italy each year from the end of March to the end of September.

Tipping In **hotels,** the service charge of 15% to 19% is already added to a bill. In addition, it's customary to tip the chambermaid .50€ per day, the doorman (for calling a cab) .50€, and the bellhop or porter 1.50€ to 2.50€ for carrying your bags to your room. A concierge expects about 15% of his or her bill, as well as tips for extra services performed, which could include help with long-distance calls. In expensive hotels, these amounts are often doubled.

In **restaurants and cafes,** 15% is usually added to your bill to cover most charges. If you're not sure whether this has been done, ask, "*E incluso il servizio?*" (ay een-*cloo*-soh eel sair-*vee*-tsoh?). An additional tip isn't expected, but it's nice to leave the equivalent of an extra couple of dollars if you're pleased with the service. Checkroom attendants expect .75€; washroom attendants .35€. Restaurants are required by law to give customers official receipts. Taxi drivers expect at least 15% of the fare.

Water Most Sicilians take mineral water with their meals; however, tap water is safe everywhere, as are public drinking fountains. Unsafe sources will be marked ACQUA NON POTABILE. If tap water comes out cloudy, it's only the calcium or other minerals inherent in a water supply that often comes untreated from fresh springs.

3

Settling into Palermo

Through all its vicissitudes, Palermo has continued to capture the imagination of world travelers. In 1768, the German romantic poet, Johann Wolfgang Goethe, had to see Palermo to add the city to his knowledge of classical culture.

In Goethe's travel diary, *Italian Journey,* he described his arrival by sea and a magnificent setting at the foot of Monte Pellegrino, the "tops of trees swaying like vegetable glow-worms" and a haze tinting "all the shadows blue." So enraptured was Goethe with his first glimpse of Palermo that the captain had to urge him to disembark. Goethe had it right: The best way to appreciate Palermo for the first time is an arrival by sea. Once the poet did go ashore, he decided that Palermo was "easy to grasp in its overall plan, but difficult to get to know in detail." That observation is still valid today.

As a city, Palermo is both loathed and adored by visitors, praised and condemned. It's a mixture of panache and poverty, a place of beauty that is hideously ugly in places, and a great city in which to wear a money belt and keep an eye on your camera. There are a lot of safer places to be in the world than Palermo after dark.

Palermo's Arab-Norman buildings have no equal on the planet, and the entire city is a treasure trove of museums (often dusty, forgotten ones) and baroque oratories. Its outdoor markets, such as raucous Vucceria, evoke North Africa and are still dominated by the influence of the Arabs who departed centuries ago.

To feel the pulse of Palermo, visit one of these markets. We are eternally fascinated by the sea creatures sold— even Jacques Cousteau would have been amazed. We sigh at the beauty of mounds of purple artichokes, piles of blood-red oranges, and pyramids of oyster-white eggplant.

Get used to the roar of traffic and the wail of police sirens. Know that that car racing down the street has only one goal for the day: to run you over. Get out of the way of those Sicilian roadrunners. Noise and pollution hang over the city as you ricochet your way among old monuments: Arab cupolas, Byzantine street markets, and Norman and baroque architectural gems that someone forgot to tear down a long time ago.

Its summers are oppressive—"not fit for habitation," in the words of one visitor, and its street scenes frenetic. Think Tangier or Algiers.

Palermo still bears the imprint of its former conquerors. What it's not is a typically European city nor even an Italian one for that matter. As one of its 700,000 residents is quick to point out, "We're Sicilian—*not* Italian."

"Yes, yes, we have crime," a city official reluctantly admits, seemingly angered that we had raised the subject. "But it's mostly petty crime. We have an underground that exists on various levels. But give us some credit. For centuries Palermo knows how to absorb its villains well."

Palermo is old, and in spite of certain "beauty marks," it looks it. The Phoenicians established a trading post here in the 8th century. In time Palermo became the Carthaginian center of Sicily. When the Roman conquest came in 254 B.C., Palermo went into decline, as the new conquerors shifted their power and trading to Syracuse on the east coast.

As the centuries moved inexorably forward, Palermo played host to what seemed like never-ending armies of invaders. The Vandals came, then the Ostrogoths, and by 831 the city had fallen to the Arabs. Although that seemed a disaster at the time, Palermo under the Arabs became one of the great emporiums of the Mediterranean, with splendid mosques and sumptuous palaces. It became the equal of Cairo in Egypt or Córdoba in Spain.

Even by the 11th century, with the Arabs in retreat, Palermo still flourished. By 1072 it had fallen to Roger de Hauteville, marking the beginning of the Norman period. Under his son, King Roger, who ruled from 1130 to 1154, Palermo entered its golden age, with Muslims, Christians, and Jews living in harmony and prosperity. There's a lot to be said for religious tolerance.

Under King Frederick, who ascended to the throne of Sicily in 1208, Palermo became the capital of the Holy Roman Empire. The grand age of Hohenstaufen rule ended in 1266 when the French Angevins came to the throne, launching a despotic rule that ended in the Rebellion of the Sicilian Vespers in 1282.

In the aftermath, the Spanish Aragonese came into power and influence in Palermo. The Aragonese preferred Naples over Palermo as a capital, and in their departure the power vacuum was filled with feudal families and religious orders.

Palermo was never to regain the power and prestige it enjoyed in its long-ago heyday. The city's decay and decline stretched on for centuries.

Then an even worse disaster descended on it in 1943, when the city was targeted for massive bombardments by Allied air forces stationed in North Africa.

In the aftermath of the war, Palermo was reconstructed haphazardly. In the postwar years the city's very name became a synonym for corruption under the Mafia. In the past 10 years the odious influence of this gang has been on the wane, but we suspect there are still plenty of aging *Godfather* types hiding out behind all those closely guarded compounds.

A number of city officials will admit (off the record, of course) that many of the funds allocated in Rome or by the European Union to "rescue" Palermo have ended up in the pockets of the Mafia. But the unheard-of actually happened some 20 years ago. A series of informers, at risk for their lives, came forward to squeal on the Mafia.

Palermo headlines blared that "the tide was turning" against the Cosa Nostra. The fight continued under Leoluca Orlando, the city's mayor from 1993 to 2001. He refused to have the city do business with companies he suspected of having links with the Mafia. Even his own Christian Democrat party disavowed him, but that didn't stop Orlando.

Along with the fight against crime, Palermo only belatedly came to realize the greatness of its architectural heritage. Interest in restoration has at long last arrived. The Teatro Massimo was restored and reopened in 1997, and old and historic quarters, such as Kalsa, are being restored and given a new lease on life with the opening of restaurants, galleries, and cafes. In Palermo, there is hope for the future.

An old-time resident, Giovanni Fatone, summed it up this way for us: "We have passion—sometimes— although it fades with age. We awake with energy but often lose strength in the scalding sun. We are warm and friendly but also rude and irksome when our mood changes quickly. We are a simple people but capable of great wisdom and sophistication when called upon. Palermo and its people are a controversial lot, and many bad things are said and written about us. But even our enemies agree on one point: We are the consumers of the pleasures of life."

1 Essentials

GETTING THERE

BY PLANE   Flights into Palermo from mainland Italy are obviously the most convenient and the fastest links. Palermo's airport, **Punta Raisi/Falcone & Borsellino Airport,** is the island's largest, with the greatest number of flights. The location is 31km (19 miles) west of Palermo on the A29 highway. To get into the city, refer to "Getting Around," below.

For more detailed information about flights into Sicily, refer to chapter 2, "Planning Your Trip to Sicily." In Palermo, you can call ℂ **091-6019250** for information about domestic flights or ℂ **091-7020111** about international connections. Most likely you will be booked on flights via Rome or Milan to your return destination.

You can catch a local airport **bus** from the airport to Piazza Castelnuovo; the fare is 6€. For the same trip, a **taxi** is likely to charge at least 35€—and more, if the driver thinks he can get away with it. It's also possible to rent a **car** at the airport (all the major firms are represented) and drive into Palermo. Allow 20 to 30 minutes—longer, if traffic is bad—to get to the center of town from the airport.

BY TRAIN   Palermo has good rail links with the rest of Sicily and also to Italy. After a 3-hour ride from Messina on the northeast coast, you arrive at Palermo's main terminal, **Stazione Centrale,** at Piazza Giulio Cesare (ℂ **091-6161844**), lying on the eastern side of town and linked to the center by a network of buses or taxis. The ticket office here is open daily from 6:45am to 8:40pm, with luggage storage available.

It's possible to book trains from major Italian cities. The most frequent bookings are from Rome, an 11-hour trip with seven trains arriving per day. Visitors in Naples most often take the ferry. You can, of course, go by train from Naples. There are about three trains daily (trip time: 10 hr.). Palermo is also hooked up conveniently to other major cities in Sicily. The train ride from Catania in the east takes 3½ hours, and there are frequent departures throughout the day. If you're in the west at Trapani, it's a 2½-hour train ride to Palermo, with 11 trains arriving daily.

If you have opted for the big rail haul from Rome, you'll pay 40€ for a one-way ticket. On-island train tickets are cheap: 12€ from Catania or Messina; 7€ from Agrigento; and 6.80€ from Trapani. For rail information for Sicily or Italy in general, call ℂ **892021.**

BY BUS   You can take a bus from Rome to Palermo, but we don't recommend it: The ride is long, dull, and boring. One bus leaves Rome daily at 6:30pm, the trip at night taking 12 hours. Palermo-bound buses leave from Rome's Tiburtina station. Information is available by calling **Segesta,** Via Balsamo 14 (ℂ **091-6167919**).

If you prefer bus travel, we'd suggest it for shorter hauls on the island itself. There are convenient links to major cities by **SAIS,** Via Balsamo 16 (ℂ **091-6166028**). From Messina, it takes 3¼ hours and from Catania 2½ hours to reach Palermo overland. Segesta also has bus links to Trapani in the west (trip

> **Tips The Next Pocket Picked May Be Yours**
>
> Palermo is home to some of the most skilled pickpockets on the Continent, so be especially alert. Don't flaunt expensive jewelry, cameras, or wads of bills. Women who carry handbags are particularly vulnerable to purse snatchers on Vespas. It's best to park your car in a garage rather than on the street; wherever you leave it, don't keep valuables inside. Police squads operate mobile centers throughout the town to help combat street crime.

time to Palermo is 2 hr.). **Cuffaro,** Via Balsamo 13 (℡ **091-6167919**), runs between Palermo and the city of Agrigento in 2½ hours.

The bus stations in Palermo (see addresses above) along Via Balsamo are adjacent to the rail station. The trip from Rome costs 38€, but most bus fares on the island are inexpensive. For example, the cost from Trapani is 6.20€; from Agrigento, 7€; from Catania, 12€; and from Messina, 13€.

BY CAR   Three *autostrade* (superhighways) link Palermo with the rest of Sicily. The most used route is A19 from Catania or A20 from Messina. From the west, A29 comes in from Mazara del Vallo. In addition, two main highways link Palermo: SS113 from Trapani in the west or Messina in the east, and SS121 from Catania and Enna in the east. Palermo is cut off from mainland Sicily. To reach it by car, you'll have to cross the Straits of Messina by ferries operated by FS, the state railway authority.

Once the ferry has landed at Messina, you still must face a drive of 233km (145 miles) to Palermo. If you're planning to drive down from Naples or Rome, as many visitors do, prepare yourself for a long ride: 721km (448 miles) south from Naples or 934km (580 miles) south from Rome.

BY SEA   This is our favorite way to reach Palermo from mainland Italy, since we always visit Palermo from Naples. In Naples the fastest and most convenient service over to Palermo is provided by **SNAV** (℡ **081-2514781**), which operates hydrofoils to Palermo. The trip takes only 5 hours and costs 52€ per person. Contrast this with a ferry operated by **Tirrenia Lines** (℡ **081-199123-199**), which takes 11 hours and costs 48€. The money you save just isn't worth it unless you're taking a car: Then you *have* to take the ferry. Schedules vary depending on weather conditions, so always call on the day of your departure even if you've already confirmed your reservation the day before.

VISITOR INFORMATION   There are **tourist offices** at strategic points, including the **Palermo airport** (℡ **091-591698**) and the main train stations (℡ **091-6165914**). The principal office is the **Azienda Autonoma Turismo,** Piazza Castelnuovo 34 (℡ **091-583847**), open Monday through Friday from 8:30am to 2pm and 2:30 to 6pm, and Saturday from 8:30am to 2pm. When you stop in, ask for a good city map and a copy of *Palermo & Provincia Live,* a bimonthly publication with lots of handy tourist information plus an events calendar.

CITY LAYOUT

The capital of Sicily has both an Old City and a so-called New City. The hardest part to navigate is the sector lying north of the rail depot. The street plan of the Middle Ages is still in effect here, and it's easy to get lost.

Two main roads cut across **medieval Palermo,** the Old City, virtually "quartering it." They are **Corso Vittorio Emanuele,** which begins at La Cala, the ancient harbor, and cuts southwest to the landmark Palazzo dei Normanni and the Duomo (the Palermo cathedral). Corso Vittorio Emanuele runs east/west through this ancient maze of streets known to the Arabs of long ago.

The Old City is split into quadrants at the Quattro Canti, the virtual heart of Palermo. This is the point where Vittorio Emanuele crosses **Via Maqueda,** an artery beginning to the west of the rail depot, heading northwest. Running roughly parallel to Via Maqueda to the east is **Via Roma,** running north from Piazza Giulio Césare. Via Roma and the much older Via Maqueda, virtually parallel streets, shoulder the burden of most of the inner city's enormous traffic.

La Kalsa, the medieval core of Palermo, lies to the southeast of the busy hub of **Quattro Canti.** The residential neighborhood of **Alberghiera** is to the southwest of Quattro Canti. This is the center of the sprawling Ballaro market. Like La Kalsa, Alberghiera was heavily bombed in World War II.

Chances are you'll have little reason to visit **Sincaldi,** the northwest quadrant, unless you want to go to the Capo market. The smallest of the districts of the quadrant is **Amalfitani,** the northeast sector. La Cala, the ancient harbor, eats up most of the space in the district.

Via Cavour divides the medieval core to the south and the **New City** to the north. In spite of its heavy traffic, the more modern section of Palermo is much easier to navigate. The heart of this grid is the double squares of **Piazza Castelnuovo** and **Piazza Ruggero Séttimo.** Palermitans call this piazza maze **Piazza Politeama** (or just Politeama). At the double square, Via Ruggero Séttimo (a continuation of Via Maqueda; see above) crosses **Via Emerico Amari.**

Heading northwest from Politeama is Palermo's swankiest street, **Viale della Libertà,** home to smart stores and tony boutiques. It is also the street of many upmarket restaurants, bars, office blocks, and galleries. Libertà races its way to the southern tip of **Parco della Favorita.**

STREET MAPS   Even with a good map, you can get lost in the maze of central Palermo. Maps called "Carta Monumentale" issued by the tourist office are sold all over Palermo. This map is updated every year or so to take into account the many changes occurring in the city as it alters and restores itself. If you purchase a map, make sure it has a street index (some don't). Otherwise, you've wasted your money.

NEIGHBORHOODS IN BRIEF

Historically, the medieval quarters of Palermo were rigidly defined. You were born into one of the city quarters, you grew up there, married, had children, and died there. What you didn't do was intermarry with a man or woman from another quarter. When this was done, it met with social ostracism. Each quarter had its own dialect, palaces, markets, and shops. From an early age, children learned the boundaries of their quarter and stayed within it. Palermo today, of course, is hardly so rigidly confined, and its citizens move throughout the city. But Palermo still has its neighborhoods, beginning with **La Kalsa.** The Saracens created this quarter. In Arabic, *Khalisa* means pure, but little was ever pure about La Kalsa. Only now is it awakening to tourism. Always an interesting section, evocative of a city in North Africa, it was viewed as extremely dangerous after dark. The opening of bars and restaurants has changed that pattern, although it's still not a place to wander blithely about at night. The center of La Kalsa was destroyed in 1943 by Allied bombers, and for years in the postwar era it remained a large bomb site. Today that bombed area has been turned into a green park, but the neighborhood still has plenty of narrow alleys and streets to get lost in. Kalsa lies to the east of Albergheria, moving toward the harbor, and to the south of Corso Vittorio Emanuele.

La Vucciria   North of Kalsa and north of Corso Vittorio Emanuele, La Vucciria moves east toward the harbor and the ancient seaport of La Cala. It is bordered to the west by the Palazzo dei Normanni and Porta Nuova and to the south by the bus terminal, Stazione Centrale. Its northern outpost is Piazza Verdi. Although famed mainly for its open-air market, Vucciria is also filled with monuments and is of major interest to the art-loving visitor to Palermo. This is the best known of all the quadrants that form the core of the medieval city. Like La Kalsa, it is still viewed as a dangerous place at night, especially along its dark maze of little alleyways. But few can resist a look at the market Leonardo Sciascia called a "hungry man's dream." In the book, *Midnight in Sicily,* Peter Robb called it "the belly of Palermo and its heart, too."

Il Ballaro   Most of this sector lies to the west of Kalsa and to the south of Il Capo, which begins north of Corso Vittorio Emanuele, the northern fringe of Ballaro. Ballaro is known mainly for its market lying to the west of Piazza Ballaro. In this district you will find one of Palermo's most elegant baroque squares, Piazza Bologni. A statue of Charles V, the emperor, stands in the heart of a rectangle of palaces decorated with coats-of-arms.

Il Capo   One of the oldest quadrants of Palermo, Il Capo lies in the northwest, east of Vucciria and directly north of Ballaro. It is entered once you have crossed north from Corso Vittorio Emanuele. It, too, is filled with decaying streets, alleys, and lanes occasionally broken by a little pocket of greenery. Our favorite square here is Piazza del Monte, whose precincts are planted with trees and which has a friendly neighborhood bar or two. The palaces are decaying, and there's not a lot of tourist interest here, but we still like to wander about with no particular goal in sight, other than to appreciate the neighborhood and wonder what lives are led behind the rotting facades of all those once-noble *palazzi* (palaces). Eventually you'll come to Porta Carini, one of the major gates left over from the Middle Ages.

Albergheria   South of Ballaro you enter this historic old district, bounded by Via Maqueda and Corso Vittorio Emanuele and lying to the northwest of the Stazione Centrale. Ripe in its decay, Albergheria is filled in part with palazzi, like all the other neighborhoods, particularly in the area that opens onto Via Maqueda. The most notable of these is the Palazzo Santa Croce, at the intersection of Via Maqueda and Via Bosco. Much of Albergheria's central area is absorbed by an open-air street market. The district is filled with a maze of narrow alleys and streets, and it also contains many fine churches (many in desperate need of funds). Several sections are very poor, and since poverty breeds crime, be sure to exercise caution both day and night. Much of the bomb damage from 1943 remains, simply because no one ever had the money to fully restore the area.

New City   As you head north of the medieval quarter, the streets grow broader but also more nondescript. The monumental and recently restored **Teatro Massimo** at Piazza Verdi marks the division between the Old City and the New City. Once Via Maqueda cuts through the medieval district, it becomes Via Ruggero Séttimo as it heads north through the modern town. This street explodes into the massive double squares at Piazza Politeama, site of Teatro Politeama Garibaldi. North of the square is Palermo's swankiest street, Viale della Libertà, shooting up toward Giardino Inglese.

GETTING AROUND

Parking is difficult in Palermo, and traffic is horrendous. There are treasures here, but getting around to see them is more than difficult.

BY BUS The modernized bus system, once you learn to work it, is the best means of getting around the attractions on the periphery of Palermo, such as Monreale or Mondello. Most central lines cross Via Maqueda and its parallel street Via Roma, going through the quadrants of the old town. Other buses run east and west along the major dividing street, Corso Vittorio Emanuele.

In the New Town, Piazza Verdi, with its landmark Teatro Massimo, is a major hub, as is Piazza Politeama.

A ride on a municipal bus costs .77€, or else you can buy a full-day ticket for 2.60€. For information, call **AMAT,** Via Borrelli 16 (© **091-321389**). Most passengers buy their tickets at tobacco shops (*tabacchi*) before boarding.

A tourist bus called **Giro Città** begins and ends its circuit at the landmark Teatro Politeama (via the Emerico Amari side). It stops at many of the major monuments of Palermo, including the Duomo and the Royal Palace. Departures are at 9am daily; tickets are sold on board, and there are no advance reservations. The cost is 11€ per person. Children under 12 are granted a 50% discount. For more information call © **091-7291111.**

BY TAXI Getting around the inner core of Palermo by bus is very time-consuming and not easy, and driving your car around Palermo is a nightmare. In most cases, taxis are the best way to get around the center of the city. Taxi stands are found at the main rail depot, at Piazza Verdi, at Piazza Indipendenza, and at Piazza Ruggero Séttimo, among other locations. The meter begins at 3.50€, and you're charged 2.25€ for the first kilometer, plus .65€ per kilometer thereafter. If you can't find a taxi on the street, call © **091-513311** or 091-513374. If you can afford it, consider renting a taxi for the day to explore Palermo attractions. Rented by the day, taxis cost 13€ per hour. Most drivers speak only a few words of English, but somehow they manage. You can request an English-speaking driver; perhaps one will be available.

ON FOOT Palermo is a city designed for walking, especially to the museums, monuments, and palaces in the medieval core. But walking is exhausting and not at all practical if you want to take in some of the attractions on the city's periphery. To go outside the center, rely on a network of buses (see above).

BY CAR Driving around Palermo can be done but is guaranteed to take years off your life. You may want to rent a car for side trips to places like Monreale, however. Car rentals can be arranged at airport desks or at offices within central Palermo. The major car-rental firms include **Avis,** Punta Raisi Airport (© **091-591684**) and Via Francesco Crispi 13 (© **091-586940**). There are two leading Italian car-rental firms. **Maggiore** (© **091-591681**) is at the airport, with a branch at the Notarbartolo Railway Station (© 091-6810801). You can also rent a vehicle from **Sicily By Car** (© **091-591250**) at the airport, or at Via Stabile 6A (© 091-581045). Car rental averages from 62€ to 70€ per day.

Then there's **parking.** Parking spaces are like gold in central Palermo. The three most convenient garages include **Garage Stazione Centrale** (© **091-6168297**) at the rail station, charging 13€ per night (closed Sun). The two other convenient parking garages—identified simply by the word GARAGE—are at Via Stabile 10 (ⓒ **091-321667**), charging 15€ per night, and at Via Libertà 102 (ⓒ **091-305512**), charging 18€ per night.

BY ORGANIZED TOUR The best tours are offered by **CST** (Compania Siciliana Turismo), 124 Via Emerico Amari (ⓒ **091-582294**). You can visit their offices and discuss your interests, and see what is available on any given day. CST arranges visits to such sights in Palermo as Monte Pellegrino or the Capuchin Catacombs, but they will also set up side trips to the Greek ruins at Segesta, or day trips to western coastal towns such as Erice and Trapani.

 ***FAST FACTS:* Palermo**

American Express American Express services are available through a local agency, at **Giovanni Ruggieri e Figli,** Emerico Amari 40 (ⓒ **091-587144**), open Monday through Friday from 9am to 1pm and 4 to 7:30pm, Saturday from 9am to 1pm. Lose your card? Call ⓒ **06-72282** at once.

Bookstore The best offerings of English-language titles are found at **Feltrinelli,** Via Maqueda 395 (ⓒ **091-587-785**), open Monday through Saturday from 9am to 7pm.

Consulates There's a **U.S. Consulate** at Via Vaccarini 1 (ⓒ **091-305857**), open Monday through Friday from 9am to 1:30pm. There's also a **United Kingdom Consulate** at Via Cavour 117 (ⓒ **091-326412**), open Monday through Friday from 9am to 1pm.

Emergencies For the police, dial ⓒ **112;** for an ambulance, ⓒ **118;** and to report a fire, ⓒ **115.** For road assistance, dial ⓒ **116.** For a general crisis, call the *Carabinieri* at ⓒ **112.**

Hospital The most convenient emergency center is found at **Ospedale Civico,** Via Carmelo Lazzaro (ⓒ **091-6062207**).

Internet Access Your best and most central bet is **Internett@mente,** Via S. Martino 3A (ⓒ **091-6121174**), which charges 2.50€ per half hour for its services. Open Monday from 3 to 8pm, Tuesday through Saturday from 10am to 8pm.

Lost Property Check with **Ufficio Stranieri,** V. S. Lorenzo Colli 271A (ⓒ **091-526037**). But property once lost in Palermo rarely turns up. The train station has its own lost-and-found: **Oggetti Rinvenuti** (ⓒ **091-6031111**) at the Stazione Centrale. Hours for both offices are daily from 9am to 1pm and from 3 to 7pm.

Luggage Storage You can leave luggage at an office in the Stazione Centrale. Open daily from 6am to 10pm; it charges 2.60€ per suitcase for 12 hours. For more information, call ⓒ **091-6033040.**

Pharmacies To locate a pharmacy near your hotel, call ⓒ **192.** Convenient pharmacies in the city center are found at the following addresses: Via Roma 1 (ⓒ **091-6162117**); Via Roma 207 (ⓒ **091-585869**); Via Mariano Stabile 177 (ⓒ **091-334482**); and Via Principe di Belmonte 110 (ⓒ **091-581771**).

Police Dial ⓒ **112.**

Post Office The main post office for Palermo is at Via Roma 322 (☏ **091-321507**), open Monday through Saturday from 8am to 7:30pm. Branches are at the train station (no phone), open Monday through Saturday from 8:30am to 1pm; and at the airport (☏ **091-6519239**), open Monday through Saturday from 8am to 1pm.

Transit Information Call the local bus company **AMAT** at ☏ **091-321333**.

Travel Agencies See **American Express** above. A budget travel–oriented agency is **Wasteels,** Via Francesco Paolo di Blasi 14 (☏ **091-7308304**), open Monday through Saturday from 7:30am to 2:30pm.

2 Where to Stay

Hotels come in all shapes, sizes, prices, and degrees of comfort, so you should not have trouble finding a room that suits both your desires and your pocketbook. You can live in first-class style in Palermo, or rather inexpensively. The city has more good and inexpensive accommodations than any other place in Sicily.

Because of the heat, July and August are the low season, whereas in such coastal resorts as Taormina those are the most expensive months to visit.

Budget hotels in Palermo are called *pensioni, locande,* or *alberghi,* and most of them lie at the southern frontiers of those two parallel streets, Via Maqueda and Via Roma. Women traveling alone will feel safer checking into hotels on one of the main arteries and not down some narrow side street in the medieval quarters which can be dark and unsafe at night.

VERY EXPENSIVE

Villa Igiea Grand Hotel ★★★   The best hotel in town, Villa Igiea, built at the turn of the 20th century, is a remarkable example of Sicilian Art Nouveau. It's in better shape and more comfortable than the also highly rated Grand Hotel et des Palmes, Palermo's other historic property. Once the private villa of the Fiorio family, whose claim to fame was coming up with the notion of putting tuna fish into a tin can, the villa hosts the moneyed elite of Sicily when they're in town for business or pleasure.

Located in the suburb of Acquasanta, 2.4km (1½ miles) north of the center and reached after you pass through a shabby district, the villa is surrounded by a park overlooking the sea. The old architecture has been preserved, including ceilings with stone vaults joining in an arch. Everywhere are genuine antiques. Large stairs lead to the good-size, often quite spacious guest rooms, which contain valuable furnishings, including comfortable old wrought-iron beds. Each room comes with a bathroom with a tub-shower combination. The villa also has a swimming pool and tennis courts. We like to wander the jasmine-scented gardens at night, admiring the ancient Greek temple near the water's edge. It's an evocative moment for Palermo.

Salita Belmonte 43, Acquasanta, 90142 Palermo. ☏ **091-6312111**. Fax 091-547654. www.cormorano.net/sgas/villaigiea/services.htm. 114 units. 207€–295€ double; 436€–567€ suite. Rates include breakfast. AE, DC, MC, V. Free parking. Bus: 139. **Amenities:** Dining room; bar; pool; tennis court; room service; babysitting; laundry. *In room:* A/C, TV, minibar, hair dryer, safe.

EXPENSIVE

Astoria Palace Hotel ★★   Chances are good that if a CEO or even a president is bunking down in Palermo, he or she will be sheltered at this government-rated

Palermo Accommodations & Dining

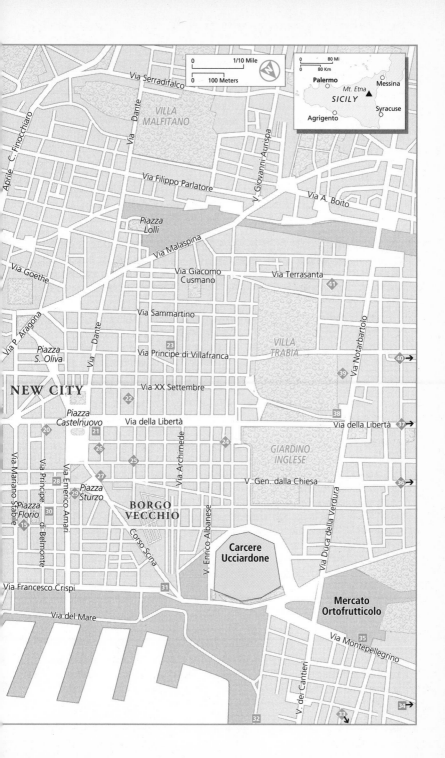

four-star selection. For sheer comfort and convenience, and not for those seeking an accommodation dripping with atmosphere, Astoria Palace surfaces as the number-two hotel in town, ranked just after the charming but less efficient Villa Igiea. "We are an island of hospitality in a brusque, modern world," the manager assured us, quite accurately. Don't let the word "palace" fool you, however. The name comes from the fact that it's a behemoth, not some classic antique. It is the largest hotel in town and the setting for many large conventions. It is our sincere hope that you won't be there during one; you'll feel more welcomed and will get better service if you don't have to share the place with hundreds of conventioneers.

The rooms have modern but elegant furnishings, and the bathrooms with tub and shower are kept in state-of-the-art condition. Not all the rooms are spacious; some are rather boxlike with just a small window. If you can afford it, we'd vote for one of the junior suites, which are far bigger and more comfortable. Naturally, the best units are those on the top floor where the view is less obstructed.

Via Monte Pellegrino 62, 90142 Palermo. (✆) **091-6282111.** Fax 091-6372178. 310 units. 166€ double; 223€ triple; 260€ suite. Rates include buffet American breakfast. AE, DC, MC, V. Bus: 139 or 721. **Amenities:** Restaurant; bar; indoor pool; fitness and beauty center; business center; valet; room service; babysitting; laundry. *In room:* A/C, TV, minibar, hair dryer.

Centrale Palace ★★ For atmosphere and comfort, we'd still give the edge to Villa Igiea or the Astoria Palace. But Centrale Palace is a close runner-up. No hotel lies as close to the Duomo, the Quattro Canti, and the monumental medieval heart of Palermo. The core of the hotel is a 17th-century private home, although guest rooms occupy adjacent buildings that are newer. The lobby is daringly painted in many of the vivid colors associated with the Italian Renaissance, such as terra cotta and intense blues.

The original palazzo was converted into a hotel in 1892 during Palermo's Belle Epoque Golden Age. In the 1990s it was taken over and severely modernized by the ubiquitous Best Western group—not always a grand upholder of tradition. Some period or Empire antiques are placed about to take the curse off the *moderno.* But many furnishings, especially those in the guest rooms, have more function than flair. Doubles are generally medium-size to spacious, with newly renovated bathrooms that mostly come with tub-and-shower combinations. The quietest rooms are on the side streets, and double-glazing on the front windows block but do not entirely keep out Palermo's horrific street noises. Our favorite perch is the top-floor dining room taking in views over the Palermo rooftops to Monte Pellegrino.

Corso Vittorio Emanuele 327 (at Via Maqueda), 99134 Palermo. (✆) **091-336666.** Fax 091-334881. www. bestwestern.com. 63 units. 206€ double; 266€ junior suite. Rates include buffet breakfast. AE, DC, MC, V. Parking 13€. Bus: 101, 102, 104, or 105. **Amenities:** Restaurant; bar; gym; sauna; room service; babysitting; laundry; dry cleaning. *In room:* A/C, TV, minibar, hair dryer.

Grand Hotel et des Palmes ★ This is the most legendary hotel in Sicily, and it's still receiving guests even though its heyday is long past. For nostalgia buffs, however, there is nothing to top it. Since the 19th century, it has sheltered some of the island's most illustrious guests, including the composer Richard Wagner, who finished *Parsifal* here. The hotel has seen enough murders, suicides of poets, romantic but off-the-record liaisons, and aristocratic intrigue to fill a book the size of *War and Peace.* A secret Mafia agent once fell from the seventh floor straight through the skyline of the hotel's great hall of mirrors. The hall of mirrors is still here, albeit no longer reflecting the greatness of a bygone era. But classy furnishings, towering pillars with gold capitals, and antique chandeliers still evoke the age in which the hotel was born. The charm of this antique *grande dame* glows on its rooftop terrace as well.

Today used largely to house tour groups, the hotel carries on nobly with such drawbacks as an absolute lack of greenery and a location along one of the busiest streets of Palermo. Management is working to revive the hotel to its former glory, but it's an uphill battle, and a great deal depends on your room assignment. While the public rooms are still glamorous, some guest rooms can be disappointingly simple. The best ones are filled with antiques and heavy Italian fabrics, and have stucco ceilings over parquet floors.

Via Roma 398, 90139 Palermo. ⓒ **091-583933.** Fax 091-331545. www.cormorano.net/sgas/despalmes. 183 units. 168€–181€ double; 289€–310€ suite. Rates include breakfast. AE, DC, MC, V. Parking 14€. Bus: 806 or 809. **Amenities:** Restaurant; bar; room service; babysitting; laundry/dry cleaning. *In room:* A/C, TV, minibar, hair dryer, safe.

Hotel Sport Club Portorais ⭐
This is the best and most appealing of the hotels near Palermo's international airport, with a location only 4.8km (3 miles) west of the check-in booths but with very little of the aircraft noise you'd expect from such a location. Painted pink, and designed like an enlarged version of a Mediterranean villa, it was built in the 1970s on a small bay lined with dark and jagged boulders. Owned and operated by the Marchese family, it functions simultaneously as a resort and as an airport hotel, welcoming overnight guests who want to avoid the traffic congestion of Palermo on the morning of their flight.

Inside the hotel is a surprisingly valuable and interesting collection of art and antiques, including 18th- and 19th-century choir stalls, painted dowry chests, and an elaborately carved *portantina,* a cramped but gilded box with horizontal poles, wherein ladies used to be carried by hardworking members of their entourages. Many of the clients here spend at least part of their day beside the terraced, oval-shaped swimming pool or at the private pebbly beach; there's a sun terrace as well. The hotel's restaurant is genuinely excellent, and a dining pavilion opens directly onto a view of the sea. Rooms are high-ceilinged and airy, with Asian art (often large-scale embroideries), tiled bathrooms (usually with showers but not bathtubs) and, in many cases, private terraces or loggias.

Via Piraineto 125, 90044 Carini (Palermo). ⓒ **091-8693458.** Fax 091-8693458. www.portorais.it. 42 units. 150€–180€ double. Rates include breakfast. Free parking. AE, DC, MC, V. **Amenities:** Restaurant; bar; pool; laundry/dry cleaning. *In room:* A/C, TV, minibar.

Massimo Plaza Hotel ⭐ *Value*
Its major competitor, Principe di Villafranca, has better rooms and facilities, but we still applaud this little palazzo for its location in the historic center in front of the Teatro Massimo. It has a tasteful but subdued elegance that we like as well. The hotel oozes Sicilian style, from its **Angle Bar,** with a drawing-room-like aura, to its welcoming atmosphere, which is both personal and helpful. It also has a breakfast room and a reading room. Most small hotels in this category in Palermo have cramped guest rooms, but the accommodations here are fairly spacious and comfortably furnished in a harmonious style, each with a tub-and-shower bathroom and a number of amenities. Rooms have been soundproofed against the curse of Palermo: traffic noise. The hotel has been completely refurbished as part of a general architectural restoration in the historic sector.

Via Maqueda 437, 90133 Palermo. ⓒ **091-325657.** Fax 091-325711. www.massimoplazahotel.com. 15 units. 160€ double; 207€ triple. AE, DC, MC, V. Parking 13€. Bus: 101 or 102. **Amenities:** Bar; room service; babysitting. *In room:* A/C, TV, fridge, safe.

Principe di Villafranca ★★★ *Finds*   Small-scale, newly built in 1998, and charming, this is the finest boutique-style hotel in Palermo. Stylish and intimate, and evoking some aspects of a well-maintained, elegant, and unfussy private home, it occupies two floors of what was originally built as a low-rise apartment house. Its Sicilian theme includes enough antiques and architectural finesse to make you think the place is a lot older than it really is. Grace notes include Oriental carpets, marble floors, vaulted ceilings, a baronial fireplace, and tasteful upholsteries, some of them silk. The hotel and some of its neighbors were built within what had been one of Palermo's most beautiful gardens, the Ferriato, owned long ago by the princes of Villafranca—hence, the name of the hotel.

Guest rooms are contemporary and well crafted, each midsize to spacious, with tile, granite, and travertine-sheathed bathrooms with tub and shower; Internet capabilities with built-in keyboards; and a welcome kind of postmodern comfort and style. Each guest room lies one floor above street level, with the ground floor devoted to reception, a bar, and an excellent restaurant, **Il Firriato,** specializing in elegant Sicilian food. In the bar, notice the valuable Liberty-era writing desk crafted by one of the luminaries of his era, Basile.

Via G. Turrisi Colonna 4, 90141 Palermo. ℂ **091-6118523.** Fax 091-588705. www.principedivillafranca.it. 34 units. 172€ double; 238€ suite. Rates include breakfast. AE, DC, MC, V. Free parking. Bus: 101 or 102. **Amenities:** Restaurant; bar; gym; room service; babysitting; laundry/dry cleaning. *In room:* A/C, TV, minibar, hair dryer, safe.

MODERATE

Jolly Hotel dei Foro Italico ★   Many hotels of charm and grace now compete for the position of the top five or six "best in town." This 1960s chain hotel, once one of the best, is now much lower on the food chain. That doesn't mean that it's fallen off in standards. It's still the same well-organized, well-run hotel it always was. Its major selling point is that it's the only hotel in the center with a swimming pool—and on an August day in Palermo, that's one heck of a selling point. Its location overlooking the sea and the Foro Italico adds to its allure.

A few steps from the Villa Giulia, the Jolly is also close to the harbor and the rail station. As was the style in Italy in the 1960s, when hotels such as this one were built, rooms tend to be small. They are comfortable, however, and well organized, with lots of built-ins, frequently renewed bed linen, and tiled private bathrooms with shower. To escape the traffic noise, ask for one of the more tranquil accommodations on the upper floors, which also have better views of the sea.

Via Foro Italico 22, 90133 Palermo. ℂ **800/221-2626** in the U.S., 800/237-0319 in Canada, or 091-6165090. Fax 091-6161441. 235 units. 132€–162€ double; 152€–182€ suite. Rates include breakfast. Half board 30€ per person. AE, DC, MC, V. Parking 11€. Bus: 139. **Amenities:** Restaurant; bar; pool; room service; laundry. *In room:* A/C, TV, minibar, hair dryer.

Palazzo Excelsior ★   No hotel in Palermo evokes the faded nostalgia of the late 19th century as effectively as this one. Built in 1892, it sits in a quiet neighborhood at the northern end of the prestigious Via Libertà, in a site that's both convenient to major boulevards and isolated. You get the sense that you're in a living museum here—the kind of appealingly dowdy and very grand venue that hasn't yet been "gussied up" by teams of 21st-century decorators. The result is appropriately grand and old-fashioned. As a recent visitor put it, "All this hotel needs is 25 million or so euros to make it the most lavish in southern Italy." Guest rooms last benefited from a renovation in the early 1990s and retain a vague Liberty-style overlay despite their modernizations. The in-house restaurant, where the staff is appropriately uniformed and formal, serves regional specialties.

Via Marchese Ugo 3, 90141 Palermo. ✆ **091-6256176.** Fax 091-342139. www.excelsiorpalermo.com. 127 units. 176€ double; 230€ suite. Rate includes breakfast. AE, DC, MC, V. Free parking. Bus: 101, 104, 107, 108, or 806. **Amenities:** Restaurant; bar; babysitting; laundry. *In room:* A/C, TV, safe in 30 units.

Politeama Palace Hotel This is a very appealing hotel, with lots of regional charm and enough touches of international modernity to make tour groups from northern Europe feel at home. Built in 1977, and set behind an angular concrete facade, it rises nine stories above a point immediately adjacent to one of Palermo's most architecturally distinctive theaters, the Politeama, in the heart of the stylish and well-heeled Via Libertà district. Inside, expect a contemporary-looking decor of polished granite, varnished hardwood, leather upholsteries, and Italian *moderno* styling. The most interesting guest rooms overlook the heroic bronze chariots on the nearby theater and the square that contains it. All rooms contain elaborate woodwork, touches of gilt, dignified (even stately-looking) friezes that evoke baronial life in 19th-century Sicily, original artworks, and small- to medium-size tiled or stone-sheathed bathrooms with tub and shower.

Piazza Ruggiero Séttimo 15, 90139 Palermo. ✆ **091-322777.** Fax 091-6111589. 94 units. 181€ double; 207€–250€ suite. AE, DC, MC, V. Bus: 101 or 102. **Amenities:** Restaurant; bar; babysitting; laundry. *In room:* A/C, TV, minibar.

President Hotel "We're not the Villa Igiea and we're not some antique palazzo, but we're reliable." Thus, the manager stated the best reason for recommending this eight-story concrete-and-glass structure rising above the harbor front. After a much-needed renovation in 2002, the President has emerged, if not presidential, at least one of the better and more moderately priced choices in town. You pass beneath a soaring arcade before entering the informal stone-trimmed lobby. The amenities are simple here but comfortable. There's little stylish about the small guest rooms, but they are well kept, as are the adjoining tiled bathrooms with tub-and-shower combinations. You needn't bother with the on-site restaurant and its clientele of tired businesspeople. All you have to do is walk out along the harbor front to find a number of fine trattorie serving excellent fish.

Via Francesco Crispi 228, 90139 Palermo. ✆ **091-580733.** Fax 091-611588. www.s-h-systems.co.uk/italy/palermo47099.html. 129 units. 103€–129€ double. Rates include breakfast. AE, DC, MC, V. Parking 5€. Bus: 139. **Amenities:** Restaurant; bar; room service; laundry/dry cleaning. *In room:* A/C, TV, minibar, hair dryer.

San Paolo Palace ★★ Rising 14 floors and built in 1990, this modern hotel offers serious competition to the Astoria Palace. Like the Astoria, San Paolo calls itself a "palace" hotel, which is hardly evocative of what it is: a large, sprawling, but welcoming high rise. In fact, if you're returning from a trattoria with too much *vino* under your belt, you might confuse the two properties. One guest told us she'd stayed in a similar hotel along the west coast of Africa, which means San Paolo could be anywhere.

Overlooking the sea, between Capo Zafferano and Mount Pellegrino, the hotel is not without its charm, its major grace note being a roof-garden restaurant. Its rooms open onto the most famous gulf in Sicily. The government gives San Paolo three stars instead of the four reserved for the superior Astoria Palace, which means its rooms are slightly cheaper, yet you get basically the same deal. Like its challenger, San Paolo attracts congresses and conventions, which are hardly ideal times to stay here. Guest rooms are extremely comfortable and not particularly stylish—but they are functional, with a wide choice of different bed arrangements, from king size to cozy "matrimonial." Located a few minutes' ride from the town center, the hotel is a favorite of business clients, a turn-off for some travelers. As for maintenance, management rightly concedes that "so far we manage with a face-lift, a tuck here and there," not the major corrective surgery of a total renovation.

Via Messina Marine 91, 90123 Palermo. ✆ **091-6211112.** Fax 091-6215300. www.sanpaolopalace.it. 274 units. 124€ double; 175€ suite. Rates include breakfast. AE, DC, MC, V. Free parking. Bus: 821 or 824. **Amenities:** Restaurant; bar; room service; babysitting. *In room:* A/C, TV, minibar, hair dryer.

Villa D'Amato ✦ *(Finds*   This little discovery, a completely renovated antique Sicilian villa opening onto the seafront, lies a 15-minute drive from the center. As a hotel, it is outclassed by Principe di Villafranca and Massimo Plaza Hotel, but it is not without its (considerable) charms. Lying in its own parklike grounds, it is especially good for motorists who don't want to battle traffic in the heart of Palermo. We like it mainly because of its gardens, a Mediterranean oasis. As you relax here, watching the plants grow, you're in Palermo but you don't seem to be. The guest rooms are completely comfortable, decorated in a sort of Italian Liberty style, yet they come off as rather plain. Small to midsize, each comes with a tiled bathroom with shower. The good Sicilian/international cuisine is another reason to book here.

Via Messina Marine 178–180, 90123 Palermo. ✆/fax **091-6212767.** www.hotelvilladamato.it/indexgb.htm. 104€ double; 113€ triple. Rates include breakfast. AE, DC, MC, V. Free parking. Bus: 224 or 225. **Amenities:** Restaurant; bar; room service; babysitting. *In room:* A/C, TV, minibar.

INEXPENSIVE

Albergo Hotel Joli   Not to be confused with a member of the Jolly chain, this is an inexpensive hotel on the third floor of a corner building on a beautiful old square, Piazza Florio. At the historic center of Palermo, it lies near the pricey Grand Hotel et des Palmes, a few blocks away from Piazza Castelnuovo. Of course, it's hardly comparable to des Palmes, which you might want to visit for a drink or a sumptuous meal. But if you're looking to save money and you don't demand elegance, this hotel offers small to midsize guest rooms, each a bit boxy and furnished simply though comfortably; compact tiled bathrooms contain shower-tub combinations. The best units come with small terraces overlooking the square. Convenient for both the port and the modern city, the hotel also lies within walking distance of most points of historic interest. Considering its heartbeat location, the Albergo is in a relatively tranquil setting.

Via Michele Amari 11, 90139 Palermo. ✆/fax **091-6111765.** www.hoteljoli.com. 30 units. 88€–98€ double; 115€–130€ suite. Rates include breakfast. AE, DC, MC, V. Bus: 101 or 107. **Amenities:** Bar; room service; babysitting; laundry/dry cleaning. *In room:* A/C, TV, hair dryer.

Albergo Mediterraneo   One of our preferred government-rated three-star hotels in Palermo sits on a narrow commercial street in a blandly modern neighborhood, within a comfortable and angular building from 1956, which was radically renovated back in 1982. The granite-sheathed lobby prefaces six floors of guest rooms with wide hallways and spacious dimensions, evoking a well-designed contemporary hospital. Rooms are bigger than you might imagine, with a sense of calm and quiet but absent of a lot of unnecessary furniture. All rooms come with private bathrooms, some with tubs, others with showers. Members of a European soccer team, say, or a family of art lovers from Paris, might check into this place; overall it's businesslike and highly recommendable.

Via Rosolino Pilo 43, 90139 Palermo. ✆ **091-581133.** Fax 091-586974. www.abmedpa.com. 106 units. 104€ double. Rate includes breakfast. AE, DC, MC, V. Bus: 101, 104, or 107. **Amenities:** Restaurant; bar. *In room:* A/C, TV, minibar, safe.

Albergo Sausele *(Value*   This family-run inn stands out amid the depressing rail-station–area hotels. It boasts high ceilings, globe lamps, strikingly clean floors, modern art, and new wooden modular furnishings. The staff is hospitable, as is the resident St. Bernard named Eva. Rooms on the street can be noisy, so light sleepers should request one overlooking the peaceful courtyard. Rooms with shower-only bathrooms are certainly small and modest but are a pleasant choice. What makes this place special are the handcrafted and antique artifacts from around the world, collected by Giacomo Sausele in his travels.

Via Vincenzo Errante 12, 90127 Palermo. ⓒ 091-6161308. Fax 091-6167525. www.hotelsausele.it. 36 units. 86€ double; 117€ triple. Rates include breakfast. AE, DC, MC, V. Parking 8€. Bus: Any to Centrale Stazione. **Amenities:** Bar; 2 lounges; room service. In room: A/C, TV, hair dryer.

Hotel Moderno ⭐ Ⓥalue   One of the city's best cost-conscious overnight options lies on the third and fourth floors of a stately-looking building that's among the grandest in its busy and highly congested neighborhood. Don't expect the same kind of grandeur inside that you see on the building's neoclassical exterior: You take a cramped elevator to the third-floor reception area, then proceed to your clean but very simple guest room, which will be on either the building's third or fourth floor. Each room comes with a tiled bathroom with shower, lots of artwork, and not a great deal of direct sunlight. In view of the oppressive heat outside, and in light of the reasonable prices, few of this hotel's repeat visitors seem to mind.

Via Roma 276 (at corner of Via Napoli), 90133 Palermo. ⓒ **091-588683**. Fax 091-588260. 38 units. 62€ double. AE, DC, MC, V. Bus: 101, 102, 103, or 107. **Amenities:** Bar. In room: A/C, TV.

Hotel Posta   The street where this hotel lies is narrow, claustrophobic, and flanked with buildings whose outsides could use a good cleaning. But the location is within a short walk from the Mussolini-era post office, several massive and very important churches, and the hubbub of a nearby street market. In spite of the unprepossessing approach to the Posta, it is a celebrated address among writers, singers, artists, and actors appearing in productions at the local landmark theaters of Palermo. The controversial playwright, actor, director, songwriter, and political activist Dario Fo (winner of the 1997 Nobel Prize for Literature) is a frequent guest at the hotel, which has been run by the same family since the early 1920s.

The Posta, renovated in 1998, is small, functional, and unfrilly, with a tiny lobby; it's an intriguing blend of hypermodern design and antique stonework. The simple, fairly spacious, and discreet guest rooms are accessible via a tiny elevator and come with small bathrooms with showers.

Via A. Gagini 77, 90133 Palermo. ⓒ **091-587338**. Fax 091-587347. 27 units. 93€ double; 180€ suite. Rates include breakfast. AE, DC, MC, V. Bus: 101 or 104. In room: A/C, TV.

3 Where to Dine

Many restaurants in Palermo lie close to the sea, from which emerges much of the bounty on the trattoria table. Pasta mixed with fresh sardines (*pasta con le sarde*), spaghetti with clams or mussels, and grilled fish and seafood are the items to order on most menus.

Most of the cuisine is Sicilian, although Palermo has more diversity than anywhere else in Sicily. Tunisian and Chinese food are the most popular foreign offerings, although you can also find Spanish, Greek, French, Italian, and even Brazilian dishes if you search hard enough. Many local dishes still show the influence of Palermo's long-departed conquerors, the Arabs.

If you're a street-food fanatic, Palermo is your kind of town. As you walk along any section of the city, you encounter peddlers touting the local specialties, such delights as *panelle* (fritters made with garbanzo or chickpea flour) and *calzoni* (deep-fried meat- or cheese-filled pockets of dough).

If you're with Mrs. Petrillo from *The Golden Girls,* and you want something authentically Sicilian, head for a food stall with a large cast-iron pot turning out fresh buns stuffed with thin strips of calf's spleen and ricotta cheese. The hot sauce that goes with it will have your tongue begging for mercy.

Desserts are also sold on the street. Some of the best concoctions are holdovers from the days of Arab occupation, including sweetened ricotta cheese with cinnamon, pistachios, candied fruit, dried fruit, and cloves.

Budget eateries crowd the Stazione Centrale, but we generally avoid these, which lean toward tourist traps. Some of the best restaurants are hidden in the medieval Kalsa sector, to which you may want to take a taxi at night to avoid walking along streets where muggings occur.

Since Palermitans tend to be late diners (but not as late as the Spanish), most restaurants don't even open until 8pm.

BREAKFAST & PASTRIES   If your hotel doesn't serve breakfast (most do), or even if it does on an a la carte menu, you might want to begin your experience in Palermo by going to almost any bar or *pasticceria* for morning coffee and pastries. Our favorites are **Bar Alba** (see below) or **Caffè Mazzara** (see "Palermo After Dark" in chapter 4).

In the Medaglie d'Oro area, a great cake shop/bar is **La Dolceria Pasticceria Coga,** Via Gustavo Roccella 56 (© **091-596944**), which turns out baked goods fresh from the oven, displayed on a large counter. One of the city's oldest and most famous cake shops, **Caffè Antico,** Via di Belmonte 115 (© **091-3292200**), in the Politeama area, bakes some of the best brioches, cakes, meringues, and croissants in Palermo and does so until midnight.

PIZZA PARLORS   The people of Palermo eat almost as much pizza as the Neapolitans. A true pizzeria serves pizza all day, and you should definitely sample the local pie, pizza Palermitana, made with bread crumbs, anchovies, pine nuts, olive oil, and cheese and sometimes such tasty ingredients as sausages, capers, olives, and fresh grilled eggplant. Our favorite pizza joint is **Italia** (see below). **Antica Focacceria San Francesco** (see below) is another tavern that has been turning out pies fresh from the oven since 1834. A word to the frugal: A pizzeria is your cheapest option for a sit-down meal in Palermo, and as such, they are packed on weekends, mostly with an under-25 crowd.

JUICE BARS   Not as plentiful as they once were, juice bars or kiosks used to line many of the city streets. They were—and some still are—an obligatory place to stop for a fruit ice. On a hot August day in Palermo, no one (in our view) has ever improved on lemon ice. For a change of pace, try a refreshing glass of sparkling water flavored with aniseed. Still carrying on the juice bar tradition is **Al Chioschetto,** Via Porta Guccia (© **091-584165**), in the Tribunali/Castellamare neighborhood. It's open 24 hours daily.

GELATERIE   These ice-cream shops are found all over Palermo, especially in the northern reaches of the city. Locals are whizzes at making ice cream, which tastes extraordinarily good even if the colors tend toward the lurid. Our favorite remains pistachio, although flavors are more varied than the rainbow. Some gelato lovers like their ice cream so much they even order it for breakfast. The concoction is called *brioche con gelato,* or ice cream in a bun.

Al Gelato 2, Via de Gasperi 15 (© **091-528299**), in the Libertà neighborhood, serves Palermo's best ice cream. It also has the vastest array of flavors of

As a city of the sea, Palermo is peopled with diners who enjoy the rich bounty of fish harvested off their coastline. The lowly sardine has a special place in their hearts, enjoying the same popularity as the codfish to the Portuguese. If you've had only tinned sardines up to now, try them fresh. The all-time favorite pasta dish in Palermo, *maccheroni con le sarde,* is made with fresh sardines and wild fennel.

any other gelateria. If you're a true ice-cream devotee and feel you've had your favorite food in all known flavors, scan the list of selections here. You're in for a surprise or two.

EXPENSIVE

La Scuderia ✦✦✦ INTERNATIONAL/ITALIAN   Dedicated professionals direct this restaurant surrounded by trees at the foot of Monte Pellegrino, 5km (3 miles) north of the city center near the stadium at La Favorita. On our latest tour of Palermo dining rooms, La Scuderia surfaced at the very top of our list. The chefs are talented, instinctive cooks, able to change the menu according to what looks good at the market. The ingredients, as always, are of top quality. Everything is beautifully presented and served with typical Sicilian courtesy. In summer the restaurant has one of the prettiest flowery terraces in town, sought after by everyone from lovers to extended families to vacationing glamour queens. The imaginative cuisine includes a mixed grill of fresh vegetables with a healthy dose of a Sicilian cheese called *caciocavallo,* stuffed turkey cutlet, beef and veal dishes, *involtini* of eggplant or veal, risotto with seafood, and *maccheroni Nettuno* (pasta studded with swordfish, sliced eggplant, and tomato sauce).

Viale del Fante 9. © 091-520323. www.orpi.it/ristoranti/sicilia/la_scuderia.htm. Reservations recommended. Main courses 10€–13€. AE, DC, MC, V. Mon–Sat 12:30–3pm and 8:30pm–midnight. Closed 2 weeks in Aug. Bus: 107 or 603.

MODERATE

Capricci di Sicilia *Value* SICILIAN   Great care goes into the traditional Palermo cuisine here, and the chef shops for only the freshest ingredients. To go really local, order *polpette* (fishballs of fresh sardines). Pasta is often flavored with sardines and broccoli, and the spaghetti with sea urchins is succulent. The swordfish roulade is always dependable. In warm weather, meals can be served in a small garden. If you've never ordered one of Sicily's most fabled desserts, *cassata Siciliana,* here is one of the best places to sample it. The central location is close to Piazza Politeama.

Via Instituto Pignatelli 6 (off Piazza Sturzo). © 091-327777. Reservations recommended. Main courses 8€–13€. AE, DC, MC, V. Sept–July daily 1–3:30pm and 8pm–midnight; Aug daily 8pm–midnight. Bus: 806 or 833.

Friends' Bar ✦ SICILIAN   About 10km (6 miles) north of Palermo, this is one of the finest restaurants in the region. Named after the four friends *(amici)* who opened it in the 1970s, it features an air-conditioned dining room and a gazebo-like indoor/outdoor structure that rises from a lush garden. A meal here is an event for many Sicilians, and a reservation (especially for the garden) might be hard to get. The antipasti, rich in marinated vegetables and grilled fish, are loaded onto a buffet table. The pastas tend to be strong, aromatic, and laced with such flavors as anchovies, fresh basil, and sardines. "After all the loves of my life have gone, and I have dried up, I can still replenish myself with Sicily's anchovies, fresh basil, and sardines," claimed the 19th-century food writer, Giovanni Taviani. Grilled swordfish, calamari, and octopus are also a savory kettle of goodies. The house wine is redolent with the flavors and sunshine of southern Italy.

Via Filippo Brunelleschi 138, Michelangelo. ℂ **091-201401.** Reservations required. Main courses 7.75€–10€. AE, DC, MC, V. Tues–Sun 12:30–3pm and 8–11pm. Closed 3 weeks in Aug. Bus: 513, 540, or 675.

La Fenice SICILIAN   On the ground floor of the historic Palazzo Notarbartolo di Rosa, near Porta Felice in the Tribunali/Castellamare neighborhood, "The Phoenix" (its English name) is a bastion of fine cuisine. But don't go there for pasta—they don't serve it, although they do offer some well-flavored rice dishes, especially a sublime rice salad. Intimate rooms with stone walls and low ceilings are placed throughout the old structure. The waiters rush about with contagious enthusiasm serving a menu that rarely varies. The chefs search out the best local ingredients, and their grilled swordfish is their masterpiece. We also like the grilled sausage *alla pizzaiola,* cooked with parsley-flavored fresh tomatoes and onions. The grilled dishes seem to go best with the Regaleali whites. After a *caffè,* go native, rinsing out your cup with anise liqueur.

Piazza Marina 52–53. ℂ **091-6162230.** Reservations recommended. Main courses 6.75€–8.30€. AE, DC, MC, V. Sept–July daily 12:30–3pm and 8pm–midnight. Aug daily 7:30pm–midnight. Bus: 103, 105, or 225.

Le Delizie di Cagliostro ★ *Finds* SICILIAN/INTERNATIONAL   The restaurant that bears his name celebrates the dubious achievements of Sicily's most successful (and ultimately, tragic) swindler, Giuseppe Balsamo (alias Count Cagliostro; 1743–95). His mystical mumbo-jumbo and sleight-of-hand looted the purses and pride of commoners and aristocrats (including Marie Antoinette) alike, earning him a respected place in the pantheon of noteworthy Sicilian rogues.

   Set close to the street traffic on a busy boulevard of a commercial neighborhood, the restaurant boasts vaulted 18th-century ceilings entirely covered with trompe-l'oeil frescoes, which may or may not (the staff wouldn't say) be contemporaneous with the scoundrel's life. Once you get beyond the overweening presence of the ghost of the count, you can sit back and enjoy the cuisine. Dishes prepared with care and market-fresh ingredients include a risotto with shrimp, cream, and curry; crepes stuffed with fresh mushrooms; and that Palermo favorite, pasta with fresh sardines. We like the home-style cooking as evoked by the stuffed calamari and the roulades of beef layered with red peppers. Vegetarians will enjoy the succulent platter of grilled vegetables, their natural flavors enhanced with olive oil and sprinklings of balsamic vinegar.

Corso Vittorio Emanuele 150. ℂ **091-332818.** Reservations recommended. Main courses 8€–13€. AE, DC, MC, V. Sun 1–3:30pm; Mon–Sat 7:30–11pm. Closed July–Aug. Bus: 101, 102, or 105.

Lo Scudiero ★★ SICILIAN   Set directly across the busy street from the Politeamo Garibaldi Theater (site of the Galleria d'Arte Moderno), this cozy and likable restaurant and brasserie (its name translates as "the Shield Bearer") is not to be confused with the grander and more expensive restaurant with a roughly similar name out in the suburbs near the soccer stadium. Honest, straightforward, and unpretentious, it's favored by locals, many of whom work or live in the nearby prestigious Via Libertà neighborhood. Fine raw materials and skilled hands in the kitchen produce such tempting dishes as grilled swordfish flavored with garlic and a touch of mint. We like the lightly cooked jumbo prawns in olive oil, fresh garlic, and tomatoes. This place gets our vote for some of Palermo's best roulades, grilled veal rolls with a stuffing of ground salami and herbs. Vegetarians can opt for the medley of grilled vegetables with balsamic vinegar and olive oil.

Via Turati 7. ℂ **091-581628.** Reservations recommended. Main courses 6.85€–12€. AE, DC, MC, V. Mon–Sat noon–3pm and 7:30–11:30pm. Closed Aug 10–20. Bus: 101 or 107.

Ma Che Bontà ⚡ *Finds* SICILIAN   On our latest visit here, our waiter was a philosopher, telling us, "The deepest mystery is always hidden in the midday sun, not in the darkness." We think he should have given credit to Nietzsche, but all was forgiven when he recommended that our party of six "leave it to me, and I will delight your palates like my quotations enrich your mind." By the third bottle of wine, our group was beyond mind enrichment. But the food was hard to forget. Surely Sicilian pasta dishes in Palermo don't get much better than this. The fettuccine arrived flavored with fresh mint, sautéed baby eggplant in virgin olive oil, and freshly caught swordfish. One platter contained two versions of ravioli, one stuffed with crabs, the other with sage-flavored mushrooms, rich cream, and butter. The tagliatelle was a taste sensation with tuna roe, almonds, pistachios, and fresh tomatoes. For a main course—that is, if you even want one—stick to the fresh fish, especially tuna in a bittersweet sauce or the freshly made swordfish roulades with an herb-flavored stuffing. "No! No! No!" everyone shouted at the suggestion of dessert and then proceeded to devour such homemade delights as the cannoli and an almond parfait with warm chocolate.

Viale Emilia 75. ℂ **091-511156.** Reservations recommended. Main courses 5.20€–7.75€. AE, DC, MC, V. Mon–Sat 1–3:30pm; daily 8–11:30pm.

Mi Manda Picone ⚡ *Finds* SICILIAN   We like to come here for three reasons: to sample the excellent and well-chosen Sicilian wines, to enjoy the tasty food at affordable prices, and to admire the facade of that Romanesque gem, Chiesa di San Francesco, rising a few steps from the restaurant's entrance.

The specialty here is wine, mostly from Sicily (450 kinds), accompanied with platters of hearty, robust food. Sit on the terrace in front of the church or retreat to a high-ceilinged, medieval-style interior whose woodsy accessories once functioned as a stable. Light snacks include stuffed and deep-fried vegetables; a marvelous flan of fava beans and pecorino cheese; fresh salads; and antipasti-style platters loaded with cured meats, cheeses, marinated fish, and vegetables. More substantial fare includes grilled tuna or swordfish steaks with capers and black pepper, and classic filets of beef braised with Barolo wine.

Via Alessandro Paternostro 59 (Piazza San Francesco d'Assisi). ℂ **091-6160660.** Reservations not necessary. Main courses 8€–11€. AE, MC, V. Wine 3.10€–7.40€ per glass. Mon–Sat 7:30–11pm. Bus: 103, 108, or 164.

Sopra I Sotto ⚡ ITALIAN/SICILIAN   One of Palermo's most avant-garde restaurants occupies a two-story storefront that's a few steps off the posh edges of the Via Libertà. Its minimalist stainless steel and ebony decor is radically different from that within more staid competitors, and includes a serpentine bar, bar stools upholstered in ostrich skin, and an upstairs dining room that manages to be ultra-modern and formal at the same time. Within a setting fashioned by Tuscany-born designer superstar Leopoldo Vezzoni, you'll dine amid black-and-white rice-paper screens and all-white slipcovers that might have been inspired by the American designer Billy Baldwin.

Menu items vary with the seasons. Expect artful preparations of Sicilian-style smoked and grilled fresh fish; a succulent spaghetti *ricci,* seasoned with sea urchins, tomatoes, and herbs; and fresh salads, including a tantalizing version made from arugula, pink grapefruit, avocados, scampi, and lobster. There might be a tendency on the part of the intensely social owner to control your venue a bit more than you want, but in light of its vivid theatricality and the dozens of social currents whirling about, you'll probably decide to take all of it in good stride.

Via XII Gennaio. (C) **091-6124736**. Reservations recommended. Main courses 10€–12€. AE, DC, MC, V. Tues–Sun 12:30–2:30pm and 8:30pm–midnight. Bus: 101, 102, 103, or 106.

INEXPENSIVE

Alla Fermata di Porta Carini ⭐ *Finds*   A Sicilian politician many years ago took us to this hidden little gem within an easy walk of Teatro Massimo. Unfortunately, he was gunned down 2 years later in a Mafia rampage, but he taught us to appreciate two local specialties. We've been coming back ever since to enjoy sea urchins *(ricci)* and tuna roe *(bottarga)*. On our last visit we noticed to our surprise several Japanese clients enjoying the same treat. Word must have spread all the way to Tokyo. The menu changes seasonally, and in fair weather you can enjoy lunch at a table outside. The decor is Sicilian rustic, which the locals refer to as *arte povera*. The fish and seafood constantly change based on what's biting—and the kitchen staff has a real way with fish. The pastas are also superb but so large that it's hard to order anything else.

Via Volturno 108. (C) **091-586024**. Reservations recommended. Main courses 7.50€–9€. AE, DC, MC, V. Mon–Sat 1–3pm and 8:30–11pm. Bus: 118, 122, or 124.

Antica Focacceria San Francesco ⭐⭐ *Kids* FOCACCIE/SICILIAN   We could never visit Palermo without at least one, possibly two, stopovers at this local favorite, a tradition since 1834, in the Palazzo Reale/Monte di Pietà district. Nearly every kid in Palermo at one time or another has feasted on its stuffed focaccia sandwiches and other inexpensive eats. High ceilings and marble floors evoke the era in which the eatery was born. The food has changed little since that time. They still serve *panino con la milza* (real hair-on-your-chest fare: a bread roll stuffed with slices of boiled spleen and melted cheese). The *panelle* (deep-fried chickpea or garbanzo fritters) are marvelous fare, as are the *arancini di riso* (rice balls stuffed with tomatoes and peas or with melted mozzarella). The specialty is *focaccia farcita* (flat pizza baked with various fillings). Or try the *sfincione* (a thick slab of pizza with onions, artichokes, tomatoes, and anchovies).

Mercato Vucciria. (C) **091-320264**. Reservations not needed. Sandwiches 3€–5€, pastas 4.50€–5.50€. No credit cards. Daily 10am–midnight. Bus: 103, 105, or 225.

Antico Caffè Spiannato ⭐⭐ PASTRIES/SNACKS   Established in 1860, this is the most plush and opulent cafe and pastry-maker in its neighborhood. Set on a quiet, pedestrian-only street, it's the focal point for hundreds of residents of the surrounding Via Libertà district, thanks to lavish displays of sandwiches, pastries, and ice creams, each intricate and elaborate, and each artfully displayed in a setting that evokes the age of Garibaldi. Buy coffee at the bar made of red porphyry and black marble, and be tempted by pastries that you might never, ever be able to duplicate in your home kitchen. If you're hungry, sit at a tiny table—either indoors or outdoors—for one of the succulent *piatti di giorno*. (These include fresh salads and grills, and succulent pastas such as spaghetti with sea urchins.) The best pastries include cannoli, *cassate*, almond cakes, and endless variations on cookies and biscuits. In the evenings there's more focus on cocktails than coffee, and on platters rather than pastries. Live music, usually in the form of a piano that's wheeled outside under a parasol, entertains the nighttime crowd.

Via Principe di Belmonte 115. ℃ 091-583231. Pastries 1€–2.75€; platters 2.85€–11€. AE, DC, MC, V. Daily 7am–1am. Bus: 101, 104, 107, or 806.

Bar Alba ⍟ SICILIAN   We were still in college when we were first taken here to sample *cassata Siciliana* on native soil. This is the famous Sicilian regional dessert of candied fruit, marzipan, and sponge cake. It's a delight if you're not afraid of a diabetic coma. The homemade ice creams deserve some sort of award. We always prefer one of their creations made with nuts, especially pistachio. The staff will dazzle you with their *frutta di Martorana* (fruits made out of almond paste). You can also go the whole hog on many of their savory dishes. For example, their *arancine* is the best in Palermo. This is a typical Sicilian specialty—a big rice ball with ham and cheese. Since 1955 the bar has been a Palermo institution, with a long counter loaded with all sorts of gourmandises. The location is at the top of Via della Libertà, near the entrance to La Favorita Park.

Piazza Don Bosco 7C. ℃ **091-309016.** Reservations not needed. Pastries 1.30€–1.60€. Main dishes 3.10€ each. AE, DC, MC, V. Tues–Sun 7:30am–10pm. Bus: 601 or 603.

Carillon SICILIAN   In the Libertà neighborhood, this well-established restaurant is a refined, tasteful choice for dining. It takes its name from the old and new music boxes used to decorate this trattoria. Some guests prefer a table on the terrace facing the street; the terrace is open year-round, as large heaters keep diners warm in winter. The dishes are properly cooked and served, and portions are large. On top of that, the service is friendly and prompt. The food has real flavor and taste, wiping from memory all the bland Italian cuisine forced on you in a lifetime. One of the most intriguing pasta dishes we recently sampled in Palermo was Carillon's spaghetti with shrimp, pumpkin flowers, and a hard ricotta cheese. Alternatively, we could have ordered spaghetti with fresh swordfish, blended with zucchini, mint, and tuna roe. As a bit of exotica, ask for grilled shrimp with strawberries (you heard that right), served with a béarnaise sauce.

Via Notarbartolo 12. ℃ 091-343666. Reservations recommended. Main courses 5.50€–7€. AE, DC, MC, V. Tues–Sun noon–3pm and 6:30pm–1am. Bus: 102, 103, or 702.

Casa del Brodo ⍟ SICILIAN   For more than a century this Palermitan institution in the Palazzo Reale/Monte di Pietà neighborhood has entertained and handsomely fed some of the island's most discerning palates, such as the late Count Giuseppe Tasca of Almerita, once Sicily's premier vintner. In its two intimate, plainly decorated rooms, it attracts an equal number of locals and visitors, its atmosphere unchanged over the years.

With a name like "House of Broth," you could well imagine that broth is its specialty. And in truth, there is no kettle of broth finer in all of Sicily than that served here. But Casa del Brodo has many other dishes to select from, too, including *macco di fave*, meatballs and tripe, a recipe that seems long forgotten in the kitchens of most Sicilians today. The one specialty we always order is *carni bolliti* (boiled meats). Trust us: It may not sound enticing, but it is a tantalizing assortment of tender, herb-flavored meats, especially good when preceded with a savory risotto with fresh asparagus.

Corso Vittorio Emanuele 175. ℃ **091-321655.** Reservations recommended. Main courses 4.65€–9€. DC, MC. V. Wed–Mon noon–4pm and 7pm–1am. Bus: 101, 104, 105, or 131.

Cin-Cin ⍟⍟ *Finds* SICILIAN/CREOLE   One of the culinary treasures of Palermo, this is a favorite spot with locals. Pronounced "chin-chin," the restaurant's name is the Italian version of the toast "Cheers" and suggests the camaraderie found here behind an unpretentious facade. The location is reached down a flight of steps off Via Libertà, in the section between the Giardino Inglese and the Politeama Theatre. You have a choice of tables in one of several rooms.

Some of the recipes have come down unchanged from Palermo's baroque period in the 19th century. "The dishes were so good then that we can't make them better," the chef confided. Come here just to sample the seafood pastas, into which all sorts of sea creatures (sea urchins, shrimp, clams, and mussels) are tossed with a succulent sauce. Sicilians often treat beef and lamb as sideshows to their antipasti, pastas, and seafood dishes, but here the chef gives full attention to turning out perfectly cooked and aromatically seasoned meats.

The owners, the Clemente family, once operated a restaurant in Baton Rouge, Louisiana, and Cin-Cin is the only restaurant in Sicily to offer such distinctly Louisiana dishes as oysters Rockefeller and chicken gumbo. Homemade Marsala and almond ice creams are a Cin-Cin specialty.

Via Manin 22, off Via Libertà. ⓒ **091-6124095.** Reservations recommended. Main courses 4€–5.50€. AE, DC, MC, V. Daily noon–3:30pm and 8pm–midnight. Closed July 12–Sept 1. Bus: 101 or 107.

Cucina Papoff ⋆ *Finds* SICILIAN   With a name like "Papoff's Kitchen," you'll think you've landed in Bulgaria. The restaurant is actually named for its Bulgarian founder, but this friendly little trattoria serves some of the most traditional of all Sicilian dishes. The location is in an atmospheric 18th-century building with stone vaulting in the heart of Palermo, near Via Libertà and Politeama Piazza, just a few steps from the newly restored Massimo Theater. The basic recipes of this place are pretty much the same as they were 200 years ago.

It was here that we became addicted to *maccu,* a creamy fava bean soup flavored with wild fennel. We also became addicted to the batter-fried cardoon florets with the nutty taste of the artichoke bottoms (only better). Stealing the recipe (but attributing it, of course), we once published it in America. The stuffed radicchio is Palermo's best, as is the exquisite rabbit in red-wine sauce. All those soul food specialties that warm a Sicilian's heart are served, including *arancini di riso* (stuffed rice balls), potato croquettes, and *caponata* (fresh eggplant salad). Want something really local? Go for sautéed wild game giblets. Unusual pasta dishes appear, including a sublime spaghetti with almond sauce, or pasta with herring and fresh fennel. Although the wine *carte* has a number of European, even American wines, opt for one of the rare Sicilian vintages that are almost never found beyond the island's shores.

Via Isidoro La Lumia 32. ⓒ **091-586460.** Reservations recommended. Main courses 6€–10€. AE, MC, V. Mon–Fri 12:30–3:30pm; Mon–Sat 8pm–midnight. Closed in Aug. Bus: 101, 102, 104, or 106.

Hirsch ⋆ *Finds* GERMAN   A meal within its cozy, wood-paneled rustic interior provides a sometimes welcome change from too constant a diet of Sicilian food. Except for the dusty sun-baked pavement outside and the palms and oleanders that line the street, you might imagine you're in Salzburg, thanks to dark-stained paneling, wrought iron, and the *Gemütlich* sense of kitsch that permeates the place. You'll find many of the time-tested Teutonic specialties inside, including sauerbraten, Wiener schnitzel, and pork cutlets with red cabbage and apple sauce, as well as more exotic fare such as ostrich steaks and barbecued filets of beef. And where else in Palermo can you order a good, fat roast goose? All of it tastes wonderful when accompanied with foaming steins of beer from the tap. Expect a table of homesick Germans to be seated at the table next to yours.

Via Damiani Almeyda 32A. ① 091-347825. Main courses 6.50€–11€. DC, MC. V. Tues–Sun 6pm–2am. Bus: 102, 103, 118, or 702.

Il Mirto e la Rosa ★ *Value* SICILIAN/VEGETARIAN   "The Myrtle and the Rose" is no longer the strict vegetarian restaurant it was when we first discovered it. True, it still serves some of the most flavorful vegetarian dishes in Palermo, made with only the very freshest harvests from the fields, but these days its customers are also treated to an array of well-prepared meat and fresh fish dishes (though little poultry). With an interesting setting in a Liberty-style building from the grand old Belle Epoque days at the turn of the 20th century, it also offers a summer terrace for dining. Its North African–inspired vegetable couscous is the best in town, as are any number of rice and pasta dishes with tantalizing sauces. We'd also rank the chef's veal Marsala as the best in Palermo. If you want generous portions and good flavor, order the delectable grilled steak Florentine. Seasonal produce is always emphasized on the menu.

Via Principe di Granatelli 30, off Piazza Florio. ① 091–324353. Reservations recommended. Main courses 5€–7€. AE, DC, MC, V. Daily noon–3:30pm and 8–11:30pm. Closed Sun in July and all of Aug. Bus: 101, 102, or 103.

Le Pergamène *Value* ITALIAN/SICILIAN   This is one of two alfresco restaurants that sit adjacent to one another at the edge of a pleasant but not-very-well-known public garden known as the Giardino Garibaldi, right at the point where the narrow streets of medieval Palermo open onto a network of 19th-century avenues and piazzas. The plastic armchairs of this restaurant are green, as opposed to the bright yellow chairs of the restaurant next door, with whom there's a friendly rivalry. The menu lists about two dozen kinds of pizza; pastas that include the ubiquitous pasta alla Norma made with eggplant, as well as a version with either smoked salmon or smoked swordfish; and main courses that focus on grilled steaks (beef, pork, and veal), roulades, and freshly caught fish. Amusingly, one of the patrons, in discussing the cuisine with us, claimed, "It's better than my mama's but nowhere near a first-class restaurant. It must be doing something right because I come here at least once a week."

Piazza Marina 48–49. ① 091-6166142. Reservations not necessary. Pizzas 3€–6.70€; main courses 4.50€–12€. Daily 5pm–2am. Bus: 103, 105, or 225.

Osteria Fratelli Lo Bizanco *Value* SICILIAN   Sicily of yesterday lives on in this no-frills eatery frequented by street vendors and stevedores, with an occasional vegetable trucker dropping in. It's not everybody's antipasti, and if we were out on a date with the queen of England we'd take her somewhere else, but we like the joint, even the rough treatment. The owner presides over the establishment with time-seasoned flair, a sort of Palermo version of the father of Eliza Doolittle in *My Fair Lady*. At a communal table on our latest visit, we were seated with a group of locals who looked as if they'd just rubbed out some annoying politician. The owner approached our table to tell us we had a choice of ravioli or spaghetti to begin with. All of the local gangsters went for the ravioli, so the proprietor informed us we could have the spaghetti. Although the ravioli looked delicious, we were highly pleased with the spaghetti alla *ragù*, not having tasted such a rich ragout sauce since we'd departed Naples. On previous visits, we've enjoyed the owner's pasta with fresh sardines, although we find his pasta with potatoes too starchy. We were recently rewarded with the sweetest tasting swordfish steak we've ever enjoyed in Sicily. Tender beefsteak is also featured, but we've had far better cuts of this elsewhere. Many diners come here to make a meal out of *pasta nero di seppia* (pasta with a medley of seafood). Our small serving of this was just enough to convince us to make a meal out of it on our next visit—that is, unless the owner sees us and demands that we have the spaghetti.

V. E. Amari 104. ℭ **091-585816.** Reservations not accepted. Main courses 3.50€–5€. No credit cards. Mon–Sat noon–3pm and 7:30–10pm. Bus: 101, 104, 106, 108, or 124.

Ristorante/Pizzeria Italia SICILIAN/ITALIAN   Set on a narrow street that funnels into the piazza that faces the elaborate 19th-century facade of the Teatro Massimo, this pizzeria-cum-taverna is fronted with an elaborate wrought-iron sign. Inside, there's a warren of three tile-floored dining rooms, forest green trim, a prominent pizza oven, and a slightly bored staff that has been churning out pizzas since 1945. Despite that, the range of pizzas is gratifying, the beer cold (and invariably, the drink of choice). Consider beginning with *bucatina* (a thick penne-style paste) with fresh sardines or else "to hell with the calories" spaghetti carbonara, followed by grilled filet steak, a North African–inspired couscous, and a medley of grilled vegetables. And if you're in the mood for spicy pizza, consider *pizza Lucifer,* spiked with red-hot peppers and pepperoni.

Via Orologio 54. ℭ **091-589885.** Reservations not necessary. Main courses 4€–9€; pizzas 3€–7€; set menu 21€. MC, V. Daily 7:30pm–midnight. Bus: 101 or 103.

Santandrea ✦ *(Finds* SEAFOOD/SICILIAN   All the bounty gathered very early that morning at the Vucciria market is prepared with skill and flavor at this chic restaurant favored by locals in the heart of La Kalsa. In fair weather you can sit out on this old square to the south of Piazza San Domenico, looking at crumbling buildings from the 19th century. Instead of handing you a menu, the waiter will recite the day's specials with obvious pleasure. Go with the mixed antipasti, which always features fresh seafood. The pasta dishes are excellent, notably thin spaghetti prepared with sea urchins, a local delicacy, or spaghetti with fresh sardines. One of the habitués at an adjoining table confided to us, "For a Sicilian, a day without fresh sardines is like a life without sex." The fresh tagliatelle in a pesto of sun-dried tomatoes, fresh zucchini leaves, and toasted pine nuts is just wonderful. The homemade desserts, especially the black chocolate mousse, are some of Palermo's most luscious.

Piazza Sant'Andrea 4. ℭ **091-334999.** Reservations required. Main courses 7€–10€. AE, DC, MC, V. Wed–Mon 1–3pm and 8pm–midnight. Closed Jan. Bus: 101, 103, 104, or 107.

Trattoria Stella ✦ *(Finds* SICILIAN   This local dive, known for its good regional cuisine, is recommended only for the adventurous. Conceal a revolver, preferably the type used by Barbara Stanwyck to kill one of her errant beaus in a *noir* film, and set out into the night through the spooky Kalsa district. You might even see the sign for the old Hotel Patria, now gone (and we can thank the gods for that). The late medieval courtyard remains, and it's one of our favorite places to be in Palermo on a summer evening. Stella is a Palermitano institution, and the recipes haven't changed since Mussolini was in diapers. The patrons would have it no other way. A former, now departed chef once told us, "The cooks in the other regions of Italy are barbarians. Only Sicilians know how to cook." The barbecued lamb is Palermo's best. You can also order *disgraziata,* a very hot, spicy pasta with eggplant, ricotta cheese, and tomatoes, or else two of the best seafood dishes, grilled calamari or swordfish.

Via Alloro 104. ℭ **091-6161136.** Reservations recommended. Main courses 5€–7.50€. AE, DC, MC, V. Tues–Sun 12:30–3:30pm; daily 8:30pm–midnight. No bus.

Exploring Palermo

4

Although relatively neglected by the casual visitor to Italy, Palermo is one of the great art cities of Italy. It may not be the equal of Venice or Florence, but it is an artistic treasure nonetheless.

Down through the ages writers have tried to capture Palermo's singular allure. Vincenzo Consolo, in his *Strolling through Sicily*, was overcome with the city's rich red earth "with springs of water where the palm grove rises tall and slender."

The oasis he wrote of is largely swept away today. In its place is one of the more difficult cities to explore in southern Italy. There's just too much traffic and pollution, and getting around in summer is an often dusty, humid affair, and even a risky one, as you try to avoid cars, buses, and motor scooters.

Yet in spite of its difficulties, for those willing to go to the trouble to uncover Palermo's hidden treasures there is much to appreciate here. In exploring Palermo, expect both sensuous sunshine and somewhat sinister shadows.

The Phoenicians were taken with the setting of Palermo way back in the 7th century B.C. They called it Ziz, which meant "flower." Palermo hasn't experienced a golden age since the 9th century when, under Arab conquerors, the city became one of the great centers of Islamic culture in the Western world.

In 1072 the Normans arrived, bringing a style that merged with the local residents into a kind of "Arabo-Norman" style.

All subsequent conquerors added their own particular style and alterations to the city's skyline and contributed other layers to Palermo's rich cultural heritage. Frederick II of Swabia arrived in 1212, ushering in a time of intellectual development and prosperity. Following the Swabians came the Angevins, until the Spaniards drove them out. In the 18th century the Bourbons of Naples arrived, embellishing everything with their baroque touch—not necessarily a good thing, as their architects and artisans destroyed much classical beauty.

Palermo spent most of the 20th century in decline, becoming a center for the notorious Mafia dons. It suffered severe damage in Allied air raids in 1943 and an earthquake in 1968. Much of its priceless medieval quarter has either been torn down or continues to decay.

Fortunately, matters are looking up these days, as more and more citizens are realizing what an artistic treasure Palermo is. Although not moving as fast as some preservationists would like, restoration is in the air.

1 The Major Attractions

You should give Palermo at least 3 days of your time, and even then you will have grasped only some of its highlights. If your time is severely limited in Palermo, we have selected the city's top 10 attractions which, on a very rushed schedule, can be visited in 2 very busy days. If you can't spare even that much

Palermo Attractions

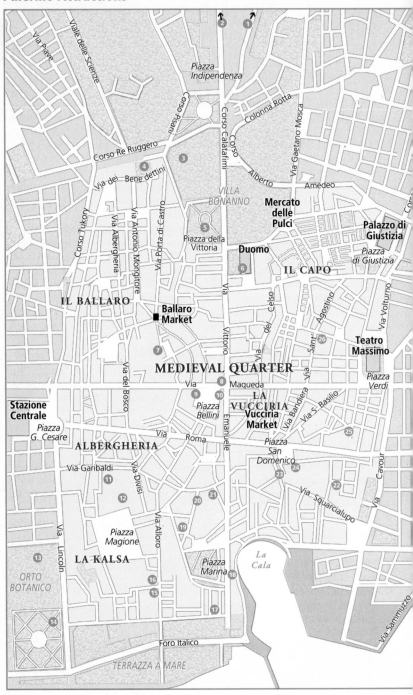

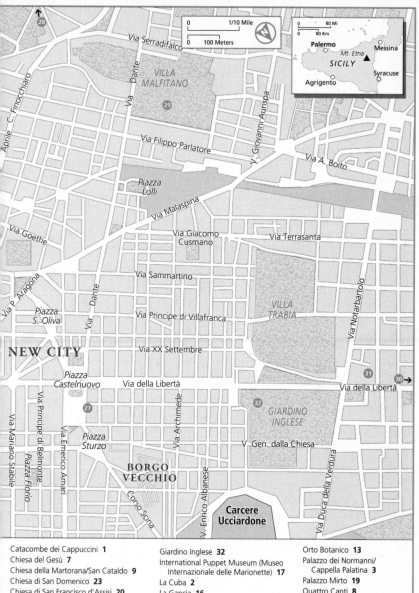

Catacombe dei Cappuccini **1**
Chiesa del Gesù **7**
Chiesa della Martorana/San Cataldo **9**
Chiesa di San Domenico **23**
Chiesa di San Francisco d'Assisi **20**
Chiesa di Sant'Agostino **26**
Chiesa S. Maria della Catena **18**
Civica Galleria d'Arte Moderne
  Empedocle Restivo **27**
Duomo **6**
Fontana Pretoria **10**
Galleria Regionale della Sicilia **15**
Giardino Garibaldi **11**

Giardino Inglese **32**
International Puppet Museum (Museo
  Internazionale delle Marionette) **17**
La Cuba **2**
La Gancia **16**
La Kalsa **12**
La Zisa **28**
Museo Archeologico Regionale **25**
Museo della Fondazione Mormino **31**
Museo Ethnografico Pitrè **30**
Oratorio di San Lorenzo **21**
Oratorio del Rosario di
  San Domenico **24**

Orto Botanico **13**
Palazzo dei Normanni/
  Cappella Palatina **3**
Palazzo Mirto **19**
Quattro Canti **8**
San Giovanni degli Eremiti **4**
Santa Cita/Oratorio del
  Rosario di Santa Cita **22**
Villa Bonanno **5**
Villa Giulia **14**
Villa Malfitano **29**

time, and have only a day for the artistic monuments of Sicily's capital, here's how the top five sights rank on a very short "A-List":

1. Palazzo dei Normanni/Cappella Palatina;
2. Galleria Regionale della Sicilia;
3. Museo Archeologico Regionale;
4. Catacombe dei Cappuccini; and
5. La Kalsa.

Palazzo dei Normanni (Palace of the Normans) ★★   This is Palermo's greatest attraction and Sicily's finest treasure trove. Allow 1½ hours and visit just this site if your time is really limited.

The history of the palace can be traced to the 9th century and the days of the Arab emirs and their harems, but probably goes back even further: The Arabs built the palace on an older Roman and Punic fortress. Over time it was abandoned by the Arabs, and the conquering Normans restored it into a sumptuous residence. The Normans came and went, and by the mid–16th century the palace was in serious decay until discovered anew by Spanish viceroys, who in 1555 began its rescue and once again turned it into a royal residence. Today it is the seat of Sicily's semi-autonomous regional government.

If you enter from Piazza Indipendenza you'll be directed to the splendid **Cappella Palatina (Palatine Chapel)** ★★★, representing the apex of the Arabo-Norman collective genius and built by Roger II from 1130 to 1140, when it was adorned with extraordinary Byzantine mosaics. You'd have to travel to Istanbul or Ravenna to encounter mosaics as awe-inspiring as these. The whole cycle constitutes the largest array of Islamic paintings to survive to the present day. Your appreciation of them, however, may be dimmed by the guardians trying to move people on their way, especially on days when too many tour-bus hordes arrive at the same time.

The chapel features a nave and two aisles divided by oval arches. The central area is surmounted by a hemispheric dome set on corner niches over a mosaic floor with walls of marble wainscoting. At the entrance to the nave is a mammoth **royal throne** encrusted in mosaics. Note the towering **Paschal candelabrum** ★ carved with figures, wild animals, and acanthus leaves, a masterpiece that has come down from the 12th century.

Covering the central nave is a honeycomb stalactite wooden *muqarnas* **ceiling** ★★, a true masterpiece and the creation of Arab artisans brought from North Africa. They depicted scenes from daily life, including animal hunts and dances. Our favorite? The depiction of a "picnic" in a harem.

The mosaics were installed to teach the story of the Bible to an illiterate people. We're especially fond of Adam and Eve, each with the "forbidden fruit" in their mouths and greedily reaching for a second luscious one. Ah, the symbolism.

There is no one set of mosaics to seek out. It is the sum total that adds to a miraculous artistic statement. Biblical scenes decorate the walls, with the image of Christ Pantocrator, surrounded by angels, on the cupola. The color of the mosaics are vivid, the style realistic, the effect sometimes achieved by gold-backed tesserae and silver mosaic tiles. This mixed inlay makes the surfaces gleam in the soft light.

The mosaics in the nave are evocative of those at Monreale's Duomo (see chapter 5). If you don't have time to pay a visit to Monreale, you'll have seen the essence of this brilliant art here. Almond-eyed biblical characters from the Byzantine world create a panorama of epic pageantry, illustrating such Gospel scenes as the Nativity. The effect is enhanced by inlaid marble as well as by pillars made of granite shipped from the East.

Expect tight security as you wander around the **Royal Apartments** ✪✪ above, because this is still a seat of government. On some days you may not gain entrance at all. When visits are possible, you enter **Salone d'Ercole,** from 1560, the chamber of the Sicilian Parliament. The salon is named for the mammoth frescoes created by Giuseppe Velasquez in the 19th century, depicting the *Twelve Labours of Hercules.* Only six panels are visible (the others concealed behind the gallery). The most dramatic and gory scene is the slaying of the Hydra of Lerna with many heads. You definitely won't want to adopt the three-headed dog, Cerberus, as your pet.

The most intriguing room of the apartments is the **Sala di Ruggero II** where King Roger himself slumbered. The room is decorated with 12th-century mosaics. Look for depictions of the peacock. Symbolically it was said that the flesh of the peacock would never rot for eternity. A charmer is the **Hall of Mirrors,** sometimes called the "Yellow Hall" because of all its stunning candelabra.

In other rooms of the Royal Apartments, one of the most splendid **courts** of Europe once held forth. Here the Western world met the mysteries of the East, as Latin scholars conversed and exchanged ideas with Arab astronomers. Regrettably, little is left of those golden days when this was the most magnificent of European medieval courts.

Piazza del Parlamento. ✆ 091-7054317. Free admission. Mon–Sat 9–11:45am; Mon–Fri 3–4:45pm; Sun 9–10am and noon–12:45pm. Bus: 104, 105, 108, 109, 110, 118, 304, or 309.

Galleria Regionale della Sicilia (Regional Gallery) ✪✪✪ This is the greatest gallery of regional art in Sicily and one of the finest art galleries in all of Italy. It's housed in the **Palazzo Abatellis** ✪, itself an architectural treasure, a Catalan-Gothic structure with a Renaissance overlay designed by Matteo Carnelivari in 1490. Carnelivari constructed the building for Francesco Abatellis, the praetor of Palermo. After World War II bombings, the architect, Carlo Scarpa, restored the palazzo in 1954.

The superb collection of Sicilian sculpture and paintings shows the evolution of the arts in Sicily from the 13th to the 18th centuries. Sculpture predominates on the main floor. Beyond room 2, the former chapel contains the gallery's most celebrated work, the *Triumph of Death* ✪✪✪, dating from 1449 and of uncertain attribution, although it's sometimes attributed to Pisanello. In all its gory magnificence, a horseback-riding skeleton, representing Death, of course, tramples his victims. The painter depicted himself in the fresco, seen with a pupil praying in vain for release from the horrors of Death. The "modernity" of this extraordinary work, including the details of the nose of the horse and the men and women in the full flush of their youth, is truly amazing, especially for its time.

The second masterpiece of the gallery lies at the end of the corridor exhibiting Arabic ceramics in room 4: the white-marble, slanted-eyed **bust of *Eleanara di Aragona*** ✪✪ by Francesco Laurana, who created it in the 15th century. This was Laurana's masterpiece.

The second-floor galleries are filled mainly with paintings from the Sicilian school, including a spectacular *Annunciation* ✪✪, the creation of Antonello da Messina. This masterpiece hangs in room 11.

In the salon of Flemish paintings rests the celebrated **Triptych of Malvagna** ✪✪ from 1510, the creation of Mabuse, whose real name was Jean

Gossaert. He depicts a Madonna and Bambino surrounded by singing angels accompanying themselves with musical instruments.

Via Alloro 4, Palazzo Abatellis. ℂ **091-6164317.** Admission 4.50€. Mon–Sat 9am–1pm; Tues and Thurs 3–7:30pm; Sun 9am–1pm. Bus: 103, 105, or 139.

Museo Archeologico Regionale (Regional Archaeological Museum)

✪✪✪ This is one of the grandest archaeological museums in Italy, stuffed with artifacts from prehistoric times until the Roman era. Spread over several buildings, the oldest from the 13th century, the museum's collection includes major Sicilian finds from the Phoenician, Punic, Greek, Roman, and Saracen periods, with several noteworthy treasures from Egypt. Even though some of the exhibitions appear shabby and the museum is definitely not state-of-the-art, its treasures are worth wading through the dust to see.

You pass through **small cloisters** ✪ on the ground floor, centered around a lovely hexagonal 16th-century fountain bearing a statue of Triton. In room 3 is some rare Phoenician art, including a **pair of sarcophagi** in the shape of human beings that date from the 5th century B.C.

On the wall in room 4 is the *Pietra di Palermo,* a black diorite slab known as the Rosetta Stone of Sicily. Discovered in Egypt in the 19th century, it was intended for the British Museum. Somehow, because of red tape, it got left behind in Palermo. From 2700 B.C., it contains carved hieroglyphics detailing information about the pharaohs, including the delivery of 40 shiploads of cedarwood to Snefru.

The most important treasure of the museum, in room 13, are the **metopes of Selinunte** ✪✪. These finds were unearthed at the temples of Selinunte, once one of the major cities of Magna Graecia (Greek colonies along the coast of southern Italy). The Selinunte sculptures are remarkable for their beauty, casting a light on the brilliance of Siceliot sculpture in general. Displayed are three magnificent metopes from Temple C, a quartet of splendid metopes from Temple E, and, in the center, a 5th-century bronze statue, **Ephebe of Selinunte** ✪. These decorative friezes cover the period from the 6th century B.C. to the 5th century B.C., depicting such scenes as Perseus slaying Medusa or the Rape of Europa by Zeus. Other scenes show Hercules fighting with an Amazon or Actaeon being transformed into a stag.

Etruscan antiquities grace rooms 14 to 17. Discoveries at the Tuscan town of Chisu shed more light on these mysterious people, when funereal *cippi* (stones) with relief decorations were unearthed. Burial urns depicted the deceased on their covers. The **Oinochoe Vase,** from the 6th century B.C., is one of the most detailed artifacts of Etruscan blackened earthenware (called *bucchero*) that is known.

Other exhibit halls on the ground floor display underwater archaeology, with the most complete collection of **ancient anchors,** mostly Punic and Roman, in the world.

Finds from Greek and Roman sites in western Sicily are to be seen on the second floor in rooms 2 and 12. Here are more artifacts from Selinunte and other ancient Sicilian sites such as Marsala, Segesta, Imera, and Randazzo. These include **funereal aedicules** (openings framed by two columns, an entablature, and usually a pediment), **oil lamps, and votive terra cottas.**

In room 7 is a remarkable and rare series of large Roman bronzes, including the most impressive, a supremely realistic **bronze Ram** ✪✪, a Hellenistic work from Syracuse. It's certainly worth the climb up the steps. Another notable work here is *Hercules Killing the Stag* ✯, discovered at Pompeii, a Roman copy of a Greek original from the 3rd century B.C. In room 8 the most remarkable sculpture is *Satyr Filling a Drinking Cup* ✯, a Roman copy of a Praxitelean original.

On the third floor is a prehistoric collection along with Greek ceramics, plus Roman mosaics and frescoes. The highlight of the collection is panels illustrating **Orpheus with Wild Animals** ✯ from the 3rd century A.D.

Via Bara all'Olivella 24. ✆ **091-6116807.** Admission 4.50€. Daily 9am–1:30pm; Tues, Wed, and Fri 3–6:30pm. Bus: 101, 102, 103, 104, or 107.

Catacombe dei Cappuccini (Catacombs of the Capuchins) ✯✯ If

you've got a secret yearning to join mummified cadavers, and your tastes lean to the bizarre, you should spend at least an hour (more if you like to walk among the dead) at these catacombs under the Capuchins Monastery.

Some 350 years ago it was discovered that the catacombs contained a mysterious preservative that helped mummify the dead. As a result, Sicilians from nobles to maids demanded to be buried here. It even became the custom on Sunday afternoon to drive out in a horse and carriage to call on Uncle Luigi and see how he was holding together. If his corpse fell apart, it was wired together or wrapped in burlap sacking. Other bodies remained perfectly preserved as in life, perhaps with a little weight loss because of dehydration.

Through a maze of dank, even somewhat spooky corridors, you can wander among the mummified bodies. Some faces are contorted as if they were posing for Edvard Munch's *The Scream.* Others look as if they'd been hanged, as a rope has been placed around many necks to hang them to the wall. Although many corpses are still remarkably preserved, time and gravity have been cruel to others. Some are downright creepy, with body parts, such as jaws or hands, missing.

At least 8,000 mummies are buried here, the oldest corpses from the late 16th century. The last corpse to be buried here was that of 2-year-old Rosalia Lombaro, who died in 1920. She still appears so lifelike that locals have dubbed her "Sleeping Beauty." The grave of Giuseppe Tommasi, prince of Lampedusa and author of one of the best-known works of Sicilian literature, *The Leopard,* was buried here in 1957. Thankfully, the body of the good prince is not embalmed but is buried in the cemetery next to the catacombs.

Capuchins Monastery, Piazza Cappuccini 1. ✆ **091-212117.** Admission 1.50€. Tours Mon–Fri 9am–noon and 1–5pm.

La Kalsa ✯✯ In Arabic, the name *Khalisa* means "pure," although that is

about the last word we'd used to describe this colorful but seedy district. Left over from the Middle Ages, the crumbling Quartiere della Kalsa is the medieval core of Old Palermo and its most intriguing neighborhood in spite of all the decay, wartime destruction, and poverty.

Located in the southwestern section of the old city, La Kalsa was designed and constructed by Arab rulers as a walled city for the emir and his ministers. Already in serious decline before World War II, La Kalsa was heavily bombed in 1943 by Allied bombers seeking to conquer Sicily from Fascist control (the neighborhood was on the bombers' radar for its strategic location near the city's port). La Kalsa in the postwar era sank into deeper misery and squalor.

When the Albanian nun Mother Teresa visited La Kalsa, she lectured the well-heeled Palermitani, telling them that since Palermo was as poor as a third-world country, "charity should begin at home." Today, after endless delays, Mother Teresa's words are finally being heard, and La Kalsa is slowly getting the restorative attention it deserves.

> **Tips Where Mafia Wannabes Get Street Smarts**
>
> La Kalsa is just as dangerous as it is fascinating. It's relatively safe to visit during the day, but even then, try not to walk around alone. Lock your valuables in the hotel safe and hang on to your wallet.
>
> More and more foreigners are visiting at night, mainly to patronize some of the newly emerging restaurants, but keep your wits about you. It's better to take a taxi to where you're going.
>
> Never wander down some dark labyrinthine street that appears deserted. Palermo's Jack the Ripper might be waiting. Just kidding: We're only trying to frighten you to be cautious. Instead of Jack the Ripper, you are more likely to encounter Jack the Mugger. These thugs, usually rejects from the Mafia, want your money or valuables more than your life, if that's any consolation.

La Kalsa is bounded by the port of La Cala on one side and Via Garibaldi and Via Paternostro to the east and west, and by Corso Vittorio Emanuele and Via Lincoln to the north and south. One of its main thoroughfares is Via Butero.

In the heart of the quarter, a good place to begin a rambling discovery is at the fancifully baroque church of **Santa Teresa alla Kalsa,** opening onto the center square, Piazza della Kalsa (✆ **091-6171658**). The church was constructed between 1686 and 1706 to the designs of Giacomo Amato. Two orders of Corinthian columns grace its stately facade. If it's open, you can visit the luminous interior to see impressive stuccoes of Giuseppe and Procopio Serpotta.

To reach Piazza della Kalsa, you enter near La Cala, the harbor, through Porta dei Greci, right off the busy thoroughfare, Foro Italico. Arm yourself with a good, detailed map, however, before venturing into the quarter.

From Piazza della Kalsa, you can walk north along Via Torremuzza until you come to **Via Alloro,** La Kalsa's main street in the Middle Ages. Head west along this street for a close encounter with the decaying district. Sadly, the street was once lined with elegant palaces, which were either destroyed, torn down, or burnt down, or are still standing, albeit most likely in a serious state of decay.

One of the grandest palaces still standing along Via Alloro is the **Palazzo Abatellis,** home today to the **Galleria Regionale della Sicilia** (p. 73).

After passing Palazzo Abatellis, you will shortly come to Via della Vetriera. At this point, head south for another close encounter with La Kalsa. This street will lead you to **Chiesa di Santa Maria dello Spasimo,** Via dello Spasimo (✆ **091-6161486**). A melancholy aura hangs over this church, originally constructed in the late Gothic style in 1506. This is the only example of the Northern Gothic style on the island. The walls went up, as did a soaring apse. But the builders abandoned the project and it was never roofed. Naturally, its interior was never finished either. Two towering ailanthus trees adopted it and now grow tall and proud. The church ruins make a marvelous venue for performances in summer.

For a final look at La Kalsa, you can head west across Piazza della Spasimo, after bidding adieu to Santa Maria dello Spasimo. This will lead you into the Piazza Magione. From here you can enjoy the facade of **La Magione** or the **Chiesa della Santi Trinità** (✆ **091-6170596**), an excellent example of a Norman church constructed in 1191 by the Cistercians. Holy Roman Emperor

Henry VI awarded it to the Teutonic Knights in 1197, and they remained in control until 1492, when Pope Innocent VIII kicked them out of Italy.

The knights are gone, but their marble funereal slabs can still be seen on the church floor. The austere interior is divided in a trio of aisles, and the beautiful cloisters date from the founding of the original Cistercian monastery. The cloisters were severely damaged when the 1943 Allied air raids bombed the church.

Chiesa di Santa Cita/Oratorio del Rosario di Santa Cita ★★★   The Oratory of the Rosary of St. Cita is a far greater artistic treasure than the church of St. Cita, on which Allied bombs rained in 1943. Only a glimmer of its former self, the church still contains a lovely **marble chancel arch** ★ by Antonello Gagini. Look for it in the presbytery. From 1517 to 1527 Gagini created other sculptures in the church, but they were damaged in the bombing. In the second chapel left of the choir is a **sarcophagus of Antonio Scirotta,** also the creation of Gagini. To the right of the presbytery is the lovely **Capella del Rosario** ★, with its polychrome marquetry and intricate lacelike stuccowork. The sculpted reliefs here are by Gioacchino Vitaliano.

On the left side of the church is the **oratory,** the real reason to visit. It is entered through the church. This was the crowning achievement of the leading baroque decorator of his day, Giacomo Serpotta, who worked on it between 1686 and 1718. His cherubs and angels romp with abandon, a delight as they climb onto the window frames or spread garlands of flowers in their pathway. They can also be seen sleeping, eating, or just hugging their knees deep in thought.

The oratory is a virtual gallery of art containing everything from scenes of the flagellation to Jesus in the Garden at Gethsemane. The *Battle of Lepanto* bas-relief is meant to symbolize the horrors of war, and other panels depict such scenes as *The Mystery of the Rosary.* At the high altar is Carlo Maratta's *Virgin of the Rosary* (1690). Allegorical figures protect eight windows along the side walls.

Via Valverde 3. ⓒ **091-332779.** Free admission (donation appreciated). Mon–Fri 8:30am–1pm; Sat 9am–1pm. Bus: 107.

Oratorio del Rosario di San Domenico ★★★   In the area of the colorful open-air market, Mercato della Vucciria, the Oratory of the Rosary of St. Dominic was founded in the closing years of the 16th century by the Society of the Holy Rosary. Two of its most outstanding members were the painter Pietro Novelli and the sculptor Giacomo Serpotta, both of whom left behind a legacy of their artistic genius in this oratory.

In allure, this oratory is the equal of the Oratorio di San Lorenzo, which also displays Serpotta's artistic flavor. The artist (1652–1732) excelled in the use of marble and polychrome, but it was in stucco that he earned his greatest fame, working here on his designs from 1714 to 1717. He decorated this second

---

Tips **Street Eats: What, You Haven't Tasted** *Babbaluci?*

Around the heart of La Kalsa, at Piazza della Kalsa, you can do as the locals do and engage in a savory treat. Several women vendors can be seen cooking and peddling *babbaluci.* A gourmet delicacy to the people of the district, these are baby snails that have been marinated in virgin olive oil, chopped fresh parsley, and garlic and sprinkled with red pepper. They are sold to passersby in paper containers called cornets.

oratory with his delightfully expressive cherubs *(putti)*, who are locked forever in a playground of happy antics.

Serpotta depicted the *Joyful Mysteries of the Rosary*, on the left and rear walls, although some of these are the work of Pietro Novelli. Themes throughout the oratory are wide-ranging, depicting everything from a *Flagellation* to *Allegories of the Virtues*. Serpotta also depicted scenes from the *Apocalypse of St. John*. Particularly graphic is a depiction of a writhing "Devil falling from Heaven." At the high altar is a masterpiece by Anthony Van Dyck, *Madonna of the Rosary* (1628). Illustrating the *Coronation of the Virgin*, the ceiling was frescoed by Pietro Novelli.

Via dei Bambinai. ℂ 091-332779. Free admission. Mon 3–6pm; Tues–Fri 9am–1pm and 3–5:30pm; Sat 9am–1pm. Bus: 107.

Oratorio di San Lorenzo ★★★ No longer as rich in treasures as it once was, the Oratory of San Lorenzo lies to the left (facing) the church of San Francesco d'Assisi. A local Franciscan order, Compagnia di San Francesco, ordered this oratory constructed back in 1569. Of extraordinary elegance, the **stucco decoration** ★★ inside is the masterpiece of Giacomo Serpotta, who worked on it between 1698 and 1710. It features a series of 10 symbolic statues, plus panels relating the details of the lives of St. Francis and St. Lawrence. Art historians have written of these wall paintings as "a cave of white coral."

Some of the most expressive of the stuccoes depict the martyrdom of St. Lawrence. Paintings alternate with statues of the Virtues. On the upper sections of the walls the nude "thinkers" evoke figures created by Michelangelo in the Sistine Chapel. In total contrast to the serene Virtues and the solemn faces of the nudes is the cavalcade of *putti*, who romp gaily, making soap bubbles or kissing each other.

Laced with mother-of-pearl, stunning mahogany **pews** are placed around the walls. They were created during the 18th century and rest on carved supports.

Near the old port of La Cala, just south of Corso Vittorio Emanuele. Via dell'Immacolatella. Free admission. Mon–Sat 9am–noon. Bus: 101 or 102.

Duomo ★★ If too many cooks in the kitchen can spoil the broth, too many architects turned Palermo's cathedral into a hodgepodge of styles. It is still a striking building, however, and well worth an hour or more of your time. Regrettably, the various styles—Greek-Roman, Norman, Arabic, Islamic—were not blended successfully with the overriding baroque overlay.

During the Norman reign in 1184, the archbishop of Palermo, Gualtiero Offamiglio, launched the cathedral on the site of a Muslim mosque, which had been built over an early Christian basilica. Offamiglio was green with envy at the supremacy of the cathedral of Monreale. As the Palermo Duomo took shape, it became an architectural battleground for what was known as "The Battle of the Two Cathedrals."

Moments **The Church That Never Was**

One of the most evocative moments you can have in Palermo is to stand in the church ruins of Santa Maria dello Spasimo on a dying summer day, watching the remains of this late Gothic building catch "fire" with the rays of the setting sun. The spirit of Raphael is evoked. He came here to paint his famous portrait of the anguish of the Madonna before the cross. But you'll have to go to the Prado in Madrid to see that masterpiece.

Fun Fact **The Mystery of the Stolen Painting**

In 1969 the art world learned in newspaper headlines that "the divine" Caravaggio's last large painting, *The Nativity,* had been stolen from the Oratory of San Lorenzo. Caravaggio created the work in 1609, and it hung over the altar until its theft. No motive for the theft has been announced, and it is believed that the painting was needlessly destroyed. The curator told us, "We keep hoping that one day it will come back to us, but as each day goes by, that hope grows dimmer and dimmer." Michelangelo Merisi (1573–1610), Caravaggio's real name, fled Rome after killing a man in a brawl in 1606. He died a year after painting *The Nativity.*

Today, the facade is closed between two soaring towers with double lancet windows. Dating from the 15th century, the middle portal is enhanced by a double lancet with the Aragonese coat-of-arms. The four impressive bell towers, or campaniles, date from the 14th century, the south and north porches from the 15th and 16th centuries.

But if anyone could be called the culprit for the cathedral's playground of styles, it is the Neapolitan architect Ferdinando Fuga, who went with the mood of his day and in 1771 and 1809 gave both the exterior and interior of the Duomo a sweeping neoclassical style. In retrospect, he should have left well enough alone. The only section that the restorers left alone were the **apses** ⊛, which still retain their impressive geometric decoration.

The Duomo is also a pantheon of royalty. As you enter, the first chapel on the right contains six of the edifice's most impressive tombs, including that of Roger II, the first king of Sicily, who died in 1154. He was crowned in the Duomo in 1130. His daughter Constance, who died in 1198, is also buried here along with her husband, Henry VI, who died the year before. Henry VI was emperor of Germany and the son of Frederick Barbarossa. Their own son, another emperor of Germany and king of Sicily, Frederick II, was also buried here in 1250, as was his wife, Constance of Aragón, who died in 1222. The last royal burial here, of Peter II, king of Sicily, was in 1342.

Accessed from the south transept, the **Tesoro,** or treasury, is a repository of rich vestments, silverware, chalices, holy vessels, monstrances, altar cloths, and, among other gems, beautiful ivory engravings of Sicilian art of the 17th century. An oddity here is the bejeweled **cap-like crown of Constance of Aragón** ⊛, designed by local craftsmen in the 12th century, and removed from her head when the tomb was opened in the 18th century. Other precious objects removed from the royal tombs are also on display here.

Piazza di Cattedrale, Corso Vittorio Emanuele. ⓒ **091-334376.** Duomo: free (donation appreciated). Crypt: 1€; treasury: 1€. Mon–Sat 9:30am–5:30pm. Bus: 104, 108, 110, 118, or 139.

2 Other Great Churches

Chiesa del Gesù Constructed in 1564, but extended and modified by several later architects, this was the first church in Sicily built by the Jesuits. Regrettably, it was another victim of the 1943 Allied air raids and had to be considerably restored at the end of World War II. Don't judge this church by its somber facade. Its **interior** ⊛⊛ is a triumph of baroque indulgence. Everywhere you look is an outstanding example of exuberant Sicilian baroque, with marble

---

Fun Fact **A Medieval Delicacy Lives On**

In the Middle Ages every convent in Palermo specialized in creating a different kind of confectionery. Many of these old recipes are gone forever. But one of the most enduring is still sold at *pasticceria* all over the city: *frutta martorana,* named after the old Benedictine convent of La Martorana. Originally this marzipan was shaped into various "fruits" and "vegetables." Today these almond paste sweetmeats resemble anything from cats to sailboats. The *frutta martorana* are most abundant in the bakeries before the feast day of All Saints in early November.

---

adornments, stucco reliefs, polychrome intarsia, and an array of paintings and sculpted works. All this overlay took centuries to complete.

The **frescoes** in the first bay of the vault of the nave are among the oldest pictorial decorations, these created by Filippo Randazzo in 1743. The presbytery and apse also contain some of the original decorations, including sculptures by Gioacchino Vitaliano. Our favorite work of art here is the brilliant **chancel decor** ⍟, the work of the Serpotta brothers. It's a romp of cherubs harvesting grapes, playing musical instruments, and holding torches or else garlands of bouquets. Seek out the second chapel on the right as you enter to view paintings of **St. Philip of Agira** and the even more expressive **St. Paul the Hermit** ⍟, both excellent examples of Pietro Novelli's work. The last figure depicted on the left in the St. Paul painting is actually a self-portrait of Novelli.

The magnificent porticoed baroque courtyard gives access to the **Biblioteca Comunale,** the public library known as "Casa Professa." Filled with ancient manuscripts and incunabula, it also displays 300 portraits of illustrious men.

Piazza Casa Professa 21. ✆ **091-581880.** Free admission. Daily 7am–noon and 5–6:30pm. Bus: 101, 102, 103, 104, or 107.

Chiesa della Martorana/San Cataldo ⍟⍟   These two Norman churches stand side by side. If you have time for only one, make it La Martorana, as it is the most celebrated church in Palermo remaining from the Middle Ages. Visit it if only to see its series of spectacular **mosaics** ⍟⍟.

Named for Eloisa Martorana, who founded a nearby Benedictine convent in 1194, this church is dedicated not to her, but to Santa Maria dell'Ammiraglio (St. Mary of the Admiral). History was made here as well: It was in this church that Sicily's noblemen convened to offer the crown to Peter of Aragon.

Today's baroque facade regrettably conceals a Norman front. You enter through a beautiful combined portico and bell tower with a trio of ancient columns and double arch openings. The bell tower is original, dating from the 12th century. Once you go inside, you'll know that your time spent seeking out this church was worthwhile. The stunning mosaics were ordered in 1143 by George of Antioch, the admiral of King Roger and a man of Greek descent who loved mosaics, especially when they conformed, as these did, to the Byzantine iconography of his homeland. It's believed that the craftsmen who designed these mosaics also did the same for the Cappella Palatina. The mosaics are laid out on and around the columns that hold up the principal cupola. We prefer to see them at their most beautiful in the morning light when the church opens.

Dominating the dome is a rendition of Christ, surrounded by a bevy of angels with the Madonna and the Apostles pictured off to the sides. Even after the passage of centuries the colors are still vibrantly golden, with streaks of spring green, ivory, azure blue, and what one art critic called "grape-red."

On a visit to La Martorana, you can obtain a key from the custodian sitting at a tiny table to your right as you enter the chapel. With this key you can enter the tiny **Chiesa di San Cataldo** next door. Also of Norman origin, it was founded by Maio of Bari, chancellor to William I. But because he died in 1160, the interior was never completed. The church is famous for its Saracenic red **golfball domes.** Sicilians liken these bulbous domes to a eunuch's hat.

Piazza Bellini 2, adjacent to Piazza Pretoria. © 091-6161692. Free admission. La Martorana: Mon–Sat 9:30am–1pm and 3:30–6:30pm; Sun 8:30am–1pm. San Cataldo: Tues–Sat 9am–5pm; Sat–Sun 9am–1pm. Bus: 101 or 102.

Chiesa di San Domenico

Although its oratory (see above) is a more intriguing artistic expression because of the delightful *putti* by Giacomo Serpotta, the Church of St. Dominic is one of the city's most remarkable baroque structures, its elegant baroque facade often depicted on postcards. It was constructed in 1640 to the design of the architect Andrea Cirrincione. The facade, however, wasn't added until 1726. Many antique buildings on the square were demolished to give this church more breathing room.

The facade rises in a trio of carefully ordered tiers, graced with both Corinthian and Doric pillars along with square pilasters that form a sort of picture frame for a statue of St. Dominic. Unlike the lavishly decorated oratory, the church has a severe interior that only emphasizes the beauty of the architecture. Its chapels, on the other hand, are richly decorated, forming a pantheon of tombs and cenotaphs of some of the more noble Sicilians, including Francesco Crispi, the former prime minister of Italy. The tomb of the painter, Pietro Novelli (1608–47), is found in the north aisle.

Adjoining is the headquarters of the Sicilian Historical Society, with its own tiny **Museo del Risorgimento,** containing mementoes of Garibaldi. The fragmented 14th-century cloister was part of the first church erected on this site.

Piazza San Domenico. © 091-584872. Free admission. Mon–Fri 7:30am–noon; Sat–Sun 7:30am–6:30pm. Bus: 101.

Chiesa di San Francesco d'Assisi

In the medieval Kalsa district, north of Via Alloro, this church remains a gem in spite of earthquakes and the devastating bombardment by Allied planes in 1943. It was built between 1255 and 1277 as a shrine to St. Francis of Assisi. The church is known for its facade with a shallow porch and zigzag ornamentation. Its **rose window** ✪ is one of the finest in Sicily, and its flamboyant **Gothic portal** ✪ is from the original 13th-century structure.

After the 1943 bombardments, restorers set about to return the interior to its original medieval appearance, removing the overlay added by decorators who found the neoclassical style more alluring. The interior today is rather austere, with a trio of cylindrical piers and wide Gothic arches. But it still has the light, airy sense of space evocative of Franciscan churches erected in medieval times.

A few notable works of art from painters and sculptors survive. In the north aisle, fourth chapel on the left, note the magnificent **arch** ✪✪, superbly sculpted by Pietro da Bonitate and Francesco Laurana in 1468. This arch was the earliest major Renaissance work in Sicily. The sanctuary has beautiful **choir stalls** carved by Paolo and Giovanni Gili in 1520.

It's best to tie in a visit to this church with a look at the Oratorio di San Lorenzo, which is virtually next door.

Piazza di San Francesco d'Assisi, off Via Paternostro. Ⓒ 091-6162819. Free admission. Mon–Sat 7am–12:30pm and 4:30–6pm. Bus: 101 or 102.

Chiesa di Sant'Agostino   Even if you don't go inside, you won't miss much. The **facade** 𝕒 is the most beautiful part of this church, which dates from the 13th century when it was financed by two prominent Palermo dynasties, the Chiaramonte and the Sciafani families. Skilled masons embroidered its elegant rose window and laid lava mosaics around the main portal. Both the portal and the distinctive rose window are in the Norman architectural style.

The interior was reconstructed with baroque adornment centuries later in contrast to the classic medieval front. Inside are the last stuccoes of followers of the Serpotta School, completed between 1711 and 1729. You can still see Serpotta's mark, a *serpe,* Sicilian for "lizard." The medieval cloister was originally built in the Catalan Gothic style, surrounding a central fountain. Lying at a corner of the cloister, the chapter house preserves many of its original 13th-century architectural features. Embedded into the wall of the stairs leading from the church's side entrance is an **ancient Roman tomb.**

Sant'Agostino lies adjacent to **Mercato di Capo,** a busy street market and one of Palermo's more intriguing sights.

Via S. Agostino. No phone. Free admission. Mon–Sat 7am–noon and 4–5:30pm; Sun 7am–noon. Bus: 225.

Chiesa S. Maria della Catena 𝕒   No church is quite as evocative as Catena at sunset. The setting sun creates dramatic colors of gold and ruby reds on its ancient facade. Situated in the old harbor district, called the *cala,* this church is from the 15th century. The name *catena,* meaning "chain," comes from the long chain that was used to close the old port at night and that was attached to the church's outer wall. The architect of this Gothic-Catalan church with Renaissance elements is believed to have been Matteo Carnelivari (1502–34).

Raised on a high flight of steps, the church's elevation is characterized by a spacious portico with a trio of arches. With its twin corner pilasters, this three-arched porch marries the Gothic with the Renaissance in its architectural style. Beneath the portico is a **trio of portals,** in bas-relief, by Vincenzo Gagini, of the most famous artistic family in Sicily.

The **interior** 𝕒 of the church is a work of beauty. A Gagini portal on the left side is graced with columns and single mullioned windows. A nave cuts through the interior with two side aisles separated by skinny Renaissance pillars. The nave was created with ribbed vaulting with side "barrel" vaults.

The church has an elevated presbytery with a trio of apses. A 14th-century Madonna and Child was discovered here in the 1980s. This work of art lies in the chapel on the right inside a 16th-century *baldacchino* (stone canopy). Wander through the east end with its beautiful, elaborate Gothic decorative elements and double columns, and even a Roman sarcophagus. At the altar, symbolic chains represent the ancient port.

Piazza delle Dogane (Corso Vittorio Emanuele). Ⓒ 091-6077111. Free admission. Mon–Fri 9am–1pm; Sun 11am–1pm. Closed Sat and Aug. Bus: 110, 118, 139, 224, 225, or 389.

La Gancia   Constructed in 1485 and dedicated to Santa Maria degli Angeli, this church stands next door to the Regional Gallery and can easily be visited at the same time. In the late Middle Ages, this was an enclave of the Franciscans. Much changed and altered over the centuries, the exterior of La Gancia contains a Gothic portal with a bas-relief on the arch. Inside, the nave is without aisles but contains a total of 16 side chapels and a marble floor in different hues.

The sculptor, Giacomo Serpotta, added baroque stucco decorations. The patterned **wooden ceiling** ⭐ is romantically painted with stars on a blue background. The chief treasure of La Gancia is a splendid **organ** ⭐⭐ by Raffaele della Valle dating from the late 1500s, making it the oldest in Palermo. At the marble pulpit, look for the **relief tondoes of the *Annunciation,*** the work of Antonello Gagini in the 16th century. As a curiosity, note the **novice monk** ⭐ peering over the top of a cornice in the chapel to the left of the main altar.

Via Alloro 27. ℂ 091-6165221. Free admission. Mon–Sat 9am–5pm. Bus: Linea Gialla (Yellow Line).

San Giovanni degli Eremiti ⭐⭐   This is one of the most famous of all the Arabo-Norman monuments still standing in Palermo. It is certainly the most romantic building remaining from the heyday of Norman Palermo. Since 1132, this church with its series of five red domes has remained one of the most characteristic landmarks on the Palermo skyline. It is located on the western edge of the Albergheria district.

In an atmosphere appropriate for the recluse it honors, St. John of the Hermits (now deconsecrated), this is one of the most idyllic spots in Palermo. A medieval veil hangs heavily in the gardens, with their citrus blossoms and flowers, especially on a hot summer day as you wander around the cloister.

A single nave divides the simple interior into two bays, surmounted by a dome. A small cupola surmounts the presbytery. The right-hand apse is covered by one of the red domes. Surrounding the left-hand apse is a bell tower with pointed windows, and it, too, is crowned by one of the church's smallest red domes.

The small **late Norman cloister** ⭐, with a Moorish cistern in the center, was part of the original Benedictine monastery that once stood here. It has little round arches supported by fine paired columns.

Via dei Benedettini 3. ℂ 091-6515019. Admission 4.50€ adults; 2€ for students, seniors, and children. Mon–Sat 9am–1pm and 3–7pm; Sun 9am–1pm. Bus: 108, 109, or 305.

3 The Best of the Palaces

La Cuba ⭐   A less elaborate version of Zisa, and not as well preserved, "Cuba" is a Sicilian derivation of the Arabic *Ka'aba,* meaning "cube" or "square-shaped structure." It has nothing to do with the Caribbean island of the same name. Built in 1180 by King William II, it was a kind of summer palace with royal gardens where the court came to escape the heat. A tall building with a rectangular plan, it is another magnificent piece of Fatimid architecture. The interior of the original structure had a hall that rose the full height of the building and was covered by a dome.

Giovanni Boccaccio made Cuba a setting in his tales of *The Decameron.* After it fell from royal use, it was privately owned, becoming a leper colony. When the Bourbons came to power, they turned it into a cavalry barracks. Today Cuba is part of a military barracks. Visitors can enter, but not photograph, the military grounds.

Corso Calatafimi 100 (in the Tukory Barracks opposite Via Quarto dei Mille). ℂ 091-590299. Admission 2€. Mon–Sat 9am–1pm and 3–7pm; Sun 9am–1pm. Bus: 105, 304, 309, 339, 364, 365, or 380.

Palazzo Mirto ⭐⭐   A visit to the nobleman's residence of the princes of Lanzi Filangeri is like taking a journey back into time. As many of the other Palermo palazzi constructed at the same time lie rotting in the sun, this one is relatively held together. Since early in the 17th century, Palazzo Mirto was the lavish abode of this prominent Sicilian family. In 1982 the last surviving family member donated the palazzo to Sicily to preserve as a memorial to a vanished era.

Pause to take in the grace of the principal facade, with its double row of balconies, open to view on Via Lungarini. No other residence in Palermo gives you a better idea of a princely residence from the 18th and 19th centuries than this one. As you enter the palazzo, to the left, magnificent **19th-century stables** feature stalls and ornamental bronze horse heads. Take a fabulous red marble staircase up to the first floor, which is still decorated as it was when the last of the princes departed.

The first of the elegant drawing rooms is the **Sala degli Arazzi,** or tapestry hall, whose mythological scenes were painted by Giuseppe Velasco in 1804. Some of the salons open onto a patio garden with a flamboyant rococo fountain flanked by a pair of aviaries. Our favorite room is the exquisite **Chinese sitting room** with its trompe l'oeil ceiling, leather-covered floor, and painted silk walls showing scenes from daily life. After dinner the princes gathered here to smoke, talk, and play cards. As a note of curiosity, the next room has a series of remarkable Neapolitan plates from the 19th century, decorated with party costumes. At masked balls each guest was assigned a plate that featured his or her costume. From the vestibule you can visit another **smoking room**, this one painted and paneled with embossed leather. For a final bit of frippery, seek out the **Pompadour sitting room**, with silk walls embroidered with flowers and a mosaic floor, elegance so divine as to be decadent.

Via Merlo 2, off Piazza Marina. ⓒ 091-6164751. Free admission. Mon, Wed, Fri, and Sat 9am–1:30pm; Tues and Thurs 9am–1:30pm and 3–5:30pm; Sun 9am–12:30pm. Bus: 103, 105, or 139.

Villa Malfitano   One of Palermo's great villa palaces, built in the Liberty style, lies within a **spectacular garden**. The villa was built in 1886 by Joseph Whitaker, grandson of the famous English gentleman and wine merchant Ingham, who moved to Sicily in 1806 and made a fortune producing Marsala wine. Whitaker had trees shipped to Palermo from all over the world planted around his villa. These included such rare species as Dragon's Blood, an enormous banyan tree and the only one found in Europe. Palermo high society flocked here for lavish parties, and royalty from Great Britain visited. In World War II Gen. George Patton temporarily stayed here as he planned the invasion of southern Italy. The villa today is lavishly furnished with antiques and artifacts from all over the world. The **Sala d'Estate (Summer Room)** is particularly stunning, with trompe l'oeil frescoes covering both the walls and the ceiling.

Via Dante 167. ⓒ 091-6816133. Admission 2.50€. Mon–Sat 9am–1pm. Bus: 103, 106, 108, 122, 134, 164, or 824.

La Zisa   Only the shell of the former Moorish palace remains, and its claims to resemble the Alhambra in Granada are so far-fetched as to be ridiculous. But an aura of *Arabian Nights* still lingers about the place. With a little imagination you can conjure up dancers who entertained the various sultans centuries ago.

Moorish craftsmen started the palace in 1166 under William I, and it was finished in 1175 for his son, William II. Zisa was the major building in a royal park that also embraced Cuba. This beautifully landscaped park was called Genoard, meaning "terrestrial paradise," and was celebrated throughout Europe in the Middle Ages (it was even known to the writer Boccaccio, who set one of his stories in his *Decameron* here). The park was fenced in so that wild animals could roam about. Unfortunately, by the 16th century, the palace's heyday was all but a memory, and it was used as a depository for objects contaminated by the plague.

The structure you see today is high and compact. Two square towers flank the short sides of the castle. With its richness long stripped away, the interior is no longer remarkable, but you can still get some impression of the former sultan's palace. On the ground floor as you enter is the **Fountain Hall,** built on a cross plan. On the second floor is a good collection of Arabic art and artifacts.

Piazza Gugliemo il Buono (near Piazza Camporeale at the end of Via Dante). © 091-6520269. Admission 2.50€. Mon–Sat 9am–noon and 3–7pm; Sun 9am–noon. Bus: 124.

4 Other Great Museums

Civica Galleria d'Arte Moderna Empedocle Restivo ★ *Finds* Located on the second floor of Teatro Politeama, this little gallery of 19th- and early-20th-century Sicilian (mostly) art seems to be a secret locals like to keep to themselves. Since 1910 the art-loving citizens of Palermo have been going to this museum to see works by their home-grown artists. Be aware that few of the artists' names will be immediately recognizable to the international visitor, and some of the art is overly romanticized and a bit sappy. A great deal is by landscapists from Palermo.

But the museum does contain works by major artists. Look for pieces by Corrada Cagli, Carlo Carrà, and Gino Severini, along with Giovanni Boldini, Antonio Mancini, and Domenico Morelli. Michele Catti, one of the finest landscape painters, is an artist of "long horizons," and his *Last Leaves* here is typical of his work. One of the most reproduced works of art from this museum is *Carusi* by Onofrio Tomaselli. The figure on the left rests while those on the right are beasts of burden with heavy loads. The Sicilian portraits of Salvatore Lo Forte are especially realistic, and Sicilian patriotism is best evoked in the works of Erulo Eruli, whose masterpiece is *The Sicilian Vesper.* From the 1930s on, the collection diminishes a bit in the remaining rooms, although Felice Casorati weighs in strongly with his memorable *Schoolchildren.* One of the most delightful sculptures is a marble *Faun* by Trentacoste.

Via Turati 10. © 091-588951. Admission 3€. Free for ages 17 and under and 66 and over. Tues–Sat 9am–8pm; Sun 9am–1pm. Bus: 101, 102, 103, 106, 108, 124, or 134.

Museo Internazionale delle Marionette (International Puppet Museum) ★★ *Kids* If you're into puppets, or *pupi* as the Sicilians say, this is the greatest museum of its kind in the world devoted to the art of the marionette. In their shiny armor and with their stern expressions, these *pupi* remain as an evocation of Norman Sicily, an era of legendary chivalry and troubadours. In the world of the puppet, the exploits of William the Bad (1120–66) and others live on, as do the legends of Charlemagne and the swashbuckling Saracen pirates.

All the puppets on display are antiques, some of them centuries old. Most were used at one time in the *opera de pupi,* or puppet opera, a local tradition fast dying out. Puppets come not only from Sicily but from other parts of Italy as well. Each puppet is handmade and painstakingly crafted right down to the smallest detail. In addition to Sicilian puppets, the collection includes puppets crafted in other parts of the world, notably Indonesia, India, and other countries from the Far East, as well as the English "Punch and Judy." The most outstanding artisan here is Gaspara Canino, who achieved fame with his theater puppets in the 1800s.

Via Butera 1. © 091-328060. Admission 3€ adults, 1.50€ children under 12. Mon–Fri 9am–1pm and 4–7pm; Sat 9am–1pm; Sun 10am–1pm. Bus: 103, 105, 139, or 225.

Museo della Fondazione Mormino   An unusual, offbeat museum, this gallery is on the second floor of the Banco di Sicilia in the historic Villa Mormino. In essence it displays the treasure trove accumulated by banking interests over the years, ranging from artwork to Greek artifacts to rare coins. The collection of Italian majolica from the 16th century to the 18th century is among the finest in Italy, and there is also a vast array of Greek vases.

Look for the magnificent but tiny Etruscan mirror with a relief of Silenus. Of equal interest is the terra-cotta statue of a young boy (case B), dating from the 3rd century B.C. Some of the artifacts removed from the Greek city of Selinunte are also displayed here, as are artifacts unearthed at the inland town of Terravecchia di Cuti, which dates to the 6th century B.C. The final section displays coins and medals, many from the 1200s.

Viale Libertà 52. ℂ 091-625519. Admission 3.50€. Mon–Fri 9am–1pm and 3–5pm. Bus: 101, 102, 702, or 704.

Museo Ethnografico Pitré   This is the attic of old Sicily, a virtual time capsule of the way life used to be lived on the island. Nearly everything that it documents has virtually been swept away in the past half century. Back in 1909, a great collector, Giuseppe Pitré, understood that the old way of life was quickly vanishing from the island, and he began to collect the tools of ordinary Sicilian life, accumulating some 4,000 objects that are today on exhibit at this museum.

Nothing is more evocative of old Sicily than the **flamboyantly decorated carts** 🟊 with their elaborate carvings and painting. Sicilians call their brightly painted carts *carretti*. In olden days, a family's social standing was judged by the decorations on their carts: the more elaborate and intricate the decoration, the more important the family.

The museum also displays an intriguing collection of Sicilian puppets and a vast array of handcrafts, ranging from ceramic holy water fonts, sundry dolls, tapestries, and painted masks, to 19th-century lace dresses and wooden *ex voto* (votive) tablets. Some of these tablets often depict the violent end of the dedicatee. Intricate examples of needlework and embroidery are also on display.

Parco della Favorita. ℂ 091-7404890. Admission 3.10€. Free for ages 17 and under and 61 and up. Sat–Thurs 9am–8pm. Bus: 101 to Stadio Partanna, then change to 614 or 645.

5 City Landmarks & Treasures

Fontana Pretoria 🟊🟊   In the heart of Palermo's loveliest square, **Piazza Pretoria** 🟊🟊, stands this magnificent fountain, the work of Francesco Camilliani, the Florentine sculptor, in 1554 and 1555. The fountain overlooks the facades of the two churches on the square, S. Caterina and S. Giuseppe dei Teatini. Surely if Camilliani had seen a lily growing in the field, he would have put gilt on it. This fountain is hardly subtle. It's adorned with depictions of allegories, the heads of animals, water, nymphs, monsters, ornamental staircases and balustrades and, of course, gods and goddesses comprising an encyclopedia of Mount Olympus. One of the statuettes guarding the ramps is the classical patroness of Sicily, Ceres, depicted with a horn of plenty. The fountain is floodlit at night, a 24-hour sight.

Quattro Canti 🟊   At the intersection of Via Vittorio Emanuele and Via Maqueda, the "Four Corners" of Palermo converge at a quartet of baroque palaces left over from the heyday of Spanish rule. The actual name of the square is Piazza Vigliena, although locals refer to it as Quattro Canti. Via Maqueda dates from the 1580s, when it converged with the ancient Via Càssaro, now called Vittorio Emanuele. The viceroy Vigliene ordered the construction of the four palaces at this crossroads, the buildings inspired by Rome's Quattro Fontane.

Each of the corners is decorated with a niche in three tiers. The first tier of each niche contains a fountain and a statue representing one of the four seasons. The second tier of each niche displays a statue of one of the Spanish viceroys: Carlos V; Felipe II, III, and IV. The third tier of each niche is dedicated to a statue of one of the patron saints of the city, Christina, Ninfa, Olivia, and Agata.

Four Corners is no longer the meeting place of Palermitani as it was in the old days. Instead of creamy white buildings, think soot-blackened gray. And be careful when admiring the former beauty of the place, or else you might be run down by a king of the road on a speeding Vespa.

6 Palermo's "Green Lungs": Parks & Gardens

A people who knew the joy of a green oasis, the Arabs introduced gardens into Palermo. The Normans extended the idea by creating parklands and summer palaces to escape the heat. Subsequent rulers created more parks. Today you can wander among gardens and greenery and encounter incredible banyan trees and other exotic plantings. If you can't visit all the parks, the most rewarding are Orto Botanico, the botanical gardens, and the Giardino Inglese, the English gardens (see descriptions of both below).

ORTO BOTANICO   Our favorite park is **Orto Botanico** ★★, Via Abramo Lincoln 2B (© **091-6173211**), the botanical gardens. We go here if for no other reason than to see the amazing **banyan tree** ★★, the tallest and most impressive specimen in the garden. Its botanical name is *Ficus magnoloides,* and this fig tree with its "aerial" roots is more than 150 years old. The gardens were laid in 1795 by Filippo Parlatore, a native botanist. The circular water lily pond from 1796 is still here.

The garden is known to botanists the world over because of the richness and variety of its plant species, which range from gigantic tropical plants to spiny kapok trees with their bottle-shaped trunks. Many of the plants were shipped in from Asia, including gigantic bamboo. Among the curiosities are the *Bombacaceae* and *Chorisias* plants shipped here in the late 19th century from South America. These have swollen and prickly trunks and in spring bloom with beautiful pink flowers that turn to a strange fruit. When it ripens, the fruit bursts open and drops its seed on the ground along with a thick "hair padding." Locals once harvested this padding and used it like horsehair.

Admission to Orto Botanico is 3.10€, and hours are Monday through Friday from 9am to 6pm and Saturday and Sunday from 9am to 1pm. Take bus no. 139, 211, 221, 224, 226, or 227.

VILLA GIULIA   Next door to the Orto Botanico, also opening onto Via Abramo Lincoln, is a public park, **Villa Giulia,** an Italianate oasis created in 1778 by Nicolò Palma and enlarged by the city in 1866. This was the city's first public park and was named for its patron, Giulia Avalos Guevara, the wife of the ruling viceroy. Goethe came this way in 1787 and had much praise for the garden, which is also called "La Flora." Its beautiful trees and flowers are in better shape than the monuments. The best-known statue is called *Genius of Palermo,* a work by Marabitti. In the park four roads converge with four Pompeiian-style niches by Giuseppe Damiani Almeyda. Sicilians call these artistic niches *prospetti.*

PARCO DELLA FAVORITA   Reached by going 2.8km (1¾ miles) north of Palermo along Viale Diana, **Parco della Favorita** is a large park at the foot of Monte Pellegrino. This was part of an estate acquired in 1799 by Ferdinand of Bourbon, who came here after he was driven out of Naples by Napoleonic troops. He ordered that the land be laid out according to his rather Victorian taste. In time it became the ruler's private hunting estate.

The fantastic **Palazzina Cinese,** or Chinese Palace, that Ferdinand ordered Venanzio Marvuglia to build for him is still standing. It was in this exotically decorated palace that the king, along with his wife, Maria Carolina, entertained Horatio Nelson and Lady Hamilton.

Note the marble fountain with a statue of Hercules. This is a copy of the celebrated *Farnese Hercules* that the king tried to abduct from Naples. Instead of the real thing, he got a copy.

In the 18th century many noble families built summer villas around the park to escape the intense heat of the city. The most famous of these is **Villa Niscemi,** Piazza Niscemi (© **091-7404859**), a venue for occasional cultural events. Di Lampedusa mentioned this villa in his novel, *The Leopard.* The villa is sometimes open on Sunday from 9am to 12:30pm; call ahead for confirmation.

VILLA BONANNO   Behind the Palazzo dei Normanni lies **Villa Bonanno** ⚘, among the most beautiful public gardens of Palermo. They are entered from Piazza della Vittoria. The city added palm trees in 1905, making the park look like an oasis in North Africa. Note the roof covering the ruins of a trio of ancient Roman houses, the only such artifacts of their kind left in Palermo. Villa Bonanno adjoins Piazza del Parlamento with its mammoth statue of Philip V of the House of Bourbon.

GIARDINO GARIBALDI   In the very heart of Palermo lies a beautiful garden, **Giardino Garibaldi** ⚘, at Piazza Marina. With their large, exposed, and trunklike "aerial" roots, stunning **banyan trees** ⚘⚘ grace this park. Fig trees and towering palms also adorn the garden.

In the 16th century Aragonese weddings and military victories were celebrated on **Piazza Marina.** Sadly, it was also the site of public executions. After a long period of neglect, Piazza Marina has been spruced up and is once again a gathering place for residents. At night it's an animated square with outdoor tables spilling from several pizzerie.

The largest palace on the square is **Palazzo Chiaramonte** ⚘, constructed in 1307 for one of Sicily's noblest and richest dynasties during the Aragonese era. Its most attractive feature can be seen on its facade—two tiers of **delightful windows** ⚘⚘ with magnificent stone inlays. The palace is sometimes open for concerts.

GIARDINO INGLESE   The **English Gardens** ⚘ lie to the north of the center, bordering Via della Libertà past Piazza Crispi. Always known as Palermo's prettiest little park, the gardens in the 1990s degenerated into a hangout for Palermo's drug-addicted population. The police have cracked down on the park and, unless conditions change, it has been returned to its former self.

The garden was designed at the end of the 19th century. It's bordered on its far side by Via Generale Dalla Chiesa, named in honor of Gen. Carlo Alberto Dalla Chiesa, who was assassinated by the Mafia here in 1982, along with his wife and chauffeur. He served 5 months in office as prefect of Palermo before he was gunned down. A plaque has been erected in his memory.

7 Especially for Kids

Palermo is not the world's most child-friendly city. Because of roaring, dangerous traffic, it is difficult to walk the city's streets, especially the narrow ones, without constantly keeping an eye out for your *bambini.*

There is one attraction that kids adore in Palermo, however, and that's the **Museo Internazionale delle Marionette (International Puppet Museum)** (p. 85). Sicilians call their famous puppets *pupi,* and they are really works of folkloric art. Puppet shows are staged here on Fridays between 5 and 6pm, and they are a delight, the finest in Europe. See if you can time your visit to see a show. Puppet shows are also presented at **Opera dei Pupi,** Via Bara all'Olivella 52 (*C* **091-3233400;** bus: 101 or 122), and at **Teatro Ippogrifo,** Vicolo Ragusi 4 (*C* **091-329194;** bus: 225). Shows, costing from 5€ to 6€ per ticket, are staged daily from 6 to 7pm, September through June only.

Each family who visits Palermo has to decide whether to take children to the **Catacombe dei Cappuccini** (p. 75), where mummified bodies and skeletons of some 8,000 Palermitans are on view. Young children in particular may be frightened by these ghoulish sights, including a baby girl who died in 1920 at the age of two, her corpse amazingly lifelike even today.

Away from the traffic, noise, and pollution of Palermo, the city's public parks are refreshing interludes for families. Especially inviting is the landscaped oasis of the **Orto Botanico,** or botanical gardens (p. 87).

Another delight for families is a trip up to **Monte Pellegrino** (p. 102), a mountain that looms over north Palermo. With its greenery and parkland, the 600m (2,000-ft.) mountain evokes Yosemite. Keep in mind that the park is likely to be crowded on Sundays with Sicilian families who come to escape Palermo's smog.

Finally, if you're in Palermo on a summer day, you might want to escape the city altogether and head for **Mondello Lido,** with its long, sandy beaches. Even on a summer night, this is the place to be, as many families can be seen walking along the water and ducking into one of the pizzerie when the kids get hungry. For more details on Mondello Lido, see chapter 5, "Side Trips from Palermo."

WALKING TOUR: OLD PALERMO

Start	San Giovanni degli Eremiti.
Finish	Piazza Marina.
Time	3 to 3⅓ hours. (Interior visits, of course, will consume far more time.)
Best Time	Daily from 8am to noon and 3 to 6pm when many of the museums and churches are open.
Worst Time	During the lunch doldrums from noon to 3pm and after dark.

Begin your tour by the iron gates protecting the palm-shaded garden surrounding:

① San Giovanni degli Eremiti

The best known of all the Arabo-Norman monuments of Palermo, San Giovanni, at Via dei Benedettini, is a short block from roaring traffic arteries difficult to navigate. (*Tip:* To avoid walking through such heavy traffic, many visitors opt to take a taxi directly to the beginning of this walking tour.) Five typically Arab domes reveal the origin of the Moorish craftsmen who constructed this monastery for Roger II in 1132. It honors St. John of the Hermits. The church's tranquil, beautiful gardens are devoted to such species as the pomegranate and rose. The gardens lead to the ruins of the original Benedictine monastery that once stood here, a structure constructed in 581 for Pope Gregory the Great.

After a visit, walk north toward the sound of roaring traffic coming from the nearby Piazza del Pinta. En route to the piazza, you'll pass a wall niche dedicated to Maria Addolorata, which is usually embellished with plants and fresh flowers.

Cross to the opposite side of Piazza del Pinta. From here, you'll see the severely dignified stone archway pierced with formidable doors, leading to:

② Palazzo dei Normanni

The chief attraction of Palermo, this mammoth palace and artistic treasure was constructed by the Arabs over the ruins of a Roman fort in the 11th century. In time it was expanded and was turned into the royal residence of Roger II, the Norman king. Much of the look of the present palace is from alterations it received from the 16th to the 17th century. The chief attraction inside is **Cappella Palatina,** a magnificent example of the Arabo-Norman artistic genius.

After a visit to this formidable monument, exit from the compound's stately entrance gate (the same one you entered), walk about 50 paces downhill, then turn left onto Via del Castione. You'll have trouble seeing a street sign at first.

From here, you skirt the Norman Palace's massive and sharply angled foundations. After 2 narrow and claustrophobic blocks, climb the first set of granite steps rising upward from Via del Castione's left side. This will lead you into a verdant garden:

③ Villa Bonanno

Imbued with the scent of jasmine and oleander, this public park separates the rear entrance of the Palazzo dei Normanni from the Duomo compound we'll be visiting soon. Dotting the garden are monuments and effigies erected in honor of such Sicilian patriots as Caetano Bucceri and Pietro Gullo. If it's a hot day, this is an idyllic place to cool off. You can walk through the garden, exiting at its opposite end, which will lead you to:

④ Palazzo Arcivescovile

Lying across the busy Via Bonello, a street of heavy traffic, only a portal survives from the palace constructed here in 1460. The present structure is from the 18th century. Originally the Museo Diocesano was founded here, housing artifacts from the cathedral and other works of art from churches about to be demolished. Since it's been closed for many years, the palace has to be appreciated from its outside.

As a slight detour from our walking tour, stroll down a narrow lane behind Palazzo Arcivescovile to the **Oratorio dei SS. Pietro e Paolo.** The interior contains stuccoes by Giacomo Serpotta and Domenico Castelli, plus a ceiling fresco by Filippo Tancredi. In repeated visits over the years, we have seen the interior of this oratory only one time. It's been closed otherwise.

On the other side of Palazzo Arcivescovile on Via Bonello is the 16th-century **Loggia dell'Incoronazione,** with ancient columns and capitals that were incorporated into

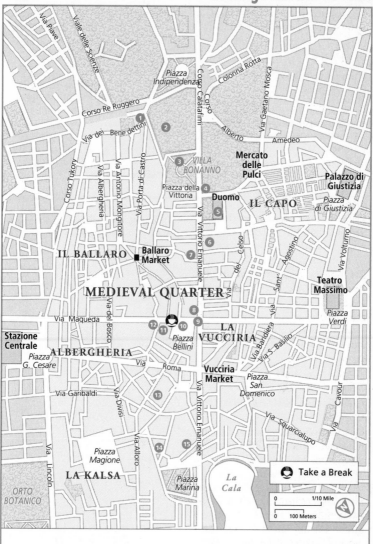

1 San Giovanni degli Eremiti

2 Palazzo dei Normanni

3 Villa Bonanno

4 Palazzo Arcivescovile

5 Duomo

6 Biblioteca Centrale
    della Regione Siciliana

7 Chiesa SS. Salvatore

8 Chiesa San Giuseppe dei Teatini

9 Quatro Canti (Four Corners)

10 Piazza Pretoria

11 Chiesa San Cataldo

12 Chiesa della Martorana

☕ Pizzeria Bellini

13 Chiesa San Francesco di Assisi

14 Palazzo Mirto

15 Piazza Marina

the present structure. The kings of Sicily used to "display" themselves to their subjects here following a coronation.

After viewing the palace, head east along the major artery, Corso Vittorio Emanuele. The sidewalk at this point becomes very narrow, barely passable, as cars roar by. In spite of the momentary discomfort, the pavement will open within a short time onto a sweeping view of the:

⑤ Duomo

At Piazza di Cattedrale, right off Corso Vittorio Emanuele, the cathedral of Palermo, dedicated to Our Lady of the Assumption, was built on the site of an early Christian basilica which was later turned into a mosque by Arab rulers. Although launched in the 12th century, the cathedral has seen many architects and much rebuilding over the centuries. The cathedral today is a hodgepodge of styles, its baroque cupola added in the late 18th century.

After a look or a visit, continue east along Corso Vittorio Emanuele on narrow sidewalks until you come to:

⑥ Biblioteca Centrale della Regione Siciliana

Once a Jesuit college called Collegio Massimo dei Gesuiti, this building today is the home of Palermo's main public library, providing shelter for more than half a million volumes and many ancient manuscripts, including several from the 15th and 16th centuries. A double arcaded courtyard is its architectural centerpiece. It is entered by the portal of the adjacent Chiesa di S. Maria della Grotta.

Continue to head east along Corso Vittorio Emanuele until you come to the intersection of Via SS. Salvatore. If it's open you can duck into the dark, shadowy recesses of:

⑦ Chiesa SS. Salvatore

Palermo has far greater churches than this, so you may settle for only a look at its facade. Built in 1682 by Paolo Amato, the church was severely

damaged during the 1943 Allied air raids but has been restored, enough so that its oval interior is frequently a venue for weddings.

Our eastward trek continues along Corso Vittorio Emanuele to a point where the street widens into a square, the Piazza Bologni. It's time to:

TAKE A BREAK
The tables of **Liberty Bar,** Corso Vittorio Emanuele 350 (✆ **091-328929**), spread out onto the square. Here you can have your fill of some excellent espresso or cappuccino, delicious ice cream as only the Italians know how to make it, or even sandwiches or a pizza.

After a refueling stop, we continue east for a short distance until we come to:

⑧ Chiesa San Giuseppe dei Teatini

Near Quattro Canti (see below), this lavishly decorated church was built by the Theatine congregation. The interior has a dancing baroque spirit, although the facade, not completed until 1844, is along more severe neoclassical lines. The cupola of the church is adorned with majolica tiles. If you go inside (hours are Mon–Sat 8:45–11:15am and 5–7pm or Sun 8:30am–1pm), you'll find a two-aisle nave. Flanking it are towering columns resting under a frescoed ceiling, holding up walls covered with a marble polychrome decoration. The main altar is constructed of semi-precious gems, and the chapels are lavishly frescoed with stucco decoration. The church was designed by Giacomo Besio of Genoa (1612–45), and was the scene of two assemblies called by Giuseppe D'Alessi during the uprising in 1647 against the ruling Spanish viceroys.

At this point of the walking tour, you are in the very heart of Old Palermo at the famous:

⑨ Quattro Canti (Four Corners)

Corso Vittorio Emanuele intersects with Via Maqueda, the latter street a famous piece of Palermitano civic planning, carved out of the surrounding neighborhood in the 16th century by the Spanish viceroy.

Architecturally, Four Corners is a melting pot of Arabo-Norman magnificence, Palermitan baroque, and the work of craftsmen of the Middle Ages. Each sculpted angle of the Four Corners celebrates seasons, a patron saint, or a Spanish viceroy.

Directly east of this "crossroads" of Palermo lies:

⑩ Piazza Pretoria

This lovely square with its beautiful but controversial fountain is Palermo's most famous. The fountain was called **Fontana della Vergogna,** or "fountain of shame," by outraged churchgoers. Originally intended for a Tuscan villa, the fountain is bedecked with nude statues and mythological monsters. This was the first landmark churchgoers saw as they left services at **San Giuseppe dei Teatini,** the church directly to the west. The eastern end of the square is flanked by **Chiesa Santa Catarina.** On the south axis stands **Palazzo Pretorio,** the city hall. Note the plaque on the front of the building commemorating Garibaldi's 1860 triumph, ending the Bourbon reign in Sicily.

Now walk to the southern edge of the Piazza Pretoria and go through the narrow gap between City Hall and the Church of Santa Catarina. In front of you will open a vista over the Piazza Bellini. At its far end rise two of the most distinctive churches in Palermo:

⑪ Chiesa San Cataldo

Standing side by side with Chiesa della Martorana (see below), this is one of two Norman churches in Palermo. With its rose-colored cupolas, the church was founded in 1154 by Maio da Bari, the despised emir of William I. After having a checkered history—in the 19th century the church was turned into a post office—San Cataldo today is the seat of the Knights of the Holy Sepulchre.

Next door to it lies:

⑫ Chiesa della Martorana

With its handsome Norman bell tower, this is the more intriguing of the two churches. It is the loveliest Greek church remaining in Sicily. It was founded in 1143 by George of Antioch, called Roger II's "Emir of Emirs." Regrettably, the linear symmetry of the original Norman church is today covered by a baroque facade.

After this intense spate of church-going, you'll probably think it's time to:

TAKE A BREAK
Pizzeria Bellini, Piazza Bellini 6 (© 091-6165691), is set directly at the base of the Church of San Cataldo, with a pleasant outdoor terrace that's shielded from the dust and congestion of the surrounding neighborhood by an evergreen hedge and latticework barrier. This is the kind of cafe where you almost fall into the chairs, then slug back a half liter of liquid refreshment. It doubles as a restaurant, in case you want a full meal, but most participants on this walking tour opt only for gelato, a coffee, or a drink. It's closed Monday.

To resume the tour, retrace your steps along Via Maqueda north to Quatro Canti. Once at these Four Corners, continue walking east along Corso Vittorio Emanuele on the street's right-hand side.

Here the neighborhood grows increasingly battered, commercial, and decrepit as you stroll along. In about 4 minutes, turn right onto Via Alessandro Paternostro, a narrow, medieval-looking street. It's reached 1 short block after Vicolo Madonna del Cassaro.

Let the Horse Lead the Way

Consider hiring one of the horse-drawn carriages that line up on the Via Maqueda at Piazza Pretoria. A 60-minute ride for up to four passengers costs 60€. In a style that's either romantic, nostalgic, or corny, depending on your point of view, it will haul you around for a view of Palermo street life and a fast overview, from the outside, of monumental Palermo. For more information about carriage tours from a driver we find cooperative, call ✆ **380-5097646.**

Walk uphill along Via Alessandro Paternostro through a commercial section of shops. In less than 4 minutes, note the intricately carved Romanesque facade of the:

⓭ Chiesa San Francesco di Assisi

This is one of our favorite churches in Palermo, thanks to its dignified simplicity and unusual combination of Romanesque and baroque detailing, plus the sense you get that it's still very much involved in the day-to-day life of this ancient parish. First constructed in the 13th century, it was destroyed by Frederick II after he was excommunicated by the pope. A new church was constructed and completed in 1277, although it's seen much alteration over the years. A 1943 Allied bombing didn't help matters either.

From the square directly in front of the church (Piazza di San Francesco d'Assisi), head east on the narrow street on the right-hand side of the church as you face it. The street is not marked. Flanking the south side of the church, walk 1½ short blocks until you reach:

⓮ Palazzo Mirto

In Old Palermo this is your greatest opportunity to visit a palace from yesterday and see close up how a Sicilian noble family lived. This palace miraculously remains as it was with its original furnishings. Of the many other palaces in the neighborhood, most are closed to the public and still not restored. This palace dates from the 18th century, having been built over earlier structures that went back to the 15th century.

After a visit, walk a few steps to the west into the broad 19th-century vistas of:

⓯ Piazza Marina

This is the largest square in Palermo. Its most significant architectural monument is **Palazzo Steri-Chiaramonte,** constructed in 1307 by one of Sicily's most influential noble families. The Chiaramonte patricians, in fact, controlled most of Sicily in the Middle Ages. The palace is built in a Gothic style with Arabo-Norman influences. In the middle of Piazza Marina is the **Giardino Garibaldi,** a beautiful park where you may want to wind down and relax, enjoying the cooling splashing waters of its central fountain.

8 City Markets & Shopping

Palermo is like a grand shopping bazaar. You'll find a little bit of everything here, including shops of high fashion. Many people seek out expert craftspeople known for their skill in producing any number of merchandise, especially beautiful coral jewelry. Embroidered fabrics are another specialty item. Some visitors come to Palermo just to purchase ceramics.

Palermo markets (see below) are the most colorful in southern Italy. At these markets all the bounty of Sicily—fruits, vegetables, fish—are elegantly displayed. Since it is unlikely you will be living in an accommodation with kitchen facilities, the markets are mainly for sightseeing, although they do offer an array of clothing and crafts as well.

For the best shopping, head for **Via della Libertà,** north of the city's medieval core within an upmarket 19th-century residential neighborhood of town houses and mid-20th-century apartment buildings that evoke some of the more upscale residential sections of Barcelona.

Within this same neighborhood, Via Principe di Belmonte is an all-pedestrian thoroughfare with many hip and elegant shops as well as fashionable cafes such as Spinnato.

The two other principal shopping streets in the old town are **Via Roma** and **Via Maqueda.**

Monday morning is the worst time to shop as nearly all the stores are closed. Otherwise, shopping hours in general are Monday through Friday from 9am to 1pm and 3:30 to 7 or 7:30pm (Sat 4–8pm).

ART

Galleria Caravello   One of Palermo's largest and busiest art galleries occupies the ground floor of a modern apartment building near the northern terminus of the Via di Libertà. It sells empty picture frames (the massively ornate and gilded kind valued by museums) as well as contemporary-looking landscapes that evoke Sicily and its vistas long after your return home. Via Marchese Ugo 64–70. ✆ **091-6251736.** Bus: 101, 102, 104, 106, 107, or 306.

BOOKS

Libreria Altro Quando   This is Palermo's most visible counterculture book-store, with a definite allegiance to things revolutionary, socialist, feminist, gay-liberated, and ecologically/politically correct. Gay books tend to be shunted off to a mezzanine in back, which is accessible via a flight of hard-to-navigate stairs. Via Vittorio Emanuele 145. ✆ **091-6114732.** Bus: 103, 104, 105, 108, 110, 139, 224, 225, 389, or 824.

Libreria Kalós   From a cool, contemplative hideaway within a walled compound in the heart of Palermo's well-heeled Via Libertà district, this shop sells books, maintains poetry readings and literary contests, sponsors chamber music concerts, and publishes some of the finest books in the world about Sicily's artistic and architectural heritage. Come here for books (mostly in Italian, less frequently in English or French) and an insight into the arts and letters of this distinct southern Italian city. Nicola Sieli, the owner and publisher of the Kalós editorial group, will usually be on hand to greet any interested reader. Via XX Settembre 56B. ✆ **091-322380.** Bus: 101 or 107.

CERAMICS

De Simone   For majolica-style stoneware, this old favorite, a family-run business, has been producing quality ware since the 1920s. They also offer some of the most tasteful ceramics and some of the finest tiles in Palermo. Most tiles are painted with scenes of Sicilian country life, including seascapes and bird-filled landscapes. They also sell porcelain dinner and tea services, along with ceramic chandeliers. While visiting the shop, you can inquire about visits to their factory at Via Lanza de Scalea 698 (✆ **091-6711005**), open Monday through Friday from 8am to 5pm. Via Gaetano Daiti 13B. ✆ **091-584876.** Bus: 103, 106, 108, or 122.

Laboratoriao Italiano di Patricia Italiano   This is the sales outlet for the most dynamic and creative ceramic artists in Palermo. Set in the fashionably well-heeled Via Libertà neighborhood, it sells inventories based on 19th-century Sicilian models, but always with a sophisticated postmodern twist. The result is a shop that's often visited by owners of nearby beach houses and condos who stock up on *jardinières,* planters, lace-edged bowls and platters, candelabra, and holders for votive candles. Prices are lower than you'd expect—usually between 5€ to 100€ for virtually anything in the store, including some surprisingly large and elaborate planters. Our favorite of the lot are the wall-mounted receptacles for holy water, priced at 36€; they show Madonnas, some of them black, "in conversation." Via Principe di Villafranca 42. ℂ 091-320282. Bus: 103.

DEPARTMENT STORES

Barone Confezioni-Abbigliamento-Corredi   In business for some 6 decades, this is the best department store in Palermo. Its focus is mainly on moderately or inexpensively priced clothing. With lots of popular labels in evidence, the store sells both sportswear and casual wear or more formal suits and dresses. Women's fashions are found on the main floor, with clothing for kids and men one floor down. Via Abramo Lincoln 146. ℂ 091-6165626. Bus: 139, 211, 221, 224, 226, 227, 231, 234, 250, or 971.

ECCLESIASTICAL OBJECTS

Postolato Liturgico   For devout Catholics visiting from parts of the world other than Sicily, this store represents a treasure trove of church-related finery (or iconography, depending on your point of view). It's staffed by an international bevy of nuns, all in white habits, all of them members of the *Paoline Piedice* (Pious Disciples of the Divine Master) order. Inventories—some of them incredibly valuable—are usually displayed behind glass in a style that might remind you of a museum. Objects include chalices, monstrances, and medallions, some made of gold, others encrusted with gemstones, as well as some of the most gorgeous liturgical robes in Italy. Objects range in price from around 12€ for a simple container for holy water to many tens of thousands of euros. Corso Vittorio Emmanuele 454. ℂ 091-6512467. Bus: 103, 104, 105, 108, 110, or 118.

FABRICS

Giuseppe Gramuglia   Traditional Sicilian decor—at least those inspired by the late 19th century—usually involves lots of fabric, in the form of heavy curtains that block out the intense sunlight, plus rich-looking upholsteries. If you want to duplicate this look in your private home, consider a visit to this store. Set at the corner of Palermo's most fashionable shopping street (Via Principe di Belmonte), it contains hundreds of bolts of fabric, in all degrees of weight and density, and in every conceivable pattern. It also sells heavy decorative ropes, fringes, and tassels. It's best to come with at least some idea of the dimensions

---

Moments **Sampling the Local Vino**

Sicily's hot climate and volcanic soil nurture a wealth of vineyards, many of which produce simple table wines. Of the better vintages, the best-known wine is **Marsala,** a sweet dessert wine produced in both amber and ruby tones. One name that evokes years of winemaking traditions, thanks to the winery's skill at producing Cerasucio di Vittoria and Moscato di Pantelleria, is **Corvo Duca di Salaparuta,** a 19th-century winery in the hills above Palermo. For information, contact the **Casa Vinicola Duca di Salaparuta,** Via Nazionale, SS113, Casteldaccia, 90014 Palermo (ℂ 091-953988). If you'd like to visit this winery, call ahead to make an appointment and get detailed directions.

(Moments Get Ready for Sugar Shock

You'll find traditional fruit-filled tarts as well as *cassata Siciliana* (tarts with ricotta-based filling) at **Fratelli Magri,** Via Isidoro Carini 42 (✆ **091-584788**). The shop also makes other types of sweets and in the summer offers gelato, but come here for the authentic high-calorie pastries. A celebration of local national confections, **I Peccatucci di Mamma Andrea,** Via Principe di Scordia 67 (✆ **091-334835**), tempts you with the bounty of Sicily's traditional fattening desserts. The best examples are pralines, *torrone, panetoni,* segments of fruit dripping with Sicilian honey, marzipan, and an age-old specialty known as *ghirlande di croccantini* (a hazelnut torte). Get ready for sugar shock and lots of local color. Bus: 122 or 124.

---

you'll need, although you can always pick out a pattern now, then let them know the quantities you'll need after your return home; they ship. Via Roma 412–414 (corner of Via Principe di Belmonte). ✆ **091-583262.** Bus: 104, 107, 122, 124, 224, or 225.

FASHIONS FOR MEN

Carieri & Carieri   This is a store for serious menswear shoppers—and if you express the slightest interest, a member of its staff is likely to "adopt" you, leading you to selections in your size and along a wide spectrum of fashion-related statements. The only thing wrong with this store is its intimidatingly large size, which might confuse you (or delight you) when you first walk in. The staff is about as upscale and attentive as any you're likely to find in Palermo, and if there aren't a lot of other customers, they're likely to descend upon you, *en masse,* to attend to your needs. The selection of suits and office wear is very extensive—the best and classiest displays in town. Via E. Parisi 4. ✆ **091-321846.** Bus: 101, 102, 104, 106, 107, 306, or 309.

FASHIONS FOR WOMEN

Le Gi di Valentino   Don't be fooled into thinking that the evening gown you buy here will be genuine (i.e., created by Valentino). What you'll get, however, is a sense of fun, "obscene" amounts of silk taffeta arranged into tarty-looking flounces, and a genuine sense of whimsy that might look fetchingly fabulous at a cocktail party or wedding reception back home. Clothes here manage to look "wenchy" and elegant at the same time, a real accomplishment if you're brave enough to wear them. Via Ruggiero Settimo 99–101. ✆ **091-324197.** Bus: 101, 102, 103, or 124.

Mötivi   The minimalist and often highly revealing clothing sold here might not be appropriate for any woman of a certain age, unless she's terribly pulled together, sexy, and well-preserved. But if you're adventurous or merely curious about what's going on in the design sense of Sicilian 20-somethings, take a look. Clothing is appropriate for the beach, for the disco, and for merely riding around in cars with boys. The venue is trendy—perhaps too much so—and at its best, fun. Via Ruggiero Settimo 109. ✆ **091-322158.** Bus: 101, 102, 103, or 124.

FRAMES

Meli   These family owners have worked for more than a century turning out handcrafted tortoise-shell frames. They also specialize in reproductions of antique picture frames made of coral along with jewel cases, stylish prints, etchings, and engravings from the 16th to the 19th century. Via Dante 294. ✆ 091-6824213. Bus: 103, 106, 108, or 122.

HAIRDRESSERS

Parrucchieri François per Uomo   Okay, so we're human too, and sometimes we stop our research for such mundane things as hair and beard trims. Here, in a setting that's decidedly working class, decidedly fair, and generally friendly, they cut hair the old-fashioned, *Don Corleone* way—with scissors, electric clippers, and a straight razor—and do a fine job at it. It's all very local, very macho, and very linked to its neighborhood—in this case a commercial district that just happens to fall alongside the path of our walking tour of Old Palermo. Since we promised the *regazzi* who work here a plug in our *guida Americana*, here's the address. And the staff is waiting for you. Corso Vittorio Emmanuele 248. ✆ 091-583860. Bus: 103, 104, 105, 108, 110, or 118.

JEWELRY

Di Bella   This is one of the better jewelry stores of Palermo, operating in a location near the old Capo marketplace. Top names in watches are featured here along with beautiful jewelry such as tastefully styled rings, necklaces, and bracelets. Via Carini 22. ✆ 091-1328031. Bus: 104 or 107.

Fiorentino   A Palermo tradition since 1890, this jeweler is still going strong, offering both traditional and contemporary designs. The jewelry is exquisite, but there's also a vast array of gift items, silverware, and watches. The fashionable set along Via Libertà shop here. Via della Libertà. ✆ 091-6047111. Bus: 101, 102, 104, 106, 107, 303, 603, 702, 704, 721, 731, or 806.

LINENS

Frette   This company's wares are highly prized by people who favor high-thread-count sheets and butter-soft linens. They have been royal purveyors of linen to everyone from the Pope to the former royal families of Italy. The shop offers sheets, tablecloths, towels, bedspreads, nightgowns, curtains, and tapestries, among other items. Via Ruggero Settimo. ✆ 091-585166. Bus: 101, 102, 103, or 124.

LINGERIE

Carezze   This is the best lingerie outlet in the city, and it sells men's underwear as well, plus a selection of swimwear for that "dressed down" look on Mondello Lido. The sales staff claims they will also outfit those persons "who use underwear as a tool of seduction." Corso Calatafimi 103. ✆ 091-6681660. Bus: 105, 304, 339, 364, 365, or 380.

LIQUEURS & JAMS

I Peccatucci di Mamma Andrea   Picture a small-scale boutique where all the merchandise evokes gemstone preciousness as well as gastronomic abundance, and you have an idea of what's sold here. It contains one of the most diverse collections of Sicilian jams, honey, liqueurs, and candies in Palermo, each artfully wrapped into the kind of gift item that would delight recipients back home. Elegant glass bottles contain liqueurs distilled from herbs or fruits you might never have thought suitable, including basil, clementines, cinnamon, almonds, myrtle, fennel, laurel leaves, figs, and rose petals. Jams and honey showcase the agrarian bounty and aromas of Sicily. There is also an array of *peccatucci* ("small sins"), utterly delightful candies made from almond paste, sugar, and liqueur, that resemble fruit (lemons, apples, pears, or clusters of grapes) or sleeping cherubs, more accurately than even the real thing. Bottles of liqueur—any of them a conversation piece—rarely sell for more than 15€ each. "Mamma Andrea," a hardworking Sicilian in her mid-50s, is devoted to perpetuating the allure of Sicilian food products to new generations of connoisseurs. 67 Via Principe di Scordia. ✆ 091-334835. Bus: 101, 102, 103, 104, 107, 122, 124, 224, or 225.

MARKETS

The Muslims were active traders, and Palermo's markets, which spill over into narrow alleys shaded by colorful awnings, still have an Arabic feel. Nothing else connects you with local life more than a visit to a bustling Palermo market.

The most famous market in Palermo—and the best—is **La Vucciria.** This is the one to visit if you have to skip all the rest. In Sicilian dialect, *vucciria* means "hubbub," or "voices," and that's what you hear here. The market spills onto the narrow side streets of Piazza San Domenico off Via Roma between Corso Vittorio Emanuele and the San Domenico Church.

This is one of Europe's great casbah-like markets, with mountains of food ranging from fresh swordfish steaks to all sorts of meat and recently harvested vegetables and fruits, reflecting the bounty of the Sicilian countryside. The array of such items as wild fennel, long-stemmed artichokes, blood oranges, giant octopus, and more, will astound you. This market trades Monday through Saturday until 2pm. Try to go before 10am when it's at its most frenetic and colorful. The markets below keep roughly the same hours.

If you're seized with market fever, you can also visit **Mercato di Capo,** a large street market that captures some of the spirit of the city's Saracen past. This market sprawls around the area of Chiesa di Sant'Agostino. Clothing stalls flank the streets of Via S. Agostino and Via Bandiera. The clothing here tends to be cheap and poorly made. More interesting is the food section off Via Volturno, which spreads along Via Beati Paoli and Via Porta Carini. The most colorful part of this market converges around Piazza Beati Paoli.

The stalls wind toward the old gate, Porta Carini, that used to be a part of the city wall surrounding Palermo. Much of the scene that takes place here still evokes the Beati Paoli stories, written in installments by Luigi Natoli

---

Moments Feasting at the Markets

We like to visit the markets not only to look at the fabulous produce, but to enjoy some of the tastiest snacks in Sicily. It's a great way to have lunch as you graze from stall to stall.

Some visitors buy and eat chopped **boiled octopus** (*purpu* in Sicilian) as they stroll along—that and delectable **artichokes** freshly brought in from the country and cooked. Of course, there is plenty of **fresh baked bread** and luscious **vine-ripened fruit** as well.

Many stalls hawk bread rolls filled with beef spleen or tripe. These are called *pani cu' la meuza.* This snack may be too ethnic for you unless you have an adventurous palate. If you do, dig in. These pani are often topped with fresh ricotta or a velvety cheese known as *caciocavallo.* Hot sauce is sprinkled on at the last moment.

You can also purchase absolutely delicious *panelle* (chickpea fritters) or *calzoni* (deep-fried meat- or cheese-filled pockets of dough).

before World War I. In Palermo, Natoli was as popular as Charles Dickens was in England.

The third great market of Palermo is **Ballarò** in the Albergheria district, found roughly between Piazza Carmine leading to Piazza Casa Professa and Piazza S. Chiazra. This is mainly a food market, with mountains of fruits and vegetables along with fishmongers and hawkers of discount clothing.

MILITARY UNIFORMS

Romano Luigi, Sartoria Civile e Militare   This shop, along with three or four shops on either side, specializes in the uniforms and paraphernalia used by members of the Italian police and *Guardia Civile*. Ironically set directly across the street from shops that specialize in church vestments for the Catholic liturgy, it's a military fetishist's dream. Not everything can be (officially) sold to a layperson (such as some aspects of an official police officer's uniform), but the selection is intriguing for anyone who ever completed a stint in the armed forces. Corso Vittorio Emanuele 453–455. ✆ 091-324457. Bus: 104, 105, 108, 110, 118, 139, 224, 225, or 389.

OPTICAL NEEDS

Ottica Stancanelli   This is Palermo's best optician, in business since 1984. You get "the works" here: permanent and disposable contact lenses, frames, sunglasses, computerized eye tests, and more. Via Oreto 330C. ✆ 091-6472978. Bus: 100, 203, 210, 220, 230, 237, or 241.

PERFUMES & COSMETICS

Limoni   When it comes to toiletries and cosmetics for both women and men, Palermo shops don't get much better than this. Affiliated with one of Italy's most popular chains, this store features a wide array of scents. Many items are suitable as gifts. Corso Tukory 222. ✆ 091-6514324. Bus: 103, 234, 246, or 318.

SPA & BEAUTY TREATMENTS

Anna Autizi Estetica   If the stress of Palermo has you feeling less than ravishing, consider a rejuvenating spa treatment at this New Age health and beauty salon. We heard about this place, just off the Via Libertà, from the extroverted clients of one of Palermo's genuinely fashionable restaurants, Sotto I Sopra, where at least three older women (each beautifully dressed and beautifully preserved) swore by Anna's blend of medical and New Age treatments. Appointments are appreciated for treatments that are conducted Monday through Saturday from 8:30am to 7pm (closed Mon in Aug). The menu includes facials, massages—either with strong and sensitive hands, or with the India-derived use of water-smoothed hot stones. Massages cost from 20€ to 80€ per hour. The philosophy is appealingly Asian, the staff is ever so charming, and as you relax, New Age music plays, captivating and soft. Via Ariosto 22. ✆ 091-6255743. Bus: 101, 102, 104, 106, 107, 309, 603, 702, 704, or 721.

STATIONERS

De Magistris   This is the biggest card and stationery store in Palermo. It has the widest selection and most tasteful designs in stationery, including all sorts of cards and gift items. Via Gagini 23. ✆ 091-589230. Bus: 103, 104, 105, 108, or 110.

9 Palermo After Dark

For such a large city, Palermo has a dearth of nightlife. In the hot summer months, the townspeople parade along the waterfront of **Mondello Lido** (see chapter 5) to cool off. Although they are improving somewhat, many Palermo areas with bars and taverns (such as La Kalsa or Alberghiera) are not safe for walking around at night. And some of the bars and taverns in the medieval core of Palermo have the lifespan of sickly butterflies. The safest places for drinking, making conversation, and meeting like-minded companions are the many bars in the deluxe and first-class hotels. They are also the most sanitary.

The liveliest squares at night—and the relatively safest because lots of people are there—are **Piazza Castelnuovo** and **Piazza Verdi.** Another "safe zone" is a pedestrian strip flanked by bars and cafes, many with sidewalk tables, along **Via Principe di Belmonte,** lying between Via Roma and Via Ruggero Settimo. Some of these bars have live pianists in summer. If you like the sound of things, drop in for a glass of wine or a beer or two.

If you're interested in the arts and cultural venues, stop by the tourist office (see chapter 3) and pick up a copy of *Palermo & Provincia Live,* which documents cafes or other venues offering live music in summer.

THE ARTS   Palermo is a cultural center of some note, with an opera and ballet season running from January to June. The principal venue for cultural presentations is the restored **Teatro Massimo,** Via Maqueda (© 091-6053515), across from the Museo Archeologico. It boasts the largest indoor stage in Europe except for the Paris Opera House. Francis Ford Coppola shot the climactic opera scene here for *The Godfather: Part III.*

The theater was built between 1875 and 1897 in a neoclassical style, and reopened after a restoration in 1997 to celebrate its 100th birthday. During the **Festival di Verdura,** from late June to mid-August, many special presentations, most often with international performers, are presented on the stage here. Ticket prices, of course, depend on the event and your seat, but they range in price from 11€ to 73€. The box office is open Tuesday through Sunday from 10am to 4pm. Bus: 101, 102, 103, 104, 107, 122, or 225.

If you have only one night for theater in Palermo, make it the Teatro Massimo. However, **Politeama Garibaldi,** Piazza Ruggero Settimo (© 091-6053315), is also grandiose, and it, too, presents a wider season of opera and orchestral performances. Again, the tourist office will have full details of what is being performed at the time of your visit. Bus: 101, 102, 103, 124.

CAFES   In the early evening, **Bar Barocco,** Corso Vittorio Emanuele 494 opposite the cathedral (© 091-16511904), is a safe haven in which to meet someone. Both visitors and inhabitants of all ages frequent this cafe Monday to Saturday from 5am (yes, that's right) to 8pm, and on Sunday from 6am to 1pm. Bus: 104 or 105.

We always like to begin our evening by heading to the century-old **Caffè Mazzara,** Via Generale Maglicco (© 091-321443). You can sample wonderful Sicilian ice cream, sip a rich coffee, or try heady Sicilian wine. You'll run into us hanging out at the espresso bar and pastry shop on the street level. The cafe is open daily from 7:30am to 11pm. Bus: 101, 102, or 103.

DANCE CLUBS   Palermo's most popular **dance clubs** lie in the city's commercial center, although one good one is in north Palermo. The city's main dance club is **Candelai,** Via Candelai 65 (© 091-327151), which charges a 4.50€ cover. Mainstream rock blasts throughout the night in this crowded complex of gyrating 20-year-olds. The club is open only Friday through Sunday from 8pm, with no set closing time.

PUBS   One of our favorite pubs in town is **Nashville,** Via Belgio 4A (© 091-522980), a good place to spend an intimate evening in fun company. You can order food here, including spaghetti or snacks, as well as drinks, beers, and even desserts. A backdrop of music such as rock, pop, and disco makes the atmosphere lively. A mainly young crowd is attracted to the precincts daily from 8pm to 1:30am. Bus: 100, 164, 529, 544, or 616.

Villa Niscemi, Piazza Niscemi 55 (② **091-6880820**), is a fun pub offering a rustic interior bar in winter, and overflowing sidewalk tables in summer. These are shaded by a "roof" of leafy trees. The pub also has a series of musical instruments. If you're the master of one (or even if you're not), you can play an instrument and hopefully entertain the patrons. Live music, such as pop, rock, jazz, blues, and what the management calls simply "Italian," is a feature on Friday. A crowd mostly from 25 to 45 years of age patronizes the joint, open daily from 7pm to 3am. It is closed on Monday in July and August. Bus: 614, 615, 645, or 837.

Agricantus, Via XX Settembre 82 (② **091-487117**), is one of the liveliest venues and pubs in town. You never know what is likely to be happening here on the night of your visit—perhaps classical music, jazz, pop, even theater. The pub attracts people of all ages daily from 8:30pm to midnight. Bus: 101or 107.

GAY & LESBIAN   Most homosexual encounters in Sicily occur on the streets, in cafes, and around squares. Gay and lesbian bars are as scarce as a virgin at the *Playboy* mansion. Gays and lesbians from ages 18 to 70 converge at **Exit,** Piazza San Francesco da Paola, 39–40 (② **348-7814698**), daily from 10pm to 3am. Live music such as rock or pop is often presented. In summer, tables are placed outside fronting a beautiful square. Bus: 122.

10 Easy Excursions

Palermo is graced with a number of satellite attractions that can easily be explored on side trips. One, Monreale, with its cathedral, is such an important sight that it is considered among greater Palermo's major attractions. Then there are the beaches of Mondello Lido to be enjoyed in summer. For a preview of what to see and do on the periphery of Palermo, refer to chapter 5, "Side Trips from Palermo."

If you don't have time to range far in your exploration, however, you can take an excursion to 600m (2,000-ft.) Monte Pellegrino, towering over the city.

MONTE PELLEGRINO ⊛

The parkland and nature preserve of the crown-shaped Monte Pellegrino looms over north Palermo. This green oasis and haven from the heat is where the Palermitani retreat on a summer day. During his visit, Goethe pronounced it "the most beautiful headland on earth." Avoid heading up this promontory on a Sunday, however, when half of the world's cars seem to have the same goal.

The mountain rises sharply on all sides except to the south. The headland here, known for its autumnal gold color, was occupied by the Carthaginian general Hamilcar Barca in the First Punic War and defended between 247 and 244 B.C. before it fell to the Romans.

You can reach the mountain from Piazza Generale Casino in Palermo, close to Fiera del Mediterraneo, the fair and exhibition grounds. From here, take Via Pietro Bonanno, following the signs toward the Santuario di S. Rosalia (see below).

After a 9-mile drive to the north, you will reach the peak of Monte Pellegrino. Along the way to the top you're rewarded with some of Sicily's most **panoramic**

⌐ *Fun Fact* The Legend of Santa Rosalia

No one knows who Santa Rosalia was for sure. She's more legend than real woman. According to legend, Rosalia was born in 1130, supposedly to a patrician Norman family said to have been descended from Charlemagne. Never a swinger, she was a very pious young lady. Unable to stand the pressures of hedonistic Palermo and its wicked ways, she fled to a cave in Monte Pellegrino in 1159 and was said to have died there in 1166. No one in Palermo knew anything about her demise, but that's the figure given.

When the Black Death swept over Palermo in 1624, the story goes, the figure of Rosalia appeared to a hunter. She directed him to her remains in the cave and ordered him to bring her bones to Palermo. She was carried in a procession through the streets and then properly buried.

After that, the plague disappeared. From then on, Rosalia—now Santa Rosalia—has been revered as the patron saint of the city.

A festival held in her honor annually on July 15 is a major social and religious event in Palermo. You can join the faithful on September 4 when the true believers walk barefooted from Palermo to the saint's sanctuary.

views ★★★, taking in the old city of Palermo and a sweeping view of Conca d'Oro, the coastline. The paved road you see today dates from the 1600s, when it was a footpath for people climbing the mountain.

The chief attraction of Monte Pellegrino is **Santuario di Santa Rosalia** (© **091-540326**), a cave where the patron saint of Palermo lived. As you near the top (past endless souvenir shops hawking kitsch), you'll approach a belvedere, dominated by a statue of St. Rosalia. If you stop here, you're treated to a **magnificent view** ★ of the sea.

Santa Rosalia holds a special place in the hearts of the Palermitani, who have affectionately nicknamed her *La Santuzza,* or little saint. You enter the sanctuary through a little chapel constructed over a cave in the hillside, where the bones (read: alleged bones) of Rosalia were found in 1624.

Goethe has already given us his approval, finding the setting "so natural and pleasing one can hardly help expecting to see the saint breathe and move about." Supposedly a niece of William II, St. Rosalia lived and died as a hermit on this mountain, retreating here in 1159.

Inside, a 17th-century statue of the saint, the work of Gregorio Tedeschi, is covered by a gilded silver mantle. Before the statue you'll find a massive pile of euros, a gift to her from the faithful. We suspect that someone else hauls in the loot at night—not the saint herself.

As a curiosity, note the thin spikes of flattened "steel cobweb" hanging from the ceiling. This isn't contemporary art. This is done to direct the water seeping from the ceiling into a container. The liquid is supposedly miraculous, and is highly prized by devout followers of the saint.

Admission is free, and the sanctuary (in theory at least) is open daily from 7:45am to 6pm. Frequent Masses may disrupt your visit.

After a visit to the chapel, note the little pathway leading to the left of the chapel. If you take it, after about 30 minutes you'll be at a clifftop promontory with a view and a statue of the saint. The pathway to the right of the sanctuary leads to the top of Pellegrino, requiring a leisurely hike of about 40 minutes. Families use the grounds and trails on Pellegrino as a picnic site.

If you're not driving, you can take bus no. 812 from Piazza Verdi in Palermo (trip time: 30 min.). You can either take the bus back or else descend from the mountain along the **Scala Vecchia,** a stepped path that winds down the mountain by the sanctuary going all the way to the Fiera del Mediterraneo fairgrounds.

5

Side Trips from Palermo

In spite of the fact that Palermo holds Sicily's greatest artistic monuments and treasures, it is also a city of noise and pollution. One of the pleasures of a visit to the island's capital is to escape it. It's a welcome respite.

At your doorstep are any number of treasures, ranging from the golden sands of **Mondello Lido** to **Ustica,** an offshore volcanic island of mysterious origins. The cathedral town of **Monreale** contains an ecclesiastical compound greater than anything in Palermo. But that's not all. You can wander at leisure through the decaying aristocratic villas of **Bagheria** and later stroll among the ruins of the Greco-Roman town of **Solunto.**

1 Bagheria: Decaying Villas

14km (8½ miles) E of Palermo

Praised by poets like Giovanni Meli and attacked by writers such as Goethe, Bagheria lies just to the east of Palermo. In the 18th and 19th centuries it became the summer retreat of the noble class who came here and built magnificent villas and great mansions to escape the scorching heat of Palermo.

The setting was one of rich agricultural lands of citrus plantations and vineyards. As family fortunes disappeared and dynasties faded, Bagheria and its villas fell into a splendid decay. Many of these still exist, evoking a scene from di Lampedusa's Sicily, but ugly modern buildings and factories have encroached on this once bucolic setting on the southern slopes of Mount Catalfano at the eastern extension of the Gulf of Palermo.

The novelist Dacia Maraini, in her memoir, *Bagheria,* recalled "the atmosphere of a summer garden enriched by lemon groves and olive trees, poised between the hills, cooled by the salt winds." For her dismal and even frightening view of the road there, see "Getting There," below.

In the latter part of the 20th century, Bagheria earned the dubious distinction of being a center of Mafia activities. You can just imagine the international deals plotted behind the decaying walls of Bagheria's heavily guarded villas.

Impressions

I lived in Sicily many years and am aware that the real problem there is the Mafia. Sicily is culturally rich, its people intelligent, capable, enterprising, imaginative. But they are terrorized by the Mafia. I know many who fled because of the difficulties there.

—Dacia Maraini, author of *Bagheria*, on the "Mafiaization" of Bagheria in particular and Sicily in general

ESSENTIALS

GETTING THERE Several trains on the Palermo/Messina line stop at Bagheria, and it also lies on the Santa Flavia-Solunto-Porticello line. Buses, operated by AST, also run here from Palermo, leaving from both the Stazione Centrale and Piazza Lolli.

By car from Palermo, it's easier to take the coastal route (113) via Ficarazzi than it is to take the trouble to get on the autostrada (A19). The road has improved since it was described by Dacia Maraini in her memoir, *Bagheria*. According to her, the highway "was not only foully potholed, but lined with the heads of bandits impaled on pikestaffs, dried by the sun, infested with flies, often with chunks of arms and legs with blackened blood sticking to the skin."

VISITOR INFORMATION The **Bagheria tourist office** is at Corso Umberto I (℃ **091-909020**), open Monday through Friday from 9:30am to 1:30pm and 4:30 to 9:30pm.

VILLA VIEWING

Villa Palagonia ★★ This is one of the most bizarre monuments of baroque decadence ever created in Europe. When Goethe came this way, he was appalled by the villa and its "bad taste and folly" as well as its "gauntlet of lunacy." It was designed in 1705 by Tommaso Maria Napoli for Francesco Gravina, prince of Palagonia. But it was hideously decorated by the prince's eccentric grandson, a hunchback, Ferdinando Gravina Alliata.

Both the interior and exterior decorations have made the villa known around the world as the "Villa of Monsters." Francesco ordered that a series of tufa statues be inserted along the top of the wall in front of the facade. Of the original 200 statues, some 60 remain. Goethe found this a *sculture grottesche,* a parade of hideous statues of human beings ("beggars of both sexes, men and women of Spain, Moors, Turks, hunchbacks, deformed persons of every kind, dwarfs, musicians, Pulcinellas"). He also commented on the depictions of animals ("deformed monkeys, many dragons and snakes, every kind of paw attached to every kind of body, double heads and exchanged heads").

In addition to his hunched back, Ferdinando was said to have a deformed mind. His wife was known to have had many lovers, and so he ordered artisans to make frightening caricatures of these men to embarrass his wife and her male harem. He didn't stop there. He also created an eccentric interior. Spikes were hidden under inviting velvet-cushioned seats. Sets of lovely Chinese porcelain were found glued together in a sticky mess of saucers, cups, and bowls.

> **Impressions**
>
> . . . the coat-of-arms of the House of Pallagonia is a satyr holding up a mirror to a woman with a horse's head. Even after having seen the other absurdities, this seems to me the most peculiar of all.
>
> —Goethe, *Italian Journey*

The decorations that so infuriated Goethe are gone today, and the entire villa, while richly evoking the glories of its baroque past, is in sad need of a major restoration. A Hall of Mirrors remains, although in disrepair. Mirrors were often built into the walls to distort the figures of visitors. Thus, the hunchback got his revenge on those who stood tall and straight.

Piazza Garibaldi (at the end of Corso Umberto I). ℃ **091-932088**. Admission 4.50€ adults, 2.25€ students and persons under 18. Apr–Oct daily 9am–1pm and 4–7pm; Nov--Mar daily 9am–1pm and 3:30–5:30pm.

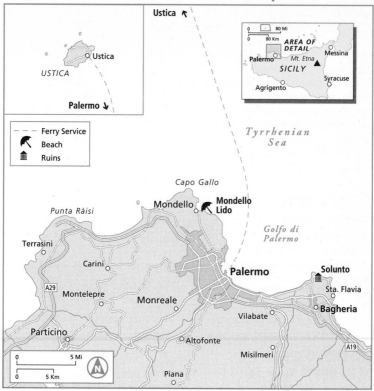

Villa Cattolica ⭐ Visit this baroque villa for a combination of antique architecture and modern art. The villa was completed in 1736 during the Ottocento vogue for ostentatious country villas. An art gallery, **Galleria Comunale d'Arte Moderna e Contemporanea,** was established here in 1973.

The villa was originally constructed by Giuseppe Bonanni Filangeri, prince of Cattolica. Most of the works in the gallery were donated by Renato Guttuso, the island's best-known modern artist. This museum offers a rare chance to enjoy the art of this neo-realist painter, born in 1912. A staunch anti-Fascist during the Mussolini era, and later anti-Mafia, Guttuso evokes Picasso in some of his works, especially when his art has been refracted into geometric shapes. Beginning in 1958, the artist fell heavily under the influence of Expressionism, abandoning realism for strong colors and daringly decisive lines. His Jazz Age portraits and still lifes evoke the 1930s, and his later works from the 1970s are startlingly sensuous. Note the portrait that Gattuso did in 1936 of French Impressionist Paul Cézanne. Gattuso died in 1987, and his sculptor friend, Giacomo Manzù, designed a surreal "blue capsule" tomb for him. Set among scrubby cacti and citrus trees in the shadow of the villa, the tomb evokes the blue of the Sicilian sky.

Also displayed in the museum are works by Domenico Quattrociocchi, a late-19th-century painter of note.

After visiting the museum, you can walk through the gardens and see Gattuso's tomb as well as a *Camera dello Scirocco,* an artificial cave built under a

Hometown Boy Makes Good: *Cinema Paradiso*

The filmmaker Giuseppe Tornatore was born in Bagheria on May 27, 1956. Before making films, he was an award-winning still photographer and later a director of TV documentaries. In 1985 he made his feature movie debut with the film *Il Camorristal (The Professor)*. But it wasn't until 1989 that he received world acclaim for *Cinema Paradiso* (aka *Nuovo Cinema Paradiso*), a nostalgic and unabashedly sentimental tribute to the influence of movies on a young boy's life, shot on location in Tornatore's hometown of Bagheria.

The film won a Grand Jury Prize at the Cannes Film Festival and an Oscar as Best Foreign Film of the Year. In 2002 Tornatore restored 52 minutes to his 1989 film and re-released it, entitled *Cinema Paradiso— The New Version*. Among other changes, the film has an entirely different, mood-altering last act. New ending or old, the director's films are said to "touch the soul of Sicily."

seignioral mansion that provided refuge on days when the scorching winds from Africa swept across the land.

Villa Consolare 9. ② **091-943902**. Admission 4.50€ adults, 2.25€ students and persons under 18. Tues–Sun 10am–8pm.

WHERE TO DINE

Il Malavoglia ★ *Finds* SICILIAN   Had we been around to greet Goethe during his visit to Bagheria, we would have invited him here for lunch—perhaps the grumpy poet would have left with a better impression of Bagheria. This is the best and most appealing restaurant in Bagheria, with a clientele that willingly travels in from Palermo. The restaurant also has a firm grip on the dining loyalties of the local community. You're greeted at the entranceway by a boat-shaped antipasti table. Long, narrow rooms, each tile-floored, radiate backwards in a baronial Sicilian style. Most of the food comes from the surrounding agricultural-rich region. The house antipasti in particular evokes this rich region. With the sea nearby, fish is prominently featured on the menu. Begin perhaps with the spaghetti with squid, its color tinted by the savory black squid ink, a real delicacy. The Palermo beefsteak, perfectly seasoned and tender, has been a justifiable favorite for years, as has the delectable filet of veal in a lemon sauce. You're reminded that you're in a setting of citrus plantations when you taste the shrimp flavored with both lemon *and* orange. Freshly caught swordfish is served with capers and olives, and the *braccioli* of pork is made heavenly with a Barolo wine sauce. The restaurant's name, incidentally, derives from an epic work *(Il Malavoglia)* by Sicilian novelist Giovanni Verga (1840–1922).

Corso Butera 9. ② **091-909172**. Reservations recommended on weekends. Main courses 7.75€–13€. AE, DC, MC, V. Thurs–Tues 7:30pm–12:30am; Sun 1–3pm.

2 Solunto: Evocative Ruins

3km (1¾ miles) NE of Bagheria, 18km (11 miles) E of Palermo

Set high on the slopes of Monte Catalfano, the ruins of the city of Solunto may not be the most impressive in Sicily, but they are evocative, and the panoramic view of the sea from here and the beautiful setting amid aromatic plants and wildflowers make the trip appealing. At a location 374m (1,227 ft.) above the bay, Solunto was the Carthaginian town of *Solus.* It had actually been founded as far back as the 8th century B.C. Along with Palermo and Mozia, it was one of three Phoenician colonies in Sicily.

In 397 B.C., Dionysius of Syracuse destroyed the city. The present ruins are from the small city that existed here in the mid–4th century B.C. In time, Solunto was captured by the Romans, its dwellers fleeing their homes sometime during the 2nd century A.D.

The conquerors would not leave poor Solunto alone, even when it was nearly empty of life. The Saracens, for reasons known only to them, practically destroyed what remained after the Roman destruction.

ESSENTIALS

GETTING THERE   Bagheria (see above) is generally the gateway for visitors going on to Solunto. On the train, Solunto is one stop beyond Bagheria on the Santa Flavia-Solunto-Porticello line. Once you get off the train, go over the tracks and head toward the sea. In 300m (984 ft.) you'll see a signpost pointing to the ruins. From here it's another 15- to 20-minute hike to the site.

Motorists generally arrive first in Bagheria. Once here (see above), Solunto is signposted from Piazza Garibaldi at the entrance to Villa Palagonia in Bagheria. You can also reach it by SS113 east from Palermo toward Porticello.

EXPLORING THE RUINS OF SOLUNTO ⚜

On the way to the **Parco Archeologico di Solunto (Solunto Archaeological Garden),** you'll pass an **Antiquarium** just inside the gate. Everything of any real value was hauled off to Palermo a long time ago, but you might stop in for a look at some artifacts removed from excavations, including bas-reliefs, statuettes, ancient coins, and architectural fragments.

Immediately to its north lie the ruins of the **Terme,** the old thermal baths, with a mosaic floor remaining. Brick supports from below held up the rooms, allowing hot air to circulate.

The Terme fronts Via della Terme. If you head north and then right, you'll be walking along the main street of Solunto, **Via Dell'Agorà** ⚜⚜. The first ruin of any interest is the so-called **Gymnasium,** actually a patrician house with a peristyle and atrium more or less intact. Partially restored in 1866, the building has a trio of Doric columns and a partial roof. Directly east of it is an even more impressive patrician house, **Casa di Leda** ⚜, with a wall frescoed with a scene of Leda and her amorous swan. This house was built around a peristyle with an elaborate cistern system for collecting rainwater. In one room you can see the remains of a fresco similar to those discovered in the ruins of Pompeii.

The large public square of **Agorà** lies east of Casa di Leda. Public life in old Solunto was centered here, and you can still see nine red clay–colored recessed rooms. Directly north of the square are the ruins of the **Odeon,** a small theater, and to its immediate east the larger ruins of what must have been an impressive **theater** in Hellenistic times, although not much remains today.

Call ⓒ **091-904557** for more information. Admission is 3.10€. The park is open Tuesday through Sunday from 9am to 5pm (closes at 4:30pm in winter).

WHERE TO DINE

Antica Pizzeria Solunto/Le Grotto/Abu Simbel SICILIAN/PIZZA   Set on the uppermost promontory of Bagheria, with views over the archaeological ruins of Solunto and the nearby hamlet of Porticello, this is the most panoramic and breezy restaurant in the district. It has an outdoors terrace and two floors of indoor space, tended by a jaded, sometimes low-energy staff. Frankly, the food and the service are both better at Il Malavoglia (see above), but the view and the ambience here go a long way toward the creation of a magical Sicilian evening.

Parco Archeologico di Solunto. (© 091-903213. Reservations not necessary. Pizzas 4.20€–7.30€; main courses 6€–14€. AE, DC, MC, V. Fri–Wed 7:30pm–1am; Sun 1–3pm.

3 Monreale & its Magnificent Cathedral

10km (6 miles) SW of Palermo

This hilltop town has one of the greatest cathedrals in all of Italy (see below). Even if it didn't, come here for the **panoramic view** 🎭🎭 over the bay, Conca d'Oro. In the distance you can see the rise of Palermo.

When the Normans ruled, the kings chose Monreale as their royal hunting ground. When William II launched the celebrated cathedral and attached a royal residence and a monastery to it, Monreale was put on the maps of the world.

Since that time, pilgrims from virtually everywhere have flocked here to see this wonder. If you have to miss all the other sights in the Palermo environs, try to schedule 2 or 3 hours of your time to make the trek to Monreale. It dwarfs other sights in this chapter and is, in fact, one of the major attractions of southern Italy.

ESSENTIALS

GETTING THERE   In Palermo, take bus no. 389, departing from Piazza Indipendenza, which drops you off at Monreale's Piazza Vittorio Emanuele 40 minutes later, depending on traffic. During the day, three buses per hour leave for Monreale, costing .80€ one-way. Motorists can approach Monreale by Corso Calatafimi from Porta Nuova in Palermo. There is no local tourist office.

MONREALE DUOMO 🎭🎭🎭: THE SICILIAN WONDER

Arabo-Norman art and architecture reached the pinnacle of its glory, beauty, and charm in this cathedral, launched in 1174 by William II. Like the grand Alhambra in Granada, Spain, the Duomo hides behind a relatively drab facade, giving little indication of the riches inside. William issued orders "to spare no expense," as he set about to out-razzle-dazzle the glory of the Cappella Palatina (Palatine Chapel) in Palermo, which was the crowning architectural achievement of his grandfather Roger II (see chapter 4 for details of that attraction).

Today the cathedral is the last and most stunning of the Norman churches of Sicily and, even more so, is viewed as one of the architectural wonders of the Middle Ages. The "command" to build this monument was said to have come to the 20-year-old Norman king in a dream where the Madonna appeared, telling him that she would direct him to a hidden stash of money with which he could erect the monument.

The facade lies between two towers, one of which was never finished. Interlacing Arabic arches crown an 18th-century classical portico. If you stand on the Via dell'Arcivescovado, you can see where the original royal palace was absorbed by the Archbishop's Palace.

Bonanno Pisano, the sculptor and architect who created the Leaning Tower of Pisa, designed the cathedral's splendid **bronze doors** 🎭🎭 in 1185. He created 46 bas-reliefs of biblical scenes from both the Old and New Testaments. Beneath a portico from the 1500s, the lateral entrance is also graced with **bronze doors** 🎭, the 1179 work of Barisano da Trani, depicting saints, battles, animals, and scenes from the life of Christ. It is through this door that you enter the Duomo.

Once you enter the golden interior, the eye doesn't know where to look first. The **mosaics** ★★★ here evoke the Cappella Palatina in Palermo, but on a much grander scale. This splendiferous cycle of 12th- and 13th-century mosaics occupies the aisles, the choir, the transepts, and all of the nave, vividly bringing to life scenes from the Old and New Testaments. Craftsmen from Venice were brought in to create some of these mosaics.

There is amazing attention to detail right down to a depiction of knives on the table at the Wedding at Cana. In

majestic splendor, ***Christ Pantocrator*** ★ dominates the middle apse. This is the most imposing of all such figures in any church on the island. There are more than 2,000 mosaics here—even more than in St. Mark's in Venice. The mosaic cycle is the second largest on earth, topped only by Istanbul's Hagia Sofia (Saint Sofia).

In the north apse, **Cappella del Crocifisso** ★ is gloriously baroqued to its teeth. The **treasury** shelters various precious objects (some venerated by religious cults) and reliquaries, along with other ecclesiastical artifacts such as vestments, silverware, and goldsmithery dating back to the Middle Ages or the Renaissance.

The plan to make this a Norman royal pantheon was never carried out, although you can see the porphyry sarcophagus of William I (d. 1166) and William II (d. 1190) before the entryway into the Cappella di San Benedetto, whose decoration dates from the 16th century.

Well worth the difficult and steep climb uphill from the cathedral is an **ascent to the terraces** ★★★. Once you reach the top, you are rewarded with a panoramic vista over the cloisters with another stunning **view of the apses** ★★. From the more elevated terrace is a **dramatic sweep** ★★ to the sea and the bay of Conca d'Oro.

Descending from the terraces, you can visit the **cloisters** ★★★, which represent the flowering of Islamic architecture in Sicily. Devout Sicilians often refer to these cloisters as a "preview of Paradise." Pointed arches link 228 twin columns, each with a different design, many decorated with mosaics or reliefs. We are particularly enchanted by the depictions of "the monsters who never were." Each of the splendid **Romanesque capitals** ★★ is imaginatively conceived and carved. The artisan who depicted Adam and Eve hiding their genitalia in shame had a sense of humor.

In the southwest corner is a **mini-cloister,** with one of the most delightful fountains in town. A dozen lionlike mouths gush water into the basin below.

Piazza Guglielmo il Buono. © 091-6404413. Free admission to cathedral. Cloisters 4.50€, treasury 2.05€, ascent to terraces 1.55€. Daily 9:30am–12:30pm and 3:30–5:30pm.

WHERE TO STAY

Baglio Conca d'Oro ★ *(Finds)*   This 18th-century paper mill at Borgo Molara was completely restored in 1998 and turned into a retreat of old-fashioned charm with 21st-century comforts. Most of the guest rooms open onto panoramas of the beautiful bay of Conca d'Oro, Monreale itself, or the Gulf of Palermo. In the antique redbrick building, the use of dark wood and Oriental carpeting adds to its allure. If you base yourself here, you'll find it convenient for exploring both Palermo and Monreale. The newly furnished, modernized guest rooms have all the creature comforts, along with small bathrooms with shower stalls.

Via Aquino 19, Borgo Molare 90126. © 091-6406286. Fax 091-6408742. www.charmerelax.com/palermo-hotel.html. 27 units. 134€–160€ double; 164€–190€ suite. AE, DC, MC, V. Located 3km (1¾ miles) from Monreale. From Palermo, take Viale Regione Siciliana and follow signs to Sciacca and N624. **Amenities:** Restaurant; bar. *In room:* A/C, TV, minibar, hair dryer.

WHERE TO DINE

Before or after your visit to Monreale, drop in at **Bar Italia,** Piazza Vittorio Emanuele (© **091-6402421**), near the Duomo. The plain cookies are wonderfully flavorful; if you go early in the morning, order one of the freshly baked croissants and a cup of cappuccino, Monreale's best. It's open Wednesday through Monday from 5am to 1am.

Peppino SICILIAN   If you're in the mood for a modest lunch or dinner, consider this simple, family-style trattoria that's positioned within a maze of narrow streets, about 4 blocks uphill (and west) from the cathedral. During clement weather, the preferred seating is on a cobble-covered outdoor terrace in front, within full view of the balconies of the neighboring houses, from which laundry hangs and dialogues develop between residents. Inside the trattoria are a large pizza oven and rolling table; a TV that's likely to be blaring the latest football matches; and the smell from straightforward dishes that many clients find very acceptable. The cuisine is typical of what you might be served at night in the private home of a middle-class local family. The chef specializes in roulades, thin slices of veal that are stuffed, rolled, and fried. The lamb (or veal) cutlets are also a worthy dish. Your best bet might be the catch of the day, which is usually grilled along with roasted vegetables. Spaghetti alla Norma is a pasta favorite (somehow eggplant always tastes better in Sicilian pastas).

Via B. Civiletti 12. © **091-6407770.** Reservations not necessary. Main courses 6.20€–7.25€. AE, DC, MC, V. Fri–Wed 12:30–2pm and 7:30pm–midnight.

Taverna del Pavone ✦ SICILIAN/ITALIAN   The most highly recommended restaurant in Monreale occupies a wood-fronted building that faces a small, cobblestone square, about a block uphill from the town's famous cathedral. Inside, you're likely to find a friendly greeting, an artfully rustic environment that's similar in some ways to an upscale tavern, and good-tasting Sicilian food. On our latest rounds, we delighted in their freshly picked zucchini flowers braised in a sweet-and-sour sauce. The special pasta of the day was a delightful *pennette* with fava bean sauce. We helped our dining partner finish off his house-made *maccheroni,* which was loaded with country cheese and absolutely delicious ("To hell with the calories"). The roulades of beef (or veal) were layered with onions and sweet red peppers, rolled, and fried for a winning combination of flavors. For dessert, the most soothing choice might be *semifreddo*—ice cream with whipped cream folded in and given extra flavor with baked almonds.

Vico lo Pensato 18. © **091-6406209.** Reservations recommended. Main courses 8.50€–14€. AE, DC, MC, V. Tues–Sun 12:30–2:30pm and 7–10:30pm.

4 Mondello: Fun at the Beach

12km (7½ miles) W of Palermo

When the summer sun burns hot, when the old men on the square seek a place in the shade, and when *bambini* tire of their toys, it's beach weather. For Palermo residents, that means **Mondello Lido.** Before this beachfront town started attracting the wealthy class of Palermo, it was a fishing village, and you can still see rainbow-colored fishing boats bobbing in the harbor. A good sandy beach stretches for about 2km (1¼ miles), filled to capacity on a July or August day. *Tip:* Some women traveling alone find Mondello more inviting and less intimidating than Palermo.

ESSENTIALS

GETTING THERE   By bus, to reach all of the locations below, take no. 806 to Mondello, leaving from Piazza Sturzo in the center of Palermo, close to Teatro Politeama. If you're driving, take Viale Regina Margherita from the northern end of Parco della Favorita, going through the dreary suburb of Pallavicino beneath the western slope of Monte Pellegrino. On your way back, you can drive from Valdesi, at the southern tip of Mondello, along the Lungomare Cristoforo Colombo toward the heart of Palermo, going via the rock-strewn coastline at the foot of Monte Pellegrino.

VISITOR INFORMATION   Contact the tourist office in Palermo (see chapter 3).

HITTING THE BEACH

As a seaside resort in Sicily, Mondello is outclassed only by Taormina. But if you're in Palermo in July and August, **Mondello Lido** ★★ is the place to be. The wide, sandy beach extends for 2km (1¼ miles) from Monte Pellegrino to Monte Gallo.

Opening onto a half-moon-shaped bay between Monte Pellegrino and Capo Gallo, Mondello is the place for showing off your most daring swimwear, for relaxing, and for living the good life, including lots of late-night partying spent staggering along with the Palermitani (most often young) from bar to bar (largely in the center around **Piazza Mondello**). Even as the sun goes down, the resort is packed in summer with city dwellers here to escape non-air-conditioned homes.

Mondello Lido holds little of historical interest. What remains of the original fishing village lies at the far north of the bay, where you can see the ruins of a tower from the 15th century—but it's hardly worth the trek up there. For artistic treasures, you'll have to visit nearby Monreale (see above) or Palermo. Between 1892 and 1910 a Belgian company built a "garden city" in Mondello in the finest Belle Epoque style. Between the wars Mondello was a snobbish retreat for the upper crust, evoking the most fashionable parts of the French Riviera. After World War II, it more democratically became a "beach for everyone."

In the center of the beach, rising from concrete piers above the surface of the water, and connected to the Sicilian "mainland" with a bridge, you can still see the *kursaal,* a whimsical bathhouse (now a restaurant, Charleston Le Terrazze; see below) designed by Rudolph Stualkret in the Art Nouveau style and adorned with sea dragons and other mythological creatures.

WHERE TO STAY

Albergo Conchiglia d'Oro *Value*   Situated a 6-minute walk inland from the Lido (beach) in a residential neighborhood loaded with bougainvillea and private homes, this well-maintained hotel has a setting that's calmer and more sedate than those of other hotels close to the oceanfront frenzy. It was built as a small inn in 1958, then expanded several times, most recently in 1978. Open year-round, it's sometimes favored by Palermo-based business travelers who

"This Thing We Have": Men of Dishonor

In Sicily, they don't call it the Mafia (from the Arabic *mu'afah* or "protection"). They call it *Cosa Nostra,* literally "our thing" but more accurately, "this thing we have." Its origins are debated, but the world's most famed criminal organization seemed to grow out of the convergence of local agricultural overseers working for absentee Bourbon landowners—hired thugs, from the peasant workers' point of view.

Members of the Sicilian Mafia (or "Men of Honor," as they like to be called) traditionally operated as a network of regional bosses who controlled individual towns by setting up puppet regimes of thoroughly corrupt officials. It was a sort of devil's bargain between the regional bosses and the national Christian Democrat Party, which controlled Italy's government from World War II until 1993 and, despite its law-and-order rhetoric, tacitly left Cosa Nostra alone as long as its bosses got out the party vote.

The Cosa Nostra trafficked in illegal goods, of course, but until the 1960s and 1970s its income was derived mainly from funneling state money into its own pockets, low-level protection rackets, and ensuring that public contracts were granted to fellow *mafiosi* (all reasons that Sicily has experienced grotesque unchecked industrialization and modern growth at the expense of its heritage and the good of its communities). But the younger generation of Mafia underbosses got into the highly lucative heroin and cocaine trades in the 1970s, transforming the Sicilian Mafia into a major player on the international drug trafficking circuit. This ignited a clandestine Mafia war that, throughout the late 1970s and 1980s, generated lurid headlines of bloody Mafia hits. The new generation was wiping out the old and turning the balance of power in their favor.

This situation gave rise to the first of the Mafia turncoats, disgruntled ex-bosses and rank-and-file stoolies who opened up and told their stories, first to police prefect Generale Alberto Dalla Chiesa (assassinated in 1982) and later to crusading magistrates Giovanni Falcone (slaughtered May 23, 1992) and Paolo Borsellino (murdered July 19, 1992), who staged the "maxi-trials" of *mafiosi* that sent hundreds to jail. It was the

appreciate the easy parking after a day in the big sweaty city. Guest rooms are contemporary, angular, and somewhat generic-looking but very comfortable, each with a small private bathroom with shower. The hotel's garden—in the midst of which is a rectangular swimming pool—is one of the largest and most appealing in Mondello. The beach is private. The in-house restaurant is large, airy, and welcoming, serving a good regional cuisine.

Via Cloe 9, 90151 Mondello, Palermo. ℭ 091-450032. Fax 091-450359. 50 units. 65€–92€ double. AE, DC, MC, V. Free parking. **Amenities:** Restaurant; bar; pool. *In room:* A/C, TV.

Mondello Palace Hotel ★★ This is the best, most appealing, and most prestigious hotel in Mondello, set on its own private beach. It is favored by resort-goers and business travelers who prefer the relative calm and peace of Mondello to the crush of Palermo. Modern, minimalist, and angular, it has an magistrates' 1992 murders, especially, that garnered public attention to the dishonorable methods that defined the new Mafia and, perhaps for the first time, began to stir true shame.

On a broad and culturally important scale, it is these young *mafiosi*, without a moral center or check on their powers, who have driven many Sicilians to at least secretly break the unwritten code of *omertà*, which translates as "homage" but means "silence," when faced with harboring or even tolerating a man of honor. The Mafia still exists in Palermo, the small towns south of it, and the provincial capitals of Catania, Trapani, and Agrigento. Throughout the rest of Sicily, though, its power has been slipping. The heroin trade is a far cry from construction schemes and protection money, and the Mafia is swiftly outliving its usefulness.

Even in Palermo, the grip of Cosa Nostra seems to be loosening. In the closing days of 2000, the city hosted a United Nations conference on combating organized crime. Palermo's mayor, Leoluca Orlando, proclaimed that his fragile city is "battling a great evil" and paid homage at the conference to those who died fighting the Mafia. As local officials have worked to fight the *mafiosi* and their corruption and stifling of Sicilian society, their efforts have been hailed as a Palermo Renaissance.

Today civic groups and schools conduct programs to help people, especially young Sicilians, loosen the stronghold of the Cosa Nostra. We never thought we'd see it in Sicily, but the **Museo Anti-Mafia,** Via Orfanotrofio 7, Central di Cultura Polivalente (✆ 091-8461255), operates in the sleepy village of Corleone, outside Palermo. Corleone, of course, is a name familiar to all *Godfather* fans. It was depicted as the home of Salvatore Rina, the "boss of all bosses." Rina lived here for nearly a quarter of a century, as Italy's most wanted man. Much of the museum's exhibits consists of photographs documenting Mafia atrocities. Admission is free, and the museum is open Tuesday through Sunday from 9am to 1pm and 3:30 to 6:30pm. GALLO buses (✆ **091-6166028**), Via Balsamo 4 in Palermo, runs buses to Corleone, a one-way ticket costing 3.85€.

appealing kind of simplicity, a hint of the 1950s-derived glamour of *La Dolce Vita,* and a crisply uniformed staff that remains amused and helpful despite the passage of time. Originally built in 1953 and reconfigured in 1982, it sits on prime real estate that's separated from the sands of the Lido only with a garden, a privacy hedge, an iron fence, and a busy oceanfront boulevard. The mix of privacy and seclusion on one side of the hedge and the crush of holiday-making flesh on the Lido is very appealing. Guest rooms are dignified, contemporary, very comfortable, and conservative. Most of the rooms contain private balconies, and the luxurious bathrooms have tub-and-shower combinations.

Viale Principe di Scalea, 90151 Mondello, Palermo. ✆ **091-450001.** Fax 091-450657. http://web.tiscali.it/mondellopalace. 93 units. 158€–201€ double; 110€ supplement for sitting room. Extra bed 58€. AE, DC, MC, V. **Amenities:** Restaurant; bar; pool; watersports; gym; room service; babysitting; laundry/dry cleaning. *In room:* A/C, TV, minibar, hair dryer.

Splendid Hotel La Torre ⭐ *Value*   Tucked away at the most distant edge of Mondello's fishing port, this postmodern building rises in stark contrast to the low-built cement buildings that for the most part line the harbor front. Inside, clean lines, oak floors, big skylights, sweeping views of the sea, and mobs of European tourists, many of them on group tours, fill the lobby. Originally built in 1959 and radically reconstructed in 1997, the hotel has a hip but busy staff and midsize guest rooms filled with comfortable, bland-looking furnishings. Each unit is equipped with an immaculately maintained tiled bathroom with a tub-and-shower combination. There are a park, a garden, and a solarium. One of the best aspects of this place is its location on a rocky peninsula jutting into the sea at the edge of Mondello harbor. Terraces wrap around the hotel, descending several steps to sweeping views over the harbor and the sands of the Lido, about a half mile away.

Via Piano Gallo 11, 90151 Mondello, Palermo. ✆ **091-450222.** Fax 091-450033. www.latore.it. 169 units. 90€–120€ double. AE, DC, MC, V. **Amenities:** Restaurant; piano bar; pool; tennis court; room service; babysitting; laundry/dry cleaning. *In room:* A/C, TV, minibar.

Villa Esperia ⭐ *Finds*   Set on a busy commercial boulevard in the center of Mondello, this charming, pleasant hotel occupies what was built around 1890 as a majestic-looking private villa. Touches of stateliness remain today, thanks to high ceilings, well-tended landscaping in a walled-in garden, and a Liberty-era decor that's more or less authentic to the late 19th century. Four of the rooms lie in a comfortable annex, originally conceived as a stable and then a garage. Rooms are small to medium-size, with vague references to the 19th century, tiled bathrooms with shower, and lots of cozy comfort. Those facing the street can be noisy, although double layers of glass, coupled with air-conditioning, keep out most of the noise. On-site is a pleasant, mostly pink restaurant, part of which extends onto a glassed-in sun terrace, which is separated from the roaring traffic outside by a verdant hedge and a layer of glass.

Viale Margherita di Savoia 53, 90146 Mondello, Palermo. ✆ **091-6840717.** Fax 091-6841508. www.hotel villaesperia.it. 22 units. 109€–115€ double. Discounts of about 20% in midwinter. Rates include breakfast. AE, DC, MC, V. **Amenities:** Restaurant; bar; pool. *In room:* A/C, TV.

WHERE TO DINE

Bye Bye Blues ⭐⭐ *Finds* SICILIAN   The editor of the newspaper *La Stampa* advised diners that if their hotel desk hasn't heard of this restaurant, they should tell the staff "to go to hell." That's carrying it a bit too far, perhaps, but savvy locals know of this place, an innocuous-looking private house that's alarmingly close to the cars that whizz through an angle of the busy street outside. The cuisine is among the finest in the greater Palermo area, though falling just short of the viands concocted at Charleston (see below). In a tranquil neighborhood of Mondello called Valdesi, this is a casual, relaxing dining room. You'll be greeted by the owners: Antonio used to work on American cruise ships, and his wife, Patrizia, inherited her love of cooking from both her mother and her grandmother, each of whom was familiar with time-tested, traditional Sicilian recipes. The kitchen takes wonderful raw materials from the surrounding countryside and shapes them into dishes filled with flavor and "passion," as they say here. The color of the food is important to Patrizia, and each dish emerges a work of art—they call it "chromatic harmony." We were won over immediately by the lentil soup with fresh squid cooked in Sicilian olive oil. The pasta with prawns was extraordinary. The soup of *frutti di mare* (fruits of the sea) was simmered to perfection. The salads get special attention here, and we were delighted with a fresh fish salad with baby artichokes. No one makes better spaghetti with mussels and zucchini, and grilled calamari is a fragrant delight. For dessert, have you ever had a watermelon gelatin tart? If that's too experimental for you, you may be won over by the hot chocolate cake.

Via del Garofalo 23. ℂ **091-6841415.** Reservations required. Main courses 7€–9€. AE, DC, MC, V. Wed–Mon 8pm–midnight. Closed Nov 1–15.

Charleston Le Terrazze ★★★ SICILIAN/INTERNATIONAL No restaurant in Mondello—or Palermo for that matter—achieves the culinary perfection of this long-established citadel of fine cuisine. The most charming building in town was built in 1913 on concrete pilings above the surface of the sea, just offshore from Mondello Lido, and connected to the "mainland" with a bridge. Conceived as an Art Nouveau, Liberty-style fantasy, and crowned with artful depictions of sea monsters, it's the setting for this most memorable and recommendable of Mondello restaurants. During clement weather, you'll dine on a wide terrace that's open to the stars; in winter, or whenever it rains, the venue moves indoors into a high-ceilinged setting that evokes the Gilded Age. Meals feature the kind of classy, elegant fare that artfully combines fish or meat with exceedingly fresh vegetables, excellent wines, and attentive, discreet service. Appetizers are full-flavored and a delight, but you may prefer to concentrate on the pastas. The marinated swordfish is done to elegant perfection, and on a summer day the prosciutto with seasonal fruit is hard to resist. The risotto with shellfish is a savory delight, as is the beautifully seasoned grilled filet of pork. Among the vegetables you can order as accompaniments are braised radicchio; spinach in cream sauce; and zucchini with *Parmigiana*. Dessert might be an almond parfait or crêpes suzettes.

Stabilimento Balneare, Viale Regina Elena, Mondello. ℂ **091-450171.** Reservations required. Main courses 10€–14€. AE, DC, MC, V. Daily 1–3:30pm and 8:30–11:30pm. Closed Wed Oct–Mar.

Trattoria La Barcaccia ★ *Value* SEAFOOD We rate this restaurant several notches above its nearby competitors because of the freshness of its fish, its air-conditioned interior, and the sheet of glass that separates diners from the noise and traffic of the narrow harbor-front street a few feet away. Inside, you'll find a Neptune-inspired color scheme of blue, white, and terra-cotta, and an impressive display of the day's catch on ice. On our last visit, the chef whipped up a tantalizing tagliatelle with lobster after we'd devoured some of his summer-fresh antipasti. The fishermen that day had come in with two different species of white fish caught in local waters: *spigola* and *sarago*. Both were grilled and seasoned to perfection. On almost any day of the year you can order calamari stuffed or sautéed. This is not a great place to order meat, although there is some beef on the menu. *Hint:* Consider the paella for two, priced (for two diners) at 31€ for a conventional version, or 51€ for a version with lobster.

Via Piano Gallo 4. ℂ **091-451519.** Reservations recommended. Main courses 6€–15€. AE, DC, MC, V. Fri–Wed 12:30–3:30pm and 7:30pm–midnight.

5 Ustica

57km (36 miles) NW of Palermo

Rising from the waters of the Tyrrhenian Sea and linked to the capital by hydrofoil or ferry, this holiday resort goes by the touristic name of "the Black Pearl of the Mediterranean." In this case, the name fits, because the volcanic island is composed of dark, petrified, rather foreboding-looking lava. The Romans, in fact, named it *ustum* ("burnt"), because it looked to them like a large black rock.

Both this turtle-shaped island and its main port are called Ustica. A visit here is a trip to unknown, offbeat Sicily. Even many Palermitans, who live a short ferry ride away, have never visited Ustica.

The village of Ustica is set on a tufa ledge between two inlets, lying in the shadow of Capo Falconara, whose summit is crowned with the remains of a fortress erected by the Bourbons.

The history of the island is ancient; it was once inhabited by the Phoenicians. In time they were followed by the Greeks, who named the island Osteodes ("ossuary"), in memory of the skeletons of 6,000 Carthaginians, mutineers who were brought here and abandoned without food or water.

Over the years Saracen pirates raided the island, carrying off the prettiest ladies. Attempts to colonize it in the Middle Ages failed because of raids by Barbary pirates. The Bourbons repopulated it in 1762 with people from the Aeolian Islands and Naples. They constructed a trio of towers to defend the island against pirates.

As late as the 1950s, Ustica was a penal colony, a sort of Alcatraz of Sicily. Antonio Gramsci, the theorist of the Italian Communist Party, was once imprisoned here. And, in one of the most secret meetings of World War II, British and Italian officers met here in September 1943 to discuss a switch in sides from Mussolini to the Allies.

Ustica is tiny, only 8.6km (2 sq. miles). The top of a submerged volcano, it is the oldest island in the Sicilian outer archipelago, even older than the Aeolian islands, one of which is Lipari, which it resembles.

Because its jagged coastline is riddled with creeks, bays, and caves, Ustica is best explored by a rented boat (see below) circling the island.

In 1987, Sicily designated part of the island a national marine park, and today its clear waters and beautiful sea, filled with aquatic flora and fauna, attract snorkelers and scuba divers from around the world. Divers are also drawn to its

---

Moments **Exploring a Watery Wonderland**

The best spots for diving are the **Grotta del Gamberi,** near Punta Gavazzi, at the southern tip of the island beyond Grotta del Tuono. Nearby is the famous **Sub-Aqua Archeological Trail** lying off the headland, Punta Gavazzi, with its lighthouse. Many anchors and even Roman amphorae can still be seen in these waters.

The best diving spot on the north coast is **Secca di Colombara,** to the west of Grotta dell'Oro. Here you can see a vast array of gorgonians and Ustica's most beautiful sponges. Finally, **Scoglio del Medico,** or "doctor's rock," lies off the west coast of the island directly north of the bay, Baia Sidoti. This outcropping of basalt, riddled with grottoes and gorges, plunges to murky depths in the Atlantic, and is a **panoramic submerged world** ★★, a seascape unequalled anywhere else in Sicily. J. Y. Cousteau claimed that the waters off the coast of Ustica were among the most beautiful he'd ever seen, ideal for both diving and underwater photography.

Booked seat 6A, open return.

Rented red 4-wheel drive.

Reserved cabin, no running water.

Discovered space.

With over 700 airlines, 50,000 hotels, 50 rental car companies and 5,000 cruise and vacation packages, you can create the perfect get-away for you. Choose the car, the room, even the ground you walk on.

Travelocity.com
A Sabre Company
Go Virtually Anywhere.

© 2002 Yahoo! Inc.

Book your air, hotel, and transportation all in one place.

Hotel or hostel? Cruise or canoe? Car?
Plane? Camel? Wherever you're going,
visit Yahoo! Travel and get total control
over your arrangements. Even choose
your seat assignment. So. One hump
or two? travel.yahoo.com

powered by **COMPAQ**

YAHOO!
Travel

ancient wrecks and the now-submerged city of Osteodes, a mile west of the island, which sank into the sea in unrecorded times.

Ustica has a population of some 1,370 islanders. Visit them in such months as June or September, which are idyllic. A trip here in July and August is so hot it's like a journey to Hades.

ESSENTIALS

GETTING THERE From Stazione Maríttima in Palermo, hydrofoils and ferries operate daily to Ustica. The ferry is the cheapest and slowest transport, costing 12€ each way and taking 2½ hours to reach the island. At a cost of 17€, the hydrofoil does it in half the time. For tickets for either transport, go to **Siremar,** Via Francesco Crispi 118 (© **091-336632**), in Palermo. In Ustica, the Siremar office is on Piazza Bartolo (© **091-8449002**). Hydrofoil service is from April to December, and ferries run year-round but not on Sundays in winter.

GETTING AROUND On Ustica you can always do as the locals do and rely on your trusty feet. Otherwise, you can take one of the orange minibuses that circumnavigate the island, hugging the coastline. These leave from the center of Ustica village daily on the hour. Figure on 2½ hours for the entire bus ride around the island, a ticket between any two points along its route costing .70€.

Arrival from Palermo is at Ustica village, the only port and home to 90% of the islanders. The heart of the village is reached by climbing a flight of steps from the harbor.

You emerge onto the main square of town—actually a trio of interlocking squares that include the piazzas of Bartolo, Umberto I, and Vito Longo. We recommend that you take care of your shopping needs before you leave Palermo. Otherwise you must buy it here—whatever Ustica has to offer is found in this area.

The summer boat excursions are run by local fishermen who not only know the most scenic beauty spots, but will also allow you time out for swimming during an island trip.

A good place for boat rentals is **Hotel Ariston,** Via della Vittoria (© **091-8449042**), which organizes sightseeing boat trips, rents boats to scuba divers, and hires out motorcycles. Its three-seater boats cost 40€ a day, gasoline not included.

The hotel staff can sign you up for a boat trip around the island, where you can see the caves and stop off at small, secluded spots for swimming. These trips last 2½ hours, costing 13€.

If you'd like to tour on your own—expect rough roads—it costs 28€ a day to hire a cycle, with gas and two helmets included.

Scuba divers can go to **Ailara Rosalia,** Banchina Barresi (© **091-8449605**), which rents boats for 50€ a day. You should bring your own scuba-diving gear, however.

VISITOR INFORMATION The tourist office is closed. However, you can visit the headquarters of **Riserva Naturale Marina (Marine National Park)** on the main square of town (© **091-8449456**). The staff here will provide information about the marine park. Hours are daily from 8am to 8pm.

FAST FACTS For a medical emergency, call *Pronto Soccorso* (© **091-9449392**). Serious cases are immediately transported to Palermo. The police or *Carabinieri* can be reached at © **091-8449049.**

ATTRACTIONS NEAR THE PORT

It's fun just to stroll around the village, taking in views of the bay, Baia Santa Maria. The little town is made more festive by a series of murals (landscapes or even portraits) that decorate the facades of the houses and buildings.

Directly south of the village stands **Torre Santa Maria,** housing the **Museo Archeologico.** The museum (no phone) is open daily from 9am to noon and 5 to 7pm and charges 3€ to enter. Its most fascinating exhibits are fragments and artifacts recovered from the ancient city of Osteodes, now submerged beneath the sea. Many of the museum artifacts, such as crusty anchors, were recovered from ships wrecked off the coast. You'll see amphorae, Bronze Age objects from the prehistoric village of Faraglioni, and contents of tombs from the Hellenistic and Roman eras.

To the east of the tower are the ruins of a Bronze Age settlement, **Villaggio Preistorico,** at Faraglioni. Excavations began in 1989 on what was a large prehistoric village dating from the 14th century to the 13th century B.C. The foundations of some 300 stone-built houses were discovered, and the defensive walls of the settlement are among the strongest fortifications of any period known in Italy. It is believed that these early settlers came over from the Aeolian Islands. Admission is free, and the site is always open.

If you walk north of Ustica village, you come to the remains of the **Rocca della Falconiera** at 157m (515 ft.). Figure on a 20-minute walk. (Along the way you'll see many cisterns, as water remains a precious commodity on Ustica, even though a desalination plant has been installed.) The defensive tower was constructed by the Bourbons to protect the island from raids by pirates. This site was first settled back in the 3rd century B.C. by the Romans. If you look toward the sea you'll see the lighthouse, **Punta dell'Uomo Morto (Dead Man's Point)** on a cliff, where a cave contains vestiges of centuries-old tombs.

From the fort you can take in a view of **Guardia dei Turchi** at 244m (800 ft.). This is the highest point on the island. That object you see in the distance, evoking a mammoth golf ball, is in fact a meteorological radar system installed by the Italian government.

The **view** ✸ from the fortress ruins stretches from the harbor to the core of the island, with the mountains of **Monte Costa del Fallo** and **Monte Guardia dei Turchi** clearly outlined.

EXPLORING THE ISLAND

Since it is the top of an extinct volcano, Ustica doesn't have sandy beaches. But as you traverse the island, you'll find jumping-off points for swimming. The biggest attraction is the grotto-lined coastline, and because distances are short, hiking is a viable option.

Wildflowers cover the island except in late July and August, when the blistering sun burns them away. You'll also see produce grown by the islanders, such as lentils, figs, capers, grapes, prickly pears, wheat, and almonds.

Of all the caves or grottoes on the island, the most celebrated and fascinating sea cave is the **Grotta Azzurra** ✸✸, the first cave south of Ustica village as you head down the coast in your boat. It's named for the more fabled cave in Capri, but both grottoes share an incredible iridescent glow from light reflections from the sea.

Almost as stunning is the next sea cave directly to the south, **Grotta Pastizza** ✸. This is a stalactite cave behind a great pyramidal rock. Directly down the coast, another grotto, **Grotta della Barche,** is also intriguing. *Barche* means "boat," and Ustica fishermen anchor in this safe haven during storms. When a garrison of 250 Bourbon soldiers occupied the island in the 18th century, the women who wanted to service them paraded around here at night.

PARCO MARINO REGIONALE ★★

The Marine National Park was created on November 12, 1986, the first marine reserve ever established in Italy. Since Ustica lies in the center of an inward current surging through the Straits of Gibraltar directly from the Atlantic Ocean, its waters are always clean and free of pollution.

Underwater photographers flock to the park to film the stunning **aquatic flora and fauna** ★★★. A splendidly beautiful seaweed, *Poseidonia oceanica,* is called "the lungs of the sea" because it oxygenates the water. There is also an array of magnificent red gorgonians, even stunning black coral.

Turtles, now that they are protected, are plentiful once again, as are red mullet, swordfish, lobster, hake, and *cernia* (a kind of sea perch). Some divers claim that they have had close encounters with grouper as big as a Fiat 500, and schools of barracuda are known to follow them around (not a comforting thought).

The park comprises three zones. **A area** extends along the western part of the isle from Cala Sidoti to Caletta and as far as 935m (1,150 ft.) offshore. Swimming is allowed here, but no boats and no fishing. **B area** extends from Punta Cavazzi to Punta Omo Morto, taking in the entire southwest to northeast coastline, and extending out into the sea a distance of 3 nautical miles. Swimming is permitted here. Finally, **C area** is a partial reserve made up of the rest of the coast. Swimming is available here, as is fishing.

HIKING AROUND USTICA

If you like to hike, you can circumnavigate the small island in about 3 to 4 hours, depending on how you pace yourself. The best hike is along the coastal path heading north of the town, where you'll see the Municipio, or island headquarters. Head left here, taking a trail along the north coast that leads past an old cemetery. This hike hugs the steep cliffs on the northern side of the island, part of the Marine Reserve, and the views are stunning.

Eventually you'll come to **Punta di Megna,** on the western coast, on the exact opposite side of the island from Ustica village. The offshore rock so appreciated by scuba divers, **Scoglio del Medico,** can be seen from here.

The road continues along the southwestern coast as far as the battered ruins of the old tower, **Punta Spalmatore,** where you can go swimming. There is no beach here, however.

Below this point, at **Punta Cavazzi,** along the southern rim of the island, is **Piscina Naturale** ★, a sheltered seawater pool and the best place on Ustica for swimming. If there are a lot of tourists on the island at the time of your visit, this "hole" is likely to be crowded with bathers in the briefest of swimwear.

At this point the route no longer follows the coast and cuts inland all the way northeast to Ustica village once again.

WHERE TO STAY

Accommodations are scarce, and they fill up quickly from April to September. In winter many places close down because of lack of business. When the hotels are fully booked, many of the islanders will rent rooms, but if you count on that, you're taking a chance. It's far preferable to arrive with a reservation. If you don't have one, go to the Piazza Umberto and start asking around for a *camera,* or room.

Hotel Diana ★ *(Finds)*   On the beach at Contrada San Paolo, this is one of the island's oldest hotels, but it's well maintained and still in good shape. Opened in 1973 at the dawn of tourism on the island, the Diana is a reliable choice. Its most attractive feature is its landscaping, with fruit trees and wild island plants. Its panoramic position allows some good views from the private terraces of its guest rooms. Rooms are only medium in size and a bit bare-bones, but they are comfortable, with good beds, marble floors, and a small, tiled bathroom with both tub and shower. The owner-manager is helpful in offering advice about setting up island tours.

Contrada San Paolo, 90010 Ustica. ⓒ/fax **091-8449109.** www.hoteldiana.too.it. 30 units. 47€–62€ double. No credit cards. Closed Oct–Mar 14. **Amenities:** Restaurant; bar; pool. *In room:* A/C, TV.

Hotel Grotta Azzurra ★★   This is Ustica's best hotel bet, lying a 5-minute walk from the center. It's modern, comfortable, and well-furnished, standing on a wide plateau above the ocean, with a steep drop to a place for swimming below. A natural grotto carved out of a cliff face below gives the hotel its appropriate name and is its most alluring feature. All of the well-appointed guest rooms, medium in size, open onto sea views. Each unit comes with a small but neatly organized private bathroom with shower. Set among lush island gardens, this hotel feels like a typical Mediterranean vacation retreat, with such resort-style amenities as sun beds, beach towels, and beach umbrellas. The most sports-oriented people check in here, as the hotel rents scooters and boats for those interested in island tours, sailing, and windsurfing. The hotel also attracts a lot of scuba divers. Even if you're not a guest, consider a meal at its restaurant, **La Cala dei Fenici,** known on the island for its refined Sicilian cuisine.

Contrada San Ferlicchio, Ustica 90010. ⓒ **091-8449396.** Fax 091-8449396. www.framon-hotels.com/grottazzurra. 51 units. 62€–114€ double. AE, DC, MC, V. Closed Oct–May. **Amenities:** Restaurant; bar; pool; hydromassage. *In room:* A/C, TV, minibar, safe.

Pensione Clelia *(Value)*   This is the most typical of Ustica's little island inns, lying off Piazza Umberto I, the main square of Ustica village. It was the very first little boardinghouse on the island to receive visitors, who began arriving in 1950 during the lean postwar years. The pensione retains some of the aura of the 1950s, although all the dark wood furnishings are well polished and the place is spotless. It is also one of the island's best bargains. Everything was renewed in 2002, and the place did need some freshening up. Guest rooms are small but comfortable, and each comes with a little bathroom with a shower stall. Plus, this is one of the few places remaining open year-round. The pensione offers a shuttle bus making trips around the island, and it also rents motor scooters and boats. The owners invite you to enjoy the lovely outdoor patio opening onto scenic views in any season.

Via Sindaco I, 29, Ustica 90010. ⓒ **091-49039.** Fax 091-8449459. www.hotelclelia.it. 14 units. 47€–88€ double; 88€–110€ triple. Prices include breakfast. AE, DC, MC, V. **Amenities:** Restaurant; bar; babysitting. *In room:* A/C, TV, minibar, hair dryer.

Villaggio Lirial Punta Spalmatore ★   Sicily's coastal towns are riddled with self-contained tourist villages, and this is the island's best such accommodation. It lies 4km (2½ miles) from Ustica village on the western coast. It is entirely surrounded by island trees and native plants. Most guests spend their days in the terraced pool area with a panoramic view of the ocean. Some guests who come from Palermo check in and don't leave the grounds until their reservation is up. The buildings rise only two floors, and accommodations are in bungalows with small but comfortably furnished guest rooms and small bathrooms containing shower stalls. The cuisine is typical resort fare, but much use is made of fresh produce when it's available on the island. Otherwise, foodstuffs have to be shipped over from Palermo. The wide difference in price depends on when you're there—the highest prices are charged in July and August.

Località Punta Spalmatore, Ustica 90010. ✆ **091-8449388.** Fax 091-8449472. www.lirial.it/spalmatore/spalmatore.htm. 399€–763€ double. Rates include full board and sports activities. AE, MC, V. Closed Sept 16–June 14. **Amenities:** Restaurant; bar. In room: A/C in some, fridge.

WHERE TO DINE

There aren't many places to dine in Ustica. Most of the little trattorie are found in the village around the trio of central squares. The hotels also offer restaurants, with roof terraces opening onto views of the water.

Da Mario USTICAN   In the very center of Ustica village on its heartbeat square, this offers good regional fare served at reasonable prices. You can sit at a table on the square, watching island life parade before you. Mario can be found in the rear, cooking a cuisine with which he is very familiar—for all we know, he learned it from his *mamma mia*. On our latest rounds, we were satisfied in every way with his homemade pasta with freshly caught swordfish. Equally good was the grilled fish—done to perfection—based on the catch of the day. On other occasions we've enjoyed roasted squid and spaghetti with fresh crabmeat. And, of course, everything tastes better when washed down with the local Albanella wine.

Piazza Umberto I, 21. ✆ **091-8449905.** Reservations recommended July–Aug. Main courses 8€–10€. AE, MC, V. Daily 12:30–3pm and 8:15–11pm. Closed Mon Nov–Mar and all of Jan.

La Rustica *Value* MEDITERRANEAN/SICILIAN   The rustic decor, which includes a wall of volcanic stones, makes this restaurant live up to its namesake. It offers good homemade food prepared with the freshest ingredients available. At La Rustica, they seem to try harder than most other island restaurants to please their foreign visitors. Your waiter will speak with a glowing face about the glories of the pasta of the day. Perhaps it will be pasta Isolana, a homemade pasta with fresh tuna, eggplant, and tomatoes. More interesting might be the homemade pasta with radicchio, fresh mushrooms, and ham. Always ask about their fresh fish of the day, which can be prepared more or less as you like it. In the evening the kitchen is known for turning out the best pizza on the island.

Via Petriera. ✆ **328-0271693.** Reservations recommended. Main courses 5€–10€; fixed-price menu 12€. No credit cards. Daily 12:30–2:30pm and 2:30–8:30pm. Closed Oct–May.

Mamma Lia ✿ USTICAN   This typically modest establishment found on the second floor of a building in the town center is Ustica's best choice for dining. It serves only island dishes, prepared whenever possible from locally grown or caught items. Fish dominates the menu, and the setting is appropriately rustic. No one puts on airs here, and the superb food is homemade, including pasta with locally caught sardines plus fennel picked from the surrounding hills. On a recent visit, we were delighted to see lobster soup on the menu, and the dish lived up to our expectations. With a bow to nearby North Africa, couscous is most often featured. The seafood depends on the catch of the day, but you can generally count on grilled swordfish to rest on your plate.

Via S. Giacomo 2. ✆ **091-8449407.** Reservations recommended in summer. Main courses 9€–15€. AE, MC, V. Daily 1–3pm and 8pm–midnight. Closed: Oct–Mar.

6

Messina & the Tyrrhenian Coast

The coastal road (A20) that runs from Messina westward to the capital at Palermo is one of the most frequented routes in Sicily. You can, of course, drive straight through to Palermo and not see a thing, but if you do, you'll miss some of the treasures of Sicily.

The coast is riddled with sandy beaches, small resorts, and villages. If you have time for only one stopover, make it Cefalù, the premier destination along the coast, with its famous Romanesque cathedral.

For those who want to cut inland to view a national park, we suggest you set aside a day to explore **Parco Naturale Regionale delle Madonie,** one of Sicily's most important nature reserves.

The best beaches lie to the east of Cefalù. They are sandy, clean, and unpolluted, though filled with visitors in July and August.

The coast also contains some of north Sicily's more impressive ruins, including those at **Himera** (near Termini Imerese) and those at **Tyndaris,** west of Milazzo.

1 Messina

233km (145 miles) E of Palermo, 683km (410 miles) SE of Rome, 469km (281 miles) S of Naples

Overlooking the Straits of Messina, with the mainland city of Reggio di Calabria across the sea and to the east, Messina lies at the foot of the Peloritani Mountains. Only 5km (3 miles) separate the city of Messina from the Italian mainland. For most passengers arriving from the mainland, the tacky industrial and port city of Messina is their gateway into the island, a shame really. But since you're here, what the hell? You might as well enjoy what Messina has to offer—and it does have some treasures if you're willing to seek them out.

Sicily's third most populous city wasn't always this dismal. Mother Nature did a better job with Messina than mankind did. However, earthquakes and warplanes have done their damage. Because it has had to be rebuilt over and over, Messina is the most modern city on the island.

Messina was founded in the 8th century B.C. by the Siculans, who named it *Zancle,* or sickle, because of its hooked promontory protecting the harbor. The Greeks from Cumae and Chalcis occupied the site in the 5th century. It fell to the dreaded Anaxilas, tyrant of Reggio, who changed the town's name to *Messána* to honor his native Messenia in the Peloponnesus.

By the 3rd century B.C. Messina had come under Roman influence. Messina's fame in the Middle Ages rested on its position as a launching pad for many of the Crusades. It was a flourishing city until the 17th century, when it lost trading privileges as punishment for protesting against the Spanish viceroys.

Messina boasts one of the deepest and safest harbors in the Mediterranean. With a population of some 275,000, Messina also is one of southern Italy's most

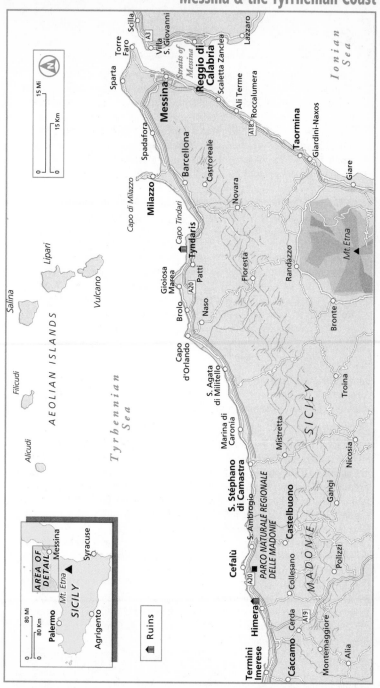

Ruins

Not-So-Fun Facts: So You Think *You've* Got Bad Luck?

Aside from the fact that Shakespeare set his *Much Ado About Nothing* in Messina, it has rarely been blessed. Get a load of these disasters.

The Black Death, or bubonic plague, swept over the city in 1743, killing more than 40,000 of Messina's population. Forty years later an earthquake struck, leveling the city. Angered at Sicilian demands for independence, the Bourbon ruler Ferdinand II bombarded Messina to a pulp in 1848. Still reeling from the blows, Messina in 1854 was swept by a cholera epidemic. It staggered back to its feet by 1894 in time for another devastating earthquake.

Messina had barely recovered when, at 5:30am on December 28, 1908, tremors shot through the city and buildings trembled. Before the day was over, some 85,000 residents were dead. The earthquake was so violent that the coast sank 20 inches into the sea.

Under the dictatorship of Mussolini, the city was rebuilt and stood rather proudly once again. It was 1943 and Italy was at war with Britain and the United States. Allied bombers were determined to knock out Messina and take Sicily as a prelude to the invasion of southern Italy. Bombs rained from the sky like raindrops falling on a roof. Messina was flattened once again.

bustling cities. Rebuilt after devastation by the 1908 earthquakes and the 1943 Allied bombings, it is a city of wide boulevards and low buildings. The structures hug the earth to prevent more danger in the event of another earthquake.

ESSENTIALS

GETTING THERE   By Boat   Messina is linked to the mainland of Italy by both hydrofoils and ferryboats crossing the Straits of Messina from either Reggio di Calabria or Villa San Giovanni. Ferries leave from Villa San Giovanni, which is 12km (7½ miles) north of Reggio and closer to Messina. Ferry services are called *traghetti*. One is state-run: **FS** (© **848-888088** in Villa San Giovanni). The other, **Caronte** (© **090-41415**), is independent. (Surprisingly, this firm is named for Charon, the horrible ferryman who transported dead souls over the River Styx to Hades—not very comforting.) Offices for both companies are at the harbor where the ferries depart. A ticket on either ferry to Messina costs 4.50€.

From Reggio, you can take either a ferry (if you have a car) or a faster hydrofoil. Hydrofoils are operated by **FS** (© **0965-29568**) and **SNAV** (© **0965-29568**), with offices right at the harbor. The trip takes 25 minutes and costs 2.60€. Ferry service is operated by **NGI** (© **0335-8427784**) and by **Meridiano** (© **0965-810414**). Ferry crossings to Messina take 40 minutes, and one-way tickets range in price from .55€ to 1.55€.

By Plane   The nearest airport to Messina is on the Italian mainland at Reggio di Calabria. The airport, **Svincolo Aeropoerto** (© **0965-640517**), lies 5km (3 miles) south of Reggio. Orange bus no. 113, 114, or 115 will take you from the Stazione Centrale in Reggio to the airport. Once you land at the airport, you can take one of the buses operated by Cavalieri, Via 1 Settembre 137 (© **090-771938**), to Messina.

By Train   Seven trains arrive daily from Rome, the trip south taking 8 to 9 hours, costing 35€ one-way. A train link from Naples takes 4½ hours, costing 23€. There are also frequent rail links to Palermo, with a dozen or more trains going between Messina and the island's capital, taking approximately 3½ hours and costing 12€ one-way. The major attraction along the Tyrrhenian coast is Cefalù. Trains from Messina go there throughout the day in 2½ to 3½ hours, costing 7.50€. There are also hourly trains between Messina and Taormina, Sicily's major resort to the south, taking 1 hour and costing 3€ each way. For rail information, call ℂ **892021.**

By Bus   This is a confused picture, as Messina has four different bus lines. For long-distance travel to Messina, we recommend the train, although **SAIS,** Piazza della Repubblica (ℂ **090-771914**), hauls in three buses per week from Naples. The trip takes a grueling 22 hours, costing 26€ one-way. More convenient might be the SAIS bus rides to Catania, departing nine times a week, taking 1½ hours, and costing 6.20€ one-way.

Many visitors in Messina use **Interbus** (ℂ **090-661754**), with offices to the left of the Stazione Centrale. A dozen buses per day run to Taormina in 1½ hours, costing 2.60€ one-way. **SAIS** (see above) also runs eight buses per day to Palermo in 3¼ hours, costing 13€.

By Car   From the mainland of Italy, follow A3 south to Reggio di Calabria, getting off at Villa San Giovanni and taking a car ferry across the Straits of Messina to Messina itself. Along the northern coast, travel the A20/SS113 east from Palermo and Cefalù. The A18 from Taormina runs north to Messina.

ORIENTATION   Messina grew around its harbor, which is shaped like a sickle. You'll see this geographic configuration as you sail into the harbor. The tip of the sickle is marked by a towering statue, *Madonna della Lettera,* atop one of the tall towers of **Forte San Salvatore,** built in 1546 in the harbor by the Spanish viceroys.

Via Garibaldi, running parallel to the sea, is the main street of Messina. It goes through **Piazza del Duomo,** the town's major square. South of this square is the second most important square in Messina, **Piazza Carducci,** site of the university, founded in 1548 and reconstructed in 1927.

To the east, the port is protected by the lighthouse known as the **Lanterna di Raineri,** on the peninsula of the same name. **Via 1 Settembre** leads from the sea to the heart of Messina. The transportation hub of Messina is **Piazza della Repubblica,** in front of Stazione Centrale. Most of the major bus lines converge

---

Tips **Rolling On, Rolling Off Across the Sea**

Train or bus travel across the Straits of Messina involves large-scale engineering on a most massive scale: Your train or bus will roll from the terra firma of the Italian mainland directly into the hold of container ships for transport across the strait. Passengers are allowed to remain within their seats on the train or bus, or they can visit a snack bar maintained on each of the ships. They can stroll around the ship's upper decks for a breath of fresh air and a view of the Port of Messina. A few minutes before landing, passengers head back to their seats on the train or bus, just before it rolls from its berth in the hold of the ship onto the highways or railway tracks of Sicily.

on this square. To reach the heart of Messina from Piazza della Repubblica, head straight across the busy square and walk directly north along Via 1 Settembre to **Piazza del Duomo,** a square crowned by Messina's cathedral.

If you come by hydrofoil or ferry from Reggio di Calabria, you'll arrive 1km (½ mile) north of Stazione Centrale on Via Vittorio Emanuele II. Those taking a ferry from Villa San Giovanni reach land 3km (1¾ miles) farther on or about 500m (1,640 ft.) north of Fiera, the site of Messina's trade fairs.

VISITOR INFORMATION   For information and a map, head to the **Azienda Autonoma per L'Incremento Turistico,** Via Calabria 301 (✆ 090-64022), near Piazza della Repubblica and Stazione Centrale. It's open Monday through Friday from 9am to 1:30pm and Monday through Thursday from 3 to 5pm.

GETTING AROUND   Most of the attractions you'll want to visit, even your hotel, most likely lie in the center and are best covered on foot. If you need to go farther afield, **ATM** buses depart from the transportation hub, Piazza della Repubblica. Bus tickets are purchased at various *tabacchi* (tobacco shops) or news kiosks throughout the city. The most useful bus is no. 79, stopping at the Museo Regionale and the Duomo. Bus tickets cost .70€ for a ticket valid for 1½ hours or 1.90€ for all day.

Taxis are found mainly at the Stazione Centrale, at Piazza Cairoli, and along Via Calabria. For a 24-hour radio taxi, call ✆ **090-6505.**

 FAST FACTS: Messina

Currency Exchange The most convenient place to exchange your own currency for euros is **Cambio/Ufficio Informazioni** (✆ 090-675234), inside the Stazione Centrale. Office hours are from 7am to 9pm daily; there are also **ATMs** in the station.

Emergencies Call ✆ **113** for the police, and ✆ **118** for first aid.

Hospitals Try **Ospedale Policlinico Universitario,** Via Valeria (✆ **090-2211**); or **Ospedale Piemonte,** Viale Europa (✆ **090-222211**).

Internet Access Your best bet is **Stamperia,** Via Cannizzaro 170 (✆ **090-6409428**), open Monday through Friday from 8:30am to 1:30pm and 3:30 to 8pm. Use of their computers costs 5.20€ per hour.

Luggage Storage A kiosk at the Stazione Centrale will store your bags for 4€ per day; it's open daily from 6am to 10pm.

Post Office The main center is on Piazza Antonello (✆ **090-6686415**). It's open Monday through Saturday from 8:30am to 6:30pm.

EXPLORING THE CITY ON FOOT

As you wander around Messina, you'll come to the ruins of the church of **Santa Maria Alemanna,** built in 1220 by the crusading Teutonic Knights. The church—or what's left of it—stands at the corner of Via dei Mille, lying off Corso Garibaldi, directly north of Via del Vespiro and to the immediate west of Piazza Cavallotti. Even though it has been allowed to wither and decay, it is one of the few Gothic churches in Sicily. The Gothic style of architecture never swept Sicily the way it did other parts of Europe, such as France or Germany. The Messinese seemed to dislike the style, and the unfinished church was left abandoned in the 15th century, although there have been a few ill-conceived attempts at restoration since then.

Chiesa SS. Annunziata dei Catalani When the Messinese saw their beloved church on this square after the 1908 earthquake, they called it a miracle. In an amazing feat, the earthquake stripped away much of the latter-day alterations and additions to the church, leaving its original 12th- and 13th-century architectural style intact. But because the quake leveled the earth on which the church sits, it seems to be sinking into the street today. Try to view the church from its western facade, where you'll see a trio of 13th-century doors.

The interior, now used as the chapel for the university, is in red, yellow, and white stone with tall Corinthian columns. The most outstanding feature is the **apse** ✪, a stellar example of the Norman composite style. A nave and two aisles run to the apse, resting under a severe, brick-built cupola. No one ever accused this church of being anything but an architectural "bastard," a kind of Arabic-Byzantine hodgepodge: Romanesque architecture blended with such Moorish features as geometrical motifs, with suggestions of the Byzantine.

In back of the church is a famous **statue of Don Juan of Austria,** the "natural" son of the Emperor Charles V and a hero in the 1571 Battle of Lepanto. Amusingly, he's depicted with his foot resting proudly on the head of the Ottoman commander, Ali Bassa. Andrea Calamech, the sculptor, carved this monument in 1572. Incidentally, an even more famous sailor sailed from Messina to take part in that battle: Miguel de Cervantes, author of *Don Quixote.* Wounded, he was brought back to Messina to recover in a hospital.

Piazza dei Catalani, Via Garibaldi. © 090-360585. Free admission. Mon–Sat 9:30–11:30am; Sun 9–11:30am.

Duomo ✪ This Romanesque and Norman cathedral has had a rough time of it since Roger II ordered it built in 1160. Henry VI, the Holy Roman emperor, attended its consecration in 1197. Earth-shaking events like the 1908 quake and a 1943 Allied firebomb didn't help. The cathedral has more or less been reconstructed from scratch, although some original architectural features remain. Critic Christopher Kininmonth called it "the postwar reconstruction of the post-earthquake reconstruction of the Norman original."

The Duomo's major happening was the wedding of Richard the Lionhearted's 15-year-old sister, Joanna, to the "divinely beautiful" Norman-Sicilian William I in 1177.

Its **central doorway** ✪ was reconstructed using fragments originally from the 15th century. The lower part of the facade is also decorated with 15th-century carvings depicting Sicilian agrarian life. The gray and pink interior has a trio of aisles divided by ogival arches and columns, resting under a trussed and painted ceiling. Many of the Duomo's treasures were re-created, using fragments pulled from the ruins after the Allied bombings.

The statue in the south aisle is of **John the Baptist** and is attributed to Antonello Gagini in 1525. Dominating the main altar is a copy of the Byzantine *Madonna della Lettera,* the original destroyed by the firebombing of 1943. A pupil of Michelangelo, Jacopo del Duca, designed the **Cappella del Sacramento** in the north apse. Spared from the destruction, it holds the cathedral's only original mosaic, a work from the 14th century that depicts the Virgin seated with saints, queens, and archangels.

The church's treasure trove is found in its **Il Tesoro,** or treasury, a two-story building displaying valuable candlesticks, chalices, and gold reliquaries. Much of the silverwork was created by artisans from Messina in the 17th and 18th centuries. Displayed for the first time in 3 centuries is the **Manta d'Oro,** or golden mantle, a special cover for the Virgin and Bambino on the Duomo's altar. The treasury's oldest object is a **lamp in a rock crystal** dating from 969.

Piazza del Duomo. (℅ **090-675175.** Free admission. Guided tours in English 2.60€. Daily 8am–12:30pm and 4–7pm.

Orologio Astronomico ✦   The Duomo is upstaged by its 60m (197-ft.) campanile, or bell tower, with its astronomical clock standing to the left of the cathedral facade. Created in 1933 in Strasbourg, France, the clock puts on "the show of shows" at noon every day. With Schubert's *Ave Maria* scraping away on a loudspeaker in a note of high camp, the bronze automata goes into action. A lion waves his banner and roars, and a cock flaps its wing and crows. Dina and Clarenza, the heroines of Messina at the time of the Sicilian Vespers, take turns ringing the bell, and Jesus pops out of the tomb for instant resurrection. Be sure to gather in the square to check out this show. The clock tells the year, the date, the phase of the moon, and the location of the planets.

Piazza del Duomo. Tower open to view 24 hr. Free show at noon.

Fontana di Orione ✦   Standing in the center of the cathedral square, this elegant fountain was the pre-baroque creation of Giovanni Angelo Montorsoli, a Florentine, in 1547. It honors Orion, the city's mythical founder, who is seen surmounting a bevy of giants, nymphs, and crocodile-wrestling *putti.* The fountain was built to honor the construction of the city's first aqueduct. The major figures represent the rivers Nile, Ebro, Camaro, and Tiber.

Piazza del Duomo. Open to view 24 hr.

Museo Regionale ✦✦   Situated in a former silk mill from 1914, this museum, north of the Duomo, is one of Sicily's finest provincial museums and contains the island's greatest collection of art from the 15th to the 17th century. Its main collection consists of art rescued from the 1908 earthquake.

Its most precious relic to the devout is found in the atrium: a **dozen 18th-century gilded bronze panels** that relate the tale of the Holy Letter. As legend has it, the Madonna sent the Messinese a boat filled with food but devoid of crew when they were experiencing a famine. The Virgin is also said to have sent along a letter containing a lock of her hair.

The museum displays many medieval and baroque treasures, including a mosaic of the Virgin and Child, known as *La Ciambretta* and dating from the 13th century. A **marble low relief of St. George** is attributed to Domenico Gagini. For us, there is nothing finer than Antonello da Messina's beautiful but damaged **polyptych** ✦✦ of the Madonna with St. Gregory, St. Benedict, and the Annunciation, from 1473. Also on exhibit are **two large masterpieces** ✦✦, the work of "the divine" Caravaggio during his sojourn in Messina from 1608 to 1609. His works represent the Raising of Lazarus and the Nativity.

Greek and Roman antiquities are on view in the newly created garden pavilion. Look for the magnificent **Senator's Coach** ✦ from 1742, with its flamboyantly painted panels. The **statues of Neptune, Scylla, and Charybdis** removed from the Fontana di Nettuno (see below) are also on display.

Viale della Libertà. (℅ **090-36292.** Admission 4.15€. June–Sept Mon, Wed, and Fri 9am–1:30pm; Tues, Thurs, and Sat 9am–1:30pm and 4–6:30pm; Sun 9am–12:30pm. Oct–May Mon, Wed, and Fri 9am–1:30pm; Tues, Thurs, and Sat 9am–1:30pm and 3–5:30pm; Sun 9am–12:30pm.

Antonello da Messina: Hometown Artist

Born around 1430 in Messina, Antonello went on to become one of the greatest masters of the Italian Renaissance and southern Italy's leading painter. Although much of his life remains a puzzle to biographers and many years have not been accounted for, it is known that the painter was very much influenced by the Flemish school, especially by the works of Jan van Eyck. Antonello was the first of the great Italian painters to master the art of painting in oil, a breakthrough that was to have an enormous impression on Giovanni Bellini, to name just one artist. What is also known is that after many travels across Europe, this brilliant artist returned to his home city of Messina in 1476, remaining there until his death in 1478.

Antonello's works are characterized by their sense of light and attention to detail. Many of his portraits show a three-quarter view of the sitter. His paintings show intense psychological depth and are remarkable in their breakthroughs in texture, shadow, and brilliant light.

In Sicily you can see masterpieces of Antonello in the Museo Mandralisca and in Cefalù at the Museo Regionale (see above).

Fontana di Nettuno   On the seafront, at the intersection of Via della Libertà and Via Garibaldi, stands this landmark fountain. It is a reconstruction of the heavily damaged fountain created by Montorsoli in 1557. The original of the muscular marble god has been in the Museo Regionale ever since the statue was "castrated" by some roaming youths from Palermo who set out to "raise hell" on their visit to Messina. The sculpture of Neptune is depicted pacifying the sea, guarding the Straits of Messina from those wicked terrors, Scylla and Charybdis. Enjoy this fountain during the day, as the port area here isn't safe at night.

WHERE TO STAY

For such a large city, Messina has a dearth of accommodations. Its budget accommodations are a disaster. In some, you might check in with luggage, but there is no guarantee your suitcase will be there when you return to your claptrap chambers.

We've recommended the only safe accommodations (see below), and although they offer comfort, they cater mainly to commercial travelers whose expense account might be greater than your vacation budget. Chances are you'll be in Messina for only 1 night and therefore won't feel the pinch too severely.

EXPENSIVE

Grand Hotel Liberty ★★★   This is the most comfortable, elegant, and appealing hotel in Messina. In fact, it's one of the finest hotels in Sicily. It originated as a battered rooming house, but in the mid-1990s, the well-recommended Framon chain closed it down for a radical 4-year renovation that transformed it from a sow's ear into one of the most elegant and beautiful hotels on the island. Throughout, you'll find rich paneling, marble-inlaid floors, ornate plasterwork that includes the most beautiful ceilings in town, and lavish stained-glass windows. Guest rooms are as plush as anything you'll find in Sicily, with marble-trimmed bathrooms with tub and shower, fine hardwoods, high ceilings, and color schemes of champagne and gold. Thanks to this and to the welcome that's extended with genuine concern to single women traveling alone, the hotel enjoys one of the highest occupancy rates (around 78%) in town. The lobby is outfitted in a turn-of-the-20th-century Liberty style that sets the style and evokes the charm of this winner.

Via I Settembre 15. *©* **090-6409436.** Fax 090-6409340. www.sicily-hotels.com/siti/framon-hotels/liberty. 51 units. 98€–108€ double; 150€–160€ suite. AE, DC, MC, V. **Amenities:** Restaurant; 2 bars; concierge; babysitting; laundry. *In room:* A/C, TV, minibar, hair dryer.

MODERATE

Jolly Hotel Messina   It isn't as architecturally dramatic, plush, or well-located as its most prominent competitor, Grand Hotel Liberty, but this boxy-looking *moderno* (ca. 1953) member of the nationwide hotel chain draws goodly numbers of loyal travelers, many of them in Messina on business. It was the first large-scale modern hotel in Messina, and until it was replaced by more artful and dramatic hotels (such as the Grand Hotel Liberty), it was the reigning hotel in town. All the rooms have double windows for insulation from the roar of traffic on the harborfront boulevard outside, and about half (including most of the doubles) open onto views of the harbor. Expect a gradual renovation of this hotel, perhaps during the lifetime of this edition, in which the rooms will be more up-to-date and contemporary-looking. Otherwise, units are clean, modern, and a bit banal-looking but very comfortable, each with a tiled bathroom with tub and shower. The in-house restaurant, specializing in fish and Sicilian wines, is recommended separately.

Via Garibaldi 126, 98100 Messina. *©* **090-363860.** Fax 090-5902526. www.jolly.it. 96 units. 129€–155€ double. Free parking. AE, DC, MC, V. **Amenities:** Restaurant; bar; room service; babysitting; laundry. *In room:* A/C, TV, minibar.

Royal Palace Hotel   Built in the 1970s, and well-recognized as a reputable and desirable hotel for business travelers, this large, boxy-looking staple of Messina's hotel scene has a high occupancy rate and contemporary styling. It lacks the high-blown style and elegance of its sister hotel, the Grand Hotel Liberty, but they're both operated by the same (Framon) chain. Scheduled for a radical renovation and upgrade during the lifetime of this edition, it's a suitable choice, thanks in part to its comfortable but slightly dated-looking guest rooms, its allegiance to streamlined, *moderno* styling, and touches that include one of the genuinely charming lobby bars of Messina. Each unit comes with a well-scrubbed bathroom with tub and shower. If cost is a concern, ask for one of the not-yet-renovated rooms (they're a bit dowdier than the more glistening newcomers), which might sell at something of a discount.

Via T. Cannizzaro 224, 98123 Messina. *©* **090-6503.** Fax 090-2821075. www.framon-hotels.com. 107 units. 158€ double; 186€ suite. Rates include breakfast. AE, DC, MC, V. **Amenities:** Restaurant; bar; babysitting; laundry/dry cleaning. *In room:* A/C, TV, minibar.

WHERE TO DINE

Baked with herbs, sautéed with garlic, or even stewed into a *pesce stucco,* swordfish *(pesce spada)* has the people of Messina hooked. The fish is plentiful in the Straits of Messina, and as you walk along the harbor, you can see the tall-masted swordfish boats *(felucche)* patrolling the narrow channel in their vessels, hoping to catch swordfish for the greedy markets of Messina. May and June are the best months for ordering swordfish.

EXPENSIVE

Jolly Restaurant dello Stretto ✿ ITALIAN/SICILIAN   Set on the ground floor of the hotel recommended above, this restaurant has the most panoramic view (in this case, of the wharves that service the ships coming in from Reggio Calabria) in town. Well-managed and contemporary, with a floor crafted from mollusk-encrusted russet marble and a sense of *la dolce vita* pizzazz, it features a display of the day's fresh fish on ice near the entrance, and a choice of up to nine kinds of mineral water. For an appetizer, select an array of smoked local fish; there's nothing better on the menu. Perfected by years of experience, the staff does very well with even a simple dish such as cream of fresh tomato soup with fresh basil. For a main dish, we were recently delighted in every way with the breast of chicken with a Sicilian citrus sauce.

In the Jolly Hotel, Via Garibaldi 126. ℂ **090-363860.** Reservations recommended Fri–Sat. Main courses 14€–18€; set-price lunch 23€. AE, DC, MC, V. Daily 1–3pm and 8–10:30pm.

La Loggia ⚶ ITALIAN/INTERNATIONAL When the town's most appealing hotel was rebuilt in the late 1990s, great care was taken to ensure a glamorous dining enclave on its uppermost floor. Today, beneath a vaulted ceiling that's richly adorned with decorative plasterwork and ringed with windows overlooking the grandiose 19th-century buildings nearby, you'll enjoy superb cuisine presented by an intensely well-trained and formally dressed staff. Much of the allure of this place derives from *maitre flambeur* Pasquale Battaglia who, from a trolley wheeled tableside, can whip together succulent versions of pastas (linguine with swordfish and shrimp, flambéed with Pernod), crepes, and flambéed fruited desserts. Other tasty choices include grilled scallops with herbs and fennel; stuffed eggplant; linguine with scampi and pesto; an especially good saffron-stuffed risotto with shrimp; pennette pasta made from "hard grain," served with bacon and eggplant; chicken breast with butter and sage; and a wide assortment of the day's freshest fish. *Note:* You might opt for a drink at the bar that prefaces the entrance to this restaurant.

In the Grand Hotel Liberty, Via I Settembre 15. ℂ **090-6409340.** Reservations recommended. Main courses 14€–19€. AE, DC, MC, V. Daily 8–10:30pm.

MODERATE

Piero *Value* SICILIAN This is one of the town's most well-recommended restaurants, with a history that goes back to 1959 and an interior that's attractively outfitted with exposed paneling, terra-cotta tile floors, and a sense of bustling good cheer and workaday efficiency. Menu items cover the range of dishes that many Sicilians remember from their childhoods, and include spaghetti with mussels and crabmeat (our favorite), pennette with scampi, spaghetti with squid ink, and pennette with fresh artichokes. Scampi is prepared any way you ask for it; risotto might be garnished with shrimp and asparagus, and fish might be prepared either on the grill, in a salt crust, or baked with artichokes. Don't overlook the luscious temptations of the antipasti table—it's a serve-yourself buffet that probably shouldn't be missed.

Via Ghibellina 119. ℂ **090-718365.** Reservations recommended Fri–Sat nights. Main courses 7.50€–20€. Mon–Sat 12:30–3:15pm and 8–11:30pm. Closed Aug.

INEXPENSIVE

Al Padrino MESSINESE/SICILIAN Part of the charm of this restaurant is its rough-edged, completely unpretentious nature, where virtually no effort has been spent on decor, and where the in-house majordomo (in this case, Sr. Pietro Denaro) dictates service rituals with an iron-fisted (and usually kindly) sense of goodwill. High-ceilinged and glaringly white, without a hint of mystery or romance, it has flourished for a quarter of a century in a dreary neighborhood of heavy industry, beside an access route to the port near the heart of town. Tables are hot and cramped, many of the clients are regulars, and the impossibly small kitchen churns out copious portions of Messinese-style food that includes a creamy homemade *maccheroni;* eggplant *al padrino* (layered with cheese and herbs); roulades of swordfish; deep-fried calamari; a mixed grill of fish; several kinds of lamb cutlets; and many different preparations of beef. Flavors are robust and hearty, and portions are large. Get ready for loud voices, an "in your face" kind of welcome, and an insight into working-class Messina at its most vivid.

Via Santa Cecilia 54–56. ℭ 090-2921000. Main courses 7.75€–11€. AE, MC, V. Mon–Fri noon–3pm and 7–11pm. Closed Aug.

Casa Savoia *(Value* ITALIAN/SICILIAN   This restaurant, established in 1996 on the site of the since-demolished Teatro della Savoia, is the best budget bet in Messina. Old-fashioned, conservative, and deeply entrenched, with a location just 4 blocks from the harbor, it's decorated with Oriental carpets and antiques, its shelves and tables loaded with unopened bottles of wine. Over the years, it has welcomed a host of actors and pop singers well known throughout Italy, including Christian di Sicca; members of the pop group Mattia Bazar; and many of the winners (from 1990, 1992, and 1996) of the Miss Italia contest. The chef specializes in swordfish, including one succulent version in which the catch is stuffed, rolled, and fried in a roulade. As the waiter placed a filet of beef in a green peppercorn sauce on our table, he said, "If you don't like it, I will take it away and bring you something else." We loved it. Beef also appeared cooked with fresh artichokes, a tempting-looking dish, as were the Milanese-style veal cutlets. A delectable homemade crescent-shaped pasta comes simply with fried zucchini and garlic browned in olive oil, a most flavorful combination.

Via XXVII Luglio 36–38. ℭ 090-2934865. Main courses 6€–12€; set-price menu 13€. MC, V July–Sept Mon–Sat 1–3pm and 7:30pm–12:30am. Closed Mon Oct–June.

Cinese Njn Hao CHINESE   One of the least expensive restaurants in Messina sits behind a prominent green-and-white sign in a residential neighborhood above the port. You'll find a cozy, wood-trimmed place that includes a brick-built bas-relief map of Italy and dozens of Chinese lanterns. The restaurant was established by expatriates of Shanghai in 2001, who prepare subtly flavored versions of pork in sweet-and-sour sauce; chicken with almonds; fried chicken with mushrooms and bamboo; steamed ravioli; shrimp-stuffed dumplings; and fried ice cream. Of course, you've had all of these dishes before, and probably in more exciting combinations, but this pocket of Asia may be a welcome relief to the palate.

Via Santa Maria Alemanna 28/34. ℭ 090-6413504. Reservations not necessary. Main courses 3.60€–7€. Set menus 6.70€–7.75€. MC, V. Daily 11am–3pm and 8pm–1am.

Il Due Sorelle *(Value* SICILIAN   Set beside the square that flanks the front entrance to Messina's town hall, this restaurant occupies a long, narrow room that contains fewer than 10 tables, with walls that are covered with wine bottles and a gracefully carved screen that rises high above the terra-cotta floor. The pair of sisters *(le due sorelle)* who established the place many years ago are long-dead, but their restaurant continues as a neighborhood staple, run (ironically) by a pair of brothers. At lunchtime, the place is loaded with municipal and local office workers, one of whom happens to be the town's mayor. The simple, unpretentious fare includes two different versions of couscous; roasted veal with roasted vegetables; chicken with sweet peppers; a *padellata di pesce* (panful of fish) with vegetables; and a full roster of house-made desserts.

Piazza Municipio 4. ℭ 090-44720. Reservations recommended on Fri–Sat nights. Main courses 9€–12€. MC, V. Mon–Fri 1–3pm; daily 8pm–midnight. Closed Aug.

Pasticceria Irrera PASTRIES   Set directly beside Messina's largest and most verdant tree-lined square, this well-known pastry shop and cafe was established in 1910, and as such has been known to most of the city residents since their childhoods. Operated by members of the Irrera family, it features a marble-covered bar serving coffee and drinks, long racks of fresh pastries, and a selection of *granita* that tastes especially wonderful on warm days. Pastries for which the establishment is widely renowned include an almond-based *Fiori di Mandorlo;* a succulent cake concocted from almonds, flour, eggs, and vanilla known as *Torta Letizia;* and a chocolate-covered version of almond paste known as *Le Amarilde.* Other items are sold only at holidays, including a Christmas version of *Stella di Natale,* and an oblong version of the above-mentioned Torta Letizia known as *Agnello Letizia.*

Piazza Cairoli 12. ℭ 090-673823. Pastries 1.50€–6€. AE, DC, MC, V. Tues–Sat 8am–1:30pm; Tues–Sun 4–8pm.

MESSINA AFTER DARK

If you're here in July or August, head for Piazza del Duomo, the central cathedral square where free concerts devoted to rock, jazz, classical music, "or whatever," are presented. Posters advertise cultural events, and the tourist office (see "Visitor Information," earlier in this chapter) has details.

If your hotel has a bar, that's often your best and safest bet for a drink. Although many bars in town aren't recommended, a few are worthy of a visit. Pubs are open all day and night until the early morning hours. **Arancia di Mezzanotte** ("Midnight Orange"), Via XXVII Luglio 111 (ℭ **090-6413185**), is the town's most popular *birreria* (beer hall), lying on a corner of Via Ghibellina between Piazza del Popolo and Piazza Cairoli. Throughout the day it draws a crowd of all ages that tends to get younger as the night wears on.

The noisiest (and most fun) *birreria* is **Le Brasserie,** Via Ugo Bassi 83 (ℭ **090-672430**), whose major drawback is that it's closed during the scorching months of June through August. Otherwise, it's always a reliable place for cold beer along with platters of affordable pastas.

The Duck, Via Pellegrino 107 (ℭ **090-712772**), is a British-style pub where you'll encounter U.S. sailors stationed with NATO forces around Messina. This pub has the fullest range of German bottled beers as well as Stones Bitter on tap. It is closed on Monday and from July 15 to September 15.

A place that always seems to be open is **Dolce Vita,** Piazza del Duomo (ℭ **090-670001**), the most central and most popular watering hole in town. Try for one of the outdoor tables so you can have a view of the Duomo bell tower. Tasty snacks are served here along with a selection of imported beers.

EASY EXCURSIONS TO THE BEACH

If streets look a little deserted in July and August, that tells you that the Messinese are hanging out at **Mortelle,** the city's beach resort, lying 12km (7½ miles)

Tips **Night Wandering: Do So at Your Own Risk**

A woman wandering the streets of Messina at night does so at her own risk. She might be abducted. Although men aren't likely to get raped, they may be mugged. The area near the Stazione Centrale, the main rail depot, is the most dangerous part of town—that and the harbor front. Some young men in Messina make their living picking the pockets of foreign men and snatching the purses of women.

north of the city. At the northeastern tip of the island, Mortelle opens onto a number of good sandy beaches. The best spots on the beach are taken early, of course. Even when the sun goes down, Mortelle continues to be busy until late at night, and you have to be careful not to get run down by cycles and scooters.

Mortelle is an easy ride from Messina on bus no. 79 or 81. The area is filled with pizzerie and bars, and in July and August open-air films are screened at 8:30 and 10:45pm at Arena Green Sky, opposite Duc Palme pizzeria.

If you find Mortelle too crowded, continue to the west, where you'll find more sandy beaches and little seaside resorts, the best of which is **Acqualadrone.**

HITTING THE BEACH

The beachfront at Mortelle is a narrow strip of pebble-strewn sand known as the **Lido del Tirreno** (© 090-31311001). Thanks to large numbers of parasols and chaise longues, as well as easy access to such beachfront restaurants as the also-recommended Dodd's Sporting Club, it's the best-accessorized beach in and around Messina. Entrance costs 2.50€ per person. Depending on its size, a day's rental of a *cabine* goes for 5.50€ to 7€, and a day's rental of a chaise longue and a sun parasol costs 3€. Parking is free.

WHERE TO STAY

Grand Hotel Lido di Mortelle   Set at the Messina end of the best beachfront in Mortelle, this government-rated three-star hotel was built in the late 1970s as the best hotel in town, a position it has retained. Guest rooms are simple and airy, outfitted in tones of blue and white and filled with holidaymakers from the region, some of whom check in with very young children. Each unit comes with a small tiled bathroom with shower. Nothing is particularly plush, but in this simple and completely unpretentious beach resort, no one really seems to mind. Access to the nearby beach is free.

S.S. 113, Mortelle, 98164 Messina. © 090-321017. Fax 090-321666. www.giardinodellepalme.it. 33 units. 74€–94€ double. DC, MC, V. **Amenities:** Restaurant; bar; pool; babysitting; laundry/dry cleaning. *In room:* A/C, TV, minibar.

WHERE TO DINE

Ristorante Sporting Dodd's SICILIAN   This is the biggest and most stylish restaurant in Mortelle, a two-story beachfront complex that encourages its guests to stay on or near the premises for an entire day. It was built in 1957 as one of the first important restaurants in Mortelle, and although competitors have moved in since then, this one still retains strong whiffs of *la dolce vita* and its sybaritic values. The complex is actually two restaurants, both of which are constantly open to sea breezes and views of the Lido. The more formal of the two is upstairs, where chefs prepare the most tempting array of antipasti in town, including a delectable carpaccio of swordfish. The cooks also base their reputations on risottos of tantalizing combinations: with "fruits of the sea," for example, or radicchio and baby shrimp. Another specialty is grilled roulade of swordfish (it's stuffed before it's grilled). Your best bet might be the catch of the day, although a savory kettle of mussels and clams is usually simmering in the kitchen. Meat courses are more limited. On the street level, directly beside the beach, is a simpler pizzeria, serving pastas, salads, and about a dozen kinds of pizza. Expect lots of wedding receptions and baptism parties on the premises—it's something of a local monument for the rites of passage of many extended families.

S.S. 113, Mortelle. © 090-321009. Reservations recommended. Main courses in restaurant 9€–13€. Pizzas 4€–10€. AE, DC, MC, V. Daily noon–3pm and 8pm–midnight.

2 Cefalù ★★

81km (50 miles) E of Palermo, 38km (24 miles) NE of Termini Imerese, 170km (106 miles) W of Messina

The major destination along the Tyrrhenian coast, the former fishing village of Cefalù has now grown into one of northern Sicily's premier stopovers. It hardly rivals Taormina in appeal, but it's trying. The town was captured in the Oscar-winning film *Cinema Paradiso*. You can tour Cefalù in half a day and spend the rest of your time enjoying its beach.

Cefalù is not only in possession of a great sandy beach, it's blessed with a Romanesque cathedral and a museum that houses Antonello da Messina's master-piece, *Portrait of an Unknown Man.*

Anchored between the sea and a craggy limestone promontory, Cefalù is a town of narrow medieval streets, small squares, and historic sights. Towering 278m (912 ft.) above the town is La Rocca, a massive and much-photographed crag. The Greeks thought it evoked a head so they named the village *Kephalos,* which in time became Cefalù.

Known to be inhabited since the 9th century B.C., Cefalù was founded by the Sikels. By the 5th century B.C., it had become the fortified western outpost of Imera. The Byzantine era saw Cefalù thriving as the seat of a Greek bishop. But Saracen raids in the 8th century drove its residents away from the sea to seek refuge on top of La Rocca. Cowering in fear, the inhabitants didn't descend again until 1131, when Roger II ordered that the town be reconstructed along with his grand design for a cathedral.

ESSENTIALS

GETTING THERE   By Train   From Palermo some three dozen trains head east to Cefalù (trip time: 1 hr.). The cost is 4€ one-way. From Messina, about a dozen trains run daily, costing 7.50€, with the trip taking about 3 hours. Trains pull into the Stazione Termini, Piazza Stazione (© **0921-421169**).

By Bus   La Spisa, Via Cavour 2 (© **0921-424301**), runs buses between Palermo and Cefalù, charging 5€ one-way for the 1½-hour trip.

By Car   Follow Route 113 east from Palermo to Cefalù, and count on at least 1½ hours of driving time (more if traffic is bad). Once at Cefalù, you park along either side of Via Roma for free or within two car parks signposted from the main street, both within an easy walk of the town's medieval core. The rate in either lot is .70€ per hour.

VISITOR INFORMATION   The **Cefalù Tourist Office,** Corso Ruggereo 77 (© **0921-421050**), is open Monday through Friday from 8am to 2pm and 3:30 to 8pm, Saturday from 9am to 1:30pm and 3:30 to 8pm, and Sunday from 9am to 1:30pm.

 FAST FACTS: **Cefalù**

Currency Exchange   Go to **Banca San Angelo** (© **0921-423922**), at the cor-ner of Via Roma and Via Giglio, near the rail depot.; it's open Monday through Friday from 8:30am to 1:30pm and 2:45 to 3:45pm. The **Banca di Sicilla,** Piazza Garibaldi (© **0921-421103**), offers 24-hour **ATM** access.

Emergencies For the police, call ✆ **0921-420104**; for first aid, ✆ **0921-424544**; and for Guardia Medica, ✆ **0921-423623** (Via Roma 15). The latter is open daily from 8pm to 8am.

Hospital The **Cefalù Hospital** is at Vis Aldo Moro at the intersection with Via Matteotti (✆ **0921-920111**).

Internet Access The most central cafe is **Bacco On-Line**, Corso Ruggero 38 (✆ **0921-421753**), across from the visitor information office; it's open daily from 9am to midnight and charges 2.50€ per half hour. Another choice is **Kefaonline**, Piazza San Francesco 1 (✆ **0921-923091**), at the intersection of Via Mazzini and Via Umberto; it's open Monday through Saturday from 9:30am to 1:30pm and 3:30 to 7:30pm and charges 5.20€ per hour.

Pharmacies The two most central drugstores are **Cirincione**, Corso Ruggero 144 (✆ **0921-421209**), open Monday through Friday from 9am to 1pm and 4:30 to 8:30pm, Saturday and Sunday from 4:30 to 11pm; and **Dr. Battaglia**, Via Roma 13 (✆ **0921-421789**), open Monday through Saturday from 9am to 1pm and 4 to 8pm.

Police Headquarters of the municipal police is along Via Roma (✆ **0921-420104**).

Post Office The Cefalù Post Office is at Via Vazzana 2 (✆ **0921-424084**). It's open Monday through Saturday from 8am to 6:30pm.

Taxis Taxis are the easiest way to get about. We don't recommend a car within Cefalù, but a car is almost vital to take full advantage of the city's history-rich environs. **Kefautoservizi** (✆ **0921-422554**) operates the taxis, most of which can be found clustered at Piazza Stazione or Piazza Colombo.

SEEING THE SIGHTS

Getting around Cefalù is easy and it's on foot—no cars are allowed in the historic core. The city's main street is **Corso Ruggero** ⊛, which starts at Piazza Garibaldi, site of one of a quartet of "gateways" to Cefalù. This is a pedestrian street that you can stroll at leisure, checking out the shops and viewing the facades of its palazzi, or old palaces, even though these are hardly comparable to those found in Palermo's medieval core.

The Romans designed a main street to bisect the village on a north-south axis. Basically that same plan is carried out today. The medieval sector is found to the west where the poor folks once lived. Noblemen and their families and the rich clergy settled in the posher eastern sector.

Across from the tourist office lies **Osteria Magno,** at the corner of Via Amendola and Corso Ruggero. Constructed in the 1300s, but massively altered over the years, this was the legendary residence of Roger II. The palace remains closed but occasionally is a venue for temporary art exhibitions. For information on what's happening there, call the tourist office at ✆ **0921-421050.**

Duomo ⊛⊛ Along Corso Ruggero, this magnificent Norman cathedral opens onto a wide square that is the center of town. Legend has it that Roger II ordered this mighty church to be constructed after his life was spared following a violent storm off the coast. Construction stretched on until 1240.

Your first impression no doubt will be that you've arrived at a fortress rather than a cathedral. Anchored at the feet of towering La Rocca, the twin-towered facade of the Duomo forms a landmark visible for miles around. Splitting the facade is a two-story portico that had to be rebuilt in the 1400s.

We prefer to stand and look at this splendid facade in the late afternoon of a dying day. It's as if the building is bathed with a golden patina, an evocative sight that will last long in your memory.

To the right of the facade on the south side, you'll find the entrance. After having been dazzled by the mosaics of Palermo's Cappella Palatina or those of the Duomo at Monreale, you may at first be disappointed, as the decoration was never completed. But press on to the apse and vault.

Here you'll find a stunning array of **mosaics** ✿✿✿ in their shimmering glory. Completed in 1148, they are the oldest Byzantine-Norman mosaics in Sicily and among the world's most brilliant. Roger himself got to enjoy them for 6 years before his death.

The *tour de force* of the cycle is the Byzantine figure of the *Pantocrator* in the apse. Few ancient portraits of Christ anywhere in the world are this brilliant. Since this was a Norman church, Christ is depicted as a blond, not a brunette. But his nose and mouth look Greek, his brows and beard black like a Saracen's. The Christ figure holds an open Bible proclaiming, "I am the light of the world: he who follows me shall not walk in darkness."

Regrettably, there's little else to see here. The Duomo seems to be in a perpetual state of restoration, hampered by lack of funds.

Piazza del Duomo. ✆ 0921-922021. Free admission. Summer daily 8am–noon and 3:30–7pm. Off-season 8am–noon and 3:30–5pm.

Museo Mandralisca ✿   We come here just to gaze at the wonder of *Ritratto di un Uomo Ignoto (Portrait of an Unknown Man)* ✿✿, the work of the great Antonello da Messina in 1465. Unfortunately, the painting is badly framed and you have to keep your distance because of a velvet rope. But this is clearly a masterpiece by the great Renaissance artist from Messina.

After being dazzled by Antonello, check out the other treasures assembled by the world-class collector, Baron Enrico Piraino di Mandralisca (1809–64). While wandering into a pharmacy one day, the baron discovered the Antonello portrait in use as a cupboard door and hastily purchased the masterpiece "for peanuts." He generously bestowed his lifetime collection on Cefalù, including all of his paintings, ancient coins and medals, artifacts unearthed at archaeological digs at Lipari, and even such esoteric delights as a Chinese puzzle in ivory. Everywhere you turn you find another treasure, such as a **4th-century-B.C. vase** ✿ depicting a tuna vendor and a customer in a heated argument. Also displayed is a remarkable collection of 20,000 shells. The baron's 6,000-volume library is also housed here.

Via Mandralisca 13. ✆ 0921-421547. Admission 4.15€. Daily 9:30am–12:30pm and 3:30–7pm.

La Rocca   If it's a dog day in August, it's a long, hot, sweaty climb up to this rocky crag, but once you're there **the view** ✿✿ is panoramic, one of the grandest in Sicily. If you're stout-hearted, count on 20 minutes to approach the ruins of the so-called Temple of Diana (it probably wasn't) and another 45 huffing and puffing minutes to scale the pinnacle.

From Piazza Garibaldi, along Corso Ruggero, a sign—ACCESSO ALLA ROCCA—will launch you on your way. In summer, we recommend taking this jaunt either in the early morning or when evening breezes are blowing.

In Cefalù's heyday, this was the site of the acropolis of Cephaloedium with a temple dedicated to Hercules on the top. Over the centuries residents from below used this zone as a stone quarry.

You'll come first to the ruins of the **Tempio di Diana,** which popular tradition has attributed as a temple to the goddess, Diana. Now consisting of mammoth trapezoidal blocks, the temple was constructed or reconstructed in various stages from the 9th century to the 4th century B.C.

As you continue to the top, you'll see the recently restored **ancient Arab** and **medieval fortifications.** From here, you can see all the way to the skyline of Palermo in the west or to Capo d'Orlando in the east. The lookout tower here, now in ruins, was called Torre Caldura, guarding an unfriendly coastline. On a clear day you can see not forever, as in the song, but a stunning view of the Aeolian Islands.

BEACHING IT

Cefalù's crescent-shaped beach is one of the best along the northern coast. Regrettably, it is always packed in summer. In town we prefer **Lido Poseidon.** At the best bar here, **Poseidon,** Lido Poseidon, Via Lungomare Giuseppe Giardino (© **0921-424646**), you can rent umbrellas for 5€ or deck chairs for the same price. It's open daily from May to September. **Splaggia Attrezzata** in town, just off the Lungomare, is another good beach, with brilliant white sand and turquoise shallows. You'll also find free showers there. Other recommended beaches are found west of town at **Spiaggia Settefrati** and **Spiaggia Mazzaforno.**

WHERE TO STAY

If you want to spend the night in Cefalù, and you have wheels, you'll find the hotels outside of town more comfortably satisfying.

Astro Hotel Originally built in a three-story format in 1969, and intelligently renovated several times since then, this is the first hotel many visitors see when they approach Cefalù from its western outskirts. Small-scale and unpretentious, with a hardworking and sensitive staff, it offers well-equipped, albeit simple, guest rooms, each with terrazzo or tile floors and a simple, modern decor with tiled, shower-only bathrooms. Hot water here means tepid. About 30% of the rooms have balconies. Parking (which is usually difficult in the traffic-clogged neighborhoods adjacent to the city's traffic-free inner core) is free and readily available within a walled-in parking lot directly across the street. The hotel lies just uphill from the private beach, and about a 12-minute walk from the city's medieval core.

Via Roma 105, 90015 Cefalù. © **0921-421639.** Fax 0921-423103. www.astrohotel.it. 30 units. 70€–120€ double. Rates include breakfast. Free parking. AE, DC, MC, V. **Amenities:** Restaurant; bar; babysitting; laundry. *In room:* A/C, TV.

Baia del Capitano ★ *Finds* Lying along the sea in a panoramic setting in an olive grove, this excellent choice stands 5km (3 miles) west of Cefalù. The architects designed the hotel to blend in with its setting. There's a private sandy beach 100m (25 ft.) from the hotel. Completely renovated in 2001, the well-run hotel offers midsize guest rooms that have comfortably modern furnishings. Five units come with tubs, the rest with showers. When you're not at the beach, you can seek a cozy retreat in the garden. There's also a sun terrace.

Contrada Mazzaforno, 90015 Cefalù. © **0921-420003.** Fax 0921-420163. www.baiadelcapitano.it. 39 units. 88€–130€ double; 108€–160€ triple. AE, DC, MC, V. **Amenities:** Restaurant; bar; pool; tennis court; room service; babysitting; laundry/dry cleaning. *In room:* A/C, TV, minibar, safe.

Kalura ★ *Kids* In a setting of palm trees, Kalura has something of a North African feel to it. This snug retreat lies 3km (2 miles) east along the coast on a little promontory, a 20-minute walk from the center of Cefalù. Follow the street signs from town to reach it. Run by the same family for nearly 3 decades, it is a friendly, inviting oasis. Guest rooms are midsize and well furnished, and most open onto a sea view. Nothing is too elaborate here, including the simple tiled bathrooms with shower stalls. The hotel also owns a private beach where the swimming is good in unpolluted waters. A special park is reserved for children, one reason that this is a very family-friendly type of place. The hotel is also the most sports conscious in the area, and can arrange excursions to nearby attractions on the island as well.

Via Cavallaro 13, 90015 Contrada Caldura. ✆ 0921-421354. Fax 0921-423122. www.kalura.it. 73 units. 145€ double. Rates include breakfast. AE, DC, MC, V. **Amenities:** Restaurant; 2 bars; pool; tennis; watersports; canoes; pedal boats; mountain bikes; children's park; room service; babysitting; laundry/dry cleaning. *In room:* A/C, TV, hair dryer.

WHERE TO DINE

If you're heading out on an excursion, perhaps to Parco delle Madonie (see below), you can secure the makings of a delightful Sicilian picnic at **Gatta Gaetano Alimentari e Salumeria,** Corso Ruggero 152 (✆ **0921-23156**)—everything except bread, which you'll find sold in many places all over town. This well-stocked deli offers the best of Sicilian cheeses and sausages, along with cured meats, to-die-for olives, and many fruits of the luscious Sicilian harvest.

You might also visit the **Pasticceria Serio Pietro,** V. G. Giglio 29 (✆ **0921-422293**), which makes the best cakes and cookies in town. The shop sells more than a dozen flavors of the most delicious gelato in town as well. Somehow the Italians always seem to make better gelato than anybody else. The drawback here? The staff never went to finishing school.

MODERATE

Al Porticciolo ✦ SICILIAN   At the seafront end of the old town, nearly adjacent to the old port, this cool, shady restaurant is set within a cavelike stone-sided room that used to be a storage point—long before the days of refrigeration—for fresh and salted fish. At lunchtime, you'll want to dine in air-conditioned comfort inside to avoid the heat, but at nighttime (when all vehicular traffic is stopped along this street), opt for an outdoor table. Previous clients have included Italy's prime minister, and a medley of actors and singers well known within Italy. The cooks search out the best of local ingredients—witness the platters of marinated or smoked fish and a *divino* tagliatelle of octopus caught from the nearby rocks. The traditional pasta with sardines—the "faithful friend" of Sicilians—is well prepared here, but we're even fonder of the mixed grill of sardines and shrimp. The cook's country-style kettle of mussel soup is just right for a seafaring town. Grilled radicchio is strangely addictive. The restaurant also serves one of the best versions of *cassata alla Siciliana* (layered sponge cake filled with ricotta cheese, chocolate, and candied fruits) we've ever tasted.

Via Carlo Ortolani di Bordonaro 66. ✆ 0921-021081. Main courses 7€–15€; set-price menus 15€–25€. AE, DC, MC, V. Daily noon–3pm and 7pm–midnight. Closed Nov to mid-Dec.

Kentia ✦✦ ITALIAN   Stylish and airy, this restaurant manages to evoke a bit more glamour, and a lot more style, than some of the less worthy competitors that have cropped up around it. It's a cool and distinguished hideaway from the sometimes oppressive sun, thanks partly to tiled floors, high masonry vaulting, white walls, and an understated elegance. In addition to its many savory dishes, the chefs prepare a daily vegetarian fixed-price menu as well as one devoted entirely to fish. We've sampled both and recommend them heartily. You can, of course, order a la carte. The finest antipasto is a trio of delectably smoked fish: salmon, swordfish, and tuna. The chef searches out the best local ingredients for a dozen pasta dishes homemade daily. The risotto marinara with mussels, clams, shrimp, and squid is super-fresh and super-good, as is the fettuccine with lobster. You'd have to walk to Messina to find swordfish as good as that grilled here. We generally stick to the *pesce del diorno* (catch of the day), which can be grilled to your specifications. For a regional dish, try the roast lamb with sausage and pork.

Via N. Botta 15. *C* **0921-423801**. Reservations recommended. Main courses 5.50€–13€. Set menus 14€–20€. Fixed-price vegetarian menu 14€; fixed-price fish menu 20€. AE, DC, MC, V. Daily June–Sept; Oct–May Tues–Sun noon–3pm and 7pm–1am.

La Brace SICILIAN   Near the Duomo, this has been a landmark restaurant in Cefalù since 1977. The Sicilian cuisine has a number of imaginative Asian touches—a surprise in this part of the world. The restaurant is located in a single, rather narrow storefront positioned on an impossibly narrow cobblestone street about a block downhill from the center of town, off Corso Ruggero.

La Brace is owned and run by a husband-and-wife team, Thea de Haan of Poland and Indonesia and Dietmar Beckers of The Netherlands. The waiters extend a friendly welcome and will even tell you what's good at the time of your visit. With a bow to Tex-Mex cuisine, chili con carne appears on the menu, but we much prefer the gratin of octopus. The filet of turkey came in a sherry sauce a little too sweet for our tastes, but we were won over by the homemade tagliatelle with porcini mushrooms. A mouthwatering specialty is *spiedini di pesce spada,* marinated swordfish that has been roasted with sweet peppers. It's served in a lemony mustard sauce. The meat specialty is tournedos La Brace, beef medallions served rare and tender and cooked with butter-laced pancetta.

The house dessert, justifiably celebrated locally, is a fresh banana doused with orange liqueur and baked, then topped with whipped cream.

Via XXV Novembre 10. *C* **0921-423570**. Reservations recommended. Main courses 5.50€–13€. Set lunch 17€–30€; set dinner 27€–30€. AE, DC, MC, V. Tues–Sun 1–2:30pm and 7–11:30pm.

Osteria del Duomo ★★ SICILIAN/INTERNATIONAL   The most sophisticated and internationally hip restaurant in Cefalù lies right in front of the town's famous cathedral, at the bottom of steps that have been trod upon by early medieval Norman knights and *La Dolce Vita* movie stars. Many of its tables sit in the open air on cobblestones, others under the beamed and vaulted ceiling of the air-conditioned interior. Its owner, Enzo Barranco, used to work for RAI (one of Italy's government-funded media groups); as such, he has always shown a knack for making the sublimely famous feel at home. The queen of Denmark dined here in the 1990s (her framed thank-you note is on display in the dining room). Other luminaries have included Italian pop entertainers Fiorella, Carmen Russo, members of rock 'n' roll band Mattei Bazar (the owners framed a napkin a member of the band illustrated on-site), director Franco Zeffirelli, and the German-born Hollywood star Klaus Maria Brandauer.

The tasty fare reflects Sicilian traditions and is fashioned with the finest ingredients. We think the chefs here top those at La Brace (Michelin's Cefalù favorite)—they will enthrall you with their smoked fish. We've found their seafood salads to be the town's best and the ideal food on a hot summer day. Serious carnivores gravitate to the truly excellent carpaccio of beef. Among the risottos, we like ours studded with fresh seafood. Veal is stuffed and rolled before it's sautéed in a roulade. Count on freshly made salads and desserts as well.

Via Seminario 3. *C* **0921-421838**. Reservations recommended Sat–Sun. Main courses 8€–15€. AE, DC, MC, V. Tues–Sun noon–midnight. Closed mid-Nov to mid-Dec.

INEXPENSIVE

Al Grabbiano SICILIAN/SEAFOOD   Unlike most of the other restaurants in Cefalù, which are tucked into hideaway alleys within the town's medieval core, this one sits directly across a quiet street from the sands of the town's most popular beach, allowing sun-kissed diners access throughout the day and evening. The venue evokes a woodsy-looking tavern or beer hall, in many cases with full-breeze access to the outdoors. It contains three distinctly different seating areas, each surrounded by heavy timbers, dark-stained wood, and exposed stone, and all interconnected via a common area with a bar, service areas, and food displays. The regular menu features regional classics, as well as dishes from other parts of the island and the mainland. Fresh fish is a menu constant, and tastes best grilled and served with fresh vegetables such as spinach or fava beans. One of our favorite items is zucchini flowers, which the chefs are skilled at either deep-frying or grilling. The mainstay of the north coast, swordfish, is served here with a tasty onion sauce. For us, no pastas in town compare to this place's linguine with fresh shrimp, clams, and mussels.

Via Lungomare Giardina 7. ℂ 0921-21495. Reservations not necessary. Main courses 4€–8.50€. AE, DC, MC, V. Daily noon–3pm and 7–11pm.

L'Antica Corte SICILIAN   The authentic Sicilian cuisine served here is market-fresh and satisfying, in spite of the restaurant's slight touristic bent. The waiters, for example, appear with red bandannas and sashes like those worn by the Saracen pirates of yore. If the weather is right, try to get one of the tables set under grapevines in the old courtyard. Otherwise, you'll find the air-conditioned tables inside a welcome relief from the heat. The pizzas are among the best in town—for a treat, try the "Drago" with spicy sausage. Among the number of tempting pasta dishes are one with hot peppers *(all'arrabbiata)* and another with small shrimp, mushrooms, and a dousing of limoncello for extra flavor. The best bet is the catch of the day, which the chefs flavor with herbs and grill as you desire it. Meat eaters might prefer a tender grilled filet of steak or the more complicated *filetto Bisanzio* in a mushroom and cream sauce.

Cortile Pepe 7, off Corso Ruggero. ℂ 0921-423228. Reservations recommended. Pizza 3.60€–8.20€; menu turistica 12€; main courses 6.20€–9.80€. AE, MC, V. Fri–Wed noon–2pm and 7–11:30pm. Closed Nov.

Lo Scoglio Ubraico (The Drunken Rock) SICILIAN   This restaurant lies high atop a rocky cliff at the edge of the old town. Walk in boldly and bypass the less desirable tables in the long and narrow dining room. Near the back, you'll find a staircase that meanders down onto a terrace perched atop jagged rocks, just above sea level. Overlooking the fortifications lining either side of the old port, the terrace is about 15m (50 ft.) downhill from the rest of the dining room. If a seat is available, this is where you should sit. Menu items are well-prepared, albeit relatively predictable in light of the roughly equivalent food served in the town's other restaurants. A tangy mussel soup might tempt you before you proceed to the mixed grill of either fish or meat. The house-style tagliatelle is understandably a local favorite, served with a well-flavored mussel and cream sauce. For meat aficionados, the chef will grill you a good filet of steak.

Via Carlo Ortolani di Bordonaro 2–4. ℂ 0921-423370. Reservations recommended. Main courses 5.20€–10€. AE, DC, MC, V. Daily July–Aug; Sept–June Wed–Mon noon–2:30pm and 7pm–midnight.

CEFALÙ AFTER DARK

Many of the townspeople like to go home, eat their catch of the day, and retire early after watching some TV. The liveliest spot in town is **Be Bop Pub, Bar & Bistro,** Via Nicolà Botta 4 (ℂ 0921-923972). The rock 'n' roll music and youthful (or at least young-at-heart) crowd in this woodsy-looking, English-style pub pull you very far away from the medieval setting of antique Cefalù. Opt for a cocktail or beer on tap, crepes, sandwiches, salads, or a plate of pasta. It's open daily from 11am to 4am, but closed every Monday between October and March. Snack items, salads, and pastas cost 1.70€ to 5€; beer 1.90€ to 4€, depending on the size.

EASY EXCURSIONS

On Cefalù's doorstep lies an array of some of Sicily's greatest attractions, including the national park **Parco della Madonie,** the ruins of ancient **Tindaris** (which date from 1500 B.C.), and the ceramic capital of **Santo Stefano di Camastra,** among many other sights.

If you're contemplating a trip, you can easily schedule 3 nights for Cefalù, allowing 1 day to explore the town and another 2 days to see the highlights of the attractions in the environs.

PARCO NATURALE REGIONALE DELLE MADONIE ★★   Since 1989 some 39,679 hectares (8,007 acres) of the most beautiful land in Sicily has been set aside as a national park. The park begins just 6km (3¾ miles) south of Cefalù. You can explore it on your own if you have plenty of time, or let **Barranco Tours** (© **0921-421525**) in Cefalù do it for you by guided bus. The staff there has preselected the beautiful spots and historic attractions for you. They call the tour "Unknown Sicily" and price it at 37€ for a full-day excursion, including a visit to the Romanesque monastery of Gibilmanna, a working Capuchin monastery with 20 monks.

The park is called a "botanic paradise," and contains more than half of the 2,600 species known in Sicily. Fauna is represented by 65% of the nesting birds and all the mammals that call Sicily home. Some of the most ancient rocks and mountains in Sicily are found here, along with some of the most spectacular peaks. Among them, **Pizzo Carbonara,** at 1,979m (6,493 ft.), is the highest mountain in Sicily outside of Mount Etna.

The park is far from a wilderness—it is inhabited and contains any number of charming villages. To reach it from Cefalù, follow the road directions south for 14km (8¾ miles) to the **Santuario di Gibilmanna.** From the belvedere at this town in front of the little 17th-century church, you can take in a **panoramic view** ★★ of the Madonie, including the peak of Pizzo Carbonara.

The Santuario di Gibilmanna is a shrine to the Virgin Mary. The Madonna is said to have shown signs of life in the 18th century when she was restoring sight to blind pilgrims and speech to a mute. Since the Vatican confirmed this claim, Gibilmanna has been one of the most important shrines in Sicily, drawing the devout.

After a view, continue southeast following the signs to **Castelbuono,** an idyllic town that grew around a *castello* constructed in the 1300s. You can stop over to visit its historic core, **Piazza Margherita.** The church here, **Madrice Vecchia,** dates from the 14th century, when it was built on the ruins of a pagan temple.

If you arrive during the lunch hour, your best bet for a bite to eat is **Romittaggio,** Località San Guglielmo Sud (© **0921-671323**), lying 5km (3 miles) south of Castelbuono. Specializing in simple but good mountain food, the restaurant is installed in a monastery from the Middle Ages. In summer you can request a table in the arcades of the cloister. Meals range in price from 25€ to 32€. The restaurant is closed from June 15 to July 15 and on Wednesdays.

The road continues south to **Petralia Soprana** ★★, at 1,147m (3,762 ft.) the loftiest town in Madonie and one of the best-preserved medieval villages of

Sicily, with narrow streets and houses of local stone. A grand belvedere is found at Piazza del Popolo, with a **stunning vista** 🌟🌟 toward Enna in the east.

You can also visit the church of **Santa Maria di Loreto,** at the end of Via Loreto, built on the site of a Saracen fortress and framed by a set of campaniles (bell towers). In back of the church is **Madonie's greatest panorama** 🌟🌟🌟, with glorious views of volcanic Mount Etna.

The next stopover is the similarly named **Petralia Sottana,** overlooking the River Imera Valley. This little village is perched on a rocky spur 1,000m (3,280 ft.) above sea level. This is the headquarters of the national park service, **Ente Parco,** Corso Paolo Alliata 16 (✆ **0921-680840**). The office is open Monday through Friday from 9:30am to 1:30pm and 3:30 to 6:30pm.

At this point, head west along S120, stopping at **Polizzi Generosa,** another hilltop magnificently situated on a limestone spur. The **view** 🌟🌟🌟 at Piazza XXVII Maggio is one of the most spectacular in Madonie, taking in its loftiest peaks and the scenic valley of the River Himera.

Here you can begin your journey back north to Cefalù, passing through little **Scillato** until you reach **Collesano,** a holiday resort where the aura of the Middle Ages still lingers.

It is deceivingly simple on its exterior, but the **Chiesa Madre,** reached by going up a flight of stairs, is filled with art treasures. The church contains masterpieces by Gaspare Vazzano, who signed his name "Zoppo di Gangi." This 16th-century painter created a **cycle of frescoes** 🌟 illustrating scenes from the lives of Jesus Christ, St. Paul, and St. Peter. He also painted another magnificent canvas, *Santa Maria degli Angeli* 🌟, in the north aisle.

After viewing Collesano, you can continue north until you reach autostrada A20, which will take you back to Cefalù, your best base for the night.

CASTEL DI TUSA   Lying on the sea, this little town is a pleasant enough stopover but only of minor interest. What makes it worth your time is a stay for the night at one of Sicily's most remarkable hotels (see below). You can also use the hotel as a base for exploring Madonie Park (see above).

The town opens onto one of the most beautiful "bayscapes" on the island. But not a lot happens here. There's room for some sea bathers, plus a handful of sleepy trattorie, but don't expect a grandiose collection of Greek ruins or a baronial motif. Despite a ruined feudal fortress that rises from the town's highest hill, Castel di Tusa might pass for an uneventful fishing village surrounded by rocky, scrub-covered landscape along the Tyrrhenian Coast. Descend a steeply inclined road from the coastal highway to a quiet half-moon-shaped harbor, whose biggest attraction is the hotel described below.

You'll really need a car for getting around the area. You can take autostrada A20 from Cefalù, which becomes the SS113 for its final stretch to Castel di Tusa, a distance of 25km (16 miles) east of Palermo. The town is more difficult to reach by train. There's a stopover at the pottery capital of Santo Stefano di Camastra (see below) on the Palermo-to-Messina run. But from there you'll have to reach Castel di Tusa, a distance of 13km (8 miles), by local train.

WHERE TO STAY

Atelier Sul Mare 🌟🌟🌟   The most unusual hotel in Sicily is now famous, thanks to massive publicity on TV stations throughout Europe. Sometimes defined as "an arts-oriented ashram," it occupies a boxy-looking, white-painted, concrete building that was erected in the 1960s as a conventional hotel with access to a nearby beach. Any vestiges of its original decor were ripped out long ago by the iconoclastic owner, Messina-born Antonio Presti, an artist's agent and self-anointed "Ambassador to Beauty." Today the hotel evokes a powerful allure that artfully combines aspects of Bauhaus architecture, Andy Warhol–style pop art, Timothy Leary–inspired psychedelics, hints of flagrant and very permissive sexuality, and goodly doses of Italian-based socialist politics.

Enter an all-black-and-white lobby, whose only adornments are hundreds of photocopies of articles about the place.

About 25 of the hotel rooms are comfortable, well-decorated, "conventional" units, each with original art, tasteful colors, and a sense of whimsy and abandon. The other 15 rooms were each decorated by an artist who lived on the premises for several months while completing the work. Examples include Luigi Mainolfi's statement about passion—a room that's entirely sheathed in terra-cotta-colored pottery shards, whose psychic heat contrasts with a big-windowed view of the very blue sea outside. The only furnishing in the room is a simple, unadorned bed that evokes some ancient fertility rite.

A guest room decorated in honor of filmmaker and gay activist Pasolini was conceived as a mud-built grotto that might remind you—thanks to the Arabic-language translation of his poetry that decorates the walls—of a miniature mosque. The effect manages to combine a sense of social outrage with psychic peace. A sinuously curved all-black room by Chilean artist Raoul Ruiz features a circular bed and a square-shaped skylight whose blasts of sunlight represent a spiritual liberty from oppressive governments and cultures. A three-sided *Sala Trinacria,* by Mauro Staccioli, outfitted only in triangular shapes and tones of black and red, evokes the shape of Sicily itself in a bizarre but thought-provoking room suitable for either a mid-life crisis or an emotional and spiritual rebirth. Each of the 15 rooms is witty, idiosyncratic, and unlike any other hotel room in Italy. You'll find a bar and restaurant on-site. Occasional classes in pottery and ceramics are held whenever enough clients sign up.

Via Cesare Battisti 4, 98070 Castel di Tusa. ℭ **0921-334295.** Fax 0921-334283. www.ateliersulmare.com. 40 units. Designer-style room 160€ double; conventional unit 120€ double. Rates include breakfast. Free parking. DC, MC, V. **Amenities:** Restaurant; bar. *In room:* A/C, no phone.

SANTO STEFANO DI CAMASTRA   Heading east of Cefalù for 33km (20 miles), you approach one of the ceramic capitals of Sicily. A visit here can easily be tied in with a trip to the previous stopover at Castel di Tusa. Santo Stefano lies 13km (8 miles) east of Castel di Tusa.

If you're driving, follow A20 east from Cefalù, which in time becomes the SS113 on its approach to Santo Stefano. The town also lies on the main rail link from Palermo/Cefalù, heading east into Messina.

Santo Stefano lies at the western end of the **Parci di Nebrodi,** one of the natural beauty spots lying to the east of Parco della Madonie (see above). Following a disastrous landslide in 1682, the town was laid out in a geometric grid said to have been copied from the gardens of Versailles in France.

On the approach roads in and out of town, you'll find dozens of vendors hawking ceramics and pottery. These wares are often stacked in "mountains" along the sides of the roads. The ceramics industry grew here because the area in the hinterlands is said to have some of the best clay in Sicily—locals claim it's "the best in Italy."

Most of the pottery styles are traditional, but others are glaringly *moderno.* Would you believe a set of tableware devoted to Princess Di? What about ceramics with illustrations from Madonna's controversial book on *Sex*—a bit much in book form but completely outrageous when translated into dishware.

In this vast array of merchandise, not all is of equal quality. Some items are even shoddily made and filled with imperfections. Examine each piece before buying it, and be prepared to haggle over prices. The local vendors expect that from you, and are skilled at overcoming your sales resistance.

If the many choices of wares overwhelm you, do as we do and head for the one shop we've found the most reliable over the years: **Ceramiche Franco,** Via Nazionale 8 (© **0921-337222**), owned by the Franco family for generations. Craftsmanship and skill go into their ceramics, which are inspired by various artistic movements in Italy, especially the Renaissance and the baroque. Hours are Monday through Saturday from 9am to 7:30pm.

Before actually buying anything, you might want to familiarize yourself with the area's wares by visiting the **Museum della Ceramica** ⍟, Via Palazzo (© **0921-331110**), which lies in the heart of town in the Palazzo Trabia, the former residence of the duke of Camastra. The restored palace itself is a thing of beauty, especially its **tiled floors** ⍟, **antique furnishings**—mainly from the 1700s—and beautifully **frescoed ceilings.** Extravagant sculptures such as *Andare,* a cluster of five "soldiers" depicted sinking into the ground, highlight the displays along with large plates and figurines. You'll learn much about how wide and varied ceramics can be and the technique and skills that go into making them. Admission to the museum is 3€. It's open from May to September Monday through Saturday from 9am to 1pm and 4 to 8pm. From October to April, hours are Monday through Saturday from 9am to 1pm and 3:30 to 7:30pm.

TYNDARIS ⍟ At Capo Tindari, approximately 85km (52 miles) from Cefalù, stand the ruins of Tyndaris, on a lonely, rocky promontory overlooking Golfo di Patti. It was known to the ancients since it was founded by Dionysius the Elder in 396 B.C. after a victory over the Carthaginians. For a long time it formed a protective union with its ally, Syracuse, until that eastern Sicilian city fell to the Romans in 256 B.C.

The most serious excavations of the site began after World War II, although digs were launched much less successfully in the 19th century.

The **view** ⍟⍟ alone is almost reason to go, stretching from Milazzo in the east to Capo Calavà in the west. On clear days you have stunning vistas of the Aeolian Islands, with Vulcano the nearest.

Tyndaris has had a rough time of it. Destroyed partially by a landslide in the 1st century A.D. , it suffered an earthquake in A.D. 365. The Arabs in the 10th century were particularly vicious in destroying its buildings.

Most of the ruins you see today date from the days of the Roman empire, including the **basilica,** whose exact function remains unknown. In rather good condition and lying just beyond the basilica is a **Roman villa.** You can still see the original mosaics on the floor.

Cut into a hill at the end of town is a wide **theater,** built by the Greeks in the late 4th century B.C. To-the-death contests between gladiators were held here in Imperial days.

The **Insula Romana** contains the ruins of baths, patrician villas with fragments of mosaics, and what may have been taverns or drinking halls. Beyond the entrance to the site on the left is a little **Antiquarium,** exhibiting artifacts dug up on the site. You can also see the ruins of defensive walls constructed during the dreadful reign of Dionysius.

The ruins are open daily from 9am to 1 hour before sunset. Admission is 2.10€ for adults, 1.05€ for students and children.

The site is also a place of pilgrimage, with the devout flocking to the **Santuario di Tindari,** containing a Byzantine Black Virgin, or the *Madonna Nera.* Legend has it that this Madonna washed up on the shores of Tyndaris centuries ago. The inscription beneath the icon reads (in English translation), "I am black but I am beautiful." Is this where the Black Panthers of the 1960s got their catchphrase? The sanctuary (℃ **0941-369003**) is open Monday through Friday from 6:45am to 12:30pm and 2:30 to 7pm, Saturday and Sunday from 6:45am to 12:30pm and 2:30 to 8pm. Admission is free.

The site is best reached by private car. From Cefalù, motorists continue east approximately 85km (52 miles) along the main coastal route (A20/SS113). Getting here by public transport can be awkward: Buses come from the little town of Patti, 6km (3¾ miles) to the west. Patti itself lies 26km (16 miles) east of Capo d'Orlando. Buses arrive and depart from a parking lot 1km (½ mile) from the ruins. A shuttle connects the parking lot with the ruins.

There is a little tourist office at the site at Via Teatro Greco 15 (℃ **0941-369184**), with limited information.

3 Termini Imerese

40km (25 miles) E of Palermo

Long known for its thermal waters, this town might merit a couple hours of your time. Although it is used mainly as a base for those wishing to take side trips from here, it does offer a few treasures.

Cáccamo, to the south, is one of the island's biggest and most magnificent bastions, and Himera, to the east, is the site of the ruins of a 7th-century-B.C. Greek settlement. For the dedicated sightseer, both Cáccamo and Himera are more rewarding than Termini Imerese itself, whose name comes from the Latin, *Thermae Himerenses,* meaning "Hot Springs of Himera." Roman soldiers often languished here, enjoying the thermal waters. Among those who came for the cure was the Greek poet Pindar. In a rather fanciful endorsement, Diodorus claimed that the springs were created by three nymphs and that Hercules was the first to enjoy the baths.

The town is split into two sectors—**Termini Bassa** (Lower Termini) and **Termini Alta** (Upper Termini). The upper town comprises most of the spa's historic center, whereas the transportation hub for the area is the lower town. Once enclosed by fortified walls, the city lost most of its charms to the creeping industrialization that followed the end of World War II, including some hideously ugly petrochemical factories.

ESSENTIALS

GETTING THERE   By Train   Trains arrive from Palermo on the main Palermo–Messina line at the rate of one every hour (trip time: 20 min.). For rail information, call ℃ **892021.**

By Bus   Buses run by **SAIS,** Via Balsamo 16 (℃ **091-6166028**), in Palermo, make frequent runs to Termini Imerese throughout the day.

By Car   From Palermo, head east along A19, the Palermo–Messina autostrada. The exit for Termini Imerese is clearly marked.

VISITOR INFORMATION   Go to the **Termini Imerese Tourist Office,** Cortile Maltese (℃ **091-8128111**), open Monday through Friday from 7:30am to 2:45pm.

Moments **Palms, Pines, Ficus & Roman Remains**

In back of the cathedral, Via Belvedere leads up to a panoramic terrace offering one of the **grandest seascapes** ★★ along the Tyrrhenian coast. The sea is set against the backdrop of Monte Calógero. From here you'll also have a vista of the lower town and the port. Try not to let the industrialization spoil this otherwise idyllic vision for you. A short walk to your left leads to the "always locked" church dedicated to **Santa Caterina d'Alessandria** in the 14th century. Continue along at this point to the park, **Villa Palmieri,** laid out in 1845 with its shade trees. Here you will see the ruins of an ancient Roman **curia.** Follow Via Anfiteatro from the park to the ruins of a **Roman amphitheater** from the 1st century A.D.

EXPLORING THE TOWN

Duomo Largely rebuilt in the 17th century, this cathedral has been much modified over the years. Its facade was designed to fit a quartet of early-16th-century statues (the present ones are copies). The facade dates mainly from 1912. Inside are some treasures, most notably 18th-century sculptures including a marble relief, *Madonna del Ponte* ★, found in the fourth chapel on the right. It was the work of Ignazio Marabitti in 1842.

In the Chapel of San Bartolomeo, look for an elaborate **Venetian rococo sedan chair,** and in another chapel, this one dedicated to the Immaculate Conception, seek out a **wooden statue** by Quattrocchi from 1799. The *Crucifix* at the main altar was painted on both sides by Pietro Ruzzolone in 1484.

Piazza del Duomo. No phone. Free admission. Daily 9am–7pm.

Museo Civico ★ Founded in 1873 in an abandoned 14th-century palazzo, this is one of the finest regional museums along the northern coast of Sicily. A visit here is like taking a class in the art, archaeology, and natural history of the area. Prehistory is even represented here, with artifacts recovered from nearby caves inhabited in Paleolithic and Neolithic times on display. A large salon is filled with Hellenistic and Roman pottery. The most precious relics are artifacts removed from the nearby ruins of Himera, including the **head of a lion** ★ that came from the Temple of Victory between 480 and 460 B.C.

A large stone slab with Arabic inscriptions may have been mounted over the gates of Termini Imerese during the days of its Saracen rule. You can also see the lead pipes used by the Romans for their plumbing (the lead eventually poisoned them), and other exhibits include columns, mosaics, reliefs, and sarcophagi. Look for a Byzantine triptych and paintings by Mattia Preti, pupil of Caravaggio. A most impressive triptych, *Madonna and Saints* ★, is by Gaspare da Pesaro from 1453.

Via del Museo Civico. ℂ **091-8128279.** Free admission. Tues–Sat 9am–1pm and 3–6pm; Sun 8am–1pm.

WHERE TO STAY

Grand Hotel delle Terme ★ This hotel from the 19th century stands right over the spring whose famous spa waters won an endorsement from Plutarch. Even today you can enjoy the curative waters that the Roman soldiers of yore did. In the basement is a thermal spa where such treatments as mud therapy are offered. Built in 1890 but renovated in 1989, the hotel offers modernized rooms with traditional furnishings, mostly in teak. Half of the guest rooms come with bathrooms with tubs, the other half bathrooms with showers. The hotel lies in the commercial center of the lower town near the port.

Piazza delle Terme 2, Termini Imerese, 90018. ℭ **091-8113557.** Fax 091-8113107. 69 units. 62€–73€ double; suite 30€ extra. AE, DC, MC, V. **Amenities:** Restaurant; bar; pool; gym; sauna; salon; room service; massage; laundry/dry cleaning. In room: A/C, TV, minibar.

WHERE TO DINE

Ristorante Pub Santi e Peccatori SICILIAN/SEAFOOD   In the heart of town, right near the cathedral square, this restaurant is the best in town (although some prefer to patronize the dining room of the Grand Hotel delle Terme; see above). Against an 18th-century backdrop, the chef prepares any number of tempting dishes for discriminating palates, often visitors from Palermo, who know of this restaurant's charm and attractively priced cuisine. Sicilians claim that the waters of Termini Imerese make the best pasta in Sicily. They may be right: We still recall a memorable spaghetti marinara with shrimp, mussels, and—as an added surprise—pistachios. Another pasta delight is fettuccine tricolore with fresh mint, tomatoes, pine nuts, mussels, and a velvety cream sauce. For a main course, we recommend the fresh fish of the day grilled with aromatic herbs. Any number of seafood dishes round out the menu. After midnight the restaurant becomes the most popular pub in town, with rock and pop music played in the background.

Piazza del Duomo. ℭ **091-8190375.** Reservations not needed. Main courses 4.50€–5.50€. No credit cards. Wed–Mon noon–5pm and 8pm–4am.

EASY EXCURSIONS

You may opt to spend less time in Termini Imerese and more hours in its environs, exploring two of the north coast's most impressive attractions: Himera and Cáccamo.

HIMERA   This is the site of a 7th-century Greek settlement, lying 15km (8 miles) east along the coast. These ruins are famous for the remains of the **Tempio della Vittoria (Temple of Victory)** ✫, lying on a coastal plain at the mouth of the Imera River off Route SS113 (signposted). Frankly, these ruins are not as impressive as those of Solunto outside Palermo (see chapter 4), and its temple is certainly less spectacular than the fabled temples of Agrigento and Segesta (see chapters 12 and 13, respectively), but they're worth an hour or so of your time.

In 480 B.C. Himera was the site of one of the major battles of Sicily. The Greeks had settled in the east, the Carthaginians in the west. The Greeks from Agrigento and Syracuse defeated a massive army led by Hamilcar, who was killed in battle. The Tempio della Vittoria was constructed to honor this Greek victory. The labor was supplied by the Carthaginians taken prisoner. The triumph was short-lived. In 409 B.C., Hamilcar's nephew, Hannibal, attacked Himera in revenge for his uncle's death. He razed the city, killing most of its inhabitants.

Himera's temple contains little more than its foundation, with no standing columns. Yet the setting and the view make it worth a visit, especially if you have the imagination to bring it alive. If your imagination fails you, you can visit a modern antiquarium that shows diagrams of how the temple looked in its heyday. The remains of two other temples are also found in this archaeological park.

From Termini Imerese you can take one of four daily buses run by **Mancini** (ℭ **091-8144497**) to the temple site, a round-trip costing 3.40€. Buses leave from the train station at Termini Imerese. The site, charging 2€, is open Monday through Saturday from 9am to 1 hour before sunset and on Sunday from 9am to 1pm. For more information, phone ℭ **091-8140128.**

CÁCCAMO   The Middle Ages live on at **Castello Cáccamo** ⊛, a huge 12th-century fortress overlooking the San Leonardo River Valley. Dominating the tranquil village of Cáccamo, this feudal castle was built by the Normans on the site of an older Saracen fortress. The entrance is from Via Termitana on a rocky spur.

With its massive towers and battlements, the gray stone *castello* looks like something Disney might have created, but it's the real thing. On a steep cliff, with views in all directions, it was basically reconstructed in the 16th century. This is the greatest fortress in Sicily and one of the most majestic in all of southern Italy.

The castle has some 130 rooms, its most impressive being **Sala della Congiura.** In 1160 the barons met here plotting to overthrow William I ("the Bad"), the Norman king. You can visit the theater hall, the court chapel, the 17th-century residence of various lords, the gatehouse, the knight's house, the keep, and the guard tower as well as the ramp wall. The castle is rather bare-bones inside, but worth seeing is the **panoramic view** ⊛ from the tower, Torre Mastra.

The castle, on Corso Umberto (☏ **091-8103248**), is open daily from 9:15am to 12:15pm and 3:15 to 5:30pm, charging no admission. It lies 12km (8 miles) south of Termini Imerese and 52km (32 miles) southeast of Palermo.

If you're driving along the Palermo–Catania autostrada, the exit for Cáccamo is signposted, a distance of 10km (6 miles) to the south. Buses bound for Cáccamo leave throughout the day from Termini Imerese's main train station.

After visiting the castle, save an hour or so to walk around the medieval village. The highlight is the main square, **Piazza Duomo** ⊛, built on two different levels. The highest part contains a spectacular complex of structures, including the 17th-century palace, **Palazzo del Monte di Pietà,** flanked on the right by **Chiesa delle Anime Sante del Purgatorio** and on the left by **Oratorio del Santissimo Sacramento.** The whole square looks like a stage set.

On the western side of the square is the town's most interesting church, **Chiesa Madre,** open Monday through Saturday from 8am to 1pm. Dating from 1090, it was largely rebuilt in the 1400s and given a heavily baroque overlay centuries later. The church contains some treasures, including a painting from 1641 by Mattia Stomer, called the *Miracle of Sant'Isidoro Agricola.*

For information, contact the **Ufficio Turismo del Commune di Cáccamo,** Piazza Duomo (☏ **091-8103248**), open in July and August Monday through Friday from 7:30am to 2pm, Thursday from 3 to 6:30pm. September to June, hours are Tuesday through Friday from 8am to 2pm, Tuesday and Thursday from 3 to 6pm.

WHERE TO DINE

Castellana *(Value* SICILIAN   This is the finest dining choice in town. But since restaurants at Cáccamo are very limited, don't get your hopes up. What you're served is hearty, filling, and affordable. The restaurant is located in the stables of the castle, which gives it a medieval aura. A number of Sicilian dishes are prepared well. Launch your repast with the very fresh antipasti or delectable smoked swordfish. The pasta selections are the best, with more than a dozen varieties prepared fresh every day. Our favorites are *penne Castellana* (pasta with mushrooms, sausage, olives, and ham), *spaccatelle con il Macco* (pasta with a fava-bean mash), or *spaccatelle* with swordfish in a mint-flavored tomato sauce with eggplant. The chefs also make 55 different pizzas.

Piazza Caduti 4. (☏ **091-8148667**. Reservations recommended on Sat. Main courses 4.20€–6€. Fixed-price menu 15€. AE, DC, MC, V. Tues–Sun noon–3pm and 5pm–1am.

7

The Aeolian Islands

The Aeolian Islands *(Isole Eolie o Lipari)* have been inhabited for more than 3,000 years, in spite of volcanic activity that even now causes the earth to issue forth sulfuric belches, streams of molten lava, and hissing clouds of steam. **Lipari** (36 sq. km/14 sq. miles) is the largest and most developed island, **Stromboli** (13 sq. km/5 sq. miles) is the most distant and volcanically active, and **Vulcano** (21 sq. km/8 sq. miles), with its brooding, potentially volatile cone and therapeutic mud baths, is the closest island to the Sicilian "mainland." The remaining islands (**Salina, Filicudi, Alicudi,** and **Panarea**) offer only bare-bones facilities and are visited mainly by day-trippers, if at all.

Despite the potential for volcanic activity, the area attracts visitors (mainly Germans and Italians) with crystalline waters that offer prime snorkeling, scuba, and spearfishing, and photogenic beaches composed of hot black sand and rocky outcroppings jutting into the Tyrrhenian Sea. The volcanoes themselves offer hikers the thrill of peering into a bubbling crater.

Ancient Greek sailors believed that these seven windswept islands were the home of Aeolus, god of the winds. He supposedly lived in a cave on Vulcano, keeping the winds of the world in a bag to be opened only with great caution. "All the winds of the world" do seem to converge here at times. When most visitors arrive in summer, however, the air is likely to be still. Until tourists began to arrive, the Aeolian Islands were one tough place to make a living. Many of its inhabitants long ago emigrated to a better life in the United States or Australia. Even today the islands remain sparsely populated.

Because of frequent ferry and hydrofoil service, the Aeolian Islands are easy to reach from the Sicilian mainland. The conquering hordes descend here in summer, with much overcrowding because of limited accommodations (hence, reservations are important). We prefer the less crowded times of late May, early June, and September. We've also made several winter visits when most tourist businesses are closed. In winter the island is sometimes bathed in brilliant sunshine. At other times the winds blow furiously, and the islands can be lashed by storms, especially between the months of October and March. The sea can be so turbulent that ferry and hydrofoil service to mainland Sicily is suspended, and you might find yourself stranded.

GETTING THERE **Ferries** and **hydrofoils** service all the Aeolian Islands from the port of Milazzo, on the northeastern coast of Sicily 32km (20 miles) west of Messina. **Società Siremar,** Via Dei Mille in Milazzo (© **090-9283242**), and **Società SNAV,** Via Rizzo (© **090-9287821**), operate ferry and hydrofoil routes.

The Milazzo–Vulcano–Lipari–Salina ferry lines leave Milazzo four to six times daily from 7am to 6:30pm. It takes 1½ hours to reach Vulcano, and a one-way ticket costs 7.25€. Lipari lies 2 hours from Milazzo; tickets cost 7.50€ one-way.

To reach Stromboli, take the Milazzo–Panarea–Stromboli line, departing Milazzo at 7am Tuesday

through Saturday, and at 2:30pm Monday, Wednesday, Thursday, Saturday, and Sunday. The Stromboli trip takes 5 hours and costs 11€ one-way.

The Milazzo–Vulcano–Lipari–Salina hydrofoil line reaches Vulcano in 30 minutes; a one-way ticket costs 12€. It takes 1 hour to reach Lipari and costs 12€ one-way. Siremar makes the trip 6 to 12 times daily from 6:05am to 7pm, and SNAV makes six runs daily from 7:30am to 7pm.

To reach Stromboli, use the Milazzo–Panarea–Stromboli hydrofoil line, which takes 2½ hours and costs 17€ one-way.

For more information about ferry and hydrofoil connections, call ℂ **081-3172999** or ℂ **199-123199** (within Italy only).

If you're driving from Messina in the east, take S113 west to Palermo until you come to the turnoff for the port at Milazzo.

1 Lipari ★★

37km (23 miles) N of Milazzo, 41km (25 miles) W of Messina

Homer called it "a floating island, a wall of bronze and splendid smooth sheer cliffs." The offspring of seven volcanic eruptions, Lipari is the largest of the Aeolians and is also the name of the island's only real town. It's the administrative headquarters of the Aeolians (except autonomous Salina). The town sits on a plateau of red volcanic rock on the southeastern shore, framed by two beaches, **Marina Lunga,** which functions as the harbor, and **Marina Corta.**

Nearly all activity is centered in Lipari town, which contains the largest concentration of tourist facilities in all the Aeolian Islands, and as such makes the best base for exploring the entire archipelago. There are also four other villages, including **Canneto,** which lies only 2km (1¼ miles) north of Lipari town. **Acquacalda** is found on the northern tip of the island. Opening onto the sea, and to the village's immediate southwest, lies **Quattropani,** which is inland. If you're heading southeast from Quattropani back to Lipari town, you will pass through the small town of **Pianoconte.**

Marina Lunga and Marina Corta lie on either side of the *castello,* or cliff-top citadel, still surrounded by walls built in the 1500s for defensive purposes. Inside these walls are the Duomo, the archaeological museum (the major sight on the island), and two decaying baroque churches.

The major artery of Lipari town, **Corso Vittorio Emanuele,** goes north-south and is the site of most of the businesses catering to visitors, including bars, banks, and trattorie.

ESSENTIALS

GETTING AROUND Ferries from Milazzo dock at the deepwater port of Marina Lunga, and hydrofoils pull in at Marina Corta. Much of what there is to see, aside from the island's scenic wonders, lies between these two small ports. Lipari is serviced by a limited bus network.

Buses leave from Marina Lunga about every hour (more frequently in summer), taking you across the island. No point on the island is less than a half-hour ride away. A bus schedule is available at **Urso Guglielmo,** Via Cappuccini 9 (© **090-9811262**), lying above Marina Lunga. Tickets costing 1.55€ are purchased onboard from the driver. Urso buses also operate tours of the island in summer from the beginning of July until the end of September. Three buses at a time leave at 9:30am, 11:30am, and 5pm, costing 3.60€ for the circuit. Along the way you'll pass the highlights of Lipari's scenery. It's also possible to summon one of the independently operated taxis, most of which are found at Marina Corta.

A final transportation option is to rent a bike (16€ daily) or motor scooter (62€ daily, not including fuel). A security deposit is required: either a large sum, a credit card, or a passport. Two rental outlets include **Da Marcello,** Via Sottomonastero, Marina Lunga (© **090-9811234**); and **Da Tullio,** Via Amendola 22, Marina Lunga (© **090-9880540**).

VISITOR INFORMATION The tourist office in Lipari is at Via Vittorio Emanuele 202 (© **090-9880095**). In July and August it's open daily from 8am to 2pm. Monday through Saturday it is also open from 4:30 to 10pm. From September to June, hours are Monday through Friday from 8am to 2pm and 4:30 to 7:30pm, Saturday from 8am to 2pm.

FAST FACTS **Ferry** and **hydrofoil** tickets are available at Siremar offices at Via Mariano Amendola at Marina Lunga (© **090-9811312**) and at the Terminal Aliscafi at Marina Corta (© **090-9812200**). Hours are Monday through Friday from 9am to 1pm and 4:30 to 7:30pm. The two major **pharmacies** are Farmacia Morsillo, Via Marina Garibaldi 72 (© **090-9811428**), and Meccio Giuseppe, Via Roma Alicudi (© **090-9889689**). Both are open Monday through Friday from 9am to 1pm and 5 to 9pm. Pharmacies operate on a rotational system Saturday and Sunday, posting the designated pharmacy in shop windows and on the doors of the drugstores themselves. For a **hospital** emergency, call © **090-98851,** for **first aid,** © **090-9885267.** For the assistance of the local *Carabinieri,* call © **090-9811333.** The **post office** is at Corso Vittorio Emanuele 207 (© **090-9811379**)

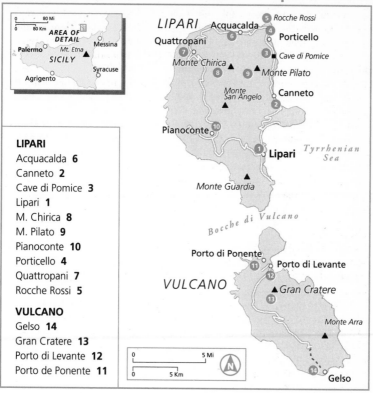

LIPARI

Acquacalda **6**

Canneto **2**

Cave di Pomice **3**

Lipari **1**

M. Chirica **8**

M. Pilato **9**

Pianoconte **10**

Porticello **4**

Quattropani **7**

Rocche Rossi **5**

VULCANO

Gelso **14**

Gran Cratere **13**

Porto di Levante **12**

Porto de Ponente **11**

and is open Monday through Friday from 8:10am to 6:30pm and Saturday from 8:10am to 12:30pm. For **Internet** access, go to Net Cafe, Via Garibaldi 61 (© **090-9813527**), open daily from 9am to 1pm and 4 to 10pm. In July and August, hours are daily from 8:30am to 5:30pm. The charge is 3.50€ per half hour. The major bank is **Banca Monte dei Paschi di Siena,** Via Torrio Emanuele 209 (© **090-9880432**), open Monday through Friday from 8:30am to 1:30pm and 2:45 to 3:45pm. An **ATM** machine on-site is available 24 hours.

EXPLORING THE ISLAND
CITADEL OR UPPER TOWN

Most of the man-made sights of Lipari are centered in this citadel area surrounded by the walls of Lipari's castle. The *castello,* or what remains of it, dates from its construction in the 16th century by the Spaniards. The citadel is approached by heading up Via Garibaldi.

You must traverse long steps cut through thick walls to reach the Upper Town. Part of the area here is an archaeological park (see below) where stratified clues about continuous civilizations dating back to 1700 B.C. have been unearthed. From these ruins, archaeologists have learned much about settlements in other Mediterranean cultures.

If you take the steps at Via del Concordato, you will climb to the **Cattedrale di San Bartolomeo,** which replaced an earlier Norman cathedral destroyed by Barbarossa on his killing rampage in 1544. A Benedictine cloister from the 1100s is all that remains from Redbeard's assault on the cathedral. Today the cathedral lies behind an impressive baroque facade and is dedicated to St. Bartolomew. A silver statue of the saint, dating from 1728, can be found in the northern transept. Charging no admission, the church is open daily from 9am to 1pm.

To the south of the Duomo you can see the archaeological ruins lying on the southern tier of the *castello,* its stones going as far back as Neolithic times. Any major finds dug up here, however, are displayed in the archaeological museum (see below). You can view some Greek and Roman burial grounds along with a contemporary Greek-style theater where concerts and ancient plays are performed in July and September (Aug is simply too scalding). The tourist office (see above) can provide all the details. **Parco Archeologico** is open from April to September Monday through Saturday from 9am to 7pm. Off-season hours are daily from 9am to 4pm. Admission is free.

Also in the Upper Town is the **Museo Archeologico Eoliano** ★★, Via del Castello (© **090-9880174**), open daily from 9am to 1:30pm and 3 to 7pm, charging an admission fee of 4.50€. This is one of southern Italy's greatest archaeological museums, housing one of the world's finest Neolithic collections, among other exhibits.

The museum is divided into two buildings. One lies just south of the cathedral in the 17th-century **Palazzo Vescovile,** or bishop's palace, and contains Neolithic and Bronze Age exhibits. The **Sezione Classica** lies on the south side of the Duomo and contains exhibits from the classical and Hellenic periods.

For ease of understanding, the collection is laid out in "time slots," beginning with the Neolithic-to-Bronze Age discoveries unearthed nearby. Here is a display of obsidian, a glasslike black volcanic rock that islanders shipped to various corners of the Mediterranean. The obsidian was crafted into blades used throughout the ancient world before it was eventually replaced by metal.

Lustrous red ceramics, known as the "Diana style," come from the last Neolithic period, 3000 to 2500 B.C. Among the other exhibits are reconstructed necropoli from the Middle Bronze Age and a 6th-century-A.D. depiction of Greek warships. The museum also houses the only Late Bronze Age (8th century B.C.) necropolis found in Sicily.

In the Sezione Classica section of the museum is a rich array of classical and Hellenic artifacts, many dug up in the nearby necropolis. Particularly noteworthy are burial urns from Milazzo dating from the 8th century B.C. and found well preserved in the lavic walls of the *castello.* Archaeologists discovered that in the 11th century B.C. Lipari islanders buried bodies in fetal positions in large jars.

The upper level of the Sezione Classica holds a stunning collection of **decorated vases** ★★, many from the ancient Roman site of Paestum. These vases, often from the 4th century B.C., depict a romp of gods and goddesses, along with satyrs and courtiers. The vases also depict scenes of daily life in ancient times, ranging from bathing scenes to sacrifices to the gods. Many of these polychrome vases are the work of an artist called **Il Pittore Liparoto,** or the Lipari Painter, from 300 to 270 B.C.

The museum contains the world's greatest collection of **theatrical masks** ★★★, displaying models unearthed in tombs from the 4th century to the 3rd century B.C. The museum owns some 1,200 of these masks. Those gruesome grins on the masks of Hercules and Hades will haunt your nightmares. Many of the masks depict scenes from Greek plays.

The final and least interesting section is the **Sezione Epigrafica** in a smaller adjoining building. This museum displays engraved stones and the remains of several Greek and Roman burial tombs.

THE LOWER TOWN

After visiting the enclosed citadel, you will have seen the best of Lipari town. The only sight of interest in the lower town is the **Parco Archeologico Contrada Diana,** west of Corso Vittorio Emanuele, the main street. Here you can see the remains of Greek walls dating from the 5th and 4th centuries B.C., as well as the ruins of several Roman villas. Ancient tombstones reveal an eerie necropolis from classical days. The burial grounds are visible off Via Marconi. The park is usually locked, so you can only stroll by and look in. Any major finds discovered here were taken to the archaeological museum in the Upper Town.

AROUND THE ISLAND

Twenty-nine kilometers (18 miles) of road circle the island, connecting all its villages and attractions. Buses run by Urso Guglielmo, Via Cappuccini (© **090-9811262**), make 10 circuits of the island per day. The trip to the little towns of Quattropani and Acquacalda, on the north coast, cost 1.55€. Closer destinations cost 1.30€. Buses leave Lipari town from Marina Lunga, opposite the service station.

The major destination is the little town of **Canneto,** 2km (1¼ miles) away, where the best beaches are found. Canneto can be reached by bus or by a 30-minute walk. It's on the eastern coast of the island, directly to the north of Lipari town. Just north of Canneto is **Spiaggia Bianca,** named for the white sand that was originally found here, although today it's rather grayish. White sand is an oddity here—the rest of the island's beaches are predominantly black volcanic sand. To reach the beach from Canneto, take the waterfront road, climbing the stairs along Via Marina Garibaldi, then veering right down a narrow cobbled path for 297m (974 ft.). Other than its beaches, nothing in Canneto need detain you.

Buses run north of Canneto, passing the **Cave di Pomice** at Campobianco, located between Spiaggia Bianca and Porticello. Other than tourism, pumice is the principal industry of Lipari. Pumice has a number of uses, ranging from a building material to an ingredient in toothpaste. Some daring visitors slide down a pumice chute directly into the waters along the north coast. The Tiviani brothers used this activity as a scene in their film classic, *Kaos,* which was based on a series of stories by Pirandello.

From Cave di Pomice you can see **Mount Pilato,** at 476m (1,562 ft.). This is the ancient crater of a volcano that last erupted in A.D. 700. Fields around this crater are the source of the pumice. You can walk to the crater, passing through barren fields locals call *Rocce Rosse,* or "the red rocks," because of the hue of the stone. A path leading to the crater from the northern tip of Campobianco stretches for 1.2km (¾ miles).

The bus stops in the village of **Porticello,** which has a beach. We suggest you avoid it, however, as it's rocky and not very special. If you do stop here, the most rewarding feature is the **panoramic view** ★★ of the other Aeolian Islands such as Alicudi, Filicudi, and Salina.

The island's northernmost little town is **Acquacalda,** or "hot water," a settlement known for its obsidian and pumice quarries. But few people go to the black sand beaches here because they're rocky and unpleasant to lie on. There's also no shade, and the sun can be fierce in July and August. Acquacalda itself is virtually a one-street town with some snack bars or waterfront dives, plus a lackluster trattoria or two.

The bus moves along the northern tier of Lipari and then heads southwest to the little town of **Quattropani,** which lies to the west of Mount Chirica at 602m (1,975 ft.). In the town you can make a steep climb to **Duomo de Chiesa**

Baraca, where the point of interest is most definitely not the "cathedral," but the **panoramic view** ⭐ from the grounds of the church. The distance between Quattropani and Acquacalda is 5km (3 miles), and some hikers prefer to traverse this route on foot, enjoying scenic vistas at every turn.

There is yet another grand view to be enjoyed before leaving Lipari. West of Lipari town, and reached by buses departing from Marina Lunga, you can visit a lookout point at **Quattrocchi** ("four eyes"). The distance is 4km (2½ miles) from Lipari town. Once at Quattrocchi you can make the steep climb to **Quattrocchi Belvedere,** where you're rewarded with one of the most **panoramic vistas** ⭐⭐ in the Aeolian Islands.

WHERE TO STAY
EXPENSIVE

Gattopardo Park Hotel ⭐⭐   Set in an 18th-century villa and enveloped by white bungalows, this is the island's most architecturally interesting hotel. In comfort, it also ranks among the top four choices on the island. Spacious terraces opening onto scenic views are yet another allure. The hotel also provides free minibus service to some of the best beaches on the island, although there is free swimming from the rocks in a bay near the hotel. For Aeolian style, this is unbeatable in Lipari, with beautifully planted grounds, tiled floors, and wood-beamed ceilings. The furnishings are a blend of antique and modern, and the best rooms are among the most comfortable in Lipari, with small, tiled, shower-only bathrooms. The dining and drinking facilities are among the island's best.

Vico Diana, 98055 Lipari. ✆ **090-9811035.** Fax 090-9880797. www.netnet.it/hotel/gattopardo. 78 units. 130€ double; 114€ per person for half board. AE, DC, MC, V. Closed Nov–Feb. **Amenities:** Restaurant; bar; room service; babysitting. *In room:* A/C, TV, hair dryer.

Giardino sul Mare ⭐   This first-class hotel lies only minutes from Marina Corta, opening onto the sea. It is a real Mediterranean resort hotel, with covered terraces for dining that are open to the breezes. Steps lead up to the smallish hotel pool, which is surrounded by chaise longues with umbrellas. Guest rooms are well groomed and comfortably furnished, with small tiled bathrooms with showers. Many European guests who stay here have told us that once they arrive, they spend all their vacation time here except for an occasional island trip. "Everything you need is here," the manager proudly told us. "Even a solarium." The drinking and dining facilities equal those of Villa Meligunis.

Via Maddalena 65, 98055 Lipari. ✆ **090-9811004.** Fax 090-9880150. www.netnet.it/conti/giardino. 46 units. 246€ double. Half board 123€ per person extra. AE, DC, MC, V. Closed Oct 30–Mar 30. **Amenities:** Restaurant; bar; pool; room service; babysitting; dry cleaning/laundry. *In room:* A/C, TV, hair dryer.

Hotel Carasco ⭐⭐   This hotel enjoys the most dramatic location in Lipari, with its own private stretch of rocks opening onto the sea and panoramic views from its bougainvillea-draped pool. The Carasco consists of two buildings linked by an addition, sitting on a lonely bluff by the sea. The cool interior contrasts with the bright heat of the outdoors; it has brown terra-cotta floors and dark-wood upholstered furniture. Each well-furnished guest room comes with a ceiling fan and rustic artifacts, with an emphasis on comfort. This hotel opened in 1971 and has stayed up-to-date ever since. Try, if possible, to get a room with one of the private balconies. Bathrooms are in fine condition and equipped with a shower or tub. Grace notes include an afternoon tea service and piano music in the lounge following dinner. The on-site restaurant is so good you might want to dine here even if you're not a guest.

Porto delle Genti, 98055 Lipari. ✆ **090-9811605**. Fax 090-9811828. www.carasco.it. 89 units. Half board 65€–110€ per person. AE, DC, MC, V. Closed Oct 13 to Easter. **Amenities:** Restaurant; bar; pool; room service; babysitting; laundry/dry cleaning. *In room:* A/C, TV, minibar.

Villa Meligunis ★★   This first-class hotel is as good as it gets in the Aeolian Islands. A restored 18th-century villa with additions, it represents the epitome of Aeolian hospitality. Less than 45m (148 ft.) from the ferry docks, the appealingly contemporary hotel rose from a cluster of 17th-century fishermen's cottages at Marina Corta. Its architectural style is Spanish Mediterranean, with a dramatic rooftop terrace overlooking the bay. It's furnished with every comfort and oozes stylish charm from its lovely fountain to its wrought-iron bedsteads used by fashion photographers as backdrops. The guest rooms are comfortably furnished with summery pieces and remain relatively uncluttered, each with a well-maintained bathroom with either a tub or shower. The hotel's name derives from the ancient Greek designation for Lipari, *Meligunia.* The on-site restaurant serves excellent regional specialties.

Via Marte 7, 98055 Lipari. ✆ **090-9812426**. Fax 090-9880149. www.villameligunis.it. 32 units. 114€–258€ double; 181€–325€ suite. Rates include breakfast. AE, DC, MC, V. Free parking. **Amenities:** Restaurant; 2 bars; pool; room service; babysitting; laundry/dry cleaning. *In room:* A/C, TV, minibar, hair dryer.

MODERATE

Hotel Oriente ★   In the historic center of Lipari town, this hotel lies only steps from the archaeological park and 300m (984 ft.) from the port. On a hot summer day, its shady garden terrace is one of the best places to be on the island. The interior is like a museum—it's stuffed with knickknacks, often artifacts that are made out of wrought iron. The rooms are light and airy, with small tiled bathrooms and showers with hydromassage. A generous breakfast is served in the Mediterranean garden amid bougainvillea and citrus blossoms.

Via Marconi 35, 98055 Lipari. ✆ **090-9811493**. Fax 090-9880198. www.hotelorientelipari.com. 32 units. 72€–129€ double; 98€–165€ triple; 123€–201€ quad. AE, DC, MC, V. Closed Oct 30–Mar 30. **Amenities:** Bar; room service; babysitting; laundry/dry cleaning. *In room:* A/C, TV, minibar, hair dryer.

Hotel Poseidon   A favorite with scuba divers, this well-run hotel lies off the main street with rooms opening onto a pleasant and inviting courtyard. The location is just 100m (328 ft.) from the sea. Scuba-diving instruction can be arranged, as can excursions to seabeds and underwater trips with a guide. Equipment rentals and cylinder refills are also offered. There is a fresh, breezy Mediterranean feel to this place, and it's a favorite of discerning travelers in general, not necessarily divers. Guest rooms are well maintained, with wicker decorations and small tiled bathrooms with showers.

Vico Ausonia 7, 98055 Lipari. ✆ **090-9812876**. Fax 090-9813295. www.hotelposeidonlipari.com. 18 units. 57€–124€ double; 78€–150€ triple. Rates include breakfast. AE, DC, MC, V. Closed Nov 15–Feb 28. **Amenities:** Bar; room service; babysitting; laundry/dry cleaning. *In room:* A/C, TV, minibar, hair dryer.

INEXPENSIVE

Villa Augustus ★ *(Finds*   In the historic center, close to the port, this hotel is surrounded by luxuriant gardens with a dramatic roof terrace overlooking the sea. It lies just 100m (328 ft.) above the sea and the main harbor and just 2km (1¼ miles) from the whitish beaches north near the pumice stone quarries. The hotel is relatively hidden from the street, reached along a narrow Aeolian island road. Rooms are comfortably and attractively furnished; preferred, of course, are those with a balcony or terrace opening onto the view. Each room comes with a small tiled bathroom with either tub or shower. Attractive features include a reading room, a piano bar, and a solarium.

Vico Ausonia 16, 98055 Lipari. ℂ 090-9811232. Fax 090-9812233. www.villaaugustus.it. 35 units. 47€–78€ double. Rates include breakfast. Closed Nov 1–Feb 28. **Amenities:** Restaurant; 2 bars; room service; babysitting; laundry/dry cleaning. *In room:* A/C, TV, hair dryer.

AT CANNETO

Casajanca *⭐ Finds* It looks like a private home, and for good reason: Before it was converted into this little inn, Casajanca was the home of Ruccio Carbone, a native son who was celebrated as "the poet" of the Aeolian Islands. The Aeolian Mediterranean–style structure has a little garden studded with tropical plantings (like palm trees) and tables and chairs. Rooms are little more than basic, midsize, motel-like accommodations, with small, shower-only, tiled bathrooms, but there is reasonable comfort here. Its friendly owners, Silvio and Massimo, provide a grand welcome to what they call "the inn of everlasting love." Furnishings mix contemporary pieces with an occasional antique.

Marina Garibaldi 115, Canneto (Lipari). ℂ **090-9813003.** Fax 090-9813003. www.casajanca.it. 10 units. 93€–155€ double; 121€–202€ triple. Rates include breakfast. AE, DC, MC, V. Closed mid-Oct to Dec 30. **Amenities:** Bar; room service. *In room:* A/C, TV, minibar.

WHERE TO DINE

E Pulera *⭐⭐* SICILIAN/AEOLIAN Owned by the same family that owns the Filippino (see below), this restaurant emphasizes its Aeolian origins. Artifacts and maps of the islands fashioned from ceramic tiles are scattered about. Some tables occupy a terrace with a view of a flowering lawn where you'll probably want to linger. Specialties include a delightful version of *zuppe di pesce alla pescatora* (fishermen's soup), *bocconcini di pesce spada* (swordfish ragout), and risotto with crayfish or squid in its own ink. Another good choices is a rich assortment of seafood antipasti laden with basil and garlic. We were recently served one of the most delightful pasta dishes we've ever tasted in the Aeolian Islands: fettuccine with yellow pumpkin, shrimp, and wild fennel. Desserts might include ricotta mousse with wild strawberries and almonds.

Via Diana. ℂ **090-9811158.** Reservations recommended. Main courses 9.50€–12€. DC, MC, V. Daily 7:30pm–2am. Closed mid-May.

Filippino *⭐⭐* SICILIAN/AEOLIAN It's a pleasant surprise to find such a fine restaurant in such a remote location. Filippino has thrived in the heart of town, near the town hall, since 1910, when it was opened by the ancestors of the family that runs it today. You'll dine in one of two large rooms or on an outdoor terrace ringed with flowering shrubs and potted flowers. Menu items are based on old-fashioned Sicilian recipes and prepared with flair. Try the *ravioloni* (large ravioli) stuffed with stone bass and served with salsa macaroni with mozzarella, prosciutto, and ricotta baked in the oven. Veal scaloppini is especially tempting when cooked in Malvasia wine (a sweet red wine typical of this area), and the array of fresh fish is broad. We especially enjoyed the *cupolette di pesce spada* with basil ("little dome" of swordfish) and the eggplant caponata. You can also spend the night here inexpensively, renting a double for 29€ to 55€ or a triple for 31€ to 65€.

Piazza Mazzini. ℂ **090-9811002.** Reservations required July–Aug. Main courses 6€–10€. AE, MC, V. Daily noon–2:30pm and 7:30–10:30pm. Closed Mon Oct–Mar.

La Nassa *⭐ Finds* SICILIAN/AEOLIAN At this enchanting family-run restaurant, the delectable cuisine of Donna Teresa matches the friendly enthusiasm of her son Bartolo, who has thousands of interesting stories to tell. The food is the most genuine and fresh you can find on the island, prepared with respect for both antique traditions and modern taste. After the *sette perle* (seven pearl) appetizer, a combination of fresh fish, sweet shrimp, and spices, you can try your choice of fish, cooked to your request. Local favorites include *sarago, cernia,* and *dentice,* as delicate in texture as their names are untranslatable. If you are more in a meat mood (not likely if you've seen the restaurant's boats coming in with delicious, just-caught fish), you can opt for Teresa's sausages seasoned with Aeolian herbs. As a dessert, try cookies with Malvasia wine.

Via G. Franza 41. © 090-9811319. Reservations recommended. Main courses 8€–16€. AE, MC, V. July–Oct daily 8:30am–3pm and 6pm–midnight; Apr–June closed Thurs. Closed Nov–Easter.

Ristorante Pizzeria Pescecane (*Value*) SICILIAN/AEOLIAN The oldest restaurant on the island is a warm, rustically furnished place. It offers tables both inside and on a terrace for warm-weather dining. It's the most centrally located restaurant in Lipari town, set right on the main street. You're greeted with a bountiful table laden with antipasti. The pasta dishes are savory, especially those made with freshly caught seafood—none better than the spaghetti with mussels, tomato sauce, and fresh parsley. *Lipparata* is the most regional pasta dish, prepared with capers, olives, anchovies, and tomatoes. Pizzas are also good, especially the Desirée, made with mozzarella, fresh tomato, and ham.

Via Vittorio Emanuele 249. © 090-9812706. Reservations recommended. Main courses 4.50€–9.30€. Fixed-price menu 13€. AE, DC, MC, V. Daily 10:30am–3pm and 6pm–midnight. Closed: Nov 1–Dec 31.

LIPARI AFTER DARK

On a summer night most of the scantily clad visitors congregate around one of the bars with outdoor tables at Marina Corta. This is the liveliest scene on the island. The early evening begins at the **Net Cafe,** Via Garibaldi 61 (© **090-9813527**) (see "Fast Facts," earlier in this section). People come here not only to surf the Web, but to enjoy drinks and snacks such as hamburgers. It also has a big-screen cable TV and a beautiful garden.

Turmalin (© **090-9811588**) is a summer dance club off Piazza Municipio near the castle. It is open nightly May through August from 11pm to 6am, charging an admission of 10€. Patrons enjoying the standard dance tunes range in age from 18 to 35 years.

Otherwise, nightlife consists of bars and more bars. One of the best is **Rusticheria Vecchia Lipari,** Corso Vittorio Emanuele 46 (© **090-9812521**), in the center of town. It offers classic Sicilian snacks such as *arancini,* little balls of fried rice filled with minced meat and tomato sauce. But it's mainly a pub filled with visitors ranging in age from 18 to 50. From May to August, hours are from 9am to 3am (9am–midnight off season). Only recorded music is played here.

Live Italian music, sometimes pop, and recorded music are featured at **Chiarra Bar,** 5 Salita San Giuseppe (© **090-9811554**), drawing both a young and middle-aged crowd. In summer it's open daily from 7pm to 4am (closes at midnight in winter). It shuts down completely in January and February.

A hard-drinking place, **Bar Caffè La Vela,** 2 Piazza San Onofrio (© **090-9880064**), is open 24 hours a day in summer, or daily from 7am to midnight off season.

2 Vulcano ✶✶✶

55km (34 miles) NW of Milazzo, 18km (11 miles) NW of Lipari

Vulcano, the ancient Thermessa, figured heavily in the mythologies of the region. The island was thought to be not only the home of Vulcan but also the gateway to Hades. Thucydides, Siculus, and Aristotle each recorded eruptions. Three dormant craters also exist on the island, but a climb to the rim of the active **Gran Cratere (Big Crater)** or Vulcano della Fosse draws the most attention. It hasn't erupted since 1890, but one look inside the sulphur-belching hole makes you understand how it inspired the hellish legends surrounding it. The 418m (1,372-ft.) peak is an easier climb than the one on Stromboli, taking just about an hour—though it's just as hot, and the same precautions prevail.

Vulcano actually boasts a trio of volcanoes, not just the Gran Cratere. The other two are Vulcano Piano and Vulcanello. Only the Gran Cratere is active, still emitting a thin fumarole, in the throes of its death.

For centuries, the island was uninhabited because of fear of the volcano. Today Vulcano is a stamping ground of the party crowd. Rich Italians from the mainland have erected fancy villas here as second homes. Vulcano's thermal baths, known for their curative powers and said to be especially helpful in relieving rheumatic suffering, also draw visitors.

The Romans had a small colony here, but the Bourbon rulers paid more attention to Vulcano. Under their reign, the whole island became a working farm, with labor provided by convicts shipped over from Lipari. A Welshman, James Stevenson, tried to bring agriculture and vineyards to the island in the 19th century, but most of his efforts failed because of a violent volcanic eruption. The last such explosive action occurred in the years 1888 and 1890, after which the volcano fell silent. Volcanologists assure us that we've heard the last major eruption from the Gran Cratere.

Vulcano is the closest island to the Sicilian mainland. Ferries and hydrofoils stop here before going on to the other islands. If the wind is blowing in the right direction, you can smell the island's prevalent sulphurous fumes. Anyone who has taken a whiff has compared that smell to a rotten egg. Surprisingly, you adjust to the smell rather quickly.

The island has the best beaches in the Aeolians, if you don't find black volcanic sands off-putting.

ESSENTIALS

VISITOR INFORMATION   The **tourist office** in Vulcano is at Via Porto di Levante (✆ **090-9852028**), and operates only from June to September. At that time it is open daily from 8am to 2pm; it is also open from 4:30 to 10pm Monday through Saturday.

GETTING AROUND   Most people walk, but a private bus, **Scaffidi** (✆ **090-9853017**), runs from the port area to Piano, a village in the southwestern interior of the island, and to Gelso at the southern tip of the island. Seven buses operate Monday through Saturday (two on Sun). Many visitors prefer to tour Vulcano by bike or motor scooter. Rentals are available at **Da Paolo,** Via Porto Levante (✆ **090-9852112**), open daily May through November from 8am to 8:30pm. Mountain bikes cost from 3€ to 5€ per day, and scooters range from 10€ to 35€.

FAST FACTS   You can exchange money at the **Banco di Sicilia** (✆ **090-98523**) at the port area. It has an ATM machine and keeps regular banking hours Monday through Friday (June–Sept only) from 8:30am to 1:30pm and 2:45 to 3:45pm. Money can also be exchanged at the **Thermessa Agency,** Via Porto Levante (✆ **090-9852230**), open daily from 6:30am to 8:30pm. You can purchase tickets on hydrofoils here as well. The **Vulcano Post Office** is found along Via Piano (✆ **090-9852230**), lying off Porto di Levante. For **medical**

services (but only June–Sept), a doctor is on call at © **090-9852220.** The island **pharmacy,** Bonarrigo, Via Favaloro 1 (© **090-9852244**), is open daily from 9am to 1pm and 7 to 9pm. The *Carabinieri* can be called at © **090-9852110.** For hydrofoil and ferry tickets, head for **Siremar,** Via Roma 74 (© **090-986016**).

EXPLORING THE ISLAND

It might be, as the ancients believed, the entrance to hell. Nonetheless, Vulcano is the most visited of the Aeolian Islands, no doubt because of its proximity to the Sicilian mainland. Only the late, great Fellini could have done justice to a film about visitors flocking here to bathe in the mud.

To reach these fabled mud baths, **Laghetti di Fanghi,** go to the docks and walk over to a 56m (183-ft.) high *faraglione,* or "stack." This is one massive pit of thick, putrid, sulphurous gunk that is said to greatly relieve certain skin diseases or rheumatic suffering.

The baths are entered along Via Provinciale, a short walk from the port. Be warned in advance that the mud discolors everything from clothing to jewelry, which is one explanation for the prevalent nudity. Expect to encounter muddy pools brimming with naked, package-tour Germans and others in summer.

Since the mud baths are also radioactive, you are warned not to stay in them for more than 10 or 15 minutes. The water from the sea bubbles up like a giant Jacuzzi nearby, and it's here that mud bathers wash off the gunk. Take care that you don't scald yourself while cleaning off the mud soup. The beach nearby isn't bad, but the aroma from the mud baths may have you holding your nose if you attempt to sunbathe here.

The baths are open from Easter to October daily from 6:30am to 8pm, charging an admission of 1€.

You can, of course, skip this muddy cauldron altogether and head directly to the beach, **Spiaggia Sabbie Nere (Black Sands Beach)** ⚓, the finest in the archipelago. Regrettably, its black volcanic sand gets so hot by midday that flip-flops or wading shoes are a virtual necessity if you plan to while away your day here. This rather dramatic beach lies on the distant side of the peninsula from Porto di Levante to Porto di Ponente. You reach it by going along Via Ponente. Porto di Ponente is just a 20-minute walk north from the mud baths.

If you tire of the black sands, leave the beach and take the only road north, which leads to **Vulcanello,** the northern tip of Vulcano. Locals call this a "volcanic pimple." It erupted from the sea in 183 B.C., spiking its way up through the earth to become a permanent fixture on the island's landscape.

Although we haven't a clue as to why they were in the area at the time, many 2nd-century celebrities of their day witnessed this eruption, among them Livy and Pliny, who left descriptions of it. As late as 1888, this toylike volcano

---

Tips **What's Where?**

A knowledge of street names is worthless, really, because there *are* no street signs. Not to worry—the locals who gather at the dock are friendly and experienced at giving directions to foreign visitors, especially since all they ever have to point out are the paths to the crater, the mud baths, and the beach. Oh, and you may want to spend time in the village center. The drab 1970s eyesore is filled with souvenir shops and snack bars.

Moments **Sunset Over Vulcano**

We like to come here with friends at sunset for one of the most memorable views in the Aeolian Islands. The setting sun turns the bay a reddish glow, lighting the towering pillars of rock that sprout in the channel separating Vulcano from Lipari. Later you can stroll over to one of the little seaside cafes for a drink.

---

erupted for the final time, creating what the islanders call a *Valle dei Mostri* ("valley of monsters") of bizarrely shaped lava fountains. Today the lunarlike field appears as if an actual sculptor had created these black lava figures.

THE GRAN CRATERE ★★★

To the south of Porto di Levante lies one of the greatest attractions in the Aeolians, the **Gran Cratere.** To reach the peak from Porto di Levante, follow Via Piano away from the sea for about 182m (597 ft.) until you see the first of the AL CRATERE signs. Once you do, follow a marked trail, and allow 3 hours to make the excursion there and back.

For your trouble in making this steep, hot climb, you'll be rewarded with **dramatic views** ★★ of some of the other Aeolian Islands. As you near the mouth of the crater you can see rivulets caused by previous volcanic eruptions. At the rim, peer down into the mammoth crater itself, whose lips measure 450m (1,476 ft.) in diameter. Vapor emissions—real sulphuric air—still spew from the crater. The steam is tainted with numerous toxins, so you may not want to hang out here too long.

SOUTH TO GELSO

Most of the activity is concentrated in northern Vulcano, but an offbeat excursion can be made by taking a bus that cuts inland to the remote, almost forgotten villages of **Piano** and **Gelso.** For details on catching one of the island buses, refer to "Getting Around," above.

Islanders who live inland are likely to reside in the remote inland village of Piano, 7km (4¼ miles) from the port. Piano lies between two peaks, **Mount Saraceno,** at 48m (157 ft.), and **La Sommata,** at 387m (1,270 ft.). There's not much here, and many of the homes are abandoned in the off season. You might decide to continue on the bus to the southernmost village of Gelso, known for its beautiful coastal scenery. Along the way you can view the inland scenery of Vulcano. At Gelso, the end of the line, you'll find some summer-only places to eat and good sea bathing. *Gelso* is Italian for "mulberry," and that and capers are the crops cultivated here.

The best beach is immediately east of Gelso. **Spiaggia dell'Asino** is a big cove reached by a steep path from the village of Gelso. Pedalos hydrocycles, deck chairs, and umbrellas can be rented from kiosks on the beach in summer.

Another little road goes to **Capo Grillo,** which has some of the best **panoramic views** ★★ on the island, with a sweeping vista of the Aeolians.

BOAT EXCURSIONS ON VULCANO

You can rent your own boat at **Centro Nautico Baia Levante,** Porto di Levante (© 090-9822197). With a boat, you can visit the hamlet of Gelso. You can also explore the caves and bays that riddle Vulcano's western shores. Boat rentals range in price from 120€ to 500€ per day, fuel not included. **Blob Center**

Tips **Beating the Heat**

Avoid midday walks to the Gran Cratere—it's unshaded and the summer sun in the middle of the day is hot enough to cook eggs on the surface. It's better to go early in the morning or late in the day. Load up on sunscreen and drinking water, and wear good, sturdy hiking shoes.

Oasy, Porto di Ponente (✆ **090-338896**), is another outfitter with boats for hire, beginning as low as 50€ per day and going up to 300€. These offices are open only from June to September daily from 8:30am to 9:30pm.

EXCURSIONS TO OTHER ISLANDS

If you'd like to use Vulcano as a base and visit other Aeolian Islands, arrangements can be made at **Centro Nautico Baia Levante,** Porto di Levante (✆ **090-9822197**), which offers both day and night excursions. Day excursions leave Vulcano heading for the islands of Lipari, Filicudi, Alicudi, and Salina. Excursions begin at 10am and last until 6pm. Because many options are available, the cost can range from 12€ to 60€ per person. Night excursions begin at 6pm and end at midnight, and the cost is the same as above. The outfitter is open from April to October daily from 8:30am to 8pm.

WHERE TO STAY

Hotel Conti ⭐ This is the second-best hotel on the island, surpassed only by Les Sables Noirs (see below). Lying only a few minutes' walk from the port where the hydrofoils and ferries pull in, the hotel opens onto the black volcanic sands of Ponente Bay. It's quite Aeolian in architecture, with luxuriant Mediterranean vegetation surrounding the main building and a series of bungalows. Inside you'll find cool tiled floors and dark wood furnishings. Accommodations are simply though comfortably furnished, and each room is midsize and comes with a small tiled bathroom with shower. All units have a private entrance opening onto the gardens. The large terraces and the solarium all open onto sea views. The restaurant, serving excellent Aeolian specialties, also opens onto panoramic views of the water.

Via Porto Ponente, 98050 Vulcano. ✆ **090-9852012.** Fax 090-9852064. www.netnet.it/conti. 67 units. 35€–83€ double. AE, DC, MC, V. Closed Oct 1–Apr 30. **Amenities:** Restaurant; bar; laundry/dry cleaning. *In room:* TV.

Hotel Eolian ⭐ *(Value)* Opening onto Ponente Bay, this hotel consists of white-sided stucco bungalows in a garden studded with palms and other tropical flora. None of the bungalows opens onto a view of the water—that's reserved for the restaurant and bar—but most guests spend their days beside the sea anyway. The structure of the hotel is in keeping with the typical Aeolian style of architecture, wherein the main building is surrounded by several bungalows, and all are set in a lush Mediterranean garden. From the restaurant and bar you can enjoy a view of some of the other islands, including Lipari, Salina, and Filicudi. Walk down from the terrace of the bar to reach the beach, where you can indulge in various watersports or rent a small boat to explore the more remote and romantic parts of the Vulcano coastline. A thermal sulphurous pool was inaugurated in 2001, and it's said to aid bodies with poor circulation. Rooms are midsize and furnished in a minimalist style; each has a tiled bathroom with a shower unit. Only two units are equipped with bathtubs.

Via Porto Levante, 98050 Vulcano. ✆ **090-9852151.** Fax 090-9852153. www.eolianhotel.com. 88 units. 57€–81€ double. Rates include breakfast. 69€–99€ per person with half board. AE, DC, MC, V. **Amenities:** Restaurant; bar; pool; babysitting; laundry/dry cleaning. *In room:* A/C, TV, minibar, hair dryer.

Les Sables Noirs ★★ This is the most elegant place to stay on Vulcano, offering a surprising level of luxury in this remote outpost. Overlooking a black sandy beach, its rooms also front a panoramic sweep of the Bay of Ponente. With its stucco and bamboo, the resort evokes the Caribbean, and you get both style and excellent service here. Accommodations are spacious and comfortably furnished, each room decorated in a typical Mediterranean style; many units open onto a wide flowering balcony. All have tiled bathrooms, about half with showers and the rest with bathtubs. There's a solarium as well. Another reason to stay here is the restaurant, which not only opens onto a broad panoramic terrace in front of the beach, but serves impressive regional specialties as well.

Via Porto di Levante, 98050 Vulcano. ② **090-9852151.** Fax 090-9852153. www.directa.net/sicilia/eolie/ hotels4/sables.html. 45 units. 83€–134€ double; 160€–217€ suite. AE, DC, MC, V. Closed Oct–Mar. **Amenities:** Restaurant; 2 bars; pool; babysitting; laundry/dry cleaning. *In room:* A/C, TV, minibar, hair dryer, safe.

WHERE TO DINE

Da Maurizio AEOLIAN/SICILIAN Known for its shady oasis of a garden and good food, this local dive lies just beyond the Siremar agency selling ferry and hydrofoil tickets to the Sicilian mainland. It's decorated in a typical Aeolian style with white walls, tile floors, and dark wooden tables. Most of the ingredients are shipped over from Sicily, although the fish is caught locally and some of the foodstuffs are grown on the island. Nothing is finer here than the macaroni with lobster. A superb pasta is made with spinach and served with fried zucchini. Seafood kabobs are also featured, made most often with swordfish or shrimp. The catch of the day is sometimes grilled and served with olives, capers, and herbs.

Via Porto di Levante. ② **090-9852426.** Reservations recommended. Main courses 8€–15€. Fixed-price menu 21€. AE, DC, MC, V. Daily noon–3pm and 7:30–11pm. Closed Nov 1 to the week before Easter.

Il Palmento AEOLIAN/SEAFOOD The big terrace opening onto the beach is a potent lure, but so is the cuisine. Although this restaurant's food never rises to the sublime, it is good, hearty fare, typical of the Aeolian Islands. There is an accurate and thorough understanding of flavor here, especially in the house specialty, spaghetti with chunks of lobster in a zesty tomato sauce. The fish soup with homemade croutons was the best we sampled in Vulcano, and that Sicilian classic, pasta with fresh sardines, was prepared admirably here, with tomato sauce, olive oil, pine nuts, and wild fennel.

Via Porto Levante. ② **090-9852552.** Reservations not needed. Main courses 6€–15€. Fixed-price menu 18€. MC, V. Daily noon–4pm and 6pm–12:30am. Closed Nov 1–Mar 30.

Ristorante Belvedere AEOLIAN/SICILIAN We like to come here for the food, of course, but we also enjoy sitting out on the beautiful terrace with a view of some of the other Aeolian Islands. The seafood dishes are typically superb; we favor the catch of the day grilled with fresh herbs and a squeeze of lemon. Grilled Sicilian lamb is another savory treat. The chef also serves tasty tagliatelle Belvedere, based on his *mamma mia's* recipe. Pasta appears again with shellfish in a white-wine sauce laced with fresh parsley. Our all-time favorite pasta here, however, is the homemade ravioli stuffed with ricotta cheese and spinach.

Via Reale 42. ② **090-9853047.** Reservations recommended. Main courses 5€–8€. AE, DC, MC, V. Daily noon–2:30pm and 8pm–midnight. Closed Oct 1–Mar 30.

Vincenzino SICILIAN/AEOLIAN This is the most appealing of the trattorie lurking near the ferry port. Known for its hefty portions and affordable prices, it serves clients in a rustic setting, feeding them well with large portions of mainly fish dishes. You might begin your meal with spaghetti Vincenzino with crayfish, capers, and a tomato sauce. Sometimes fish is shaped into roulades, particularly the swordfish, or else it might appear in a seafood salad. We're especially fond of the risotto *alla pescatora,* with crayfish, mussels, and other sea creatures. Another good choice is the house-style macaroni with ricotta, eggplant, fresh tomatoes, and herbs. From October to March, the menu is limited to a simple array of platters from the bar.

Via Porto di Levante. (*C*) 090-9852016. Reservations recommended. Main courses 7€–9€. Fixed-price menu 14€. AE, DC, MC, V. Daily noon–3pm and 8–11pm.

VULCANO AFTER DARK

One of your best bets for a drink in the evening is **Ritrovo Remigio,** Porto di Levante, open daily from 6am to 2am. It offers terrace seating, its tables overlooking the port at Porto di Levante where the ferries and hydrofoils from the mainland come in. In addition to its soothing cocktails, it serves excellent pastries and velvety-smooth gelato.

The best nightlife—in fact, virtually the island's only nightlife—is found at **Cantine Stevenson,** Via Porto di Levante ((*C*) **090-9853247**), the former wine cellars of James Stevenson, a virtual Renaissance man who did much to change the face of Vulcano. Born in Wales, Stevenson's many interests led him here, where he exported sulphur and pumice. In 1870 he purchased most of the island, indulging in agriculture and planting the first vineyards. Here, in his former wine cellars, live music is heard nightly—whether folk, Sicilian, pop, rock, jazz, or blues. More than 600 types of wine are sold, a glass beginning reasonably at 3.50€. The old-style cantina, with seats outside in summer, is open April through September daily from noon to 3am, and attracts visitors of all ages.

3 Stromboli ★ ★ ★

This is the most famous island of the Aeolians for the simple fact that its volcano is still active. The volcano, its single cone measuring 926m (3,038 ft.), has caused the island to be evacuated several times, although today the island maintains a small population and attracts summer visitors.

The island has two settlements. **Ginostra,** on the southwestern shore, is little more than a cluster of summer homes with only 15 year-round residents. **Stromboli,** on the northeastern shore, is a conglomeration of the villages of Ficogrande, San Vincenzo, and Piscita, where the only in-town attraction is the black-sand beach. You won't see volcanic eruptions from any of these villages, because they occur on the northwest side of the volcano.

The entire surface of Stromboli is the cone of a sluggish but still-active volcano. Puffs of smoke can be seen during the day. At night along the **Sciara del Fuoco (Slope of Fire),** lava glows red-hot on its way down to meet the sea with a loud hiss—a memorable vision that might leave you feeling a little too vulnerable.

The main attraction is a steep, difficult climb to the lip of the 92m (3,000-ft.) **Gran Cratere.** The view of bubbling pools of ooze (which glow with heat at night) is accompanied by rising clouds of steam and a sulphuric stench.

The most distant island in the archipelago, Stromboli achieved notoriety and became a household word in the United States in 1950 with the release of the Roberto Rossellini *cinema vérité* film starring Ingrid Bergman. The American public was far more interested in the love affair between Bergman and Rossellini than in the film. Although tame by today's standards, the affair temporarily ended Bergman's American film career, and she was even denounced on the Senate floor.

Movie fans today are more likely to remember Stromboli from the film version of the Jules Verne novel *Journey to the Center of the Earth,* starring James Mason.

ESSENTIALS

VISITOR INFORMATION   You're on your own. There is no local office.

GETTING AROUND   Although several agencies at the port hawk deals in summer ranging from cruises to boat trips, **Strombolandia,** Via Marina (© **090-986390**), is the most reliable. It's open daily from 9am to 1pm and 3 to 7pm, but only from Easter to September. Boat rentals for tours around Stromboli begin at 130€ a day (fuel extra). You can also rent a scooter here for 18€ a day (fuel extra). The staff can arrange boat excursions to Vulcano. Excursions leave at 6am and return at midnight, costing 24€ per person with a guide. An excursion from Stromboli to Panarea costs 35€ per person with a guide. It leaves Stromboli at 10am and returns at 6pm. The Stromboli excursion to Filicudi and Alicudi begins at 10am and ends at 6pm, costing 70€ per person.

The agency can also book you on boat trips around Stromboli, calling at Ginostra and Strombolicchio. Trips last 3 hours and cost 13€ per person. Trips at night to see Sciara del Fuoco last 2 hours, 20 minutes, costing 15€. Most of these boat excursions leave from the beach at Ficogrande.

FAST FACTS   To book **hydrofoil** or **ferry** rides, head for the offices of **Siremar** (© **090-986016**) or **SNAV** (© **090-986003**), both lying along the harbor road at the port and easy to spot. Boats arrive from Milazzo from April to September only. It's possible to book hydrofoil tickets on SNAV from Stromboli direct to Naples for 57€ to 62€ per person one-way. On the other hand, Siremar offers boat trips year-round from Stromboli to Naples at 32€ to 35€ per person. The local **pharmacy** is Farmacia Simone, Via Roma (© **090-986713**), open daily from 8:30am to 1pm and 4:30 to 9pm, and daily in August from 8am to midnight. The Stromboli **Post Office** is at Via San Vincenzo (© **090-9812735**), open Monday through Saturday from 8:10am to 1:20pm.

EXPLORING THE ISLAND

Climbing the volcano is the big deal here (see below); otherwise, there isn't much to see in the town. Film buffs can follow Via Vittorio Emanuele to the **Chiesa di San Vincenzo,** a church so unremarkable it barely merits a visit. However, just two doors down on the right, near the Locanda del Barbablu, is the **little pink house** where Ingrid Bergman and her director and lover, Roberto Rossellini, "lived in sin" during the filming of the 1949 flick *Stromboli.* The house can only be viewed from the outside.

CLIMBING THE VOLCANO

The cone of the volcano, **Gran Cratere** ★★★, can be visited with a guide. In fact, the law states that you can climb the slope *only* with a guide. The island's authorized guide company is **Guide Alpine Autorizzate** (© **090-986211**), which charges 24€ to 36€ per person to scale the volcano. Guides lead groups on a 3-hour trip up the mountain, leaving at 6pm and returning at midnight. The trip down takes only 2 hours but you're allowed an hour at the rim.

We don't recommend taking the trip during the day—it's far less dramatic then. About halfway up is a view of the **Sciara del Fuoco** ★. In daylight the glow of this trail of molten lava is barely discernible, but at night its fiery red is striking. The volcanic explosions at night are also far more dramatic.

OTHER ATTRACTIONS

On the northeast coast is a striking rock, **Strombolicchio,** a steep basalt block measuring 43m (141 ft.). It is reached by climbing steps hewn out of rock. Once at the top you're rewarded with a **panoramic view of the Aeolians** ★★, and on a clear day you can see as far as Calabria on the Italian mainland.

WHERE TO STAY

La Locanda del Barbablu ★ *Finds*   This is a quirky choice, a charming little isolated Aeolian inn with only a few rooms, standing against turn-of-the-20th-century breakfronts. Rooms are small but comfortably furnished, often with four-poster beds encrusted with cherubs and mother-of-pearl inlay. A wide terrace opens onto dramatic views of the volcano and the sea. All units have well-maintained bathrooms with shower-tub combinations. The restaurant is worth a visit even if you're not a guest.

Via Vittorio Emanuele 17–19, 98050 Stromboli. ℂ **090-986118.** Fax 090-986323. 6 units. 60€–110€ double. AE, DC, MC, V.

La Sirenetta Park Hotel ★★   This is the island's finest accommodation, a well-maintained and well-run, government-rated four-star hotel. It has an idyllic location on the Ficogrande Beach in front of Strombolicchio, the towering rock that rises out of the waters at San Vincenzo. The hotel is also the best equipped on the island, with a scenic terrace, a nightclub, and a. restaurant serving the best cuisine of any hotel here. Guest rooms are attractively furnished, with tiled floors and an airy feeling. All rooms come with private tiled bathrooms—half with showers, half with tubs. The hotel is justly proud of having the island's best pool as well, complete with hydromassage. Facilities include a fitness center and a dive center that also offers water skiing, sailing, and windsurfing.

Via Marina 33, 98050 Ficogrande (Stromboli). ℂ **090-986025.** Fax 090-986124. www.netnet.it/hotel/lasirenetta. 60 units. 220€ double in summer. Rates include breakfast. 280€ double with half board; 260€–390€ suite with half board. Off-season discounts. AE, DC, MC, V. Closed Nov 1 to mid-Mar. **Amenities:** Restaurant; 2 bars; pool; tennis court; fitness center; watersports; room service; massage; laundry/dry cleaning. *In room:* A/C, TV, minibar, hair dryer, safe.

WHERE TO DINE

Il Canneto AEOLIAN   This is a very typical island restaurant constructed in the old style with white walls and dark tables of solid wood. Among the local trattorie, it's nothing fancy, but it's one of the more reliable joints in town. The specialty of the kitchen is always fish caught in local waters. A delectable pasta is large macaroni with minced swordfish or whitefish cooked in a light tomato sauce with fresh herbs. Swordfish roulades are also prepared with a certain flair here. The summer diners are often more exotic than the fish on the platters.

Via Roma 64. ℂ **090-986014.** Reservations recommended. Main courses 9€–14€. AE, MC, V. June–July daily 12:30–2:30pm; May to mid-Oct daily 7pm–midnight. Closed off season.

La Locanda del Barbablu ★ SICILIAN/ITALIAN   This *locanda,* or inn, has enjoyed a certain renown since the early 1900s when sailors used to stop here for some R&R en route to Naples. It's still going strong and still serving a mainly Sicilian cuisine with some specialties from Venice and Naples thrown in. Today the place is rather chic and has a lovely garden. The food is classically Italian, with no experimentation whatsoever—we are certain that the cooks' grandmothers made the very same dishes. That doesn't mean they're not good. On the contrary, they are often excellent, especially the recently sampled *ravioli di melanzane,* fried ravioli stuffed with eggplant and covered with a tomato sauce.

We have enjoyed *matarocco* here. This is pasta flavored with tomato sauce, garlic, pine nuts, and fresh basil and parsley. That old Sicilian reliable, *pasta con le sarde,* pasta with fresh sardines, is a savory meal, as is filet of tuna baked in cloves and cinnamon and given extra flavor with hot peppers.

Via Vittorio Emanuele 17–19. ℂ 090-986118. Reservations recommended in summer. Main courses 6€–9€. AE, DC, MC, V. Daily 7:30–11:30pm. Closed Nov 1–Feb 1.

Punta Lena ⭐⭐ AEOLIAN   The island's best cuisine is served at this old Aeolian house tastefully converted into a 17-seat restaurant, with a terrace opening onto the sea. The restaurant lies on the beach, a 10-minute walk from the center of town. Much of the cuisine is based on the use of fresh fish, and there is a genuine effort here to cook with fresh products whenever possible. We recently dropped by to sample the spaghetti Stromboliana made with fresh anchovies, wild fennel, fresh mint, and tomatoes and topped with toasted croutons. Except for the croutons, it was an excellent dish, as was the gnocchi *alla Saracena,* with whitefish, capers, olives, and tomatoes. The chef loves spaghetti as much as Rudolph Valentino did, and the pasta named for the silent-screen star appears with freshly caught little shrimp and sautéed zucchini. Stick to whatever the fishermen have brought in that day—just ask one of the friendly waiters. The restaurant also stocks the island's widest selection of wines.

Marina Ficogrande. ℂ 090-986204. Reservations recommended. Main courses 8€–14€. AE, DC, MC, V. Daily noon–2:30pm and 7–11pm. Closed Nov 1–Mar 31.

Trattoria Ai Gechi di Mirabito AEOLIAN   Everything here is homemade—each dish has that *mamma mia* touch. This typical Aeolian trattoria is warm and airy and serves familiar dishes. You sit on wooden Mediterranean chairs as you enjoy the aromas wafting from the kitchen. The menu focuses on freshly caught fish. The homemade pasta of the day we recently sampled was made with tomato sauce, capers, onions, garlic, parsley, and lemon zest. We followed that with fish cooked in white wine and flavored with fresh herbs. This is one of the few restaurants on island that remains open year-round.

Via Salina 12. ℂ 090-986213. Reservations recommended. Main courses 8€–10€. AE, DC, MC, V. Aug daily 7:30pm–2am; Sept–July daily 12:30–2:30pm and 7:30pm–2am.

STROMBOLI AFTER DARK

As the sun sets and the volcano lights up the sky, it seems that everyone heads for the island's most popular bar, **Bar Ingrid,** at Piazza San Vincenzo (ℂ **090-986385**). Naturally, it's named for Ingrid Bergman and stands in remembrance of that ill-fated Rossellini movie that no one went to see but that everybody here still talks about. Drinks, beer, rolls, and sandwiches are the casual offerings, but mainly people come here to be seen or to see others. It's open 6 days a week from 6pm to 2am. It closes Monday one week, Sunday the next week.

The next most popular bar is **Il Malandrino,** Via Marina (ℂ **090-986376**), where you can hang out, drink, and even order a pizza. It's open 6 days a week from 5:30pm to 3am. It closes Monday one week, Sunday the next week, a rotation it jointly maintains with Bar Ingrid.

For live music, head over to **La Tartana,** Via Marina 33 at Ficogrande (ℂ **090-986025**), opening onto the beach. It's open from June to September from 9pm to 2am, attracting a crowd 18 to the early thirties in age. Patrons come here to dance to disco music or enjoy live pop groups. La Tartana is part of La Sirenetta Park Hotel, right near the port.

8

Taormina & Mount Etna

Sicily's greatest resort, **Taormina,** and its fiercest attraction, **Mount Etna,** can be combined in one powerful trip. Besotted with the glories of Taormina, with its panoramic views of the bays beyond and Mount Etna looming in the background, such writers as Goethe and D. H. Lawrence spread word of its charm.

Taormina was built on a cliff, Monte Tauro, overlooking the sea. To the surprise of many first-time visitors, Taormina has no beach of its own. To reach the sands you must take a steep descent down the hill. But the medieval charm of Taormina makes a stay high on the hill well worth your time.

Although many older visitors prefer to visit in the winter when the hordes have departed, the official high season lasts from April to October. If you are seeking a holiday by the beach and prefer to enjoy Taormina only on day trips, then **Giardini-Naxos** is your best choice. It has more style and flair than many beach resorts in Sicily, which, frankly, tend toward the tacky. Seen from the terraces of Taormina, Giardini-Naxos opens onto a wide, curving bay with a beach that is justifiably one of the most popular on the entire island.

There are many excursions to take from Taormina, including a visit to the even loftier **Castelmola** and to the **Alcantara Gorges.** But nothing lures visitors quite like Mount Etna, the highest volcano in Europe. It's a potential menace, however: The entire coast of eastern Sicily is dominated by this volcanic peak, which continues to blow its top, sending deadly lava flows in all directions. The main crater is still dangerously active, as people visiting Sicily in the summer of 2001 discovered, when Etna put on what was described as an "awesome, dramatic display" of volcanic fireworks. As this book was going to press, Etna was at it again, opening up a new crater near Catania and spewing mile-high columns of smoke and ash into the air.

1 Taormina ★ ★ ★

53km (33 miles) N of Catania, 53km (33 miles) S of Messina, 250km (155 miles) E of Palermo

Taormina was just too good to remain unspoiled. Dating from the 4th century B.C., it hugs the edge of a cliff overlooking the Ionian Sea. The sea and even the railroad track lie below, connected by bus routes. Looming in the background is Mount Etna, an active volcano. Noted for its mild climate, the most beautiful town in all of Sicily seems to have no other reason to exist than for the thousands upon thousands of visitors who flock here for dining, bar-hopping, shopping, and enjoying the nearby beaches.

International visitors pack the main street, Corso Umberto I, from April to October. After that, Taormina quiets down considerably. In spite of the hordes that descend in summer, Taormina has remained charming, with much of its medieval character intact. It's filled with intimate piazzas and palazzi dating

Taormina

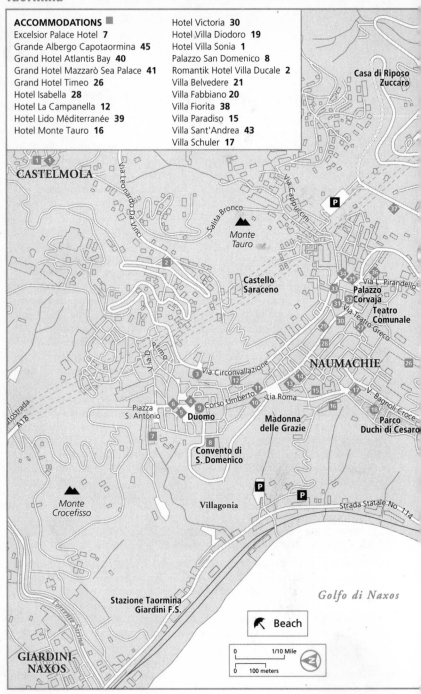

ACCOMMODATIONS

Excelsior Palace Hotel **7**
Grande Albergo Capotaormina **45**
Grand Hotel Atlantis Bay **40**
Grand Hotel Mazzarò Sea Palace **41**
Grand Hotel Timeo **26**
Hotel Isabella **28**
Hotel La Campanella **12**
Hotel Lido Méditerranée **39**
Hotel Monte Tauro **16**
Hotel Victoria **30**
Hotel Villa Diodoro **19**
Hotel Villa Sonia **1**
Palazzo San Domenico **8**
Romantik Hotel Villa Ducale **2**
Villa Belvedere **21**
Villa Fabbiano **20**
Villa Fiorita **38**
Villa Paradiso **15**
Villa Sant'Andrea **43**
Villa Schuler **17**

Casa di Riposo Zuccaro

CASTELMOLA

Monte Tauro

Castello Saraceno

Palazzo Corvaja

Teatro Comunale

NAUMACHIE

Via Circonvallazione

Piazza S. Antonio

Corso Umberto

Duomo

Madonna delle Grazie

Parco Duchi di Cesaro

Convento di S. Domenico

Monte Crocefisso

Villagonia

Strada Statale No. 114

Stazione Taormina Giardini F.S.

Golfo di Naxos

GIARDINI-NAXOS

Beach

0   1/10 Mile
0   100 meters

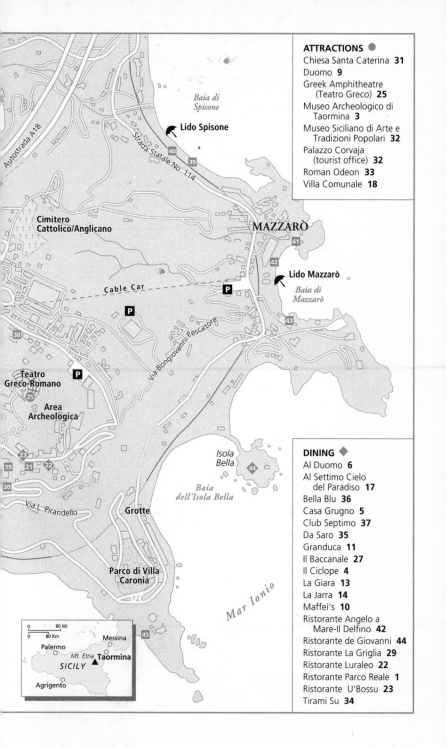

ATTRACTIONS ●
Chiesa Santa Caterina **31**
Duomo **9**
Greek Amphitheatre
  (Teatro Greco) **25**
Museo Archeologico di
  Taormina **3**
Museo Siciliano di Arte e
  Tradizioni Popolari **32**
Palazzo Corvaja
  (tourist office) **32**
Roman Odeon **33**
Villa Comunale **18**

*Baia di
Spisone*

Lido Spisone

Autostrada A18

Strada Statale No. 114

**Cimitero
Cattolico/Anglicano**

MAZZARÒ

Lido Mazzarò

*Baia di
Mazzarò*

Cable Car

Via Bongiovanni-Pescatore

**Teatro
Greco-Romano**

**Area
Archeologica**

Via L. Pirandello

*Isola
Bella*

*Baia
dell'Isola Bella*

Grotte

**Parco di Villa
Caronia**

Mar Ionio

DINING ◆
Al Duomo **6**
Al Settimo Cielo
  del Paradiso **17**
Bella Blu **36**
Casa Grugno **5**
Club Septimo **37**
Da Saro **35**
Granduca **11**
Il Baccanale **27**
Il Ciclope **4**
La Giara **13**
La Jarra **14**
Maffei's **10**
Ristorante Angelo a
  Mare-Il Delfino **42**
Ristorante de Giovanni **44**
Ristorante La Griglia **29**
Ristorante Luraleo **22**
Ristorante Parco Reale **1**
Ristorante U'Bossu **23**
Tirami Su **34**

0   80 Mi
0   80 Km
Messina
Palermo
Mt. Etna **Taormina**
SICILY
Agrigento

from the 15th to the 19th century. You'll find a restaurant for every day of the week, and countless stores sell everything from fine antiques to cheap trinkets.

You can always escape the throngs during the day by seeking out adventures, perhaps climbing Mount Etna, walking to the Castelmola, or making a day trip to Syracuse (see chapter 10). In summer you can hang out at the beaches below the town (although Taormina itself isn't right on a beach). At night you can enjoy jazz and disco or just spend time in a local tavern or restaurant.

Lots of people contributed to putting Taormina on the map. First inhabited by a tribe known as the Siculi, it has known many conquerors, such as the Greeks, Carthaginians, Romans, Saracens, French, and Spanish. Its first tourist is said to have been Goethe, who arrived in 1787 and recorded his impressions in his *Journey to Italy*. Other Germans followed, including a red-haired Prussian, Otto Geleng. Arriving at the age of 20 in Taormina, he recorded its beauties in his painted landscapes. These landscapes were exhibited in Paris and caused much excitement—people had to find out for themselves whether Taormina was really that beautiful.

Another German, Wilhelm von Gloeden, arrived to photograph not only the town but also nude boys crowned with laurel wreaths. His pictures sent European high society flocking to Taormina. Von Gloeden's photos, some of which are printed in official tourist literature to this day, form one of the most enduring legends of Taormina. Souvenir shops still sell the pictures which, considered scandalous in their day, seem tame—even innocent—by today's standards.

In von Gloeden's footsteps came a host of celebs hoping to see what all the excitement was about: Truman Capote, Tennessee Williams, Marlene Dietrich, Joan Crawford, Rita Hayworth, and Greta Garbo. Always in disguise, sometimes as "Harriet Brown," Garbo used Taormina as a vacation retreat from 1950 until her last mysterious arrival in 1979. Garbo and many other stars stayed at a villa on the road to Castelmola owned by Gayelord Hauser, the celebrated dietitian to Hollywood stars of the golden age. In time, another wave of stars arrived, including Elizabeth Taylor and Richard Burton, Cary Grant, and the woman who turned Grant down, Sophia Loren.

ESSENTIALS
GETTING THERE   You can make **rail** connections on the Messina line south. It's possible to board a train in Rome for the 8-hour trip to Messina, where you make connections on to Taormina. Call ⓒ **848-888088** for schedules. There are 26 trains a day from both Messina and Catania; trips from both towns take 1 to 1½ hours and cost 2.85€ one-way. The Sicilian Gothic train station for Taormina/Giardini-Naxos is a mile from the heart of the resort, below the town. Buses run uphill from the station every 15 to 45 minutes (schedules vary throughout the year), daily 9am to 9pm; a one-way ticket costs 1.25€. You can also take a taxi for 10€ and up.

In addition, you can take the train as far as Messina and then hop a Taormina-bound **bus.** There are 15 a day, taking 1½ hours and costing 2.60€ one-way. More details are available by calling **Interbus** at ⓒ **0942-625301.**

By **car** from Messina, head south along A18. From Catania, continue north along A18. If you're arriving by car, the main parking lot is **Lumbi Parking,** Contrada Lumbi, which is signposted off the Taormina Nord Autostrada junction. There is another garage at **Mazzarò Parking** along Via Nazionale in Mazzarò, in the vicinity of the cable-car station lying off the coastal road. For 24-hour parking, count on paying anywhere from 12€ to 15€.

VISITOR INFORMATION   The **tourist office** is in the Palazzo Corvaja, Piazza Santa Caterina (© **0942-23243**), open Monday through Saturday from 8am to 2pm and 4 to 7pm. From this office, you can get a free map, hotel listings, bus and rail schedules, and a schedule of summer cultural events staged at the Greek amphitheater. Information is also available at a branch office at Via Tysandros 54 (© **0942-51010**), keeping the same hours as the parent branch.

SPECIAL EVENTS   The Greek Amphitheater (see below) offers regular **theatrical performances** from July to September. In addition, churches and other venues are the settings for a **summer festival of classical music** from May to September. Each July an **international film festival** is held in the amphitheater.

GETTING AROUND   Within the heart of Taormina, use your trusty feet to get about. If you're venturing off on day excursions, a network of buses goes to such places as Giardini-Naxos or Mount Etna.

The more distant parts of Taormina are linked by minibus leaving from the terminal at Via Luigi Pirandello in town and costing .50€ for a one-way ticket. Most visitors use the minibus that goes from the terminal to Madonna della Rocca, since it passes most of the major hotels. Service is daily from 8am to 7:05pm.

Taxi ranks are found at Piazza Vittorio Emanuele and at Piazza San Pancrazio. These are used primarily if you're leaving the heart of Taormina and venturing into its hinterlands. A typical fare—say, from the center of Taormina to Madonna della Rocca—is 10€.

Instead of relying on a bus, many visitors prefer to rent a car in Taormina and explore at their leisure. A good local company is **Auto Europe** (© **800-334440**); reservations should be made in advance in high season. In Taormina you can visit its offices at Via Apollo Arcageta 4 (© **0942-21252**).

Vehicles rent for between 63€ and 220€ per day with unlimited mileage. Cars can be picked up in one Sicilian location and returned to another if you plan to explore beyond Taormina, perhaps taking a trip south to Syracuse and Agrigento.

Cable cars from Taormina up above run to the beaches below at Mazzarò, next to the Mazzarò car park. Service is daily in summer from 8am until 1:30am (shuts down at 6pm in winter). A single ticket costs 1.60€, a round-trip ticket 2.70€.

Many athletic visitors prefer to travel around Taormina and the coastal area on mopeds. **Autonolo "City,"** Piazza Sant'Antonio 5 (© **0942-23161**), arranges rentals of scooters for 24€ daily, or Vespas for 38€ daily. Hours are from March to October daily from 8am to noon and 4 to 8pm.

 FAST FACTS: Taormina

American Express A travel agency, **La Duca Viaggi,** Via Don Bosco 39 (© **0942-625255**), handles Amex clients Monday through Friday from 9am to 1pm and 4 to 7:30pm. However, the most comprehensive travel agency in Taormina is not the Amex one but **Dr. Silvestri Travel Bureau,** Corso Umberto I, 143–145 (© **0942-23052**). Established in 1905, it offers services ranging from car rentals and airline tickets to foreign currency exchange and day-trip bus excursions. It's open Friday through Wednesday from 9am to 1pm and 4 to 8pm.

Currency Exchange There are dozen of possibilities, especially at the banks along Corso Umberto I and Via Pirandello. The most convenient center with ATMs is **Cambio Valute,** Corso Umberto I, 224 (© **0942-24806**), near Piazza Sant'Antonio. The office here is open Monday through Saturday from 9am to 1pm and 4 to 8pm.

Emergency Dial © **113** or 0942-23232.

Hospital Serving the entire Taormina area is **Ospedale San Vincenzo,** Piazza San Vincenzo (© **0942-5791**).

Internet Access The best place to go is the **Internet Café,** Calle Umberto I, 214 (© **0942-628839**), charging 1€ per hour.

Left Luggage A kiosk inside the Taormina–Giardini-Naxos train station is open daily from 8am to 9pm, and charges 4€ per piece of luggage over a 24-hour period.

Medical In an emergency, call **Guardia Medica** (© **0942-625419**), open Monday through Friday from 8am to 8pm, Saturday and Sunday 24 hours.

Pharmacy The most central drugstore is **Farmacia Ragusa,** Piazza Duomo 9 (© **0942-23231**), open only Thursday through Tuesday from 8:30am to 1pm and 5 to 8:30pm. However, it posts a schedule of other pharmacies open at other times. This list changes weekly on a rotational system.

Police Dial © **112** for help.

Post Office The **Taormina Post Office** is at Piazza Sant'Antonio (© **0942-23010**), at the top end of Corso Umberto I in the vicinity of the hospital. Hours are Monday through Friday from 8:15am to 1:30pm and 4 to 7pm, Saturday from 8:15am to 1:30pm.

EXPLORING THE AREA

Many visitors to Taormina come for the beach, although the sands aren't exactly at the resort. To reach the best and most popular beach, **Lido Mazzarò** ★★, you have to go south of town via a cable car (© **0942-23605**) that leaves from Via Pirandello every 15 minutes. A one-way ticket costs 1.50€. This beach is one of the best equipped in Sicily, with bars, restaurants, and hotels. You can rent beach chairs, umbrellas, and watersports equipment at various kiosks from the beginning of April to October. To the right of Lido Mazzarò, past the Capo Sant'Andrea headland, is the region's prettiest cove, where twin crescents of beach sweep from a sand spit out to the minuscule **Isola Bella** islet. You can walk here in a minute from the cable car, but it's more fun to paddle a boat from Mazzarò around Capo Sant'Andrea, which hides a few grottoes with excellent light effects on the seaward side.

North of Mazzarò are the long, wide beaches of **Spisone** and **Letojanni,** more developed but less crowded than **Giardini,** the large, built-up resort beach south of Isola Bella. A local bus leaves Taormina for Mazzarò, Spisone, and Letojanni, and another heads down the coast to Giardini.

The **Greek Amphitheater (Teatro Greco)** ★★★, Via del Teatro Greco (© **0942-23220**), is Taormina's most visited monument, offering a view of rare beauty of Mount Etna and the seacoast. In the Hellenistic period, the Greeks hewed the theater out of the rocky slope of Mount Tauro, and the Romans remodeled and modified it greatly. What remains today dates from the 2nd century A.D. The conquering Arabs, who seemed intent on devastating the town, slashed away at it in the 10th century. That left us with a rather sparse and dusty ruin, more spare looking and less evocative than the Greek theater in Catania. Today, Taormina's Greek theater is the site of the annual Taormina film festival. On the premises is an antiquarium containing artifacts from the classical and early Christian periods.

Between April and September, hours are daily from 9am to 7pm; from October to March, daily from 9am to 4pm. Admission is 4.50€ adults, 2€ ages 18 to 25. Entrance is free for persons over 65 and under 18. The ruins lie on the upper reaches of Taormina, near Grand Hotel Timeo.

Behind the tourist office, on the other side of Piazza Vittorio Emanuele, is the **Roman Odeon,** a small theater partly covered by the church of Santa Caterina next door. The Romans constructed this theater around A.D. 21, when Taormina was under their rule. Much smaller than the Greek theater and with similar architecture, it was discovered in 1892 by a blacksmith digging in the area. A peristyle (colonnade) was also discovered here, perhaps all that was left of a Greek temple dedicated to Aphrodite.

Chiesa Santa Caterina, Piazza Santa Caterina, off Corso Umberto I (② **0942-23123**), was consecrated to St. Catherine of Alexandria (exact consecration date unknown). It might have been built in the mid–17th century, and the sacristy could have been constructed even earlier. The facade of the sacristy contains two small windows decorated with seashells, the same motif used on the architrave of its doors. This church, with its severely dignified exterior, sits on a piazza that abuts the highest point of the town's main street, Corso Umberto I. Inside are baroque detailing, a trussed wood-beamed ceiling, and a sunlight-flooded airiness. Chiesa Santa Caterina is the temporary replacement for Taormina's cathedral, which will be closed for some time. Admission is free; the church is open daily from 9am to noon and 4 to 7pm.

Farther along the main drag, **Corso Umberto I** ★, you arrive at Piazza del Duomo and the **Duomo (cathedral)** of Taormina. Built around 1400 on the ruins of a church from the Middle Ages, this fortress cathedral has a Latin cross plan and a trio of aisles. The nave is held up by half a dozen monolithic columns—three on each side—in pink marble. A fish-scale decoration graces their capitals in

---

 Where Garbo's Big Feet Trod the Sands

The district's most appealing beach club, **Beach Club Paradiso,** Via Lungomare, Letojanni (② **0942-36944**), lies at the most easterly end of the beachfront of Letojanni, a sea-fronting hamlet that receives lots of traffic from hotel residents of Taormina above. It was built on the site of a villa (ca. 1920s) that was the lair of Dr. Gayelord Hauser, a dietitian and confidant of a long list of Hollywood stars that included Greta Garbo. Come here for a half or full day, relax beside a freshwater pool, enjoy a meal at the pleasant restaurant, or swim in the sea on a gravel beach under supervision by a registered lifeguard. Platters of well-prepared food in the open-air restaurant cost from 8.50€ to 15€. At least some of the clients here might be registered guests at Taormina's Villa Paradiso, with which this beach club is associated, and which maintains shuttle service from Taormina. The club is open from June to October only, daily from 9am to 6pm. The entrance fee of 9€ includes all-day use of a chaise longue and parasol.

honor of the island's maritime tradition. The ceiling of the nave is an attraction, its wooden beams held up by carved corbels decorated with Arabian scenes. The main portal was reconstructed in 1636, with a large Renaissance-inspired rosette sculpted on it. The Duomo is currently closed for renovations and may remain so for some time. For information, call (② **0942-23123.** The cathedral's role has been assumed by Chiesa Santa Caterina (see above).

Taormina's newest museum, **Museo Archeologico di Taormina,** in the Palazzo Badia Vecchia, on Via Circonvallazione ((② **0942-620112**), is set on the site of the ancient and ruined Roman baths. It is a repository for the hundreds of archaeological remnants discovered during excavations in and around the city. Expect pottery shards and lingering artifacts of the ancient Roman world. Admission is 2.60€; it's open Tuesday through Sunday from 9am to 1pm and 4 to 8pm.

The Palazzo Corvaja, one of the most famous palaces in Taormina, contains not only the tourist office but the **Museo Siciliano di Arte e Tradizioni Popolari (Museum of Art and Popular Traditions),** Piazza Santa Catarina at Corso Umberto I ((② **0942-23243**). The museum consists of interconnected rooms filled with 18th-century oil portraits, woodcarvings, painted glass, brightly painted donkey carts, and embroidery. The most charming pieces in the collection are secular portraits of the mid-19th-century Sicilian bourgeoisie, in particular family portraits that are naive and crude. Entrance to the ground floor of the palace (also the town's tourist office) is free. Admission to the museum costs 2.60€. It's open Tuesday through Sunday from 9am to 1pm and 4 to 8pm.

The site of the best temporary art exhibitions is the Palazzo di Santo Stefano, containing the **Fondazione Mazzullo,** Corso Umberto I, 242–246 ((② **0942-610273**). Entrance is free, but dates and opening times vary (check with the tourist office; see above). Many of the exhibitions focus on the history of Taormina; others are showcases for modern art. Constructed for the dukes of Santo Stefano, the palace dates from the 15th century. Among the materials used to build the palace is a rather stunning mix of black lava and white Syracuse stone.

A sightseeing oddity in Taormina is **Villa Comunale,** sometimes called **Parco Duca di Cesarò** ✦✦, Via Bagnoli Croce, off Corso Umberto I. One of the most beautiful little parks in all of Sicily, the gardens were the creation of Lady Florence Trevelyan in the late 19th century. This Scottish lady was "invited" to leave Britain after a well-publicized romance with the future king, Edward VII, son of Victoria. As an avid bird-watcher, she built various amusements in the garden, including a fanciful stone-and-brick pavilion that might have been conceived as a teahouse—it's ivy colored, small in scale, and open to the breezes. A large variety of flowering plants and shrubbery, much of it exotic, stud the gardens, which are open daily from 8:30am to 7pm, charging no admission. In winter, closing time is 6pm.

Another garden in Taormina is the **Giardino Púbblico (Public Garden),** Via Bagnoli Croce. The flower-filled garden overlooking the sea is a choice spot for views and a nice place to relax. You can order drinks at a bar in the park. The garden is open from dawn until dusk.

From Taormina, you might set out for the nearby village of **Castelmola** ✦, 3km (2 miles) northwest. It's worth a trip: This is one of the most beautiful places in eastern Sicily, and you'll have a panoramic view of Mount Etna if the day is clear. You might also visit the ruined *castello* on the summit of Mount Tauro, about 3km (2 miles) northwest of Taormina along the Castelmola road. If you like walking, you might prefer to hike there, following a footpath. The summit is at 390m (1,280 ft.). Once there, you'll see the ruins of a former acropolis, but most people simply come for the panoramas.

FARTHER AFIELD TO THE ALCANTARA GORGES

To see some beautiful rapids and waterfalls, head outside of town to the **Gole dell'Alcantara** ★ (© **0942-985010**), a series of gorges. Uncharacteristically for Sicily, the waters are extremely cold (but quite refreshing in Aug). During most conditions, it's possible to walk up the river from May to September (when the water level is low), although you must inquire about current conditions before you do. From the parking lot, take an elevator partway into the scenic abyss and then continue on foot. You're likely to get wet, so take your bathing suit. If you don't have appropriate shoes, you can rent rubber boots at the entrance. Allow at least an hour for this trip. From October to April, only the entrance is accessible, but the view is always panoramic. It costs 2.50€ to enter the gorge daily from 9am to 5pm. If you're driving, head up SS185 some 17km (11 miles) from Taormina. To get there by bus, take **Interbus** (© **0942-625301**) for the 20-minute trip departing from Taormina at 9:30am. There's only one bus back, which leaves at 2:25pm. The round-trip fare is 4.50€. You can also go by taxi from Taormina, but you'll have to negotiate the fare with your driver. If you'd like a taxi, call Franco Nunzio at © **0942-51094.**

SHOPPING

Shopping is easy in Taormina—just find **Corso Umberto I,** the main street, and go. The trendy shops here sell everything upscale, from lacy linens and fashionable clothing to antique furniture and jewelry. If you're a little more adventurous, veer off the Corso and search out the little shops on the side streets.

Bar Pasticerria A Chemi   Everything in this brightly lit store comes from Sicily, including the ice cream, and many of the elaborate inventories are made on the premises. The array of candies, many made from almond paste, is amazing. Expect sugared orange slices *en confit;* at least four kinds of *torrone* (nougat) including black, white, and a version made with pistachios; local honey fortified with slices of dried fruit; and every conceivable kind of marzipan. Bottled Sicilian liqueurs are also available, including a worthy collection of Marsalas and an almond-flavored dessert wine. Corso Umberto I, 102. © **0942-24260.**

Casa d'Arte Forin   The Venetian family who operates this store sells antique prints featuring bucolic scenes of the Sicilian countryside and the Ionian Sea. They also have some excellent reproductions of antique jewelry and antique furnishings, with an emphasis on Sicilian and Venetian pieces. Corso Umberto I, 148. © **0492-23060.**

Ch'ien   Small-scale, upbeat, and hip, this is a stylish and sophisticated gift shop whose inventories reflect the whimsy and taste of owner Alessandra Martorana. Look for lamps in leopard-skin patterns, plastic handbags that might have been held by Twiggy on a psychedelic 1960s holiday in Miami Beach, carved boxes from China and India, housewares, and garden ornaments, all of them permeated with a Zen-like sense of calm. Via Bagnoli Croce 53. ℂ **0942-628722.**

Carlo Panarello   This shop features an entire range of merchandise, offering a good choice of Sicilian ceramics, plus deluxe umbrellas, tablecloths, and an eclectic mixture of antique furnishings, paintings, and engravings. Corso Umberto I, 122. ℂ **0942-23910.**

Gioielleria Giuseppe Stroscio   This is the best outlet for antique gold jewelry from 1500 to the early 1900s. It also sells a good selection of modern jewelry. We've seen a more helpful staff, however. Corso Umberto I, 169. ℂ **0942-24865.**

Giovanni di Blasi   Ceramic stores are found all over Sicily, but this is one of the best in terms of quality and design. It specializes in the highly valued "white pottery" of Caltagirone. Corso Umberto I, 103. ℂ **0942-24671.**

Il Quadrifoglio   Here, you'll find a rich collection of amber jewelry from the Dominican Republic and the Baltic, antique jewelry from estate sales throughout Sicily, antique porcelain from Dresden, and papier-mâché masks that might be suitable for Carnevale in Venice. The venue is artsy, antiquey, and charming, with lots of appealing objects. Corso Umberto I, 153. ℂ **0942-23545.**

La Torinese   Loaded to the rafters with the agrarian bounty of Sicily, this delicatessen was established in 1936 by—you guessed it—a one-time resident of Torino. Its combinations of cheese, sliced meats, patés, breads, jams, and pastries might form the foundation of a picnic you'd enjoy on any of the city's panoramic outcroppings. Famous people have been so commonplace here over the years that the owners have virtually stopped reacting to, say, Hollywood starlets shopping for their off-the-record companions. There's also an impressive collection of wines, liqueurs, and grappas. Corso Umberto I, 59. ℂ **0942-23321.**

Oggettistica e Arredi   The inventory at this store includes mostly brass and, to a lesser extent, silver, reproductions of art objects from the 18th and 19th centuries. We prefer the good replicas of brass door knockers that cost between 35€ and 85€. Massive and finely detailed, they're so close to the genuine article that you're hard-pressed to tell them apart. Via Fratelli Ingegnere 4 at the corner of the Corso Umberto I. ℂ **0347-6066148.**

WHERE TO STAY

The hotels in Taormina are the best in Sicily—in fact, they're the finest in Italy south of Amalfi. All price levels and accommodations are available, from sumptuous suites to army cots.

If you're coming primarily to hit the beach, at least in July and August, consider staying at **Mazzarò**, 5km (3 miles) from the center, and trekking up the hill for the shopping, nightlife, and dining. Mazzarò is the major beach and has some fine hotels (see the Grand Hotel Mazzorò Sea Palace, below). A bus for Mazzarò leaves from the center of Taormina every 30 minutes daily from 8am to 9pm (the return-trip schedule is the same). The one-way fare is 1.50€. Otherwise, we recommend that you stay in Taormina—it has far more charm and attractions than anything down by the sea.

The curse of Taormina hotels in summer is the noise, not only of traffic but of visitors who turn the town into an all-night party. If you're a light sleeper and you've chosen a hotel along Corso Umberto, ask for a room in the rear. You might not get a view, but at least you should get a good night's sleep.

If you're driving to the top of Taormina to a hotel, call ahead to see what arrangements can be made for your car. Also ask for clear directions—the narrow, one-way streets can be bewildering once you get here.

VERY EXPENSIVE

Grand Hotel Timeo ★★ Hidden in a tranquil private park full of cypresses and magnolias just below the ancient Greek Amphitheater, the Timeo opened in 1873 and has hosted everyone from King Umberto II to Liz Taylor and Richard Burton. It's perched at the eastern edge of Taormina, on a precarious but panoramic terrace that seems completely flooded with light and panoramas upward to the Greek Amphitheater and down across Taormina to the sea. A prestigious member of the Framon chain, it evokes a stately but comfortable 19th-century neoclassical villa that manages to be lighthearted and baronial at the same time. It lacks the manorial sobriety and dignity of the Palazzo San Domenico, and has none of its ecclesiastical overlays. You get the feeling that the Timeo was built purely for pleasure, and it carries the aura of a sophisticated and very secular private villa. Guests are treated to a winning combination of old-world elegance and contemporary conveniences. All the rooms are spacious and well furnished, with large marble bathrooms with tub and shower. Guest rooms, accessible via claustrophobic-looking corridors, are usually large and sometimes have vaulted ceilings, well-crafted plaster bas-relief friezes, and comfortable furniture—discreet but a bit blandly modernized. Guests are greeted with a fruit basket or a bottle of dessert wine on arrival. All rooms have balconies with a view of the snowcapped peak of Mount Etna or the sea. Room nos. 301 to 316 enjoy the widest panorama. The hotel has a private beach with lounge chairs, umbrellas, and other amenities; the staff will arrange tee times at nearby golf courses. Because it's so close to the monument, local archaeological authorities are still doing battle with the hotel in court, refusing its right to dig a swimming pool so close to the Greek ruins.

Via Teatro Greco 59, 98039 Taormina. (✆ **0942-23801.** Fax 0942-628501. www.framonhotels.com. 87 units. 284€–366€ double; 465€–547€ suite. Rates include breakfast. AE, DC, MC, V. Free parking. **Amenities:** Restaurant; piano bar; concierge; car-rental desk; shuttle service to the beach; room service; babysitting; laundry. *In room:* A/C, TV, minibar, hair dryer, safe.

Palazzo San Domenico ★★★ This is one of the greatest hotels of Italy, with a pedigree so impressive that it evokes a national monument. Having housed such illustrious guests as François Mitterand, Winston Churchill, and hundreds of outrageously decadent celebrities, it's the envy of most of the other hoteliers of Taormina. Set in the heart of the resort's oldest neighborhood, it originated in the 14th century as a semi-fortified Dominican monastery. Today, after generations of meticulous upgrades, it's surrounded by walled-in terraced gardens lit at night by flickering torches that evoke a sort of medieval mysticism.

In many ways, it's a miracle that this place functions as a hotel at all: It boasts greater amounts of public space per overnight guest than any other hotel in Sicily, delightfully divided among vast reception rooms, two Romanesque courtyards, hideaway chapels, and vaulted monastic-looking hallways as long as football fields. Add to this a rambling set of interconnected paneled salons and scads of valuable antiques, and you have plenty of material for a romantic holiday in a unique setting.

Don't expect the interior of this place to look cutting-edge and glossy, or as if a team of decorators just finished moving in the furniture: What you get are massive and dignified areas outfitted with museum-quality antiques that have

Moments **When the Monks Come Out at Night**

We suggest that if you stay at San Domenico, take a walk through the ecclesiastical-looking hallways, chapels, and courtyards late at night, when things are eerily empty and quiet, and when torches flicker exotically in the gardens. That's when the resident ghosts (two or three) are said to make their appearances. It's the most mystical and otherworldly experience available in any hotel in Sicily.

been in place for at least 75 years, a genuinely impressive patina, and a physical setting that no one would ever dare modernize. The result is Old World, high class, unglossy, and old-fashioned in the most appealing sense of the word.

Guest rooms lie in either the old monastery part of the hotel, where furnishings are severely dignified and very comfortable, or in the somewhat more opulent "newer" wings, those added in 1897, which evoke the Gilded Age and its aesthetics a bit more richly. All accommodations have richly accessorized bathrooms with shower/tub combinations. Views extend out over the bougainvillea, palms, and citrus trees in the garden to the sea. Unlike its biggest competitor, the Grand Hotel Timeo, the San Domenico has a swimming pool (the only heated one in town), which was artfully carved into the slope of the hillside below the gardens.

Piazza San Domenico 5, 98039 Taormina. ℂ **0942-613111.** Fax 0942-625506. www.sandomenico.thi.it. 108 units. 274€–423€ double; from 700€ suite. Rates include breakfast. AE, DC, MC, V. Free parking outside; 3 spaces inside (summer only) 15€. **Amenities:** Excellent restaurant (with outdoor terrace dining and views); piano bar; heated pool with a view; concierge; room service; babysitting; laundry. *In room:* A/C, TV, minibar, hair dryer, safe (in most rooms).

EXPENSIVE

Excelsior Palace Hotel ★★ This government-rated four-star hotel in Taormina is used more aggressively by tour groups (especially Boston-based Grand Circle Travel) than virtually any other hotel in town. It's set on a rocky ridge in the lower reaches of Taormina, midway between a busy piazza and an isolated, somewhat dusty garden that slopes steeply down to a swimming pool. Part of the allure of this place derives from its outrageous facade (ca. 1903), which artfully mimics the grand Moorish architecture you might expect in Marrakesh, complete with ogival arches and geometric zigzags. Most of the rather formal-looking guest rooms were renovated and upgraded in 2001, inspired by late-19th-century models. Older, not-yet-renovated rooms are a bit more bland but equally comfortable. All guest rooms come with private bathrooms, some with shower, some with tub. There's a solarium on the grounds.

Via Toselli 8, 98039 Taormina. ℂ **0942-23975.** Fax 0942-23978. www.taohotels.com/excelsior. 88 units. 206€ double. AE, DC, MC, V. **Amenities:** Restaurant; bar; pool. *In room:* A/C, TV.

Hotel Isabella Only one other hotel, the Victoria, enjoys a location directly on the main street of Taormina, and of these, the Isabella is the better-rated of the two. Small-scale, well-upholstered, and chic in a way that only a boutique hotel can be, it welcomes visitors with a lobby that might remind you of a living room, with well-padded upholsteries and a peaches-and-cream color scheme. Established in 1985 and renovated in 2001, it pleases you with a decor inspired by a sun-flooded country house in England. Guest rooms are cozy, not particularly large, and plush, some with views over the all-pedestrian hubbub of the town's main street, and all with tiled bathrooms with shower. On the rooftop is a solarium.

Corso Umberto I, 58, 98039 Taormina. ℂ **0942-23153.** Fax 0942-23155. www.gaishotels.com. 32 units. 200€–300€ double. Rates include breakfast. AE, DC, MC, V. **Amenities:** Restaurant; bar; free access to beach club with watersports, sunning, and swimming. *In room:* A/C, TV, minibar, hair dryer, safe.

Hotel Monte Tauro   This hotel is built into the side of a hill rising high above the sea. Renovated in the early 1990s, each room has a circular balcony with a sea view, often festooned with flowers. Most rooms are midsize, each furnished to a high standard, with tiled bathrooms with shower-tub combinations. The social center is the pool, whose cantilevered platform is ringed with dozens of plants.

Via Madonna delle Grazie 3, 98039 Taormina. ℂ **0942-24402.** Fax 0942-24403. www.hotelmontetauro.it. 100 units. 277€ double; 342€ junior suite. Rates include breakfast. AE, DC, MC, V. Closed Jan 15–Mar. **Amenities:** Restaurant; 2 bars; pool; room service; babysitting; laundry/dry cleaning. *In room:* A/C, TV, minibar, hair dryer, safe.

Hotel Villa Diodoro ★   This is one of Taormina's better hotels, with tasteful design through and through. There are sunny spots where you can swim, sunbathe, and enjoy the view of mountains, trees, and flowers. The vistas of Mount Etna, the Ionian Sea, and the eastern coastline of Sicily are reason enough to stay here. The guest rooms are elegant and comfortable, with wrought-iron headboards, terra-cotta floors, balconies, and compact tiled bathrooms with shower-tub combinations. A shuttle bus makes a half-dozen runs per day (June–Oct) to the beach at nearby Lido Caparena.

Via Bagnoli Croce 75, 98039 Taormina. ℂ **0942-23312.** Fax 0942-23391. 99 units. 168€–260€ double. Rates include breakfast. AE, DC, MC, V. Free parking. **Amenities:** Dining room; lounge; pool; room service; laundry. *In room:* A/C, TV, minibar, hair dryer, safe.

Romantik Hotel Villa Ducale ★★   This restored old villa boasts magnificent views of the Mediterranean, the town, and Mount Etna. Villa Ducale sits on a hillside, a 10-minute uphill walk from the center, in a quiet setting in the hamlet of Madonna della Rocca (midway between the heart of the resort and high-altitude Castelmola). It's a charming and romantic choice. Each guest room has a veranda with a sea view, antique Sicilian decor with terra-cotta floors and wrought-iron beds, and a compact tiled bathroom with a shower-tub combination. The service is warm and helpful. Breakfast is usually served on an outdoor terrace with a gorgeous view.

Moments **An Evening Promenade**

We like to stroll at twilight along Corso Umberto I until we reach the resort's most charming small square. **Piazza IX Aprile** overlooks the sea with the **grandest panoramas** ★★ of Mount Etna looming in the background. One side of the square is open, its other three sides enclosed by the 17th-century church of San Giuseppe, San Agostino (converted into a library), and Torre dell'Orologio from the late 1600s. Choose any of the bars with tables outside. Piazza IX Aprile is the favored rendezvous point for the young men of Taormina to meet ladies—a temporary visitor from abroad, perhaps?

Via Leonardo da Vinci 60, 98039 Taormina. ☎ **0942-28153.** Fax 0942-28710. www.hotelvilladucale.it. 15 units. 155€–238€ double; 310€–413€ suite. Rates include buffet breakfast. AE, MC, V. Parking 7€. **Amenities:** Lounge; shuttle service to the beach; room service; laundry. *In room:* A/C, TV, minibar, hair dryer, safe.

MODERATE

Villa Belvedere   With a friendly reception, professional maintenance, and old-fashioned style, this hotel near the Public Garden offers the same view enjoyed by guests at more expensive hotels nearby. Guests congregate on the cliffside terrace in the rear to enjoy the view of Sicilian skies, the Ionian Sea, the cypress-studded hillside, and smoldering Mount Etna. The small to midsize guest rooms feature functional furniture with a touch of class. Most rooms have slivers of balconies from which to enjoy views over the neighboring Public Garden to the sea, and the top-floor rooms have small terraces. Each unit comes with a compact, tiled bathroom, most of which have shower-tub combinations. The hotel is located near the cable car and the steps down to the beach.

Via Bagnoli Croci 79, 98039 Taormina. ☎ **0942-23791.** Fax 0942-625830. www.villabelvedere.it. 47 units. 93€–176€ double. Rates include breakfast. MC, V. Parking 5.50€. Closed late Nov to mid-Dec and mid-Jan to early Mar. **Amenities:** 2 bars; pool; room service; laundry. *In room:* A/C, TV, hair dryer, safe (in some).

Villa Fabbiano ★★ *Finds*   Only Villa Ducale and Grand Hotel Timeo enjoy the same tranquility and romantic position as this house situated in a mock castle, which attracts some of the most discerning guests in Taormina. Its chief allure is a terrace roof garden, and it's a charmer in every way. The staff, the service, the accommodations, and the price combine to make this a little gem. Within an hour the staff will get to know you and your needs. The furnishings are well chosen for comfort, tradition, and style, and each guest room is beautifully furnished and inviting. All come with a neatly tiled private bathroom with tub or shower. The cuisine is first rate. We count the days until we can return.

Via Pirandello 81, 98039 Taormina. ☎ **0942-626058.** Fax 0954-23732. www.villafabbiano.com. 27 units. 135€–185€ double; 285€–325€ suite. MC, V. Closed Nov–Mar. Parking 6€. **Amenities:** Restaurant; pool; room service; babysitting; laundry/dry cleaning. *In room:* A/C, TV, minibar, hair dryer, safe.

Villa Paradiso ★ *Finds*   This charming boutique hotel originated in 1921 when the grandfather of the present owner bought a villa originally built in 1892 by Florence Trevelyan, an heiress, horticulturist, and niece of one of Britain's most famous historians, D. H. Trevelyan. Today, it's the impeccably maintained domain of a dignified local patriarch, Signore Salvatore Martorana. Set within a warren of narrow streets, immediately adjacent to the town's most beautiful public gardens, the Paradiso contains tastefully furnished public rooms outfitted with antiques, fine art, and good reproductions. Each of the cozy, individually decorated guest rooms has a balcony and conservative, comfortable furnishings, and a tiled bathroom with (in most cases) a shower-tub combination. Between June and October, the hotel offers free shuttle-bus service, and free entrance to the also-recommended **Paradise Beach Club,** about 6 km (4 miles) to the east, in the seaside resort of Letojanni. The hotel's excellent restaurant (Al Settimo Cielo del Paradiso), on its panoramic rooftop, is separately recommended in "Where to Dine," later in this chapter.

Via Roma 2, 98039 Taormina. ☎ **0942-23922.** Fax 0942-625800. 35 units. 130€–180€ double; 166€–216€ junior suite. AE, DC, MC, V. Parking 12€. **Amenities:** Restaurant; bar; lounge; room service. *In room:* A/C, TV, hair dryer, safe.

INEXPENSIVE

Grande Albergo Capotaormina ★★★   Only a very creative architect could have transformed this barren cape into a dramatic oasis of comfort, and that is exactly what noted architect Minoletti did in the late 1960s with this hotel. The result is the most avant-garde architectural statement in or around Taormina—an oasis of comfort and poshness within a spectacularly inhospitable natural setting. Surrounded by the Ionian Sea on three sides, and by the coastal highway on the fourth, and with a layout that resembles an irregular pentagon, the hotel contains five floors with wide sun terraces. Rambling public areas are outfitted in cherry-wood paneling and colors inspired by the sea. Elevators take you through 46m (150 ft.) of solid rock to the beach and to a large, free-form swimming pool far below the level of the hotel, directly adjacent to the sea. Guest rooms are handsome and well-proportioned, each with roomy tiled bathrooms with tub and shower, and wide glass doors opening onto private terraces.

Via Nazionale 105, 98039 Taormina. ℂ **0942-572111.** Fax 0942-625467. www.capotaorminahotel.com. 200 units. 208€–360€ double; 394€–980€ suite. AE, DC, MC, V. **Amenities:** 3 restaurants; 3 bars; pool; seawater Jacuzzi; sauna; watersports program (supplemental charge) including deep-sea fishing and scuba; golf; tennis; salon; room service; massage; laundry/dry cleaning. *In room:* A/C TV, minibar, hair dryer, safe.

Grand Hotel Atlantis Bay   This is the newest government-rated five-star hotel along the Taormina coast, with its own private beach. Associated with the genuinely excellent Mazzarò Sea Palace, but with a less experienced management and a less gifted staff, it blends artfully into a landscape of pebbly beachfronts and sea-fronting cliffs, invisible from the road except for a view over its roofline. Great care was taken during the hotel's reconstruction for an ecologically sensitive approach to the natural surroundings. The result is a jagged and earthy-looking combination of rough-hewn stones, terra-cotta tiles, and primal colors and textures that don't stand out when viewed from afar. There's something stylish and postmodern about this youthful, sports-oriented hotel, with its bubbling aquariums and neo-Roman accessories in the lobby, and comfortable, midsize guest rooms, many with terraces and all with tiled bathrooms with tub and shower. Only time will tell, however, whether it will live up to its high expectations, or whether it will always remain in the shadow of its better-established and more solidly grounded sibling (see below).

Via Nazionale 161, 98030 Taormina Mare. ℂ **0942-618011.** Fax 0942-23194. www.atlantisbay.it. 86 units. 274€–388€ double; from 370€ suite. AE, DC, MC, V. **Amenities:** 2 restaurants; 2 bars (1 with a pianist); pool; fitness center; concierge. *In room:* A/C, TV, minibar, hair dryer.

Grand Hotel Mazzarò Sea Palace ✦✦✦   The leading hotel in Mazzarò opens onto the most beautiful bay in Sicily and has its own private beach. Completed in 1962, it has been renovated frequently since, most recently in the mid-1990s. From the coastal highway, you won't be able to see very much of this spectacular hotel—only a rooftop and masses of bougainvillea. You'll register on the top (4th) floor, then ride an elevator down to sea level for access to a stylish, airy set of marble-sheathed public rooms, each evoking a sea palace with touches of whimsy that Neptune himself might have appreciated. The allure of this government-rated five-star deluxe hotel is reinforced by a location directly on a charming, intimate, half-moon–shaped bay. It's very elegant, richly furnished, genuinely charming, and well staffed. Big windows let in cascades of light and offer views of the coast. The guest rooms are well furnished, filled with wicker and veneer pieces along with original art and wood or tile floors; most have panoramic views. The bathrooms are clad in marble, each with a shower-tub combination.

Via Nazionale 147, 98030 Mazzarò. ℂ **0942-24004.** Fax 0942-626237. www.mazzaroseapalace.it. 88 units. 274€–388€ double; 429€–558€ suite. Rates include breakfast. AE, DC, MC, V. Parking 16€ nearby. **Amenities:** Restaurant; bar; pool; fitness center; room service; babysitting; laundry/dry cleaning. *In room:* A/C, TV, minibar, hair dryer, safe.

Hotel La Campanella   This hotel is rich in plants, paintings, and hospitality. It sits at the top of a seemingly endless flight of stairs, which begin at a sharp curve of the main road leading into town. You climb past terra-cotta pots and the dangling tendrils of a terraced garden, eventually arriving at the house. The owners maintain clean and simple guest rooms, each containing potted plants and homey touches. The tiled bathrooms are tidy and come with showers and tubs.

Via Circonvallazione 3, 98039 Taormina. ⓒ **0942-23381.** Fax 0942-625248. 12 units. 75€ double. Rate includes breakfast. No credit cards. **Amenities:** Lounge. *In room:* Hair dryer.

Hotel Lido Méditerranée ⭐   Less stylish and a bit more dowdy and dated than some of the government-rated five-star palace hotels that lie within a 3-minute drive along the coast, this solidly reliable four-star hotel offers less expensive rates than those around it. Originally built in 1968 and renovated a few times since then, it resembles a private villa. It's draped with bougainvillea and positioned next to a gravel beach. Guest rooms are simple and unpretentious, reminiscent of a slightly dated beachfront hotel in the Caribbean, and usually have balconies or terraces.

Via Nazionale, 98030 Taormina Mare (Spisone). ⓒ **0942-24422.** Fax 0942-24774. www.taorminahotels.com. 72 units. 156€–196€ double. AE, DC, MC, V. Closed Nov–Easter. **Amenities:** Restaurant; piano bar; room service; babysitting; laundry/dry cleaning. *In room:* A/C, TV, minibar.

Hotel Victoria   It's unusual to find a good government-rated two-star hotel in Taormina, and this one is conveniently positioned smack in the middle of the nighttime action, on the town's all-pedestrian main street. It was established in 1885 within a 300-year-old, four-story building that has been frequently upgraded and improved over the years. Its most famous clients have included Oscar Wilde and, several decades later, industrialist Olivetti, who stayed here in the 1920s. All but a few of the rooms have air-conditioning, and eight have minibars. Rooms are accessible via a flight of stone steps and are high-ceilinged, well-maintained, and comfortable, with hints of manorial style. Each has a shower-only, tile-sheathed private bathroom. Rooms overlooking the Corso Umberto I get more light but also more noise.

Corso Umberto I, 81, 98039 Taormina. ⓒ **0942-23372.** Fax 0942-623567. www.albergovictoria.it. 22 units. 93€–103€ double. AE, MC, V. Closed Jan–Feb. *In room:* TV.

Villa Fiorita ⭐ *Value*   This small inn stretches toward the Greek theater from its position beside the road leading to the top of this cliff-hugging town. Its imaginative decor includes a handful of ceramic stoves, which the owner delights in collecting. A well-maintained flower garden lies alongside an empty but ancient Greek tomb whose stone walls have been classified a national treasure. The guest rooms are arranged in a steplike labyrinth of corridors and stairwells, some of which bend to correspond to the rocky slope on which the hotel was built. Each unit contains a piece of antique furniture and tiled bathrooms with shower, and most have private terraces.

Via Luigi Pirandello 39, 98039 Taormina. ⓒ **0942-24122.** Fax 0942-625967. 26 units. 112€ double; 138€ suite. Rates include breakfast. AE, MC, V. Parking 12€. **Amenities:** Lounge; pool; room service. *In room:* A/C, TV, hair dryer, safe.

Villa Sant'Andrea ⭐ *Finds*   Staying here is like going to a house party at a pretty home. The atmosphere and tasteful refurbishment draw return visits by artists, painters, and other discerning guests. The Sant'Andrea lies at the base of the mountain, directly on the sea, and opens onto a private beach. The guest rooms are well maintained and comfortable, although size and decor vary. Many have balconies or terraces with sea views. The tiled shower-only bathrooms are small but have adequate shelf space. A cable car, just outside the front gates, runs into the heart of Taormina.

Via Nazionale 137, 98030 Taormina Mare. © 0942-23125. Fax 0942-24838. www.framon-hotels.com. 80 units. 216€–308€ double. Rates include breakfast. AE, DC, MC, V. Parking 15€. **Amenities:** 2 restaurants; bar; boat rental; room service; babysitting; laundry/dry cleaning. *In room:* A/C, TV, minibar, hair dryer, safe.

Villa Schuler ★ *Value* We'd be happy to return here again and again. Filled with the fragrance of bougainvillea and jasmine, this hotel offers style and comfort at a good price. Family-owned and -run, it sits high above the Ionian Sea, with views of snowcapped Mount Etna and the Bay of Naxos. The hotel is only a 2-minute stroll from Corso Umberto I and about a 15-minute walk from the cable car to the beach below. The guest rooms are comfortably furnished, with well-maintained bathrooms with shower-tub combinations, and many have a small balcony or terrace with a view of the sea. Breakfast can be served in your room or taken on a lovely terrace with a panoramic sea view. The service is impeccable.

The most luxurious way to stay here is to book the garden villa suite with its own private access. It's spacious and beautifully furnished, with two bathrooms (one with a Jacuzzi). The villa comes with a kitchenette, patio, private garden, and veranda, and costs from 200€ per day for two, including breakfast.

Piazzetta Bastione, Via Roma, 98039 Taormina. © 0942-23481. Fax 0942-23522. www.villaschuler.com. 26 units (most with shower only). 110€ double; 144€ junior suite. Rates include breakfast. AE, DC, DISC, MC, V. Parking 10€ in garage; free outside. **Amenities:** Bar; lounge; room service; laundry; library. *In room:* A/C, TV, hair dryer, safe.

CASTELMOLA: HIGH-ALTITUDE ESCAPIST'S RETREAT

Hotel Villa Sonia ★ *Finds* Built in 1974 on the site of an old villa, this hotel lies a short walk downhill from Castelmola's town square. The best-rated and most appealing hotel in Castelmola, it was built on a ridge almost immediately beside the winding road that accesses the village, with spectacular views out over both the front and back of the hotel. Few remnants of the original villa remain in place today: What you see is a stylish brick-and-stone structure carefully terraced into the hillside, with public areas that are bigger and more numerous than the limited number of guest rooms would imply. Rooms here contain modern lines and touches of manorial Sicilian style, including wrought-iron headboards, and about half have private terraces. Each is equipped with a tiled bathroom with a tub or shower. The restaurant here (Ristorante Parco Reale) is especially noteworthy—it's the best in Castelmola and is recommended separately in "Where to Dine," later in this chapter. Shuttle-bus transfers run twice a day from the hotel to central Taormina.

Via Porta Mola 9, 98030 Castelmola. © 0942-28082. Fax 0942-28083. www.tao.it/intelisano. 36 units. 119€–170€ double; 170€–270€ suite. Rates include breakfast. AE, DC, MC, V. Free parking. **Amenities:** Restaurant; bar; pool; fitness room with sauna; babysitting; laundry. *In room:* A/C, TV, minibar, safe.

WHERE TO DINE
VERY EXPENSIVE

Casa Grugno ★★★ MODERN SICILIAN/INTERNATIONAL The most creative and exciting restaurant in Taormina is making a bold and bright statement about modern Sicilian cuisine that's being carefully watched by other restaurateurs. Andreas Zangerl is the Austrian-born chef, whose former duties involved running the kitchens aboard some of the most upscale cruise ships in the world, where price was not an issue and where heads of state would arrive with their entourages. That's something of the impression you get at this increasingly famous restaurant, where the snows of the Austrian Tyrol seem to mingle with the torrid Sicilian scrublands. The venue, a stone-sided house, built by a Catalonian family during the Spanish occupation of Taormina, contains a bar, an ocher-colored dining room outfitted like a trompe l'oeil rendition of Carnevale in Venice, and a walled-in outdoor terrace ringed with plants. The hip and alert young (largely European) staff gets excellent supervision from the town's most successful maître d'hotel, Stephano Lo Guidice.

The sublime cuisine draws from a pan-European sensibility that translates artfully into an upscale Sicilian idiom of enormous charm. The set-price menus—including an all-Sicilian set menu and an even more appealing pair of "tasting menus"—reveal the kitchen's finesse at its most impressive. One or the other might include tuna steak with sweet-and-sour onion and mint sauce; fusilli pasta with pasta *alla Trapanese* (with pulverized almonds, tomatoes, and chile peppers); sardines *becca fino* served with bread crumbs, orange peel, and raisins; roasted pigeon with lentils from the offshore island of Pantelleria; shellfish soup with saffron and chile peppers; and a perfect and impeccable version of Parmesan eggplant that might be the most deliciously fragrant dish in this part of town. This is reinvented Sicilian cuisine at its finest, a haute cuisine that's proudly emerging to compete with the best regional cuisines of Europe.

Via Santa Maria de Greci. © 0942-21208. Reservations recommended. Main courses 14€–23€; set-price menus 40€–52€. AE, DC, MC, V. Daily 7:30pm–midnight.

EXPENSIVE

La Giara ★★ SICILIAN/ITALIAN   Glossy, airy, and reminiscent of Rome during the heyday of Gina Lollobrigida, La Giara evokes a warmed-over *la dolce vita*. It's an accomplished standard that's been eclipsed by the more hip, more cutting-edge Casa Grugno (see above). The restaurant is elegant and almost excessively formal, and has remained predictably stable since its founding in 1953. Views sweep from the veranda, with its outdoor tables, onto the bay of Taormina. The staff is discreet and extremely "grand hotel" in their uniformed dress codes. The kitchen turns out flavorful dishes that make the most of fresh ingredients grown in the southern sunshine of Italy. The Art Deco ambience is also inviting—with marble floors and columns shaped from stone quarried in the fields outside Syracuse. The pastas are meals in themselves, and we're especially fond of the ricotta-stuffed cannelloni served with zucchini cream au gratin; the tagliolini with savory lemon-and-shrimp sauce; and the ravioli stuffed with pesto-flavored eggplant and covered with tomato sauce. The fresh fish of the day is grilled to perfection, and meats are cooked equally well.

Vico la Floresta 1. © 0942-23360. Reservations required. Main courses 18€–22€. AE, DC, MC, V. Apr–July and Sept–Oct Tues–Sun 8:15–11pm (Nov–Mar open only Fri–Sat; Aug open daily).

Maffei's ★ *Finds* SICILIAN/SEAFOOD   Maffei's is very small, with only 10 tables, but it serves the best fish in Taormina. Every day the chef selects the freshest fish at the market, and you simply tell him how you'd like it prepared. We often choose the house specialty, swordfish *alla Messinese*, braised with tomato sauce, black olives, and capers. The *fritto misto* (a mixed fish-fry with calamari, shrimp, swordfish, and sea bream) is made superbly light by good-quality olive oil. Among the succulent desserts are velvety lemon mousse and crepes flambé stuffed with vanilla cream.

Via San Domenico de Guzman 1. © 0942-24055. Reservations required. Main courses 7€–8€. AE, DC, MC, V. Daily noon–3pm and 7pm–midnight. Closed early Jan to mid-Feb.

MODERATE

Al Duomo ✿ SICILIAN/MESSINESE   Known for its outside terrace dining, this restaurant prepares its dishes using the freshest local produce and regional ingredients. It's an attractive place, with brickwork tiles and inlaid marble tables. The romantic terrace provides a view of the square and the cathedral. Try the stewed lamb with potatoes and red Sicilian wine. The fried calamari is sautéed in extra-virgin olive oil and not overcooked. Another great dish is *rissolé* of fresh anchovies. For dessert, taste a typical almond cake or a Sicilian *cassata*.

Vico Ebrei 11. ✆ 0942-625656. Reservations required. Main courses 8€–16€. AE, DC, MC, V. Nov–Mar Mon–Sat noon–2:30pm and 7–11pm; Apr–Oct Thurs–Mon noon–2:30pm and 7–11pm.

Club Septimo ✿ INTERNATIONAL/ITALIAN   In addition to its excellent cuisine, this restaurant and club offers a sweeping view of Taormina and the Ionian Sea and is framed with reproductions of ancient Roman columns. The restaurant lies on the winding road leading downhill from Taormina, between Campo Sportiva (a soccer field) and Parcheggio Lumbi, the public parking lot. This place has a ritzy feel, especially if you get a table on the terrace overlooking the Ionian Sea. On a clear night, the view of the bay embraces the distant coast of Calabria on mainland Italy. The setting is one of the most beautiful in Taormina, with large terraces and age-old trees. Menus present classic and modern cuisine ideas almost in equal measure. Among the more stimulating dishes we recently sampled was swordfish with a surprise addition of mussels and "other creatures of the sea," served with sliced potatoes and given an aromatic touch of saffron. Small shrimp were spiced with strong, flavorful Sicilian cheese and sautéed lightly in an olive oil sauce. A platter of smoked fish came with a citrus-and fruit–flavored olive oil sauce and hot toasted bread.

Via San Pancrazio 50. ✆ 0942-625522. Reservations required. Main courses 7.50€–14€. AE, DC, MC, V. June–Sept daily 7:30pm–midnight (or later).

Il Ciclope *Value* SICILIAN/ITALIAN   This is one of the best of Taormina's low-priced trattorie. Set back from the main street, it opens onto the pint-size Piazzetta Salvatore Leone. In summer, try to snag an outside table. The meals are fairly simple, but the ingredients are fresh and the dishes well prepared. Try the fish soup or Sicilian squid. Or go for entrecôte Ciclope or grilled shrimp. Most diners begin with a selection from the *antipasti di mare,* a savory assortment of seafood hors d'oeuvres.

Corso Umberto I, 203. ✆ 0942-23263. Main courses 5.50€–13€. AE, DC, MC, V. Thurs–Tues noon–3pm and 6:30–10:30pm. Closed Jan 10–Feb 15 and Wed Oct–May.

Ristorante La Griglia ✿ SICILIAN   One of the city's newer restaurants evokes an age that's much older, thanks to a cool, shady location within the thick stone walls of what was in the 1600s a private palazzo. Our favorite seats are those against the most distant back wall. There windows overlook a steep drop-off into one of Taormina's oldest streets, a ravinelike alleyway known as Via Naumachia, whose walled edges were built by the ancient Romans. (If you ask, a waiter will take you to the restaurant's rear entrance, to an iron staircase extending high above its cobblestones and verdant trees.) Food is well-prepared and the setting is comfortable and country-elegant. The restaurant's cooks prepare one of the best selections of Sicilian antipasti in town. Or you might start with one of the classic island pastas—we enjoyed one prepared with swordfish caught off the coast and cooked with baby eggplant. The chef will be happy to prepare grilled fresh vegetables for the vegetarian. There's a wonderful wine list.

Corso Umberto I, 54. ℂ **0942-23980.** Reservations recommended only for dinner during midsummer. Main courses 9€–15€. AE, DC, MC, V. Wed–Mon noon–2:30pm and 7pm–1:30am.

Ristorante Luraleo (Value) SICILIAN/INTERNATIONAL Luraleo offers excellent value. Many diners choose to eat on the flowery terrace, where pastel tablecloths are shaded by a vine-covered arbor. If you prefer to dine indoors, there's a rustic dining room with tile accents, flowers, evening candlelight, racks of wine bottles, and a bountiful antipasti table. The grilled fish is a good choice, as are pastas (such as homemade macaroni with tomato, eggplant, and basil), regional dishes, and a tender, herb-flavored steak. Risotto with salmon and pistachio nuts is a specialty.

Via Bagnoli Croce 31. ℂ **0942-24279.** Reservations recommended. Main courses 15€–25€. DC, MC, V. Daily 10am–3pm and 6pm–midnight. Closed Wed in winter.

INEXPENSIVE

Al Settimo Cielo del Paradiso ★ (Value) It's far from being the most famous or popular restaurant in Taormina, but in some ways it's our undisputed budget favorite, thanks to a high-altitude view that seems to sweep over half of Sicily, superb food, and a sense of chic inspired by the most extravagant days of *la dolce vita*. To reach it, take an elevator from the marble-floored lobby of the also-recommended hotel, then dine on a rooftop where Orson Welles and John D. Rockefeller IV once dined, and where you'll see a surprising number of couples return to celebrate wedding anniversaries. Salvatore Martorana is the owner and impresario here, orchestrating dishes that are likely to include well-crafted versions of pennette or risotto with salmon; succulent salads of grilled giant prawns served with a limoncello sauce; roulades of grilled swordfish layered with vegetables and herbs; and a wide selection of very fresh fish prepared any way you want. There's a catch here. You must enter the restaurant between 8 and 9pm, as it has the shortest opening times of any place along the coast.

On the top floor of the Hotel Villa Paradiso. Via Roma 2. ℂ **0942-23922.** Reservations recommended. Main courses 7.20€–11€. AE, DC, MC, V. Daily 8–9pm.

Bella Blu ★ SICILIAN/INTERNATIONAL This chic international rendezvous is a restaurant and pizzeria, as well as a piano bar and disco. In addition to offering fine cuisine, Bella Blu is one of the most entertaining places to be in Taormina after dark. Located a 150m (492-ft.) walk from the center of Taormina, the place has a rich, luxurious aura. Its menus and fine food are based on the freshest of local ingredients. "We like to prepare our food at the moment," the chef assured us, "so that everything will be fresh." The chef specializes in barbecued and grilled meat flavored with fresh herbs, as well as fresh fish, much of it plucked from the Ionian Sea. Our mixed grill of fish could not have been fresher—and the olive oil was virgin and the main seasoning little more than fresh lemon. Other Sicilian favorites include homemade pasta with fresh sardines in a savory tomato sauce with wild fennel and pine nuts.

Via Luigi Pirandello 28. ℂ **0942-24239.** Reservations required June–Aug. Main courses 5€–10€. Fixed-price menu 15€. AE, DC, MC, V. Daily 6:30–11pm.

Da Saro SICILIAN This popular and often crowded restaurant is favored by neighborhood locals as well as mainly European visitors. Much of its charm derives from the animated staff (many of whom are members of the same family), who show an inordinate pride in the quality of its genuinely flavorful cuisine. The neighborhood that contains it, near the Grande Arco Porta Messina, isn't particularly fashionable, and commercial traffic roars by on the street outside. But that doesn't detract from the genuinely delicious flavor within—for example, try the spaghetti Don Giuliano, concocted from olives, tuna, olive oil, and tomatoes. Other choices include stuffed peppers, grilled eggplant, and roasted green peppers in oil; prosciutto with olives; and a memorable *frittura* (mixed grill) of fish and calamari. As you dine, ceiling fans slowly spin, and the garrulous staff might take a genuine interest in where you're from.

Via Costantino Patricio 24. (C) 0942-23934. Reservations not necessary. Main courses 7.50€–12€. AE, DC, MC, V. Daily noon–3pm and 7–11pm. Closed Wed Oct–Feb.

Granduca ★ (Finds ITALIAN/SICILIAN

This is the most atmospheric choice in town, and it also serves an excellent, carefully executed cuisine. You enter through an antiques store with potted plants and various art objects. Even more alluring is the terrace with its panoramic views. In fair weather, request a table in the beautiful gardens. The competent cookery always focuses on the quality of its ingredients. Our favorite pasta here is spaghetti alla Norma (with tomato sauce, eggplant, and ricotta cheese). If you want something truly Sicilian, ask for pasta with sardines. Pasta also comes with a savory kettle of freshly caught mussels and clams. The best meat dish is the grilled roulades, or meat rolls. At night various pizzas are baked to perfection in a wood-fired oven.

Corso Umberto I, 172. (C) 0942-24983. Reservations recommended. Main courses 7.50€–12€. AE, DC, MC, V. Daily 12:30–3pm and 7:30pm–midnight. Closed Tues in winter.

Il Baccanale SICILIAN

This trattoria/grill serves what islanders called *Cucina Tipica Siciliana,* cooking they prefer to all others, even when job opportunities send them to such faraway places as Milan or even America. A slightly better dining venue than its many competitors that flank it on all sides, this eatery lies at the end of a pedestrian-only street. It's the Taormina equivalent of a French bistro, with checkered tablecloths, prints of wine and grape arbors, and a bustling kitchen visible on an upper balcony. The 30 or so tables spill onto the piazza in front.

Piazzetta Filea 1 (Via Di Giovanni). (C) 0942-624390. Reservations recommended. Main courses 8€–13€. MC, V. Daily noon–3pm and 6–10pm. Closed Thurs Oct–Mar.

Ristorante U'Bossu SICILIAN/MEDITERRANEAN

Vines twine around the facade of this small restaurant in a quiet part of town. Amid fresh flowers, wagon-wheel chandeliers, prominently displayed wine bottles, and burnished wooden panels, you can enjoy a meal pungent with the aromas of an herb garden. Start with the complimentary *bruschetta* (grilled bread with oil and garlic or tomato). Specialties include pasta *con la sarde* (with sardines) and *involtini di pesce spada* (swordfish roulades), and there's a groaning antipasti table. The restaurant is decorated with a folkloric scene from *Cavalleria Rusticana,* and the chef has paid homage to the famed opera by naming his best pasta dish *maccheroni alla Turiddu,* after the principal character (it contains tuna, olives, capers, onions, wild herbs, tomatoes, and fennel). For dessert, nothing can top the zabaglione with fresh strawberries.

Via Bagnoli Croce 50. (C) 0942-23311. Reservations recommended. Main courses 7€–13€; fixed-price menu 11€. V. Tues–Sun noon–3pm and 6pm–midnight. Closed Nov 10–Mar 1.

Tirami Su ★ (Value SICILIAN

This is one of the most frequently praised inexpensive restaurants in Taormina, drawing appreciative comments from a wide variety of residents and visitors, as well as managers of hotels in cities as far away as Messina. It's small and basic-looking, lying beside a noisy commercial street that's so busy and so impossibly narrow you might fear for your life as you approach or leave it, especially if you've had a bit too much wine. Within an environment accented with murals, and tables and shelves loaded down with the bounty of a Sicilian harvest, you'll enjoy dishes that include a filet of beef with mushrooms and cream sauce; swordfish roulades; a savory fish soup; and a Palermo-style entrecôte with croquette potatoes. The spaghetti with seafood is, according to the raves of overfed and fully satisfied diners, wonderful. We concur.

Via Costantino Patricio. ℂ **0942-24803.** Reservations recommended. Pizzas 5.50€–6.50€. Main courses 8.50€–13€. AE, MC, V. Wed–Mon noon–3pm and 7:30–11pm.

AT MAZZARO: TAORMINA BY THE SEA

Ristorante Angelo a Mare-Il Delfino MEDITERRANEAN/ITALIAN This late-19th-century structure is in Mazzarò, about 5km (3 miles) from Taormina and a 2-minute walk from the cable-car station. From the flower-filled terrace, you enjoy a view over the bay. The decor and the menu items are inspired by the sea and carefully supervised by the chef/owner. Mussels *Delfino* (cooked with garlic, parsley, olive oil, and lemons) and house-style steak (with fresh tomatoes, onions, garlic, capers, and parsley) are specialties. Other good choices are roulades of fish, cannelloni, *risotto pescatore* (fisherman's rice), and anchovies roasted with basil.

Via Nazionale. ℂ **0942-23004.** Reservations recommended. Main courses 6.20€–12€. AE, DC, MC, V. Daily noon–3pm and 6pm–midnight. Closed Nov–Mar.

AT ISOLA BELLA

Ristorante da Giovanni SICILIAN/ITALIAN Perched precariously between the coastal road and the cliff that drops vertiginously down to the sea, this restaurant enjoys a view that sweeps over the peninsula of Isola Bella. You'll find yourself in a glassed-in dining room that's simple and airy, and accented with blue tile floors and very few adornments other than the view. Menu items are well-prepared and flavorful, and include a fish soup that might win the approval of Neptune, as well as a mixed grill of fish that was caught that morning by fishermen working the Ionian Sea. For our pasta fix, we gravitate to pennette with succulent crabmeat. Meat aficionados should find the veal scaloppine with white wine sauce heartwarming.

Isola Bella. ℂ **0942-23531.** Reservations recommended. Main courses 7.90€–17€. AE, DC, MC, V. Tues–Sun 12:15–3pm and 8–11pm.

AT CASTELMOLA

Ristorante Parco Reale ★ *Finds* SICILIAN/INTERNATIONAL Artful, romantic, candlelit, and panoramic, and set within the previously recommended Hotel Villa Sonia, this is the best restaurant in Castelmola, offering lots of international pizzazz. Some members of the staff are Australian, with an offbeat sense of humor that might contribute to your understanding of this very Sicilian venue. Within an airy and rambling dining room awash with displays of wine and rolling food trolleys, you'll enjoy freshly prepared and good-tasting dishes. The risotto with fresh mushrooms we recently sampled was worthy of that prepared in a fine restaurant in Lombard, where the dish originated. The grilled catch of the day is done to perfection and the preferred choice of most discerning diners. On the constantly changing menu, we've enjoyed such dishes as air-dried beef with carrots julienne and macaroni with garlic, tomatoes, and bits of ham. A veal escalope is made especially alluring when it's cooked in almond wine.

Fun Fact The Case of the Bouncing Check

Like Tennessee Williams, the author Truman Capote used to visit Taormina to finish his novel *Answered Prayers*. One drunken night at the San Domenico, he closed a deal to purchase the offshore island, Isola Bella. Actually, it's a gloriously conical peninsula—small, ringed with sand, and absolutely beautiful. The asking price from a local landowner was $10,000. Everyone was happy with this amazing deal until the check was returned from New York marked "insufficient funds."

In the Hotel Villa Sonia, Via Porta Mola 9, Castelmola. (C) 0942-28082. Reservations recommended for dinner in midsummer. Main courses 8€–15€. AE, DC, MC, V. Daily 12:30–2:30pm and 7–10:30pm.

TAORMINA AFTER DARK

Sicilian cities aren't known for their nightlife. The best, and certainly the most sophisticated, after-dark amusements can be found in Taormina. The resort is also the best spot in Sicily for gay and lesbian visitors. Incidentally, drinks here are more expensive than in all the bars of Sicily.

Many visitors are content to spend their evenings at cafe tables on outdoor terraces. The most popular form of evening entertainment is the *passeggiata,* or promenade, along the Corso Umberto I. Join it—it's fun.

You might also catch a bus to Giardini-Naxos (see below) for a waterfront stroll in the evening. Most bars and clubs stay open here until way past midnight, at least in the summer months.

For a nightlife adventure, one of the most popular activities in Taormina is to take a CST bus tour, **Etna Tramonto,** for a sunset trip to the slopes of Mount Etna. Buses run from June to October only; a one-way trip costs 55€ per person. Call (C) **0942-625301** for tickets and information daily from 6:40am to 8:30pm. Departures are Monday and Wednesday from the bus terminal along Via Luigi Pirandello, leaving Taormina at 3pm and returning at 10:30pm. The tour features a guide and a Jeep excursion to the crater; food is not included in the price.

Bar at the Palazzo San Domenico   A (relatively) inexpensive way to see the inside of one of Italy's most legendary hotels is to drop by here for a drink one night. Within a sprawling labyrinth of public areas—some of which evoke the Gilded Age, others the inner sanctums of medieval monasteries—you can order drinks between 9pm and midnight and listen to the live music of a pianist. Bar service is technically available every day from 4 till 11:30pm, but the place is at its most romantic after 9pm, when flickering torches illuminate gardens that might have come from the pages of the New Testament. Piazza San Domenico 5. (C) 0942-613111.

Bar San Giorgio   Perched on the main square of the village, immediately adjacent to a rocky drop-off guaranteed to induce vertigo, this might be the only building in the town's historic core that was able to beat the local building codes and alter its otherwise medieval-looking architecture. The result is a boxy, glass-sided upper story that looks like something from the German Bauhaus, but with Sicilian views that sweep over the surrounding hills. Many visitors opt for coffee or gelati on the ground-floor cafe, but if you prefer to sit awhile in contemplation, simply negotiate the impossibly steep flight of steps that clings to the building's exterior to reach the upper story. The place serves only coffee, sandwiches, and drinks. It's open daily, year-round, from 7:30am to midnight. Via Porta Mola 9, Castel-mola. ℂ 0942-28228.

Bella Blu　When the entire town is having fun on a summer day, you can almost bet that the most fun is generated by the high-energy 20- and 30-somethings who flock to this previously recommended restaurant/pizzeria. It's one of the most elegant and popular piano bars and dance clubs in town. "What kind of music do you normally feature?" a waiter was asked. His reply: "We're at the rocky end of things. Normal isn't a word to use for us." The disco is open only on Saturday from 11pm to 2:30am; the piano bar is also open only on Saturday from 9pm to 2am. Via Luigi Pirandello 28. ℂ 0942-24239. No cover.

Café Marrakech　Its name reminiscent of a late-night Marlene Dietrich movie from the 1930s, this is a popular hot spot. The patrons? In the words of one habitué, "The club attracts a delightful mixture of the flotsam and jetsam of America and North Europe." Naturally, the cafe leans heavily on its Moroccan theme, even sporting Sahara-like tents. Against a backdrop of recorded music, the night is filled with hot young men and women sizing each other up. The club keeps erratic opening hours; call before you go. Piazza Garibaldi. ℂ 0942-625692.

Caffè Wunderbar　We always begin our evening here, as Tennessee Williams did on his yearly visits to Taormina. This bar/cafe lies in the center of the resort on Taormina's main street, opening onto a panoramic view of the bay and Mount Etna beyond it. For some reason, this has been the favored cafe of many visiting celebrities, including Greta Garbo and Rainer Werner Fassbinder. Sicilian ice creams and *granite* (traditional crushed ice drinks) are served at outdoor tables or inside an elegant salon, where the soft notes of a cafe concert might be playing. The cafe is open daily from 8:30am to 2:30am; closed on Tuesday from November to February. Piazza IX Aprile 7 (Corso Umberto I). ℂ 0942-625302.

Club Septimo　With some of the loveliest terraces in Taormina, this well-attended nightclub plays disco music all night long to a crowd, mostly European, in their twenties to forties. Fashion shows and other gala evenings are often staged here. The interior contains all the strobe and ultraviolet lights you'll ever see. Some of the resort's most daring apparel can be seen here in the evening, the later the wilder. The disco is open from June to September daily from midnight to 5am. Offseason, it is open only on Saturday and Sunday during the same hours. Via San Pancrazio 50. ℂ 0942-625522. Cover 8€–13€.

La Cisterna del Moro　The focal point of this restaurant/pub is a stone-sided cistern, built during the Middle Ages by the Arabs, that's set deep within a basement used for wine storage. A staff member will show it to you if you ask, but you're more likely to be drinking, eating, and talking on the upper floors. Located a few steps downhill from Corso Umberto, on a narrow alleyway, the club is most fun after 8pm. A restaurant is attached to the pub, set on a terrace layered in bougainvillea. It serves 25 kinds of pizza (including a version with grilled radicchio, smoked cheese, and bacon), each priced between 3€ to 8€. Both McFarland and Heineken are on tap here, and beer is the preferred drink. La Cisterna is open for meals Tuesday through Sunday from 12:30 to 3pm and 7:30pm to midnight, and as a pub it's open Tuesday through Sunday from 12:30pm to at least 3am. Via Bonifacio 1. ℂ 0942-23001.

Mocambo Bar This is our favorite outdoor bar in Taormina. It occupies an enviable location on the town's main square, midway between two churches and a medieval watchtower, smack in the center of the resort's evening hubbub. It was established during the peak of *La Dolce Vita* (1952), when Truman Capote and Tennessee Williams held court at sidewalk tables, relating their respective indiscretions to anyone who cared to listen in. You can opt for a seat on the piazza throughout the year, weather permitting, but during colder weather many visitors migrate inside, where a satirical mural showing a busy night at the Mocambo Bar (by artist Christian Bernard) and an oversized display of alarmingly realistic photos of late-19th-century *contadinos* by Wilhelm von Gloeden seem to spark conversational energies. There's live piano music every evening between 9pm and 12:30am. It's open daily in the summer from 8pm to at least 2am; in winter it's open Saturday and Sunday only from 9pm to 12:30am. Piazza IX Aprile 8. ✆ **0942-23350.**

Morgana Bar Named after the seductive fairy (Morgan la Fée) of Camelot days, who lured valiant knights to their doom, this ultra-hip, cutting-edge bar is tucked into one of the narrow alleyways running downhill from Corso Umberto I. Centered around a semicircular bartop, it spills onto a candlelit terrace whose lighting is guaranteed to make any man look alluring or any woman fabulous. Don't expect this place to even begin to hop until around midnight, when an almost instantaneous flush of clients pours new energy through the place. The clientele is international, attractive, and pan-European, and mating games between the regulars and incoming holidaymakers sometimes get serious. It's open nightly from 9pm to 5am. Scesa Morgana 4. ✆ **0942-620056.**

O-Seven Irish Pub One of our favorite bars in Taormina is a woodsy, sudsy affair on a piazza that abuts the town's main street, a few steps from the town's architectural centerpiece, Piazza 9 Abrile. High-ceilinged and airy, and staffed with attractive Europeans, it welcomes 20- and 30-somethings from throughout the world, many of whom flirt and philosophize with one another over foaming mugs of beer. From June to September, it's open daily from 4pm to 6am; from October to May, it's open Thursday through Tuesday from 5pm to 2am. Largo La Farina 6 (corner of Corso Umberto I). ✆ **0942-24980.**

Re di Bastoni Favored as a cramped and convivial hideaway by local Sicilians, this music bar employs a cosmopolitan staff that might include a Russian emigré or Polish beauty or two. The seats are claustrophobically close together, and the music—either recorded or live—after around 10pm gets impossibly loud, as it reverberates off sienna-colored walls, a beamed ceiling, and oversized paintings. Clients come here with an almost joyful kind of abandon, usually late at night, sometimes with their pets, and always with their fetishes, to slurp down strawberry caipirinhas (7€ each), the widely acknowledged house specialty of celebrity bartender Giusseppe. The bar is open Tuesday through Sunday from 10am to 3am. Sandwiches are the only food served here. Corso Umberto I, 120. ✆ **0942-23037.**

Shatulle Cozy and convivial (and often cramped), this counterculture night bar was established by an Austrian several years ago, who gave it the German name *Shatulle*, or "jewel box." It occupies a site on an intimate-looking piazza several steps downhill from Corso Umberto I. Although most of the youngish guests opt for seats outside, some venture into the chrome- and mirror-trimmed bar inside. This bar and the also-recommended Ziggy's/Perroquet (see below) are the self-acknowledged gay, or gay-friendly, hangouts of Taormina. You'll find a mix of clients from throughout Europe, as well as nonconformist locals who sometimes drive long distances just to be in a tolerant and bemused setting. Year-round, it's open daily from 5pm to 4am. Piazza Paladini 4. ℂ 0942-626175.

Tout Va If you can get past the unfriendly management, this club attracts a wilder, younger crowd than most of the previous offerings. Down by the water, the open-air club features panoramic views and boogies into the wee hours. It's a sort of ill-defined disco and nightclub, often with live music, where the beer and wine flow. Most of the patrons are in their twenties and thirties, with a smattering of customers on the shady side of 40. The cover varies depending on the evening's events, ranging from 10€ to 20€, including a first drink. Via Luigi Pirandello 70. ℂ 0942-23824.

Ziggy's Bar/Disco Le Perroquet Eastern Sicily's most prominent gay bar occupies a peaceful, contemplative site just across the piazza from the entrance to the Palazzo San Domenico Hotel. During clement weather, many patrons opt to sit outside amid potted plants and vines. Inside, leopard-skin chairs and banquettes accessorize walls and ceilings covered with frescoes (ca. 2001) of *putti* and *cherubini* as they cavort coyly and/or indiscreetly. Entrance to Ziggy's Bar is free; it's open daily from 8pm to 2am. The disco is open much less frequently, only on Friday and Saturday nights between July and September. Entrance to the disco, during the rare moments it's open, costs 10€, and includes the first drink. Piazza San Domenico. ℂ 0942-24808.

2 Giardini-Naxos

5km (3 miles) S of Taormina, 47km (29 miles) N of Catania, 54km (34 miles) S of Messina

Many first-time visitors to Taormina are disappointed when they find they have to commute from its hotels to the beach. At Giardini-Naxos you can walk from your hotel room to the sands in short order. You can reach this resort by the sea in just 30 minutes by taking the Giardini-Naxos bus from the hilltop of Taormina.

The beach here opens onto the bay, lying between Capo (Cape) Taormina in the northwest, sweeping down to Capo Schisò in the south. Its point formed by an ancient lava flow from Mount Etna, Capo Schisò was the natural landfall for mariners rounding the toe of Italy on their way from eastern Mediterranean ports.

Thucydides tells us that Naxos was founded in 735 B.C. by Chalcidians under the leadership of the Athenian Thucles, who was the first Greek (or so it is believed) to land on Sicilian soil. From their base at Naxos, the Greeks branched out to take over more parts of Sicily for colonization. The colony at Naxos thrived until Dionysius of Syracuse destroyed it in 403 B.C. Even if you're staying in Taormina, you should set aside some time to visit the archaeological garden that remains here (see below).

Over the years, beach development has been so great at Giardini-Naxos that the resort today competes with Taormina for visitors, although it lacks the older resort's medieval charm. Since the 1960s, it's been a large holiday resort, catering mainly to package-tour operators from the north of Europe. (As a local said, "Taormina has the class, we have the sands.") Indeed, all the trappings of tourism are evident in this once-tranquil fishing village today, with its many public sports facilities and amusement parks, handcraft shops, antiques stores, several dozen hotels, trattorie, and beachside bars.

Much of the resort continues to function even during its short winter when the winds can blow cold. But for Europeans who have survived a winter in the frigid north, Giardini-Naxos has balmy Mediterranean weather most any time of year.

For the location of Giardini-Naxos, see the map "In and Around Mount Etna," in the next section of this chapter.

ESSENTIALS

Giardini-Naxos has a long main street, **Lungomare,** that runs parallel to the sea.

Interbus (© 0942-625301) runs buses daily every half hour from the terminal in Taormina along Via Luigi Pirandello; a one-way ticket costs 1.20€. Service is from 8am to midnight.

Giardini-Naxos shares the same rail depot as Taormina (see above). Motorists driving from Taormina take the SS114 south. From Messina, follow Autostrada A18 south, exiting at the turnoff for Giardini-Naxos.

The **Giardini-Naxos tourist office,** Via Tysandros 54 (© 0942-51010), is open Monday through Saturday from 8:30am to 2pm and 4 to 7pm.

EXPLORING ANCIENT RUINS

In a setting of citrus trees and prickly pears, on the headland of Capo Schisò, lie the ruins of the **Naxos excavations** ✦, the site of the first Greek colony in Sicily. This site has been inhabited since 735 B.C., and has gone through the various tribulations of all such colonies, thriving and prospering until conquered and devastated—only to rise again out of the ashes.

If you're driving, head out on Via Naxos, which becomes Via Stracina. The ancient site lies in the dusty, barren scrubland above Giardini-Naxos. The actual excavations lie behind a rusted and dented iron fence facing the uphill (land-ward) side of the main road leading into Giardini-Naxos. Inside you'll find the repository of artifacts that remained after Dionysius of Syracuse razed the city to the ground in 403 B.C.

This is not Pompeii, so don't be disappointed. What the tyrant didn't raze to the ground, centuries of builders carted off for other structures. Little remains today except some structural foundations and the pavement stones of ancient streets.

The best of what was dug up is displayed in the **Archaeological Museum** on two floors of an old Bourbon-built fort. Terra-cotta and architectural fragments abound. Note the little altar dating from 545 B.C. and adorned with sphinxes in relief. The most evocative artifact is a statuette of Aphrodite Hippias from the 5th century B.C. As a curiosity, one exhibit displays objects removed from a surgeon's grave, including a strigil, a speculum used to examine injuries, and tiny ointment jars. The site is open daily from 9am to 1pm and 4 to 8pm; admission is 4.15€. Persons 17 and under enter for free. For information, call © 0942-51061.

WHERE TO STAY

Arathena Rocks Hotel ✦ Value   Charming and individualized, this govern-ment-rated three-star hotel contains one of the most appealing collections of dec-orative art objects along the Taormina coastline. They include bas-reliefs, sculptures, candelabra, wrought-iron balustrades, gilded baroque door frames, and hand-painted tilework tastefully assembled into a complete whole. The overall effect is that of a whimsically cheerful, well-organized private villa that happens to rent out guest rooms. Built in the early 1970s atop a jagged sea-facing strip of eroded lava rocks, it has compensated for its lack of a sandy beach with a terraced swimming pool, masses of potted flowers, and patches of greenery rising from crevices in the rocks. The rock-studded beach is private. Rooms are smallish to midsize, cozy, and clean, and many contain balconies or loggias. About half the bathrooms contain showers, the rest bathtubs.

Via Calcide Eubea 55, 98035 Giardini-Naxos. ℂ **0942-51348.** Fax 0942-51690. 92€–98€ double. Rates include breakfast. AE, DC, MC, V. Free parking. Closed Nov–Easter. **Amenities:** Restaurant; bar; pool; free shuttle-bus transfers to and from Taormina. *In room:* A/C in half, TV.

Hellenia Yachting Club ★★   Set in the heart of Giardini-Naxos, closer to the town's bars than some of its competitors, this is a gracefully modern and elegant hotel whose public areas have some of the most lavish marble decoration anywhere, often with hints of classical Greek antiquity. Built in 1978 and radically upgraded in 2000, it contains touches of gilt, a sun terrace that's punctuated with a pleasant but not overly large swimming pool, and black lava steps that descend to a private gravel beach. The place has the aura of a private club—perhaps one in Greece that welcomes an English, nautically-minded clientele. Be warned in advance that the guest rooms are not as opulent as the lobby would imply. Each room has a sparsely furnished, somewhat cold, decor, with glossy hints of 18th-century French styling. Each is equipped with a well-maintained private bathroom with tub or shower, and half have private balconies.

Via Jannuzzo 41, 98035 Giardini-Naxos. ℂ **0942-51737.** Fax 0942-54310. www.hotel-hellenia.it. 112 units. 139€–211€ double. Rates include breakfast. Free parking. AE, DC, MC, V. **Amenities:** Restaurant; 2 bars (piano and poolside [June–Sept only]); pool; tennis nearby; fitness room; room service. *In room:* A/C, TV, minibar, hair dryer, safe.

Hotel Sabbie d'Oro   The on-site restaurant (see below) is genuinely charming and more alluring than the hotel that administers it. Nonetheless, this simple hotel is acceptable in every way, though it's hardly grand. Built in 1990, and named after the public beach (Sabbie d'Oro/Golden Sands) that lies just across the street, this narrow-fronted, government-rated three-star hotel is clean, only a bit battered, and completely unpretentious. Each room has a tile-covered bathroom with showers but no bathtubs.

Via Schisò 12, 98035 Giardino-Naxos. ℂ **0942-51227.** Fax 0942-56913. www.tao.lit/sabbie. 36 units. 140€–156€ double. Rates include breakfast. AE, DC, MC, V. Parking: 10€. **Amenities:** Restaurant; bar; concierge; laundry. *In room:* A/C, TV, minibar, hair dryer, safe.

Sant Alphio Garden Hotel ★   This is the biggest, best-accessorized, and most opulent hotel in Giardini-Naxos. Built in 1979 at the northern edge of the resort, it's airy, well-managed, and richly accessorized in a style that evokes the scope and imagination of Las Vegas. Its centerpiece is a large, free-form outdoor pool, with lavish landscaping and a swim-up sunken bar, that's set directly adjacent to the best-looking cluster of swimming pools along the Taormina coastline. Developed by Sebastiano Puglia, a U.S. citizen and part-time resident of Long Island, New York, it's outfitted in contemporary-looking tones of navy blue and white, with touches of chrome and an appealing and jazzy combination of Sicilian and European styling. Bedrooms range from midsize to spacious, each with a well-maintained bathroom with shower or tub. Most visitors opt to spend at least a week here, decompressing from overburdened schedules in other parts of (usually northern) Europe. Come here for a retreat, with the understanding that the medieval attractions of Taormina are just an easy taxi ride away. A private beach lies within a 3-minute walk; and tennis, horseback riding, and golf are available through outside concessions.

Marina di Recanati, 98030 Giardini-Naxos. © **0942-51383.** Fax 0942-53934. 124 units. 108€–220€ double. Rates include breakfast. AE, DC, MC, V. Free parking. **Amenities:** 2 restaurants (1 poolside); 2 bars; outdoor pool with sunken bar; spa with indoor heated pool; fitness center; Jacuzzi; sauna; steam room; massage; 24-hr. room service. *In room:* A/C, TV, minibar, hair dryer.

Villa Mora ★★ *Finds*   "There's a small hotel," as the song goes, and it's sitting across from the beach and the waters of the Ionian Sea. A friendly, welcoming couple take special care of Villa Mora guests. Most of the units contain private balconies opening onto the bay. Furnishings range from antique writing desks to painted trunks, giving the place a cozy ambience. Guest rooms are midsize and invitingly comfortable; each has a bathroom with tiled shower. The staff takes pride in the aromatic Sicilian cuisine served here, mainly fish and vegetables, using locally grown ingredients.

Via Naxos 47, 98030 Giardini-Naxos. ©/fax **0942-51839.** www.hotelvillamora.com. 17 units. 68€–83€ double. Rates include breakfast. Half board (required in Aug) 54€ per person. MC, V. Free parking. Closed Dec 20–Mar 1. **Amenities:** Restaurant; bar; room service; laundry/dry cleaning. *In room:* Ceiling fan, TV.

WHERE TO DINE

La Cambusa ★★ SICILIAN/SEAFOOD   Since the 1980s, this restaurant has attracted the gastronomes and romantics of Giardini-Naxos, thanks to an indoor/outdoor setting with a view that sweeps over the beach, the coastline, and hundreds of fishing craft and yachts bobbing at anchor. After dark, the allure is enhanced with dozens of flaming torches that add an undeniable, often primal, feel to the place. From the harbor-front street that accesses it, you'll only see the chimneys of a low-slung concrete building. Its charms don't become visible till you're inside, where the well-trained staff, color scheme of blue and white, and bubbling lobster tanks create a relaxed ambience. In Giardini-Naxos, the cuisine doesn't get better than this even at Sea Sound, which is almost the equal of this place. Menus present classic and modern ideas in equal measure. For a zesty pasta, opt for fusilli with tuna and capers. The spaghetti with clams is savory, but we can never resist a platter of local smoked fish in Sicily—and we certainly don't here. Linguine with whitefish sounds dull but isn't. The cooks prepare a spectacular *zuppe di pesce* (fish soup) with olive oil, lemon juice, and fresh oregano.

Via Schisò 3. © **0942-51437.** Reservations recommended evenings in midsummer. Main courses 8.50€–15€. AE, DC, MC, V. Daily 12:30–3pm and 7:30pm–midnight. Closed Tues mid-Sept to May and Nov–Mar.

Ristorante Sabbie d'Oro SICILIAN   Amicable and laid-back, this restaurant sits in a covered open-air pavilion adjacent to both the beach and the hotel that manages it. In a setting that evokes a woodsy tavern, near tables loaded with grappas and shelves filled with wine, you sit beneath a ceiling draped with fishnets and nautical bric-a-brac. Using first-rate raw materials, the cooks, though not world class, are attentive and caring with their cuisine. You can enjoy such dishes as a curious marriage of beef and clams; pennette pasta with swordfish and almonds; macaroni with eggplant and fresh tomatoes; and delectable platters of assorted smoked fish.

Via Schisò 12. © **0942-52380.** Reservations recommended Sat–Sun. Main courses 8€–14€. AE, DC, MC, V. Daily noon–3pm and 7–11pm.

Ristorante Sea Sound ★★ SICILIAN/SEAFOOD   From a position beside a commercial street in the center of Giardini-Naxos, immediately adjacent to the Hellenic Yacht Club Hotel, you'll walk for at least 4 minutes along a private footpath flanked by morning glories and other flowering vines. Just when you suspect you've made a wrong turn, you'll suddenly see a tucked-away low-rise concrete bungalow adjacent to the sea. Its focal point is a concrete terrace, on either side of which rise walls adorned with cheerful pottery. Something about the angles of those walls, and the concrete base on which they sit, replicate an echo chamber, a setup that makes the sound of waves reverberate more loudly than they might otherwise. Overall, the place is charming, humorous, and very pleasant. A staff member will carry an oversized tray loaded with samples of the day's catch to your table. Ranging from smoked tuna to salmon or swordfish, the antipasti selection is the best in the area. You can also start with a savory kettle of mussels and clams in a garlic sauce. More than a dozen different pastas are made daily, including spaghetti *alla bottarga* (with tuna roe) and a risotto with fresh seafood. Meat choices are limited, but dishes such as veal scaloppine in Marsala sauce and the grilled filet of beef are competently made. We always opt for the catch of the day or else a tasty grilled swordfish caught in the Straits of Messina.

Via Jannuzzo 37A. ℂ **0942-54330.** Reservations recommended. Main courses 11€–20€. AE, DC, MC, V. Daily 12:30–2:30pm and 7–11:30pm. Closed late Oct to late Mar.

3 Mount Etna ✦✦

23km (15 miles) SW of Taormina; 31km (19 miles) N of Catania, 60km (37 miles) S of Messina

Looming menacingly over the coast of eastern Sicily, **Mount Etna** is the highest and largest active volcano in Europe—and we do mean active. The peak changes in size over the years but is currently in the neighborhood of 3,292m (10,800 ft.). Etna has been active in modern times (in 1928, the little village of Mascali was buried under its lava), and eruptions in 2001 and 2002 rekindled Sicilian fears. In October 2002, the air was thick and dirty over eastern Sicily as Mount Etna once again spewed out columns of ash that blackened skies as far away as Tripoli on the coast of North Africa. Although lava flowed down both sides of the mountain, at press time no villages were endangered.

Etna has figured in history and in Greek mythology. Empedocles, the 5th-century B.C. Greek philosopher, is said to have jumped into its crater as a sign that he was being delivered directly to Mount Olympus to take his seat among the gods. It was under Etna that Zeus crushed the multiheaded, viper-riddled dragon Typhoeus, thereby securing domination over Olympus. Hephaestus, the god of fire and blacksmiths, made his headquarters in Etna, aided by the single-eyed Cyclops.

The Greeks warned that whenever Typhoeus tried to break out of his prison, lava erupted and earthquakes cracked the land. That must mean that the monster nearly escaped on March 11, 1669, the date of one of the most violent eruptions ever recorded—it destroyed Catania.

Visitors will have to decide whether you wish to ascend Mount Etna from the northern or southern approaches. We prefer the north-facing side, partly because it's cooler, much more beautiful, and much richer in wildflowers that thrive in the volcanic soil. Also, the north side is more heavily forested. The south side, because of the eruptions during the last decade, is mostly covered with barren-looking lava flows that resemble a desert. Its access routes are more crowded, and its views less appealing. Nonetheless, many visitors to Catania come up Etna's south side (for more details, refer to chapter 9).

If you decide to come up the north side, simply take the highway to its end, Piano Provenzana, which stops at a complex of Alpine-inspired, wood-sided

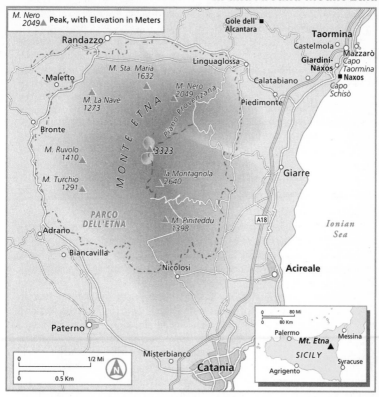

M. Nero
2049▲ Peak, with Elevation in Meters

chalets selling souvenirs and clothing. During the heat of a Sicilian summer, they appear visibly out of place, but in winter, because of the high altitude (2,700m/8,858 ft.), they function as the centerpiece of a small-scale but thriving ski colony. The ski facilities include five downhill slopes and a network of cross-country ski trails.

It is from this artificial-looking Alpine hamlet of Piano Provenzana that you buy tickets for bus excursions to the top of Mount Etna. The round-trip excursions last 2 hours each, and cost 37€ per adult, 26€ per child under 16. Departures are whenever business merits, but during the summer, buses usually leave every hour.

The bus tours are loaded with bio-curious, bio-conscious folks from throughout Europe, especially France, who snapshot away as the specially equipped bus (more like an armored car) winds its way laboriously uphill, through gravel beds and rocky, much-eroded gullies, past barren, lichen-covered gray-green landscapes. Frankly, it's not all that exciting or spectacular. At the top, the bus parks near a seismic exploration station, which is mostly abandoned, and guests walk a bit farther to a point near the top, across gravel-covered landscapes of great brutality. There's no fire and brimstone to see—if there is, and if the crater is active, all bus ascensions are immediately discontinued.

In Taormina, **CST,** Corso Umberto I, 101 (© **0942-23301**), organizes tours to Etna 5 days a week in summer Monday through Friday. The tours cost 25€

to 55€ per person. The office is open Monday through Saturday from 8:45am to 12:45pm and 4 to 7:30pm; it's closed on Saturday from October to April.

A road around the foot of the volcano takes you through magnificent country where the rich soil has spawned many plantations and vineyards. Pistachio trees and prickly pears are commonplace. If you're driving around Etna in the morning, you can usually see the volcano, although it is often hidden in mist after lunch.

THE FOOTHILLS OF MOUNT ETNA

The village of Linguaglossa, 18km (11 miles) west of Taormina, is the best center for excursions to Mount Etna. From here you can access Piano Provenzana at 1,800m (5,906 ft.), the main ski resort on Etna with five ski lifts. It's at Piano Provenzana that four-wheel-drive vans are organized for those wanting to go on excursions to Etna's dangerous summit. Many hikers walk from Piano Provenzana to the cone of Etna in about 3 hours, following the track used by the shuttle vans.

LINGUAGLOSSA

Before climbing the mountain, you may want to linger in the village of Linguaglossa. Built from black volcanic lava, it is traversed by a main street called Via Roma. At the most distant end of this street lies the 17th-century church **Chiesa Madre Madonna della Grazie,** capped with an iron cross and opening onto Piazza Matrice.

Via Roma is covered with large and very heavy black lava cobblestones. It begins at the **Chiesa di San Francesco de Paola,** known for its lavish baroque frescoes and plasterwork. The church rests on a foundation of chiseled volcanic rock. Via Roma continues to the 17th-century Duomo, which is also known as **Chiesa della SS. Annunziata.** The pink stucco–sheathed and stately looking **Town Hall (Il Municipio)** opens on Piazza Municipio overlooking a Liberty-style monument dedicated to the Italian dead in World War I.

The tourist office, **Associazione Turistica Proloco Linguaglossa,** Piazza Annunziata 5 (℃ **095-643094**), is open daily from 9am to 12:30pm and 4 to 5:30pm. Inside, you'll find a desk distributing brochures and pamphlets for attractions in the area, and a mini-display that showcases the local geology, including insights into its abundant lava flows.

A bus from Giardini-Naxos (see above) leaves for Linguaglossa daily at 2:55pm. If you're driving from Taormina to Linguaglossa, take A18 south. After 12km (7½ miles), take the exit marked FIUMEFREDDO. After 815m (2,674 ft.), turn left and follow SS120 into Linguaglossa.

WHERE TO DINE

Chalet della Ginestre SICILIAN   As you navigate your way uphill through the scrubby pine forests and occasional snows of the north slope of Mount Etna, this isolated, cement-sided chalet is a welcome sight. Set 9km (5½ miles) from the uppermost terminus of the highway, it was built in 2000 and offers a clean, cozy, weatherproof venue for a fortifying meal or drink. There's a wide-angled view over the surrounding valleys from this restaurant, Food items include mixed grill of meat; roulades of beef; asparagus with risotto, butter, and sage; and roasted veal. The food is satisfying and filling, nothing more.

Strada Mareneve, Km 10.8. ℃ **0347-8180990**. Reservations not necessary. Main courses 5€–8€; set-price menu 19€. No credit cards. Oct–Feb daily 12:30–4pm; Mar–Sept daily 12:30–4pm and 8–10pm. Closed 2 weeks in Nov.

Ristorante La Betulle ITALIAN   Everything about this restaurant (indestructible wooden furniture, easy-to-mop tile floors, a tavern-style coziness, and big windows overlooking the mountains) might remind you of ski resorts in Alpine climes farther to the north. That was the intention in this surreal context of a Sicilian ski resort. The food is satisfying and served in generous portions—the rib-sticking fare you so much appreciate in cold climates. Look for home-made soups, fresh salads, pastas, grilled meats, and the occasional fresh fish.

Etna Nord (Linguaglossa). © 095-643430. Reservations not required. Main courses 7.80€–12€. Daily noon–3pm and 7–9pm. Closed Nov.

RANDAZZO

After you explore Linguaglossa and Mount Etna, continue west to another intriguing "volcano town," Randazzo, 20km (13 miles) away on Route 120. Amazingly, this town built of lava and with a history going back into antiquity has never been destroyed by the volcano. Most of its destruction came from man when the Germans made Randazzo their last stand of resistance in August 1943. That dubious honor caused Randazzo to be bombed by the Allies.

Some visitors arrive in Randazzo on the Circumetnea train, which originates outside Catania (see chapter 9) and partially encircles the volcano to Riposto on the Ionian coast. If you choose to travel this way, Randazzo is a good place to break for lunch.

The **tourist office** in Randazzo is at Via Corso Umberto I, 193 (© **095-7991611**), open daily from 9am to 1pm and 3 to 7pm.

Seeing the Sights

The "black town" of Randazzo, built of lava, holds its own intrigue because of its unusual look, but it does have some monuments worth exploring.

Chief of these is **Chiesa di Santa Maria** ✮, Piazza della Basilica 5 (© **095-921003**), open daily from 10am to noon and 4 to 6pm; free admission. It's a study in contrasts, its building materials of black lava contrasting with its white trim. Its black-and-white tower is a prime example of brilliant Sicilian masonry. The church dates from the 13th century and contains a three-story south portal, reached by two flights of stairs, which is built in the Catalan Gothic style and is of later origin (15th c.). The interior opens onto impressive black lava columns.

The other notable church, **Chiesa di San Martino,** Corso Umberto I (© **095-921003**), is open daily from 10am to noon and 4 to 6pm, with free admission. Its bell tower, or **campanile** ✮, is from the 13th century, although the church was reconstructed in the 17th century. The tower is impressive in that it is built of black-and-white stone, a dramatic contrast to the church, whose facade is adorned with reliefs of martyrs and saints.

Where to Stay

L'Antica Vigna ✮ *(Kids)*   At a point 4km (2½ miles) southeast of Randazzo, this is a stunningly situated little hotel of charm lying at the foot of the volcano. You reach it by traveling the SS120 out of Randazzo. The hotel is actually a converted farm built at the turn of the 20th century, and it's surrounded by 3 hectares (32 acres) of cultivated olive trees.

Guests are treated to such farm produce as wonderful cherry or blackberry jams served with your morning bread. The farmyard menagerie includes horses along with the inevitable Sicilian goats. The place is ideal for families with children; there's even a small park set aside for them, as well as some bunk beds. Guests are housed in small villas that comfortable and furnished with everything from kitchens to fireplaces. Each unit comes with a small bathroom with tub.

Località Monteguardi Est., 95036 Randazzo. ℂ **095-924003.** Fax 095-923324. 10 units. 44€ per person (includes half board). No credit cards. **Amenities:** Restaurant. *In room:* No phone.

Where to Dine

Trattoria di Veneziano SICILIAN   Randazzo's most substantial and elegant restaurant is separated from the town's medieval zone by a deep valley, along the bottom of which runs a busy boulevard. It's set on the ground floor of an airy, modern, plant-filled building decorated in tones of Chinese red. The restaurant was established in 1953 by members of the Veneziano family, the best and most ardent spokespersons for the good food and charm of Randazzo, having entertained most of the pop or political celebrities who have visited this town. Among the well-prepared menu items are grilled tenderloin steaks, grilled and smoke-cured ham, salted codfish, grilled sausages, and either rigatoni or papperdelle with fresh mushrooms.

Via Buonaventura s/n. ℂ **095-921418.** Reservations not necessary. Main courses 6€–7.75€. AE, DC, MC, V. Tues–Sun noon–3:30pm and Tues–Sat 7–11:30pm.

9

Catania

Often neglected by visitors in their race toward Taormina, the baroque art city of Sicily deserves at least a day or two—and hopefully more—of your time. The capital of the eastern part of Sicily and its second largest city after Palermo, **Catania** ★★ has had a tormented history of conquest and devastation by nature. It's also one of the richest repositories of baroque architecture in Europe, with treasures well worth seeking out.

The city has suffered natural disasters throughout the centuries. Much of the history of Catania is linked to its volcanic neighbor, **Mount Etna.** It has also been a victim of earthquakes. In 1669, the worst eruption in Catania's history occurred when Etna buried much of the city under lava that literally ran through the streets. Catania had hardly recovered when a massive earthquake leveled much of the city in 1693, creating an economic crisis.

But the people of Catania bounced back, creating an even better city and rebuilding in the harmonious baroque style. Many of the buildings were fashioned from the black lava that had rained down upon it. An aura of the 18th century still lingers over much of the heart of Catania as a direct result of the city's rebuilding program.

Even though much of the city today is in decay, its art treasures, church museums, and Roman ruins make it a rewarding stopover—that and the chance to meet, argue with, converse with, and dine with the Catanian people.

Of course, looming in the background is that menace of a volcano, Mount Etna. If you didn't take our suggestion and visit Etna from a base in Taormina (see chapter 8), you can do so from the southern slopes, with a base in Catania (see below). But make sure the volcanic activity has quieted down before you go; in late 2002 Etna was again raining ash and lava down near Catania.

The chapter concludes with our surprise destination: a side trip to **Acireale.** As Sicilian cities go, Acireale is a mere infant, having been founded in 1326. Built on streams of lava, the little city stands on cliffs above the sea and is filled with wonders, especially around its monumental inner core.

1 Essentials

52km (32 miles) S of Taormina, 60km (37 miles) N of Syracuse

Standing in the ominous shadow of Mount Etna, Catania is a city of lava. A bustling port opening onto the Ionian Sea, Catania is called the "city of black and white." White plaster and marble and black lava form major parts of its architectural adornment.

Catania is the second-largest city in Sicily, with a population of 380,000. It's a lively place, and the seat of a bishop and a great university. In deference to its hometown boy, **Vincenzo Bellini** (1801–35), Catania boasts one of Italy's grandest opera houses, where you can hear the operas and the eternal arias of this virtuoso composer.

Its second hometown boy who made good was **Giovanni Verga** (1840–1922), acclaimed as Italy's greatest writer after Manzoni. Known for his naturalistic fiction, he wrote such masterpieces as *Vita dei Campi* and *Mastro Don Gesualdo.*

If we can believe the historian Thucydides (he wasn't always right), Catania was founded in 729 B.C. It's had a rough go of it ever since. In 403 B.C., Dionysius of Syracuse sold off its citizens into slavery. Its patron saint, Agatha, in 253 B.C. had her breasts lopped off and has been carrying them around on a platter ever since—at least in artistic depictions of herself. That was the penalty she suffered for turning down the advances of the Roman praetor, Quintianus. Catania grew up on the Laestrygonian Fields known in Book 10 of the *Odyssey* as the home of the cannibalistic Laestrygones.

The Catania you see today, a city of wide boulevards, is a direct result of those disasters. **Battista Vaccarini** (1702–68), the famous architect, was assigned the task of rebuilding. He decided to turn it into "the city of the baroque," since that was the fashionable architectural statement of the time. Many famous artists were commissioned, including Alonzo di Benedetto, Antonino and Francesco Battaglia, Giovanni Vaccarini, and Stefano Ittar. Fragments of solidified black lava were used extensively. This lava, and the way it was positioned into the masonry, gave added strength to the walls of various buildings. The result was so successful that in the 18th and 19th centuries Catania was a mandatory stopover for those rich dandies making the "Grand Tour" of Europe. Regrettably, the Allied bombing raids of 1943 did much to destroy or damage many monuments.

Grime and neglect have also taken their toll. Today Catania is often called "the most degraded city of Europe," largely because of the decay of its once-beautiful historic core. Urban flight from Catania to the suburbs is common, with residents leaving behind an inferno of garbage, the despair of poverty, and crime. In fact, Catania vies with Palermo for the dubious distinction of "crime capital of Sicily." Sicilians living elsewhere on the island generally express disdain for Catania. As one old gentleman in Messina told us, "I don't much care for the place and never like to be seen on the streets there. If I go at all, it is under the cloud of darkness so my wife won't find out."

Yet, in spite of its crime and poverty, the city's industry and burgeoning economy have earned it the appellation of "the Milano of the South." And the inner city has seen improvements in recent years, including a few brightly restored antique buildings.

Our verdict on Catania? You'll either love it or hate it. We're among its devotees because we don't judge a city by whether it's pretty or not or even by whether it's well kept. We gravitate to places that bustle with life, and Catania is blessed with plenty of that. In what some critics have called a "rotting urban carcass," we have found joy in its people, pleasure in its food, and spiritual fulfillment in its artistic treasures.

There is no greater symbol of Catania, a city wiped off the map at least seven times, than the hideously ugly but endearing puce-colored elephant in front of the Duomo. It's made entirely of lava spewed from Etna. Somehow this tough little elephant is an appropriate mascot for Catania itself. By its very toughness, it symbolizes the city's ability to bounce back from one disaster after another, or even to create art from the lava that destroyed it.

Catania is a cauldron in summer, one of the hottest cities in Italy, with temperatures known to shoot up to 104°F (40°C). Winters are mild, but the best time to visit is spring or autumn.

GETTING THERE   By Plane   Flights from across Italy arrive at **Aeroporto Fontanarossa** (© 095-340505), 7km (4½ miles) to the south. Major links are via Palermo, Naples, and Rome.

The major carriers flying into Catania include the market leader, **Alitalia.** Call © **800/223-5730** in the U.S. In Italy call © **8488-65641** for information on domestic links in Italy. You can also fly in on **Meridiana** (© **06-478041**) from Milan (not Rome or Naples). **Air Europe** (© **800-454000**) offers services from Milan or Venice. A taxi into the center of the city costs around 16€. You can also take an Alibus to the Stazione Centrale, or rail depot, in the heart of Catania. Bus departures between the two points are every 20 minutes from 5pm to midnight. A ticket costs the same as a ride on a city bus (see "Getting Around," below).

Many people fly into Catania but choose to skip the city and go on to Taormina. If that fits you, you can catch a bus just outside the airport that will take you into Taormina in about an hour, for 4€ one-way.

By Train   Arrivals are at the **Stazione Centrale,** Piazza Papa Giovanni XXII (© **095-7306255**). Catania is a 10-hour train ride from Rome, with four trains arriving daily, costing 35€. Catania also enjoys links with all the major cities of Sicily: Palermo (trip time: 3½ hr.), costing 12€; Agrigento (trip time: 4 hr.), costing 9.30€; Messina (trip time: 2 hr.), costing 4.95€; and Taormina (trip time: 1 hr.), costing 2.85€. For rail information in general, call © **892021.**

By Bus   There is no central bus company; all operate independently and in total chaos. Companies are found on Via D'Amico across from the Stazione Centrale. The most useful for visitors include **SAIS Trasporti** (© 095-536201), running 11 buses per day to Agrigento (trip time: 3 hr.), costing 9.85€ one-way; and **SAIS Autolinee** (© 095-536168), running 27 buses per day to Messina (trip time: 1½ hr.), costing 6.20€, and 17 buses per day to Palermo (trip time: 2¾ hr.), costing 12€.

By Car   From Messina, which will probably be your gateway into Sicily, take A18 south passing Taormina and continuing on to Catania.

VISITOR INFORMATION   Tourist offices are found at the Stazione Centrale, Piazza Giovanni XXIII (© **095-7306255**), and at Via Cimarosa Domenico 10 (© **095-2503129**), both open daily from 8am to 8pm. There is also a branch at the airport (© **095-7306266**), open daily from 8am to 8pm.

CITY LAYOUT

Catania was rebuilt using anti-seismic measures. Its major boulevards were made straight and wider, virtually eliminating anything that had existed from medieval Catania. Broad piazzas punctuate many streets. The aim was to have streets wide enough to allow Catanians to escape in case lava flows through the streets again.

In recent years, unchecked growth has sent Catania crawling up the southern slopes of the ferocious Etna and sprawling across the fertile lands of the Simeto River.

The old center of the city is the **Piazza Duomo** (see later in this chapter) with the fountain of the ancient elephant previously mentioned. Splitting Catania in two parts is its main street, **Via Vittorio Emanuele II,** which begins east at **Piazza del Martini** running west past Piazza Duomo.

Running on a north-south axis, **Via Etnea** ✦ is the grand boulevard of Catania that runs north from Piazza Duomo for 3km (1¾ miles). Along this avenue you'll find the best shops, restaurants, and boutiques. Eventually Via Etnea reaches **Villa Bellini,** the beautiful public gardens.

In western Catania, **Via Crociferi** is the city's street of the baroque. Catania's most gracious avenue is flanked by churches and palazzi.

GETTING AROUND   Traffic is not quite as horrendous as in Palermo, but it's still the second worst in Sicily. Don't even attempt to use a car. Go by bus or taxi. Most of the historic treasures in Catania can be covered on foot.

By Bus   **AMT (Azienda Municipale Transport)**, Via Plebiscito 747 (✆ **095-7360247**), operates a good network of buses, branching out across the city. Tickets cost .80€ and are valid for 90 minutes. A ticket valid for a day goes for 2€. You can purchase tickets at *tabacchi* (tobacco stands) and news kiosks. *Tip:* If you take circular bus no. 410, you'll be treated to a round-trip of all the major sightseeing attractions and points of tourist interest for only the cost of a one-way bus fare. The service is run only by appointment; call ✆ **095-73660226**.

By Metro   The very limited subway system has trains running every 15 minutes to a half hour daily from 7am to 8:45pm, costing .80€ for a ticket valid for 90 minutes. Metro tickets, like bus tickets (see above), are available from newspaper kiosks and tobacco shops. Metro service runs from Stazione Centrale at Platform 11 south to Catania Porto and north and northwest all the way to Catania Borgo, the terminus for the Stazione Circumetnea via Caronda 490.

By Taxi   **CST** (✆ **095-330966**) operates a 24-hour taxi service. Taxi ranks are found at the Stazione Centrale and Piazza Duomo.

FAST FACTS: Catania

American Express In Catania, Amex is represented by **La Duca Viaggi,** Viale Africa 14 (✆ **095-7222295**), Monday through Friday from 9am to 1pm and 4 to 7:30pm, Saturday from 9am to noon.

Currency Exchange Most banks lie in the center along Corso Sicilia, including **Banca Deutsche,** Corso Sicilia 51 (✆ **095-325-831**), open Monday through Friday from 8:30am to 1:30pm and 2:30 to 4pm; and **Banca Banco di Sicilia,** Corso Sicilia 8 (✆ **095-32368111**), open Monday through Friday from 8:30am to 1:30pm and 2:30 to 4pm. There are also currency exchange offices at the train station and at the American Express office (see above).

Emergencies Call ✆ **113**. For **first aid,** dial ✆ **095-7594371. Guardia Medica** is at Corso Italia 235 (✆ **095-377122**).

Hospital The major hospital is **Garibaldi,** Piazza Santa Maria el Gesù (✆ **095-759-1111**).

Internet Access Your best bet is **Hi-Tech Café,** Via Antonino di Sangiuliano Giovanni 230 (✆ **095-312324**), open Monday through Saturday from 9:30am to 1pm and 4 to 7:30pm, charging 2.60€ per hour.

Pharmacies These are found all over town; ask at your hotel for the one nearest you. A night pharmacy is **Croceverde,** Via Gabriele D'Annunzio 43 (✆ **095-441-662**), open daily from 4pm to 1am.

Police Dial ✆ **112** or 095-7306711.

Post Office The main **Catania Post Office** is at Via Etnea 215 (✆ **095-7155111**), next to the Villa Bellini Gardens. Hours are Monday through Friday from 8:15am to 7:30pm, Saturday from 8:15am to 1pm.

2 Where to Stay

EXPENSIVE

Excelsior Grand Hotel ★★★ No other hotel in Sicily so gracefully manifests the flowing sense of *la dolce vita* modernism as Catania's leading hotel. It's the establishment that brought postwar tourism to Catania with a stately and monumental facade, built in 1954, that's almost a mirror image of the Palazzo di Giustiza (Municipal Courthouse) (ca. 1953), which lies immediately across Piazza Verga, the biggest and most impressive square in Catania. A radical renovation and upgrade in 2001 retained the best aspects of this hotel's retro, age-of-Sputnik design, and added zillions of new grace notes.

Expect a *moderno*-style lobby in perfect taste, with a resident pianist, deep and comfortable settees, and the kind of bar you'd expect in a posh hotel on Rome's Via Veneto. Half of the bedrooms overlook Piazza Verga and faraway Mount Etna. These standard double rooms are called deluxe rooms, and each comes with a loggia-style balcony. The remainder ("superior rooms") are just as large, plush, and comfortable, but they face the back of the hotel and in most cases don't have balconies. Bathrooms are sheathed in marble, with big mirrors and plenty of room. The deluxe rooms contain showers, while the superior units and suites come with tubs as well. The in-house restaurant—**Le Zagare**—is recommended below.

Piazza Verga, 95129 Catania. (✆ **095-7476111.** Fax 095-537015. www.thi.it. 176 units. 99€–233€ double; 202€–506€ suite. Free parking. Rates include breakfast. AE, DC, MC, V. Bus: 443, 457, 721, or 722. **Amenities:** Restaurant; American-style piano bar; steam room; babysitting; laundry/dry cleaning; e-mail facilities in the lobby. *In room:* A/C, TV, minibar, hair dryer, safe.

Sheraton Catania ★ This seaside resort lies in Cannizzaro, 5.6km (3½ miles) north of Catania's center. Set across the highway from the sea, and originally built in 1983, it offers a *moderno* lobby accented with fountains set into artificial grottos, potted plants, Lucite-trimmed balustrades, and a low-rise atrium that fills the interior with sunlight. This is not a "showcase" Sheraton (it's a member of the Sheraton franchise, but owned by a local investor), and its links to the international chain are relatively loose. It looks a bit dated when compared to more recently renovated places such as the Excelsior, in the heart of town. But it's appealing and comfortable, graced with a surprising number of modern paintings. Guest rooms, accessible via a labyrinthine set of low-ceilinged hallways, have big windows, a sense of 1980s design, and generous space. Each comes with a well-polished tiled bathroom with a tub-and-shower combination.

Via Antonello da Messina 45, 95020 Cannizzaro-Catania. (✆ **095-271557.** Fax 095-271380. www.sheraton catania.com. 170 units. 214€ double; 410€–430€ suite. DC, MC, V. Free shuttle bus to town center. **Amenities:** 2 restaurants; bar; outdoor pool; tennis court; fitness center; business center; salon; room service. *In room:* A/C, TV, minibar.

Villa del Bosco ★★★ No other hotel in Catania so gracefully exemplifies the aristocratic life of a land-owning family in Sicily during the early 19th century. Stately looking and symmetrical, the Bosco is set behind a high wall that separates it from a suburban neighborhood, 5km (3 miles) south of Catania's historic core. It was originally built in 1826 as a private home, then radically renovated, always in keeping with the original style, in the mid-1990s. The result is a dignified boutique hotel rich with antiques and a sense of another time, a client list that has included both Whitney Houston and Ray Charles, and lots of European politicians.

Catania Accommodations & Dining

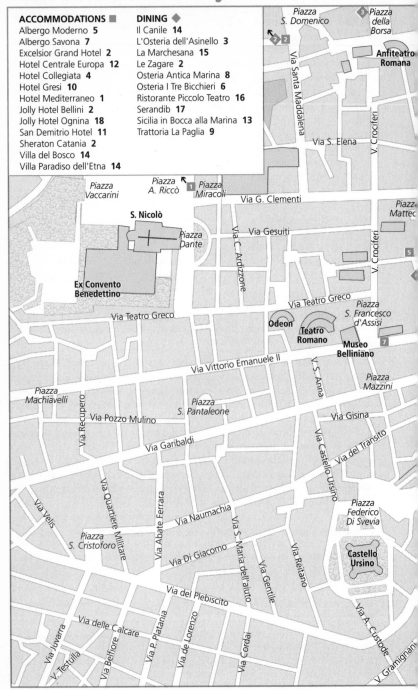

ACCOMMODATIONS ■
Albergo Moderno **5**
Albergo Savona **7**
Excelsior Grand Hotel **2**
Hotel Centrale Europa **12**
Hotel Collegiata **4**
Hotel Gresi **10**
Hotel Mediterraneo **1**
Jolly Hotel Bellini **2**
Jolly Hotel Ognina **18**
San Demitrio Hotel **11**
Sheraton Catania **2**
Villa del Bosco **14**
Villa Paradiso dell'Etna **14**

DINING ◆
Il Canile **14**
L'Osteria dell'Asinello **3**
La Marchesana **15**
Le Zagare **2**
Osteria Antica Marina **8**
Osteria I Tre Bicchieri **6**
Ristorante Piccolo Teatro **16**
Serandib **17**
Sicilia in Bocca alla Marina **13**
Trattoria La Paglia **9**

Piazza S. Domenico

Piazza della Borsa

Anfiteatro Romana

Via Santa Maddalena

V. Crociferi

Via S. Elena

Piazza Vaccarini

Piazza A. Riccò

Piazza Miracoli

Via G. Clementi

Piazz Mattec

S. Nicolò

Piazza Dante

Via Gesuiti

Via C. Ardizzone

V. Crociferi

Ex Convento Benedettino

Via Teatro Greco

Via Teatro Greco

Piazza S. Francesco d'Assisi

Odeon

Teatro Romano

Museo Belliniano

Via Vittorio Emanuele II

V. S. Anna

Piazza Mazzini

Piazza Machiavelli

Via Recupero

Piazza S. Pantaleone

Via Gisina

Via Pozzo Mulino

Via Garibaldi

Via del Transito

Via Castello Ursino

Via Velis

Via Quartiere Militare

Via Abate Ferrara

Via Naumachia

Via S. Maria dell'aiuto

Piazza Federico Di Svevia

Piazza S. Cristoforo

Via Di Giacomo

Via Gentile

Via Reitano

Castello Ursino

Via del Plebiscito

Via A. Custode

Via delle Calcare

Via Juvarra

V. Testulla

Via Belfiore

Via P. Platania

Via de Lorenzo

Via Cordai

V. Gramignani

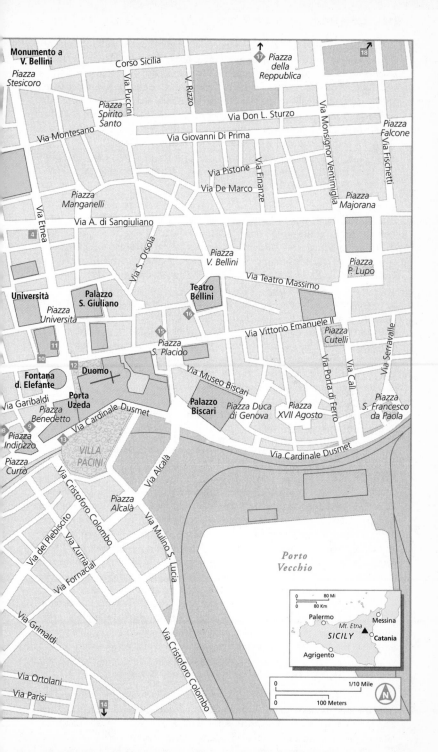

Monumento a
V. Bellini

Piazza
Stesicoro

Corso Sicilia

Via Puccini

V. Rizzo

Piazza della Reppublica

Piazza
Spirito
Santo

Via Don L. Sturzo

Via Giovanni Di Prima

Via Montesano

Via Pistone

Via De Marco

Via Finanze

Via Monsignor Ventimiglia

Piazza
Falcone

Via Fischetti

Piazza
Manganelli

Piazza
Majorana

Via A. di Sangiuliano

Via S. Orsola

Piazza
V. Bellini

Via Teatro Massimo

Piazza
P. Lupo

Via Etnea

Università

Palazzo
S. Giuliano

Teatro
Bellini

Piazza
Università

Piazza
S. Placido

Via Vittorio Emanuele II

Piazza
Cutelli

Via Serravalle

Fontana
d. Elefante

Duomo

Via Museo Biscari

Via Porta di Ferro

Via Calì

Porta
Uzeda

Piazza
Benedetto

Via Cardinale Dusmet

Palazzo
Biscari

Piazza Duca
di Genova

Piazza
XVII Agosto

Piazza
S. Francesco
da Paola

Via Garibaldi

Piazza
Indirizzo

Piazza
Currò

VILLA
PACINI

Via Cardinale Dusmet

Via Cristoforo Colombo

Piazza
Alcalà

Via Alcalà

Via del Plebiscito

Via Zurria

Via Mulino S. Lucia

Via Fornacia

Porto
Vecchio

Via Grimaldi

Via Cristoforo Colombo

Via Ortolani

Via Parisi

0   80 Mi
0   80 Km

Palermo

Messina

Mt. Etna

SICILY

Catania

Agrigento

0   1/10 Mile

0   100 Meters

N

211

At great expense, lavish baroque frescoes were added to the walls of some of the public areas, including the elegant dining room. The hotel's social center is a richly furnished, elaborately detailed salon, with a bar at one end and a service staff that's quick to give you a drink. Guest rooms are elegant and pretty, with four-poster beds, small- to midsize tiled or stone-sheathed bathrooms with tub and shower, and the sense of fragility you might expect in a private home. Its artfully frescoed breakfast room is the most beautiful in Catania.

The in-house restaurant, **Il Canile,** is recommended below.

Via del Bosco 62, 95125 Catania. © 095-7335100. Fax 095-7335103. www.hotelvilladelbosco.it. 33 units. 197€ double; 275€–320€ suite. AE, DC, MC, V. Bus: 129, 314, or 421. **Amenities:** Restaurant; salon-style bar; outdoor pool; laundry. *In room:* A/C, TV, minibar.

Villa Paradiso dell'Etna ★★ *Finds*   If you need to stay near the Fontanarossa airport, you might want to spend the night here, 11km (7 miles) from Catania. This elegant hotel lies on the slopes of Mount Etna, between the towns of San Giovanni La Punta and Viagrande. Surrounded by gardens, the hotel was opened in 1927 and has been restored to its former glory. Journalist and entrepreneur Cosimo Mollica Alagona launched the villa, wanting to take advantage of the beautiful surroundings that had won the praise of such writers as Goethe and Maupassant. Over the years the villa became a vacation retreat for artists and other dignitaries. The villa's original furnishings are still here, and the atmosphere of the past lives on splendidly. Guest rooms are beautifully and comfortably furnished; all have views of Etna. Antique Sicilian furnishings, traditional upholstery, and old prints grace each room. The suites have hydromassage baths, and most bathrooms have tubs, the rest showers. The villa also features a wine cellar, a panoramic roof garden, and disco on summer Sundays.

Via per Viagrande 37, 95030 San Giovanni La Punta. © 095-7512409. Fax 095-7413861. www.paradiso etna.it. 34 units. 217€ double; 336€ suite. Rates include breakfast. AE, DC, MC, V. From Catania, follow the Catania–Messina motorway in the direction of Etna and San Gregorio. At the yellow signs leading to Le Zagare shopping center, the hotel is signposted. **Amenities:** Restaurant; piano bar; lounge; pool; tennis court; fitness center; sauna; massage; room service; laundry/dry cleaning. *In room:* A/C, TV, minibar, hair dryer, safe.

MODERATE

Alberto Savona   A definite cut above the also-recommended Hotel Centrale Europa, which sits across the street, this solid, well-located hotel lies a 2-minute walk from the Duomo. Converted into a hotel about a century ago, it has three upstairs floors devoted to thick-walled, quiet guest rooms with comfortable, severely dignified furniture and high ceilings. Each room was renovated in 2001. Although some have views of the cathedral, room nos. 102 and 104 are among the most interesting, with views over a medieval-looking courtyard dotted with potted plants. You'll access the rooms via an elegant and grandiose flight of marble-capped stairs flanked with elaborate wrought-iron railings. Each unit comes with a boxlike bathroom with shower unit. One of the best aspects of this place is the plush, carefully paneled bar, complete with deep armchairs, soaring ceiling vaults, leather sofas, and plenty of dignified style. It doubles as a breakfast room.

Via Vittorio Emanuele 210, 95124 Catania. ©/fax 095-326982. 30 units. 110€–130€ double. AE, DC, MC, V. Bus: 1-4, 2-5, 3-6, or 457. **Amenities:** Bar; laundry service. *In room:* A/C, TV, minibar.

Hotel Mediterraneo ★   Well designed and unpretentious, with three stars from the local tourist authorities, this is one of Catania's newest hotels. A century ago, there was an inn on this site. In April 2002, after a well-planned reconfiguration by celebrity architect Romeo Francesco, it was reincarnated as a member of the Best Western hotel chain. You enter a blue-floored lobby whose best features include a tactful, hardworking staff and dramatic murals inspired by the great masterpieces of the Italian Renaissance. Guest rooms are predictably angular, simple, and uncomplicated, with big windows and bathrooms with tub-and-shower combinations.

Via Dottor Consoli 27, 95124 Catania. © **800-5281234** or 095-325330. Fax 095-7151818. www.hotel mediterraneo.it. 64 units. 125€–135€ double. Rates include breakfast. Parking 10€–18€ per day, depending on vehicle size. Bus: 431. **Amenities:** Lobby cafe and bar; laundry/dry cleaning. *In room:* A/C, TV, minibar.

Jolly Hotel Bellini   This is the older (ca. 1959), more central of Catania's two Jolly Hotels, sporting only three government stars, a low ranking for a chain more noted for its four- and five-star properties. Detractors find it a wee bit dated; we find it comfortable, well maintained, and, despite a few remaining touches of retro-dowdiness, an acceptable choice. All the rooms come with a boxlike bathroom with shower stall.

Piazza Trento 13, 95129 Catania. © **095-316933**. Fax 095-316832. www.jollyhotels.it. 159 units. 129€–155€ double. Rates include buffet breakfast. Bus: 421, 443, 721, or 722. **Amenities:** Restaurant; bar; room service; laundry/dry cleaning. *In room:* A/C, TV, minibar, safe (in some).

Jolly Hotel Ognina ⭐   Set at the point in Catania where the city devolves into the seaside strip of beach resorts that eventually lead to such towns as Acireale, this boxy-looking but well-respected, government-rated three-star hotel is favored by business travelers. A somewhat blasé staff will check you into medium to smallish contemporary-looking guest rooms, outfitted with bland but comfortable furniture and color schemes of blue and white. About 21 of the units have views over the harbor. Each unit comes with a well-maintained private bathroom with shower. There's no restaurant on-site, but a respectable choice of dining options lie within a few minutes' drive or walk.

Via Messina 626–628, 95126 Località Ognina Catania. © **095-7528111**. Fax 095-7121856. www.jolly hotels.it. 56 units. 155€ double. Rate includes breakfast. Free parking. AE, DC, MC, V. Bus: 334 or 448. **Amenities:** Bar. *In room:* A/C, TV, minibar.

INEXPENSIVE

Albergo Moderno   This government-rated three-star hotel is set halfway up a flight of steps leading to the Church of San Placido, near a cluster of nightlife recommendations (among them Bar Nievski), a 10-minute walk from the cathedral. A pair of elevators take you to clean, unpretentious guest rooms, each *moderno,* reminiscent of 1960s styling and accessories, and with cool-to-the-touch terrazzo floors. The rooms were renovated in 2002 by crews who deliberately left the airport-lounge styling intact. All units come with tiled bathrooms with shower.

Via Alessi 9, 95124 Catania. © **095-326250**. Fax 095-326674. www.albergomoderno.it. 18 units. 93€ double. AE, MC, V. Bus: 454. **Amenities:** Breakfast lounge. *In room:* A/C, TV, safe.

Hotel Centrale Europa   This age-old government-rated two-star hotel occupies a site that's closer to the cathedral than any other hotel in town. It has been here since 1900, still evoking a battered but genteel pensione whose staff has seen thousands of art lovers and business travelers coming and going on their exploration of Catania and its architectural treasures. You register in a small lobby filled with sepia-toned photos of old Catania. Rooms are very simple and bland-looking, having few frills but acceptably comfortable furniture. More than half the rooms overlook the Duomo and the historic buildings around it. Each room is equipped with a bathroom, half with showers, the other half with tubs. No meals of any kind, not even breakfast, are served, but the Caffè Duomo (featured as part of our walking tour of Catania) lies a few steps away.

Finds   A Farmhouse Retreat in the Shadow of Etna

With Mount Etna rising ominously in the foreground, **Azienda Trinità**, 34 Via Trinità, 95030 Mascalucia (ⓒ/fax **095-7272156**; www.azienda trinita.it), is a rural farm dating back to 1609. It lies near the little Etnean town of Mascalucia, renowned for its 16th-century churches. The setting is a botanical park where Etna's lava breeds a collection of indigenous and exotic plants.

Visitors can stay on the farm or in one of the newly built apartments. Guest rooms are midsize and cozy, each with a small bathroom with shower; they come with air-conditioning and TVs, and have wooden ceilings with traditional wooden furniture. Guests are invited to have their fill from the garden's citrus trees, prickly pears, persimmons, walnuts, chestnuts, and summer fruits. Meals are prepared with old Sicilian recipes using as much locally grown produce as possible, including the farm's own citrus fruit, olive oil, artichokes, zagara honey, mandarin liqueur, and baked olives. Half board costs 44€ per person. From the center of Catania, follow the road signs to Tangenziale Ovest. Go along this road until you see the exit to Gravina. From here, follow the street signs to Mascalucia Etna.

Via Vittorio Emanuele 167 (Piazza Duomo), 95124 Catania. ⓒ **095-311309**. Fax 095-317531. 17 units. 70€ double. AE, MC, V. Bus: 1-4, 2-5, 3-6, or 457. *In room:* A/C, TV.

Hotel Collegiata ⭐ *(Finds)*   Most of the floors in this 17th-century building are devoted to private apartments, except for two, which contain a series of large, high-ceilinged guest rooms that, however spartan-looking, are bigger than you'd expect, airy, and comfortable. Each unit comes with a small bathroom with a shower stall. The setting is close to one of Catania's most beautiful churches, La Collegiata, a short walk from the Duomo. The staff is hip and friendly.

Via Vasta 10 (at the corner of the Via Etnea), 95100 Catania. ⓒ **095-315256**. Fax 095-322848. www.col.net.mt/collegiate/index.htm. 14 units. 73€ double. Rates include breakfast. AE, DC, MC, V. Bus: 448, 449, or 457. *In room:* A/C, TV.

Hotel Gresi   Small-scale and lacking any bona-fide amenities, this would be nothing more than a tucked-away set of rooms fashioned from a once-private apartment except for the fact that the painted ceilings are as lavishly frescoed as those in any hotel in town. You'll pass through a stately-looking courtyard to reach the place, take a small elevator to the third floor, and register in a high-ceilinged anteroom whose painted ceiling is only one of many more to come. Most of the frescoes date from around 1850 in a style so lovely as to place them in almost surreal contrast with the hotel's simple furniture. Each unit is equipped with a small bathroom with shower stall.

Via Pacini 28, 95124 Catania. ⓒ **095-322709**. Fax 095-7153045. 23 units. 65€ double. AE, DC, MC, V. Bus: 1-4 or 7. **Amenities:** Breakfast lounge. *In room:* A/C, TV.

San Demetrio Hotel ⭐ *(Finds)*   Small-scale, personalized, and deeply idiosyncratic, this hotel occupies one of the upper floors of a grandiose building near the cathedral; it shares the floor with the branch of the local bureaucracy that fines motorists for parking and traffic violations. (To reach the entrance to the hotel, you pass somewhat scary-looking government offices, traverse a courtyard, and take an impossibly claustrophobic elevator to an upper floor.) The hotel was converted from a private apartment in 2000, and it still evokes a private home. It is graced with some of the most beautiful ceiling frescoes of any hotel in Catania. The appealing paintings on the walls are done in a "post-Renaissance kind of modernism." Room no. 22 is particularly charming, but the others compete worthily with early-19th-century (or earlier) grace notes. In contrast, room furnishings are spartan. Each room has a private bathroom with a shower stall.

Via Etnea 55, 95124 Catania. (℃)/fax 095-2500237. www.hotelsandemetrio.com. 7 units. 78€ double; 104€ triple; 128€ quad. Rates include breakfast. MC, V. Free parking. Bus: 448, 449, 457, 722, or 733. **Amenities:** Room service; babysitting; laundry/dry cleaning. In room: A/C, TV, hair dryer.

3 Where to Dine

EXPENSIVE

Le Zagare ★★ CONTINENTAL/SICILIAN   When an army of designers renovated the dining room of the Excelsior Grand Hotel in 2001, they took pains to retain the original lines of its *dolce vita* decor (ca. 1954). The result is a genuinely elegant Grand Hotel–style dining experience complemented by an army of staff members, superb food, and access to an outdoor terrace lined with flickering candles and flowering shrubbery. Menu items are a cut above the standardized fare served in other hotel dining rooms. The best examples include braised scorpionfish in a green-olive sauce; superb sautéed medallions of lobster with fried endive; scalloped lamb in an aromatic breaded crust with leek slices in a curry sauce; and a delightful glazed loin of pork with a celery and apple stew flavored with green pepper. A meal here always digests better when it's followed with an after-dinner drink at the hotel piano bar.

In Excelsior Grand Hotel, Piazza Verga. (℃) 095-7476111. Reservations recommended. Main courses 18€–25€. AE, DC, MC, V. Daily 12:30–3pm and 7:30–11pm. Bus: 443, 457, 721, or 722.

Osteria I Tre Bicchieri ★★★ CONTINENTAL   This is the finest and most appealing restaurant in Catania. Established in 2000 in partnership with one of the best-respected wine merchants (Benanti, Inc.) in Sicily, it welcomes visitors to a location on a narrow, quiet street about 2 blocks northwest of the cathedral. Be warned in advance that it contains two dining venues, one a well-conceived wine tavern **(Cantina)** in a woodsy-looking room near the front entrance. The real culinary vision of the place is found in a carefully choreographed gastronomic citadel—three high-ceilinged vaulted rooms outfitted in a graceful 18th-century style—that you reach by walking through the Cantina and through the kind of sliding, high-security door you might have expected in a bank vault.

Part of the success of this place derives from the culinary vision of Naples-born *wunderkind* chef Laquinangelo Carmine, whose creativity is fast becoming a legend among local gastronomes. The chef has a magic combination of inventiveness and solid technique. There's no regional pasta better than farfalle with baby squid and baby octopus, swimming in black squid ink with seasonal vegetables. Potato gnocchi comes with spinach and sea urchins in a reduction of fish sauce and *fines herbes*. An amazing dish is a grand platter of Mediterranean fish swimming in fish broth and perfumed with onions. Where can you get a good salad from the foot of a wild boar? Here it comes with lemon-flavored tripe and fava beans. Delight in steamed medallions of sole, shrimp, and *triglia* (a local saltwater fish) in a spinach-flavored cream sauce, served with a chilled salad of new potatoes and lemon-flavored chive sauce. Glasses of wine include at least 1,000 Italian vintages, many from Sicily.

Well-prepared food in the Cantina costs 6€ to 13€ and includes platters designed to go well with the wine. The Cantina offers fondues, steak tartare with salad, carpaccios, pastas, grilled steaks, and both sweet and salted crepes.

Note to wine experts: Make it a point to drop into this restaurant's wine boutique. Maintained at enormous expense and expertly staffed, it sells both popular and very rare vintages by the bottle and, best of all, it maintains a resident expert wine steward who really knows what he's talking about.

Via San Giuseppe al Duomo 31. ℂ 095-7153540. www.osteriaitrebicchieri.it. Reservations required. In gastronomic restaurant, main courses 16€–25€; set-price menu 45€. AE, DC, MC, V. Mon–Sat 1–3 pm and 8:30–11pm. Bus: 443, 457, 721, or 722.

MODERATE

Il Canile SICILIAN/CONTINENTAL   Elegant and traditional, and set in the Villa del Bosco hotel (see above), this restaurant is very appealing. You can dine in a richly frescoed interior room or take a seat on an outdoor terrace overlooking the stars, without a hint of Sicilian traffic. Menu items include a *risottini* of porcini mushrooms from the slopes of Mount Etna. We sampled our finest seafood pasta in Catania here and went on to devour a succulent filet of sea bream under an oven-crispy potato crust. The restaurant's name, which translates as "The Kennel," is taken from the pair of 18th-century stone dogs that stand near its entranceway.

In the Villa del Bosco hotel, Via del Bosco 62. ℂ 095-7335100. Reservations recommended. Main courses 13€–15€. Daily 1–2:30pm and 8–11pm. Bus: 129, 314, or 421.

INEXPENSIVE

La Marchesana ★ *Value*   The charm of this place lies in its well-managed simplicity, the genuinely friendly welcome from the staff at the bar near the entrance, and the simple but flavorful cuisine. Outdoor tables fill part of the quiet street during nice weather; otherwise, you can dine in a high-ceilinged vaulted dining room that manages to stay cool even on very hot days. The Didio family, well versed in welcoming diners from the English-speaking world, prepare dishes that include a mixed fish-fry; a succulent spaghetti with squid, cuttlefish, shrimp, and tomatoes; and delectable pastas, risottos, and freshly made salads.

Via Mazza 4–8 (at the Piazza San Placido). ℂ 095-315171. Reservations recommended on weekends. Main courses 7.75€–12€. AE, DC, MC, V. Wed–Mon 12:30–5pm and 7:30pm–12:30am. Closed 2 weeks in Aug. Bus: 1-4.

L'Osteria dell'Asinello SICILIAN   Small, cozy, and completely unpretentious, this is the kind of family-run trattoria to which the neighborhood hotels often refer their clients. It's set behind a hard-to-decipher sign on an undistinguished-looking piazza in a quiet residential neighborhood rarely visited by foreigners. Inside the cramped but cozy interior, you'll find wall-hung ceramic plates, tile floors, a generously stocked antipasti buffet, and an iced display of the day's fresh fish. Begin with any of five different kinds of pasta; seafood risotto; spaghetti with clams; veal cutlets Milanese; or roulades of either swordfish or veal. The restaurant's trademark shows a Sicilian-style donkey cart pulled by an *asinello* (donkey) wearing a battered straw hat.

Piazza San Domenico 22–23. ℂ 095-312203. Reservations not necessary. Main courses 7€–9.50€. AE, DC, MC, V. Mon–Sat noon–3:30pm and 7pm–midnight. Closed 1 week in Aug.

Osteria Antica Marina SICILIAN   Only a handful of other restaurants convey as effectively the earthy, grimy, teeming maze of humanity that hauls food in and out of central Catania. Established just after World War II and sheathed with wooden panels, this osteria is set amid the densest concentration of open-air food stalls in town, two labyrinthine blocks south of the cathedral, on a piazza that by day teems with food merchants, but by night is calmer and quieter. You'll be separated from most of the hysteria outside by plate-glass windows and air-conditioning, but at the same time you'll get a sense of the freshness and variety of raw material just a few steps away. It's a good bet that more than a few locals have dragged visitors from other parts of Europe into this bustling neighborhood to show off the local color. (French actress Catherine Deneuve was one such visitor.) Menu items include ultra-fresh versions of homemade pasta, garnished (you guessed it) with various forms of seafood and shellfish; jumbo prawns with almond sauce; linguine with sea urchins; every imaginable kind of grilled gilled creature in the Mediterranean; and very fresh cuts of beefsteak, pork, veal, and lamb.

Alla Pescheria di Catania, Via Pardo 29. ✆ **095-348197.** Reservations recommended. Main courses 7€–11€. AE, DC, MC, V. Thurs–Tues 1–3pm and 8pm–12:30am. Bus: 1-4, 2-5, or 3-6.

Ristorante Piccolo Teatro INTERNATIONAL   Set a few steps from the Teatro Massimo, this is a cozy, wood-sheathed pub whose battered panels and prominent bar might remind you of an Italian beer hall. It's never open for lunch but instead attracts after-work business and a pre-theater crowd of young hipsters and hipster wannabes. Expect mugs of beer and dishes that include fresh fish (especially variations of swordfish), risottos, and hot-weather favorites such as octopus salads and sorbets. "A dish for the gods," as one habitué described it, is spaghetti with sea urchins, eggs, and extra-virgin olive oil given additional flavor by fresh parsley, garlic, and hot peppers. Pennette with swordfish is made enticing by the addition of eggplant, fresh mint, pine nuts, and hot peppers.

Via Michele Rapisardi 6–8. ✆ **095-315369.** Reservations not needed. Main courses 7€–15€. AE, DC, MC, V. Wed–Mon 8pm–12:30am. Bus: 14.

Serandib *Value* INDIAN   Set in an upscale residential neighborhood near the Piazza Verga and the Excelsior Hotel, this is one of the few East Indian restaurants in Catania, and as such, it's a welcome change from a too-constant diet of Sicilian cuisine. It evokes a rustic Italian tavern, except for the Sri Lankan and Indian clientele that travels here from all parts of the city. There's only one option: a fixed-price menu that includes flavorful versions of dishes such as well-prepared chicken curry, chicken tandoori, biryani rice, and fruit salad.

Via Aloi 50. ✆ **095-530671.** Fixed-price menu 11€. MC, V. Tues–Sun 12:30–3pm and 7–1:30pm. Bus: 334, 443, 457, 721, or 722.

Sicilia in Bocca alla Marina SICILIAN   Set near the Porta Uzeda, facing the Villa Pacini park, this restaurant is tucked into a soaring vaulted space beneath the cluster of buildings that flank the cathedral. To reach the dining room, you'll pass through an anteroom where the day's catch is laid out on ice in a style that evokes a local market. The venue looks as old as the ancient Roman world, although a staff member told us that the high lava-rock vaults date from the 1700s, when the place was used as a warehouse and stables for the cathedral complex above it. The only complaint we have about this restaurant is an almost defiantly dour staff, but if you don't expect cheerfulness, you'll get well-prepared and very fresh cuisine in a dining venue favored by many local residents. The best items include spaghetti with clams; ~~linguine with cuttlefish~~ and shrimp; spaghetti alla Norma; grilled beefsteaks; and a goodly assortment of fresh fish hauled in that day.

Via Dusmet 31–35. (✆) **095-2503135.** Reservations not necessary. Main courses 7.50€–9.50€. AE, DC, MC, V. Tues–Sun 1–3pm and 8pm–midnight. Bus: 431N or 457.

Trattoria La Paglia _Finds_ SICILIAN At the site of the lively fish market, you can enjoy the most authentic Catanian dining experience. If you like your food ethnic and your atmosphere hale and hearty, this is the place. The fish is the freshest in town. It often happens that if you don't like the day's offerings, one of the staff will step out to the market and buy a fish you like, cooking it to your specifications. Start, perhaps, with an excellent pasta in fresh bean sauce called _la triaca pasta_. Another savory opening is _sarda al beccafico_ (sardines fried in bread crumbs with pecorino cheese). We're also fond of the spaghetti whipped with sea urchins in an extra-virgin olive oil with fresh garlic. One local dish that's highly favored is _tonno con cipollata_ (broiled tuna with onions and a dash of vinegar). Most of the dishes are based on the sea, and the atmosphere is very rustic.

Via Pardo 23. (✆) **095-346838.** Reservations required Fri–Sat. Main courses 4€–7€; fixed-price menus 16€–26€. MC, V. Mon–Sat 12:30–2:30pm and 8–11pm. Bus: 457.

4 Seeing the Sights

Duomo 🖈 In the center of the city, the cathedral of Catania is dedicated to the memory of the martyred St. Agatha. Originally, the Duomo was ordered built by Roger I, the Norman king, but it was destroyed in the earthquake of 1693 and had to be reconstructed. Its **facade** 🖈 is its most enduring architectural legacy, the work of Battista Vaccarini (1702–68), who redesigned the city after the earthquake. For the granite columns of the facade, the architect "removed" them from the city's Roman amphitheater. Only the lovingly crafted medieval apses, each made from lava, survived the devastation of that earthquake.

Many opera fans come here to pay their respects at **Bellini's tomb,** guarded by a life-size angel in marble. It's to the right as you enter the Duomo through its right door. The words above the tomb are from _Sonnambula_ and in translation read, "Ah, I didn't think I'd see you wilt so soon, flower."

In the **Norman Cappella della Madonna,** also on the right, precious metals envelop a magnificent Roman sarcophagus and a statue of the Virgin Mary carved in the 1400s. This chapel also contains the ashes of the Aragonese kings—Frederick II, Louis, and Frederick III. To the right of the choir is the **Cappella di Sant'Agata,** to whom the cathedral is dedicated. In the sacristy is a fresco depicting the horrendous eruption of Mount Etna in 1669. The fresco is said to have been created in 1774.

Piazza Duomo, Via Vittorio Emanuele II 163. (✆) **095-320044.** Free admission. Daily 7am–noon and 4:30–7pm. Bus: 448, 449, 457, 722, or 733.

Piazza Duomo The cathedral (see above) is not the only attraction on this landmark square. Lying in the very heart of Catania, the Piazza Duomo was also created by the city's planner, Vaccarini. The baroque elegance of Catania's heyday lingers on in this square.

The symbol of the city, the **Fontana dell'Elefante** 🖈🖈, its mascot, was created in 1735. It was obviously inspired by Bellini's monument in Rome's Piazza Minerva. The elephant was hewn from black lava spewed forth by Mount Etna. The platform on which the elephant stands is Byzantine. The elephant is a beast

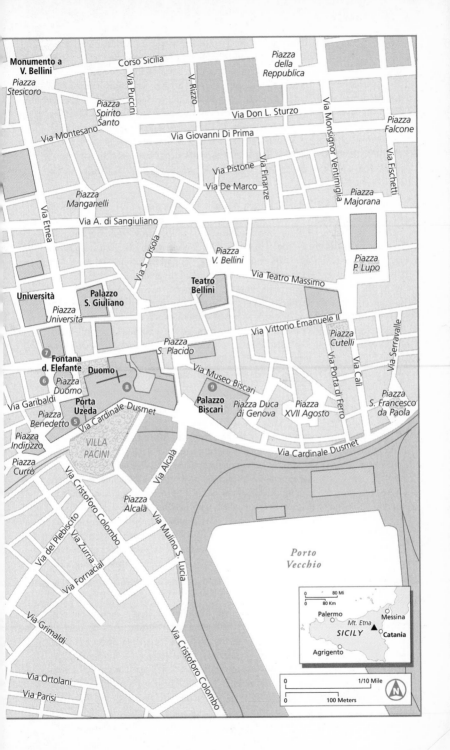

in 1835. Signatures in the guest book read like a who's who of international musicians and include Carlo Muti and Pavarotti. Many of the mementos of his life were donated by Rossini, a devoted latter-day fan of Bellini's brilliant *bel cantos*. Exhibits inside lay out the chronologies of his life, including the years of completion of such titanic works as *La Straniera* (1829); *Sonnambula* (1831); the always-divine *Norma* (1831); and two versions each of *I Puritani* and *I Cavalieri*, both operas destined for performances in Paris and Naples, respectively (1835). If you're an opera fan, you will likely find this museum thrilling. If you're not, it might be passed through, in all its dusty magnificence, more quickly.

Piazza San Francesco 3. ℂ **095-7150535**. Free admission. Daily 9am–1pm; Tues–Thurs 3–6pm. Bus: 1-4, 2-5, or 3-6.

Museo Emilio Greco ★   Larger, plusher, and more obviously well-financed than either the Bellini or the Verga museums, with which it's frequently compared, this second-story museum showcases the oil paintings and engravings of Sicilian artist **Emilio Greco** (1913–95). His fame is mostly derived from accolades he received in New York and Tokyo, not from adulation heaped upon him by other Sicilians. Of the trio of museums in the immediate neighborhood, this is the one that's least visited by Catanians. Many locals are not that familiar with Greco, whose abstract nude forms contrast vividly with the lavish display of baroque architecture, as seen in the facade of the Church of San Francesco and visible immediately across the piazza from some of the windows of this museum. Sure, we admire Emilio Greco, but we couldn't help but wonder why works by other Sicilian artists weren't also on display in this magnificent space.

Piazza San Francesco 3. ℂ **095-325706**. Free admission. Mon, Wed, and Fri–Sun 9am–1pm; Tues and Thurs 3–6pm. Bus: 31.

Casa di Verga   This is a memorial to Sicily's national poet, **Giovanni Verga** (1840–1922), who lived and wrote here for many years. Verga was a firebrand who wrote with poignancy about the plight of underpaid workers during the Industrial Revolution. You'll have to be very alert to the nuances of his writing, however, to appreciate the battered, dusty, and not-particularly-well-stocked museum that occupies the rooms where he completed some of his works. Much of the place is preserved as Verga left it. Climb a flight of worn, badly marked stairs for access to the limited roster of memorabilia associated with his life. Despite the artist's powerful literature, you might leave with a sense of sadness that the local municipality has neglected this museum as obviously as it has. We recommend this place only for avid literary enthusiasts—much more interesting, with a staff that's more emotionally involved with its subject matter, is the Bellini Museum a few blocks away.

Via Sant'Anna 8. ℂ **095-7150598**. Admission 2€ adults, 1€ ages 18–25. Free for ages 17 and under. Tues and Thurs–Sat 8:30am–1pm; Wed 2:30–5pm. Apr–June Sun 8:30am–1pm. Bus: 1-4, 2-5, or 3-6.

Museo del Giocattolo (Museum of Childhood) *Kids*   New, relatively unpublicized, and almost chaotically disorganized, this museum is devoted to the whimsical fancies of children. Defining itself as a "permanent laboratory" of human psychology, it offers exhibits and programs designed to both entertain and shape the creativity of children and their psyches. It's partly publicly funded and partly privately supported through donations. The place is so confusing, the staff so unhelpful and inarticulate (even in Italian), that you may feel like Alice in Wonderland. Exhibits include dolls, doll houses, electric train sets, and whimsical sculptures, many displayed beneath lavishly ornate frescoed ceilings from the late 18th or early 19th century.

Where Gladiators Battled Lions

Lovers of antiquity should head for the Piazza Stesicoro, Via Vittorio Emanuele 260 (© **095-7150508**), for a very evocative site, the ruins of a **Roman amphitheater** dating from the 2nd century A.D. Because of shifting land, the ruins lie below street level, although the gladiator tunnels are still visible. This is one of the largest of all Roman amphitheaters; it is believed that some 17,000 spectators were once entertained here by blood games. Only a tiny part of the theater survives, so you'll have to use your imagination to conjure up the ancient gore. The reason? The Ostrogoths, not devotees of Roman glory, used the amphitheater as a quarry. In fact, the Goths found the Roman gladiator contests too vicious and completely outlawed them. They converted the stones into churches and public monuments. The site is open daily from 9am to 1:30pm and 3 to 7pm. Admission is 2€ for adults, 1€ for students or ages 17 and under.

In the Palazzo Bruca, Via Vittorio Emanuele 201. © **095-320111**. Admission 3.50€ adults, 2€ for ages 3–12. Free for ages 2 and under. Tues–Sun 10am–6pm. Bus: 448, 449, 457, 722, or 733.

Palazzo Biscari Today a private home, this is the most impressive palazzo in the city. To visit, you must call first and make an appointment. Constructed after the 1693 earthquake, the palace flowered in the mid–18th century as the home of Ignazio Paternò Castello, prince of Biscari, "the Renaissance man of Catania," who held a passionate interest in art, archaeology, painting, music, and literature. When Goethe and others doing the Grand Tour of Europe passed through Catania, they pronounced Palazzo Biscari the city's grandest attraction.

Partially constructed on the city's old fortress wall, the palace dances with a wealth of *putti* (cherubic angels) and caryatids. Balconies are formed by both *putti* and cartouches, the stunning work of Francesco Battaglia and his son, Antonino. In the courtyard is a grand stairwell, and on the second floor are the major reception rooms. The room at the far end has frescoes by Sebastiano Lo Monaco.

Prince Biscari installed an archaeological museum in his palace, but the collection has been moved to Castello Ursino (see below). Classical music concerts are sometimes staged in the palace's sumptuous interior (check with the tourist office).

Via Museo Biscari 10–16. © **095-321818**. Free admission (donations appreciated). Call to reserve a visit. Bus: 1-4, 457, or 733.

Castello Ursino & Museo Civico West of Piazza Duomo, this castle was once the proud fortress of Frederick II in the 13th century. When it was originally built, the grim-looking fortress, surrounded by a moat, stood on a cliff overlooking the Ionian Sea. But Mount Etna's lava has shifted the land over the centuries. Now landlocked since the mass south of here was reclaimed from the sea, Castello Ursino is reached by going through a rough neighborhood where caution is recommended.

The castle is built on a square plan with a keep 30m (99 ft.) high on each corner and semicircular towers in the middle on each side. If you walk along the perimeter of the castle, you can still see the old moats and even some Renaissance windows imbedded in the south side.

Moments   Something Fishy This Way Comes

One of the largest, most bustling, and certainly most colorful fish markets *(pescheria)* in the Mediterranean is held Monday through Saturday morning in a narrow warren of streets behind the Duomo. We doubt if even the late Cousteau could identify some of these creatures from the murky depths. "If it swims, we Catanians eat it," a local fishmonger told us

Octopus, squid, eels, shellfish, and other writhing, twitching creatures are sold here. You can buy fresh mussels and sea urchins to eat on the spot. Vegetable and fruit stalls also spill into the offshoot lanes. The bloody butchers' tables surely inspired the paintings of the late Francis Bacon.

The castle's *pinacoteca* (library) has an interesting (though hardly spectacular) series of paintings that date back to the 1400s, extending all the way to the 1800s. Most of the work is from Sicily or southern Italy, including Antonello de Saliba's polyptych of the **Madonna Enthroned with Saints Francis and Anthony** 👁; De Saliba was a pupil of the legendary Antonello da Messina. One of the best-known Catanian artists was Michele Rapisardi, who is represented by two lovely studies: the **Head of the Crazed Ophelia** and a **depiction of the Sicilian Vespers.** Surely the saddest *Grieving Widow* in all of Catania was that depicted by another home-grown artist, Giuseppe Sciuti. The art of Lorenzo Loiacono is also worth noting for his vivid, even theatrical efforts.

Housed inside are Prince Biscari's **archaeological collection** (see above), along with **objects from San Nicolò Monastery,** and some of the best **Sicilian painted carts** on the island.

Piazza Federico di Svevia. 📞 **095-345830.** Free admission. Tues–Sat 9am–12:30pm and 3–6pm; Sun 9am–1pm. Bus: 422, 428, or 429.

Chiesa di San Nicolò All'Arena   This is the largest and spookiest church in Sicily, stretching for 105m (345 ft.) with transepts measuring 42m (138 ft.). The cupola is 62m (204 ft.) high. Begun in 1687 by Giovanni Battista Contini, it was reconstructed in 1735 by Francesco Battaglia. Stefano Ittar designed the dome; the facade, with its mammoth columns, was left unfinished in 1796 but remains impressive. Catanians call it "mastodonic" because the pillars stick up like tusks. The interior of the church is large but rather bare-bones. A beautiful 18th-century organ with 2,916 pipes is found behind the main altar. A meridian line was laid in the transept floor in 1841 to catch the sunlight precisely at noon. But because of the shifting volcanic land, today it catches the sun at 12:13pm. Sadly, the church will never be completed. Sporadic renovations try to keep it propped up, but the efforts seem doomed to failure.

The adjoining **Monastereo di San Nicolò All'Arena** is the second-largest monastery in Europe, rivaled only by Mafra, outside of Lisbon. This old Benedictine complex, dating from 1703, is part of Catania University, but frankly, it's in really bad shape. Depending on conditions at the time of your visit, you may or may not be able to visit it.

Piazza Cavour. 📞 **095-438077.** Free admission. Thurs 5–7:30pm; Sun 11am–1pm. Bus: 429 or 432.

Moments **The Green Lung of Catania**

Escape from the city heat and congestion to **Villa Bellini** ★, the "Central Park" of Catania, reached by heading north along Via Etnea. Planted with such exotics as Brazilian araucavias, the park sprawls over several hills. This is one of the most attractive public parks in Sicily, and for some reason maintenance is higher here than it is in most of Catania's public monuments or gardens. The Catanians claim that the fig tree planted in this park is the world's largest. Unique in Italy is the floral clock and calendar on the hillside. Stand on a hill here and be rewarded with a panoramic view of Mount Etna.

WALKING TOUR **HISTORIC CATANIA**

Start	Castello Ursino.
Finish	Piazza Università.
Time	4½ hours, including brief visits inside churches and monuments.
Best Times	Morning before noon when the food market is at its busiest.
Worst Times	After dark when the alleyways of the old town are unsafe.

Begin your tour amid the palms and palmettos of the piazza in front of the massive and forbidding-looking

❶ Castello Ursino

Built on ancient Greek foundations, its soaring, severe-looking interior has some of the biggest and most impressive stone vaulting in Catania. The inside is devoted to a municipal museum that contains everything from archaeological remnants to 19th-century landscapes and portraits. When the *castello* was built in 1239, it directly fronted the sea, although since then, lava flows from Etna raised the ground level to the point where it now lies some distance inland. Look for patterns of both menorahs and crosses set into the medieval masonry, a hallmark left by the masons.

After your visit, with your back to the *castello*, walk kitty-corner (diagonally) to the right, across Piazza Federico de Svevia, heading to a point immediately to the left of the iron fence that fronts the railway tracks. Pass through an alleyway that funnels

into an unnamed triangular piazza, and from there continue onto Via Auteri. At Via Auteri 26, note the 18th-century facade of the privately owned **Palazzo Auteri.** Said to be haunted, and long ago divided into private apartments (none of which can be visited), it's just one example of the many grand buildings dotting this historic neighborhood. From Via Auteri, turn right onto Via Zappala Gemelli, site of the beginning of Catania's

❷ Outdoor Fish, Meat & Produce Market

We can't even begin to describe the cornucopia of sights, sounds, and smells that rise from this warren of narrow streets. Pay attention to your footing: Don't slip on the slime from fish guts, discarded and rotting vegetables, or whatever, and continue walking downhill, through the souks, to the bulk that rises on the right-hand side of Via Zappala Gemelli, the:

❸ Chiesa Santa Maria dell'Indirizzo

Its elegant baroque facade—punctuated with a garish-looking neon sign declaring VIVA MARIA—stands above a square (Piazza dell'Indirizzo) that rises above that part of the food market specifically dedicated to meats, a sight that might horrify any dedicated vegetarian. This is not a showcase church destined for the art books or tourist trade. It's the parish church of the meat- and fish-market district, with an evocatively battered interior, crumbling stucco, a small-to-medium-scale format, and scads of dusty-looking baroque/rococo ornamentation inside. Opening hours are erratic, but are usually daily from 8am to noon and 3 to 6pm.

After your visit, walk to the church's southern side (the one on the left as you face it from the teeming meat market outside). Here, separated from the square by an iron fence, lies the ancient Roman ruins of the:

❹ Terme dell'Indirizzo

Constructed by the ancient Romans of black volcanic rock and terra-cotta brick, with only a few of its original vaults and arches still intact, these baths are best admired from the outside of the fence. Look also for a tiny domed Greek-cross building, constructed of black lava. It's virtually never open except for qualified archaeologists, and then only under the strictest of circumstances. It's the ugliest monument on this tour—and the rocks have been cited as unsafe for climbing.

After your visit to the ruined Roman baths, descend along basalt cobblestones in front of the Church Santa Maria dell'Indirizzo. They lead downhill into the bowels of the rest of the food market. The largest open space in the food markets—a mass of parasols, blood, humanity, and grime—is the **Piazza Pardo** (also known as the Via Pardo), at the edge of which is the hard-to-see facade of a highly recommended restaurant (see "Where to Dine," earlier in this chapter), **Osteria Antica Marina.** With your back to the restaurant, turn left, noting the massive and soaring archway, built of dark lava

rock, on either side of which the food market teems wildly. It's the:

❺ Porta Carlo V

Punctuating the entranceway to the indoor section of the city's food markets, this is one of the rare structures of Catania that survived the earthquake of 1693. Pass beneath it (a fish vendor will probably nod his or her greetings as you go by; one even warned us to be careful of our wallets); then turn left. After a few steps, you'll emerge into the open air again, into an all-neoclassical, traffic-free square filled with more food vendors selling, in this case, fish. Your map might identify it as the Piazza A. di Benedetto, but there is no sign. Most of the buildings that surround you at this point date from the early 1600s. At the distant edge of this piazza, at the top of a short flight of stone steps, is a small stone obelisk marked **Fontana dell'Amenano.** Built in 1867, it marks the location of a powerful underground river.

❻ Fontana dei 10 Canales (Fountain of the 10 Rivers)

This is visible at the bottom of a steep masonry-sided chasm from the obelisk's rear side. For years, it was the only water source in this teeming neighborhood, and many local residents remember when a flood of water from this underground canal was diverted, thanks to conduits and channels, to an aboveground curtain of water used liberally by everyone in the food market. Today, because of urban renovations and difficulties with the plumbing, the waters remain mostly underground. From here, walk to the top of the previously mentioned stone steps for a view over the:

❼ Piazza Duomo

At the edges of this piazza sit several of the monuments visited as part of this walking tour. But before your visits, look left (westward) along the wide upward-sloping vista of the:

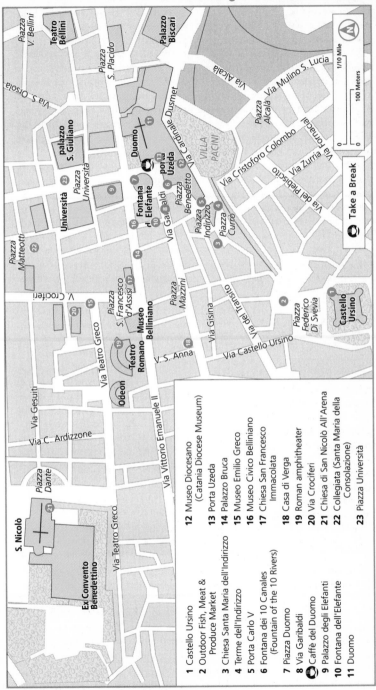

1 Castello Ursino
2 Outdoor Fish, Meat &
   Produce Market
3 Chiesa Santa Maria dell'Indirizzo
4 Terme dell'Indirizzo
5 Porta Carlo V
6 Fontana dei 10 Canales
   (Fountain of the 10 Rivers)
7 Piazza Duomo
8 Via Garibaldi
   Caffè del Duomo
9 Palazzo degli Elefanti
10 Fontana dell'Elefante
11 Duomo

12 Museo Diocesano
   (Catania Diocese Museum)
13 Porta Uzeda
14 Palazzo Bruca
15 Museo Emilio Greco
16 Museo Civico Belliniano
17 Chiesa San Francesco
   Immacolata
18 Casa di Verga
19 Roman amphitheater
20 Via Crociferi
21 Chiesa di San Nicolò All'Arena
22 Collegiata (Santa Maria della
   Consolazione)
23 Piazza Università

⑧ Via Garibaldi

At the most distant point on the street's faraway horizon, beyond the masses of people and cars, note the decorative triumphal arch that was built to celebrate the marriage, in 1768, of the Spanish king Ferdinand de Bourbon and Princess Carolina of Austria. About a century later, in 1862, it marked the processional route of Garibaldi for his triumphant entrance into Catania during the agonizing process of unifying Italy into a coherent political whole. The event marked Garibaldi's utterance, for the first time, of what eventually became a unifying political slogan, *"O Roma, o morte"* ("Give me Rome or give me death"). Now, prepare yourself to:

TAKE A BREAK
Caffè del Duomo, Piazza Duomo 12 (℅ 095-7150556). This is the most charming of the several cafes flanking the Piazza Duomo. Built in the late 1800s, it has a marble countertop, an inlaid marble floor, hints of the Belle Epoque, and a lavish *tavola calda* (hot table) adjacent to the bar. Here, you can choose from at least 15 different snack items, any one or two of which might compose a satisfying snack or even lunch. Most are priced at between 1€ and 2€. The cafe also sells some of the most artful and beautiful almond candies in Catania, shaped like berries, pears, apples, or whatever. For a quick pick-me-up at the bar, order an espresso, or do as the locals do: Ask for seltzer water that's doctored with a tantalizingly small scoop of fruit-flavored *granita*. The cafe is open daily from 5:30am to midnight.

After your refueling stop, walk across Piazza Duomo to the:

⑨ Palazzo degli Elefanti

Today this palace is the Municipio, or town hall, of Catania. From its central balcony, Mussolini once gave one of his crowd-pleasing rabble-rousing speeches. If it's open, walk into the building's central courtyard, where you'll see lava-rock foundations; bas-relief wall friezes dedicated to Catania's patron saint (St. Agatha); and a pair of 18th-century ceremonial coaches that are used every February to carry Catania's ecclesiastical and secular dignitaries (including the mayor) down the city thoroughfares for the Festival of St. Agatha. If the security guard allows it (usually they do), proceed into the second or innermost courtyard as well. Here, note the wall-mounted 19th-century copy of an ancient Greek sundial. Proud Sicilians claim that the ancient Romans learned the art and science of sundials from the Greek colonists of Sicily. Regrettably, unless you're on official civic business, the rest of city hall is usually closed to casual visitors.

After your visit, cross the Piazza Duomo and take time to admire:

⑩ Fontana dell'Elefante

This fountain was created from black lava and is Catania's most famous and photographed monument. It stands on a Byzantine platform and carries on its back an ancient Egyptian obelisk covered with hieroglyphics. On top of that is an iron ornament that includes, among other symbols, a cross devoted to the patron saint, Agatha.

⑪ Duomo

Begun by King Roger in 1902 and rebuilt by Caccarini after the earthquake, this cathedral used many ancient monuments of Catania in its construction, including stones from Roman theaters. Pause to admire its lugubrious baroque facade with granite columns. Norman apses can be viewed from Via Vittorio Emanuele. Inside, the church was built over the ruins of a vaulted Roman bath, and a Romanesque basilica lies under the Duomo's nave. The cathedral is a pantheon of some Aragonese royalty.

After you exit from the cathedral, turn immediately left (with your back to the Duomo's front entrance) and walk a few steps to a building that functioned for many generations as a seminary for theologians and is now the:

⑫ Museo Diocesano (Catania Diocese Museum)

Located at Via Etnea 8, this museum gives you a view of the ornaments and an insight into the lavish traditions associated with one of Sicily's most powerful undercurrents of religious ecstasy, the Cult of St. Agatha. Inside, you'll find photographs of modern-day religious processions, and the massive silver sledge that holds the iconic effigy of St. Agatha hauled through the streets every February as part of the mystical rites associated with this powerful cult.

After your visit, with your back to the entrance of the Diocese Museum, turn left and walk a few paces to the south, passing beneath the massive ceremonial stone portal known as:

⑬ Porta Uzeda

Originally built by Sicily's Spanish overlords during the early 18th century, this archway contains some interesting shops selling folkloric pottery. On its opposite side is a pleasant and verdant park, **Villa Pacini,** where you might decide to rest for a few moments with the older people and children.

Now retrace your steps back into Piazza Duomo, walking diagonally across it toward Via Vittorio Emanuele, which flanks its northern edge. Continue westward. A point of minor interest you'll find en route lies at Via Vittorio Emanuele 175, immediately adjacent to the Hotel de l'Europe.

Here, note the **hidden doorway,** crafted from wood, whose panels were painstakingly designed by a long-departed craftsperson to look like a continuation of the stone mullions of the building that contains it.

Continue walking west along the Via Vittorio Emanuele to one of Catania's quirkiest and most idiosyncratic museums. Concealed behind a massive wall and an imposing doorway is the:

⑭ Palazzo Bruca

Located at Via Vittorio Emanuele 201, the palace contains the **Museo del Giocattolo (Museum of Childhood).** For a more detailed review of this museum, refer to "Seeing the Sights," earlier in this chapter. This once private and still elegant palace is prefaced with an enormous walled-in sloping courtyard punctuated in the center with a heroic, heavily muscled fountain of Hercules. If you're in the mood for another refueling stop, consider the museum's on-site cafe (its hours are erratic). Expect pastries, cold drinks, and the like. Your drinks or snacks can be consumed either on a panoramic rooftop reached by stairs or in the street-level entrance area.

After your visit, exit back onto Via Vittorio Emanuele, and continue walking westward past some lesser churches and lots of baroque facades. Stop at the point where the street opens onto Piazza San Francesco, site of three important attractions, each noted below. You'll recognize the square thanks to the contemporary-looking statue that rises from its center devoted to Cardinal Dusmet, a 19th-century benefactor of Catania's poor. The inscription on its base translates as "Because we have bread, we give it to the poor." The three attractions flanking the square include:

⑮ Museo Emilio Greco

Located at Piazza San Francesco 3, this archive-cum-museum displays the major artistic contributions of Catania citizen **Emilio Greco** (1913–95). He is most famous for his grand sculpture. For more information, refer to "Seeing the Sights," earlier.

Accessible via the same entranceway on the western edge of the square is the more interesting:

⑯ Museo Civico Belliniano

The great **Vincenzo Bellini** (1801–35) was born in this house on Piazza San Francesco. It's still standing and displays his memorabilia, including portraits of the composer of *Norma*. For details, refer to the review earlier under "Seeing the Sights."

Facing both of these museums at the eastern edge of Piazza San Francesco is:

⑰ Chiesa San Francesco Immacolata

Note that the most interesting art objects inside this church are the massive, richly gilded candelabra (six of them, most at least 3.3m/11 ft. high and incredibly heavy) proudly displayed in the nave. Carved at the beginning of the 20th century and almost ridiculously massive, they're carried on the shoulders of the faithful during the Feast Day of St. Agatha. The largest and heaviest of them was carved in 1913, gilded in 1935, and donated to the church and to St. Agatha by the city's bakers' guild.

After your visit, continue walking westward along Via Vittorio Emanuele, turning left in 2 short blocks onto Via Santa Anna. On that street, you'll find the small-scale baroque facade of the tiny Chiesa Santa Anna (it's almost always closed to casual visitors) and, a few buildings later, on the left, the former home of one of Sicily's most famous writers:

⑱ Casa di Verga

Known for his naturalistic fiction, **Giovanni Verga** (1840–1922) became one of Sicily's greatest writers. Though his fame diminished toward the end of his life, he was celebrated in his day, making friends with such greats as Emile Zola. Much of Catania turned out for his 80th birthday, where Luigi Pirandello appeared as orator. For details of the building at Via Sant'Anna 8, go to "Seeing the Sights, earlier in this chapter.

Retrace your steps to Via Vittorio Emanuele and turn right, back toward the Piazza San Francesco. En route,

along that street's northern edge, see the deceptively modern-looking stone entrance to one of Catania's proudest and most cherished archaeological treasures, the:

⑲ Roman amphitheater

Draped with ivy, and overlooked by the windows of an encircling ring of 17th-century buildings and apartments, this charming and evocative theater at Via Vittorio Emanuele 260 is an ancient oasis concealed in the midst of an urban neighborhood whose traffic and congestion seem light-years away. During classical times, it held as many as 17,000 spectators for plays and—to a lesser extent—water games, when boats would float on waters funneled in from then-nearby streams and aqueducts. It was also a site for gladiator contests. Ironically, part of the theater's graceful half-moon–shaped seating structure is blocked with a black-lava stone bridge added during the early 17th century as the base for the since-demolished Via Grotte, once a densely populated street within this residential neighborhood.

Via Grotte, most of its bridgelike foundations, and all of its buildings were demolished in the 1950s by Catania's historic buildings committee as a means of returning the ancient theater to some semblance of its original purity. Vestiges of the street remain within the circumference of the Roman theater, however, cutting surreally across one edge of the theater's sweeping crescent-shaped bleachers.

Since Via Grotte was demolished, some former residents of the neighborhood have returned from prolonged sojourns in North America, Australia, or Argentina, and have been shocked to find their childhood playgrounds (the Via Grotte and its offshoots) no longer in place. Ghosts are rampant here. Come with stamina, a good sense of balance, and strong walking shoes. Sandals are not recommended because of the steep, uneven steps, which lead visitors through ghostly tunnels that wind their way through and beneath the bleacher stands.

A smaller theater, the **Odeon,** is accessible near the back side of the Roman theater. To reach it, follow signs from the theater, and walk sharply uphill through some tunnels and steep vaulted stairs.

After your visit, return to Piazza San Francesco, stand in front of its mammoth church, and turn uphill to face the lowest end of one of the most richly embellished baroque streets in Catania:

⑳ Via Crociferi

Above its downhill entrance is a soaring stone bridge, **L'Arco San Benedetto,** which allowed nuns, many of whom were in seclusion, to access the buildings on either side of this street during the convent's heyday in the 17th to 19th centuries. Via Crociferi is so authentically baroque that it has been filmed by, among others, Franco Zeffirelli, in his cinematic tale of love gone awry during the baroque age, *Storie di une Copinere.* In order of their appearances on this fabled but relatively short street, you'll see the following churches, convents, or monasteries: (1) **San Benedetto,** (2) **San Francesco Borgia,** (3) **San Giuliano,** and others whose facades aren't marked with name or number.

Three blocks from where you first entered Via Crociferi, turn left onto Via Gesuiti. Walk 4 blocks (or, if you're tired, merely glance at it from afar) to reach Piazza Dante and the mammoth, never-completed:

㉑ Chiesa di San Nicolò All'Arena

The biggest church in Sicily was never completed and it's almost ringed in scaffolding to keep it from falling down. Immediately adjacent is an abandoned monastery once intended as a library. Surrealistically large, this complex is Catania's symbol of the folly of large-scale projects gone awry. For more information, refer to "Seeing the Sights," earlier in this chapter.

Retrace your steps to Via Crucifero, turn left for about a block, then turn right (downhill) onto Via San Giuliano. You'll be walking down the steep slope of a dormant volcanic crater that's associated with the geology of nearby Mount Etna. After 2 blocks, turn right onto Via Etnea and walk 2 short blocks. On the right you'll see a church with a baroque and distinctive concave facade. It's dearly beloved to many Catanians, many of whom attended religious celebrations here during their childhoods:

㉒ Collegiata (Santa Maria della Consolazione)

This royal chapel from 1768 is one of the masterpieces of the Catanese late baroque style, based on plans by Angelo Italia. The facade was completed by Stefano Ittar, and the vaults inside were frescoed by Giuseppe Sciti.

After your visit, continue walking for another block south along Via Etnea to the:

㉓ Piazza Università

This elegant and symmetrical urban piazza is often the site of political rallies and demonstrations. One side is devoted to the back of the previously visited Municipio (town hall), the other side to the symbolic headquarters of the University of Catania. The university was founded in 1434, but the bulk of it lies in a modern educational complex 3km (2 miles) to the east, in Catania's suburbs. The square was constructed at the request of the duke of Camastra. It's dominated by the **Palazzo Sangiuliano,** which Vaccarini built in 1745, and by the main university building, **Palazzo dell'Università,** which was finished at the end of the 1700s. One of the richest libraries in Sicily—maybe the richest—is housed in the **Università degli Studi di Catania,** founded by Alphonese of Aragon in 1434.

5 Shopping

Il Dolci de Nonne Vincensa   Come here for marzipan and almond-based candies, made from recipes developed generations ago. You'll pay about 7€ per pound, and each candy comes artfully wrapped and intensely caloric. The shop is on a quiet piazza, across from the main facade of the San Placido church. Piazza San Placido 7. ✆ 095-7151844. Bus: 3-6, 259, or 334.

L'Artigianato Siciliano   Chances are you'll eventually wander beneath the Porta Uzeda during your stay in Catania, either as part of our walking tour or as part of your logical exploration of the Piazza Duomo, which it fronts. Beneath it are vaulted spaces loaded with the fancifully hand-painted pottery skillfully made in Caltanizzetta, a city in central Sicily that has churned out tons of the stuff during the past centuries. Look for gaily decorated serving dishes, candelabra painted like members of the 19th-century bourgeoisie, and all manner of art objects. Via Etnea 2 (beneath Porta Uzeda). ✆ 095-345360. Bus: 448, 449, 457, 722, or 733.

Marella Ferrera   Catania-born Marella Ferrera is the most successful and famous women's clothing designer to emerge from Sicily, a "look-maker" of note in an industry that—at least in Italy—is more frequently centered in Milan. An intelligent 40-something, Ferrera wears simple black pantsuits at fashion shows where her models are much more exotically dressed. She's known for clothing that makes women look like goddesses or lionesses, sometimes with outrageous flounces or appropriately inappropriate slits in indiscreet places. Her post-Valentino look has women paying prices that begin at about 800€ for a ready-to-wear pantsuit, and from 3,100€ for couture. The shop evokes a cross between an Italian garden and a boudoir, with antique chests bursting with bolts of lace, and paintings that evoke dream sequences, in a style that might have been inspired by Salvador Dalí. Viale XX Settembre 25-27. ✆ 095-446751. Bus: 443, 721, or 722.

6 Catania After Dark

Lapis, a monthly bulletin issued by the tourist office, and available at hotels and bars throughout Catania, documents any special concerts or festivals, movies, or nightclubs (such as they are).

If you have only 1 night in Catania, and you're a music lover, head for the **Teatro Massimo** ⭐ (sometimes called Teatro Bellini in honor of the hometown composer). It's at Piazza Teatro Massimo, Via Perotta Giuseppe 12 (✆ **095-7306111**). Some of Italy's best operas and concerts are presented here from December to June, with tickets costing from 10€ to 35€. To us, nothing is grander than hearing Bellini's *Norma* or *La Sonnambula* on its home turf. The box office is open Monday through Friday from 9:30am to 12:30pm and also Tuesday through Friday from 5 to 7pm. Bus: 417, 429.

Pubs and dance clubs rule the night. **Royal Pub Ceres,** Via San Giuseppe al Duomo 17–21 (✆ **095-7152294**), is on a block northwest of the Duomo. This woodsy-looking English pub comes complete with a carved Victorian-style bar and a crowd of good-looking people under 35. Its reputation for beers on tap is unequalled in Catania. The venue sometimes spills onto the narrow street outside. The place rocks daily from 7am (for that early libation) to 2am. Bus: 448, 449, 457, 722, or 733.

In the same vicinity, the other popular after-dark rendezvous occurs at **Mr. Bahia Pub,** Via Alessi 14 (✆ **095-2500083**), also on a narrow street a 5-minute walk northwest of the Duomo. This is a wide-open and airy nightclub whose architects inserted stainless-steel bartops and catwalks into an older, stately building. The result is a bustling room suitable for drinks, disco-ing, snacking, or meeting the scads of 20- and 30-somethings who flood in here late at night. Part of the venue moves onto the quiet piazza outside. The bar makes about 40 kinds of cocktails. It's open Friday through Wednesday from 5:30pm to 3am, and closes for 2 weeks in August. Bus: 448, 449, 457, 722, or 733.

Bar Nievsky, Scalinetta d'Alessi 13 (© **095-313792**), is the most visible of Catania's limited number of counterculture bars, where—if labels like this were still fashionable today—Marxists, Communists, anarchists, and leftists of any ilk feel genuinely welcome. It's also the self-acknowledged haven for bikers, radical feminists, gay liberationists, avant-garde painters, and counterculturists of virtually any flavor. Dotted with posters of Che Guevara and art-conscious graffiti, it sprawls across a multilevel, multifloored labyrinth of early-20th-century rooms. Entrance is via a flight of steps from the Chiesa San Placido, a 5-minute walk northwest from the Duomo. Most people come here to drink, but the bar also serves macrobiotic salads and sandwiches. Bus: 448, 449, 457, 722, or 733.

7 Side Trips from Catania

The looming menace of **Mount Etna** attracts those who did not explore the volcano from its northern tier (see chapter 8). In addition to Etna, the town of **Acireale,** like Catania, is adorned with baroque treasures—but here you can enjoy the sights without the traffic and the people.

MOUNT ETNA ★★★

Few who visit Catania can resist the temptation to explore Europe's most active volcano, menacing Mount Etna, northwest of the city. At 3,292m (10,800 ft.), it is the highest volcano in Europe and one of the largest in the world. Taormina (see chapter 8) is the base for exploring it from the north. Catania is ideal for flirting with this still-active volcano (spewing smoke and ash as recently as late 2002) from the southern tier.

For a good view of this ferocious mountain, take one of the trains that circumnavigate the base of the volcano. Trains are boarded at Via Caronda 350 (© **095-932181**) in Catania off Viale Leonardo da Vinci. A tour from Catania, lasting 3 hours, 20 minutes, costs 5.15€ per person.

A **bus** leaves from the Stazione Centrale in Catania at 8:30am daily bound for Rifugio Sapienza (see below). The bus returns to Catania in theory at 4:45pm—but always check schedules locally, as they vary. The round-trip costs 3.60€ per person.

You can also **drive** one of the many southern approaches to Etna from Catania. The quickest and most convenient route is to head northwest of Catania by following the road signs to Tangenziale Ovest. Drive along this road until you see the exit to Gravina. At Gravina, continue northwest along the road directing you to Mascalucia. Once there, you will see signs pointing to Nicolosi. At Nicolosi, follow a small road to the north for the final lap to Rifugio Sapienza.

At either Rifugio Sapienza, a little village on the southern slope of Mount Etna, or in the little town of Nicolosi, you can book guided Jeep tours of Mount Etna for a cost of 38€. The trip takes 2 to 3 hours, depending on location conditions. This tour takes you as close as you can get to the top without walking. Tickets can be purchased at the office, **Funivia dell'Etna** (© **095-911158**), in Nicolosi Monday through Friday from 9am to 1pm and 5:30 to 8pm, Saturday from 9am to 1pm. Nicolosi is connected with Rifugio Sapienza by frequent shuttle-bus service. You can also purchase tickets in Rifugio Sapienza at the office at **Contrada Cantoniera** (© **095-915321**), open daily from 9am to 4pm.

More private tours can also be organized at Rifugio Sapienza. For information on these, call the **tourist information office** in Nicolosi at Via Garibaldi 63 (© **095-911505**).

From Rifugio Sapienza, it's also possible to hike up to the **Torre del Filosofo (Philosopher's Tower)**, at 2,920m (9,580 ft.). The trip there and back takes about 5 hours. At the tower you'll have a panoramic sweep of Etna, its peaks and craters hissing with steam. This is a difficult hike and not for the faint of heart. The climb is along ashy, pebbly terrain, and once you reach the tower, you have another risky 2-hour hike to the craters. The craters can erupt unexpectedly (as they did in the early 1990s, killing 11).

Tours should only be taken with a guide who knows current conditions. If Etna shows signs of erupting or even "belching," guided tours are suspended. Of course, you can continue on alone. But make sure you've got your will and life insurance in order. On the return from Torre del Filosofo to Rifugio Sapienza, you pass Valle de Bove, the original crater of Etna.

ACIREALE

Lying 16km (10 miles) north of Catania, this makes for one of the most satisfying day trips along the eastern coast of Sicily. Many people find Acireale more interesting than those rather dull lava fields of Mount Etna.

Overlooking the Ionian Sea, Acireale lies in a fertile valley of Mount Etna surrounded by citrus groves. The town stands on seven streams of lava and has long been known for its hot springs and spa facilities. Like Catania, it is a city of the baroque, with many of its greatest treasures from the 17th century. The same 1693 earthquake that destroyed Catania also did major damage in Acireale.

The "Aci" in the town's name comes from the mythical river said to have been created in the wake of the death of Acis, the handsome youth in love with the graceful Nereid Galatea. Acis was, according to the story, slain by the jealous Polyphemus, the savage of Cyclops.

To reach the town, most visitors arrive by car driving north of Catania until you see the cutoff to the right leading to the sea and Acireale. Buses also run throughout the day from Catania.

Before walking about the town, you can stop at the **Acireale Tourist Office,** Via Scionti 15 (© **095-891999**), for a town map. Hours are Monday through Friday from 8am to 2pm and Tuesday and Thursday from 4 to 7pm.

SEEING THE SIGHTS

Piazza del Duomo 🟊 is the monumental baroque heart of Acireale, containing its most impressive attractions. Filled with gelato parlors and cafes, the square is dominated by its **Duomo** (cathedral; see below). Another important church, **Basilica dei Santi Pietro e Paolo,** also calls the square its address. The church is identified by its landmark bell tower. Although it was constructed in the 17th century, its facade is from the 18th century. The church's greatest artworks are the beautiful frescoes and paintings of **Pietro Paolo Vasta** (1697–1760), a home-grown artist. Charging no admission, the church is open daily from 8am to noon and 4 to 7pm. For more information, call © **095-601834.**

With its lavish tiled and cusped bell towers, the restored **Duomo** 🟊 is a favorite subject of picture postcards. It is much larger than Pietro e Paolo and still retains its fine baroque portal, which leads you into the larger interior with frescoed vaults. Originally built in the late 16th century, the church has suffered abuse from

Etna, and the present building has been vastly altered and reconstructed, mainly in the 18th century. In the interior at the east end are beautiful frescoes by Pietro Paolo Vasta (see above). In the right transept is the Cappella di Santa Venera, dedicated to the patron saint of Acireale. Hours are daily from 8am to noon and 4 to 7pm; call ℂ **095-601797** for more information. Admission is free.

The 17th-century **Palazzo Comunale** is a rather bizarre example of the Spanish/Sicilian baroque style. Its wrought-iron balconies are held up by depictions of monsters and gargoyles. The entrance to the palace is on Via Lancasteri right off the Piazza del Duomo. Admission is free; it is open Monday through Friday from 8am to noon.

A final church worth visiting is **Basilica di San Sebastiano** ★, Piazza Vigo (ℂ **095-601313**), one of the loveliest of all the baroque churches on the island. We prefer it to the treasures of the Duomo. It boasts a **magnificent balustrade facade** ★, adorned with statues representing scenes from the Old Testament. Most were created by G. B. Marino. In the interior you can inspect the various chapels. In the transept and chancel are frescoes by Pietro Paolo Vasta (there's that name again). Vasta depicted episodes from the sad life of St. Sebastian, the saint to whom this church is dedicated. Get to the church by way of Corso Vittorio Emanuele just beyond Piazza del Duomo. Admission is free, and it is open daily from 8am to noon and 4 to 8pm.

Other than Piazza del Duomo, the second most impressive baroque square of Acireale is **Piazza San Domenico,** lying at the end of Via Cavour. Dominating this small square is the splendid baroque facade of the **Church of San Domenico.** The most beautiful building on the square is the 17th-century **Palazzo Musmeci,** celebrated locally for its graceful wrought-iron balconies and rococo windows.

Since the days of the Greeks and most definitely the Romans, the sulphur-rich Etna "volcanic waters" have lured visitors to Acireale. The tradition continues at **Terme di Acireale,** Via della Terme 61 (ℂ **095-601508**). Every illustrious person passing through Sicily in the 18th and 19th centuries seems to have taken the waters here, including Richard Wagner. Many still do. No longer government-run, the bathing establishment is now independently operated. There is talk—so far, just that—of modernization. The waters here are said to have miraculous powers to treat rheumatism, gynecological disease, skin diseases, and periodontal diseases. You can also come for massages and mud treatments, each costing 21€. The facility is open for treatments daily from 7am to 12:30pm.

SHOPPING

Most islanders who visit Acireale go home with marzipan, as the town is famous for this confection. The best are sold at **El Dorado,** Corso Umberto 5 (ℂ **095-601464**), open Monday through Friday from 6am to midnight. It also makes the town's best chocolate cakes and sells cannoli filled with a cream made of pistachios and hazelnuts. Its competitor is also good: **El Castorina,** Piazza del Duomo (ℂ **095-601546**). Go there for *cassata Siciliana,* the island's most celebrated cake, made with ricotta and chocolate and a bit of marzipan. You might also order its divine *granita di mandorle* (almond granita). The shop is open Monday through Saturday from 7am to 1am.

WHERE TO STAY

Aloha D'Oro ★   When the owners constructed this hotel in 1968, they decided to use materials and techniques evocative of the old farmhouses surrounding Mount Etna. Architectural grace notes include wooden windows, arches, towers, handmade tiles, and plenty of wrought-iron adornments. This offbeat and very comfortable choice is one of the better stopovers between Taormina and Catania. The complex includes a main building, called the *castello,* and another 33 accommodations in outlying units. We opt for a room with a view, which in this case means in the rear, looking out onto views of the Ionian Sea and a government-protected nature reserve. Units come with neatly tiled bathrooms, half with tubs, the other half with showers. The hotel is within walking distance of a good sandy beach and the thermal baths.

Via dei Gasperi 10, 95024 Acireale. ⓒ **095-7687001.** Fax 095-606984. www.hotel-aloha-com. 119 units. 88€–170€ double; 138€–220€ junior suite. Rates include breakfast. AE, DC, MC, V. Free parking. **Amenities:** Restaurant; bar; 2 pools; sauna; room service; babysitting; laundry/dry cleaning. *In room:* A/C, TV, minibar, hair dryer.

Grande Albergo Maugeri ⭐ *Value* Close to the Duomo, this is your best bet for an overnight stopover in the heart of town. Rated four stars by the government, the hotel opened in the spring of 2001 across from Villa Garibaldi Park. Many guests we encountered here were using Acireale instead of Catania or Taormina as a base for exploring Mount Etna. The hotel is the most up-to-date accommodation in town, with midsize, traditionally furnished guest rooms. All of the units contain modern private bathrooms, half with showers, the rest with bathtubs. Its restaurant serves the best hotel cuisine in Acireale. Many guests check in to enjoy the **Maugeri "Well-Being" Center,** offering any number of spa treatments from massages to therapy pedicures.

Piazza Garibaldi, 95024 Acireale. ⓒ/fax **095-608666.** www.sicilytourist.com/hotelmaugeri. 45 units. 154€ double; 93€ per person half board. AE, DC, MC, V. Free parking. **Amenities:** 2 restaurants; bar; room service; laundry/dry cleaning. *In room:* A/C, TV, minibar, hair dryer.

WHERE TO DINE

All'Antica Osteri SICILIAN/PIZZA A rustic restaurant with wooden furniture, this restaurant-cum-pizzeria prepares an array of local delicacies and specializes in grills, especially grilled seafood from the Ionian Sea. The chefs cook with skill, dedication, and passion, turning out such dishes as *maccheroni All'Antica Osteria* (homemade pasta flavored with a creamy pesto, Parmesan cheese, and fresh tomatoes). Spaghetti *alla Pietro* is especially delightful, prepared with shellfish, garlic, and parsley. *Stocco* is a white fish cooked *alla Messinese*—with carrots, potatoes, raisins, celery, and pine nuts. The small, well-priced wine list offers some local gems.

Via Carpinati 34. ⓒ **095-7634135.** Reservations recommended. AE, DC, MC, V. Main courses 6.10€–7.25€. Fixed-price menu 13€–20€. AE, DC, MC, V. Daily noon–4pm and 7pm–2am.

Moments **The Images of Lost Dreams**

The town of Acireale is known for its puppet shows and theater. Sicilian families journey here to give their kids a treat. (Most adults enjoy the shows, too.) Although the art of Sicilian puppetry is rarely seen today, Acireale still carries on this ancient tradition. Shows are staged at **Teatro dell'Opera dei Pupi,** Via Nazionale 195 (ⓒ **095-606272**), from July to September on Thursday and Sunday at 9 and 10:30pm. Tickets, which cost 10€, must be purchased just before the show, as there is no box office open during the day.

Al Molino SEAFOOD/SICILIAN   A restaurant devoted to fish, this local favorite lies adjacent to an antique water mill on the Lungomare, the boardwalk along the sea. The location is a short walk from the center of Acireale. There's a small garden with a wooden grape arbor from which vines dangle, creating an evocative atmosphere. Inside, the decorations are appropriately nautical. You'll probably sit under a polished teak steering wheel from a large fishing boat or yacht. Of course, since the menu is based on fresh fish, it can vary from night to night. You might begin with Acireale's best bowl of fish soup or a homemade pasta made with fish. Raw marinated shellfish is another specialty. Using old-fashioned recipes, the restaurant is better than ever.

Via Molino 106. *C* 095-7648116. Reservations recommended. Main courses 7€–9€. AE, DC, MC, V. Thurs–Tues 1–3pm and 8pm–midnight. Closed 15 days in Nov or Dec.

La Grotta di Carmelo ★★ SEAFOOD/SICILIAN   Here's a chance to dine in a cave with a rock-face wall—hence, the name of the joint. Much of the structure was built from black lava rock from Mount Etna. But this is no touristy gimmick. Its tables are in demand more than any other in town, in large part for its excellent fresh seafood, much of it plucked from the Ionian Sea. Start your meal with a savory bowl of freshly made fish soup; it doesn't get much better than this. Our pasta favorite is homemade and served with squid ink along with tomatoes, garlic, olive oil, and red hot peppers. For a main course, the cooks are experts at grilling fish to your specifications. Simply select from the catch of the day and tell the waiter how you want it cooked. (***Note:*** Locals tend to eat fish cooked less than the average American cooks it.) A selection of delicately steamed fish with lemon and olive oil is memorable. Desserts, wine, and service are first rate.

Via Scala Grande 56. *C* 095-7648153. Reservations required. Main courses 8€–12€. AE, MC, V. Wed–Mon 1–3pm and 8–11pm. Closed Oct 15–Nov 1.

L'Oste Scura SICILIAN/MEDITERRANEAN   This is the warmest, coziest, and friendliest trattoria in town, and it also serves good food. The innkeeper, Carmelo Muscolino, insists on it. He runs this charming little dive next to the Basilica di San Sebastiano. The kitchen both experiments and uses time-tested recipes from grandma's day. Five pastas arrived for our large party, and we sampled a little of each, finding it hard to pick a favorite. Fusilli *alla Catanese* came with anchovies, peas, and tomatoes; pasta *dell'Oste* with cherry tomatoes, fresh basil, red hot peppers, garlic, and lemon zest; pasta *Acciughe e Mollica* with anchovies, garlic, and red hot peppers; linguini *mare* with scampi and fresh Etna mushrooms; and finally, there was spaghetti with sea urchins and roe. Other selections include meats grilled over lava stones. The list of liqueurs is seemingly endless, made from everything from fennel to figs.

Piazza L. Vigo 5–7. *C* 095-7634001. Reservations recommended. Main courses all 8€. AE, DC, MC, V. Thurs–Tues 12:30–3pm and 8pm–1am.

10

Syracuse & the Southeast

One of the centers of ancient Western civilization, southeastern Sicily is a sightseeing mecca filled with glorious, evocative ruins. The area's chief town is **Syracuse,** one of the most important cities of the ancient world of Magna Graecia (Greater Greece).

We'll even go out on a limb and suggest that if you're forced to choose between Agrigento (see chapter 12) and Syracuse, opt for "Siracusa," whose wealth and size were once unmatched by any other city in Europe.

Those with extra leisure time should also explore the baroque city of **Noto** and its surrounding sites, populated by Bronze Age people between 2,000 and 1,500 B.C.

Today, many of the sights of this sunbaked land are decaying. Noto, especially, is in peril. Earthquakes have caused massive damage to monumental, centuries-old buildings. But a trip through towns that knew great glory centuries ago is one of the most rewarding jaunts to take in Sicily, not to mention all of Italy.

1 Syracuse ✮✮✮ & Ortygia Island ✮✮✮

182km (110 miles) S of Messina, 87km (52 miles) S of Catania, 330km (198 miles) SE of Palermo, 256km (154 miles) E of Agrigento

Of all the Greek cities of antiquity that flourished on the coast of Sicily, Syracuse (Siracusa) was the most important, a formidable competitor of Athens. In its heyday, it dared take on Carthage and even Rome.

Colonists from Corinth founded Syracuse on the Ionian Sea in about 735 B.C. Much of its history was linked to despots, beginning in 485 B.C. with Gelon, the tyrant of Gela, who subdued the Carthaginians at Himera. Syracuse came under attack from Athens in 415 B.C., but the main Athenian fleet was destroyed and the soldiers on the mainland were captured. They were herded into the **Latomia di Cappuccini** at Piazza Cappuccini, a stone quarry. The "jail," from which there was no escape, was particularly horrid—the defeated soldiers weren't given food and, packed together like cattle, were allowed to die slowly.

Dionysius I was one of the greatest despots, reigning over the city during its greatest glory in the 4th century B.C., when it extended its influence as a sea power. But in A.D. 212, the city fell to the Romans under Marcellus, who sacked its riches. In that attack, Syracuse lost its most famous son, the Greek physicist/mathematician Archimedes, slain in his study by a Roman soldier.

Although the ruins of Syracuse will be one of the highlights of your trip to Sicily, the city itself has been in a millennia-long decline. Today it's a blend of often unattractive modern development (with supermarkets and high-rises sprouting along speedways) and the ruins of its former glory, a splendor that led Livy to proclaim it "the most beautiful and noble of Greek cities."

Syracuse & the Southeast

0 80 Mi
0 80 Km
Palermo
Messina
Mt. Etna
SICILY
Syracuse
Agrigento
AREA OF DETAIL
Brucoli
Villasmundo
Augusta
Megara Hyblaea
Golfo di Augusta
Pedagaggi
Melilli
Sortino
Peninsola magnisi
Marina di Melilli
Ferla
Sta. Panagia
Cassaro
124
Solarino
Belvedere
Castello Eurialo
Syracuse (Siracusa)
Floridia
Palazzo Alacreide
Canicattini Bagni
A18
Peninsola della Maddalena
Lido Arenella
Cava Grande Del Cassible
Ognina
Villa Vela
Cassibile
Testa dell'Acqua
287
Fontane Bianche
S. Corrado di Fuori
Castelluccio
115
Avola
Monte Renna
Noto
Calabernardo
Villa Del Tellaro
Lido di Noto
E45
S. Paolo
Eloro
Golfo di Noto
Rosolini
Riserva Naturale di Vendicari
Ispica
Ionian Sea
S. Lorenzo Vecchio
Marzamemi
Pozzallo
Pachino
Capo Passero
Beach
Portopalo di Capo Passero
Capo delle Forniche
0 5 Mi
0 5 Km
N

A lot of what you'll want to see is on the island of **Ortygia,** which is filled with not only ancient ruins but also small crafts shops and dozens of boutiques. From the mainland, Corso Umberto goes to the Ponte Nuova, which leads to the island. Parking is a serious problem on Ortygia, so if you drive, park in one of the garages near the bridge and then walk over and explore the island on foot. Allow yourself at least 2 hours to explore, plus another hour to shop along the narrow streets. You'll also want to sit for half an hour or so on **Piazza del Duomo,** off Via Cavour. This is one of the most elegant squares in Sicily.

The ancient sights are a good half hour's walk back inland from Ortygia, past a fairly forgettable shopping strip, so you might want to take a cab (they're easily found at all the sights). You'll find buses on Ortygia at Piazza Pancali/Largo XXV Luglio. The harbor front is lined with 18th- and 19th-century town houses.

Syracuse is a cauldron in summer. Do as the locals do and head for the sea. The finest **beach** is about 19km (2 miles) away at **Fontane Bianche;** bus nos. 21 and 22 leave from the Syracuse post office, Piazza delle Poste 15. If you're driving, Fontane Bianche lies to the south of the city (it's signposted); take SS115 to reach it. The same buses will take you to **Lido Arenella,** only 8km (5 miles) away but not as good a beach.

ESSENTIALS

GETTING THERE   From other major cities in Sicily, Syracuse is best reached by **train.** It's 1½ hours from Catania, 2 hours from Taormina, and 5 hours from Palermo. Usually you must transfer in Catania. For information, call ✆ **892021.** Trains arrive in Syracuse at the station on Via Francesco Crispi, centrally located midway between the Archaeological Park and Ortygia.

From Catania, 17 SAIS **buses** daily make the 1¼-hour trip to Syracuse. The one-way fare is 4.15€. Phone **Interbus** (✆ **0931-66710** in Syracuse or 095-536168 in Catania) for information and schedules.

By **car** from Taormina, continue south along A18 and then on E45, past Catania. Although trip time depends on traffic, allow at least 1½ hours.

VISITOR INFORMATION   The **tourist office** is at Via San Sebastiano 45 (✆ **0931-67710** or 0931-65201), and there's a branch office at the entrance to the Archaeological Park. Both are open from June to September, Monday through Saturday from 9am to 1:30pm and 3:15 to 6:15pm, Sunday from 9am to 1pm. From October to May, hours are Monday through Friday from 9am to 1:30pm and 3:15 to 6:15pm.

SPECIAL EVENTS   Some of the most memorable cultural events in Sicily are staged in May and June of even-numbered years, when actors from the Instituto

---

Moments   **Syracuse from the Sea**

On every visit, we like to see this ancient city the way the Greeks first came upon it—from the sea. Motor launches operated by **Selene** (✆ **0931-790132**) take you on a **panoramic trip** ★★ around Porto Grande and Ortygia. The trip lasts an hour, and the scenes of the ancient ruins are evocative and inspiring. The most memorable boat trips are around twilight, when the monuments are floodlit. Somehow, when the lights are on, the ruins don't look like ruins any more, but real buildings.

Nazionale del Dramma Antico present **classical plays** by Aeschylus, Euripides, and their contemporaries. The setting is the ancient Greek Theater (Teatro Greco) in the Archaeological Park, beneath the open sky. Tickets cost about 23€. For information, schedules, and tickets, write or call **INDA,** Corso G. Matteotti 29, 96100 Siracusa (© **0931-67415).**

CITY LAYOUT   The chief attraction, **Isola di Ortygia,** is linked to mainland Syracuse by a bridge, **Ponte Umbertino. Corso Umberto** is the city's main street, running from this bridge directly to the train station and crossing **Piazza Marconi,** a square from which most of the buses depart. One of the other main streets is **Via Montedoro,** which runs parallel to and to the immediate north of Corso Umberto.

Other than Ortygia, Syracuse's grand attraction is the **Parco Archeologico della Neapolis.** From the heart of Syracuse, this garden of ruins is reached by heading north along **Corso Gelone.**

If you'd like to drive along the boulevard fronting the Ionian Sea, head up the **Dionisio Grande** for some panoramic scenery. This route will also take you to the **Latomia dei Cappuccini,** one of the most ancient of the limestone quarries, or *latomie,* that supplied blocks of limestone for the construction of the major buildings and monuments of Syracuse.

Off Via Cavour is **Piazza del Duomo,** one of the city's most elegant squares. A 5th-century temple that the Greeks dedicated to Athena became in time a Christian cathedral, or duomo.

From Piazza del Duomo, **Via Picherali** heads southwest to the sea and the **Fountain of Arethusa,** a freshwater spring beloved by the ancient Greeks, who claimed that this was where the nymph Arethusa was turned into a fountain.

One of the main streets of Syracuse, **Via della Maestranza,** is a sightseeing attraction in its own right, and it's also the oldest street in town. It passes the island's most aristocratic residences, mostly baroque in architectural style. The two most interesting palaces, which can be admired from the outside, are **Palazzo Interlandi Pizzuti,** at no. 10, and **Palazzo Impellizzeri,** at no 17.

On the southernmost tip of Ortygia rises **Castello Maniace,** named in honor of George Maniakes, the Byzantine who with aid from Norman soldiers captured the city from the Muslims. Rebuilt by Frederick II in 1239, this castle is now a military barracks and is off-limits to the public. You can sail by the castle, however, if you take a boat tour (see box, "Syracuse from the Sea," above).

GETTING AROUND

Syracuse is served by a network of **buses** following circular routes, which means that many places will be quite a ways from a bus stop. Buses leave from the center of Syracuse for Piazza della Posta, which lies across the bridge on Ortygia Island. The best place to catch a bus in Syracuse proper is Piazza Marconi (also called Foro Siracusiano). The most frequented buses are nos. 21 to 23, which also stop at the rail depot.

Sometimes it's better to call a **taxi;** dial © **0931-69722.** The taxi fare from the train station to Ortygia, for example, is about 8€.

We're fond of **biking** along Ortygia Island. You can rent a bike for 10€ a day at **Dove/Where,** Via Maestranza 69 (© **0931-61916).** You can also rent a scooter for the day for 30€.

FAST FACTS: **Syracuse**

Emergency Dial ✆ **113.**

Internet Your best bet is **w@w: Web and Work,** Via Roma 18 (✆ **0931-465960**), in Ortygia. It is open Monday through Saturday from 10am to 10pm, Sunday from 6 to 10pm. The charge is 3€ per half hour or 5€ per hour.

Luggage Storage A kiosk in the train station along Via Francesco Crispi is open from 7am to 10pm, charging 3.90€ per piece of baggage.

Medical For a medical emergency, **Guardia Medica,** Contrada La Pizzuta 20 (✆ **0931-484629**), is open Monday through Friday from 8pm to 8am and Saturday and Sunday from 2pm to 8am. The regular hospital is the **Ospedale Generale Provinciale,** Via Testaferrata (✆ **0931-724111**), lying near the end of Corso Gelone.

Pharmacy Go to **Farmacia Zecchino,** Viale Zecchino 199 (✆ **0931-783384**), open Monday through Saturday from 8:30am to 1pm and 4:30 to 8pm. In the window, a list of pharmacies open at night is posted. Pharmacies operate on a rotational system.

Police Call ✆ **0931-481511.**

Post Office The **Syracuse Post Office** is at Riva Posta 15 (✆ **0931-464358**), open Monday through Friday from 8am to 7:40pm, Saturday from 8am to 1:30pm. There is also a currency exchange here.

SEEING THE ANCIENT SIGHTS

Take bus no. 1 to reach these sights.

Parco Archeologico della Neapolis ★★★   Syracuse's Archaeological Park contains the town's most important attractions, all on the mainland at the western edge of town, to the immediate north of Stazione Centrale where the trains pull in from other parts of Sicily, including Messina and Taormina. The entrance to the park is down Via Augusto.

On the Temenite Hill, the **Teatro Greco (Greek Theater)** ★★★, Viale Teocrito, was one of the great theaters of the classical period. Hewn from rock during the reign of Hieron I in the 5th century B.C., the ancient seats have been largely eaten away by time. But you can still stand on the remnants of the stone stage where plays by Euripedes were mounted. The theater was much restored in the time of Hieron II in the 3rd century B.C. Today, the Italian Institute of Ancient Drama presents classical plays by Euripedes, Aeschylus, and Sophocles. In other words, the show hasn't changed much in 2,000 years.

Outside the entrance to the Greek Theater is the most famous of the ancient quarries, **Latomia del Paradiso (Paradise Quarry)** ★★, one of four or five from which stones were hauled to erect the great monuments of Syracuse in its glory days. Upon seeing the cave in the wall, Caravaggio is reputed to have dubbed it the "Ear of Dionysius" because of its unusual shape. But what an ear—it's nearly 60m (200 ft.) long. You can enter the inner chamber of the grotto, where the tearing of paper sounds like a gunshot. Although it's dismissed by some scholars as fanciful, the story goes that the despot Dionysius used to force prisoners into the "ear" at night, where he was able to hear every word they said. Nearby is the **Grotta dei Cordari,** where rope-makers plied their craft.

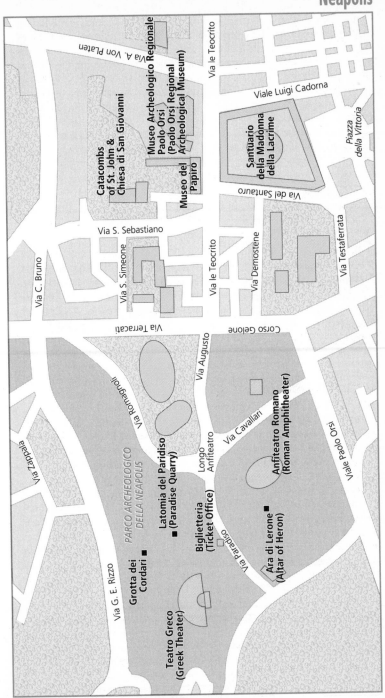

Via A. Von Platen

Via le Teocrito

Viale Luigi Cadorna

Piazza della Vittoria

Catacombs of St. John & Chiesa di San Giovanni

Museo Archeologico Regionale Paolo Orsi (Paolo Orsi Regional Archeological Museum)

Museo del Papiro

Santuario della Madonna della Lacrime

Via del Santauro

Via S. Sebastiano

Via S. Simeone

Via le Teocrito

Via Demostene

Via Testaferrata

Via C. Bruno

Via Terracati

Corso Gelone

Via Romagnoli

Via Augusto

Via Cavallari

Viale Paolo Orsi

Via Zappala

PARCO ARCHEOLOGICO DELLA NEAPOLIS

Latomia del Paridiso (Paradise Quarry)

■ **Grotta dei Cordari**

Via G. E. Rizzo

Teatro Greco (Greek Theater)

Longo Anfiteatro

Biglietteria (Ticket Office)

Via Paradiso

■ **Ara di Lerone (Altar of Heron)**

Anfiteatro Romano (Roman Amphitheater)

A rather evocative but gruesome site lies on the path down into the Roman amphitheater. The **Ara di Lerone,** or Altar of Heron, was once gigantic and used by the Greeks for sacrifices involving hundreds of animals at once. A few pillars still stand as well as the mammoth stone base of this 3rd-century-B.C. monument. The longest altar ever built, it measured 196m by 23m (653 ft. by 75 ft.).

The **Anfiteatro Romano (Roman Amphitheater)** ★ was created at the time of Augustus. It ranks among the top five amphitheaters left by the Romans in Italy. Like the Greek Theater, part of it was carved from rock. Unlike the Greek Theater with its classical plays, the Roman Amphitheater tended toward gutsier fare. Gladiators (prisoners of war and "exotic" blacks from Africa) faced each other with tridents and daggers, or naked slaves were whipped into the center of a battle to the death between wild beasts. Either way, the victim lost: If his opponent, man or beast, didn't do him in, the crowd would often scream for the ringmaster to slit his throat. The amphitheater is near the entrance to the park, but you can also view it in its entirety from a belvedere on the road.

Via Del Teatro (off the intersection of Corso Gelone and Viale Teocrito). © 0931-66206. Admission 4.15€. Apr–Oct daily 9am–6pm; Nov–Mar daily 9am–3pm.

Museo Archeologico Regionale Paolo Orsi (Paolo Orsi Regional Archaeological Museum) ★★★   One of the most important archaeological museums in southern Italy surveys the Greek, Roman, and early Christian epochs in sculpture and in fragments of archaeological remains. Crafted from glass, steel, and Plexiglas, and designed as an ultramodern showcase for the objects unearthed from digs throughout Sicily, this is the kind of museum that reinvigorates your appreciation for archaeology, its rewards, and its implications. Its stunning modernity is in direct contrast to the sometimes startling portrait busts and vases unearthed throughout Sicily. Laid out like a hexagon, and interconnected in a series of honeycomb-shaped cells, the museum is set in a garden dotted with ancient sarcophagi. Photographs of lonely beaches and fields near the site where the objects were found convey a sense of irony.

Section A takes us back before the dawn of recorded history. We're always fascinated by the skeletons of prehistoric animals found here, including dwarf elephants. Many artifacts have been dug up to illustrate life in Paleolithic and Neolithic times. Look for the stunning red-burnished **Vase of Pantalica** ★.

Section B is devoted to Greek colonization. We can wander for hours here and always find something of fascination and intrigue. The celebrated **Landolina Venus** ★★ is seen here, without a head but alluring nonetheless. After all these centuries, the anatomy of this timeless Venus is still in perfect shape. A Roman copy of an original by Praxiteles, the statue was found in Syracuse in 1804 by Saverio Landolina. When he visited the town in 1885, Guy de Maupassant fell in love with this Venus and left a vivid description of her.

Megara Hyblaea was one of the ancient Doric colonies of Syracuse. Although it's not the equal of the Landolina Venus, the singular limestone block of a **Mother-Goddess** ★ suckling twins dates from the 6th century B.C. and was recovered from a necropolis.

Section C brings the sub-colonies and Hellenistic centers of eastern Sicily alive once more. It's a hodgepodge of artifacts and fragments from the era, including votive terra-cottas, cinerary urns, sarcophagi, and vases from Gela. Interspersed among some rather dull artifacts are stunning creations, such as an enthroned male figure from the 6th century B.C., a horse and rider from the same era (believed to be part of the decoration of a temple roof), a terra-cotta goddess from the late 6th century B.C., and a miniature 6th-century-B.C. altar with a relief depicting a lion attacking a bull. You can also seek out three rare wooden statues from the 7th century B.C. (found near Agrigento).

In the gardens of the Villa Landolina in Akradina, Viale Teocrito 66. © **0931-464022**. Admission 4.50€. Tues–Sat 9am–1pm; Mon and Wed 3:30–6:30pm.

Museo del Papiro Near the Paolo Orsi museum (see above), these galleries devoted to papyrus are unique in Italy. That's because Syracuse has the only climate outside the Nile Valley in which the papyrus plant can flourish. Since the days of antiquity, the plant, *Cyperus papyrus,* has been cultivated outside Syracuse along the banks of the Clane River.

The word "paper," of course, comes from papyrus. But the plant has far more uses than making paper. Papyrus was used to construct lightweight boats or to make ropes, trays, and baskets. It was also used to create wigs and was a fabric for clothing (papyrus sandals were all the rage in ancient Egypt). The most delicate part of the stalk might once have served as food.

This gallery illustrates the plant's various transformations into utilitarian objects. The most intriguing exhibit is of documents dating from the era of the pharaohs, featuring fragments from the Egyptian *Book of the Dead.* A display of papyrus fans is also on view, as are the most featherweight of boats.

Viale Teocrito 66. © **0931-61616**. Free admission. Tues–Sun 9am–1pm.

Catacombe di San Giovanni (Catacombs of St. John) ★★ Evoking the more famous Christian burial grounds along Rome's Appian Way, the Catacombs of St. John contain some 20,000 ancient tombs, honeycombed tunnels of empty coffins that were long looted of their "burial riches" by plundering grave robbers.

In Roman times, Christians were not allowed to bury their dead within the city limits, so they went outside the boundaries of Syracuse to create burial chambers in what had been used by the Greeks as underground aqueducts. The early Christians recycled these into chapels. Some faded frescoes and symbols etched into stone slabs can still be seen. Syracuse has other subterranean burial grounds, but the Catacombs of St. John are the only ones open to the public.

You enter the "world of the dead" from the **Chiesa di San Giovanni,** now a ruin. St. Paul is said to have preached on this spot, so the early Christians venerated it as holy ground. Now overgrown, the interior of the church was abandoned in the 17th century. In its heyday it was the cathedral of Syracuse, and the first bishop of Syracuse, St. Marcian, was flogged to death on the site in 254.

The church's roots go back to the 6th century, when a basilica stood here, but it was eventually destroyed by the Saracens. The Normans reconstructed it in the 12th century, but in 1693 an earthquake destroyed it. From the ruins a baroque church was built, but that was left in ruins by the earthquake of 1908. All that remain are roofless Norman walls and about half of the former apse. A beautiful rose window is still visible on the facade of the Norman church.

Underneath the church is the **Cripta di San Marciano (Crypt of St. Marcian),** constructed on the spot where the martyr is alleged to have been beaten to death. His Greek-cross chamber is found 5m (16 ft.) below the ground.

Warning: Make sure that you exit well before closing. Two readers who entered the catacombs after 5pm were accidentally locked in and managed to escape only after a harrowing ordeal of wandering around in the dark.

Piazza San Giovanni, at end of Viale San Giovanni. © **0931-36456**. Admission 3.50€. Free for ages 17 and under. Daily 9am–12:30pm and 2:30–5pm. Closed Feb.

Castello Maniace **12**
Fonte Arethusa **13**
Latomia Dei Cappuccini **4**
Museo Archeologico Regionale
Paolo Orsi **3**
Palazzo Bellomo **11**
Palazzo Beneventano del Bosco **16**
Palazzo del Senato **17**
Palazzo Impellizzeri **9**
Palazzo Interlandi Pizzuti **10**
Palazzo Lanzo **8**
Parco Archeologico della Neapolis **2**
Piazza Archimede **8**
Piazza del Duomo **15**
Piazza Pancali **6**
Santa Lucia **14**
Santa Lucia al Sepolcro **5**
Teatro Greco (Greek Theater) **1**
Templo di Apollo **7**

Santuario della Madonna delle Lacrime   The "Our Lady of Tears" sanctuary is one of the most bizarre monuments or churches in all of Sicily. Designed to evoke a gigantic teardrop, the structure was created by two Frenchmen, Michel Arnault and Pierre Parat, in 1994. It houses a statue of the Madonna that supposedly wept for 5 days in 1953. Alleged chemical tests showed that the liquid was similar to that of human tears.

Although criticized by architectural purists, the contemporary conical structure dominates the skyline, rising 74m (243 ft.) with a diameter of 80m (262 ft.). The **interior** ✿ is rather amazing. You might get dizzy looking up at the vertical windows stretching skyward to the apex of the roof. Pilgrims still flock here.

Lacrime is new, but just to the south of the sanctuary, on Piazza della Vittoria, you can stand and see the fenced-off excavations of an array of ancient Greek and Roman houses and streets.

Via Santuario 33. ✆ 0931-64077. Admission 1.55€. Daily 9am–12:30pm and 4–6pm.

Santa Lucia al Sepolcro   The original church here was constructed on the site where in 304 St. Lucy (Santa Lucia) was said to have been martyred. Dating from the Byzantine period, the church was vastly altered in the 12th century and completely reconstructed in the 17th century. Beneath this sanctuary is a vast labyrinth of dank catacombs dating from the 3rd century, most of which, even today, have not been explored and are closed to the public. You can, however, visit the sanctuary. The famous Caravaggio painting depicting the burial of Santa Lucia once hung here but is now in the Palazzo Bellomo museum.

Indeed, there isn't much left to see of this church since all its former treasures have been hauled off. The doorway and apses are from Norman days, and a lovely rose window is from the 14th century. A granite column to the right of the presbytery marks the spot where Syracusans believe Santa Lucia suffered decapitation. Under the reign of Frederick III in the 16th century, the present ceiling was constructed with painted beams, reproducing a thick constellation of "stars" alternating with rose petals and small crosses.

Adjacent to the basilica and linked to it by a spooky underground catacomb built in the 12th century is a little baroque chapel containing the tomb of the martyred saint. She is long gone, however. In 1039 the Byzantine general, Giorgio Maniace, ordered that her corpse be sent to Constantinople. During the Crusades the Venetians claimed the remains and shipped them back to Venice, where they remain today.

A marble statue placed under the sepulcher's altar is of particular, though morbid, fascination. From May 6 to 8, 1735, eyewitnesses reported that this statue miraculously "sweated" profusely.

The sanctuary lies at the northern end of one of the loveliest squares in Syracuse, Piazza Santa Lucia. The piazza is lined on three sides by rows of trees.

Via Gignami 1. ✆ 0931-67946. Free admission. Daily 9am–noon and 4–7pm.

EXPLORING ORTYGIA ISLAND ✿✿✿

Ortygia, inhabited for many thousands of years, is also called the *Città Vecchia* (old city). It contains the town's Duomo, many rows of houses spanning 500 years of building styles, most of the city's medieval and baroque monuments, and some of the most charming vistas in Sicily. In Greek mythology, it's said to have been ruled by Calypso, daughter of Atlas, the sea nymph who detained Ulysses (Odysseus) for 7 years. The island, reached by crossing the Ponte Nuova, is about a mile long and half again as wide. Take bus no. 21 or 23.

Heading out the Foro Italico, you'll come to the **Fonte Arethusa** ✷, also famous in mythology. The river god Alpheius, son of Oceanus, is said to have fallen in love with the sea nymph Arethusa. The nymph turned into this spring or fountain, but Alpheius became a river and "mingled" with his love. According to legend, the spring ran red when bulls were sacrificed at Olympus.

At Piazza del Duomo, the **Duomo** ✷ (cathedral) of Syracuse, reached by heading down Via Minerva from Piazza Archimede, illustrates more than any other structure in town the changing colonizations and architectural styles that have dominated the city over the centuries. The present cathedral incorporates architectural fragments from a temple honoring Athena dating from the 5th century B.C. In its heyday, this Greek temple was spoken of in revered tones by the people of the Mediterranean. A visitor in the 1st century B.C., Cicero spread its glory and wrote of its lavish adornments in gold and ivory. For miles at sea, sailors could see the golden statue of Athena shining like a beacon. Twenty-six of the temple's **Doric columns** ✷ are still in place.

In 1693, an earthquake caused the facade to collapse, and in the 18th century the cathedral was rebuilt in the baroque style by Andrea Palma, the Palermo architect.

In the first bay on the right, look for a **beautiful font** ✷ fashioned from a Greek marble krater. It is held up by seven rather stunningly carved 13th-century wrought-iron lions. The Duomo is also rich in statues adorning its chapels, including one honoring patron saint Lucia. As you enter the cathedral, the first chapel on the right is dedicated to "St. Lucy"; the ornate reliquary in the glass case on display is said to contain a piece of her left arm.

Admission to the Duomo is free, and it's open daily from 8am to noon and 4 to 7pm.

The irregular **Piazza del Duomo** ✷ is especially majestic when the facade of the cathedral is dramatically caught by the setting sun or when floodlit at night. Acclaimed as one of the most beautiful squares in Italy, it's filled with fine baroque buildings. They include the striking **Palazzo Beneventano del Bosco,** with its lovely courtyard. Opposite it is the **Palazzo del Senato,** with an inner courtyard displaying a senator's carriage from the 1700s. At the far end of the square stands **Santa Lucia,** another church (but one that hardly competes with the Duomo).

The other important landmark square is **Piazza Archimede,** with its baroque fountain festooned with dancing jets of water and sea nymphs. This square lies directly northeast of Piazza del Duomo, forming the monumental heart of Ortygia. It, not the cathedral square, is the main piazza of the old city. On this piazza, original Gothic windows grace the 15th-century **Palazzo Lanza.** As you move about Ortygia, you'll find that Piazza Archimede is a fine place from which to orient yourself. Wander the narrow streets wherever your feet will take you, and when you get lost, you can always ask for directions back to Piazza Archimede.

Palazzo Bellomo ✷✷   This elegant 13th-century palace is today the home of the **Museo Regionale di Arte Mediovale e Moderna,** which contains one of the great art collections of Sicily. The art dates from the high Middle Ages through the 20th century. It's located next to St. Benedict's Church close to Fonte Aretusa.

The palazzo is from the Swabian era and was enlarged in the 15th century by the powerful Bellomo family. The art is arranged chronologically on two floors, illustrating the painting and decorative arts of southeast Sicily. Much of it comes from art treasures rescued from deconsecrated monasteries or churches.

The Tears of an Abandoned Mistress

One of the most evocative boat rides in and around Syracuse is along the **River Cyane,** lying 5km (3 miles) west of the city along Via Elorina. From May to September, a 2-hour boat trip takes you to the source of this river. Here you will see a pool that, according to legend, was formed by the tears shed by Cyane, a nymph attending her mistress, Persephone, who was abducted by Hades (Pluto in Roman mythology), leaving Cyane alone.

Along the way you can see clusters of papyrus plants. The original plants were a gift from Ptolemy to Hieron II. On the way to the river's source, the boat goes by the meager ruins of **Olympeion,** a temple erected at the end of the 6th century.

Boat rentals cost between 8€ and 15€ per person, depending on how many passengers are on board. For tickets and information on departure times, call ✆ **0931-69076.** To reach the departure site, take bus no. 21, 22, or 23 from Piazza della Posta and get off at Ponte delle Fiane.

We like to come here to gaze upon two exquisite masterpieces: ***The Burial of St. Lucia*** (1608) ✮ by the "divine" Caravaggio, and Antonello da Messina's exquisite ***Annunciation*** (1474) ✮. Caravaggio, the master of light, created a stunning canvas of grieving figures, graced with the serene expression of the martyr and the raw nudity of the gravediggers. The saint's death sleep was meant to signify her glorious rebirth in heaven. Though damaged, Da Messina's *Annunciation* remains powerful in its imagery and majesty.

On the ground floor of the palazzo is an array of sculpture from the Middle Ages and the Renaissance, the most outstanding of which are from the Gagini school, including the **tomb of Giovanni Cardinas** by Antonello Gagini, and a masterful ***Madonna of the Bullfinch*** by another family member, Domenico Gagini. Look for the 17th- and 18th-century **Sicilian carriages** in the loggia.

The collection of **Sicilian decorative arts** ✮ is full of charm and whimsy. It includes marble intarsia panels, ecclesiastical objects, 18th-century statuettes, church vestments, antiques, terra-cotta figurines by Bongiovanni Vaccaro, ceramics, and silver- and goldsmithery.

Via Capodieci 16. ✆ 0931-69511. Admission 2.50€. Tues–Sat 9am–2pm; Fri–Sat 3–7pm; Sun 9am–2pm.

Tempio di Apollo   At the Piazza Pancali on the island of Ortygia, this Greek temple dating from the 6th century B.C is the oldest peripteral (having a row of columns on each side) Doric temple in the world. The inscription says that the temple honors Apollo. However, after Cicero came to Syracuse, he wrote that the temple was dedicated to Artemis. Whatever: The temple faced a rocky future—first it was turned into a Byzantine church before the Saracens took over and converted it into a mosque. Later, under Norman rule, it was turned back into a church. On a square across the bridge to Ortygia, the fenced-off ruins can be viewed at any time.

SHOPPING

Galleria Bellomo   Set in a one-room structure across the narrow medieval street from the Museo Bellomo, this is an art gallery with a twist. It sells colorful still lifes and landscapes painted on papyrus that's manufactured on the premises. Part of the charm of this place involves a free demonstration of how a water-logged reed (papyrus) is soaked, pressed, and layered between linen sheets to painstakingly produce the substance upon which the day-to-day business of ancient Egypt was conducted. The laboriously manufactured papyrus, painted with scenes, costs between 5€ for a simple postcard and 800€ for an original work of art suitable for framing. Via Capodieci 15. ✆ **0931-61340.** Bus: 21 or 22.

Enoteca Capriccio This well-recommended shop inventories the town's largest collection of Sicilian wines, with a good selection from the Piedmont and Tuscany as well. They're displayed within a pair of rooms lined with boxes and shelves of wine, with bottles priced from 4€ to around 100€. The most sought-after wines include a 1988 "Regaleali" cabernet sauvignon, priced here at around 100€ per bottle. Via Dell'Amalfitania 11. ✆ **0931-464918.** Bus: 21 or 22.

Old Times/Davies of London Antiquario This shop's entrance is set on the innermost rim of an antique courtyard, immediately adjacent to the Ortygia Island branch of Syracuse's tourist office. Inside is a wide array of mostly English art objects and porcelain, hauled down to Syracuse from estate sales in Britain by an expatriate who fell in love with southern Sicily many years ago. Via Maestranza 33. ✆ **0931-60977.** Bus: 21 or 22.

WHERE TO STAY

The best place to stay here is on Ortygia, at either the Grand Hotel or the Albergo Domus Mariae (see below). The island has far more character and charm than "mainland" Syracuse. On the downside, both of these hotels might be booked to capacity, especially in the summer. In that case, we've included some backup choices.

EXPENSIVE

Grand Hotel ★★★ Originally built in 1905, with an interior that was ripped apart and radically upgraded in 1995, this is the best and most appealing hotel in Syracuse, with a mix of modernity and old-world charm that's very appealing. It's set directly on the waterfront, near Ortygia's main access bridge to the Italian "mainland," in a stately four-story building containing lots of inlaid marble and polished Belle Epoque hardwoods. The vaulted cellar contains a bar with comfortable sofas and a collection of remnants—some museum-quality—unearthed from this site during long-ago excavations. Guest rooms are contemporary and comfortable, with color schemes of beige and champagne. In some of the suites, duplex setups include interior staircases of polished steel. Units boast state-of-the-art bathrooms with shower-tub combinations. The in-house restaurant, **La Terrazza,** is separately recommended below. The bus station lies only 100m (328 ft.) away.

Viale Mazzini 12, 96100 Siracusa. ✆ **0931-464600.** Fax 0931-464611. www.grandhotelsr.it. 58 units. 208€ double; from 260€ suite. Rates include breakfast. AE, DC, MC, V. Free parking. **Amenities:** Restaurant; 2 bars; babysitting; laundry/dry cleaning. *In room:* A/C, TV, radio, minibar, hair dryer, safe.

Grand Hotel Villa Politi ★ For many decades after its inauguration in 1862, the Grand Hotel Villa Politi (not to be confused with Syracuse's separately recommended Grand Hotel) was one of the three most elegant and sought-after hotels in Sicily, rivaled at the time only by Palermo's Villa Igiea and Taormina's Palazzo San Domenico. By around 1900, the Politi was a major stop on the Grand Tour of Italy as defined by wealthy English and German travelers, a widely recognized monument of the highest quality. Today, thanks in part to a series of badly planned

Syracuse Accommodations & Dining

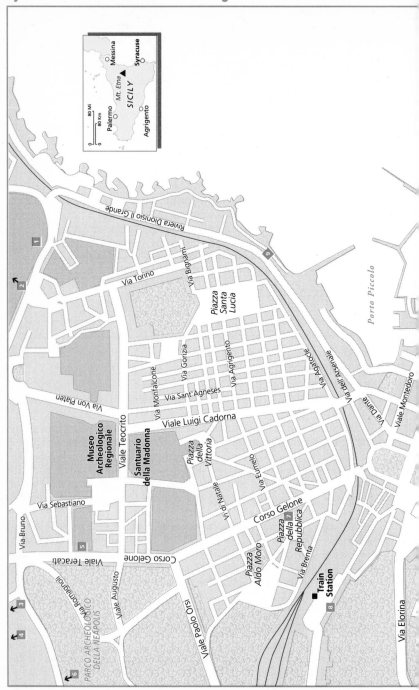

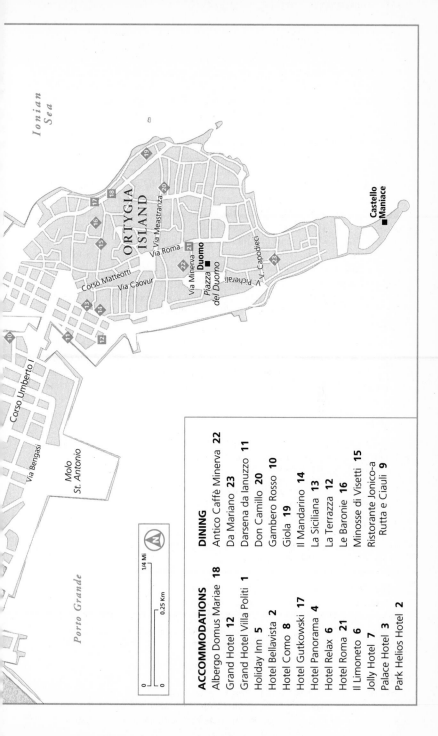

Ionian Sea

ORTYGIA ISLAND

Corso Matteotti
Via Caovur
Via Roma
Via Meastranza
Via Minerva
Duomo
Piazza del Duomo
Via Minerva
Picherali
V. Capodieci

Castello Maniace

Corso Umberto I

Via Bengasi

Molo St. Antonio

Porto Grande

0   0.25 Km
0   1/4 Mi

ACCOMMODATIONS
Albergo Domus Mariae **18**
Grand Hotel **12**
Grand Hotel Villa Politi **1**
Holiday Inn **5**
Hotel Bellavista **2**
Hotel Como **8**
Hotel Gutkowski **17**
Hotel Panorama **4**
Hotel Relax **6**
Hotel Roma **21**
Il Limoneto **6**
Jolly Hotel **7**
Palace Hotel **3**
Park Helios Hotel **2**

DINING
Antico Caffè Minerva **22**
Da Mariano **23**
Darsena da Ianuzzo **11**
Don Camillo **20**
Gambero Rosso **10**
Giola **19**
Il Mandarino **14**
La Siciliana **13**
La Terrazza **12**
Le Baronie **16**
Minosse di Visetti **15**
Ristorante Jonico-a
Rutta e Ciauli **9**

enlargements and renovations, it's a lot less elegant and prestigious than it once was, evoking, at least from the outside, either a hospital, a battered public school or, worse, an outbuilding of one of Italy's hundreds of government bureaucracies. But if you know what you're getting before you come, *and* if you understand some of its background and history, you'll probably be content to stay on its unusual premises. The hotel is awkwardly located in a residential neighborhood that's connected by roaring boulevards, after a 10-minute drive, to Syracuse's Archaeological Park, and that has a lot less of the baroque splendor you'll easily find on Ortygia Island. Its building site is immediately above what was used thousands of years ago as a rock quarry (the historic "Latomie dei Cappuccini"). The result is bizarre, even surreal, incorporating a dry, dusty garden with a deep chasm almost at the hotel's foundation, all of it surrounded by the somewhat unsightly urban encroachments of the mid-20th century. Despite frequent renovations, most of the rooms reflect the somewhat dowdy tastes of what might have been someone's well-heeled but not widely traveled Sicilian aunt: carefully embroidered lace curtains, high ceilings, comfy beds, and a definite sense of the south Italian bourgeoisie. Some rooms have modern Jacuzzis in their tiled bathrooms, and some include a genuinely valuable antique desk or table as part of the furnishings. Overall, the hotel lacks the excitement and good location of, for example, the Grand Hotel on Ortygia Island.

Via MP Laudien 2, 9610-0 Siracusa. ⓒ 0931-412121. Fax 0931-36061. www.villapoliti.com. 180€–232€ double; 346€ suite. Rates include breakfast. AE, DC, MC, V. Free parking. Bus: 1 or 4. **Amenities:** Restaurant; bar; pool. *In room:* A/C, TV, minibar, hair dryer, safe.

Holiday Inn ⭐ Originally built in 1965 as an AGIP hotel, this box-shaped structure is set between a large gas station and the eastern edge of the Parco Archeologico. Everything about it was designed for quick and uncomplicated access for business travelers and, as such, it offers reasonably good value without a shred of historic association or antique charm. Guest rooms are chain-motel efficient, each with a writing desk, an adequate amount of space, tiled shower-only bathrooms, and bland but efficient international styling.

Viale Teracati 30, 96100 Siracusa. ⓒ **0931-440440.** Fax 0931-67115. www.holiday-inn.com/siracusaitaly. 83 units. 184€ double. AE, DC, MC, V. Free parking. Bus: 8. **Amenities:** Restaurant; bar; laundry/dry cleaning. *In room:* A/C, TV, minibar, safe (in some).

Hotel Roma ⭐ A block from the city's magnificent cathedral, this government-rated four-star hotel opened in the late 1990s in the much-renovated shell of a hotel that was originally built in the 1880s. Enter a lobby whose vaulted ceiling is crafted from chiseled stone blocks and ringed with Belle Epoque columns. After registration, head for one of the well-appointed, very comfortable guest rooms. These usually have elaborate marquetry floors, bathrooms sheathed in blue-toned tiles, original lithographs, and comfortable furniture vaguely inspired by Art Deco models. Only a few of the bathrooms contain tubs; most offer a modern shower instead. About four of the rooms have computers. Overall, this is a fine hotel choice, with a location in the heart of monument-laden Ortygia Island.

Via Minerva 10, 96100 Siracusa. ⓒ 0931-464626. Fax 0931-465535. www.hotelroma.sr.it. 45 units. 180€ double; 233€ junior suite. AE, DC, MC, V. Parking 5.25€ per day. Bus: 21 or 23. **Amenities:** Restaurant; bar; laundry/dry cleaning. *In room:* A/C, TV, minibar.

MODERATE

Albergo Domus Mariae ⭐ *Finds* Clean, impeccably honest, and well-respected, this small-scale hotel originated in 1995 when a Catholic elementary school was transformed into a decent, well-managed lodging. It's owned by an order of Ursuline nuns (Le Sorelle de Orsoline), and although the desk staff and porters are likely to be laypersons, its manager is a hardworking, habit-clothed member of the order. This is the only hotel in Syracuse with its own chapel (a modern, cell-like affair laden with Catholic symbols) and a reading room that's a genuinely contemplative site for R&R. There's also a rooftop terrace for sun-bathing. Rooms are fairly priced and well-scrubbed, with modern furniture and a no-nonsense approach to decorating. Each has a tiled bathroom with a shower (no tubs). Know in advance that there will be no attempt to foist religious educa-tion on you if you choose to stay here—for most purposes, it's a conventional hotel, without any evangelistic mission. *Note:* The signs that indicate this place are so small as to be almost invisible, especially if you're driving along the waterfront promenade that flanks it. Here's a tip: It's set directly across a tiny waterfront piazza from the baroque facade of San Filippo Neri Church.

Via Vittorio Veneto 76, 96100 Siracusa. ℰ/fax **0931-24854.** www.sistemia.it/domusmariae. 17 units. 120€–130€ double. Rates include breakfast. AE, DC, MC, V. Free parking. Bus: 20. **Amenities:** Restaurant; laundry/dry cleaning. *In room:* A/C, TV, minibar.

Jolly Hotel   A major stop for tour groups, the six-story Jolly is part of the chain that's Italy's answer to Holiday Inn. You get no surprises, just your basic motel room (albeit slightly worn), with good beds and a small tiled bathroom. At least the view of the sea is panoramic. The location is on a dull but busy shop-ping street, about a 20-minute walk from Ortygia.

Corso Gelone 45, 96100 Siracusa. ℰ **800/221-2626** in the U.S., 800/237-0319 in Canada, or 0931-4611111. Fax 0931-461126. www.jollyhotels.it. 100 units. 119€–155€ double. Rates include breakfast. AE, DC, MC, V. Free parking. **Amenities:** Restaurant; lounge; room service; laundry. *In room:* A/C, TV, minibar, hair dryer, safe.

Palace Hotel   Not as well known as the previously recommended hotels, this is a completely modern, completely comfortable, and welcoming hotel, with rather luxurious architecture and interior furnishings. It's located in the new shopping and residential area of Syracuse, 4km (2½ miles) from the city center. Built in 1994, it offers a streamlined, tasteful decor. The midsize guest rooms are traditionally furnished. Only 18 units have bathrooms with tubs; the rest have bathrooms with modern showers. Maintenance is high, and the service is among the best in town. The place, however, doesn't quite escape the curse of a businessperson's hotel.

Viale Scale Greca 201, 96100 Siracusa. ℰ **0931-491566.** Fax 0931-756612. 85€–153€ double; 134€ junior suite. Rates include breakfast. AE, DC, MC, V. Free parking. **Amenities:** Restaurant; bar; room service; laundry/dry cleaning. *In room:* A/C, TV, minibar, hair dryer.

Park Helios Hotel   It's architecturally uninspiring in its *moderno* statement, except for the private balconies, but this hotel is a solid, reliable choice for Syra-cuse. It offers airy, comfortably furnished guest rooms, each with traditional modern furnishings set on tiled floors. Most of the bathrooms come with show-ers, although a few have bathtubs. The service is good here, though we found the restaurant rather mediocre. For the money, though, the place isn't a bad choice.

Via Filistro 80, 96100 Siracusa. ℰ **0931-412233.** Fax 0931-38096. parkhotel.helios@tin-it. 182 units. 93€ double. AE, DC, MC, V. Free parking. **Amenities:** Restaurant; bar; pool; room service; babysitting; laundry/dry cleaning. *In room:* A/C, TV, minibar, hair dryer.

INEXPENSIVE

Hotel Bellavista   Family-owned and -run, this hotel lies in the commercial center, close to the archaeological zone. There's an annex in the garden for over-flow. The spacious main lounge has leather chairs and semitropical plants. The guest rooms are informal and comfortable; most are furnished with traditional pieces and have sea-view balconies. All units have tidily kept bathrooms with shower units.

Via Diodoro Siculo 4, 96100 Siracusa. © **0931-411355.** Fax 0931-37927. www.sistemia.it/bellavista. 47 units. 93€ double. Rates include breakfast. AE, MC, V. Free parking. **Amenities:** Restaurant; lounge; gym; sauna; room service. *In room:* A/C, TV.

Hotel Como ★ *Value* This small hotel, not far from the historic core, is one of the city's best bargains. It lies in the square at the train station and is convenient for those arriving on trains from Catania. It's little more than a utilitarian hotel, but many of the rooms are quite spacious and comfortably furnished. Each guest room comes with a small tiled bathroom with shower. Since some of the accommodations are triples, this is a favorite with vacationing families, often from other parts of Sicily. Plus, its low-slung design and sense of style set the place apart from a typically tacky train station hotel.

Piazza Stazione 13, 96100 Siracusa. © **0931-464055.** Fax 0931-464056. www.hotelcomo.it. 20 units. 94€ double; 116€ triple; 148€ suite. AE, DC, MC, V. Parking: 10€. Bus: 22 or 23. **Amenities:** Bar; laundry/dry cleaning. *In room:* A/C, TV, safe in 5 units.

Hotel Gutkowski Modern, simple, unpretentious, and with a distinct sense of being alive to the creative, cutting-edge arts scene of Syracuse, this small, cost-conscious hotel opened in 1999. It occupies a waterfront town house on Ortygia. Its owner and founder is the English-speaking Polish-Sicilian entrepreneur Paola Pretsch. Don't expect any particular luxury, as everything here is simple and utilitarian and a bit less comfortable than rooms at the nearby (and also-recommended) Domus Mariae. It nonetheless has a welcoming atmosphere. Only four bathrooms contain tubs; the rest have showers. The only meal served is breakfast in a spartan-looking room next to the reception desk.

Lungomare Vittorini 26, 96100 Siracusa. © **0931-465861.** Fax 0931-480505. www.guthotel.it. 14 units. 88€ double. Discounts of 10% available Oct–Mar. Rates include breakfast. AE, DC, MC, V. Free parking. Bus: 21 or 22. **Amenities:** Laundry. *In room:* A/C, TV, minibar.

Hotel Panorama Near the entrance to the city, on a rise of Temenite Hill, this bandbox-modern hotel sits on a busy street about 5 minutes from the Archaeological Park. It's not a motel, but it does provide free parking. The small guest rooms are pleasant and up-to-date, with comfortable but utilitarian furniture and small tiled bathrooms with showers.

Via Necropoli Grotticelle 33, 96100 Siracusa. © **0931-412188.** Fax 0931-412527. 51 units. 62€ double. Rates include continental breakfast. AE, MC, V. Free parking. Bus: 12. **Amenities:** Lounge. *In room:* A/C, TV.

Hotel Relax This Mediterranean-style hotel lies 2km (1¼ miles) from the center in a rather tranquil residential area. The hotel offers a garden, a swimming pool, and a large solarium, making it a good choice on a summer day for those who don't want to lodge directly in the center of hot, dusty Syracuse. Guest rooms are light and airy and furnished in a minimalist yet comfortable fashion. About half the bathrooms are equipped with modern showers; the rest have bathtubs. Suites are a good buy here, but there are only two and they must be reserved in advance. Since you're away from the city center, you can dine here at night on the typical but quite good Sicilian and international cuisine.

Viale Epipoli 159, 96100 Siracusa. © **0931-740122.** Fax 0931-740933. www.hotelrelax.it. 59 units. 99€ double; 148€ suite. Rates include breakfast. AE, DC, MC, V. Free parking. Take any bus marked BELVEDERE. **Amenities:** Restaurant; bar; pool; room service; laundry/dry cleaning. *In room:* A/C, TV.

Il Limoneto ★ *Kids*   What a discovery! This place brings you close to the heart of Sicily. Set in 6 hectares (5 acres) of orange groves and orchards, this tranquil retreat lies 9km (5 miles) from the center of Syracuse along SP14 Mare-Monti. You can lodge at this estate and visit not only Syracuse but Noto (see later in this chapter) and Ragusa (see chapter 11). Much of the food served here is grown on the grounds, including oranges, vegetables, grapes, and olive oil, and guests are invited to pick their own fruit. The homemade pastas are one of the reasons to check in. The hotel chef, Adele, was kind enough to give us her secret recipe for spaghetti alla Norma (made with eggplant). We enjoyed the hotel's house-party atmosphere, with guests gathering in the evening for wine, conversation, and even Sicilian poetry. If you like the outdoors, this is the best choice in the area. They offer an aerobics class, and even archery taught by an instructor. Guest rooms, in a farmhouse-rustic style, are comfortably furnished. Families prefer to check into one of the rooms with a mezzanine, stashing the kids upstairs. Each bathroom comes with a tiled shower.

Via del Platano 3, 96100 Siracusa (Contrada Magrentino). ℂ 0931-717352. Fax 0931-717728. limoneto@ tin.it. 8 units. 35€ double. Rates include breakfast. Dinner 16€ per person extra. DC, MC, V. Free parking. Take the Palazzolo bus from Syracuse's central station. **Amenities:** Restaurant. *In room:* A/C in 2 units, no phone.

WHERE TO DINE

If you're in need of a full meal, you have all the choices below. But if you're seeking only a drink, a snack, or coffee, head for the elegant **Antico Caffè Minerva,** Via Minerva 15 (ℂ **0931-22606**), in the vicinity of the Duomo or cathedral. It's open Thursday through Tuesday from 7am to 1am.

Only a few of the restaurants below lie on a bus line.

EXPENSIVE

La Terrazza ★ ITALIAN/SICILIAN   Set on the top floor of Ortygia's highest-rated hotel, this restaurant features a *dolce vita* ambience, formal service, and big-windowed views that sweep from the outdoor terrace way, way across Syracuse's bay. There's something festive about this place, and the fine food includes starters like smoked salmon with mint sauce; jumbo shrimp with citrus sauce; and an antipasti platter containing smoked turkey. Equally alluring are the main courses such as risotto with monkfish and saffron or the superb grilled filet of sea bass flavored with fresh Sicilian herbs. The cuisine is admirably authentic and satisfying, prepared with the freshest of ingredients.

On the top floor of the Grand Hotel, Viale Mazzini 12. ℂ 0931-464600. Reservations recommended. Main courses 10€–16€. AE, DC, MC, V. Daily 12:30–2:30pm and 7:30–10:30pm.

Ristorante Jonico-a Rutta e Ciauli ★ SICILIAN   This is one of the best restaurants for typical Sicilian cuisine and wines. It's right on the sea, with a panoramic view, not far from Piazzale dei Cappuccini. The decor is pure Liberty (Art Nouveau) style. The antipasti array is dazzling, and the homemade pasta dishes are superb—try pasta *rusticana*, with eggplant, cheese, ham, and herbs (ask one of the English-speaking waiters to explain the many variations), or spaghetti with fresh tuna and herbs. Swordfish appears here in roulades with raisins, pine nuts, and bread crumbs. Meat specialties include *bistecca Siciliana* (tender beef with pulverized tomatoes, eggplant, onions, white wine, and local cheese); sliced veal with eggplant, tomatoes, onions, and slices of local cheese; and savory fish stew. The dessert specialty is *cassatine Siciliane* (mocha-chocolate ice cream capped with sprinkles of coffee-flavored chocolate, all floating in a lake of English custard). A roof garden has a pizzeria serving typical Sicilian pizza.

Riviera Dionisio il Grande 194. ℂ **0931-65540.** Reservations recommended. Main courses 5.15€–7.75€; pizza 3.10€–6.50€. AE, MC, V. Wed–Mon noon–3pm and 8–10:30pm.

MODERATE

Don Camillo ⭐ SEAFOOD/SICILIAN   This is one of the city's finest dining rooms, built on the foundation of a 15th-century monastery that collapsed during an earthquake in 1693. The cuisine is among the most creative in town—the owner speaks of his food "as an evolution of island cuisine." Located near the historic center, this rather classy joint offers lighter versions of heavier and time-tested Sicilian recipes. If you're a devotee of sea urchins (and not everyone is), the delectable morsels are particularly fresh-tasting here. Sea urchins also appear in *spaghetti delle sirene,* which contains shrimp as well. All kinds of freshly caught fish are served, and your catch of the day can be prepared almost any way you like it. Full of atmosphere, the place boasts an interior filled with vaulted ceilings and potted plants. More than 450 different brands of wine are offered.

Via Maestranza 96. ℂ **0931-67133.** Reservations recommended. Main courses 9€–11€. AE, DC, MC, V. Daily 12:30–2:30pm and 7:30–10:30pm. Closed Nov.

Gambero Rosso SICILIAN/MEDITERRANEAN/SEAFOOD   Near the bridge to the Città Vecchia, this large restaurant is in an old tavern. The dining room extends from the restaurant onto a terrace dotted with potted flowers and shrubs that faces the port. Two reliable choices are *zuppa di pesce* (fish soup) and *zuppa di cozze* (fresh mussels in a tasty marinade). The Sicilian cannelloni are good, too. The meat dishes feature a number of choices from the kitchens of Lazio, Tuscany, and Emilia-Romagna.

Via Eritrea 2. ℂ **0931-68546.** Reservations recommended. Main courses 5€–12€. AE, MC, V. Fri–Wed 11am–3pm and 7:30pm–midnight. Bus: 12 or 23.

La Siciliana ⭐ *Value* SICILIAN   Well recommended by many of Syracuse's local newspapers, and popular because of its good food and reasonable prices, this restaurant originated in the 1920s as a simple *tavola calda* (hot-table snack bar). Today, it occupies a site along a dignified residential street near the northern tip of Ortygia Island, and includes sidewalk tables. The interior has a wood-burning pizza oven and dozens of framed photographs of the hardworking labor force of the city during the early 1900s. The dozen or so varieties of pizza on offer are superb—so much so that many local residents phone in for takeout service, then wait near the dining room for their order to be ready. More elaborate meals might include well-prepared versions of *cavatelli a modo nostro* (pasta with ham, cream, peas, and olives); spaghetti alla Norma with eggplant; grilled cutlets; mixed grills of either fish or meat; and grilled swordfish with herbs and capers.

Via Savoia 17. ℂ **0931-68944.** Reservations recommended only Fri–Sat night. Main courses 6€–12€; pizzas 3.10€–4.15€. DC, MC, V. Tues–Sun 10am–4pm and 6pm–midnight. Bus: 20.

Minosse di Visetti ⭐ *Finds* ITALIAN   This well-run restaurant is more dignified, more formal, and a lot more sedate than many of the quasi-hysterical restaurants that compete with it on Ortygia Island. It's set on an obscure alleyway in the heart of town, occupying a trio of paneled dining rooms filled with the aroma of the kitchen's well-prepared food. The restaurant entered the annals of local history in 1993, when it was selected as the dinner venue for the Pope on the occasion of his inauguration of the Our Lady of Tears sanctuary (see "Seeing the Ancient Sights," earlier in this chapter). The chef immediately wins your praise when he serves you a plate of fresh mussels with little cherry tomatoes. The spaghetti with seafood is marked by intense, refined flavors. Try the grilled filets of tuna with a zesty pizzaiola sauce. A delicious lemon sole comes in lemon sauce, and the chefs make one of the best-tasting fish soups, *zuppe di pesce,* in town.

Via Mirabella 6. ⟳ **0931-66366.** Main courses 8.20€–16€. MC, V. Tues–Sun noon–3pm and 7–11pm. Closed 2 weeks in July. Take any minibus leaving Piazza delle Poste and get off at Via Mirabella.

INEXPENSIVE

Da Mariano SICILIAN   Set on a very narrow cobble-covered alleyway, much too narrow for a car, a short block downhill from the Museo Bellomo, this hide-away restaurant has simple plastic tables and chairs, red-checkered tablecloths, and a good reputation with the desk staff at several of Ortygia Island's hotels. Established in 1996, it offers only 70 seats in a cavelike warren of vaulted rooms that you might find either charmingly intimate or impossibly claustrophobic. The chef's use of fresh ingredients is a compelling reason to dine here. We recently sampled a delightful homemade cavatelli with a wild boar sauce. Many dishes, such as grilled baked rabbit, Sicilian tripe, and perfectly sautéed calves' liver, are full of good old country flavor. The roast lamb arrived tender and aromatic with fresh island herbs. The grilled filets of swordfish were immensely tasty, as was a farfalle pasta with braised radicchio.

Vicolo Zuccala 9. ⟳ **0931-67444.** Reservations recommended. Main courses 5.50€–7.80€. MC, V. Wed–Mon 1–3pm and 8–11:30pm. Closed 3 weeks in July. Bus: 21 or 23.

Darsena da Ianuzzo ITALIAN/SICILIAN   Well located, almost immediately adjacent to the older of the two bridges leading from the Sicilian "mainland" to Ortygia Island, this is a stylish and well-liked dining enclave that overlooks the artfully ratty harbor-front life giving Ortygia such color. The style is *la dolce vita moderno.* We've enjoyed some good meals here, but be forewarned: This is not the friendliest oasis in town. Only time-tested local recipes are served. One specialty is a savory fish soup; another is spaghetti in a mass of little sea urchins. Another excellent dish is *conchigliette al ragù di pesce,* or minced fish in a rich tomato sauce. A covered veranda overlooks the Ionian Sea.

Riva Garibaldi 8. ⟳ **0931-66104.** Reservations recommended. Main courses 6€–8€. AE, DC, MC, V. Thurs–Tues noon–3pm and 7:15–11pm.

Giola SEAFOOD/PIZZA   This restaurant occupies the street level of a 250-year-old palace in Città Vecchia, overlooking the sea, a 10-minute walk east of the cathedral. Despite its understated decor and inexperienced staff, it serves a memorable cuisine. Many specialties emerge from the fragrant kitchen, including a wide array of homemade pastas, a cheese-laden crespelline of the house, pasta with sardines, spiedini with shrimp, and a selection of pungent beef, fish, and veal dishes. Two pasta dishes sampled on a recent visit were beautifully conceived: ravioli *di pesce alla salsa Norma* (stuffed with fish in a sauce laced with eggplant) and spaghetti with delectable sea urchins. There's also a pizzeria on-site.

Via dei Tolomei 5. ⟳ **0931-66386.** Reservations recommended. Main courses 6€–11€. AE, DC, MC, V. Tues–Sun 12:30–3pm and 7:30pm–midnight. Bus: 21 or 23.

Il Mandarino CHINESE   After too constant a diet of Sicilian food, you might take a cue from the many locals who pack into this elegantly outfitted Chinese restaurant for a change of culinary venue. Its exterior is gaily and charmingly decorated with twinkling lights that might remind you of Chinese New Year, even in the glare of midsummer. Inside, you'll find red and gold lanterns and big tables that seem to correspond exactly to the size of large and extended Sicilian families. The menu (written entirely in Italian) is instructive: It tells you how to use chopsticks; gives a lengthy introduction to the cuisines of

Asia; shows photos of every conceivable variation on the menu items; and even gives thumbnail sketches of the signs of the Chinese zodiac. Among the best menu items are squid and prawns on a hot iron platter; pork in hot chili sauce; and myriad preparations of duck, pork, chicken, and beef.

Via Savoia 12. (✆ **0931-22898.** Reservations not necessary. Main courses 4.50€–6.50€. AE, MC, V. Daily noon–3pm and 7:30pm–midnight.

Le Baronie ⭐ *Finds* SICILIAN   Expatriate Americans and longtime friends of ours living in Syracuse turned us on to this delightful trattoria in an old Sicilian villa. Laid out like a hexagon, and connected in a series of honeycomb-shaped cells, it's set in a garden dotted with ancient sarcophagi. It offers both patio and interior dining. The restaurant serves traditional island cuisine but adds many creative touches. The result is highly personal, inventive food. Try tucking into gnocchi *alla tancredi* (with radicchio, Parmesan, cream, butter, and virgin olive oil). Our favorite pasta here—and it's a delight—is linguine *del vicere* (with those trusty urchins again, plus olive oil, garlic, and Parmesan). The chefs take justifiable pride in their *pesce spada d'Almeria* (swordfish steaks served in a sauce made of green pepper, butter, and brandy).

Via Gargallo 24. (✆ **0931-68884.** Reservations recommended. Main courses 6.85€–10€. DC, MC, V. Tues–Sun noon–3pm and 7:30pm–midnight.

SYRACUSE AFTER DARK

Much of the nightlife here takes place in satellite villages in summer, particularly along the coast. Unless specifically stated, some of the clubs keep irregular hours. Check before heading to one of the hot spots, especially those out of town.

In Syracuse itself, you can visit **La Nottola,** Via Gargallo 61 (✆ **0931-60009**), on a small street near Via Maestanza. This is a stylish jazz club/piano bar/disco, attracting a well-dressed younger crowd.

Buio Bar, Via Delle Vergini 14 (✆ **333-9854177**), is run by its likable owner (Fabbio Modicano). He's proud of the way his bar survived the "Ortygian wars," when the neighborhood around it was slowly gentrified from a run-down slum into one of Syracuse's most appealing historic neighborhoods. Hip and alert to the pop-culture trends in the north of Italy, this is one of the best bars and hangout joints of Syracuse. It offers a woodsy-looking pub ambience with posters of Jack Daniels and reggae great Bob Marley, comfortable armchairs, a changing array of paintings by local artists (all of which are for sale) and, every evening after 10:30pm, live music. If you're looking for insight into counterculture Syracuse, this is definitely the place. It's open daily from 10:30am to 4am.

Peter Pan Caffè Letterario, Via Castello Maniace 46–48 (✆ **0931-468937**), is a cocktail bar and wine tavern that even has books, giving it some claim to fame as a "literary cafe." Many patrons are students from the local university, and its young guests lounge on comfortable sofas. It occasionally features live music, especially jazz and pop. The Peter Pan is open from June to September daily from 7pm to 3am; from October to May, daily from 4:30pm to 3am.

Doctor Sam, Piazza San Rocco 4 (✆ **0931-483598**), along with the also-recommended Buio Bar, is the premier counterculture bar of Syracuse, with a hip, youthful, and high-energy clientele that tends to be interested in tattoos, motorcycles, piercings, Rastafarian music, rock 'n' roll and—under the right circumstances—romance. Come here for a view of *la dolce vita* as reinterpreted by 21st-century hipsters with a full-fledged appreciation for all aspects of Western pop culture. From April to September, the bar is open nightly from 7pm till 4am. From October to March, it's closed on Wednesday.

Besides the most popular hangouts, Buio Bar and Peter Pan, Syracuse has a number of other worthy bars and cafes, including **Bar Bonomo,** Corso Gelone 48 (℃ **0931-67845**), which is more of a bar/bakery. The aroma of fresh bread will direct you to the place. Its gelato is some of the best in town.

Another spacious bar and gelateria, **Baro Ortigia,** Largo Aretusa 2–3 (℃ **0931-64312**), is near Syracuse's most famous fountain. Come here for all kinds of drinks, snacks, and excellent, velvety gelato. Tables overflow onto the square in fair weather, which is most of the time.

Also in the vicinity of the fountain is a fashionable bar, **Lungo la Notte,** Lungomare Alfeo (℃ **0931-65042**), open only at night, that attracts a young clientele. It's in a panoramic setting overlooking the harbor.

ON THE OUTSKIRTS

The region's best disco is **Fontana Bianca,** Viale Dei Lidi (℃ **0931-753633**), 18km (11 miles) southwest of the town center and open from June to September. It contains a walled garden, a pool that at night seems mostly ornamental, and a crowd that's older than you'll find at the student hangouts closer to the town center. Another option is the **Discotecca Malibu,** Via Elorina 172 (℃ **0931-721888**), about 6km (3½ miles) southwest of town on SS115, where a younger crowd dances all night at a seaside pavilion that evokes its California namesake.

In midsummer, head for the **Sporting Club Terrauzza,** Via del Galeone (℃ **0931-714647**), centerpiece of the village of Terrauzza. Located about 10km (6 miles) southwest of Syracuse, it's where vacationers at the local beaches show up to mingle with local 20-somethings.

SIDE TRIPS FROM SYRACUSE

Although much of the environs of the city of Syracuse are polluted with industrial sites, including ugly oil refineries, there are some fruits to be plucked from the tree as you "branch" out into the hinterlands. The best of what there is follows. For specific locations, refer to the "Syracuse & the Southeast" map on p. 239.

CASTELLO EURIALO ✦   This boat-shaped structure is one of the most evocative and formidable Greek fortresses to have survived from ancient times, lying 9km (5½ miles) northwest of Syracuse along Via Epipoli, in the Belvedere district. The castle was adapted and fortified by Archimedes, the famous mathematician who was born in Syracuse in 287 B.C.

The castle was considered impregnable, but such was not the case. The Romans conquered it without a struggle. The approach road crosses the **Wall of Dionysius,** which once stretched for 27km (17 miles) across the Epipolae high plateau, enclosing the northern tier of Syracuse. Two parallel walls were built of limestone blocks, the center filled with rubble. The walls, launched by Dionysius the Elder in 401 B.C. after the Athenian siege, were finished in 385 B.C.

As you survey the ruins, know that they are the most complete of any Greek military work extant. Three ditches precede the west front of the fortress. The main castle consisted of a keep, the barracks, and cisterns (they were prepared for long sieges). A warren of underground passages was cut through the fortress. From the castle precincts, you can enjoy a **panorama** ✦ back to Syracuse.

Take bus no. 11, 25, or 26 from the Archaeological Park to reach the site, which is open daily from 9am to sunset, charging no admission. For more information, call ℃ **0931-711773.**

MEGARA HYBLAEA   If you don't suffocate passing through the industrial horror, *Zona industriale,* with its polluting oil refineries, you'll reach ancient Megara

Hyblaea, near the major port of Prilo along the coast of southeastern Sicily. The Greeks built the city to open onto the Gulf of Augusta, whose shoreline now contains the largest concentration of chemical plants in Europe. Pollution has killed nearly all marine life in the bay, and the air in this area is contaminated.

Should you be a serious-enough archaeologist, and if you have persisted this far, you'll come upon the ruin of what was Megara Hyblaea, 16km (10 miles) to the north of Syracuse and reached along SS114. Yellow signposts direct you to the excavations, which are open Monday through Saturday from 9am to 2pm and Sunday from 9am to 1pm; admission is free.

The Megarians arriving in ships from Greece founded Megara Hyblaea in the 8th century B.C., making it one of the oldest of all Greek settlements in Sicily. It was leveled by the tyrant, Gelon, in 483 B.C. By 340 B.C., the ruler, Timoleon, founded a second city. But that, too, fell to conquerors, this time the Romans in 214 B.C. Serious excavations of the site began in 1949 and continue to this day.

Outside the old town walls are the remains of a necropolis. After a look, you can walk into the heart of the ruins, exploring foundations of buildings from both the Archaic periods (indicated by red iron posts) and the Hellenistic era (green posts). Of particular interest is a Hellenistic house from the 4th century B.C. (the entry is marked by iron steps). Nearly two dozen chambers were arranged around two patios.

To the left of the old *agora,* or marketplace, are the ruins of Hellenistic baths, with a boiler still discernible in the rubble. Nearby is a small Doric temple in bad shape, which dates from the 4th century B.C. You can also view the Hellenistic west gate with its two square towers.

Although Megara Hyblaea is the finest and most complete model of an Archaic city still extant, all the valuable artifacts dug up here have been transferred to the museums of Syracuse.

2 Noto ★ ★

31km (19 miles) SW of Syracuse, 55km (34 miles) E of Ragusa

Justifiably the most popular day trip from Syracuse is to the little town of Noto, which is set amid olive groves and almond trees on a plateau overlooking the Asinaro Valley. Noto dates from the 9th century and knew a Greek, a Roman, a Byzantine, an Arab, a Norman, an Aragonese, and even a Spanish culture before 1692, when an earthquake destroyed it. The town was constructed somewhat like a stage set, with curvilinear accents and pot-bellied wrought-iron balconies. Many Sicilian artists and artisans have worked hard to rebuild the town into a baroque gem with uniform buildings of soft limestone.

Mercifully, traffic has been diverted away from the main street, **Corso Vittorio Emanuele,** to protect its fragile buildings, on which restoration began in 1987—and not a moment too soon. Your best approach is through the monumental **Porta Reale (Royal Gate),** crowned by three symbols—a dog, a swan, and a tower, representing the town's former allegiance to the Bourbon monarchy. From here, take **Corso Vittorio Emanuele,** going through the **old patricians' quarter.** The rich-looking, honey-colored buildings along this street are some of the most captivating on the island. This street takes you to the three most important piazzas (see below).

ESSENTIALS
GETTING THERE   By Train   Noto is reached by trains (usually nine per day) heading southwest from Syracuse, which has good rail connections with the

rest of Italy. The ride takes 30 minutes and costs 2.10€ one-way. The train station lies along Via Principe di Piemonte, a 20-minute walk west of the historic core. For schedules, call ℭ **0931-892021.**

By Bus   You can also reach Noto by **Interbus** (ℭ **0931-66710**), leaving Syracuse at the rate of 11 buses per day; the trip takes 50 minutes and costs 3€ one-way. The bus station is on Piazzale Marconi, near Giardini Pubblici just east of the center, a 5-minute walk to Porta Reale and the main street, Corso Vittorio Emanuele.

By Car   Head southwest along Route 115.

VISITOR INFORMATION   To get your bearings, stop first at the **tourist office** at Piazza XVI Maggio, Villetta Ercole, in front of San Domenico Church (ℭ **0931-573779**), to pick up a map and some tips about exploring the town on foot. From May to September, office hours are daily from 9am to 1pm and 3:30 to 6:30pm; from October to March, hours are Monday through Friday from 8am to 2pm and 3:30 to 6:30pm.

WALKING THROUGH A BAROQUE CITY

The main thoroughfare, **Corso Vittorio Emanuele,** cuts through a trio of squares, each with its own church. The main axis begins at **Porta Reale,** a giant gateway to Noto patterned on a Roman-style triumphal arch, except this one dates from the 19th century instead of ancient times. The three squares are Piazza Immacolata, Piazza Municipio, and Piazza XVI Maggio.

If it's a hot day you can rest in the **Giardini Pubblici,** immediately to the right of Porta Reale opening onto Viale Marconi. These public gardens are filled with swaying palm trees and masses of flowering bougainvillea. Don't bother trying to figure out all those local figures honored by marble busts. Even most of the people of Noto today have forgotten these guys of dubious achievement.

Heading west on Corso Vittorio Emanuele, you first approach **Piazza Immacolata,** dominated by the facade of **Chiesa di San Francesco all'Immacolata** (ℭ **0931-573192**), which contains notable artworks rescued from a Franciscan church in the old town. The major work of art here is a painted wooden *Madonna and Child* from 1564, believed to be the work of the artist Antonio Monachello. The church rests behind a handsome facade designed by Vincenzo Sinatra (no relation to Ol' Blue Eyes). The most impressive aspect of this church is the grandiose flight of steps leading up to the building. The church is open daily from 8:30am to noon and 4 to 7:30pm; admission is free.

Immediately to the right of the church as you face it is the **Monastereo del Santissimo Salvatore,** which can be admired from the outside. The building, today a seminary, is characterized by windows adorned with "potbellied" wrought-iron balconies. The elegant tower—perhaps designed by Rosario Gagliardi—is the hallmark of its fine, long, 18th-century facade.

The next square is **Piazza Municipio** ✪, the most majestic of the trio. It's dominated by the **Palazzo Ducezio** (ℭ **0931-98611**), a graceful town hall with curvilinear elements enclosed by a classical portico, the work of architect Vincenzo Sinatra. The upper section of this palace was added as late as the 1950s. Its most beautiful room is the Louis XI–style **Hall of Representation** *(Salone di Rappresentanza),* decorated with gold and stucco. On the vault is a Mazza fresco representing the mythological figure of Ducezio founding Neas (the ancient name of Noto). The custodian will usually allow you a look around on the ground level during regular business hours; admission is free.

Like Venice, a City in Peril

The collapse of the dome of the Duomo in 1996 sent a dangerous signal racing through this little baroque city. After literally centuries of decay and neglect, the monuments of Noto are in grave danger. Complicating matters, much of the regional material—white tufa stone—is soft and not meant to last the ages like marble; unless it is constantly maintained, it can rapidly deteriorate. The only reason many of the buildings of Noto are still standing is because of wooden supports, and for some buildings it looks as if scaffolding is here to stay. Noto is hampered by lack of money, even though restoration is proceeding—but at a snail's pace, in some critics' view. What's the hope? That Noto will be approved as an addition to the World Heritage Site list, sponsored by UNESCO. This would mean funds for ongoing restoration. Until enough money is found, Noto continues to decline, with many of its most precious monuments in peril.

On one side of the square, a broad flight of steps leads to the **Duomo,** flanked by two lovely horseshoe-shaped hedges. The cathedral was inspired by models of Borromini's churches in Rome and was completed in 1776. In 1996, the dome collapsed, destroying a large section of the nave, and it's still under repair.

On the far side of the cathedral is the **Palazzo Villadorata,** graced with a classic facade. Its six **extravagant balconies** 𝄢𝄢 are supported by sculpted buttresses of galloping horses, griffins, and grotesque bald and bearded figures with chubby-cheeked cherubs at their bellies. The palazzo is divided into 90 rooms, the most beautiful being the **Yellow Hall** *(Salone Giallo),* the **Green Hall** *(Salone Verde),* and the **Red Hall** *(Salone Rosso),* with their precious frescoed domes from the 18th century. The charming **Feasts Hall** *(Salone delle Feste)* is dominated by a fresco representing mythological scenes. In one of its aisles, the palazzo contains a *pinacoteca* (picture gallery) with antique manuscripts, rare books, and portraits of noble families. The building is under renovation and its status can change suddenly; check locally with the visitor center before heading here or call ⓒ **0931-835005** for up-to-date information. Currently, the building is open Monday through Saturday from 9am to 1:30pm and 3:30 to 6:30pm; admission is 1.55€. Guided tours in English are available for 3.10€.

The final main square is **Piazza XVI Maggio,** dominated by Rosario Gagliardi's convex facade of **Chiesa di San Domenico** 𝄢, with two tiers of columns separated by a high cornice. The interior is filled with polychrome marble altars but you'll have to take our word for that, as the church appears to have been shut indefinitely. It's in really bad shape. At least you can admire its facade. Directly in front of the church is a public garden, the **Villetta d'Ercole,** named for its 18th-century fountain honoring Hercules.

Right off Corso Vittorio Emanuele is one of Noto's most fascinating streets, **Via Nicolaci** 𝄢, lined with magnificent baroque buildings.

In summer, Noto is also known for some fine **beaches** nearby; the best are 6km (3½ miles) away at **Noto Marina.** You can catch a bus at the Giardini Pubblici in Noto. The one-way fare is 1.30€. Call ⓒ **0931-836123** for schedules.

WHERE TO STAY

Camere Belvedere   At the highest elevation of the historic district, this elegant stone structure opens onto the "balcony of the city," a short walk from the crumbling Duomo. From its terrace, you're treated to a panoramic view of the baroque city, and on a clear day, you can see all the way to the seashore at Noto Marina and up to Portopalo, the extreme southeastern tip of the island. Constructed of ancient stones from other buildings, the belvedere is traditional all the way. Its guest rooms are sparsely furnished yet comfortable, resting for the most part under wood-beamed ceilings. The furnishings were handcrafted of solid wood. Even though it's in the middle of a town, there is a rustic, country aura to the place. Each unit comes with a small private bathroom with shower.

Piazza Perelli Cippo 1, 96017 Noto. ℭ 0931-573820. Fax 0931-573820. www.camerebelvedere.com. 4 units. 44€–49€ double. No credit cards. Free parking on street. **Amenities:** Bar; breakfast room. *In room:* A/C, no phone.

La Sumalia Residence   This ancient rural mansion, a real discovery, lies less than 1km (½ mile) from the center of Noto in the hills. From its panoramic perch, a view of the Gulf of Noto and the town unfolds. The property has been restored and renovated to receive guests, with a number of its original architectural features intact. The property dominates a valley of 9 hectares (23 acres) planted with almond and olive trees along with carob plants. Breakfast is served on a terrace taking in the view. Resting under wooden beams, rooms are small and filled with rustic, comfortable furnishings. Each is equipped with a small bathroom with a shower unit. Guests can use the communal kitchen.

Contrada San Giovanni, 96017 Noto. ℭ/fax 0931-894292. www.lasumasumalia.com. 5 units. 45€–60€ double. Rates include breakfast. AE, DC, MC, V. Bus departs from Piazza Marconi in Noto for Contrada San Giovanni. **Amenities:** Bar. *In room:* A/C, TV, no phone.

Villa Caniselle ⭐ *(Finds*   Surrounded by lush Mediterranean vegetation, this offbeat discovery offers you the chance to stay in a restored 19th-century farmhouse just a 10-minute walk from the historic core of Noto. You enter a world of peace and tranquility here. The property has been restored with sensitivity, with tasteful decorations throughout. All guest rooms have private entrances through a terrace or a patio. The lounge in the garden is also used as a reading room, and the public lounges display local handcrafts. Guest rooms are small but beautifully kept, each with a small bathroom with shower.

Via Pavese 1, 96017 Noto. ℭ 0931-835793. Fax 0931-837700. www.villacanisello.it. 6 units. 50€–70€ double. No credit cards. Free parking. **Amenities:** Bar; breakfast room. *In room:* A/C in some (ceiling fan in others), TV, fridge, no phone.

Villa Favorita/Villa Giulia ⭐ *(Finds*   These two 18th-century residences have been beautifully restored and filled with modern comforts while retaining their original architectural details. Lying between Noto and Noto Marina (the beach area), they provide the best-equipped lodgings in the area. Under the same management, and very similar in style, they actually lie 10km (6¼ miles) apart, but on the same road. Villa Favorita contains 39 rooms, Villa Giulia 34. The properties let you experience how elegant dons and landowners of yesteryear lived in this part of Sicily. Palm trees grace the grounds, and the look is one of elegance and serenity. Guest rooms, are comfortably though somewhat austerely furnished. Each unit comes with a small, tiled bathroom with either tub or shower. The dining rooms are handsomely appointed, and the cuisine of regional and international dishes is some of the best in the area.

Contrada Falconara, 96017 Noto. ℂ **0931-812912.** Fax 0931-812812. www.hotelvillafavorita.it. 73 units. 100€ double. AE, DC, MC, V. Free parking. May–Sept a bus leaves Piazza Marconi in Noto and heads for Marina di Noto, stopping at both hotels. **Amenities:** Restaurant; bar; pool; room service. *In room:* A/C, TV.

Villa Mediterranea ✦   This is your best bet if you'd prefer to visit historic Noto on a day trip but stay on the best beach while you're in the area. Right along the seafront, this cozy hotel stands in its own gardens with a swimming pool. You can also go through a private gate to reach the beach. The public lounges are stylishly furnished, and the midsize guest rooms contain comfortable beds and tiled floors. In the tradition of beach hotels, there is no attempt to overly decorate here. Each unit comes with a tidily kept private bathroom with shower.

Viale Lido, 96017 Noto Marina. ℂ **0931-812330.** Fax 0931-812330. www.villamediterranea.it. 15 units. 68€–104€ double. AE, DC, MC, V. Free parking. Closed Nov 1–Dec 19 and Jan 8 to mid-Mar. **Amenities:** Bar; pool; room service; laundry/dry cleaning. *In room:* A/C, TV.

WHERE TO DINE

Il Barocco ✦ SICILIAN   What is probably the most whimsical, charming, and lighthearted of Noto's restaurants occupies what was built in the 1700s as the stable block for a historic palace nearby. Tables sit beneath gracefully vaulted ceilings, beside walls that former clients have "autographed" in heavy markers with often personalized messages for the extroverted owner, Graziella. Some of these autographs elicit immediate recognition from virtually everyone in Italy: They include singers and pop entertainers Pippo Baudo, Katia Ricciarelli, and Lucio Dalla, and political commentator Vittorio Sgarbi. Seafood is well handled, especially a delightful plate of calamari and a *fritto misto* (mixed fry) of shrimp and fish. Textural contrasts show to good effect in a tender filet of beef in a robustly enriched green peppercorn and balsamic vinegar sauce, and in a dish of escalopes of veal whose flavor is only enhanced by a white-wine sauce.

Via Cavour 8 (at corner of Ronco Sgadari). ℂ **0931-835999.** Reservations recommended. Main courses 7€–10€. Set-price menu 8€. MC, V. Daily noon–3:30pm and 5–11:30pm.

La Buco ✦ *Finds* SICILIAN   Of the several restaurants we recommend in Noto, this is one of the easiest to reach, positioned as it is only a few steps downhill from the town's main thoroughfare, Corso Vittorio Emanuele. Descend (carefully) a flight of modern marble steps into a simply furnished interior that's kept cool by thick masonry walls and a location that's partially below the street's grade. We first arrived here on a spring day and were treated to the best plate of deep-fried zucchini blossoms we'd ever had in Sicily. The menu incorporates all the mainstays for fish eaters. Japan meets Sicily in the plate filled with slices of raw swordfish marinated in a citrus sauce. An order of fresh slices of grilled tuna was a delight in its simplicity and goodness. Frequently a house specialty, linguine comes in a savory shellfish sauce riddled with fresh mussels and shrimp, among other children of Neptune. Meat eaters don't get the same loving care fish devotees do, although our filet of steak was perfectly cooked, emerging on our table in a pepper-flavored cream sauce.

Via Giuseppe Zanardelli 17. ℂ **0931-838142.** Reservations recommended. Main courses 7€–12€. MC, V. Sun–Fri noon–3:30pm and 7pm–midnight.

Neas *Value* SICILIAN   Reach this family-run restaurant by walking through a medieval-looking courtyard, then pass into a duet of vaulted rooms whose stonework was set in place during the 1730s. There's outdoor seating if you want it, but during the heat of a Sicilian day, most diners opt for the restaurant's cool inner recesses. The most typical of Sicilian dishes in Noto are served here. Just because they're typical doesn't mean they aren't good—quite the contrary. We launched our most recent meal with a plate of roasted sardines, and after lunch a hungry cat followed us through the old town. We also took delight in pennette pasta garnished with swordfish and clams.

Via Rocco Pirri 30. ⓒ 0931-573538. Reservations not necessary. Main courses 6.20€–12€. AE, MC, V. Tues–Sun 10am–3pm and 7pm–midnight.

NOTO AFTER DARK

Café Sicilia   Small-scale, cozy, and prefaced with outdoor chairs and tables, this is Noto's most enduring cafe-bar. Part of its allure comes from architectural adornments in place since 1892, and a clientele that seems reluctant to take its coffee or drinks anywhere else. Beer costs 1.30€ to 3€, and some absolutely luscious pastries, including a bomb-shaped *savarin al Marsala,* are priced at about 1.30€ each. Jars of Sicilian honey and liqueurs are available for sale. Corso Vittorio Emanuele 125. ⓒ 0931-835013.

La Fontana Vecchia   Set at the monumental end of Noto's main walkway, this popular and well-positioned bar has a huge outdoor terrace and a reputation for being mobbed most evenings after sunset. Established in 1996, but with a turn-of-the-20th-century design that might make you think it's much older, it has a helpful and good-looking staff, a winning collection of *granite* (including raspberry and almond flower) that taste fantastic when a scoop is dissolved in soda water, and a wide selection of cocktails. It's open daily from 7am to midnight (Apr–Sept) and daily from 7am to 10pm (Oct–Mar). 150 Corso Vittorio Emanuele. ⓒ 0931-839412.

SIDE TRIPS FROM NOTO

Those visitors with an extra day or two can use Noto as a base for side trips ranging from wonderful nature preserves, including Cava Grande del Cassibile, to ruins evoking the heyday of Magna Graecia.

CAVA GRANDE DEL CASSIBILE ★★   The "Grand Canyon of Sicily" is a bit of a misnomer, but this remote section of the Iblei mountain range attracts hikers and nature buffs. To reach the site, drive north of Noto for 19km (12 miles) on Route 287 in the direction of the town of Palazzolo Acreide. When you reach the village of Villa Vela, with its Art Nouveau villas, you will be near the gorge's site. A little secondary road is signposted to Cava Grande. Go to the end of the road where there is a car park with a stunning **panoramic vista** ★ over the Cava Grande gorge: a canyon 250m (820 ft.) deep and some 10km (6¼ miles) long between towering limestone cliffs.

The ancients used the gorge as a burial ground, and thousands of tombs have been discovered here, dating from the 11th to the 9th century B.C. The most important artifacts were removed and taken to Syracuse museums.

If you descend into the gorge, allow at least 45 careful minutes. Figure on doubling your time for the climb back. The most stunning aspect of Cava Grande is a series of **natural rock pools** ★ that were created by the Cassibilie River over many a century. You can swim, if you like—we recently noted several nude bathers from Germany doing just that. On a hot August day, it's almost the most refreshing place to be in inland Sicily. The site is always open.

ELORO   The countryside surrounding this ancient city is lonely and lovely today, but it was one of the first cities founded by Syracuse back in the 7th century B.C. The location, overlooking the sea, is even more idyllic because it lies on a hill near the mouth of the Tellaro River.

What remains today only vaguely suggests what the little city must have looked like in its heyday. The ruins are in the early stages of excavation. So far, a bit of the ancient city walls have been unearthed. You can also see the ruins of a temple dedicated to Demeter (in Roman mythology, Ceres). In the direction of the river lie the ruins of a theater which have also been dug out. From the earth emerged the north gate, with its foundations of flanking towers. The foundation of a temple believed to have been dedicated to Asclepius can also be viewed.

The admission-free site is open Monday through Saturday from 8am to 1 hour before sunset. To reach it by car, drive 11km (7 miles) southeast of Noto. Follow the signposts to the beach town of Noto Marina. Eloro lies immediately to the south.

VILLA DEL TELLARO　In 1972 a Roman villa dating from the second half of the 4th century A.D. was discovered with some of its magnificent polychrome mosaics still intact. Its location is 7km (4 miles) west of the principal Noto/Pachino highway beside the Tellaro River. It is believed that in its heyday, this villa was as richly adorned as the celebrated Villa Romana del Casale in the vicinity of Piazza Armerina (see chapter 11).

Constructed around a square peristyle, the building was obviously occupied by someone who had a lot of money and a taste for the exotic. The mosaics depict everything from the slaying of animals during a hunt to erotica.

Only the most serious archaeologists may want to seek out this place, which lies near the village of Caddeddi, signposted 1km (½ mile) off the main road. The ruins of the villa lie beneath a farmhouse. The on-site farmer will show you through; a tip is expected. If you drop in, arrive at a reasonable hour (9am–4pm).

RISERVA NATURALE DI VENDICARI 𝒜𝒜　Created as a government-protected nature reserve in 1984, this stretch of coast south of the River Tellaro is one of the beauty spots of southeastern Sicily. Open daily from 9am to dusk, with free admission, it covers 574 hectares (1,418 acres) of lovely marshland that is an oasis for migratory birds and serious birders from all over the world. Guides are available at the office (℃ **0931-462452**) at the park entrance.

What you see depends on the season. In winter all sorts of ducks can be spotted, ranging from the mallard to the red-crested pochard. In fall, you'll spot the white egret, the black stork, and even a European flamingo. Most birds only check in and then fly away to other climes, with the exception of the black-winged stilt, the Kentish plover, and the reed warbler, which all breed here.

The reserve is always open but it's best to go in the early morning or closer to twilight, when you are able to see more birds nesting; don't forget binoculars. To get here from Noto, drive southeast to the coast. Once there, take the road south—signposted PACHINO—until you come to the marked entrance to the reserve.

If you first visited Eloro (see above), continue driving south for 5km (3¾ miles) where you'll see the **Torre Vendicari,** an abandoned Norman tower. This artifact from Sicily's conquerors of yesterday overlooks a beautiful crescent of golden sand near old salt pans. It's a great place to log some time on the beach.

Motorists with the time can continue all the way to the extreme southeastern tip of Sicily at **Capo Passero.** You'll pass first through the pleasant little town of Pachino before reaching the cape, which lies 7km (4⅓ miles) south of Pachino. An important tuna fishing grounds, the cape rewards you with a **panoramic view** 𝒜𝒜 out to sea. Dominated by a lighthouse, the cape was known as *Pachynus* to the ancients, forming the southeast "horn" of Sicily.

11

Ragusa & Piazza Armerina

Few foreign visitors cut into the inland trails of central Sicily to discover the treasures they hold. Sicily's coastline, with its Greek ruins, ancient cities, and fabulous beaches, is just too alluring, especially on a hot summer day. But even a short visit will give you a taste of the mountainous interior of this fascinating island, a land that is more representative of traditional Sicily than its port towns and villages.

In this short jaunt we penetrate the wilds of central Sicily to discover one of the grandest Roman villas ever unearthed. Celebrated for its stunning mosaics, **Villa Romana del Casale,** outside the town of **Piazza Armerina,** is definitely worth the trek inland. It's one of the highlights of antiquity and may be Sicily's greatest single man-made attraction.

For another look at inland Sicily, visit the two cities of **Ragusa Superiore** and **Ragusa Ibla.** After Noto, Ragusa Ibla is one of the most stellar examples of the Sicilian baroque.

1 Ragusa ⊛

267km (166 miles) SE of Palermo, 138km (86 miles) E of Agrigento, 104km (65 miles) SW of Catania, 79 km (49 miles) SW of Syracuse

Ragusa is really two towns in one: an upper town, **Ragusa Superiore,** mapped out after a devastating earthquake in 1693, and **Ragusa Ibla,** constructed on an isolated spur. Ibla, in glaring contrast to the modern city, is one of the best-preserved old towns in Sicily, and well worth a day of your valuable time. The two parts of town are linked by a steep winding road or else by steps. Even if Ragusa Ibla weren't fascinating, the site would make an interesting trip because of the craggy valley that separates the two towns. It is a vista of winding pathways and plant-filled cliffs.

From the twin towns, panoramas of the countryside unfold. The landscapes around Ragusa are among the most memorable (and eerie) in Sicily. Many are crisscrossed with low-lying stone walls, pieced laboriously together without mortar, and lying in impoverished solitude beneath the punishing and unflinching sun. These are the landscapes most often evoked in Sicilian literature and cinema, an oft-filmed terrain that has positioned Ragusa and its outlying districts in the forefront of Italian filmmaking.

If all this weren't enough, you can take a 30-minute, 7.5km (4½-mile) drive to **Marina di Ragusa,** a thriving beach resort. Many visitors prefer to anchor here, visiting Ragusa Ibla for the day. Unlike the historic core of Ragusa Ibla, Marina di Ragusa is relatively modern, with its long, narrow, and unusually sandy beach strip. A boardwalk is lined with shops, bars, and restaurants. A party atmosphere prevails there in summer when, by 10pm, the action is just getting started.

ESSENTIALS

GETTING THERE From the east, Syracuse is often the rail gateway into Ragusa, with a dozen trains per day making the 2-hour journey for a cost of

6.70€ one-way. It's also possible to take one of three trains per day from Palermo; the 5-hour trip costs 13€ one-way.

Ragusa also has a bus link with Syracuse. Seven buses a day make the 2-hour run at a cost of 5.40€ one-way. The train and bus stations in Ragusa are at Piazza del Popolo and the adjoining Piazza Gramsci.

Motorists touring southeastern Sicily who visited our last stopover in Noto (see chapter 10) can continue southwest along Route 115 to the town of Ispica, at which point the highway swings northwest toward Ragusa.

VISITOR INFORMATION   The **Ragusa Tourist Office,** Via Capitano Bocchieri 33 (© **0932-221511**), is open Monday through Friday from 9am to 1:30pm and Tuesday and Thursday from 3 to 6:30pm.

FAST FACTS   The local hospital, **Ospedale Civile,** Via da Vinci (© **0932-600111**), services the area. For a **medical emergency,** dial © **118.** Call the **police** at © **112,** and for a **general emergency** dial © **113.** The **Ragusa Post Office,** Piazza Matteotti (© **0932-624043**), is open Monday through Saturday from 8:15am to 6:30pm.

GETTING AROUND   If you don't want to make the steep climb linking Ibla with Superiore, you can take city bus no. 3 departing from in front of the cathedral or from Piazza del Popolo and costing .55€ for a one-way ticket. It's a hairraising ride. The bus lets you off in Ibla at Piazza Pola or Giardino Obleo, most central for exploring the medieval and baroque town.

EXPLORING THE TWO TOWNS

If your time is very limited, you can skip the upper town (Ragusa Superiore) and occupy all your hours in Ragusa Ibla, as the older town holds far more intrigue. Those with more time can hike through the upper town, looking for the attractions that follow.

RAGUSA SUPERIORE

The long main street, **Corso Italia,** cuts through the upper town and makes for Ragusa's best promenade.

The main attraction of the upper town is **Cattedrale di San Giovanni,** Via Roma 134 (© **0932-621658**), dating from the 18th century and dedicated to St. John the Baptist. Pause on the elegant square in front of the cathedral and look uphill to admire its decorative facade, which is made asymmetrical by a campanile on its western side. Its front elevation contains a wide terrace. Inside, the decor is ornate, especially the stucco decorations in the cupola. The Latin cross interior is notable for its two orders of pillars, each made of locally quarried asphaltite. Admission is free; the cathedral is open daily from 9am to noon and 4 to 7:30pm.

Museo Archeologico Regionale Ibleo, Palazzo Mediterraneo, Via Natalelli (© **0932-622963**), lies off Via Roma, within an easy walk of the Duomo, near the Ponte Nuovo bridge. The museum is rich in artifacts unearthed from ancient colonies in the province. The collection is at its best in remnants of the civilization that flourished in Grecian days at Rovine di Camarina, 16km (10 miles) northwest of Marina di Ragusa. Assaulted by the Carthaginians, the colony was finally leveled by the Romans as early as 598 B.C. Some of the artifacts at the museum in Ragusa are from a temple here once dedicated to Athena. A *kore,* for example, was found at this temple site. (A *kore* is an ancient Greek statue of a clothed young woman standing with feet together.) Various necropolis reconstructions hold great interest. Hours are daily from 9am to 1:30pm, and admission costs 2.10€.

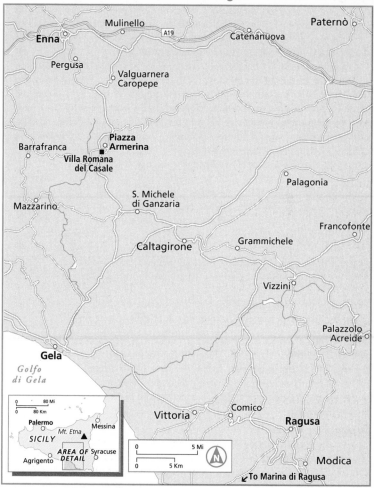

RAGUSA IBLA ★★

We prefer to reach the old town by taking a long stairway, **Santa Maria delle Scale** ★, heading down from Ragusa Superiore to the historic core of Ibla. Take this walk for the **panoramic vistas** ★★ alone, some of the finest in southeastern Sicily.

All right, so the town is in deep decay, and some of it looks relatively inhabited, but it's a nostalgic remnant of yesterday. Wander its narrow streets, checking out its crumbling baroque palaces. We were once tempted to purchase a palazzo here and restore it to its former glory (the prices are most reasonable).

Continue walking east until you come to the **Duomo di San Giorgio** ★, Piazza del Duomo (© **0932-220085**), which is open daily from 9am to noon and 4 to 7pm; no admission fee. Characterized by an impressive neoclassical dome, this is one of the best examples of Sicilian baroque in the south of Sicily, dating from the 18th century. Rosario Gagliardi, who gained fame for his architectural work in Noto, designed the facade of this cathedral as a trio of tiers, and it looks like nothing so much as a glamorous wedding cake. Each level holds up gradually narrowing Corinthian pillars that are pierced by jutting cornices. The columns were added in the 19th century. After all that show-biz drama outside, the interior comes as a disappointment, as it's quite plain.

Continuing east from the Duomo, you come to the **Chiesa di San Giuseppe** ✦, Via Torre Nuova 19 (© **0932-621779**), open daily from 9am to noon and 4 to 7pm, charging no admission. Because of the facade's similarity to that of the Duomo, this church is attributed to Gagliardi (see above), though it may have been the work of an imitator. It dates from 1590, and its oval-domed interior contains beautiful galleries. The locally mined pavement is quite striking, crafted of black asphalt interspersed with majolica tiles. Among the notable artworks is a painting, the *Glory of St. Benedict,* by Sebastiano Lo Monaco (1793).

You can continue walking all the way east through Ragusa Ibla until you reach some beautiful public gardens, **Giardino Obleo** ✦, which are studded with religious buildings, notably **Chiesa di San Giacomo,** dating from the 14th century. It was struck by a 1693 earthquake, and much of the damage was never repaired. If it's open, you'll get to see a beautiful **triptych** ✦ by Pietro Novelli, depicting the Madonna flanked by St. Agatha and St. Lucy. You may have to take our word for how lovely it is, because most visitors find the doors locked.

At the edge of the gardens, enjoy the **panoramic view** ✦ sweeping across the Valley of Irminio. The gardens are the perfect place for a picnic and can be visited daily from 8am to 8pm; there's no admission fee. Some visitors use the shady benches in the gardens for siestas on hot Sicilian afternoons.

SHOPPING

Antica Drogherie   Long ago, the building that contains this shop sold medications, salves, and ointments. Today, you'll see a wide selection of all-Sicilian wines, liqueurs, candies, honeys, jams, jellies, and gift items, all displayed inside a very old building reeking of Sicilian character and authenticity. Corso XXV Aprile 59. © **0932-652090.**

WHERE TO STAY
RAGUSA SUPERIORE

Mediterraneo Palace ✦   A healthy hike from the center of medieval Ragusa, this government-rated four-star hotel is a boxy concrete structure, but it's the finest lodging for miles around. It offers a high level of comfort, with the best rooms in town. All guest rooms are attractively and comfortably furnished, each coming with a tiled bathroom with bathtub and shower. The decor is so modernized and minimalist that you could be anywhere from Nigeria to Alaska. Those who like to eat in will find a good restaurant and drinking facilities on-site.

Via Roma 189, 97100 Ragusa. © **0932-621944.** Fax 0932-623799. www.mediterraneopalace.it. 92 units. 115€ double; 230€ suite. AE, DC, MC, V. Parking 7.50€. **Amenities:** Restaurant; bar; room service; laundry/dry cleaning. *In room:* A/C, TV, minibar, hair dryer.

Montreal   In the modern part of Ragusa, a hellish climb from the medieval quarter, this completely renovated, bandbox contemporary hotel is short on style but big on creature comforts. The location, 10 minutes by car from the baroque-style Ragusa Ibla, the historical center, is at the corner of Via San Giuseppe and Corso Italia. Guest rooms are without frills but contain strong, sturdy pieces of furniture. Each comes with a small tiled bathroom, most with shower although several contain bathtubs. The Montreal is a favorite with businesspeople visiting Ragusa to hawk their wares.

Via San Giuseppe 8, 97100 Ragusa. © **0932-621133.** Fax 0932-621133. www.chshotels.com/ragusa.htm. 50 units. 83€ double; 100€ triple. AE, DC, MC, V. Parking 6€. **Amenities:** Restaurant; bar; room service; laundry/dry cleaning. *In room:* A/C, TV, minibar.

MARINA DI RAGUSA

Eremo della Giubiliana ★★ *Finds*   About a quarter mile inland from the barren highway, midway between Ragusa (7km/4½ miles to the north) and Marina di Ragusa, this stone estate is set in dignified and sun-blasted solitude against a landscape crisscrossed with low limestone walls. Maintained by local tenant farmers for at least a thousand years, the walls enclose grazing lands for cows and sheep. No other hotel we've seen in Sicily is as deceptive in the way it contrasts a baronial, severely dignified, even desiccated-looking exterior with a walled-in compound of verdant greenery and lighthearted posh. Inside the compound, expect water fountains, lemon and almond trees, a kitchen garden burgeoning with life, and a truly unusual restaurant that's recommended separately under "Where to Dine," below.

To enter the compound (which functioned as a fortified monastery during the 1400s), you navigate some signposted country roads that meander between the above-mentioned stone walls, across a parched landscape that hasn't changed much in 300 years. After shouting your name into a microphone, you and your car will be "buzzed" in through massive iron gates that swing open, soundlessly, to reveal a walled-in world that might have been the home of a forbidding Sicilian *don* during the 18th or 19th centuries. Today it's a warm, historically poignant hotel of discreet luxury and meticulous architectural detail. The creative mind responsible for its status today as an inn is a much-respected local architect, Salvatore Mancini, who lives on-site while pursuing his local practice. Guest rooms are cozy, midsize, and as artfully authentic as rooms in a private home. Each unit comes with a private bathroom with shower.

This is the only hotel in Sicily that maintains a private airstrip. One-day airborne excursions to offshore islands such as Lampedusa and Pantelleria cost 750€ for up to three passengers, with a chauffered private car and lunch on the islands included.

Contrada Giubiliana, 97100 Ragusa. © **0932-669119.** Fax 0932-633891. 11 units, with 5 self-contained cottages scheduled for construction during the lifetime of this edition. 204€ double; 400€ suite. Rates include breakfast. Half board 250€ for 2 persons. AE, DC, MC, V. From Ragusa, take SP25 southwest toward Marina di Ragusa. Eremo is signposted at Km 7. **Amenities:** Restaurant; bar; pool; laundry/dry cleaning. *In room:* A/C, TV.

Hotel Terraqua   This is the most appealing hotel in the seaside resort of Marina di Ragusa. Configured as a cement-and-glass cube dotted with loggias and balconies, it was built in the 1980s, and identifies itself mainly as a beachfront hotel with clean rooms and frequent breezes. It usually shows its guests a good, albeit somewhat anonymous, holiday. Don't expect any personalization from the staff—they're familiar with hordes of holiday-makers coming and going. But as a base for the exploration of the neighborhood, including Ragusa Ibla, the hotel is a worthwhile choice. Guest rooms have white tile floors, color schemes of blue and white, and a beach-going simplicity. Each unit is outfitted with a small bathroom with shower. The hotel is not directly on the sands of the beach—it's inside its own walled garden, a 5-minute walk from the water (use of sun umbrellas and chaise longues is free). It's one of the most laid-back members of the distinguished Framon chain, whose administration of some of the most prominent palace hotels of Sicily is well known and widely appreciated. It also has the best and biggest swimming pool in town—and perhaps in this part of Sicily.

Via delle Sirene 35, 97010 Marina di Ragusa. © **0932-615600.** Fax 0932-615580. www.framon-hotels.it. 77 units. 130€–174€ double; 229€ junior suite. Rates include breakfast. AE, DC, MC, V. Free parking. **Amenities:** Restaurant; bar; outdoor pool; tennis court; outdoor Jacuzzi; babysitting; laundry/dry cleaning. *In room:* A/C, TV, minibar.

WHERE TO DINE
RAGUSA SUPERIORE

La Pergola ✮ SICILIAN   This restaurant offers the finest dining in the modern town of Ragusa. An elegant restaurant with marble floors and comfortable chairs, it is decorated in a style evocative of the late 19th century, with a Belle Epoque aura. Dishes are full of flavor and prepared with a certain flair, as exemplified by the swordfish in a lemon sauce with capers and toasted pine nuts. Succulent ravioli is filled with porcini mushrooms and chestnuts along with a light ricotta cheese and a whiff of marjoram. A homemade pasta dish is cooked with swordfish in an eggplant sauce, and the best tortellini in town is served here with fresh shrimp and a saffron sauce.

Contrada Selvaggio. © **0932-686430.** Reservations recommended. Main courses 6.80€–12€. Fixed-price menus 25€–30€. MC, V. Wed–Mon noon–2:30pm and 8–11:30pm.

RAGUSA IBLA

Il Barocco SICILIAN   The name comes from the elaborate baroque-style doorway, crafted in the 1600s, that dominates the restaurant's small, high-ceilinged dining room. (In fact, you might get the vivid impression that the restaurant and its open-to-view stainless-steel kitchen are rather uncomfortably crammed into the anteroom of a very grand palazzo or church.) Today, tiles from Caltagirone and wrought iron decorate the interior. Plastic tables and chairs spill onto the pavement in front. Don't confuse this restaurant with a gelateria (ice-cream shop) with the same name and management about a block downhill. Menu items are not as artful or creative as what you'll find at either of Ragusa's more prestigious eateries (Il Duomo and Locanda Don Serafino), and the staff can be blasé, but food items are flavorful and filling. The best examples include filet steak "chateaubriand" for two; a mixed grill of meats or fish; lamb cutlets; and a dessert specialty of orange mousse.

Via Orfanotrofio 29. © **0932-652397.** Reservations recommended. Main courses 5€–11€. AE, DC, MC, V. Thurs–Tues 12:30–2:30pm and 7:30pm–midnight.

Il Duomo ✮✮ SICILIAN   Set on an impossibly narrow street, uphill and about a block behind the cathedral, this is generally considered the finest restaurant in Ibla. Inside, a quintet of small rooms are outfitted like private parlors in a 19th-century country-Victorian style, some with views that sweep over the dry, scrub-covered hillsides of southern Sicily. Come here for the intensely patriotic cuisine of Ciccio Sultana, a native *Ragusano* who commits himself passionately to the perpetuation of old-time Sicilian traditions every evening. Several varieties of bread are baked on-site each day, using old-fashioned, increasingly hard-to-find strains of wheat. (Sultana travels to faraway Caltagirone at least once a week to get them.) Tables and trays display at least 20 types of olive oil in every possible hue of green, gold, or amber, and if you ask for help, a staff member will advise you on which variety is best with which particular bread or platter. Many of the dishes here make ample use of such local products as cherry tomatoes, pistachios, bitter almonds, wild fennel, and mint.

On our most recent visit we were dazzled by *gnocchi farciti al formaggio Ragusano* (gnocchi with a Ragusan cheese, zucchini, cream, and fresh mussels). One of our favorite pastas is *ravioli di sugo di maiale in salsa di ricotta* (ravioli in a tomato sauce and pork served with ricotta). A delectable cutlet of the "black pork" of Nebrodi is stuffed with bread crumbs, cheese, and salami, a savory enticement. Menus are based on the changing seasons.

Via Bocchieri 31. ⓒ **0932-651265.** Reservations recommended. Main courses 9€–17€. Fixed-price menus 40€–45€. AE, DC, MC, V. Tues–Sun noon–2:30pm; Tues–Sat 7–11pm. Closed: Oct 1–15.

La Bettola SICILIAN Old-fashioned and traditional-looking, and a short walk through narrow winding streets from the town's cathedral, this restaurant shows few hints of any changes that might have been made since the days of Mussolini. That, coupled with the 1940s-era decor, provides much of its charm. During clement weather, it arranges tables, chairs, and parasols on a large piazza in front, amid potted flowers and ample doses of old-fashioned Italy. On a recent visit, the chef told us to "leave matters in my hands." His hands turned out to be capable indeed, as our party was treated to a homemade penne with fresh ricotta cheese, followed by a tender, herb-infused chicken breast, delectable roulades stuffed with ham and onions and, as a finale, the catch of the day.

Largo Camerina 7. ⓒ **0932-653377.** Reservations recommended. Main courses 6.20€–7€. MC, V. Mon–Sat 12:30–2:30pm and 7:30–11:30pm.

Locanda Don Serafino ★★★ SICILIAN This is one of the finest restaurants in southern Sicily. It's set in the cellars of a 17th-century palace in a labyrinth of intricately vaulted cellars that were once used for storage. The temperature remains cool in summer and temperate even on the coldest days of winter. Established in 2000, it's a relative newcomer to Ragusa's restaurant scene, but already one that's enormously respected throughout the region. Any of the lavishly decorated tables inside would present a charming venue for lunch or dinner, but the most prestigious, and awe-inspiring, is the venue at the deepest and most distant part of the labyrinth, a monastic-looking stone-sided room lined with wines selected personally by restaurant owner and wine entrepreneur Giuseppe LaRosa. (He tours the great restaurants of New York City every other year for ideas he can bring to Ragusa.) If you dine here, know in advance that film director Berlusconi has already beat you to it, enjoying dishes that include, among others, *zuppe di pesce Don Serafino,* a dish that has flourished in an associated restaurant every year since it was first created in 1953. Swordfish is but one of the delicious main courses, as is ravioli with a porcini mushroom sauce. Every day fresh fish is brought in and cooked to perfection. Other savory main meat courses include herb-and-garlic-infused lamb cutlets.

Via Orfanotrofio 30. ⓒ **0932-248778.** Reservations recommended. Main courses 13€–18€. AE, DC, MC, V. Wed–Mon 12:30–2:30pm and 5:30–11:30pm.

MARINA DI RAGUSA

Eremo della Giubiliana SICILIAN Even if an overnight stay at this previously recommended hotel isn't practical, we heartily recommend it for its fine cuisine, its eerily antique location, and the almost tangible presence of the ghosts of other eras that seem to wander the surrounding fields. The setting is inside a walled compound that originated in the 1400s as a fortified monastery and later evolved into a manorial private home for some very tough and tenacious landowners. Meticulously restored in the 1990s to its full limestone glory by a local architect, and permeated with a discreet poshness, it serves well-prepared meals in a high-ceilinged room whose massive timbers are supported by soaring masonry arches. Lunches are relatively simple, consisting of a medley of omelets, salads, and *focaccia*—artfully crafted sandwiches stuffed with, among other things, smoked or marinated fish, prosciutto, or local cheeses. Dinners are more elaborate, featuring orecchiatta with walnut sauce; roasted quail with spices; couscous; carpaccio of tuna; grilled fish; and very fresh salads usually culled from the hotel's walled-in garden. Come here as much for the sightseeing as for the food, and make an effort, at least, to see the surrounding landscapes in the glare of day.

Contrada Giubiliana. © **0932-669119.** Reservations recommended. Lunch platters 4€–8.50€. Main courses 7.50€–9€. Fixed-price Sun lunch 21€. AE, DC, MC, V. Daily 12:30–2pm and 7:30–10pm.

Ristorante/Pizzeria La Falena *Value* SICILIAN   Short on style but good in the kitchen, this restaurant is a rustic trattoria known for its fresh fish. It also serves tasty pizzas. Attracting a beach-loving crowd, it offers dining inside or out. The food is home-style, and the reception is most welcoming. One gentleman from Tuscany, Ovidio Sgatti, told us he comes here every summer with his family, and that he can personally testify to the authenticity and quality of the food. We quickly agreed with him after sampling pasta with little shrimp and arugula. Our table was also impressed by the tortellini with ham and cream, and especially by the savory rice dish of fresh shrimp, mussels, virgin olive oil, and garlic.

Via Porto Venere. © **0932-239321.** Reservations required Sat–Sun. Main courses 5€–10€. AE, DC, MC, V. Wed–Mon 12:30–2:30pm and 7:30pm–12:30am. Closed Jan.

RAGUSA AFTER DARK
RAGUSA IBLA

Antichi Sapori   This quirky, idiosyncratic bar has a loyal clientele of local clients and occasionally attracts a fun, beer-loving crowd of night owls who appreciate the night air and one another's company. Most customers stand or sit on a stone-floored terrace immediately adjacent to the church of SS Annunziata, a few steps below a busy traffic artery where cars (as you might by now expect in Sicily) drive too fast. The inside is tiny and cramped, and if you approach them wrong, the staff can be defensive and short-tempered. Try to overlook its shortcomings and consider coming here for a *Warsteiner,* and perhaps a dialogue with a local resident. The club is open Friday through Wednesday from 8pm to 2am. Via Orfanotrofio 9. © **0339-1148707.**

Belle Epoque   Set in a tucked-away corner of the square directly in front of the cathedral, this place will welcome you for either daytime gelato or nighttime beer and cocktails. It's owned by an extended family. Ice creams are *artigianale* (homemade) and are likely to include *nocciola* (hazelnut), *pesca* (peach), and *arancia* (orange). Depending on its size, gelato costs from 1.05€ to 2.10€. From July to September, the Belle Epoque is open daily from 7am to 1:30pm. The rest of the year, it's closed on Wednesday. Via Convento, near Piazza Duomo. © **0339-7528402.**

MARINA DI RAGUSA

Charleston Pub   Attracting a more earthy, mature, and sophisticated clientele than the Victoria Pub (see below), this attractive nightspot has a glossy, marble-covered bar top, a hip and attractive staff, and an undeniable sense of fun. A short list of salads and platters is available, priced at between 2.50€ and 10€, but most people come for the beer, the cocktails, and the whiff of bemused glamour that sometimes permeates this place. It's open daily in summer from 7pm to 5am. Between November and March, it's closed every Monday. Lungomare Andrea Doria 4. © **0338-981670.**

Victoria Pub   Set directly across the street from the beach, this is the largest pub in Marina di Ragusa and, thanks to the owner's aggressive policy of collecting pop memorabilia from London and New York/New Jersey, it's one of the most whimsically decorated. The pseudo-Victorian decor includes pithy quotes from William Shakespeare, expired New Jersey license plates, the kind of junk you might find rejected at an auction on the English Riviera, and banners advertising everything from Jack Daniels to Newcastle Ale. The crowd here tends to be young, slightly manic, on the make, and into rock 'n' roll, so if those parameters appeal to you, bop in for a wee dram. Between April and October, the pub is open nightly from 10am to 4am, although between November and March, it's open only on Friday and Sunday from 4pm to 3am, and Saturday from 10am to 4am. Lungomare Andrea Doria 20. ℂ **0339-240-9247.**

2 Piazza Armerina

84km (52 miles) SW of Catania, 181km (113 miles) SW of Messina, 164km (102 miles) SE of Palermo, 103km (64 miles) NW of Ragusa, 134km (84 miles) NW of Syracuse

Art lovers journey from all over Europe and America to see the ruins of an extraordinary Roman villa at Casale (see below), basing themselves in the little town of Piazza Armerina. Once known only as "Piazza," the town gets its name from Colle Armerino, one of a trio of hills on which it was constructed. The town is actually two-in-one: the original "Piazza," a village that dates from the heyday of the Saracens in the 10th century; and a 15th-century "overflow" town that extended to the southeast as early as the 15th century.

Graced with impressive but decaying palazzi (mansions), the town itself is worth a visit for at least an hour or two (see below), although most tour buses rush through here delivering their passengers directly to Villa Romana.

ESSENTIALS

GETTING THERE   One bus a day from Syracuse makes the 3-hour trip for 7.25€ one-way. Seven buses per day leave from Ragusa, our last stopover, making the 3-hour journey at a cost of 5.40€ one-way.

If you're driving from Ragusa, where we launched our inland tour of Sicily, continue north along Route 194 following the signs to the town of Caltagirone. At the town of Vizzini, continue northwest along Route 124 to Caltagirone. From here the road will be signposted northwest all the way to Piazza Armerina.

VISITOR INFORMATION   The **Piazza Armerina tourist office,** Via Cavour (ℂ **0935-680201**), is open Monday through Friday from 8am to 2pm. On Wednesday, it is also open from 3 to 6:30pm.

GETTING AROUND   If you've arrived in Piazza Armerina by bus, you can take yet another bus (no. B) to reach the Roman villa at Casale. **Piccola Società Cooperative** (ℂ **0935-85605**) runs buses daily from 9 to 11am and 4 to 6pm to the site (trip time: 15 min.). A one-way ticket costs 1.50€.

SEEING THE SIGHTS

Piazza Armerina is set on a plateau some 700m (2,297 ft.) above sea level. The city as we see it today was founded during the Norman era, its historic **medieval quarter** ✦ graced with many beautiful churches, the most impressive of which is the Duomo (see below), crowning the highest point in town at 720m (2,364 ft.). Today Piazza Armerina is filled with mansions showing both baroque and Renaissance architectural influences. You're free to wander at will.

Head for the **Duomo,** Via Cavour (© **0935-680214**), which is open daily from 8:30am to noon and 3:30 to 7pm, charging no admission. With its maze of narrow streets, the old town sprouted around this cathedral. The bell tower you see is from 1490, a surviving architectural feature of an even earlier church. The present building was inaugurated in 1627, the facade dating from 1719 and the dome from 1768. The facade is adorned with pilasters and columns, and the grand central door is surmounted by a large, square window topped by an eagle.

The interior is a vision of white and blue and is spacious and filled with light. Among the best-known works of art here is the ***Virgin delle Vittorie*** ⭐, above the main altar at the far end of the nave in a 17th-century tabernacle. It is believed to have been given by Pope Nicholas II to Count Roger, ruler of Sicily. Dating from 1455 is an **impressive wooden cross** ⭐ on view in the small chapel to the left of the chancel. Its back depicts a scene of the Resurrection which has been much reproduced in art books on Sicily.

Villa Romana del Casale ⭐⭐⭐   The Roman mosaics discovered here are celebrated among scholars of antiquity. Lying 6km (3½ miles) from Piazza Armerina, this magnificent villa is one of the largest dwellings of its kind to have survived from the days of the Romans. Its 40 rooms are "carpeted" with 11,340 sq. m (37,800 sq. ft.) of some of the greatest, most magnificent mosaics in western Europe.

It is obvious that a wealthy patrician built this mansion, and some scholars have even suggested that it was the hunting lodge of Maximanus, the "co-emperor" of Diocletian. The exact date of the villa's construction is hard to ascertain, however—perhaps the end of the 3rd century A.D. or the beginning of the 4th century. The complex was destroyed by fire in the 12th century and over the years was buried in mudslides. Parts of the villa were unearthed in 1881.

Many of the mansion's walls are still standing, but most visitors come here to take in the mosaics on the villa's floors and the surviving wall paintings. Many of the scenes depicted in the mosaics are mythological. Since this was a hunting lodge, many of the tableaux involve the pursuit of wild animals. Some of these animals were captured alive and shipped to Rome to entertain spectators at the Colosseum.

Rooms branch out from a central courtyard, or peristyle. Among the discernible rooms still left are the **Terme, or steam baths,** which supplied water and also heated the villa with steam circulating through cavities in the floors and walls. In the **Sala delle Unizioni,** slaves are depicted massaging the bodies of their masters.

The Peristylium, directly east of the peristyle, contains the splendid **Peristylium mosaic** ⭐⭐, which can be viewed on all sides of the portico. It's a romp of birds, plants, wild animals, and more domesticated creatures such as horses.

Adjoining it is the **Salone del Circo** ⭐⭐, the narthex (portico) of the Terme. Its name comes from the scenes of the Roman circus depicted in its mosaics. The chariot race at Rome's Circus Maximus can clearly be seen.

Directly south of the peristyle is the **Sala della Piccola Caccia** ⭐⭐⭐, "The Room of the Small Hunt," with mosaics depicting everything from a sacrifice to the goddess of the hunt, Diana, to the netting of a wild boar.

To the immediate left or west of the peristyle is the **Ambulacro della Grande Caccia** ⭐⭐⭐, "The Corridor of the Great Hunt," measuring 60m (97 ft.). The mosaics discovered here are among the most splendid from the ancient world. One of the most dramatic scenes is of all species of wild animals, ranging from the rhino to the elephant to the antelope, being loaded onto a ship.

In a salon at the northwestern corner of the peristyle is the most amusing room of all: **Sala delle Dieci Ragazze,** or "The Room of the 10 Girls." Wearing strapless two-piece bikinis, the young women are dressed for gymnastic exercises. Their outfits would be appropriate for a beach in the 21st century. The young women are depicted performing such stunts as discus throwing or playing ball.

Directly north of the peristyle is the **Triclinium** ★★★, a large central space that spills into a trio of wide apses. This was probably the dining area, and it's known for its magnificent rendition of the Labors of Hercules. In the central apse the mosaics depict "the Battle of the Giants," five mammoth creatures in their death throes after being attacked by the poisoned arrows of Hercules.

Among the final salons to visit is the **Vestibolo del Piccolo Circo** ★★ or "Vestibule of the Small Circus," depicting circus scenes such as chariot racing; and the **Atrio degli Amorini Pescatori** ★★, with mosaics illustrating fishing scenes.

In conclusion, **Cubicolo della Scene Erotica** ★ features a polygonal medallion depicting a panting young man locked in a tight embrace with a scantily clad seductress. Yes, there is a gratuitous bottom shot.

The site is open daily from 8am to 30 minutes before sunset. Admission costs 4.50€.

WHERE TO STAY

Mosaici da Battiato (see "Where to Dine," below), also rents rooms.

Hotel Ostello del Borgo   This small hotel in the historical center occupies a wing of the ancient monastery of San Giovanni, once filled with Benedictine nuns and dating from the 14th century. It is the most atmospheric place to stay in the area. The owners have kept it up to date, and it's filled with basic comforts, including small to midsize rooms, each well maintained and each equipped with a small tiled bathroom with shower. All the sights, including several restaurants, lie within easy reach of the front door.

Largo San Giovanni 6, 94015 Piazza Armerina. ℂ **0935-687019.** Fax 0935-686943. 20 units. 52€ double. Rates include breakfast. MC, V. **Amenities:** Breakfast room. *In room:* TV, no phone.

Park Hotel Paradiso   This modern hostelry is in the best location for those who want to be close to the main attraction in the area, Villa Romana del Casale, with its fabulous mosaics. Surrounded by a forest, and lying right outside of town, this is a well-kept building. It offers comfortably furnished, midsize guest rooms, each with a tiled bathroom with either shower or hydromassage tub. The hotel also has good on-site dining and drinking facilities so you don't have to wander around Piazza Armerina at night. The location is 1km (½ mile) beyond Chiesa di Sant'Andrea.

Contrada da Ramaldo, 94015 Piazza Armerina. ℂ **0935-680841.** Fax 0935-684908. 56 units. 90€ double; 120€ suite. Rates include breakfast. AE, DC, MC, V. Free parking. **Amenities:** Restaurant; 2 bars; pool; gym; room service; laundry/dry cleaning. *In room:* A/C, TV, minibar, hair dryer.

WHERE TO DINE

Mosaici da Battiato SICILIAN   This classic countryside restaurant lies 3km (1¾ miles) outside Piazza Armerina on the road to Mirabella. Unless a tour group has stopped off here (a frequent occurrence), this is a good place to order some of the best homemade Sicilian dishes in the area. We recently began with a delectable pasta, *pennette dello chef,* made with rich cream, fresh tomatoes, and mushrooms. It was followed by a veal scaloppini also served with fresh mushrooms.

The *rigatoni alla Norma* is another succulent pasta, this one made with eggplant recently harvested in the country along with vine-ripened tomatoes. Most plates of food are reasonably priced except the copious meat platter of grilled specialties—for trenchermen only. The restaurant also rents 24 well-maintained, simply furnished guest rooms, each with a private, shower-only bathroom. A double costs 44€. Built in 1990, the inn is a three-story building west of the center en route to the famous mosaics.

Contrada Casale Ovest. ✆ 0935-685453. Reservations recommended. Main courses 5€–6€. Fixed-price menu 15€. MC, V. Open 24 hrs. Closed Nov 20–Dec 27.

Trattoria La Ruota SICILIAN   This rustic restaurant was created from a defunct water mill. Opt for a table on the open-air terrace. In an atmospheric setting, you are served a typical Sicilian lunch (the only meal offered) evocative of the plains of central Sicily. Everything is homemade, and the food is free of preservatives. "It's good, country cooking," the chef told us, and we concur. We launched our most recent repast with *tagliatelle alla Boscaiola* (pasta with minced beef in a zesty tomato sauce laced with cream, with fresh peas and mushrooms). Another tasty offering was the stewed rabbit with olives, capers, and tomatoes. The chef also specializes in grills, notably herb-flavored pork chops and homemade grilled pork sausages.

Contrada Casale Ovest. ✆ 0935-680542. Reservations recommended. Main courses 4.65€–7.25€. Fixed-price menus 10€–14€. AE, MC, V. Fri–Wed noon–3pm.

12

Agrigento & Selinunte

Two of the great cities of Magna Graecia—or what's left of them—can be explored along Sicily's southern coast. Both **Selinunte** and **Agrigento** knew greater glory than they experience today, but the remains of what they used to be are still relatively rich in spite of the looters and conquerors who have passed through. Of the two, Agrigento is the far greater attraction.

Once known as the Greek city of Akragas, Agrigento has seen many conquerors in its day, from the Romans to the barbarian invasions, followed by the Byzantines and Arabs. The year 1087 saw the arrival of the Normans.

Agrigento's remarkable series of Doric temples from the 5th century B.C. are unrivaled except in Greece itself. All the modern encroachments, especially the hastily built and often illegal new buildings, have seriously dimmed the glory of Agrigento, but much is left to fill us with wonder.

Selinunte, in contrast, was never built over as Agrigento was, and holds extensive remains of the acropolis, though none quite equal the charm of Agrigento's Valley of the Temples.

As you stand in the midst of a carpet of mandrake, acanthus, capers, and celery growing wild at Selinunte, you'll have to work hard to imagine what the city must have looked like at the apex of its power.

1 Agrigento ✶✶✶ & the Valley of the Temples ✶✶✶

129km (80 miles) S of Palermo, 175km (109 miles) SE of Trapani, 217km (135 miles) W of Syracuse

Agrigento's amazing **Valley of the Temples (Valle dei Templi)** is one of the most memorable and evocative sights of the ancient world. Greek colonists from Gela (Caltanissetta) called this area Akragas when they established a beachhead in the 6th century B.C. In time, the settlement grew to become one of the most prosperous cities in Magna Graecia. A great deal of that growth is attributed to the despot Phalaris, who ruled from 571 to 555 B.C. and is said to have roasted his victims inside a brass bull. He eventually met the same fate.

Empedocles (ca. 490–430 B.C.), the Greek philosopher and politician (also considered by some the founder of medicine in Italy), was the most famous son of Akragas. He formulated the theory that matter consists of four elements (earth, fire, water, and air), modified by the agents of love and strife. In modern times the town produced playwright **Luigi Pirandello** (1867–1936), who won the Nobel Prize for Literature in 1934.

Like nearby Selinunte, the city was attacked by war-waging Carthaginians, beginning in 406 B.C. In the 3rd century B.C., the city changed hands between the Carthaginians and the Romans until it finally succumbed to Roman domination by 210 B.C. It was then known as Agrigentium.

The modern part of Agrigento occupies a hill, and the narrow casbah-like streets show the influence of the conquering Saracens. Heavy Allied bombing during World War II necessitated much rebuilding. The result is, for the most part, uninspired and not helped by all the cement factories in the area. But below the town stretch the long reaches of the Valley of the Temples (Valle dei Templi), where you'll see some of the greatest Greek ruins in the world.

Visit Agrigento for its past, not for the modern incarnation. However, once you've been awed by the ruined temples, you can explore the *centro storico,* with its tourist boutiques hawking postcards and T-shirts, and enjoy people-watching at a cafe along Via Atenea. When it gets too hot (as it so often does), flee to a beach at nearby **San Leone.**

ESSENTIALS

GETTING THERE   The **train** trip from Palermo takes 1½ hours and costs 7€ one-way. There are 11 trains daily. The main rail station, **Stazione Centrale,** Piazza Marconi (② **892021**), is downhill from Piazzale Aldo Moro and Piazza Vittorio Emanuele. From Syracuse by rail, you must first take one of nine daily trains to Ragusa; the 2½-hour trip costs 6.50€ one-way. Three trains a day make the 3½-hour trip from Ragusa to Agrigento at a cost of 8.50€ one-way.

Interbus (② **0922-596490**) runs four **buses** per day from Palermo, the trip taking 2 hours and costing 6.70€ one-way. The company also has service from Syracuse, the trip taking 5 hours and costing 14€ one-way.

By **car** from Syracuse, take SS115 through Gela. From Palermo, cut southeast along S121, which becomes S188 and S189 before it finally reaches Agrigento and the Mediterranean. Allow about 2½ hours for this jaunt.

VISITOR INFORMATION   The **tourist offices** are at Via Cesare Battisti 15 (② **0922-20454**) and at Via Empedocle 73 (② **0922-20391**). Both are open Monday through Friday from 8am to 2pm.

SPECIAL EVENTS   The **Settimana Pirandelliana** is a week-long festival of plays, operas, and ballets staged in Piazza Kaos at the end of July and August. The tourist office (② **0922-20454**) can supply details; tickets cost 7.50€ to 15€.

GETTING AROUND   Agrigento is serviced by a network of orange **TUA buses** (② **0922-412024**). A ticket selling for .80€ is valid for 1½ hours. Bus no. 2 or 2/ runs to the beach at San Leone, where you'll find hotels and restaurants (see our recommendations below). Bus nos. 1, 2, and 2/ make frequent runs to the Valley of the Temples, and bus no. 11 goes to Pirandello's House.

For **taxi service** in Agrigento, call ② **0922-21899** or 0922-26670.

FAST FACTS   The **Ospedale Civile,** San Giovanni XXII (② **0922-492111**), services the greater area. The most central drugstore is **Farmacia Averna Antonio,** Via Atenea (② **0922-26093**), open daily from 9am to 1:30pm and 5 to 8:30pm. For Internet access, go to **Libreria Multimediale,** Via Celauro 7 (② **0922-408562**), off Via Atenea, 2 blocks from Piazza Moro. It's open Monday through Saturday from 9am to 1pm and 4:30 to 8:30pm, charging 3.10€ per hour. The **post office** is at Piazza Vittorio Emanuele (② **0922-551111**), open Monday through Friday from 8:10am to 6:30pm and Saturday from 8:10am to 1:20pm. In an **emergency,** call ② **113** or the *Carabinieri* at ② **0922-596322.**

WANDERING AMONG THE RUINS

Many writers are fond of suggesting that the Greek ruins in the **Valley of the Temples (Valle dei Templi)** be viewed at dawn or sunset, when their mysterious aura is indeed heightened. Regrettably, you can't get very close at those times. Instead, search them out under the cobalt-blue Sicilian sky. The backdrop is idyllic, especially in spring, when the striking almond trees blossom into pink.

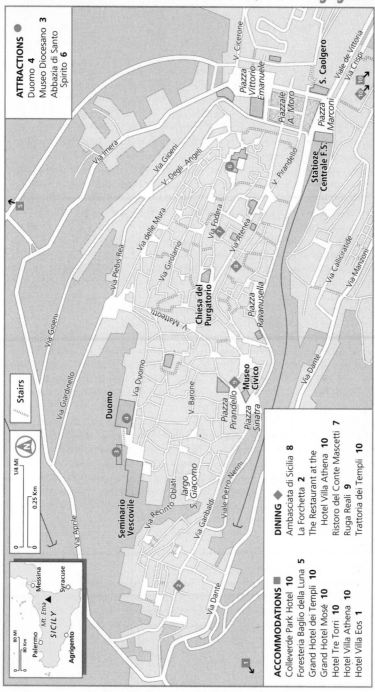

Agrigento

ATTRACTIONS ●
Duomo **4**
Museo Diocesano **3**
Abbazia di Santo
Spirito **6**

ACCOMMODATIONS ■
Colleverde Park Hotel **10**
Foresteria Baglio della Luna **5**
Grand Hotel dei Templi **10**
Grand Hotel Mosé **10**
Hotel Tre Torri **10**
Hotel Villa Athena **10**
Hotel Villa Eos **1**

DINING ◆
Ambasciata di Sicilia **8**
La Forchetta **2**
The Restaurant at the
Hotel Villa Athena **10**
Ristoro del Conte Mascetti **7**
Ruga Reali **9**
Trattoria dei Templi **10**

Stairs

0   1/4 Mi
0   0.25 Km

SICILY
Palermo
Mt. Etna
Messina
Syracuse
Agrigento
0   80 Mi
0   80 Km

Via Cicerone
V. Cicerone
Piazza Vittorio Emanuele
Piazzale A. Moro
Piazzale Marconi
S. Caolgero
Viale de Vittoria
V. Crispi
Stazioze Centrale F.S.
Via Imera
Via Gioeni
Via Degli Angeli
V. Prandello
V. Prandello
Via Fodera
Via Artenea
Via Callicratide
Via Manzoni
Via delle Mura
Via Plebis Rea
Via Girolamo
Piazza Ravanusella
Via Dante
Chiesa del Purgatorio
V. Matteotti
Via Gioeni
Via Gioeni
Via Giardinello
Via Duomo
Duomo
V. Barone
Museo Civico
Piazza Sinatra
Piazza Prandello
Seminario Vescovile
Via Recinto Oblati
Largo S. Giacomo
Via Garibaldi
Viale Pietro Nenni
Via Aprile
Via Dante

283

Ticket booths are found at the west and east entrances (© **0922-497341**); tickets cost 4.50€ for adults, 2€ for children under 16. Hours are Sunday and Monday from 9am to 1:30pm, Tuesday through Saturday from 9am to 1:30pm and 2 to 7:30pm.

Board a bus or climb into your car to investigate. Riding out the Strada Panoramica, you first approach (on your left) the **Temple of Juno (Tempio di Giunone)** ★★, erected sometime in the mid-5th century B.C., at the peak of a construction boom honoring the deities. Many of its Doric columns have been restored. As you climb the blocks, note the remains of a cistern as well as a sacrificial altar in front. The temple affords good views of the entire valley.

Temple of Concord (Tempio della Concordia) ★★★, which you'll come to next, ranks with the Temple of Hephaestos in Athens as the best-preserved Greek temple in the world. With 13 columns on its side, six in front, and six in back, the temple was built in the peripheral hexastyle. You'll see the clearest example in Sicily of an inner temple. In the late 6th century A.D., the pagan structure was transformed into a Christian church, which might have saved it for posterity, although today it's been stripped down to its classical purity.

Temple of Hercules (Tempio di Ercole) ★★ is the oldest, dating from the 6th century B.C. Badly ruined (only eight pillars are standing), it once ranked in size with the Temple of Zeus. At one time the temple sheltered a celebrated statue of Hercules. The infamous Gaius Verres, the Roman magistrate who became an especially bad governor of Sicily, attempted to steal the image as part of his temple-looting tear across the island. Astonishingly, you can still see black sears from fires set by long-ago Carthaginian invaders.

Temple of Jove or Zeus (Tempio di Giove) ★ was the largest in the valley, similar in some respects to the Temple of Apollo at Selinunte, until it was ruined by an earthquake. It even impressed Goethe. In front of the structure was a large altar. The giant on the ground was one of several telamones (male caryatids) used to support the largest Greek temple in the world and one of the most remarkable.

The so-called **Temple of Castor and Pollux (Tempio di Dioscuri),** with four Doric columns intact, is composed of fragments from different buildings. At various times it has been designated as a temple honoring Castor and Pollux, the twin sons of Leda and deities of seafarers; Demeter (Ceres), the goddess of marriage and of the fertile earth; or Persephone, the daughter of Zeus and the symbol of spring. *Note:* On some maps, this is called Tempio di Castore e Polluce.

The temples can usually be visited daily from 9am until 1 hour before sunset. City bus nos. 8, 9, 10, and 11 run to the valley from the train station in Agrigento.

MORE ATTRACTIONS

The **Museo Regionale Archeologico (Regional Archaeological Museum)** ★, near San Nicola, on Contrada San Nicola at the outskirts of town on the way to the Valle dei Templi (© **0922-401565**), is open daily from 9am to 7:30pm. Admission is 4.50€. Its most important exhibit is a head of one of the telamones (male caryatids) from the Tempio di Giove. The collection of Greek vases is also impressive. Many of the artifacts on display were dug up when Agrigento was excavated. Take bus no. 8, 9, 10, or 11.

Casa di Pirandello (Pirandello's House), Contrada Caos, Frazione Caos (© **0922-511102**), is the former home of the 1934 Nobel Prize winner, known worldwide for his plays *Six Characters in Search of an Author* and *Enrico IV.* He

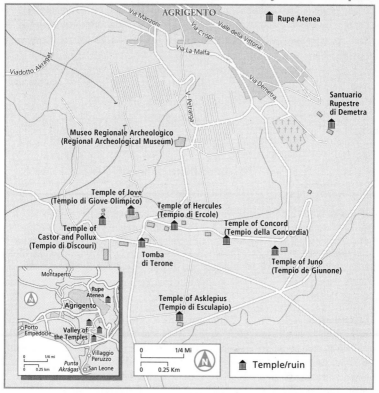

died 2 years after winning the prize and its attendant world acclaim. Although Agrigentans back then might not have liked his portrayal of Italy, all is forgiven now, and Pirandello is the local boy who made good. In fact, the Teatro Luigi Pirandello at Piazza Municipio bears his name. His *casa natale* is now a museum devoted to memorabilia pertaining to the playwright's life. His tomb lies under his favorite pine tree ("One night in June I dropped down like a firefly beneath a huge pine tree in the garden"). The tomb lies a few hundred yards from the house and grounds, which are open Monday through Saturday from 8:30am to 1pm and 4 to 7pm. Admission is 2.50€. The birthplace lies outside of town in the village of Caos (catch bus no. 11 from Piazza Marconi), just west of the temple zone.

THE CHURCHES OF AGRIGENTO

Abbazia di Santo Spirito ★ There is one good reason to venture into the tacky modern city itself. Although this 13th-century church is rotting away, it is still a worthy goal, as you'll realize when you stand at its impressive Gothic entrance surmounted by a rose window. The single nave is adorned with a baroque interior of fantastic stucco work with **four high reliefs** ★ believed to have been created by Giacomo Serpotta. The scenes depict *The Adoration of the Magi, The Nativity, The Presentation of Christ at the Temple,* and *The Flight into Egypt.* Take the exit to the right of the facade to look at the cloisters. Here you'll note a **lovely entrance** ★ into the chapter house, lined with Gothic arcades. A handsome doorway leads through a pointed arch. On each side are elaborate windows in the Arabo-Norman style. The nuns in the adjoining convent still sell a sweet confection called *kus-kus,* composed of chocolate and pistachio nuts.

Via Porcello at Via Santa Spirito. (€) 0922-20664. Free admission. Tues–Sat 9am–1pm and 4–7pm; Sun 9am–1pm. No bus.

Duomo ✪   Founded in the 12th century, the cathedral of Agrigento has faced rough times. There are still remnants from the early Norman days, particularly the windows, but most of the church was reconstructed in the 13th and 14th centuries. It was vastly restored in the 17th century, and later rejuvenated from the effects of a landslide in 1966. The bell tower or campanile is graced with a series of Catalan Gothic single lancet windows. The tower is from 1470 but it was never completed, which gives the cathedral a strange, disturbing look, as if it were the victim of a windstorm. The **beautiful interior** ✪ rests under an **impressive wooden ceiling** ✪, the tie beams adorned with scenes from the lives of various saints. This work was carried out in the 16th century. The Duomo itself is dedicated to a Norman, San Gerlando, the town's first archbishop. His tomb is set in the right wing of the transept. Guides are fond of positioning you under the apse, where you can clearly hear even the whispers of people at the other end of the nave 80m (262 ft.) away. Standing in odd contrast to the rather somber chapels is the choir, a baroque romp of angelic angels and golden garlands.

Piazza Don Minzoni, off Via del Duomo. (€) 0922-27595. Free admission. Tues–Sun 10am–1pm and 4–6pm. No bus.

SHOPPING

We recently found some great buys at **Castello,** Via Atenea 44 ((€) 0922-21769). Come here for stylish Italian-designed men's shirts, available in a wide array of patterns ranging from vivid paisleys to subdued all-whites, grays, or blues. Shirts cost from 25€ to 50€ each, and are distributed by a nationwide chain with boutique-style branches in at least 35 other cities.

WHERE TO STAY
VERY EXPENSIVE

Foresteria Baglio della Luna ✪✪ *Finds*   In 1995, one of the most historic medieval sites in Agrigento was richly and meticulously restored by a local antiques dealer, Dr. Ignazio Altieri. The country inn that resulted has housed some of the most glamorous names in European media, members who appreciate its isolation from the crowds and its stylish ways. The first impression you'll get is of a squarish medieval tower, ringed with a protective wall, in a well-landscaped compound that rises above a dusty landscape west of Agrigento. Originating in the 1200s as a watchtower, then rebuilt in the 1500s by Emperor Charles V, it eventually evolved into an aristocratic manor house that controlled hundreds of acres of the surrounding fields and orchards. In the 19th century even Viollet-le-Duc, the world-famous French architect who restored the cathedral of Paris, took a hand in its restoration. From the dusty, sun-blasted landscape outside, you enter an immaculately maintained cobble-covered courtyard, off of which lie the midsize, stylishly decorated rooms. Each evokes a romantic lodging in an upscale private home, and many have antique headboards, blue tilework, flowered upholsteries, and marble-clad bathrooms with showers and tubs. Some have faraway views of Agrigento's Greek temples. Villa Athena (see below) may have a closer view of the temples, but this hotel far surpasses it in charm and hospitality. To miss the experience of dining in the hotel's restaurant, **Ristorante Il Dehor**—the very best in this part of Sicily—would be unfortunate.

Note: Unless they've been allowed by local zoning restrictions to add bigger signs, the place is hard to spot from the SS640. Look for the squarish medieval tower on the northern edge of the SS640, about 4.8km (3 miles) west of Agrigento, and turn off at the exit marked SPIAGGIA DI MADDALUSA.

Contrada Maddalusa (S.S. 640), Valle dei Templi, 92100 Agrigento. ℰ **0922-511061.** Fax 0922-598802. www.jpmoser.com/foresteriabagliodellaluna.html. 24 units. 243€–295€ double; 346€–501€ suite. Half board 45€ extra per person. AE, DC, MC, V. Bus: 1 or 3. **Amenities:** 2 restaurants; room service; babysitting; laundry/dry cleaning. *In room:* A/C, TV, minibar, hair dryer.

EXPENSIVE

Hotel Villa Athena ★ *Overrated*   This 18th-century villa rises from the landscape in the Valley of the Temples, less than 3km (2 miles) from town. It's worn and overpriced and in dire need of an overhaul, but its location at the archaeological site is so dramatic we like to lodge here anyway, if only to see the ruins lit up at night from our hotel room. The guest rooms are clean, with little style, and the tiled bathrooms have shower-tub combinations and aging but still functioning plumbing. Ask for a room with a view of the temple, preferably one with a balcony. The perfect choice would be no. 205, which frames a panorama of the Temple of Concord. During the day, guests sit in the paved courtyard, enjoying drinks and the fresh breezes. Even if you're not staying here, try to walk through the garden at night for an amazing view of the lit temple. You can also park here during the day and take a 10-minute walk along a trail to the temples.

Frankly, this could be a great hotel but it needs a major overhaul. The staff is known for being the unfriendliest in Agrigento, yet the setting is so compelling that there are those of us who can overlook both drawbacks. At any rate, it remains the most popular and most famous hotel in Agrigento—be sure to reserve at least a month in advance—although celebrities now check in elsewhere. In its heyday, you could see such "golden age" Italian stars as Sophia Loren and Marcello Mastroianni checking in, even the president of Italy. Because of its incomparable location and because of its drawbacks, this is the only hotel in this guide that rates both a star and an overrated icon.

Via Passeggiata Archeologica 33, 92100 Agrigento. ℰ **0922-596288.** Fax 0922-402180. 40 units. 207€ double. Rates include breakfast. AE, DC, MC, V. Free parking. Bus: 2 or 2/. **Amenities:** Dining room, 2 bars; pool; room service; laundry/dry cleaning. *In room:* A/C, TV, minibar.

MODERATE

Colleverde Park Hotel ★★   Sheathed in a layer of ocher-colored stucco, this is one of our favorite hotels in Agrigento, partly because of its large and verdant garden, partly because of its polite and helpful staff, and partly because of a location that's convenient to both the ancient and medieval monuments of Agrigento. Renovated in 1992, it has the finest hotel garden in town, a labyrinth of vine-covered arbors and terra-cotta terraces with views of the faraway Greek temples, and enormous sheets of white canvas stretched overhead as protection from the glaring sun. The hotel's eminently tasteful glass-sided restaurant is the site of many local wedding receptions. The decor throughout the hotel is discreetly elegant and upscale, providing a genuine refuge from the hysteria that sometimes permeates Agrigento, particularly its roaring traffic. Guest rooms have white tiled bathrooms (all with shower-tub combinations), lots of exposed wood, charming artwork, and big windows that in some cases reveal views of the temples of Concordia and Juno.

Via Panoramica dei Templi, 92100 Agrigento. ℰ **0922-29555.** Fax 0922-29012. www.colleverdehotel.com. 48 units. 129€–145€ double. Rates include breakfast. AE, DC, MC, V. Free parking. Bus: 1, 2, or 3. **Amenities:** Restaurant; bar; laundry/dry cleaning. *In room:* A/C, TV, minibar, safe.

Grand Hotel dei Templi ★ Don't confuse this relatively sedate and conservative government-rated four-star hotel, which was originally built as a member of the upscale Jolly Hotel chain, with the more radical-looking three-star Grand Hotel Mosé next door. Originally built in an airy, high-ceilinged style in the mid-1970s, it's dignified and a lot more restrained, with less of a "let's party with *or* without the kids" motif, than what you'll find next door. There's a swimming pool surrounded by a wall on the premises, a tactful and reserved staff, and guest rooms that are contemporary-looking and comfortable—simple to the point of being a touch banal. Each unit comes with a small private bathroom with shower and tub. Public areas—large, high-ceilinged, and extremely tasteful—evoke the best design standards of *la dolce vita* years.

Via Leonardo Sciascia, Villaggio Mosé, 92100 Agrigento. ⓒ 0922-610175. Fax 0922-606685. www.itali-aabc.it/az/ghdeitempli. 146 units. 155€ double. Rates include breakfast. AE, DC, MC, V. Free parking. Bus 3/. **Amenities:** 2 restaurants; bar; outdoor pool; room service; babysitting. *In room:* A/C, TV, minibar.

INEXPENSIVE

Grand Hotel Mosé ★★ This government-rated three-star hotel (not to be confused with the more formal four-star Grand Hotel immediately next door) is a well-designed architectural oddity that evokes a touch of Las Vegas—or at least the way that the Nevada resorts might have reinvented Agrigento's Valley of the Temples. It sits beside the main traffic artery of Mosé Villaggio, a modern suburb stretching to the north of medieval Agrigento. Sheathed in stucco with the same honey tones of the sandstone used to build the Valley of the Temples, it's theme-ish and imaginative, with a highly responsive staff and a bubbly kind of zest that can be a lot of fun. Guest rooms are simple and stripped down—tasteful, colorful, and slightly spartan-looking, like something you might expect in a Club Med. Most of the units have tiled floors, wrought-iron headboards, and touches of manorial Sicilian flair. The most dramatic are the units on the hotel's rooftop, which are designed on the outside like mud-walled huts in a North African casbah, and which inside evoke a simple officer's barracks on the edge of the Sahara. Each unit comes with a tiled bathroom with shower. The oval, free-form pool is one of the best and most appealing in Agrigento—an azure oasis that artfully sets off the terra-cotta tiles and honey-colored stucco of the rest of the hotel.

Viale Leonardo Sciascia, Villaggio Mosé, 92100 Agrigento. ⓒ 0922-608388. Fax 0922-608377. www.jas hotels.com. 99€–118€ double. Rates include breakfast. AE, DC, MC, V. Free parking. Bus: 3/. **Amenities:** Restaurant; bar; pool; boutiques; babysitting; laundry/dry cleaning. *In room:* A/C, TV, minibar.

Hotel Tre Torri Though it's near an unattractive commercial district 7km (4½ miles) south of Agrigento, this is among the area's busiest hotels. Behind a mock-medieval facade of white stucco, chiseled stone blocks, false crenellations, and crisscrossed iron balconies, Tre Torri is a favorite with Italian business travelers. The small guest rooms are comfortable, with modern furnishings and compact tiled bathrooms with shower units.

Strada Statale 115, Viale Canatello, Villaggio Mosè, 92100 Agrigento. ⓒ 0922-606733. Fax 0922-607839. www.mediatel.it/public/tre-torri. 118 units. 104€ double. Rates include breakfast. AE, DC, MC, V. Free parking. Bus: 3. **Amenities:** 4 restaurants; 3 bars; nightclub; 2 pools; fitness center; sauna; room service; laundry/dry cleaning. *In room:* A/C, TV, hair dryer.

Hotel Villa Eos ★ √Value Small and personalized, but isolated in a barren stretch of land between the SS640 and the sea about 4.8km (3 miles) southwest of Agrigento, this hotel evokes a rambling, contemporary-looking private home, thanks partly to its well-meaning staff and small scale. Named after Eos, the deity responsible for the arrival of dawn, it sits in an oasis of greenery with views over the sea. Its clientele generally opts to bathe in the hotel swimming pool rather than head for the beaches, all of which require a taxi or bus ride. Rooms are simple, modest, and comfortably furnished. Some, but not all, have mini-bars. Although each unit contains a small, tiled bathroom, only one bathroom comes with a tub; the rest contain showers. If you happen to come from New York, check out the business cards and commemorative banners decorating the reception area: Many represent high schools, politicians, and church groups in the New York area, particularly Staten Island, which sends some of its residents here every year on holiday. Frankly, the hotel is best for visitors with cars—its isolated position and small scale may guarantee peace and quiet, but the location is something of an inconvenience if you want to avail yourself of the area's many nearby attractions and dining options.

Contrada Cumbo, Villaggio Pirandello. ℰ **0922-597170.** Fax 0922-597188. 10 units. 90€–104€ double. Rates include breakfast. Free parking. AE, DC, MC, V. Bus: 1. **Amenities:** Restaurant; bar; pool; tennis court; babysitting; laundry/dry cleaning. In room: A/C, TV.

AT THE BEACH RESORT OF SAN LEONE

Dioscuri Bay Palace ★★   The setting is more lavish than those of many nearby competitors, and this is a good choice if you want to be housed in comparative luxury close to Agrigento's beachfront. A member of Sicily's well-recommended Framon chain, this modern hotel rises three floors above a small bay at the northwestern tip of the seaside boardwalks of Agrigento's waterfront resort of San Leone. Rooms are contemporary and comfortable, with tiled bathrooms and shower-tub combinations.

Lungomare Falcone e Borsellino 1, 92100 San Leone (Agrigento). ℰ **0922-406111.** Fax 0922-411297. www.framon-hotels.it. 102 units. 170€ double; 211€ suite. Rates include breakfast. AE, DC, MC, V. Bus: 2 or 2/. **Amenities:** 2 restaurants; 2 bars; outdoor pool; Jacuzzi; car-rental desk; room service; babysitting; laundromat; pharmacy. In room: A/C, TV, hair dryer, safe.

Hotel Akragas   This is one of the most appealing budget-priced hotels of San Leone. Boxy-looking, it sits on the busy main road leading from Agrigento into San Leone, a brisk ¾-mile walk from the beachfront. It isn't particularly near the water, and other than its restaurant, it has very few amenities, but in light of its reasonable prices, no one seems to care. It originated in the early 1950s and was completely rebuilt in the 1990s. Expect a pleasant place that's completely unpretentious, family-friendly, and conducive to low-key holidays near the beach. Rooms are spartan, clean, and comfortable, with small tiled bathrooms with showers but no bathtubs. The restaurant here is substantial, and some guests take all their meals on-site. Set-price menus cost 28€ per person.

Viale Emporium 16–18, 92100 San Leone (Agrigento). ℰ **0922-414082.** Fax 0922-414262. hotelakragas@cibero.it. 12 units. Sept–July 68€ double. Rate includes breakfast. In Aug, half board required at 100€ double, with breakfast and either lunch or dinner. AE, DC, MC, V. Free parking. Bus: 2 or 2/. **Amenities:** Restaurant. In room: A/C, TV.

WHERE TO DINE

Ambasciata di Sicilia ★ SICILIAN   This restaurant has been a city staple since the end of World War I, when a local family decided to celebrate the cuisine and color of their native Sicily in the form of this intensely vernacular trattoria. Today, the owner is Rosalba Schembri, who perpetuates the local color in a cramped setting accented with panels from antique donkey carts, boldly frescoed ceiling beams, and marionettes salvaged from some long-ago street performance. When the weather's nice, the preferred seats are outside on four separate dining platforms built with planks and stout timbers on the steeply sloping alleyway. (Some clients have commented that the flocks of birds that fly over the city rooftops far below are among the most soothing and mystical sights in Agrigento.) Menu items are based on the cuisine of the 19th century. Stellar examples include beef roulades with two kinds of cheese; an excellent sampling of antipasti *(antipasti rustico);* and linguine *al'Ambasciata* (prepared with meat sauce, bacon, calamari, and zucchini).

Via Gianbertoni 2, off Via Atenea. (C) 0922-20526. Reservations not required. Main course 5.50€–16€. AE, MC, V. Sept–July Tues–Sun 12:30–3:30pm and 7–11:30pm. Daily in Aug (same hours). Closed 2 weeks in Nov.

La Forchetta SICILIAN/AGRIGENTESE   This pleasant and unpretentious restaurant sits directly on the piazza in front of the golden sandstone facade of the Chiesa San Francesco (ca. 1788), 1 block down a steep flight of stairs from the town's main pedestrian thoroughfare, Via Atenea. In clement weather, tables are strewn across the square in front, but whenever it rains or gets cold, dining is limited to only 10 tables that completely fill a modest, pine-sheathed room decorated with grainy-looking photographs of Agrigento around 1911. Prices are low, portions are generous, and the cuisine focuses on the kind of two-fisted agrarian specialties that have fed many generations of field and construction workers. Hearty examples include roasted lamb, roasted sausage, at least six different kinds of fresh fish, pasta with swordfish and herbs, and pan-fried pork cutlets. Even better than the pork is a *cotolette si agnello arrosto* (tasty, herb-flavored—with lots of garlic—roasted lamb chops). Any of these can be accompanied by a local wine. All buses coming into town stop nearby, as La Forchetta is in front of the bus depot.

Piazza San Francesco 11. (C) **0922-596266.** Reservations recommended Fri and Sat nights. Main courses 5.25€–6.50€. AE, MC, V. Mon–Sat 1–3:30pm and 7pm–midnight.

The Restaurant at the Hotel Villa Athena CONTINENTAL   The formally dressed staff here tends to be brusque, despite a long tradition of welcoming visitors from far away. But the site can be so magical, at least for first-timers to Agrigento, that a midsummer dinner on its outdoor terrace can be an unforgettable experience unaffected by food, staff, weather, or circumstances. If you opt for lunch here, it will be served in a crescent-shaped stone-and-stucco building whose curtains are usually closed against the noon-day glare. But it's at dinner that the true magic emerges, especially in midsummer, when reservations are required: Views sweep from the torch-lit, flower-dotted terrace to the nearby Temple of Concordia (which literally looms before you) in ways unmatched by any other restaurant or hotel in Agrigento. In fact, whenever the city of Agrigento wants to impress representatives from the Italian Parliament or the world of Italian fashion, the dinner that's held to celebrate their arrival is invariably conducted at this restaurant.

Chefs here are far superior to the waitstaff. Begin, perhaps, with a duet of smoked salmon and swordfish or else a fresh, well-flavored shellfish salad. The chef's special risotto for some odd reason is called "mother-of-pearl" and is made with pumpkin flowers, lobster, zucchini, and vodka. Every day a fresh catch from the sea is brought in—we are especially fond of the filet of sea bass flavored with saffron. Tasty grilled meats are flavored aromatically with herbs. A "fantasy" of ice creams and sherbets is served to end the repast.

Via Passeggiata Archeologica 33. (C) 0922-596288. Reservations required. Main courses 9€–18€. AE, DC, MC, V. Daily 12:30–2:30pm lunch; 7:30–9:30pm dinner (till 10pm June–Sept). Bus: 2 or 2/.

Ristoro del Conte Mascetti ☆ *Finds* SICILIAN   Much of the charm of this unusual restaurant comes from its location on a very old mini-piazza, about a block steeply uphill from the Via Atenea, in the heart of medieval Agrigento. In winter, tables are hauled inside into what was built about 250 years ago as a stable for cows and horses, now romantically illuminated with candles and scented with dried bundles of Mediterranean herbs. Part of the fun of a meal here involves finding it: Look for Via Bentivagna, which leads uphill from a point directly opposite Via Atenea 141. (The grotesque carvings on the doorway at Via Bentivagna no. 3, visible during your uphill trek, might make you smile.) You'll appreciate the cuisine of co-owners Sonia Messina and Ilphonso Indelicato. They concoct a wonderful homemade tortellini stuffed with fish and eggplant, and excel in fettuccine with shrimp in a mint sauce. The filet of beef is grilled "down Argentine way," and a swordfish caught in the Straits of Messina comes with capers. The catch of the day might be a whitefish cooked with fresh tomatoes and onions and seasoned with fresh oregano.

Vicolo Lo Presti 19. ⓒ 0922-24600. Reservations not necessary. Main courses 7.25€–15€. AE, MC, V. Mon–Sat 1–2:30pm and 7pm–midnight. Closed 10 days in Sept. Bus: 1, 4, 5, or 6.

Ruga Reali SICILIAN   Tables here spill onto one of Agrigento's most beautiful squares, high in the medieval center's upper zones, a short walk downhill from the cathedral, where there aren't a lot of other restaurants. We usually prefer the outdoor terrace here, but if it's cold, rainy, or unbearably hot, descend into one of the nearby cellars, built in the 1400s as a stable, where other tables await. Dishes are flavorful, well-prepared, and appetizing, and include pasta with squid ink and shrimp; veal piccata with Marsala; sausage with lemon juice and pistachios; and steamed calamari with green peas. The restaurant's name comes from the district of medieval houses, stables, and palazzi (the Ruga district).

Piazza Pirandello (Piazza Municipio), Cortile Scribani 8. ⓒ 0922-20370. Reservations not required. Main courses 6.50€–12€. Set-price menu 13€. AE, DC, MC, V. Thurs, Fri, and Sun–Tues noon–3pm; Thurs–Tues 8pm–1am. Daily for lunch and dinner mid-July to Aug.

Trattoria dei Templi ☆ SICILIAN   Charming, discreet, and extremely well-managed, this restaurant sits at the bottom of the hill between medieval Agrigento and the Valley of the Temples. Inside, you'll find brick-trimmed ceiling vaults over tile-covered floors, a polite crowd of diners from virtually everywhere in Europe, and excellent food that's served on hand-painted china emblazoned with the restaurant's name. Menu items, served with efficiency by a staff of young, well-trained waiters, include *cavatelli valle dei Templi tipa Norma* (pasta with eggplant and cheese); *panzerotti della casa* (big ravioli stuffed with whitefish and served with a seafood sauce); fettuccine *alla' gramaglia* (with swordfish, eggplant, and tomato sauce); and local fish with Sicilian herbs, white wine, lemon juice, capers, olives, and orange zest.

Via Panoramica dei Templi 15. ⓒ 0922-403110. Reservations recommended. Main courses 10€–16€. AE, DC, MC, V. Daily 12:30–3pm and 7:30–11pm. Closed Sun July–Aug and Fri Sept–June. Bus: 1, 2, or 3.

AT THE BEACH RESORT OF SAN LEONE

Il Pescatore ☆   Set directly on the waterfront of Agrigento's beach resort of San Leone, this is the most famous of the 10 or so restaurants that flank it on either side. It's noted for its skillful preparations of fish, and also for a rough-and-tumble staff whose brusqueness is legendary but which, almost perversely, has added to the restaurant's fame. (In other words, if your feelings get hurt by the staff, you won't be alone: Every hotel concierge in Agrigento knows about the rudeness of the staff here and has learned, over the years, to recommend it only to clients they think are thick-skinned or savvy enough to handle it!) The restaurant's interior is more beautiful than you might expect, thanks to its division into four separate dining rooms, each capped with high, sometimes beamed ceilings and flanked with Romanesque-style columns and capitals salvaged from older, perhaps early medieval, buildings. The owners, movers, and shakers at this place are the Sicily-born brothers Pasquale and Salvatore Matracia, who are far, far from being shy about expressing their opinions or emphasizing the culinary honors they've won for their fish preparations. Spaghetti with baby clams is always a smooth lead-in to a meal here, as is the *zuppa di cozze* (a kettle of fresh mussels). Homemade bucatini comes with fresh sardines whipped into the pasta, and sole meunière is featured regularly.

Lungomare Falcone e Borsellino, San Leone. ⓒ 0922-414342. Reservations recommended. Main courses 10€–13€. AE, DC, MC, V. Tues–Sun 12:30–3:30pm and 7:30–11:30pm. Bus: 2 or 2/.

Leon d'Oro SICILIAN/FISH   Set in a cement-sided modern building that originated as a garage and car-repair shop, this restaurant is uncomfortably close to the busy boulevard that funnels most of the traffic from Agrigento into the beach resort of San Leone. Undistinguished-looking by day, it reveals a festive-looking interior that's one of the most respected restaurants in town. Signs on the front offer promises that the restaurant and its staff are fully capable of offering: *IL PESCE, IL VINO, LA SICILIA.* Expect savory dishes based on time-tested recipes often handed down from the chefs' mothers, who in turn learned these recipes from their own mothers. Our favorite dish here is *rotolini Emporium* (pasta with shrimp, tomatoes, fresh vegetables, and a pecorino cheese sauce). An unusual meat dish is the filet of beef served with a carob pesto flavored with fresh herbs.

Via Emporium 102, San Leone. ⓒ 0922-414400. Reservations recommended. Main courses 6€–13€. AE, DC, MC, V. Tues–Sun 12:30–3:30pm and 7:45–11:30pm. Closed 2 weeks in Nov (annual variations). Bus: 2 or 2/.

Ristorante Il Dehor ⭐⭐⭐ SICILIAN/INTERNATIONAL   Set within the thick medieval walls of the Foresteria Baglio della Luna Hotel (see earlier in this chapter), 5km (3 miles) west of Agrigento, this is the finest restaurant in Agrigento, and one of the six best in all of Sicily. Its excellence is the work of chef Damiano Ferraro, an Agrigento-born, London-educated culinary genius who has reinvented aspects of traditional Sicilian cuisine in ways that elicit rave reviews from discerning diners from throughout Europe. Of the three separate dining areas, one is an outdoor terrace. The other two (for summer and winter, respectively) are ringed with important 19th-century paintings and tapestries acquired by the hotel owner, Ignazio Altieri, in the course of his career as an art appraiser and antiques dealer.

The 39€ set menu is traditional Sicilian and a bit cliché-ridden, but the 45€ tasting menu truly shows off the genius of this most talented chef. The appetizers are the best along the southern coast of Sicily—just wait until you sample the octopus and shrimp with new potatoes in a bisque flavored with escargot butter, or the sea scallops with king prawns on cannellini beans with candied lemon in a sea urchin sauce. We could return here every night for the pastas, such as the tortellini of spiny lobster in a *jus* of summer truffles or the cannelloni of scampi on a leek fondue with a curry *jus* of clams and fresh herbs. Wild salmon is served in a consommé of cherry tomatoes with little ravioli of melted fennel and chopped garlic. Desserts don't get much better than the chocolate fondant with a pistachio parfait and two sauces.

Foresteria Baglio della Luna Hotel, Contrada Maddalusa (S.S. 640), Valle dei Templi 92100. ☎ **0922-511061.** Reservations required. Main courses 14€–16€; set-price menus 39€–45€. AE, DC, MC, V. Daily 12:30–2pm and 7:30–9:30pm. Bus: 1 or 3.

2 Selinunte

122km (76 miles) SW of Palermo, 113km (70 miles) W of Agrigento, 89km (55 miles) SE of Trapani

Guy de Maupassant called the splendid jumble of ruins at Selinunte "an immense heap of fallen columns, now aligned and placed side by side on the ground like dead soldiers, now having fallen in a chaotic manner." Regardless of what shape they're in, the only reason to visit Selinunte is for its **ruins,** not for the unappealing modern towns (Mazara del Vallo and Castelvetrano) that have grown around it.

One of the superb colonies of ancient Greece, Selinunte traces its history to the 7th century B.C., when immigrants from Megara Hyblaea (Syracuse) set out to build a new colony. They succeeded, erecting a city of power and prestige adorned with temples. But that was calling attention to a good thing. Much of Selinunte's history involves seemingly endless conflicts with the Elymi people of Segesta (see chapter 13). Siding with Selinunte's rival, Hannibal virtually leveled the city in 409 B.C. The city never recovered its former glory and ultimately fell into decay.

GETTING THERE

From Palermo, Trapani, or Marsala, you can make rail connections to Castelve-trano on the southern coast of Sicily, 23km (14 miles) from the ruins. Once at Castelvetrano, you board a bus for the final lap of the journey to Selinunte. Rail fares are reasonable; a one-way ticket from Palermo to Castelvetrano, for exam-ple, costs only 4.15€ each way, the trip taking 2 hours.

Lumia buses (☎ **0922-20414**) also run to Castelvetrano from the cities of Agrigento, Marsala, and Trapani. Since schedules vary, call for information. Buses arrive in Castelvetrano in front of the rail depot. From here you must go the rest of the way by a bus operated by **Autoservizi Salemi** (☎ **0923-981120**); the one-way fare for the 20-minute trip is .77€.

Selinunte is on the southern coast of Sicily and is best explored by **car** because public transportation is awkward. From Agrigento, take Route 115 northwest into Castelvetrano; then follow the signposted secondary road marked SELI-NUNTE, which leads south to the sea. Allow at least 2 hours to drive here from either Palermo or Agrigento.

VISITOR INFORMATION

For information on the site, visit the **Selinunte Tourist Office,** Via Caboto Giovanni (☎ **0924-46251**), near the archaeological garden. It's open Monday through Saturday from 8am to 2pm and 3 to 8pm, Sunday from 9am to noon and 3 to 6pm.

EXPLORING THE ARCHAEOLOGICAL GARDEN ★★

Selinunte's temples lie in scattered ruins, the honey-colored stone littering the ground as if an earthquake had struck (as one did in ancient times). Some sec-tions and fragments of temples still stand, with great columns pointing to the sky. From 9am to 2 hours before sunset daily, you can walk through the monument zone. Some of it has been partially excavated and reconstructed, as much as is possible with the bits and fragments remaining. Admission is 4.50€.

The temples, in varying states of preservation, are designated by letters. They're dedicated to such mythological figures as Apollo and Hera (Juno); most date from the 6th and 5th centuries B.C. Near the entrance, the Doric **Temple E** contains fragments of an inner temple. Standing on its ruins before the sun goes down, you can look across the water that washes up on the shores of Africa, from which the Carthaginian fleet emerged to destroy the city. **Temple G,** in scattered ruins north of Temple E, was one of the largest erected in Sicily and was also built in the Doric style. The ruins of the less impressive **Temple F** lie between Temples E and G. Not much remains of Temple F, and little is known about it.

After viewing Temples E, F, and G, all near the parking lot at the entrance, you can get in your car and drive along the Strada dei Templi west to the Acropoli. You can also walk there in about 20 minutes. The site of the western temples was the **Acropoli,** which was enclosed within defensive walls and built from the 6th century to the 5th century B.C.

The most impressive site here is **Temple C.** In 1925, 14 of the 17 columns of Temple C were re-erected. This is the earliest surviving temple of ancient Selinus, built in the 6th century B.C. and probably dedicated to Hercules or Apollo. The pediment, ornamented with a clay Gorgon's head, lies broken on the ground. Temple C towers over the other ruins and gives you a better impression of what all the temples might have looked like at one time.

Also here is **Temple A** which, like the others, remains in scattered ruins. The streets of the Acropoli were laid out by Hippodamus of Miletus along classical lines, with a trio of principal arteries bisected at right angles by a grid of less important streets. The Acropoli was the site of the town's most important public and religious buildings, and it was also the residence of the town's aristocrats. If you look down below, you can see the site of the town's harbor, now overgrown. After all this earthquake damage, you can only imagine the full glory of this place in its golden era.

WHERE TO STAY NEARBY

The site of the ruins contains no hotels, restaurants, or watering holes of note. Most visitors come here on a day trip while they're based elsewhere. But there is a handful of accommodations in the seafront village of Marinella, about a mile east of Selinunte. To reach Marinella, you'll travel along a narrow country road.

Hotel Alceste This white-sided concrete structure is about a 15-minute walk from the ruins. A 1998 renovation added new furniture to the guest rooms, which have small tiled bathrooms with shower-and-tub combos. Most visitors, however, stop only for a visit to the plant-filled courtyard, where in summer there's musical entertainment, dancing, cabaret, and theater. In July and August, the hotel hosts what may be the highest percentage of academics on-site than in any other hotel in Sicily; they come from universities throughout the world. The somewhat shy and very kind owner, Drazio Torrente, is charming, as is his family. The big, airy, bustling restaurant is open daily for lunch and dinner, and is sometimes filled with busloads of visitors from as far away as Milan. Main courses cost from 4€ to 6.50€. *Note:* The hotel is occasionally closed for periods in winter.

Via Alceste 21, 91022 Marinella di Selinunte. ℂ **0924-46184.** Fax 0924-46143. 30 units. 75€–85€ double. Rates include breakfast. AE, DC, MC, V. **Amenities:** Restaurant; lounge; room service; laundry. *In room:* A/C, TV, hair dryer, safe.

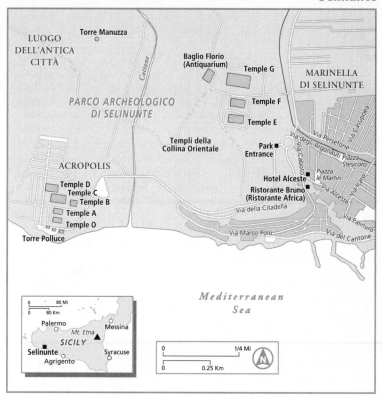

WHERE TO DINE NEARBY

Hotel Alceste, recommended above, is also a good choice for dining.

Ristorante Bruno (Ristorante Africa) SICILIAN   Set across the street from the Hotel Alceste, in a very clean, cement-sided building completely open to the air and sunlight of the quiet neighborhood surrounding it, this restaurant serves excellent food and the best antipasti in town. The result of a holiday romance oh-so-many years ago, it's managed by Swiss-born and multilingual Ester Weidmann and her Selinunte-born companion, Bruno Veneziano, who jointly prepare excellent fish and an always-refrigerated antipasti buffet with the kind of salads, fish, and vegetable offerings that tempt many diners to make it a meal unto itself. Pizzas are also appealing, with two dozen choices, including a "pizza Africa" laden with mozzarella, tuna, onions, and pepperoni.

Via Alceste 24, Marinella. ✆ **0924-46456.** Reservations not necessary. Pizza 2.80€–7€; main courses 5.50€–9.50€. AE, DC, MC, V. Fri–Wed noon–2:30pm and 7:30–11:30pm. Open daily July–Aug. Closed Nov–Feb.

13

Western Sicily

In the early days of 20th-century tourism to Sicily, the western part of the island was easily dismissed. On our first visit a long time ago, we were even discouraged from going there by a tourist official in Palermo. "What is there? A few Greek ruins and maybe some Mafia boys running about? Stay in Palermo, where we will wine and dine you."

Even today, most foreign visitors land in the east. But we have come to regard the western coast as one of our favorite areas for discovery. Much of Sicilian history was shaped along these shores, and much is left that is ancient, including the magnificent ruins at **Segesta,** whose temple has remained virtually intact for 2,500 years.

No hilltop medieval town, not even Taormina, equals **Erice.** And in spite of unfortunate modern building on its periphery, **Trapani** still has a historic core with a jumbled maze of narrow streets. **Marsala,** to the south, is known as the center for the making of world-famous dessert wines.

1 Segesta ★★

30km (19 miles) E of Trapani, 75km (47 miles) SW of Palermo

There's only one reason to come to Segesta: to see a single amazing temple in a lonely field. For some visitors, that's reason enough because it's one of the best-preserved ancient temples in all Italy. The trip here takes about an hour from Palermo, and makes a good brief stop en route to Trapani (see later in this chapter).

Segesta was the ancient city of the Elymi, a people of mysterious origin who are linked by some to the Trojans. As the major city in western Sicily, it faced conflicts with the rival power nearby, Selinus (Selinunte). From the 6th century to the 5th century B.C., there were near-constant hostilities. The Athenians came from the east to aid the Segestans in 415 B.C., but the expedition ended in disaster, eventually forcing the city to turn for help to Hannibal of Carthage.

Twice in the 4th century B.C., Segesta was besieged and conquered, once by Dionysius and again by Agathocles (a particularly brutal victor who tortured, mutilated, or made slaves of most of the citizenry). Segesta, in time, turned on its old but dubious ally, Carthage. Like all Greek cities of Sicily, it ultimately fell to the Romans.

GETTING THERE   Nearly a dozen **trains** per day make the run from Trapani (see later in this chapter) to the depot at Segesta, Segesta Tempio. A one-way ticket costs 2.50€. The station is only a 1km (½-mile) walk from the Doric temple. Segesta is also reached by **AST bus** (✆ 0923-31020), leaving from Piazza Montalto in Trapani; the 25-minute ride costs 2.50€.

Motorists can take the autostrada (A29) running between Palermo and Trapani. The exit at Segesta is clearly marked.

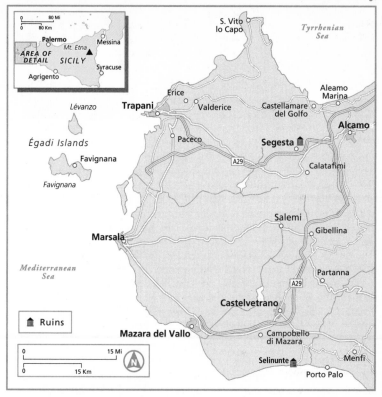

A JOURNEY INTO ANTIQUITY

The **Tempio** ⟨★★★⟩, or **Temple of Segesta,** is one of the world's most perfectly preserved survivors from the days of antiquity. For those who have had to be satisfied seeing only a sprinkling of columns in Sicilian archaeological gardens, this full temple stands on a 304m (997-ft.) hill, on the edge of a deep ravine carved by the Pispisa River. Here is a temple of scope and dimension, with its columns relatively intact.

The site is made all the more majestic by the deep valley that envelops it. In the fading gold and pink sunlight of a Sicilian afternoon, you can stand here and absorb the full view, the setting framed by the distant peaks of Monte Barbaro and Monte Bernardo. It is perhaps the most **magnificent view** ⟨★★★⟩ in all Sicily.

Constructed in the 5th century B.C., the well-preserved temple is supported by 36 Doric columns that in turn support its entablatures and pediments. Because the interior architectural elements are lacking, professors of antiquity believe that the temple was never finished because of a war with Segesta's archenemy, Selinunte.

The site is open daily from 9am to 7pm; admission costs 4.15€ for adults and 2.10€ for children under 18. The ticket office closes an hour before the temple park closes.

After visiting the temple, you can take a bus to the large **Teatro** ⟨★⟩ or theater at the top of Mount Barbaro at 431m (1,414 ft.). The one-way fare costs 1.05€, and buses depart at the rate of two per hour during the day.

Dating from the 3rd century B.C., the theater was constructed during the Hellenistic period. A semicircle with a diameter of 63m (207 ft.), it was hewn right out of the side of the mountain, its stage facing north. In ancient days, the theater could hold as many as 4,000 spectators, and the site is still used for the staging of both modern and classical plays presented from mid-July to early August every other year.

2 Erice ★★★

96km (60 miles) SW of Palermo, 14km (8½ miles) NE of Trapani, 45km (28 miles) NW of Marsala, 330km (205 miles) W of Messina

Originally established some 3,000 years ago, Erice is an enchanting medieval city. From its thrilling mountaintop setting, two sheer cliffs drop 743m (2,478 ft.) to vistas across the plains of Trapani and down the west coast of Sicily. On a clear day, you can even see Cape Bon in Tunisia, but the Sicilian aerie of Erice is often shrouded in mist that only adds to its mystique (or misery, especially in winter, when temperatures can plummet below Sicilian norms and snow and hail are not uncommon).

Erice is a lovely place to spend an afternoon wandering the medieval streets, with their baroque balconies and flowering vines, and drinking in the vistas. The southwest corner of town contains the **Villa Balio gardens,** originally laid out in the 19th century. Beyond the gardens, a path winds along the cliff's edge up to Erice's highest point, the **Castello di Venere,** today little more than crumbling Norman walls surrounding the sacred site where a temple to Venus once stood.

ESSENTIALS

GETTING THERE   If arriving by **train** from Palermo, you pull into the station at Trapani (see later in this chapter). **AST buses** (✆ **0923-21021**) depart from Piazza Montalto in Trapani at the rate of 11 per day, heading for Erice. Service is daily year-round from 6:40am to 7:30pm, the trip lasting 50 minutes and costing 1.80€ one-way.

Motorists can reach Erice from Trapani by heading out the Via Fardella to the end of the street. At some point near the end of the wide boulevard, you'll see signs pointing the way to Erice. Follow A29 all the way to Erice.

DISCOVERING A MEDIEVAL TOWN

Erice's chief attraction is the **medieval town** ★★★, although there are some individual points of interest worth seeking out as you make your way along its cobblestone streets. The historic core of Erice forms a triangle, with the southeastern corner framed by the **Castello di Vevere** (see below). In the southwestern corner is the **Chiesa Matrice,** near Porta di Trapani, the best place to park your car before you walk into the medieval center. The access road to Erice affords **panoramic vistas** ★★ of Trapani plains and the sea.

After leaving Porta di Trapani, your first discovery is immediately to the northeast. **Chiesa Matrice di Erice,** Via Vito Carvini (✆ **0923-869123**), is the main church of Erice. Not quite a cathedral, it was constructed in 1314, using stones from the ancient Temple of Venus that once stood here. Its merlon-topped walls speak of the church's former role as a fortress and a place of worship. The rose window on the church facade is a thing of beauty, as is its Gothic porch.

If you climb the church's campanile, or bell tower, you are rewarded with a stunning view across the Gulf of Trapani to the Egadi Islands. Ordered built by

Frederick of Aragon, the former watchtower has impressive Gothic mullioned windows. The church is open Monday through Friday from 9:30am to 12:30pm and 3:30 to 5:30pm, Saturday and Sunday from 9:30am to 1pm and 3:30 to 6pm.

As you walk north after a visit to the church, you can follow **Mura Elimo Puniche** ✸, the Elimo Punic walls constructed by the Elimini (8th–6th c. B.C.) around the northeastern flank of Erice. Any attack on the town had to come from this direction, which was exposed. The best-preserved part of the walls lies along Via dell'Addolorata stretching from Porta Carmine to Porta Spada, which is at the far northern end of the massive fortifications.

At Porta Spada, the end of your "wall walk," you'll find yourself at **Chiesa di Santa Orsola,** a church constructed in 1413 with its original Gothic rib-vaulting still on view in the nave. Directly to the east of this church is the **Quartiere Spagnola.** Launched in the 17th century but never finished, this "Spanish Quarter" building is no grand sight, but a **panoramic vista** ✸ unfolds from here over the Bay of Cofano.

In the historic core of Erice stands the **Museo Civico Antonio Cordici,** Piazza Umberto I at Corso Vittorio Emanuele (✆ **0923-860048**), open Monday through Friday from 9am to 1:30pm; there's no admission fee. Named for a local historian, Antonio Cordici (1586–1666), the building originally was a library dating from 1867. Its initial stock came from suppressed convents in the area. In its entrance hall is a magnificent relief of the ***Annunciation*** ✸ by Antonello Gagini, one of his most impressive pieces of art and dating from 1525. The museum upstairs displays the more intriguing artifacts from archaeological digs in the area, including a small Attic head of Venus dating from the 5th century B.C.

Heading east, you come first to **Giardino del Balio** ✸, initially constructed by the Normans as a forward defense for their castle (see below). The gardens take their name from Baiulo, a former Norman governor who lived in a building on this site. The present gardens, with their ilexes and box hedges, were mapped out in 1870 by Count Agostino Pepoli. On the summit of a hill, the gardens open onto one of the most **spectacular views** ✸✸ in western Sicily, embracing the peaks of Monte Cofano, with distant views of the Egadi Islands. On a clear day you can see all the way to Cap Bon in Tunisia, a distance of 170km (106 miles). Entrance to the gardens is free, and they are always open.

Saving the best for last, we come to **Castello di Venere,** or Castle of Venus, built on top of Mount San Giuliano, on the same spot where in ancient times a temple to the goddess stood. Dating from the 12th century, the present *castello* was constructed as a defensive fortification by the Normans. Massive and majestic, it became the seat of Norman authority in the west. It's still encircled by mammoth medieval towers. Above the entrance to the castle, note the coat-of-arms of Charles V and an original Gothic window. The castle provides an even more **memorable view** ✸✸✸ than does the adjoining Giardino del Balio. You can see the plains of Trapani and the Egadi Islands to the southwest. In fair weather, you can even view the offshore island of Ustica (see chapter 5).

After all that looting, burning, and destruction this castle has witnessed over the centuries, little is left of the ruins. But that view makes it worthwhile. The castle is open daily from 9am to 8pm year-round, with no admission fee.

SHOPPING

Altieri 1882   Small and charming, this shop lies a few steps uphill from the heart of Erice, Piazza Umberto I. Inside, you'll find coral jewelry, silver picture frames, and Sicilian pottery, some of it produced locally. Via Cordici 14. ✆ 0923-869431.

Bazar del Miele   There are hundreds of food shops in Sicily, and several dozen in and around Erice, but in our memory, this is one of the most impressive. Everything inside this aromatic boutique comes from Sicily, and a few are esoteric even by local standards. You'll find racks devoted to Sicilian honey (15 different aromas, including many from local hives); a half-dozen preparations of anchovies, including filets that are wrapped around almonds; Marsala wines, arranged by vineyard, year of production, and degree of sweetness; and liqueurs (including a pale-green one made from fermented pistachios). The array of cheeses and almond-based candies is the most comprehensive in town. Via Cordici 16. ✆ 0923-869181.

Ceramica Ericina   Erice craftspeople are as famous for their rugs as they are for their ceramics. This is basically a ceramics store, the wares painted with scenes of Sicilian life or daily life in Erice. We also found the best selection of multicolored Erice carpets here. These rugs are highly valued and rigorously hand-woven, the most traditional colors being red, yellow, and blue. Sometimes the colors are broken up with even brighter hues, creating an Arabian aura, with both floral and geometrical designs in zigzags and diamonds. There is also a good selection of Sicilian lace. Via Vittorio Emanuele 7. ✆ 0923-869140.

Gal'Arte   One of Erice's most unusual shops—and the subject of several local newspaper articles—sits on the town's main square, selling exotic handblown glassware. When you enter, you're likely to be greeted with New Age music and a blast of super-hot air streaming from the studio of the town's most famous glassblower (French-born Arnaud Mercier), who shapes bowls, sculptures, and ornaments as you watch, in ways that—at least to neophytes—seem miraculous. Art objects range in price from 3€ to 160€. Piazza Umberto I. ✆ 0923-8695084.

Nino Marchese   The pottery and stoneware sold here is of a more monumental stature, with more historical antecedents, than what's available in competing shops nearby. Most items are faithful copies of religious and "portrait" porcelain from 18th-century Sicily. Look for wall-mounted containers for holy water, votive candles, and vases and water pitchers molded and painted to resemble Moors, Sicilian noblemen, poets, and troubadours. Corso Vittorio Emanuele 39. ✆ 0923-869660.

WHERE TO STAY
EXPENSIVE

Hotel Elimo ✦   Set in the lower reaches of Erice's historic core, a few steps from the also-recommended Hotel Moderno, this arts-conscious hotel was built 400 years ago as a private palazzo. Since its transformation in 1986 into a hotel, it has been managed by Carmelo Tilotta, a descendant of the original family that built it. Its public areas include an appealing combination of old frescoed ceiling beams, antique masonry, Oriental carpets, and contemporary-looking leather sofas, all nestled around a library-style TV den that adds considerable coziness to the venue. The best views sweep over the golden plains of western Sicily, seen through the enormous glass windows of the hotel restaurant, which juts onto a terraced ledge in back. We prefer this hotel's conventional guest rooms, which tend to be large and have well-styled modern furniture. Avoid the duplex suites, which some visitors find uncomfortably claustrophobic. In the main building, guest rooms come with tiled bathrooms with tub and shower; in the annex, the bathrooms have showers.

Via Vittorio Emanuele 75, 91016 Erice. ✆ 0923-869377. Fax 0923-869252. 21 units. 170€ double; 196€ suite. AE, DC, MC, V. **Amenities:** Restaurant; bar; laundry/dry cleaning. *In room:* A/C, TV, minibar.

MODERATE

Hotel Baglio Santa Croce ★ *Finds*   This is a most delightful discovery and, for many, the most tranquil, idyllic way to enjoy the pleasures of historic Erice without staying in the crowded center. Not far from town, this converted farmhouse dates back to 1637 and lies on the slope of Mount Erice, opening onto the Gulf of Cornino. The original architectural materials, including wooden beams, have been retained. The atmosphere is one of charm and grace, as is the hospitality extended to visitors from all over the world. Guests meet each other in the delightful terraced gardens with panoramic vistas. Guest rooms are simply but comfortably furnished with tiled floors and wooden beams, along with olive-wood pieces and wrought-iron beds. Each unit comes with a small tiled bathroom with shower. The on-site restaurant serves good Sicilian-style country cooking.

SS187, Km 300 (Contrada Ragosia), 91019 Erice. ℂ **0923-891111.** Fax 0923-891192. www.bagliosan tacroce.it. 24 units. 96€–112€. Rates include breakfast. AE, DC, MC. Free parking. Located 2km (1.2 miles) east of Valderice on N187. **Amenities:** Restaurant; bar; laundry/dry cleaning. *In room:* TV.

Hotel Moderno ★   It's cozy, it's warm, and it has a lot of charm, but don't let this hotel's name fool you: The kind of modernism it was named for dates from just after World War II, when a 19th-century stone house and, later, the 14-room annex across the street were converted into one of central Erice's most appealing hotels. Rooms in the annex are bigger than those in the hotel's main core, and if you opt for a unit there, you'll be given a key to its usually locked front door for unrestricted access day and night. (A desk attendant holds court in the hotel's main building 24 hr. a day, and no front door key there is necessary.) Regardless of their location, guest rooms have hints of 19th-century styling, an occasional antique, and bentwood, brass and, in some cases, wicker furniture; about a dozen of the rooms open onto private balconies or terraces. All units come with immaculately kept tiled bathrooms with tub-shower combos. If you arrive on a cold day in winter, you are likely to be welcomed by a blazing fire. Many antiques and local handcrafts, such as antique dressers and brass bedsteads, were used to give the hotel more intimacy and take the curse off the name "Moderno." The on-site restaurant is highly regarded.

Via Vittorio Emanuele 67, 91016 Erice. ℂ **0923-869300.** Fax 0923-869139. modernoh@tin.it. 41 units. 93€–114€. Rates include breakfast. AE, DC, MC, V. Free parking. **Amenities:** Restaurant; bar; babysitting; laundry/dry cleaning. *In room:* A/C, TV, minibar.

La Pineta ★ *Finds*   On the north side of Erice, this inviting small hotel stands inside a park of about 2 hectares (5 acres). Guests are surrounded by flora, including flowering shrubs and tall trees. La Pineta lies within the ancient Elymian-Punic walls of the old city, and is the only centrally located hotel with private parking in traffic-congested Erice. Even if you don't stay here, try to visit its restaurant (see below), one of the finest in the area and known for its Sicilian regional cuisine. In the main building are two restaurants; on the grounds are private cottages with terraces. From many of these terraces, views of the Tyrrhenian Sea, Mount Cofano, and the Gulf of Cornino unfold. A private bus takes guests to the harbor and the train depot. The guest rooms are furnished in a snug and cozy way, with simple but comfortable wooden pieces and tiled floors. Each unit comes with a small tiled bathroom with shower.

Viale Nunzio Nasi, 91016 Erice. ℂ **0923-869783.** Fax 0923-869786. www.lapinetaerice.it. 23 units. 80€–115€ double; 114€–155€ triple. Rates include breakfast. AE, DC, MC, V. Free parking. **Amenities:** Restaurant; bar; laundry/dry cleaning. *In room:* TV, minibar, hair dryer.

INEXPENSIVE

Hotel Belvedere San Nicola ☆ *Kids*   Positioned about 731m (2,398 ft.) downhill from the fortifications that surround medieval Erice, this inn stands in an isolated location that slopes down to views over the shoreline of Trapani. The hotel markets itself as a family-friendly country inn that's less expensive than hotels in Erice's historic core. Built in 2000 immediately adjacent to a community of Mediterranean-style town houses (mostly second homes and timeshares for holiday-making north Europeans), it resembles a postmodern version of a thick-walled, big-windowed farmhouse. None of the compact, tile-floored guest rooms has air-conditioning, but thanks to Erice's high altitude and constant breezes, you don't need it. Some rooms have high, sloping ceilings, and all have an efficient, no-frills styling. The social center is the large outdoor swimming pool.

Contrada San Nicola, 91016 Erice. ✆ **0923-860124.** Fax 0923-869139. www.pippocatalano.it. 10 units. 78€ double. Rate includes breakfast. AE, DC, MC, V. **Amenities:** Restaurant; bar; pool; horseback riding grounds; *bocce* court; children's playground. *In room:* TV, hair dryer.

Hotel Ermione ☆ *Kids*   Opening onto panoramic views of the Egadi Islands, this dramatically perched hotel lies only 700m (1,297 ft.) from the heart of Erice. Builders in the 1960s chose this breezy location to erect a hotel overlooking the Tyrrhenian Sea, and today most of the midsize guest rooms open onto these vistas. Units have tiled private bathrooms, most with showers, a few with tubs. Because many of the accommodations are triples or quads, this is an ideal family choice. Old-style Sicilian furniture—not necessarily antiques—grace the public areas. You can park your car in the free lot, then take a complimentary hotel van into the center of Erice. With its beautiful views of the sea, the hotel's restaurant is a worthy choice even if you're not staying here.

Via Piuneta Comunale 43, 91016 Erice. ✆ **0923-869138.** Fax 0923-869587. www.ermionehotel.com. 47 units. 67€–83€ double; 87€ triple; 103€ quad. Rates include breakfast. AE, DC, MC, V. Free parking. **Amenities:** Restaurant; bar; pool; room service; laundry/dry cleaning. *In room:* TV, minibar in some.

WHERE TO DINE

Monte San Giuliano ☆ *Finds* SEAFOOD/TRAPANESE   To reach this garden hideaway, negotiate your way through a labyrinth of narrow stone alleys that begin a few steps downhill from Erice's Piazza Umberto I, then pass through an iron gate and wander beyond stone walls and shrubbery to the restaurant's terraces and dining rooms. The setting is very rustic, typical of Erice. The freshest and finest seafood in Erice is served here. That the Arabs once ruled the land is evidenced in the seafood couscous—and it's just as good here as you get on the coast of North Africa. Our favorite pasta is something to savor: *busiate* (a homemade pasta) made with *pesto alla Trapanese,* which in this case means garlic, basil, fresh tomatoes, and—surprise—almonds.

Vicolo San Rocco 7. ✆ **0923-869595.** Reservations recommended. Main courses 7.50€–13€. AE, DC, MC, V. Tues–Sun 12:15–2:45pm and 7:30–10pm. Closed Jan 7–21.

Osteria di Venere TRAPANESE/SICILIAN   This local dive has a staff not trained in the social graces, but it serves excellent regional cooking. In one room, a mix of visitors and locals feast nightly off the fat of the land. Start, perhaps, with the homemade pasta of the day. It's often made with a spicy sauce of garlic, tomatoes, fresh basil, and toasted almonds in the Trapanese style. The chef's namesake pasta, *alla Venere,* is made with fresh tomatoes and eggplant prepared with swordfish and a surprising touch of mint. The menu is based mainly on meat in the winter, with fish predominating on summer menus.

Via Roma 6 at Piazza San Giuliano. *©* **0923-869362.** Reservations required. Main courses 5€–13€. DC, MC, V. Thurs–Tues 12:30–2:30pm and 8–10:30pm.

Ristorante La Pineta TRAPANESE/SICILIAN   This charming restaurant in La Pineta hotel is set in a park with outdoor tables. The regional cuisine served here, based on the freshest of local ingredients, is a potent lure. The menu reflects a concise, focused attention on flavorful combinations, often derived from decades-old recipes. The *spaghetti alla Bottarga* is the most savory pasta, prepared with tuna, extra-virgin olive oil, garlic, and parsley. A runner-up is *brucoli alla Nostromo,* homemade pasta served in a sauce peppered with swordfish, eggplant, tomatoes, and fresh mint. The inevitable *involtini alla Sicilian* also appears on the menu here—roulades of beef with aromatic herb seasonings.

La Pineta hotel, Viale Nunzio Nasi. *©* **0923-869783.** Reservations required in Aug and on holidays. Main courses 5€–12€. AE, DC, MC, V. Daily 12:30–2:30pm and 7:30–9:30pm. Closed Mon Oct–June and Jan 7–Feb 28.

Ulisse SICILIAN   Enter this airy indoor/outdoor dining room by walking up a series of ramps and stairs that seem to go on forever, past hidden pockets of cultivated greenery loaded with hibiscus and palmettos. At the top of your climb, you reach a dining room lined with paintings by local artists, many of which highlight the architecture and panoramas in and around Erice. Pizzas are available here, but only at dinnertime, and they're less popular than the well-prepared fresh fish, meat, and pasta platters for which the place is best known. On our most recent rounds, we had the best spaghetti with lobster we've enjoyed in western Sicily. A pasta favorite with locals are those wide noodles, pappardelle, served with fresh mushrooms. The chef's special pasta is *pasta Ulisse,* flavored with herbs, tomatoes, and chunks of eggplant. The venue is definitely family-managed, as evidenced by the daily presence of several generations of the same hardworking family.

Via Chiaramonte 45. *©* **0923-869333.** Reservations not required. Main courses 6.20€–15€. AE, DC, MC, V. Fri–Wed noon–3pm and 8pm–midnight. Daily June–Aug.

PASTRIES

Erice is renowned throughout Sicily for its pastries. These delectable goodies were carefully refined over the years by nuns based in Erice convents from the 14th to the 18th century, and the recipes have been handed down from generation to generation. Even if you're dining in one of the restaurants in the central core, skip dessert and head to the two best pastry shops in town.

Pasticceria Grammatico   Maria Grammatico is a former nun who became famous in Italy when she wrote a book, *Bitter Almonds,* the story of her life. Co-authored with Mary Taylor Simeti, the book told of her recollections and recipes from a Sicilian girlhood growing up in a convent. There she learned to craft such sweet confections as marzipan. Her almond creations have made her celebrated in these parts, especially her crunchy almond cookies, rum-filled marzipan balls, and confections fashioned from chocolate-covered almond paste. The almond paste creations are works of art, shaped into a variety of forms such as whimsical animals. The pastry shop also sells liqueurs such as a green, minty Marsala.

Via Vittorio Emanuele 14. *©* **0923-869390.** Pastries from 1€. No credit cards. Daily 7am–10pm.

Pasticceria Michele II Tulipano ⭐   This is the most spectacular bakery in Erice, with a stand-up coffee and drink bar where you can eat the goods on-site. Established on the town's main street in the early 1980s, it devotes itself to the intricately decorated pastries, many flavored with almonds or chocolate, that have made southern Italy famous. The most spectacular pastry we had in all of Sicily was a *casatella,* a deep-fried beignet (fritter) stuffed with sweetened ricotta cheese, that's typical of the Trapani region. It tastes best with espresso and perhaps a glass of almond-flavored water.

Via Vittorio Emanuele 10–12. © 0923-869672. Pastries from 1€. No credit cards. Daily 7:30am–9pm (until 2am July–Aug).

3 Trapani

100km (64 miles) SW of Palermo, 31km (19 miles) N of Trapani, 14km (8½ miles) SW of Erice, 150km (94 miles) NW of Agrigento

The major city along the western coast of Sicily, Trapani may be your gateway to the west because of its superior transportation links to the rest of Sicily and its easy road links with Palermo.

Trapani lies below the headland of Mount Erice, with the Egadi Islands visible most days off its shore. Trapani is also the capital of its own province, which embraces the medieval hill town of Erice (see above). This most westerly of Sicilian provinces covers a land of great natural beauty, including a coastline that has many long beaches of white sand such as the one at San Vito lo Capo.

The city stands on a sickle-shaped promontory stretching into the sea. Its economy is based largely on fishing and winemaking along with salt mining, with tourism growing annually. A maze of narrow streets makes up its historic core, but it has none of the charm of Erice. If you have only 1 day for the west, time is better spent in Erice to the north. But if you have an extra day, consider devoting it to historic Trapani, once a Phoenician outpost. Trapani's most dubious reputation is as a major Sicilian center of the Mafia.

Drepanon, as it was once called, was the key port in the Carthaginian defense of the island at the time of the Punic Wars. The Romans, led by Catulus, captured the city in 241 B.C., marking its decline. It regained some of its lost prestige during the 9th century when the Saracens landed to conquer it. Three centuries later they were followed by the Normans.

It was here in 1272 that Edward I of England pulled into port fresh from the Crusades to learn that he'd inherited the throne. More conquerors were to come, including Peter of Aragon, who landed here in 1282.

Architecturally, the worst blows to Trapani were the Allied bombardments in 1940 and 1943. The entire historic district of San Pietro was razed. Regrettably, the new Trapani bounced back with the building of several ugly modern blocks—think Soviet Union in the heyday of the Cold War. As a result of all this destruction, Trapani has fewer historic sights to visit than most Sicilian cities of its size. But there are some nuggets.

GETTING THERE   By Plane   Not a very busy airport, **Florio Airport** (© 0923-842502) is serviced by daily flights from Rome and the offshore island of Pantelleria. It's located in Birgi on the road to Marsala, 15km (9 miles) from the center of Trapani. Buses are timed for the arrivals and departures of airplanes, and leave from Piazza Malta.

By Train   Most trains, at the rate of 16 per day, make the 2-hour run from Palermo; a one-way ticket costs 6.80€. There are also 16 trains per day from Marsala, taking 30 minutes at a cost of 2.30€ one-way. Trains pull in at the **Piazza Stazione** (© 0923-28071), where luggage storage is available. For general rail information in Italy, call © **892021.**

By Bus   AST (© 0923-21021) runs buses to Erice, departing from Piazza Montalto in Trapani. Buses head for Erice at the rate of 11 per day, taking 50 minutes; the one-way ride costs 1.80€.

By Ferry   Trapani is a major embarkation point for ferries and hydrofoils *(aliscafi)*. Most departures are for the offshore Egadi Islands of Marrettimo, Levanzo, and Favignana. Service is also available to Ustica, Pantelleria, and even Tunisia in North Africa. Ferries depart from the docks near Piazza Garibaldi. Service and tickets are available from **Siremar** (© 0923-545455) and **Ustica** (© 0923-22220).

By Car   From Palermo, follow A29 all the way southwest into Trapani. From Marsala, head north along Route 115 to Trapani.

VISITOR INFORMATION   Not very helpful, the **Trapani Tourist Office,** Piazza Saturno (© 0923-29000), is open Monday through Saturday from 8am to 8pm, Sunday from 9am to noon.

FAST FACTS   Your hotel will point you to the nearest **pharmacy.** In Trapani all drugstores are open Monday through Saturday from 9am to 1:30pm and 4:30 to 8pm. Pharmacies operate on a rotational system for night hours, with at least one open every night of the week. Every pharmacy posts a notice on its door as to what pharmacy is maintaining night hours. More serious **medical** needs are attended to at **Ospedale Sant'Antonio Abate,** Via Cosenza, in the northeast of the city (© 0923-809111). For **Internet** access, head to **Phone Center GGE,** Stazione Marittima (© 0923-549840), where the rate is 2.50€ per hour. The **Trapani Post Office** is at Piazza Vittorio Veneto (© 0923-28914), open Monday through Saturday from 8:20am to 6:30pm. The biggest and best **travel agency** in Trapani is **Francesca Badalucco,** 91 Via Ammiraglio Staiti (© 0923-542470). It lies across the street from Trapani's harbor front, at which ferryboats make frequent excursions to and from the Egadi Islands. The agency knows all the boat schedules and can sell tickets from Trapani to any of Sicily's offshore islands. It also sells boat tickets from, say, Palermo to Genoa, or from Palermo or Trapani to Corsica in France.

EXPLORING TRAPANI

Most visitors head first for the *centro storico* ✿, the medieval core lying on the headland jutting into the sea. The most ancient part of this "casbah" was constructed in a typical North African style around a tightly knit maze of narrow streets. Originally these streets lay behind protective walls that guarded against sudden invasions from the sea.

The most intriguing street is **Via Garibaldi** (also known as Rua Nova, or "New Road"). The Aragonese laid out this street in the 18th century, and it's flanked with churches and palaces. The best shops in the old town line **Via Torrearsa,** which leads down to a bustling **Fish Market** *(pescheria)* where tuna—caught in waters offshore—is king. The spacious central square, **Piazza Vittorio Emanuele,** laid out in 1869 and planted with palm trees, is a relaxing oasis.

The pedestrianized main street of Trapani is **Corso Vittorio Emanuele,** sometimes called "Rua Grande" by the Trapanese. Many elegant baroque buildings are found along this street, which makes for a grand promenade. At the eastern end of the street rises the **Palazzo Senatorio,** the 17th-century town hall, done up in pinkish marble.

Along this street you can visit the **Cattedrale** (© 0923-432111), open daily from 8am to 4pm with no admission fee. The 1743 facade is by Giovanni

Biagio Amico. Built on the site of an earlier structure from the 14th century, the cathedral is dedicated to San Lorenzo (St. Lawrence). Artworks inside include a *Crucifixion* by Giacomo Lo Verde, a local artist, on the building's south side (4th altar). At the second altar on the north side is a painting of St. George by Andrea Carreca.

Another important church is **Chiesa Santa Maria del Gesù,** on Via San Pietro, with a facade that incorporates both Gothic and Renaissance features, dating from the first half of the 16th century. Its major work of art is a beautiful *Madonna degli Angeli* (Madonna with Angels), a glazed terra-cotta statue by Andrea della Robbia. Regrettably, the church is often closed. An attendant rudely told us, "We are a church, *not* a museum."

Another worthy church that seems perpetually closed is **Chiesa di Sant'Agostino,** Piazzetta Saturno, adjacent to the tourist office. This church is known for its lovely rose window from the 14th century, and even more so for occasional concerts staged here. Ask at the tourist office for details.

Another church in the heart of old town, **Chiesa del Purgatorio,** is in the 17th-century baroque style. This church, in theory at least, is open daily from 8:30am to 12:30pm and 4 to 8pm, charging no admission fee. It lies across from Stazione Marettima, 1 block up from Via Giglio from Piazza Garibaldi. The entire atmosphere of this church remains medieval, with suffocating incense and otherworldly music. It houses the single greatest treasure in Trapani, however: the *Misteri* ⚘, 20 life-size wooden figures from the 18th century depicting Christ's Passion. Every bloody detail, including the Crucifixion, is shown.

A once major attraction, **Torre di Lingny,** built in 1671 as a defensive bastion on the tip of Trapani's "sickle," and a major landmark, has closed its doors "for a very, very long time"—so we were told.

Villa Margherita lies between old and new Trapani. These public gardens offer a welcome respite from a day of tramping the cobblestoned streets. Fountains, banyan trees, and palms rustling in the wind make for an inviting oasis. In July a festival of opera, ballet, and cabaret, **Luglio Muscale Trapanese,** is staged here. Shows start daily during that month at 9pm. Inside the park gates, a kiosk sells tickets for 5€. For more information, call ℂ **0923-21454.**

Modern Trapani has two sights worth a visit; otherwise, you can skip it without cultural deprivation. **Santuario dell'Annunziata** ⚘ is a 14th-century convent whose cloisters enclose the major museum of Trapani (see below). The 14th-century church was forever altered in the 18th century by new decorators, although its Gothic portal remains, surmounted by a lovely rose window. The **chapels** ⚘⚘ are a treasure and include two dedicated to the fishermen of Trapani who risk their lives daily to harvest the sea. The major chapel to seek out is the **Cappella della Madonna,** with its sacred Virgin and Bambino, attributed to Nino Pisano in the 14th century. The bronze gates to the chapel are from 1591. On its left flank is **Cappella dei Marinai,** a tufa structure crowned by a dome and built in the Renaissance style.

Adjacent to the church is Trapani's major museum: **Museo Nazionale Pepoli** ⚘, Via Conte Agostino Pepoli 200 (ℂ **0923-553269**), open daily from 9am to 12:30pm, charging an admission fee of 4€. The former Carmelite convent has been converted into a showcase of regional art that emphasizes archaeological artifacts but also has a worthy collection of statues and coral carvings. The artistic Gagini family is more well-represented here than any other artist. Especially striking is *St. James the Greater* by Antonello Gagini. The **folk art figurines** are noteworthy, including a brutal depiction of the biblical legend of

Herod's search for the Christ Child. Other works of art include a moving 14th-century *Pietà* ⍟ by Roberto di Oderisio and some impressive triptychs by anonymous artists, including *Maestro del Polittico di Trapani* ⍟ from the 15th century.

WHERE TO STAY

Albergo Messina This is one of the cheapest hotels we're willing to recommend in all of Sicily, and although its entrance might look forbidding, it's actually a warm, hospitable refuge that's maintained by a religiously devout family for whom cleanliness is indeed next to godliness. To reach it, you'll pass through a majestic 18th-century courtyard that's accessible from Trapani's main commercial thoroughfare, then climb a labyrinthine set of steps (they get more and more narrow as you go up) to a warren of rooms on the building's third floor. Here, amid potted plants and framed portraits of venerated saints, members of the Messina family will show you high-ceilinged guest rooms, each with a tiled floor, monastic-looking furniture, and a sink. None has a private bathroom, but adequate facilities are accessible in the corridors. Virtually no amenities are available here (and at these prices, would you expect any?). If you want to experience Sicily at prices that went out of fashion in the 1960s, in a hotel that's in something of a time warp from 35 years ago, this pensione might be it.

Corso Vittorio Emanuele 71, 91100 Trapani. ✆ **0923-21198.** 9 units, none with private bathroom. 15€ double. No credit cards. No phone.

Crystal Hotel ⍟ A member of the well-respected Framon chain, this is the most architecturally dramatic and urban-style hotel in Trapani. Constructed in the early 1990s, it's the most distinctive ultramodern building in town, characterized by an all-glass facade that curves above a piazza directly in front of the town's railway station. (Staff is quick to point out that very few trains come into Trapani every day—and the neighborhood, partly because of that, is very quiet.) Guest rooms are comfortable and efficiently organized, with clean, well-conceived styling. Each unit comes with an immaculately kept, tiled private bathroom with shower. Overall, this is a worthy hotel choice, and a modern refuge in the midst of an otherwise antique city.

Piazza Umberto I, 91100 Trapani. ✆ **0923-20000.** Fax 0923-25555. www.framon-hotels.com. 70 units. 124€–150€ double; 207€ suite. Rates include breakfast. AE, DC, MC, V. Free parking. **Amenities:** Restaurant; bar; babysitting; laundry/dry cleaning. *In room:* A/C, TV, minibar, safe.

Hotel Russo Newer buildings have since taken over this hotel's role as the town's preeminent hotel, and by many standards the design (ca. 1950) and five-story ocher-fronted facade looks slightly outmoded. But a quick view of its art-filled lobby, and a quick understanding of its solid sense of respectability, make you feel you're about to sleep in one of the most deeply entrenched hotels in western Sicily. There are marble or tile floors throughout, an amusing set of frescoes (giggling cherubs) in the breakfast room, and a sense of old-fashioned Trapani everywhere. Rooms are clean, comfortable, and without any particular sense of drama or theatricality—and in many cases, thanks to the hotel's popularity, fully booked. Each unit comes with a small tiled bathroom with shower.

Via Tintori 4, 91100 Trapani. ✆ **0923-22163.** Fax 0923-26623. 35 units. 68€ double. AE, DC, MC, V. **Amenities:** Babysitting; laundry/dry cleaning. *In room:* A/C, TV.

Hotel Vittoria On the waterfront road, a short distance from the center of town, this hotel is less preferable to the Crystal but is acceptable in every way. The second-best hotel in town stands on a corner and is a well-built, solid structure lacking any particular architectural charm or style. Nevertheless, it is exceedingly comfortable, and the staff is helpful. Guest rooms are midsize and furnished in a minimalist way, though the beds are inviting, and each unit comes with a small bathroom. Only three bathrooms contain tubs; the rest have showers.

Via Francesco Crispi 4, 91100 Trapani. ⓒ **0923-873044.** Fax 0923-29870. www.hotelvittoriatrapani.it. 65 units. 73€ double. AE, DC, MC, V. Free parking. **Amenities:** Breakfast lounge, bar; room service. *In room:* A/C, TV, minibar, hair dryer.

WHERE TO DINE

Ai Lumi Tavernetta ⭐ SICILIAN   Many locals accurately cite this artfully rustic tavern, established in 1993 on the ground floor of what used to be an important family-owned palazzo, as one of Trapani's best restaurants. It's positioned 2 blocks from the cathedral and features a long, narrow dining room capped with a series of medieval-looking brick arches. During the 17th century it functioned as a stable, but today the venue is filled with wines from virtually everywhere, dark-stained furniture, and a clientele that includes actors, politicians, and journalists. And, thanks to thick masonry walls and air-conditioning, it's a cool retreat from the blazing heat outside. The cuisine grows more proficient each time we visit. Dishes full of flavor include *tagliata* with strips of filet steak and arugula, or roast lamb in a citrus sauce. Taking a page from a classic recipe, local rabbit is larded and then roasted. Tuna caught off the coast is most often grilled and flavored with onions and a dash of balsamic vinegar. Our seafood pasta came with shrimp and calamari that tasted so fresh they could have just leapt from the boat. Fava beans and fresh tomatoes make the dish a treat.

Corso Vittorio Emanuele 75. ⓒ **0923-872418.** Reservations recommended Fri and Sat nights. Main courses 6.50€–15€. Sept–June Mon–Sat 1–3:30pm and 8–11pm. Daily in Aug (same hours). Closed July.

Ristorante da Peppe SICILIAN   Well-prepared and often convivial meals are served in this one-room restaurant where large murals and a color scheme of blue-green alternates with varnished wood and white plaster. Menu items feature a well-rehearsed, oft-repeated medley of mostly Sicilian dishes that includes spaghetti with clams or squid and squid ink; three kinds of couscous, including a version with fish; risotto paella (a Sicilian adaptation of the famous dish of Valencia, Spain); and a time-honored favorite, *spaghetti rustica,* with swordfish, tuna, salmon, dried tomatoes, Abruzzi herbs, and bread crumbs.

Via Spalti 50. ⓒ **0923-28246.** Reservations recommended Fri–Sat nights. Main courses 6€–13€. AE, DC, MC, V. Daily 1–11pm.

Taverna Paradiso ⭐ SICILIAN   This tavern was established in 1996 in a very old warehouse set directly on the seafront. It's artfully decorated with rustic artifacts that show off the antique masonry to its best advantage. This is the town's most elegant and prestigious restaurant. At least part of its clientele comes here to discuss business deals; the rest visit because the food is excellent and prices are not nearly as high as you might expect from a restaurant of this quality. The setting is richly evocative—a warren of medieval-looking stone rooms cheerfully and stylishly decorated. Care and precision go into every dish, especially the house specialties: a maritime version of the North African couscous, and spaghetti with tangy sea urchins. A marvelous pasta dish comes with lobster, shrimp, and fresh artichokes. The ubiquitous roulade of swordfish is a favorite among locals. In winter, well-flavored versions of meat and poultry are likely to be featured when fish catches are slim because of rough waters.

Lungomare Dante Alighieri 22. ⓒ **0923-22303.** Reservations recommended. Main courses 9€–13€. AE, DC, MC, V. Mon–Sat noon–3:30pm and 8–11pm. Open daily (same hours) in Aug.

4 Marsala

134km (83 miles) NW of Agrigento, 301km (187 miles) W of Catania, 124km (77 miles) SW of Palermo, 31km (19 miles) S of Trapani

Evoking a North African town with its tangle of narrow streets and alleys, Marsala is the home of the world-famous Marsala wine, a rival of port and Madeira. The wine was first popularized in 1770 when an Englishman, John Woodhouse, came ashore from a British ship that had been forced to anchor here during a violent storm. Woodhouse headed for a local tavern, and the rest is history.

The name Marsala dates from the port's occupation by the Saracens, who called it *Marsa el Allah,* or "Port of God." But it was the Carthaginians who founded the town on Cape Lilibeo (also called Cape Boeo) in 396 B.C. after fleeing nearby Mothia, which had been destroyed by armies from Syracuse. Marsala then fell to the Romans after a siege that lasted a decade (250–241 B.C.). The year 47 B.C. saw the arrival of Julius Caesar, who pitched camp here en route to North Africa.

One of the most famous events in Italian history occurred here on May 11, 1860, when Garibaldi and his brigade of 1,000 red-shirted men arrived to liberate Sicily from the Bourbons.

In 1943 Marsala sustained heavy damage from Allied bombers before their land invasion of Sicily.

Today Marsala is a thriving little town on Cape Boeo, the westernmost tip of Sicily. Many of its hotels and restaurants are filled with businesspeople trading in Marsala wine. Although Erice (see earlier in this chapter) is a more popular attraction, Marsala merits a day if you can spare it.

GETTING THERE   At least 15 **trains** per day run south from Trapani Monday through Friday, 10 on Saturday, and 11 on Sunday, the trip to Marsala taking 30 minutes; the one-way fare is 2.35€. For schedules, call ✆ **892021. Buses** for Marsala leave from Piazza Montalto in Trapani at the rate of four per day, the trip taking 55 minutes, a one-way ticket going for 2.60€. For bus schedules, call ✆ **0923-21021. Motorists** head south from Trapani along Route 115.

VISITOR INFORMATION   The **Marsala Tourist Office,** Corso 11 Maggio 100 (✆ **0923-714097**), is open Monday through Saturday from 8am to 1:45pm and 2:10 to 8:10pm, Sunday from 9am to noon.

GETTING AROUND   Bus no. 5 services most of the addresses in the heart of Marsala. For a **taxi,** call ✆ **339-5497849.**

FAST FACTS   In an **emergency,** call the *Carabinieri* (police corps) at ✆ **0923-951010** or **112.** The most convenient **drugstore** is the **Marsala Pharmacy,** Corso 11 Maggio 126 (✆ **0923-953254**), open Sunday through Friday from 9am to 1:30pm and 4:30 to 8pm. When this drugstore is closed—for example, on a Saturday—a notice is posted listing what other pharmacies are open. For **medical care,** the **Guardia Medica** (✆ **0923-782343**) is at the Hospital San Biagio, Via Colocas 10 (✆ **0923-782343**).

EXPLORING THE TOWN

The heart of this wine-producing town is the **Piazza della Repubblica,** site of the Chiesa Madre (see below) and the Palazzo Senatorio, dating from the 18th century and nicknamed "Loggia."

Branching off from this square is the main street, **Corso 11 Maggio,** flanked by the town's most splendid palazzi. In the heyday of the Roman empire, this street was called *Decumanus Maximus.* From Piazza della Repubblica, **Via Garibaldi** heads south to **Porta Garibaldi,** a magnificent gateway crowned by an eagle. Garibaldi is honored because it was at Marsala that he and 1,000 volunteers, dressed in red shirts, landed from Genoa. Their aim was to overthrow the Bourbon rulers, thus liberating the "Kingdom of the Two Sicilies."

The largest church in Marsala is **Chiesa Madre,** Piazza della Repubblica (✆ **0923-716295**), open daily from 7:30am to 9pm, charging no admission fee. Constructed originally during the Norman occupation, it was massively rebuilt in the 1700s. The original church here was dedicated to St. Thomas à Becket. The dome collapsed in 1893 and was partially reconstructed in the 20th century. The facade is decorated with statues and flanked by two small campaniles (bell towers), completed as late as 1956. The three-nave interior is graced with slender pillars and contains many art treasures, including 15th- and 16th-century sculptures by the Gagini brothers. Seek out, in particular, the lovely *Madonna del Popolo* in the right transept, a 1490 creation of Domenico Gagini..

In back of the Chiesa Madre is the entrance to **Museo degli Arazzi,** Via Garraffa 57(✆ **0923-712903**), open daily from 9am to 1pm and 4 to 6pm; admission costs 1.05€. Its main attraction is a collection of eight big **Flemish tapestries** ✦ made in Brussels between 1530 and 1550. They were a gift from Antonio Lombardo (1523–95), the archbishop of Messina, who was born in Marsala. He received them as a present from Philip II when he was the ambassador to the Spanish court. The tapestries depict such scenes as the capture of Jerusalem and the war fought by Titus against the Jews in A.D. 66 to 67. Art lovers come from all over the world to admire these skillfully created tapestries.

Marsala's other major museum, **Museo Archeologico di Baglio Anselmi,** lies at Lungomare Boéo (✆ **0923-952535**) and is open daily from 9am to 1:30pm, and also Wednesday, Friday, Saturday, and Sunday from 4 to 7pm. Admission is 2.10€. The museum is installed in a former warehouse for bottles of Marsala. Its chief attraction is the remains of a **Punic ship** ✦ discovered in 1971 off Isola Longa, north of Marsala. The well-preserved poop, found in a seabed, measures 35m (115 ft.) long. It was artfully reconstructed in 1980, and it's amazing to believe that a vessel that sank on its maiden voyage during the First Punic War is still around in any form. Once manned by 68 oarsmen, this is the only known such war vessel ever uncovered. The ship may have been constructed for the Battle of the Egadi Islands in 241 B.C. On display are objects rescued from the sunken vessel, such as a sailor's wooden button or corks from the amphorae.

Open for a look 24 hours a day is the **Insula di Capo Boeo,** lying at the end of Viale Vittorio Emanuele. Here are the ruins of a trio of Roman *insulae* (apartment complexes), including that of a spacious villa dating from the 3rd century B.C. Around the *impluvium* (basin built into the floor) you can see a quartet of mosaics depicting "The Battle of the Wild Beasts." Also here are the ruins of *terme* (baths) and salons containing mosaics. The head of Medusa is clearly visible.

SHOPPING

Farmacia Fici   One of the oldest, continuously operating pharmacies in Sicily was established on this site in 1773 and still displays some of its original architectural adornments. You'll find it a 2-minute walk from the Chiesa Madre, behind an elaborately carved wooden facade. It retains a sense of its old-fashioned roots despite the modern medicines that fill part of its interior. 70 Via XI Marzo. ✆ **0923-953058**.

Don't Even Mention Port in This Town

If you'd like to watch Marsala grapes crushed and turned into the town's "sweet nectar," Marsala wine, head for the **Cantine Florio,** Lungomare Via Florio (✆ **0923-781111**), which offers free guided tours of the winery. The 30-minute tours are on Monday or Thursday at 11am and again at 3:30pm, with another tour on Friday at 11am.

Devotees of Marsala also flock to **Cantina Sperimentale Istituto Regionale della Vite e del Vino,** Via Trapani 218 (✆ **0923-737511**), open daily from 7:30am to 2pm and also on Tuesday and Wednesday from 3 to 7pm. You are allowed to sample a number of experimental wines here.

WHERE TO STAY

Delfino Beach Hotel   Although not fully complete, this is the closest thing to a large-scale resort in Marsala. Set 5km (3 miles) south of town, behind a neobaroque facade across a busy highway from the beach, it was designed as a compound of cement-sided buildings within a walled garden, centered on a splashy-looking core that evokes a highly theatrical stage setting. Regrettably, part of the original dream here went sour, and there's a sense of incompleteness about the place, thanks to scaffolding that never seems to be dismantled, piles of sand, cement mixers, and occasional clouds of dust.

Plans originally called for the construction of 100 guest rooms and enough amenities to afford the hotel a government-rated four-star status, but in its present state, tourist authorities gave it only three stars. The hotel restaurant (recommended below)—which is better maintained and more pulled together than the hotel itself—and its beachfront lie a dusty 10-minute walk across the busy coastal highway from the hotel's core. Frankly, despite the swimming pool, whose design evokes a pool in Las Vegas, and nearby access to the beach, we prefer the accommodations at the Hotel President (see below), closer to the center of town.

Lungomare Mediterraneo 672, 91025 Marsala. ✆ **0923-751076.** Fax 0923-751303. www.delfinobeach. com. 50 units. 83€–114€ double. Rates include breakfast. AE, DC, MC, V. **Amenities:** Restaurant; bar; pool; laundry. *In room:* A/C, TV, minibar.

Hotel Acos   This boxy-looking government-rated three-star hotel was originally built in 1959 as a member of the now-defunct AGIP hotel chain. It's set in back of a gas station on one of the town's busiest boulevards, on the south side of Marsala's commercial core. Favored by business travelers, it has a serviceable but not at all stylish lobby with a cramped coffee bar in one corner, and an unpretentious restaurant (the **San Carlo**) immediately adjacent. The small to midsize guest rooms were renovated in 2000 and feature efficient contemporary furniture and tile-covered bathrooms, usually with shower-tub combinations.

Via Mazara 14, 91025 Marsala. ✆ **0923-999015.** Fax 0923-999132. 41 units. 75€ double; 98€ suite. Rates include breakfast. AE, DC, MC, V. **Amenities:** Restaurant; bar; laundry. *In room:* A/C, TV, minibar.

Hotel President ⍟   Modern and pleasingly designed, this is Marsala's best and most prestigious hotel, with a whiff of jazzy insouciance that might have been inspired by Vegas. You may be surprised to learn that this favorite stopover of business travelers is rated only three stars by the local tourist authorities, since it looks very much like it deserves four. The entrance is prefaced with a row of palms; inside, a sheathing of travertine marble adds a touch of sober dignity. Guest rooms are located in two five-story towers, each connected at its base with a granite-floored lobby strewn with leather-upholstered sofas and chairs. Guest rooms are comfortable, sunny, and relatively large, each with a bathroom that— with three separate kinds of marble sheathing and shower-tub combinations— looks like a testimonial to the stonemason's art.

Via Nino Bixio 1, 91025 Marsala. ℂ **0923-99333.** Fax 0923-999115. 128 units. 98€ double and suites. AE, DC, MC, V. **Amenities:** Restaurant; 2 bars (1 with live piano music); pool; health club; room service. *In room:* A/C, TV, minibar.

WHERE TO DINE

Fonte d'Oro ⭐ SICILIAN   Charming and small in scale, this local favorite was established in 1999 and is directed by two Marsala-born partners, Massimo and Omar, who place a huge emphasis on the freshness and quality of the fish they serve. In some ways, it's one of the insider-ish hipster restaurants of Marsala, having hosted many of the pop and rock 'n' roll singers who come to town. The setting is a long, narrow, high-ceilinged room with a bar at its distant end, a stone facade, and a genuinely friendly welcome from the hardworking staff. A platter loaded with ice and a selection of the day's fish is often brought directly tableside for your inspection (and education). The best menu items include a *fritto misto* (mixed fry of fish), grilled swordfish, squid or octopus with mint sauce, and squid delectably stuffed with minced veal and pork (a house specialty).

Via Curatolo. ℂ **0923-719586.** Reservations recommended. Main courses 4.50€–9€. MC, V. Daily 11:30am–3pm and 7pm–midnight.

Ristorante Delfino ⭐ FISH/SICILIAN   This restaurant lies adjacent to the beachfront and across the highway from the hotel that bears the same name. It was established in the 1960s and has done rip-roaring business ever since. The setting is a very large, always bustling series of terrazzo-floored, slightly battered dining rooms, with a row of large windows and a terrace overlooking the sea. A huge array of antipasti, plus a steamy hardworking kitchen that's open to view, greet visitors as they enter. The fish soup is the best in town, but the homemade bucatini in a tuna and mint sauce may be your starter of choice. Several kinds of carpaccio, often flavored with balsamic vinegar, are presented nightly. The chef is justifiably proudest of his wide variety of fresh fish, much of which is exhibited in a display case near the entrance.

Delfino Beach Hotel, Lungomare Mediterraneo 672, 91025 Marsala. ℂ **0923-998188.** Reservations not necessary. Main courses 7.75€–16€; pizza 3€–5.50€; set menu 13€. AE, MC, V. Daily 8:30am–11pm. Closed Tues Oct–Mar.

Tenuto Volpara ⭐ *Finds* SICILIAN   Follow a labyrinth of winding country roads, then pass between a stately pair of masonry columns to reach Marsala's quintessential country inn—a jumble of light, noise, and energy in an otherwise quiet and isolated rural setting 5.6km (3½ miles) south of the city center. Vast and echoing, with one of the largest dining rooms in western Sicily, it was rebuilt (in a much-expanded form of the original) in 1993 on the site of a ruined country tavern that had been here for centuries. Many of your fellow diners might be here as part of wedding receptions and baptisms, and you'll probably find yourself dodging cameras and cascades of rice during the ongoing festivities that add to this place's sense of fun.

You'll dine beneath soaring stone arches. Our party took comfort in the filet steak braised in a red Barolo wine sauce and the rabbit roasted with fresh herbs. Homemade sausages served roasted with an herb-flavored liqueur were a delight, as was the fettuccine with fresh mushrooms. Our favorite pasta here is the wide-noodled pappardelle *rustico,* with broccoli, pine nuts, bacon, and cream. The dessert specialty is *zabina,* a pastry richly laced with ricotta cheese.

Situated in an annex somewhat removed from the brouhaha surrounding the restaurant are **18 motel-style guest rooms,** each trimmed in stone and featuring a tile-covered bathroom (with shower only), air-conditioning, minibar, TV, and phone. With breakfast included, a double costs 62€.

Contrada de Volpara. ℂ **0923-984588.** Reservations recommended Fri–Sat nights. Main courses 4.20€–9.30€; set-price menu 17€. AE, DC, MC, V. Daily 1:30–3pm and 8:30pm–midnight. Closed Mon Oct–Mar.

IN THE ENVIRONS

Trattoria delle Cozze Basirico ⍟ *Finds* SEAFOOD   Set on the southern outskirts of the town of Mazara del Vallo, about 5km (3 miles) from the center, in one of the few all-wooden buildings in town, this restaurant might remind you of an oversized railway car that just happens to serve vast amounts of seafood to hundreds of diners every night throughout the summer months. Don't expect grandeur; this is a gutsy, two-fisted place whose walls are open to the sea breezes, where even the occasional billionaire who ventures in leaves all his pretensions at the door. Furniture consists of nothing more than hard-backed benches and battered trestle tables, and the overworked staff is coyishly clad in exaggerated versions of sailor costumes. There are no printed menus here: You give your order to a fast-talking waiter, who will tell you that the only options are selections from the buffet-style antipasti table, several different preparations of mussels, and steamed octopus that's served either in a lemon or a light tomato sauce. Drinks of choice include wine or beer, a suitable accompaniment for the restaurant's widely acknowledged specialty, mussels. Mazara del Vallo is reached by heading southeast of Marsala along Route 115 for 22km (13½ miles).

Litoranca Bocca-Torretta. ℂ **0923-942323.** Reservations not accepted. Main courses 7€–20€. AE, DC, MC, V. May–Sept daily 8pm–midnight. Closed Oct–Apr.

Appendix: Sicily in Depth

Sicily is a land unto itself, proudly different from the rest of Italy in its customs and traditions. On the map, in fact, the toe of the Italian boot appears poised to kick Sicily away from the mainland, as if it didn't belong to the rest of the country. The largest of the Mediterranean islands, it's separated from Italy by the 4km (2½-mile) Straits of Messina, a dangerously unstable earthquake zone, making the eventual construction of a bridge doubtful.

Although the island's economy is moving closer to those of Europe and the rest of Italy, its culture is still very much its own. Its vague Arab flavor reminds us that Sicily broke away from the mainland of Africa, *not* Italy, millions of years ago. Its Greek heritage lives on. Although there are far too many cars in Palermo, and parts of the island are heavily polluted by industrialization, Sicily is still a place where life is slower, tradition is respected, and the myths and legends of the past aren't yet forgotten.

Sicily has been inhabited since the Ice Age, and its history is full of natural and political disasters. It has been conquered and occupied over and over: by the Greeks in the 6th to 5th centuries B.C., then the Romans, the Vandals, the Arabs (who created a splendid civilization), the Normans, the Swabians, the fanatically religious House of Aragón, and the Bourbons. When Garibaldi landed at Marsala in 1860, he brought an illusion of freedom, soon dissipated by the patronage system of the Mafia. Besides the invaders, the centuries have brought a series of plagues, volcanic eruptions, earthquakes, and economic hardships to threaten the interwoven culture of Sicily.

The land has a deep archaeological heritage and is full of sensual sights and experiences: verdant vineyards and fragrant citrus groves, horses with plumes and bells pulling gaily painted carts, masses of blooming almond and cherry trees in February, Greek temples, ancient theaters, complex city architecture, and aromatic Marsala wine. In summer the *sirocco* (hot wind) whirling out of the Libyan deserts dries the fertile fields, crisping the harvest into a sun-blasted palette of browns. Beaches are plentiful around the island, but most are rocky, crowded, or dirty. The best are at Mondello, outside Palermo, and around Taormina in the east.

1 The Natural Environment

Of all the islands of the Mediterranean, Sicily is the largest, spread across 40,965km (25,460 miles), and lying halfway between Gibraltar and the Suez Canal. It is surrounded by several archipelagos, the most important of which are the Aeolian Islands (see chapter 7), with such touristed spots as Stromboli, Lipari, and Vulcano. Other island groups include Egadi, Pantelleria, and Pelagie, the latter centered at Lampedusa.

Bounded by the Tyrrhenian Sea to its north, the Sicilian Sea to its southwest, and the Ionian Sea on its eastern coast, Sicily is separated from southern Italy by the Straits of Messina. Though it's the country's largest region, Sicily is only the fourth highest in population.

Sicily enjoys a Mediterranean climate—it's the first part of Italy to heat up in the spring and the last to grow chilly in winter. It also suffers the longest, hottest summers, with July a scorcher.

An island of rivers, Sicily is also volcanic, the most threatening menace being Mount Etna on the eastern coast. Some of the islands in the various archipelagos also have volcanoes, notably Stromboli, but most are long dormant.

The island is split by four mountain groups. First and foremost are the so-called "Sicilian Alps," the Apennines, actually a continuation of the same mountain range that begins in Calabria on the mainland. These mountains stretch along the north coast, beginning at the Straits of Messina and going west to the Torto River. The Apennines are divided into a trio of ranges, including Peloritani, Nebrodi, and Madonie. Of all three, we recommend at least an exploration of Madonie, the most fascinating for touring.

Another mountain range is found in western Sicily to the west of the Platani and Torto rivers. The third member of the trio lies at the core of Sicily, looking out to the coast of North Africa 140km (87 miles) away, scene of so many embarkations of island conquerors. The southern and western half of Sicily, in terms of topography, is more similar to the Atlas Mountains of North Africa than the Sicilian mainland.

> **Impressions**
>
> *To have seen Italy without having seen Sicily is not to have seen Italy at all, for Sicily is the clue to everything.*
>
> —J. W. Goethe

The ancient Greeks, among the first major settlers, called Sicily *Trinacria,* or triangle, because of its triangular shape. The island coastline covers much ground, a distance of 1,000km (621 miles). The smoothest and most uninterrupted flank stretches from the Straits of Messina to the Gulf of Palermo, overlooking the city of Palermo, Sicily's capital. The southern coast begins in the southeast at Capo Passero on the Golfo di Noto and heads west along the Golfo di Gela, coming to an end at Capo Lilibeo south of Marsala of winemaking fame.

The eastern coast, opening onto Mare Ionio or the Ionian Sea, begins at Capo Passero and heads north to Messina, bypassing the cities of Catania and Syracuse. Gólfo di Catania is the most important body of water in the east, providing the island's largest plain with a seafront.

As the coastline nears Messina, it becomes a series of towering cliffs broken up by a network of craggy inlets. For the visitor, the most stunning sea- and landscapes are found around the resort of Taormina and the small city of Acireale, north of Catania.

FLORA & FAUNA   The deforestation of the island since as far back as Roman times has been a disaster. Once rich in forests that provided it with abundant water, Sicily had vast tracts of woodland razed over the years to turn the island into the grain belt of the Roman Empire. This massive deforestation has left Sicily with a more foreboding climate—hot and dry.

The ancient Greek settlers brought with them the cultivation of the **grape** and the **olive tree.** The Arab conquerors brought **date palms** from Africa and encouraged the cultivation of **citrus groves.**

Typical Mediterranean flora is found all over the island, including the **strawberry tree** and **myrtle. Broom bushes** set the countryside alive in spring, with miles of sunflower-yellow coloring. The **spiny shrub,** the so-called "bastard olive," grows wild almost everywhere.

Island fauna have been horrendously affected by the gradual deforestation of Sicily. Other than **sheep** grazing in country fields, it is rare to see much wildlife as you travel the country roads of Sicily. Along the coast, of course, there is still plenty of birdlife, notably **cormorants** and **seagulls.** The **viper** is the only poisonous snake on the island, frightening tourists as it suns itself at various archaeological sites in summer.

The western coast dwellers of Sicily, who for centuries have depended on the mammoth schools of **tuna** for their livelihoods, are now facing diminishing returns. Huge Japanese trawlers in international waters are capturing more and more of these fish for shipment to the markets of Tokyo.

2 History 101: Past & Present

EARLY COLONIZERS

Of the Mediterranean, Plato wrote that conquerors flocked to its coastline like "frogs gathering at a pond"—an apt comparison for Sicily itself. Much of the history of this largest of Mediterranean islands is unknown. Perhaps many tales from the *Odyssey* were set in what is now Sicily, adding to its allure as a land of myth and legend.

For 6,000 years conquerors from both Europe and Africa have tried to turn Sicily into a colony. Sicilians are so used to foreign occupation that the most nationalistic of islanders even today believe they are living under "occupation" by mainland Italy and under the control of Rome.

Archaeology provides much of the evidence of early colonization. Of course, indigenous people already existed on Sicily when the Greeks arrived, the way that Native Americans inhabited North America before the arrival of the ships of Columbus. The Siculi people, for whom Sicily was named, came from the Calabria peninsula on the mainland, settling in the east and southern central parts of the island. Tribes of Sicani from Iberia occupied the western frontiers, and the people of Elimi, claiming descent from the Trojans, inhabited the medieval hilltop town of Erice on the west coast.

Arriving from Carthage, the Phoenicians—the last of the preHellenistic invaders—settled into Solunto near present-day Palermo. The ruins of their settlement can be explored today (see chapter 5). The Phoenicians also founded Palermo,

DATELINE

- **734 B.C.** Corinthians found Syracuse.
- **480 B.C.** Syracusans overrun the Carthaginian beachhead at the Battle of Himera.
- **415 B.C.** Athens sails a Great Armada against Syracuse but is defeated.
- **409 B.C.** Carthage attacks and destroys Selinunte and Himera.
- **211 B.C.** Syracuse sacked as Romans declare victory.
- **535** Belisarius annexes Sicily to the Eastern Roman Empire.
- **827** Saracens' invasion of Sicily launched.
- **1032** Roger seizes Palermo, launching the Norman dynasty.
- **1190–97** Henry, a Hohenstaufen, rules Sicily after defeating the Normans.
- **1231** Frederick II issues the anti-feudal Constitution of Melfi.
- **1282** A rebellion—the so-called Sicilian Vespers—breaks out in Palermo, spreading across the island.
- **1302** Peace treaty between the Angevins and the Aragonese gives Sicily to the Spaniards.
- **1513** Spanish Inquisition introduced.
- **1693** Earthquake destroys much of eastern Sicily, including Catania.
- **1713** Treaty of Utrecht assigns Sicily to House of Savoy.
- **1734** Spanish reclaim Sicily under Bourbon king, Charles I.
- **1812** A liberal constitution spells the doom of the feudal system.
- **1816** Ferdinand abrogates constitution, creates Kingdom of the Two Sicilies.
- **1860** Garibaldi's forces chase out the Bourbons, as Sicilians vote for unification.
- **1908** Earthquake in Messina takes 80,000 lives.

continues

the capital of Sicily, calling it *Panormus*. The Chalcidians landed in the east to establish what is modern-day Messina, and the Megarians founded the colony of Megara Hyblaea, the ruins of which can be explored north of Syracuse, once you pass through an industrial blight.

In time these tribes came in for Hellenization. Naxos, near today's Taormina, was launched around 735 B.C. by mariners, a group of Chalcidians from Greece. You can explore these ruins today (see chapter 8). Around the same time (734 B.C.), the Corinthians laid the first stones on the island of Ortygia, calling their city *Syracoussai*, which in time became today's Syracuse.

- 1943 Allied armies under Patton and Montgomery capture Sicily from the Nazis.
- 1946 Sicily granted limited independence.
- 1951 A massive immigration from the island begins, eventually totaling one million Sicilians.
- 1980s–1990s In spite of a campaign against it by the government, the Mafia maintains a strong influence on the island.
- 2002 Mount Etna announced itself once again, belching smoke and fire and threatening tourist facilities near Catania.

North of Syracuse, Megara Hyblaea was founded in 728 B.C., followed in 628 B.C. by the founding of Selinunte, still among the great archaeological ruins of Sicily. The last of the great Greek cities, Agrigento, was founded in 581 B.C., its Valley of the Temples today remaining one of the great attractions of southern Italy (see chapter 12).

The growing power of Carthage in North Africa brought fear to Sicily. By the 7th century B.C., Carthage had allied itself with the Phoenicians against the Greek settlers. The colonies of Magna Graceia, or Greater Greece, thrived on trade. As the Greek colonies grew more powerful in Sicily, they fought each other out of greed and jealousy—all of which laid the groundwork for the "rule of the tyrants."

THE RULE OF THE TYRANTS

In ancient times, the word "tyrant" described men who grabbed power instead of inheriting it, as in a royal lineage. Tyrants ruled over the Greek city-states of Sicily. The year 480 B.C. proved pivotal in the island's history. That was when the Carthaginians mounted a massive attack on the western possessions of Greece, including Sicily. Hamilcar, the African commander, sailed into Sicily on the northern coast with an army of 300,000 mercenaries carried in 3,000 transport ships. The Carthaginian general besieged Himera outside Termini Imerese, and the tyrant of the area, Thereon, appealed to Syracuse for help. Syracuse sent 55,000 men marching across the heart of Sicily. Hamilcar asked for help from Selinunte on the south coast.

The Carthaginians fell for a variation of the old Trojan Horse trick, mistaking the Syracuse forces for reinforcements from Selinunte. When their ranks opened, some 150,000 soldiers were slain and their ships torched. As a result, the winner of that battle, Gelon, the tyrant of Syracuse, became a towering figure in the Greek world. Seven decades would pass before Carthage would return to pillage Sicily.

The defeat of the Carthaginians led to a golden age for Sicily, as such classical figures as Archimedes, Theocritus, and Empedocles became household names. Plato and Aeschylus dropped in from Greece. The largest of the Greek temples were constructed in Agrigento, the biggest amphitheater in Syracuse. The period of growth and expansion was set back only by infighting among the city-states.

Syracuse was clearly the dominant power in Sicily, so much so that it dared challenge the supremacy of Athens itself. In response, in 415 B.C. Athens sent the largest armada ever assembled to subdue Syracuse. The Great Expedition from the east met with failure, and 7,000 soldiers from Athens were taken prisoner. The great city of Syracuse reached the apex of its power.

THE REVENGE OF CARTHAGE

The grandson of the defeated Hamilcar, the great Hannibal, arrived on the southern coast of Sicily with his mercenaries in 409 B.C., seeking revenge over his ancestor's defeat at Himera on the northern coast. He destroyed what had been a great city, Selinunte, its modern-day ruins a testament to his victory. Selinunte faded into history forever.

Hannibal then headed north to seek his revenge against Himera, where his grandfather had been defeated. He won a great victory and tortured and murdered all the male survivors of Himera.

Hannibal came back in full force once again and in 406 B.C. destroyed Agrigento (then called *Akragas*). At the time Akragas was surpassed only by Syracuse in power and influence. During the siege a plague swept through his camp, and Hannibal succumbed to it. His successor, Himilkon, took over for the Carthaginians, offering his son, Moloch, as a sacrifice to the Gods to show he meant business. After 8 months of siege, Akragas fell to the Carthaginians.

Blaming the generals in Syracuse for the defeat of Akragas, a demagogue, Dionysius, seized power in 405 B.C. and became one of the most famous of all the tyrants. The Carthaginians moved on Syracuse, but the plague swept over their forces and the remaining army returned to Africa.

THE ROMANS IN SICILY

The Grecian hold over Sicily was coming to an end. With Carthage subdued, a new menace rose to threaten imperial Sicily: Rome. Sicily was largely spared during the First Punic War (264–241 B.C.), but the people of Syracuse sided with Carthage during the Second Punic War in 213 B.C. For this, the newly emerged powers of Rome did not forgive Sicily, and in 211 B.C. the Romans conquered the island. In its defeat, Sicily became a "sub-colony," and the formerly proud inhabitants of the island became slaves or servants, living in poverty. Slave revolts broke out periodically but were brutally suppressed by the Romans, who used the island as a breadbasket after felling its trees.

In the 3rd century A.D., when Sicilians were finally granted citizenship in the Roman Empire, it was a little late. The barbarians from the north were on the march.

BARBARIANS, BYZANTINES & THE SARACENS

As the Roman Empire collapsed to the invading Visigoths in A.D. 410, Sicily came under increasing attack from the Vandals, who launched warships from the coastline of Tunisia. The barbarian invasion of the island was short-lived, but for a while Sicily was temporarily reunited with Italy under the Ostrogoth Theodoric.

In A.D. 535 Belisarius, the Byzantine general, occupied Sicily. Amazingly, for a brief time in A.D. 663 Syracuse became the center of the eastern Byzantine empire.

Known collectively as the Saracens, the Arabs, Berbers, and Spanish Muslims had become increasingly attracted to the prize of Sicily. By 700 the island of Pantelleria had fallen to them. By 827 a full-fledged Arab invasion of Sicily was successfully mounted. Their landing was at Mazara del Vallo, in the south. Four years later Palermo fell to the Saracens, and by A.D. 965 the invading African forces had moved east to the Straits of Messina.

The Arabs made Palermo the capital of their new Sicilian empire, decorating it with gardens, mosques—some 300 in all—palaces, and domes. Unlike the Roman occupation, Sicily actually prospered under the Arab rulers, who made substantial breakthroughs in agriculture, introducing citrus trees, date palms, cotton, and other crops. Even religious tolerance was practiced, and many Christians abandoned their faith to Muslim beliefs.

But the Saracen rule, like so many others, would be short-lived. Because of internal Arab bickering, the Byzantine general, George Maniakes, decided that Sicily once again was ripe to be plucked. Although his forces never got much beyond Syracuse, a new menace loomed: The Normans were about to move in on Sicily, an island they regarded as a glittering prize.

THE MEN OF THE NORTH

If a traveler should wonder why there are so many blondes in Sicily today, it's because of the Norman conquest of the island. In 1061 an Arab emir in Messina called on Roger Hauteville for help in putting down a rebellion among fellow Saracens. Big mistake. The Normans came, they saw, and they conquered, although it took them another 3 decades to subdue the entire island.

Amazingly, the Normans sometimes enlisted the aid of the resident Arabs to fight other Arabs. At one of the series of bloody battles, the Normans ended up firmly entrenched in Palermo, making it their capital in 1072.

Although the Normans were to stay less than a century, ruling with a series of five kings, they left an architectural legacy that remains a distinctive feature on the Sicilian landscape, especially in Palermo. Sometimes they took over an already existing Arab mosque and turned it into an "Arab-Norman" style of church. By 1200 the Arabic language was fading, giving way to French and Italian.

Count Roger or Roger I (1031–1101) launched the Norman-Sicilian dynasty. He was followed by Roger II (1105–54), one of the great kings of Europe in the Middle Ages, who brought together some of the most creative forces in the Mediterranean and who was also a big patron of the arts. In addition, he extended his Sicilian kingdom to embrace parts of North Africa, southern Italy, and Malta. Weaker kings, such as William the Bad (1154–66), followed.

THE REIGN OF THE HOHENSTAUFENS

When the Norman king, William II (1166–89)—called William the Good—died in 1189 at the age of 36, the throne went to Tancred, his illegitimate son. The ascension to the throne was challenged by King Henry VI, a German Hohenstaufen, or Swabian. Tancred hung on until his death in 1194, surviving a sacking of Messina in 1190 by Richard the Lion-Hearted on his way to join the Third Crusade.

William III succeeded Tancred, but the Hohenstaufen fleet docked at Messina, and the short-term king was imprisoned and would eventually die in a castle. Henry (later to become the Holy Roman Emperor Henry VI) was declared king of Sicily in 1190.

Henry was to die of dysentery in 1197, the throne passing to Frederick I of Sicily, his son, who was only 3 years old. His mother, Constance, ruled for him. When he grew up, he proved to be a strong king, especially against such island rebels as the Arabs. As a promoter of science, medicine, and law, he was called *Stupor Mundi,* or "Wonder of the World." Under Frederick, Palermo became the most important city in Europe, a cultural center with no equal in the Western world. In 1231 he issued the anti-feudal Constitution of Melfi, stripping the barons of much of their power. At his death in 1250, Sicily entered a period of decline.

A French pope eventually awarded the title of King of Sicily to Charles of Anjou, the brother of Louis IX, the French king. Under Charles, in 1266 Angevin forces fought and beat the armies of the Hohenstaufen rulers. Once in power, Charles of Anjou launched a punishing attack against those islanders who had supported the Hohenstaufens.

THE WAR OF THE VESPERS

The abject poverty and the stern rule of the Angevins sparked an uprising, known as the Sicilian Vespers, which began on Easter Sunday 1282. What sparked the uprising is not known for certain. One story has it that a gang of French troops raped a teenage girl; another that a French soldier insulted a local woman in Palermo.

At any rate, the tolling of a church bell for evening services, or Vespers, at the Chiesa di Santo Spirito set off a riot. Every French soldier in sight was slaughtered, the rebellion fanning out to eventually cover the island. Any Frenchman unable to pronounce the word *cicero* correctly was massacred.

There were many patriots, to be sure, but the general rioting and slaughter was also a time for many islanders to settle old scores with their enemies. A group of noblemen called upon Peter of Aragon for help. He landed in Traipani 5 months after that initial violent outbreak on Easter Sunday. In only a few days he was proclaimed king.

The actual War of the Vespers was fought between the armies of Aragon and the forces of Angevin, who used Naples as their base. It was to last for 21 years. Slowly but effectively, Spain tightened its noose around Sicily. The rope would not be untied for 5 centuries.

RULE BY THE SPANIARDS

In 1302 the Peace of Caltabelotta concluded the war between the Vatican-leaning Angevins and the imperial Aragonese. Sicily was divided into two kingdoms, the Angevins retaining the territories in mainland Italy (such as Naples), but with Sicily itself going to the Spaniards. The Aragonese kings, based in Palermo, would rule the island directly until 1458.

Isolated in the Mediterranean, Sicily virtually "sat out" the great artistic and cultural movements sweeping mainland Europe in the 14th and 15th centuries. The Renaissance of Italy had virtually no impact in forgotten Sicily. Only one great artist arose from this depression: Antonello da Messina (1430–79), who had been inspired by Flemish art during his travels to the north.

If anything, feudal bonds were tightened as Sicily drifted back into the Middle Ages. The Spanish Inquisition, introduced to Sicily in 1513, virtually silenced any inquiring minds.

THE 17TH & 18TH CENTURIES

As Spain drifted into its own long decline in the 17th and 18th centuries, so did its colony of Sicily, ruled by indifferent viceroys. Political corruption was rampant throughout the land.

In the hinterlands of Sicily, brigand bands, protesting against vast estates and their cruel owners, rose up to strike back. Calling themselves the *Mafia,* these outlaws butchered livestock, burned crops, and slaughtered local bailiffs to protest the outmoded feudal system.

As if the feudal system and its inherent evils weren't enough, in the 17th century Sicily was plagued by natural disasters. Mount Etna erupted in 1669, causing massive damage to the east coast and destroying Catania. The eruption was followed in 1693 by earthquakes along the same coastline, which killed about 5% of Sicily's population. Sicily was also struck by outbreaks of the plague.

Politically, the island became a pawn among the powers of Europe. After the death of Charles II of Spain in 1700, that country was plunged into the Wars of the Spanish Succession. In 1713 Sicily passed into the hands of the House of Savoy, according to the terms of the Treaty of Utrecht. In 1720 it was traded to the Austrians for Sardinia.

The Spanish came back in full force in 1734, reclaiming Sicily and placing it under the Bourbon king Charles I (1734–59). Charles I was to visit Sicily only once. In time he gave up the kingdom to assume the title of King Charles III of Spain. He was followed by Ferdinand IV, who held power as Ferdinand IV of Naples in 1806. The island's so-called noblemen, living parasitically off the people of Sicily, tightened their feudal grips on the island, as new ideas unleashed by the French Revolution brought in winds of change.

THE COMING OF NAPOLEON

The little colonel, Napoleon, never actually invaded Sicily, although his rearranging of the maps of Europe had an impact on the island. When Napoleon conquered Naples in 1799, Ferdinand IV was forced out when the crown went to Napoleon's brother, Joseph. Ferdinand fled to Sicily, where he was protected by British troops. Under pressure from the island commander of British forces, Lord William Bentinck, Ferdinand was compelled in 1812 to draw up a constitution for Sicily similar to that which governed Britain.

This document spelled the death of the feudal life, as a two-chamber Sicilian Parliament was formed in Palermo. The court established in Palermo was to be free of the one presiding in Naples.

Once Napoleon was defeated in 1815, Ferdinand went back to Naples and abrogated the constitution. The British departed, and Ferdinand assumed control again, declaring himself Ferdinand I, King of the Two Sicilies (that is, Naples and Sicily) in 1816. He repealed all reforms.

In protest, Sicily rebelled, but the rebellion was put down with the aid of mercenaries from Austria. Ferdinand died in 1825, and conditions only worsened under Ferdinand II (1830–59), who was named *Re Bomba* after his 5-day bombardment of Messina to quell insurrections there and in Palermo in 1848. In spite of the failures of the rebellions, the spirit of revolution remained. By 1860, the name Garibaldi was being whispered across the island.

REVOLT & THE ARRIVAL OF GARIBALDI

On April 4, 1860, an island-wide revolt against the Bourbon regime broke out. Seizing upon the news, the revolutionary leader, Giuseppe Garibaldi, decided the time to strike was at hand. Along with his famous *mille,* 1,000 red-shirted soldiers, he arrived at Marsala on the west coast of Sicily on May 11, 1860. He set about to conquer the island, aided by the peasants who joined his army.

A Bourbon army of 15,000 soldiers was defeated at Calatafimi on May 15, and within 2 weeks the capital at Palermo had fallen. By the time Garibaldi declared victory at the port of Milazzo on July 20, the Bourbons were in serious retreat. For the first time since 1282, Sicily was no longer under the yoke of the Bourbon regime.

On October 21 of that same year, an island-wide referendum was conducted. The results were staggering. Some 99% of the voters had opted to follow Garibaldi's plan and unify with mainland Italy. Many poor Sicilians not allowed to vote were cynical of the results, viewing the Piedmontese House of Savoy as the new "occupier" of the island.

FASCISM & WARS

Under the House of Savoy, Sicily indeed found itself in the same poor position it had endured over the centuries under many conquerors. The so-called aristocracy remained firmly in charge of the economy, and the peasants got nothing, not even the right to vote. In 1866 Turin crushed a rebellion in Palermo, just as previous rulers had done.

The *Mafiosi,* which later became the dreaded Mafia of the 20th century, acted as regent for the bailiffs, or landowners, extracting exorbitant rents from the peasant farmers. In desperation, some 500,000 Sicilians felt compelled to leave the island to settle in Australia or North or South America. Many of these people came from Messina, which was devastated in the earthquake of 1908, with some 80,000 lives lost.

The 20th century brought more grim realities, with the Italian conquest of Libya in 1912, followed by World War I, which devastated the economy of Sicily and took the lives of many of its young men.

The aftermath of World War I, which Italy lost to the Allied victors, was followed in 1922 by the emergence of Benito Mussolini, who had gained power in Rome. The island of Sicily was anything but his bastion of power, so the Italian dictator decided to crack down on Sicily's *Mafiosi,* a move that simply drove the criminals underground.

Mussolini sent his agent, Cesare Mori, to restore law and order to Sicily. To do so, Mori won the support of the landed gentry. To reward these large estate holders for their help, he reversed all agrarian reforms of the past decades. Amazingly, by the 1920s Sicily found itself plunged back into a feudal system.

By the 1930s Mussolini took a page from the ancient Roman conquerors' playbook and came to regard Sicily as a breadbasket to feed his armies in his quest for empire. Wheat production on the island increased but at great expense to the land, which suffered from erosion and soil depletion.

Suddenly, Sicily found itself caught up in a new war, World War II. Softening it for an invasion with aerial bombardments, the allies attacked most of Sicily's major cities. Catania, Messina, and Palermo were heavily bombed.

In July of 1943 General Patton and the American Seventh Army landed at Gela on the southern coast, as Montgomery's British forces put ashore at a point to the east. The Sicilians offered little resistance, but the Nazis fought back with venom, hoping to delay the Allied advance until they could move their men and equipment across the Straits of Messina into Calabria.

Palermo fell to the Allied advance, followed by Messina. On September 3, as the Germans escaped to southern Italy, Sicilian authorities signed an armistice with the Allies, becoming the first region of Italy to fall to the Allies, long before the invasion of Normandy in 1944. Amazingly, the Allies were greatly helped by the Mafiosi, who were eager to rid Sicily of the Fascists who had tried to wipe them out.

49TH STATE FOR THE U.S.?

With the devastation of World War II behind it, Sicilians reviewed their modern link with the Italian mainland, with thousands deciding the union had been a disaster. A Separatist movement gained hold, demanding complete independence for the island.

Sicilian Communists called for massive land redistribution. In an unlikely marriage, the landed gentry allied itself with the Mafia to keep a lid on "dangerous left-wing uprisings" throughout the land.

In 1946, bowing to pressure, the government in Rome agreed to give Sicily limited independence. Regional autonomy called for Sicily to have its own assembly and president. The role would be similar to what Scotland enjoys with England.

Many of the Separatists were even lobbying to be linked to the United States, becoming the 49th state. But with the coming of the elections of 1951, the Separatists faded into history.

For most of the latter part of the 20th century Sicily was dominated by the Christian Democrats. This is the party more or less of the Catholic church, with center-of-right leanings—a very conservative bunch. In an unspoken, almost hidden alliance, the Christian Democrats worked with the Mafia, as *clientilismo*—political patronage—became the rule of the land. Many a developmental fund ended up in the pocket of a Mafia don.

Even in the late 20th century and early 21st century, the Mafia remained a strong influence on the island, in spite of a campaign against it by the governments presiding in the 1980s and 1990s.

While it is estimated that some one million people left Sicily over a 20-year period beginning in 1951, today North Africans in hopes of a better life arrive by the boatload on such southern-tier islands as Lampedusa and Pantelleria.

3 Art & Architecture 101

For decades scholars have claimed that if you want to uncover the history of Western civilization, you need look no further than the island of Sicily. The original melting pot is a showcase of art and architecture of the Mediterranean, as each conqueror brought a different style and artistic statement to the island over 10,000 years of history. From the earliest graffiti found in caves to the glorious Doric temples at Agrigento to the pinnacle of Sicilian baroque in Catania, each wave of civilization has left its mark. Sometimes the styles of two different occupiers have been uniquely blended—witness the marriage of Arabic and Norman art and architecture into an "Arabo-Norman" style.

The bad news is that much of Sicily's artistic legacy has been damaged by volcanic explosions, earthquakes, and a range of man-made forces, from Hannibal's invading troops from North Africa to the Allied bombardments of 1943, which routed the Nazi occupiers. Much that remains is threatened by decay.

The Mafia hasn't helped either. The looting of the island's treasures for sale abroad to wealthy, anonymous buyers has taken a vast toll on Sicily's artistic heritage.

PREHISTORIC ART

Artists have been at work in Sicily since prehistoric times, as rock paintings and graffiti discovered at Palermo and Messina reveal. Even in the Neolithic period, the first indigenous cultures, such as those who settled Lipari, were turning out artful ceramics and terra-cotta items, many of which remain to this day (see the Museo Archeologico Eoliano in Lipari, chapter 7).

The most remarkable **cave paintings** were those found at Grotta del Genovese on Levanzo, one of the Egadi Islands off the western coast of Sicily. Discovered by accident in 1949, Paleolithic wall paintings and Neolithic drawings are anywhere from 6,000 to 10,000 years old. Most of the drawings are of wild animals, such as deer and horses. Even the mighty tuna traditionally found in these waters (until the Japanese started overharvesting them) show up here.

THE LEGACY OF THE GREEKS

From the 8th century on, the Greeks settled Sicily in waves, leaving great contributions to architecture before they were replaced by other conquerors. Much of their heritage was destroyed by pillagers, but much remains to delight us. The Greeks left a legacy of some of the best-preserved **temples** in the Western world, especially those at Agrigento in the Valley of the Temples, those in the ruined city of Selinunte, those in the archaeological gardens at Syracuse, and (best of all) the magnificent and still-standing Temple at Segesta. The temples constructed in Sicily were more innovative than those of classical Greece.

The archaeological museums of Sicily are filled with artifacts from the Greek occupation: **painted ceramics** and **amphorae, sculptures** and **metopes,** and **bronzes** and **carved ornaments** for temple buildings.

The apogee, however, of Greek architectural contributions to Sicily is the **Doric temple,** which stood on a three-stepped base, its inner chamber housing a statue of the god to whom the temple was dedicated.

THE COMING OF THE ROMANS

Unlike the Greeks, the Romans did not leave a great artistic legacy in Sicily, except for the **Roman villa (Villa Romana)** at Casale, outside the town of Piazza Armerina (see chapter 11). The vast polychrome floor mosaics at this 40-room villa from the 3rd century A.D. are worth the trek across Sicily. Other traces of Roman architecture can be found in the amphitheaters of Taormina and Syracuse, as well as in Syracuse's Christian catacombs.

ARTISTIC FLOWERING UNDER THE NORMANS

Subsequent conquerors such as the Byzantines and the Arabs made little artistic impact on Sicily until invited back by later conquerors, the Normans. The Byzantines transformed Greek temples into Christian basilicas, and the Arabs built palaces, private residences, and religious buildings with such Asian characteristics as domes piercing the roofs. The Arab-Norman artistic expression—called the Arab or "Arabo-Norman" style—represented a flowering of art and architecture.

From the 11th century on, the Normans began to transform Sicily, and much of their achievement remains today. This trio of different cultures—Norman, Arabic, and Byzantine—created what came to be called the "Sicilian Romanesque" style.

The Normans erected **cathedrals, or** *duomos.* Their achievements—the cathedrals at Monreale and Cefalù and the Palazzo dei Normanini in Palermo—remain among the greatest sightseeing attractions on the island today.

Roger II (1131–54) launched the first major Sicilian cathedral at Cefalù, using a Latin cross plan with a chevron pattern. Pointed arches and angled columns particular to Sicily, as opposed to mainland cathedrals, still characterize this landmark church. The mosaic decorations in its interior alone would make this one of Sicily's greatest churches.

The mosaics in the cathedral at Monreale are even more stunning and beautiful. It was at Monreale that Sicily reached the apex of its contribution to medieval art in Europe. The Monreale duomo also contains the most examples of Norman sculpture on the island, more than 200 colonnettes with twin capitals. Each of these capitals is graced with a singular composition.

Palermo also has a splendid cathedral and important **churches** of the period, such as Martorana and San Giovanni degli Ermeti, along with the Arab-influenced **palaces** of La Cuba and La Zisa.

But the Normans lavished the most attention on the seat of their power, the mammoth Palazzo dei Normanni in Palermo. This sumptuous palace became the seat of the Hauteville dynasty. Using a palace originally constructed by the Arabs in the 9th century, the Normans greatly extended it between 1132 and 1140. The crowning architectural glory of this palace is the **Cappella Palatina (Palatine Chapel),** with its Arab-inspired cupola and a stunning modern honeycomb ceiling based on Arab designs.

With the passing of the Normans and the arrival of the Hohenstaufen rulers in the 13th century, the great flowering of Sicilian art slowly died. The Hohenstaufens were more interested in fortifications and castles than in art. The Dark Ages of Sicilian art had descended on the island and would last for 4 centuries.

SICILY SLEEPS THROUGH THE RENAISSANCE

At the height of the Renaissance, Sicily remained under Spanish occupation. That may explain why Sicily virtually slept through the Renaissance, which began in Florence and swept across the rest of Italy. Although no great architectural heritage remains in Sicily from this era, painting and sculpture dominated the artistic firmament, revealing mainly Spanish but also Flemish influences.

Sicily's greatest artist, **Antonello da Messina** (1430–79), emerged during this period, initially inspired by the Flemish school and later showing the influence of his encounters with Piero della Francesca and Giovanni Bellini in Venice. One painting more than any other exemplifies his work: *Portrait of an Unknown Man,* in the Cefalù Museo Mandralisca. His other notable works, the greatest of Renaissance art in Sicily, are the *Polyptych of St. Gregory* in the Museo Reginale in Messina and the *Annunciation* in the Palazzo Bellomo in Syracuse.

The **Gagini family** of sculptors and architects moved down from Lake Lugano and had an enormous impact on Sicily. The founding father of the Gagini school was Domenico Gagini (1420–92), who often worked in conjunction with his son, Antonello, born in Palermo in 1478. Their sculpture still adorns many of the churches of Palermo, and a Gagini school flourished in Sicily until the mid-1600s.

THE EXPLOSION OF THE BAROQUE

The baroque style swept Sicily, awakening the island from a long slumber since the Normans departed centuries ago. That observer of all things Italian, Luigi Barzini, saw the baroque as a metaphor for "a frenzied search for consolation and revenge against crude and overbearing foreign devils."

The baroque came into vogue as a result of a devastating earthquake in 1693 in eastern Sicily that leveled such cities as Catania. The style of their reconstruction was baroque, whose founding father in Sicily was **Rosario Gagliardi** (1700–70). He designed the magnificent **Cattedrale San Giorgio** at Ragusa Ibla. Islanders combined the Spanish-inspired version of the baroque with Sicilian decorative and structural elements to create their own unique style.

The baroque city that emerged after the earthquake in Catania was created in part by **Giovanni Battista Vaccarini** (1702–69), who devoted 3 decades of his life to pulling a new Catania out of the ashes.

Noto, in southeastern Sicily, is another city that was rebuilt in the baroque style after the earthquake. The unity of the baroque style here remains unequaled anywhere else on the island.

In Palermo in the west, the baroque style came under the influence of Spanish dons who preferred *Spagnolismo,* or a love of ostentation. The **Quattro Canti crossroads** of the city remains today as the most lavish example of the dons' taste for overly adorned squares and streets. Private palaces, or *palazzi,* were also richly adorned, with sculptures ranging from angels to nymphs to gargoyles.

The master of the Palermitan oratories, **Giacomo Serpotta,** born in Palermo in 1656, specialized in adorning church oratories with molded plasterwork in ornamental frames. You can see one of his masterpieces today, Palermo's **Oratory of the Rosary** in the church of Santa Zita—about which the author Paul Duncan once claimed: "You can almost hear the chortling, farting and giggling of the *putti.*"

CONTEMPORARY ART

Now that the 20th century has ended, it can safely be said that few books will be written on modern art and artists in Sicily. The one exception is **Renato Guttuso** (1911–87). Painting in a style often called "visceral," Guttuso became renowned around the world for his nudes, landscapes, and still lifes. The visitor to Palermo today need drive just outside the city to the **Galleria Comunale d'Arte Moderna e Contemporanea** at the town of Bagheira (see chapter 5) to see the best examples of Guttuso's work as well as his on-site tomb.

4 La Cucina Siciliana

Good food is one of the main reasons to go to Sicily, especially now that the so-called "Mediterranean diet"—a cuisine comprised of fresh vegetables, fruit, fish, and olive oil—is being touted as healthy fare. But few heart-healthy diets are as enchanting as Sicilian fare, whether served up in modest trattorie or star kitchens.

A MELTING-POT CUISINE

Island fare is a blend of the cuisines of Sicily's many conquerors and cultures. The lush citrus groves around Catania were originally planted by the Arabs. Even those magnificently intricate pastries and rich desserts are a direct result of the Arab invasions, which brought a taste of North Africa to the shores of Catania.

In time, subsequent invaders, including Norman rulers and Spanish viceroys, left their own legacy of "aristocratic food," often as part of huge banquets ornately prepared by enormous staffs and served by a legion of servants. These extravagant excesses were in direct contrast to the diet of the fishermen, the land-tillers, and other working people who set a simple table based mainly on fish and the rich, bountiful harvest of vegetables from the Sicilian countryside.

THE TYPICAL SICILIAN DIET

Sicily is blessed with some of the finest raw culinary materials in Italy. Using this incredible array of fresh ingredients from the sea and field, the chefs of Sicily fashion a delectable display of enticing platters, many of them better and more original than those found anywhere on the mainland of Italy.

SICILIAN STARTERS   Sicilian antipasti make a fine meal by themselves. Our favorite opening to a meal is the island specialty, *caponata,* eggplant and caper salad. It's made with eggplants, sweet bell peppers, cauliflower, fresh tomatoes, olives, fat capers, onions, and celery in a sweet-and-sour sauce of vinegar and sugar.

Another savory starter is *arancini di riso,* little rice balls stuffed with peas, cheese, and meat, then coated with bread crumbs and deep-fried. These rice balls are strangely addictive, as is **bottarga,** the dried and salted roe of gray mullet or tuna, which is pressed into loaves, cut into paper-thin slices, dressed with lemon-laced virgin olive oil, and served.

We could begin any meal in Sicily with an **insalata di mare,** a deluxe seafood salad of boiled squid, tasty bits of octopus, fat shrimp, and chopped fresh vegetables with a dressing of olive oil flavored with lemon juice or vinegar.

PASTA ALLA SICILIANA   For your *primi,* or first course, especially if you skipped the antipasti, you're treated to delicious pasta and rice dishes and even couscous, the latter deriving from Sicily's centuries-old links with North Africa. Most pasta dishes are adorned with fresh fish or vegetables, such as **spaghetti alla Norma,** pasta with eggplant.

Fishermen in particular love the classic **pasta con le sarde,** a simple but savory pasta with fresh sardines, served in a tomato sauce and wild fennel and given added zest with raisins, pine nuts, and capers.

Instead of the relatively mild Parmesan, many islanders sprinkle a particularly strong cheese *(caciocavallo)* on their pasta dishes. For us, there is nothing finer than **spaghetti alle vongole veraci.** This pasta is served with fresh clams steamed in wine with garlic, fresh parsley, and olive oil.

VEGETABLES & FRUIT   Luscious **vegetables,** used liberally in pastas and main courses, include vine-ripened tomatoes, spring-green zucchini, yellow onions, tangy capers, fat garlic cloves, many varieties of olives, multicolored peppers, and broccoli—each among the most flavorful in Italy.

On a visit to a citrus grove on the slopes of Mount Etna north of Catania, we were treated to some of the sweetest-tasting and most vividly colored **blood-red oranges** known to humankind (and we've lived in both Florida and California).

BOUNTY OF THE SEA   Naturally, **fresh fish and crustaceans**—including sea urchins, mussels, cockles, and whitebait—are the dominant feature at most tables. The traditional **musseddu,** salted and fried tuna, is used to flavor many salads. The most popular fish dishes are tuna from the west and swordfish from the Straits of Messina. For most gastronomes, fish is best served *alla griglia* (simply grilled) or else *arrosto* (roasted). After a sea harvest, you'll find what might be the world's best **zuppa di cozze** (mussel soup) resting in a bowl in front of you. Or try **cozze alla marinara,** fresh mussels steamed in wine with garlic and parsley. **Involtini di pesce spada,** grilled roulades of swordfish, are covered with bread crumbs and sautéed in olive oil. Sicilians are also fond of **anchovies,** using them in such dishes as **sfincione,** thick island pizza topped with anchovies, onions, and tomatoes. Many Sicilians don't consider *sfincione* pizza, but it's still sold in focaccerias, in bakeries, or perhaps from street vendors, but never in a pizzeria.

MEAT   Traditionally, the Sicilian cuisine is based largely on vegetables and the catch of the day harvested from coastal waters. But you can also fill your plate with marvelous **meat specialties,** including our favorite, a simple but tasty concoction called **costoletta alla Siciliana** (thinly sliced veal with Parmesan and chopped garlic), which is dipped in bread crumbs and sautéed. One of the better-known meat dishes is **falsomagro,** meaning "false lean." This rich, bountiful dish, a family favorite, is composed of a large slab of beef wrapped around Sicilian sausages, perhaps prosciutto, raisins, pine nuts, grated cheese, and even a boiled egg or two. The treat is tied with a string and stewed in a savory tomato sauce.

One Sicilian dish now served around the world is **pollo alla Marsala** (chicken in Marsala wine). A variation on this famous dish is veal Marsala, which originated among western Sicily's English families living here in the 19th century.

Some form of *involtini* appears on almost every Sicilian menu. This is a roulade that can be made from grilled or roasted chicken or sliced beef stuffed with a vegetable or meat filling. Sometimes a leafy vegetable such as radicchio is added to the meat filling.

SWEET STUFF   One of the most succulent of the byproducts derived from the sweet blood-red oranges (and from Sicily's tangerines, lemons, and figs as well) is *frutta candita,* a sugared and preserved confection that explodes with flavor in your mouth and that is well worth the effort of taking home with you. Equally tempting are the fabulously lifelike **replicas of pears, grapes, or apples** concocted from almond paste and sugar. The colors used in their fabrication and the realism with which they're crafted make them appear as if they had just been picked. In some cases, for added realism, the artisans add hints of a tiny bruise or blemish in each of the confections, partly for charm, partly for whimsy, and partly, we think, to show off their skills. Many of these techniques were origi-nally developed by monks or nuns in monasteries or convents during the 17th and 18th centuries.

Sicilians are also known for their **ice cream,** often produced in exotic flavors. (Have you ever had a velvety, creamy mulberry?) Right on the street from a ven-dor, you can order in summer a *granita di anguri,* a delectable, slushy water-melon ice. Sicily makes some of the best *granita* in the world, using purées of fresh fruit pulp—and not just watermelon, but *limone* (lemon), *fragola* (straw-berry), and *pesca* (peach), among other flavors. Of course, they also do splendid chocolate, coffee, and vanilla flavors.

Islanders point with justifiable pride to their desserts, one of the high points of dining in Sicily. Nothing is grander than a *cassata alla Siciliana,* Catania's most famous cake. It's a layered sponge cake sweetened with Marsala or orange liqueur and filled with ricotta cheese, chunks of chocolate, and candied island fruits. A different cake, *cassata al galleto,* is made with a vanilla-flavored frozen custard and, perhaps, candied fruits, chocolate bits, hazelnuts, or pistachios.

Finally, never leave Sicily without sampling one of its classic *cannolo,* a crunchy tube of pastry filled with ricotta and studded with candied fruits, bits of chocolate, and the inevitable pistachios.

THE WINES OF SICILY

Sicily is celebrated for its wines. Sicily's most famous wine, **Marsala,** comes from the west coast in a city of the same name. This is Sicily's version of port or sherry. Marsala is a fortified wine whose alcoholic content is about 20%. A typical Marsala is amber yellow in color with wonderful depths of orange. With its spe-cial bouquet, it has a pleasing fragrance, both velvety and fruity, coming in both "brut" and sweet versions.

Moscata wines usually carry the designations *della Zucco, di Noto,* or *di Pan-telleria* (an offshore western island). Moscata is made from the Muscat grape, which is sometimes fortified with Zibibbo or Corinto. Most often it is a golden or light amber dessert wine. It can also be sparkling—then it's called *spumante.*

Malvasia wine is associated with the volcanic island of Lipari. It is golden yel-low, turning to amber, with a delightful aroma, both generous and strong. **Nov-ello** is the island's nouveau wine, sold just months after the grapes are harvested and pressed. This is a red wine, both robust and fruity. *Faro,* the name meaning "lighthouse," is a wine produced around Messina. With a fine bouquet, it is a vivid ruby red, with a nutty flavor. It's a good wine for roasts.

Index

FROMMER'S® MEMORABLE WALKS

Chicago
London

New York
Paris

San Francisco
Washington, D.C.

FROMMER'S® GREAT OUTDOOR GUIDES

Arizona & New Mexico
New England

Northern California
Southern New England

Vermont & New Hampshire

SUZY GERSHMAN'S BORN TO SHOP GUIDES

Born to Shop: France
Born to Shop: Hong Kong,
  Shanghai & Beijing

Born to Shop: Italy
Born to Shop: London

Born to Shop: New York
Born to Shop: Paris

FROMMER'S® IRREVERENT GUIDES

Amsterdam
Boston
Chicago
Las Vegas
London

Los Angeles
Manhattan
New Orleans
Paris
Rome

San Francisco
Seattle & Portland
Vancouver
Walt Disney World®
Washington, D.C.

FROMMER'S® BEST-LOVED DRIVING TOURS

Britain
California
Florida
France

Germany
Ireland
Italy
New England

Northern Italy
Scotland
Spain
Tuscany & Umbria

HANGING OUT™ GUIDES

Hanging Out in England
Hanging Out in Europe

Hanging Out in France
Hanging Out in Ireland

Hanging Out in Italy
Hanging Out in Spain

THE UNOFFICIAL GUIDES®

Bed & Breakfasts and Country
  Inns in:
  California
  Great Lakes States
  Mid-Atlantic
  New England
  Northwest
  Rockies
  Southeast
  Southwest
Best RV & Tent Campgrounds in:
  California & the West
  Florida & the Southeast
  Great Lakes States
  Mid-Atlantic
  Northeast
  Northwest & Central Plains

Southwest & South Central
    Plains
  U.S.A.
Beyond Disney
Branson, Missouri
California with Kids
Chicago
Cruises
Disneyland®
Florida with Kids
Golf Vacations in the Eastern U.S.
Great Smoky & Blue Ridge Region
Inside Disney
Hawaii
Las Vegas
London

Mid-Atlantic with Kids
Mini Las Vegas
Mini-Mickey
New England and New York with
  Kids
New Orleans
New York City
Paris
San Francisco
Skiing in the West
Southeast with Kids
Walt Disney World®
Walt Disney World® for Grown-ups
Walt Disney World® with Kids
Washington, D.C.
World's Best Diving Vacations

SPECIAL-INTEREST TITLES

Frommer's Adventure Guide to Australia &
  New Zealand
Frommer's Adventure Guide to Central America
Frommer's Adventure Guide to India & Pakistan
Frommer's Adventure Guide to South America
Frommer's Adventure Guide to Southeast Asia
Frommer's Adventure Guide to Southern Africa
Frommer's Britain's Best Bed & Breakfasts and
  Country Inns
Frommer's Caribbean Hideaways
Frommer's Exploring America by RV
Frommer's Fly Safe, Fly Smart
Frommer's France's Best Bed & Breakfasts and
  Country Inns
Frommer's Gay & Lesbian Europe

Frommer's Italy's Best Bed & Breakfasts and
  Country Inns
Frommer's New York City with Kids
Frommer's Ottawa with Kids
Frommer's Road Atlas Britain
Frommer's Road Atlas Europe
Frommer's Road Atlas France
Frommer's Toronto with Kids
Frommer's Vancouver with Kids
Frommer's Washington, D.C., with Kids
Israel Past & Present
The New York Times' Guide to Unforgettable
  Weekends
Places Rated Almanac
Retirement Places Rated